Som the Frontier

❖ ❖ ❖

A PAKISTAN JOURNAL

Noor Khan's book is so rich and varied and swashbuckling! A semi-equestrian pirate love adventure—a convert to Islam in a land of Islam, yet he clearly doesn't come off as a saint. The crazy thing about the story is it seems like it was meant to happen to him, maybe because he doesn't go down the road of sensationalism—even though it is a pretty mad story.

*Okay, it's got the guns and dope and woman and he's not averse to the breaking of a few taboos, although the thing that came across for me is the heart and impulse and life. **And the life of Pakistan, close up and engaged.** However things are, he just seems to go for it head-first! Which is why, I guess, the story is such an eye-opener into Pakistan.*

*To be honest, two pages into it made me want to hop on a flight to Pakistan. And at the end, I was ready to pick up the sequel... but to be truthful, I was happy my imagination was trying to conjure up whatever happened next... **Very cool book!***

Sean Foley, Visual Anthropologist/Afghan Box Camera Project (2012)

---

*Cover: Suliman Hills, above Khyber Pass (looking back on Afghanistan) 1982 — Mirza A. Khan
insert: Phandar Valley, Hindu Kush, Northern Pakistan, 1989 — Noor M. Khan*

Some Time on the Frontier
A Pakistan Journal

❉   ❉   ❉

For Nasreen, who couldn't see beyond the borders of her own life

For Noor, who couldn't see beyond the borders of his own illusion

And for **ALLAH**,

Who has power over all things

❉   ❉   ❉

For Frank,

Hope you enjoy my little travel tale

Noor Khan

Noor Mohammad Khan

COLOR PHOTOGRAPHS ONLINE
(Internet links)

See the photos that appear in this book in color and chronological order at:
www.pbase.com/noorkhan/00journalphotos
See the author's photographs of Pakistan, Afghanistan, & India plus the horse trip
described in this book online at:
www.pbase.com/noorkhan

The song *'Nasreena'* at (end of chapter 6) can be heard online at:
www.youtube.com/watch?v=TfHz4jX7nZ8

❄   ❄   ❄

Dear Reader,

*I hope you will enjoy reading my book. I think it shows a side of Pakistan not normally portrayed in books plus quite an intriguing story of romance. You can read some sample chapters plus view all the photos that appear in the book in color (and more) at www.pbase.com/novel . Your feedback is enjoyable to me and you can contact me through the guestbook on my pbase site www.pbase.com/noorkhan/profile or my Facebook page (**Some Time on the Frontier-A Pakistan Journal**). Also if you have a book club that would like to read my book and wish to have further discussion do not hesitate to contact me, I would be delighted to talk to you.*

❄   ❄   ❄

First Edition 2009. This printing January 2016
Published by Noor Mohammad Khan
Printed in the United States of America
All rights reserved.
Copyright © 2008 by Noor Mohammad Khan.

ISBN 1440415978

EAN-13 9781440415975

Peshawar Pakistan

(Northwest Frontier Province)

❖ ❖ ❖

1988

*P*eshawar was the seat of activity for Afghan *mujahideen* fighting across the border in Afghanistan. When they weren't fighting and dying in Afghanistan they were roaming the bazaars of Peshawar. Bombings and political intrigues were the norm. It was a time of *aid-wallahs*, ex-pats, journalists and spies, living mostly in University Town (simply called *Town*) outside of Peshawar City (old city) on Jamrud Road, leading to the Khyber Pass and Afghanistan. Heroin factories abounded just outside the city in Tribal Territory and across the border in neighboring Afghanistan.

This story takes place in this environment and in this time, but only has passing concerns with these matters. I lived in Peshawar City, in Hashtnagri, in the house of Bibi Ji (a local PPP* leader and of a respected and prominent *Sayid* family). One could say this story is about Pakistan, though parts of Pakistan most travelers don't get to tread—a diary, a travelogue of sorts.

It covers from January 1988 to November 1991, starting with a visit to Hira Mandi, the infamous red-light and *nautch* district in Lahore, known for it's exotic wickedness, to prayers in the Shrine of Data Baba ** and at the majestic Badshahi Mosque. It tells of a five month, 1000 mile horse expedition through the Hindu Kush, the Hindu Raj, the Karakoram and Himalayan Mountains from Peshawar to Chitral, Kalash (Kafiristan), Gilgit, Kaghan Valley and Azad Kashmir; witnessing the world's highest polo match on the Shandur Top; delays by road blocks in the Karakorams; crossing the Babu Sar Pass; and intermingling with migrating *Gujars* and *Koochies*.

I was involved in the Pashtu music recording scene in Peshawar, though only bits of that come out in these journals. Running through this story of life in Pakistan is my ongoing relationship with a Pathan courtesan and her family residing in Lahore; afternoons spent lounging on a *charpoy* visiting friends at a Pathan *'house of pleasure;'* an evening shootout with Punjabi pimps; smoking *charras* with *malangs* and policemen. All roads traveled brought me back to her side in Lahore.

In the second half of the story there is an entertaining brief interlude taking place in Thailand and a wild month abroad fringing on insanity staying with Waziri taxi drivers in the desert outside of Dubai on a crazed search for my paramour after her disappearance from Lahore. Back home in Pakistan my search for a wife, including chaperoned meetings with several girls on the Frontier.

Finally our relationship caused me to be kidnapped to Bajaur Agency (Tribal Territory) where I found myself miles off the paved road in a mud fort a short walk from the Afghanistan border chained to a *charpoy* with her.***

---

*   *Pakistan People's Party—political party of Zulfigar Ali Bhutto (later Benazir Bhutto)*
** *Syed Abul Hassan Ali Ibn Usman of Hajvery, more commonly known as Data Gunj Baksh, one of the most important religious leaders who brought Islam to the subcontinent.*
*** *The slight government control is limited to the paved road in Tribal Territory*

A Pashtu Poem

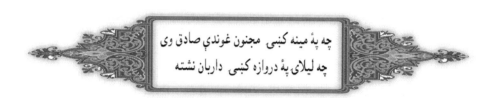

"Che pa meena ki, Majnoon ghunday, sadiq vee
Che Layla pa darwaza ki, darbon neeshta."

"When you are in love, like Majnoon
When Layla is at the door, there is no guard"
Rahman Baba *

* *Abdul Rahman Mohmand* (1653-1711) popularly known as *"Rahman Baba"* was called the "Nightingale of Pakhtoonkhwa," the Pashtu speaking region of Afghanistan and Pakistan. Rahman Baba is a legendary Pashtu Sufi poet. His poetry places him alongside Khushal Khan Khattak for his contribution to Pashtu poetry and literature. His mausoleum/shrine and *mazar* (tomb) is located on the outskirts of Peshawar in Hazarkhawni.

Contents

❊   ❊   ❊

❊

SOME NOTES AND EXPLANATIONS

❖ It is my sincere wish that none of the sentiments expressed in the following pages be offensive to Pathan people *(Pukhtun Ghirrat)*, women, or to the good people of Pakistan (or Pakistanis in general). It must be said that the majority of this was written (and experienced) under extreme pathos and the outermost extremities of obsessed and insane love.

❖ This is not a history of Pakistan. I am not a historian nor an academic. The bits of history appearing herein are purely coincidental. Nor is this an anthropological or cultural study, though I imagine a fair amount of that finds its way in here as well (including a detailed glossary). I did not study Pakistani culture and tradition; I merely found myself living it. One could say it was a gradual progression, a natural osmosis. This is the story of my life in Pakistan, circa 1988-1991, as seen through my eyes, the only ones I have.

❖ I hope no friends are offended by what is written here. The people depicted here are all real people whom I love dearly, portrayed as they are. As with any friends dearly loved, sometimes there may be differences of opinions, but the love is always there. In only a few instances did I change a name or two.

❖❖❖ **Please note that the smoking of *charras* in this novel does not have the same connotations as it does in Western countries. It is more akin to people in the West having a beer or two. In Pakistan alcohol is the big taboo... and besides, I didn't inhale.** ❖❖❖

"A great rock is not disturbed by the wind;
the mind of a wise man is not disturbed by either honor or abuse."
Gautama Buddha

Badshahi Mosque

Forward by the author - 2009

Pakistan is a country much in the news nowadays and much maligned. It is a beautiful country with wonderful, warm, hospitable people.

This story is basically my private diaries, collected and organized in 1993-94, when all was still fresh in my memory. I could have rewritten some of the story without so many personal, painful details, although at the time it was written I felt it was such a fascinating view into a world that so few Westerners (or even Pakistanis) have tread that I decided to omit nothing! _**No holds barred!**_ Definitely parts of Pakistan and events one doesn't read about in your usual travel novels!

This story occurred more than twenty years ago. There are things I did that I might not necessarily repeat, yet nothing I'm ashamed for having lived at the time. Incredible adventures in Pakistan and an intriguing, maybe scandalous relationship run throughout this story. The times that were do not come again.

Looking back, the truth does seem rather harsh at times. I could have changed her into just a *nautch* (dancing) girl, but *'the profession'* is so different in Pakistan and both are interwoven. As her mother told me, it was their *zot* (caste); her mother had done it, as had her mother before her, and her mother's mother before her. Yet she was a Muslim girl, of a Muslim culture, with many Islamic values and views. She believed it was her *taqdeer* (predestination) where and what she was born into, as it was my *taqdeer* to fall in love with her. She was a *'family girl'* by many standards, doing housework and looking after family and children. She wouldn't have thought of going outside the house without a *chaddar* to cover her head. She was more modest and family orientated than so many Western woman I have seen.

It all seems so different to me. Am I only naive? When we look into that special set of eyes we have no choice where God will cast us. From the moment she walked into that room in Lahore and I looked into her mesmeric eyes, I cannot forget her. Prostitute or queen, it was not my choice.

All is God's will.

This is how it happened and this is how I present it to you....

Noor Mohammad Khan

San Francisco, 2009

❖ ❖ ❖

This book is a true story taken from my journals and diaries. Any similarities to any fictional work is purely coincidental. Only an occasional name has been changed to protect some privacy.

In telling this story it is not my intention to demean anybody, nor the country of Pakistan or the Islamic faith (both subjects very dear to my heart).

Special Thanks

Thanks to my good friend Jara Mali for the inspiration to take this book the 'final furlong'... and to all the other fine folks who helped along the way. Special thanks to my dear daughter, Odessa, for her time spent in first copy edits and advice. Never could have done it without you!

Amy Hawes (who appeared out of my past) for her editing effort and Maqadus Begum for her helpful edits. And Ayesha, another surprise from the past, for her painstaking editorial skill and for use of some of her photos.

Also thanks to my brother Mirza (a lion of *Allah*) for encouraging me to write it all down and for teaching me about horses (sometimes against my will). Some of the "snaps" may even be his handiwork.

Self protrait taken with a small Rolli 35 camera placed on a step

In Peshawar City

Chapter 1
ON A LARK
(Forbidden Fruit)

 I had first gone to Lahore on a lark. It was with one of the few foreign friends I had in Pakistan, an English journalist. I had been in Pakistan's ancient Mughal city often before as a stopping off and overnight watering spot on journeys between Afghanistan and India but never just to Lahore—*the garden city*. Never just for the sake of being in Lahore.

And it was more than just for the sake of being in Lahore that we were there. Of course we wanted to see the sights of Lahore, a historic city, the capitol of the Punjab for nearly a thousand years. The Mughal emperor Akbar had held his court there for fourteen years from 1584 to 1598. He built the Lahore Fort at that time as his imperial residence. A city famous for its beautiful mosques, tombs, gardens, the fort, and the rich variety of its many storied and intriguing bazaars. One of these bazaars, the infamous Hira Mandi, we were especially keen on investigating.

We had heard many interesting tales about Hira Mandi, literally *the diamond market*.* The *nautch* houses of dancing girls, and as Pakistanis themselves say, 'loose character women' are there. In more direct words the red light district. This mecca of the senses has been known since Mughal times, maybe before. Sensual pleasures are as old as sin, and as seductively enticing. Historically patronized by maharajahs and men of power, it has also been a place where female-lonely men could come to get a sight and a taste of the forbidden. Forbidden fruit is the sweetest, is it not?

In olden days it seethed with sensuality. Prostitution was condoned here until the mid-seventies when certain religious parties pressured ex-Prime Min-

---

* *The word Hira means diamond in Urdu and was used by locals to describe the beauty of the girls in the market. The people called the courtesans who worked in the area as "Hiras" (diamonds). But it is a misconception that the name of Hira Mandi has anything to do with the beauty of girls in the market. The bazar was named Hira Mandi by Maharaja Ranjit Singh as a tribute to one of his ministers, Hira Singh.*

ister Zulfigar Ali Bhutto to openly crack down on immorality. *

Now in these days of *Islamization* this time-old art is much more restrained. Prostitution is illegal and women are banned from dancing in public. The area of Hira Mandi (also known as Shahi Mohallah—The Royal Neighbourhood) is now heavily patrolled by Pakistani vice cops. But the action still exists and can still be found on several back streets that run behind the Badshahi Mosque. Only now we had to be careful our ethnic research wouldn't land us in the hands of the law.

Police in groups patrol the area on foot or stand around watching the public; smoking cigarettes and chatting, waiting it seems for some flagrant example of moral decadence. No cars are allowed to leave the area without being checked to see if girls are being smuggled out of Hira Mandi. Yet these visual deterrents seem to have little effect. An unspoken laissez faire—'Look, but don't touch.' By 10:00 P.M. the narrow streets are crammed with strolling men, cruising, looking for action, Pakistani style. Men that is, only men... and of course, in the business establishments are the girls....

The girls you see in all shades of satins and silks, sparkling in sequins and rhinestones. Filmy Punjabi *shalwar kameez* and smoky flowing gossamer thin *dupattas*, heavily made up and glittering golden bejeweled. They sit in upper-story windows and balconies, looking down, looking enticing. Some sit and smoke, taking their ease, not paying any attention to the men walking below gazing up at them longingly. Others beckon coyly with *surma*-rimmed luminous eyes sparkling, their red, voluptuous lips mouthing unheard half-imagined words of encouragement.

This warren of winding streets is a remnant of another age. The houses lean haphazardly against one another. Stairways and dimly lit passageways lead to the various rooms. Downstairs the musicians are warming up—mostly dark skinned swarthy Punjabis, gold loop earrings and greasy black hair, plump from years of sitting and plying their trade, lips and rotted teeth stained dried blood red with *betel* juice.

Tabla, dholak, sitar, harmonium, sarangi and tambourine. The shimmering sounds of the *ghungrughan* (leather leggings covered with rows of small shiny brass bells fastened to the dancing girls' ankles). With gracefully arched bare feet they stomp out the rhythms, dancing to the accompaniment of the pulsing drums. Fat madames sitting on plush cushions, faces painted, ostentatious rings on corpulent fingers, silver filigreed *paan* boxes by their sides, watch the doorways for potential customers.

By 11:30 the dancing starts. The hypnotizing beat of the drums and *dholaks* mix and carry down the streets. In front of the houses the drone of the *harmoniums*, the plaintive whine of a sitar or wail of the *sarangi* can be heard calling their individual melodies. The fronts of the *kothas* (dancing rooms) are open on the bottom floor and brightly lit behind veils of transparent smoke-like fabrics of many hues.

---

* *Bhutto was later executed by President-General Mohammad Zia ul-Haq after Zia seized control of the government in 1976*

The street is a surging press of massed humanity. Vendors, beggars, food, lights, colors, smells—cars slowly inching between. The pounding of drums and the ringing of bells bedazzle our senses. We change money on the street from one of the many money changers with their glass covered card table size cases filled with wads of crisp new rupee notes. Ones, fives, and tens, held together with thin rubber bands stretched to the breaking point. Money to shower the dancing girls, the key to keep them spinning. It's never free to enter these rooms and sometimes more expensive to leave.

We walk up and down the streets, gazing in, trying to pick some girls we like. We linger in front of an establishment, watching. The madame leans on her golden brocaded cushion and spits blood red *paan* juice into a shiny silver spittoon.

"Come in sons," she croons.

We step up and cross the smooth linoleum covered floor to sit on richly stuffed cushions. The girls are dressed in beautifully bright scintillating satins. Gold nose rings and jangling golden earrings and chains. Long thick luxurious hair, plaited down shimmering satin covered backs, silken gold or silver tassels twisted into the ends.

The room we have picked has only two dancing girls, though some houses have as many as half a dozen. As long as we keep showering them with money they keep dancing. A barely teenaged girl brings us *chai*.

The dancers are caught up in the tempos of the drums, twirling, their glittering hair plaits streaming out behind them. They dance up to us, suggestively gyrating in our faces and laps, the smell of their flowers and perfume intoxicating. As they coax us more we carelessly toss the remainder of the money we've changed. Larger notes are drawn from our pockets. They rub up to us, plucking the money from our pockets and off our laps. It's loud and garish, ethereal, very ethnic, and from my experiences in Pakistan over the last twelve years a sumptuously surreal flash from the past—entertainment of the maharajahs.

Living in an Islamic country is great. It's my choice. Being a Muslim, I wouldn't have it any other way. I like the culture, the unity, the brotherhood, the respect and awareness of God. But being raised on the Western ideals of romance, it does seem Islam and the culture doesn't leave much room for a romantic relationship in Pakistan. As to what I've seen, it's practically impossible to have a girlfriend here, that is a woman as a friend, let alone a romantic relationship. Most people I've met can't relate to platonic relationships between men and women.

Marriage is the only way, and love isn't the main factor in a marriage here. It's the family unit, the clan, the tribe that is important. Most marriages are arranged by the family. Divorce is very uncommon and rather unacceptable. It isn't so easy to make a mistake in marriage and then divorce your way out. Not many children suffer the broken home syndrome here. This is what I see.

Now, as two (foreign) Peshawari bachelors, I must admit that besides the temptation of seeing a colorful, exotic leftover relic of another era we were intrigued to suss out, as they say, "the world's oldest profession." Does it still exist here in Lahore? In Islamic Pakistan? Out of curiosity. Out of adventure. Out of cultural research. To see if we could 'get laid.' We figured we'd give it a go, even though neither of us had much experience in, how one would say, whoring.

We were told though, dancing is at night in Hira Mandi. Any other business is conducted during the day.

Our first day walking in Hira Mandi we are approached on the streets several times by agents—sleazy Punjabi junky types. Dirty and slovenly.

"You want to go?" they say in Urdu, coming up and walking beside us.

"Where?" we naively answer.

"Girls! Nice young girls. You want to go?"

Too sleazy. Maybe dangerous. This is *THE ISLAMIC REPUBLIC OF PAKISTAN*. Walking in Hira Mandi isn't like cruising Sunset Strip back in Los Angeles. Here, if the police catch you involved in more than just looking it could spell real trouble, jail or a flogging. For a foreigner most likely deportation. This isn't America. I don't want to think about it too much. Being green in this field even in the countries of our birth we assuredly don't know the ropes here. What can happen? We keep an eye over our shoulders for police or plainclothes followers. Maybe the agent will set us up with the police. I don't know yet how the game is played.

In a Pathan tea house we meet one young, slick, well dressed, clean looking agent. He tells us if we want girls to come back in the morning. It is already afternoon and getting much too close to the night.

The next morning, in the name of cultural research, and by now mostly just plain curiosity, we go back to the Pathan tea house. Our agent isn't there. We sit in the smoky, cramped stall drinking *qawah* and watching the clientele. They mostly seem to be junky types, burnt out and wasted by the years, miles or other substances. The pungent acrid smell of heroin mixed with cheap tobacco hangs heavily in the air. We're dedicated to our research though and we end up with a sleazy, stubbly-chinned agent.

He takes us to a house. We sit in the front room. A young man comes into the room to greet us. Then a girl comes in. She's Pathan. She isn't bad looking, though she appears to have just woken up. There is no trace of makeup on her sleepy face and her jet black hair is disheveled. The fellow who greeted us tells us she is his wife. My companion and I exchange glances. We agree to leave. No inspiration here, no feeling, no magic for sure.

We leave to wander the dark, narrow, cobbled lanes of old Lahore. I go to the Badshahi Mosque for the *Juma* (Friday) prayer. The Badshahi Mosque (Emperor's Mosque) is the congregational mosque built by the Emperor Aurangzeb (Alamgir), great grandson of Akbar, in 1673-4, to the west of Lahore Fort. It has one of the largest open courtyards of any mosque in the Islamic world, capable of accommodating over 55,000 worshipers. The architecture and design of the Badshahi Mosque is closely related to the Jama Masjid in Delhi, India, which was built in 1648 by Aurangzeb's father and predecessor,

14

Emperor Shah Jahan. A few thousand pray the *Juma* prayer.

We then go back to the tea house for one last try. We sit and drink more *qawah*. Our agent from yesterday comes in. We finish. He pays for our tea and we go. The three of us walk to the end of Hira Mandi where we get into a *rickshaw* and head out of the old city toward the outskirts of town. We are conversing with him in *Urdu* and *Pashtu.* He is Pathan, but my limited Pashtu doesn't feel adequate. I don't know Lahore, don't know where we are. Eventually we come to a dead end dirt alley with a *shamiyana* tent blocking the way. We leave the *rickshaw* and squeeze between the tent and a brick wall, following the agent through a wooden doorway and down three steps into a room.

The room is furnished with big, upholstered chairs and a double bed with a wooden headboard inlaid with floral designs in fine brass. A rainbow colored Afghan knit bedspread covers it. There is a bureau with a mirror on it against the wall. Another doorway leads into a garden. We sit on the cushioned chairs across from the bed. The agent sits on the end next to my friend. Two girls come in to sit in front of us. Another two are standing at the garden door.

The agent is telling us the price but I can only stare at the girl sitting in front of me on the edge of the bed. I fall right into her deep dark liquid pool eyes. Her hair, dark and damp, falls in long moist ringlets over her shoulders. She's drying it with a towel over her shoulder. She is dressed in pure white satin.

My heart is immediately caught in her silvery, sparkling smile and large, luminous eyes. There seems to be some instantaneous spark between us. I look at the other three girls, but all I can see now is this girl with the dark glistening eyes and inky, silken, hair surrounded in a vision of white satin. She seems to be in charge. I'm not sure if she is even for the picking, but it's too late. She's my only choice....

"What do you think about the price?" my friend asks me. "It is rather dear."

It is more than we had imagined it would be, but by now I'm in a world where money has no real value.

"I like her," I state, without taking my gaze off the girl in front of me. "If you want one of the others, go ahead. If she is available, I'm ready."

I look at her and smile. She smiles back into me.

"Do you like?" the agent says.

"I like her," I say.

"She doesn't work, she only negotiates." He tells me, "This is her family's business. Which girl do you like?"

"Still I like her" I repeat.

He speaks to her in Pashtu. She gives a silvery laugh and leaves the room. I look at the agent and he says "Wait."

Soon we're sitting in the room together, alone on the bed. She gets up to close the door. I don't know what to expect. I put my vest with my money and passport on the far corner of the bed. I'm not sure if somebody may sneak in to snatch it while we're involved. I don't want to take chances. Maybe the police will come in? This is all so new to me.

She sits on the bed next to me and takes my hand. I stroke my other hand along her satin covered leg. She smiles into my eyes. She's warm, soft and sleek. I can't keep from falling into her lustrous eyes.

Falling forever.

In Peshawar City

Chapter 2

The Dark Eyes

"Every Saint Has a Past, Every Sinner Has a Future"

Mid-February, 1988
Peshawar

Dark eyes.
Long dark hair.
Visions of white satin.
A girl with no name.

In a haze. In a daze. What have I gotten into? What has gotten into me? Twenty minutes with a nameless Pathan girl and my mind is running crazy around her. Her flashing smile and shimmering laugh. The silvery sound of her sweet voice.

It could be interesting, it would be convenient. Bachelor life for me in Peshawar occasionally does get stale. It would be so nice to have a female friend. A relationship? Dare I hope? Am I crazy to entertain such a thought? An impossible romance one can touch. Sometimes you just don't realize how swiftly something can hit. Isn't it said "Love only devours the starving?"

I'm driven to go back to Lahore to find her again before it burns a hole in my mind. It seems so impossible, but then I'm living in Asia, something that once also seemed impossible for me. To make the break from the place my body happened to be born in. Isn't life a constant series of breaks? Change? Life is change. Who's to say what is impossible? That is for God to say. I could say this does seem rather improbable. How tragically romantic. How doomed. How unplanned.

I've been thinking about her constantly. Confusion. Should I go find her or just forget it? Is it too dangerous?

*T*wo weeks later and I'm back in Lahore. Another grueling ten-hour Flying Coach jostle on GT Road. GT Road stands for the Grand Trunk Road, though nowadays I imagine it could easily be taken as *'Grand Truck Road.'* It leads from Calcutta, India, to the approach of the Khyber Pass, hence practically to my doorstep. From the gateway of Central Asia to the Bay of Bengal, it connects the far reaches of a lost empire.

Lahore is 280 miles from Peshawar as the Flying Coach flies. Well, it's only flying if your eyes are closed and you can think of yourself as flying in an unbelievable mass of turbulence. The Flying Coach is the transportation of the middle class and the only air conditioned service that plies this wretched excuse for a highway.

I know in an advanced country 280 miles of highway doesn't sound all that formidable, but on GT Road it's not the distance that gets you, it's the road itself. The paving, in ill repair and full of potholes, rattles your kidneys and threatens to snap the extra strength shock absorbers of the Flying Coaches.

In a few improved spots the road is freshly paved, four lanes and divided, though most of it is still two undivided lanes of sheer madness cutting its swathe across Pakistan. Trucks, buses and tractors, all garishly painted and flag festooned are decorated with colorful intricately cut plastic designs, clocks over the windscreen (on the outside), model jet planes, palm tree cutouts (over the cabs), clattering silver chains and pendants dangling off the front bumpers and cut out filigreed chrome work. Graceful flowing Arabic script, invocations to Allah or the Prophet Muhammad (PBUH) in all colors. Decorated and caked tapestries of color and jangling flying designs. Cars, mini vans, and the more sedate Japanese manufactured Flying Coaches vie with motorcycles, *tongas*, bullock carts, camels, water buffalos, donkeys, bicycles and pedestrians.

Whoever is going fastest, with the loudest horn blaring has the right of way, squeezing down the middle of the road. Other traffic jostles along the edges. At night it isn't unusual to come up behind an unlit, slowly crawling bullock or donkey cart. At the last moment, when the driver of the speeding vehicle finally sees the slowly advancing cart, they must swerve to the middle of the road to avoid it. Hopefully there isn't another speeding vehicle performing the same maneuver on the opposite side. *'Khudai meriban day.'* (God is Kind) As long as they clear an oncoming vehicle by a coat of paint, no problem, though it isn't unusual to see the burnt out skeleton of a Flying Coach wrapped around a tree or flipped over on the side of the road.

Leaving Peshawar at 11:00 P.M. the night bus stops in *Pindi* around 1:30, then a roadside mosque for morning prayer at 6:00 somewhere about an hour out of Lahore around the town of Gujranwala.

And so I find myself again in the Pathan tea house in Hira Mandi. It's 9:00 in the morning and chilly. I'm wrapped in a blanket, wearing a jet-black and silver-gray striped turban. The agent from last time isn't here. There is an old man with a ragged turban and a ragged wife. The cigarette that dangles from his slack mouth reeks with the acrid stink of heroin. We talk....

From my dress and language he thinks I'm a Kabuli. He's an Afghan, probably anxious to talk to somebody from home. He tells me he came to Lahore 19 years ago and has been here ever since, now a wasted old addict with a wasted life.

He prepares another cigarette, sucking the finely pulverized gray powder up out of a *rupee* note and into the loosened tobacco of the cheap cigarette. Gray and pulverized like his life has become I prophetically think. I look into his craggy face and bleary eyes as he translates my Farsi into guttural Pashtu for the *chai wallah.* I need to find my agent. I need to find out about a special house, about a special Pathan girl.

Bad news he says. Police trouble. That agent went back to Peshawar. Nobody in the tea house can tell me any information about a house with Pathan girls. All the junkyard agents say the same thing. Punjabi girls... young, nice, and no problems.

Not what I came for. I leave.

Walking in Hira Mandi I'm approached by several sleazy agents but I keep walking, thinking, hoping beyond hope that maybe my information is wrong and I will see my agent. Finally out of disappointment, a sense of adventure, and a need for accomplishment after spending the entire night on the bus to get here I do follow one agent. He's dirty and unshaven, a plaid wool muffler wrapping the top of his mangy, close cropped stubbly head. Seems a regular code of dress. A dubious looking and smelling cigarette dangles from his yellow, rotten toothed mouth.

We journey up many narrow and dimly lit back streets, the four story ancient brick buildings closing in on the street and blocking out the hazy morning sunlight. We double back into Hira Mandi, obviously to avoid any police followers. We slip into a house and up several flights of uneven ill lit brick stairs. I sit in the front room on a large over-stuffed couch. A tall girl wearing heavy dancing-girl makeup, yellow satin *shalwar kameez* and golden jangling ornaments and a golden nose ring sits next to me. She leans into me breathing sweetly and seductively.

Negotiations are difficult as they only speak Punjabi and Urdu, neither of which I speak very well, but the money is no problem and is understood. The girl is pretty and I am turned on by nose rings. I breathe in the heavy scent of her available perfumed body. But she isn't my nameless lost Pathan girl whose image has been tormenting me these past weeks. I'm there briefly, she's not what I came for and by noon I'm back on a Flying Coach bound for Peshawar.

Not finding her has only inflamed my burning desire. I'm falling deeper and deeper, seemingly without any control, completely overwhelmed by a brief encounter with a nameless stranger.

Two weeks later and I'm drawn to Lahore again. I'm in Hira Mandi at the same Pathan tea house. The old Afghan man is still there smoking his powdered death. I look at his wife's sunken face. She gives me a compassionate toothless grin. I guess there isn't much left for them anyway. Another day in Lahore, another cigarette.

As I drink my *qawah* a young neat looking Pathan sits next to me. His youth, combed hair and tidy clothes contrast him with the burnt out empty shell inmates of the tea house.

"You want to go see after tea?" he asks me.

I tell him I am looking for a house with Pathan girls which is located outside of Hira Mandi. I describe the agent who took me there a month before. He knows him.

"Aurangzeb is still in Peshawar. I don't know when he is coming back," he informs me. "I'm not sure which house he took you to but I do know some Pathan houses and they are not in Hira Mandi."

"I'm looking for a special girl."

"These are all special girls," he tells me grinning.

"No. One special girl. I was with her a month ago, but I don't know her name or where the house was I went to."

He pays for my tea and we leave the tea house. The *rickshaw* goes in the same general direction we went last time. It's hard to tell from the back of the tiny cramped rickshaw. We stop in a dead end dirt street. Seems the same only this time there is no *shamiyana* wedding tent.

We enter through a blue metal doorway into a courtyard surrounded by brick white-washed walls, bushes and bougainvillea running alongside. In the back is a veranda and a few doorways leading into the house. Another doorway also leads into a room at the front of the house facing the street. Some girls and children are about but nobody pays me much attention. I stand and wait while they wake someone sleeping on a *charpoy* under a blanket in the front room. She pulls a purple-blue *chaddar* over her head and shoulders and goes out. The *charpoy* is moved and I am ushered inside.

Yes! The same room I was in a month ago! There is the bed and headboard with the rainbow colored Afghan spread. I'm sitting in one of the chairs lining the wall across from it again. I see the dresser with the mirror I adjusted my turban in last time before I left.

The agent sits next to me. The girl with the purple-blue *chaddar* comes in and sits at my other side. She looks at me as she draws on the cigarette between her lips. She has a gold nose ring in the left side of her nose, three small gold balls jangling down from it.

"I want a special girl," I tell her, now armed with a month's work of Pashtu cramming—all the special lines I figured I would need. "I was here last month with her. I'm looking for that girl. She's very special to me."

"What is her name?" the girl asks me.

"I don't know."

"You don't know her name? I think I know which one you are talking about." She smiles. "She has gone to her village."

"Is she coming back?"

"No. She's gone," she says and she laughs at my disappointed expression. "You don't recognize me? I am that girl."

I gaze at her closely now, curiously surprised. Now it's falling into place. Only my memories are of blacks and whites, damp hair and sleek satin. Now my vision is one of browns and goldens, wrapped in blue. My English friend's girl from last time comes into the room. After greeting me, she asks,

"How is your friend? He didn't come?"

"He's fine. No. He stayed in Peshawar."

"He didn't like?" she laughs.

"No, not exactly."

"You like?"

I look into the deep dark eyes of the girl in blue. She smiles back. Now I can recognize her, her smiling flashing eyes. I smile back. My gaze never leaving her, I say to the other girl,

"I like her. I came from Peshawar to find her."

"Did you find her?" she asks.

"Yes I did."

"God is kind."

"*Insha'Allah.*"

She leaves the room, as does the agent. I'm alone with my fantasy.

"I came from Peshawar two weeks ago to find you, but I couldn't. I went back to Peshawar with a sad heart. I've been thinking about you ever since I met you."

"You don't have my address?" she asks.

"No. I don't even know your name."

She leaves me alone in the room in anticipation. She comes back and hands me a scrap of paper with Urdu writing scrawled on it.

"It's the address here," she explains. "Come anytime, but before 9:00 at night. Any day. No agent."

"That's good. Now tell me (by the way), what is your name ?" I gaze at her starry eyed. She lights a cigarette and exhales a cloud of bluish white smoke. She looks at me....

"Nasreen," she says, smoke swirling around our heads.

"Nasreen," I repeat, marveling that I finally know my dream's name. "I was here two weeks ago to see you Nasreen, but nobody in Hira Mandi could help me find you. I didn't even know your name. I was so very sad. I went back to Peshawar but my mind kept eating circles around you. I knew I had to come again and try to find you."

"Why did you want to find me?"

"Because my heart likes you. You are special to me. I can't forget you."

"I'm glad."

"Why?"

"I just am."

She bends close to me, cigarette smoke on her breath. I take the cigarette from her lips and drop it on the brick floor. With her smile she pulls me close. Her cotton *kameez* is cool and smooth as I run my hands up her back. With my hands in her thick, luxurious hair I hold her close to me. We fall back on the bed and merge into an embrace that I know I can never leave. I can't believe we're here together again like this! Her skin is warm, soft, smooth and sleek. I'm in a dream I don't want to wake from.

Later I'm lying on the bed, alone in her afterglow. She returns with a two-year-old baby girl. She gives me a cup of tea. We play with the baby.

"Is she yours?" I ask.

"No. She's my sister's. Her name is Shahbo," she says, kissing the baby's face.

"Does your sister do this work?"

"No... *toba, toba*," she says with such a cute frown as she touches her earlobes.*

I give the baby a toffee. Nasreen takes it from the child's mouth, biting it in half so it isn't so big. Easier for the child to suck on. The remaining half has shattered in her mouth. The flecks of candy glisten like glass slivers on her lips. She puts a piece in my mouth. We laugh as I suck the sweet fragments off her long, slender fingers. I lick the cartoon tattoo wrapper and put it on the baby's little wrist. I kiss her nose.

Nasreen sees my cup is empty. "Do you want more tea?" she asks.

"*Meribani*," I say politely (thanks-no thanks).

"No *meribani*," she says forcefully. "Drink more tea!"

She takes the baby out of the room and brings me more tea. With a flick of her delicate wrist she closes the curtain and shuts the door. We sit back on the bed. My legs are stretched out in front of me. She curls up next to me, her long legs over mine.

"Is it true in *Amerika* brothers and sisters do this work (sex)?" she asks from nowhere.

"Yes, sometimes. Sometimes fathers and daughters, mothers and sons," I tell her. "But not often."

"*Toba, toba*," she gasps. "Do brothers marry sisters?"

"It is against the law," I say.

"*Al-hamdu-lillah*. Is it true that in *Amerika* there are no thieves?"

"No. Where did you hear that?"

"Ummm, I just heard it."

"It is wrong talk."

"Well then, leave it."

We move on to discussing Islam, a common ground.

"In Islam now, I have only one problem," I tell her.

"What problem?" she wants to know.

"*You!*" I say, squeezing her butt. We laugh.

"It's okay," she tells me. "In this world everybody does this work or some other sin. Only God is without sin."

Well, now that is one way of looking at it. We can lie here together in each other's arms and she talks seriously of God, sin and repentance. She lights a cigarette and takes a few puffs.

"Nasreen," I ask apprehensively, "are you married?"

---

* **Toba** means repent, 'God forbid.' Toba is usually said accompanied with a tugging on the earlobes with the thumb and first finger (from the Indian sub-continent up into Central Asia).

"Yes," she says. "I have a husband."

Gulp... I think, exhaling my smoke in a hurry.

"What work does he do?" (am I being naive at this point or just trying to make conversation with the limited Pashtu I know?)

"This," she says, signifying with a wave of her hands that she means the house. "Why?"

"That's not good," I tell her.

"Not good? Why?"

"Well, good for me. I got to meet you. I like you. But for you I think not good."

"Good for you? Why not for me?" she smiles at me. Is it a Western or just a male double standard?

"I like you, so in that it's good for me. But for you... do you like this kind of work?"

"I like you," she laughs and pulls me close to her. "Well then?" she signals with her eyes as she playfully tugs on the drawstring of my pants.

"I'd like," I say. "But I didn't bring much money."

"Don't worry. No one will know."

The thought that she is married is now running through my mind, but I cannot refuse her warm embrace. She crawls on top of me. I lay back and watch a spider crawl across the ceiling to a fly entrapped in its web.

I relax and surrender to the warmth of our bodies.

GT Road, Peshawar City

Out my window in Gari Saidan

Karimpura Bazaar (with Shaheen Bazaar branching off to left)

Chapter 3

Peshawar to Lahore

*B*ack in Peshawar more and more thoughts of this girl fill my time and mind. I am working hard to improve my Pashtu—to be able to express to her my feelings. I wake before dawn to the *Azan*. Before I can complete one breath her name is there in my head... *Nasreen*. Even in the mosque it's hard for me to chase her from my mind. **Allah** *Akbar,* God is Great.

Problems?

I'd say so. A husband. Can I do that? Why not? I'm playing outside any rules I've ever known. What kind of husband is it that can sell his wife like that? Surely not one who deserves her.

Who's making the rules anyway? I don't know where it will go or where it can go. I don't know what she is open to. I do know I could love her if she would love me too. God, I want her so, her heart and soul. Am I crazy to want to follow this impossible, maybe dangerous dream? I'm compelled.

Her husband is a problem in my mind. At this point it's still just business with him, but the way I act about her I keep thinking he is bound to get upset. Maybe I just don't know how these type of people think. Obviously he thinks differently than I. I could never do what he does. Also the thought of being so in love with a married woman is rather difficult for me. It doesn't feel right, but then this is a different situation, isn't it? What kind of marriage is theirs anyway?

Her profession? Another problem on my mind. It is difficult being in love with a *'that kind of girl,'* knowing other men can be with her in the same intimate ways I am. Sometimes it feels like unfaithfulness, then I have to remember it is only her job. Is it hypocritical to take advantage of the situation? If she weren't there I would never have met her in the first place so how can I really complain about her work? For the time being I'll have to just live with it.

Language? My Pashtu is coming along. I've never needed it so badly.

Sometimes I wonder, how did I ever get into this? Most of the time though I can only think of Nasreen. By my sixth visit to Nasreen's house I had figured I had it all down. I hadn't yet realized there would be nothing routine in this affair....

As I come around the corner of her street I see in front of the house a large red and blue striped *dari* (rug) with a dozen men sitting there. A fellow I know from her house is squatting on a pile of bricks and rubble at the corner.

"What has happened?" I ask.

"Baba has died." Baba was her husband's father, the head of the house. The head pimp. My new girlfriend's husband's father.

"What? When?" I ask, surprised.

"Yesterday."

"Why? Which problem?"

"Sick. Heart attack. Now dead."

I walk to the rug and shake hands with the husband. We all raise our hands, palms out in front of our faces in supplication, and repeat a prayer for the deceased. This is repeated as each new member arrives to offer condolences and upon each member's departure. Prayers for the departed soul. I guess Baba will be needing them.

I sit next to the husband on the rug and he repeats the story I had heard on the corner. On his left hand I notice the large scrolled gold ring I remember seeing on Baba's hand. On his other hand is a silver and lapis lazuli ring I had given to Nasreen. Not a complete surprise. After giving it to her she had told me he liked it. He can take whatever he likes from her. That is the way it's played.

At noon the husband tells me to go with his brother. As I climb on the back of his motorcycle I hear the husband explaining to the guests that I am not a Kabuli (I'm still wearing my turban) but an American Muslim from Peshawar. I don't know where we are going but it seems at present I'm in the grip of this family. I assume I should listen to her husband if I want to see her again. After all he is the head of the family now.

The brother takes me to the same house my English friend and I had first gone to with the sleepy uninspiring girl. It seems a lifetime away now. The same fellow lets us in. We sit in a room, smoke, drink sweet *lassi* and talk. There is a Punjabi girl lounging on the *charpoy* upon which I sit. She is under a fluffy and colorfully patterned quilt, only her head, her black disheveled flossy hair and her smooth bare golden shoulders showing.

"You like this girl?" Nasreen's brother-in-law asks me. She pushes her quilt covered knees into the small of my back. I look at her laying there as she takes a puff on a cigarette. She stretches and smiles at me.

"Yes. Why not?" I say, being polite.

"You want her?" he asks.

She closes her eyes, blowing smoke out from between her sensual full pouted available lips. Can I refuse her?

"No thank you. That isn't what I came for. I came all the way from Peshawar because I want to see Nasreen. I like her. She is special to me."

"This girl is special. Lay with her and you will like her too," he replies. The girl looks at me from under her long lashes, smiling seductively.

"No. I only have room in my heart for one special girl."

"There is no work in our house now. Baba has died."

"I understand that. I can wait."

"You want to see Nasreen? I can bring her here for you tonight at 7:00," he tells me. This sounds strange, hard to believe, but I did travel the entire night only to see her.

"How can this be? Didn't your father just die?"

"She's not my sister!"

"I know. Isn't she your brother's wife?"

"No. She is only a relative, our cousin."

I'm happy at this information, yet more confused than ever. The brother of the man Nasreen tells me is her husband says she isn't married to his brother, she is only a cousin. The brother tells me I should go back to their house if I don't want to do business with this Punjabi girl. As I approach the corner by her house, a fellow I have never seen before is standing there.

"Baba is died," he tells me. "At this house is no work."

"I know," I explain. "I was here earlier. I don't care. I just want to see Nasreen. I don't care about work! I've come all the way from Peshawar. I just want to see her, to say *salaam* and give her a present I have brought from Peshawar. Then I will go. Baba's son told me to wait here."

"Who is he to say? I am the oldest son! I am in charge now!"

He latches on to me like a leech latching on to the scent of blood, pulling me on the string of her name. I follow.

"There is a house close by. A very nice house with a very nice young girl. Looks completely *Englaise*. You will like. You will forget Nasreen."

Now I'm more confused. He says he's Baba's oldest son. So he must be in charge of the house. And he wants me to forget Nasreen. Okay, what choice do I have right now? Might as well check it out. Isn't this how I first found her anyway? I wish I could forget her. I can feel the pain coming already. The pain of utter attachment.

We walk through some back streets to a house. *Deja vu*, a wedding tent in front like the first time I was at her house. We go up an outdoor spiral wrought iron staircase and enter an upstairs apartment. The room is richly carpeted. We sit on the floor with a woman in her mid-fifties, sagging under forty years of makeup. The girl comes into the room and sits next to me. She is young, maybe seventeen. Her complexion is light, her hair auburn. She's wearing a sparkling nose ring and more than a splash of makeup.

Oh, but I love Nasreen's wild, natural look—her dark, deep, brown, gypsy eyes. I'm her prisoner. The prison of her eyes. I seem to be falling deeper and deeper into the web of loving her. These people are also Pathans. The fellow who brought me wants me to hurry up and pay.

"A minute," I say. "Let me think."

I'm torn. I don't know. I look at the girl. She looks at me shyly. She has a nice smile and she is pretty. Except for her nose ring and the Pashtu she speaks she could have been someone I had gone to high school with in California growing up, so 'English' does she look.

"What does she think?" I ask.

"What does it matter what she thinks? Just give the money and enjoy!"

Another man comes in from another room and sits with us. He has thick black hair and a heavy moustache, heavy features. I look at him. We've seen each other before when I was at Nasreen's house earlier.

"Do you want this girl?" he asks.

"I want to know what she thinks about this." Am I just being naive?

"She is afraid of you," he chuckles.

Humm, it seems perverted, though I do want to ease the pressure on my heart and mind that this growing obsession with Nasreen is causing.

"How much?" I ask.

The girl smiles and looks down, now coy. The older woman tells me the price. The fellow I've come with quickly adds, "And one hundred rupees for me."

"Why should I give you any money?" I ask him. "Last week I loaned Baba 1200 rupees. Nasreen was in the room, she knows. If you are Baba's son, then

27

you owe me 1100 rupees yet."

"Him? Baba's son?" the other man laughs, surprised. "He's not of their family. He's not Baba's son. He lied to you. He's just an agent."

"Just a pimp!" I scream at him. "You lying scum! Forget it!"

I was going for this girl because I had thought with Baba's oldest son not wanting me around, wanting me to forget Nasreen, the whole scene was rather pointless. Now I find out he's not even related. Then there may be hope. I don't really want to forget her. I can't.

"I didn't come here to just have sex with any girl. I came here to see Nasreen. She is my friend. My heart likes her heart. I'm going back to her house. You get out of here *banchod!*" I scream at the pimp, shoving him toward the door.

"I made a mistake coming here." I tell them. "I thought he was Baba's son. That he didn't want me at their house. I didn't come for a girl, I wanted to see Nasreen. I am sorry."

"She's not nice?" the woman asks me. "You don't like?"

"No, she is very nice," I tell her. And she is. "But I came here from Peshawar to see Nasreen. This damned pimp lied to me."

"Here," I say, handing the girl a 100 rupee note, "This is your present. I am sorry about the mistake."

She takes the pink 100 rupee note from my hand with a smooth plucking motion and hands it directly to the older lady, who stuffs it down her bra. The man and I talk. He assures me this isn't his line of work (I'll listen to anything to be with her again) but he does happen to have been friends with Baba and the family. I know I need some kind of help. I tell him how I feel about Nasreen. He again tells me she isn't married. More uncertainties, but I like him, as I would anyone seeming remotely on my side. I trust him, to an extent.

"Let us go back to her house. I will help you with her mother and the family," he proposes.

"Okay! Let's go!" I'm ready and open to the idea.

We come around the corner to her house. There she is, standing in the doorway of the house next door with another girl. Their *chaddars* are over their shoulders and covering their hair. Her back is to us.

"You're lucky. It's her standing there," my friend says.

"Yes, I know it is. Yes, I know."

She sees me round the corner with this dark haired man and the pimp, who has latched onto us again just as we rounded the corner. She's curt with the man when he speaks. I don't hear what he is saying, I can only look into the abyss of her eyes. We get rid of the pimp, walk the distance to the house, and step down into the front *behtak*. We sit on the bed and are served *pilau* and tea.

"Shall I get them in here for you to talk to?" he says.

"Sure," I say. That is why I came in the first place, isn't it?

He parts the curtained doorway and steps out into the yard.

Nasreen comes into the room, looking upset. She has been crying and doesn't look great, her face swollen and puffy, but I still see her as my Nasreen. It's enough. By now I'm a bit blown out myself. House to house, girl to girl, this story and that, and now here I am facing her.

"What do you want to say?" she asks, standing there limply in front of me.

"How are you? I'm sorry about Baba," I say, "yes I understand it is not a good time right now, can I come back? I just wanted to see you."

She listens. I'd like to take her in my arms and comfort her. I don't even know if she can relate to that kind of sympathy. The mother comes in the room. A big, fat, Pathan woman with large, gold hooped earrings and a colorful scarf tied around her head making her appear as a gypsy. She also has been crying, her eyes rimmed in red. I tell her I came from Peshawar just to see Nasreen.

"Nasreen isn't working because of the death of Baba," she needlessly explains to me.

"I know," I repeat. "I only wanted to see her and say *'salaam'* and that *'I'm sorry about Baba.'* For you too, mother. I also want to know if I have your permission to come back. I know this isn't a good time. I've brought her a present."

I hand Nasreen a small, square, wrapped box—a nose ring I had thrilled over while purchasing in the gold bazaar of Peshawar. She nonchalantly hands the unopened box to a man standing, I now notice, behind her—the one she claims to be her husband. Well, okay, this is his show. What can I do? The mother asks if I want the 1200 rupees I had loaned Baba last week back now. Nasreen must have told her.

"No, not if I can come again. The money can stay with you," I tell her. "Your other son said I could meet with Nasreen tonight, but why, I can't understand."

The mother laughs through her tears. "Who is he to say? He's crazy! Don't listen to his talk." Then she looks at me sternly. "You did a *program* (had sex) with a girl in the other house?"

"No," I tell her. "I came from Peshawar to see Nasreen. She's special for me. Very special. I didn't come just to lay with her. I wanted to see her. My heart's choice is Nasreen. I can wait for her. Now I am also sad about Baba. I'm sorry to your family. To you."

Nasreen looks at me and smiles through her tear glistening eyes. She repeats to the mother what I have just said, it being easier for her to understand my faulted Pashtu than the mother.

"Ah, he is a proper Muslim," the mother smiles. Even in this house religion, Islam, runs strong and deep. It is important. It does seem somewhat ironic to the Western side of my mind. Saving myself from one prostitute for her niece and maybe daughter-in-law who is also in the profession. To the Eastern side of my mind, which is the side forward, it seems perfectly normal.

"You can come in eight to ten days," the mother tells me.

I'm not sure if there is a special set of rules governing this kind of situation or not but I'll go along with what the woman says; she appears to be in charge of the situation. It is sooner than I had expected, but how was it said, *'Needs must, when the Devil drives'*?

I look at Nasreen, "I'll come in ten days then, but I want your and your family's permission."

"I will see you then, we will meet," she smiles. "*Insha'Allah.*"

She and the mother leave the room. My friend remains. A few other male relatives come in and sit down. We chat. The supposed husband comes in and sits across from me. We look into each other's eyes in the silence. I think he is her husband unfortunately. He offers me tea. He knows my story—how I became a Muslim when I was living in Afghanistan and now live in Peshawar; that I am an American, though I've left my country and my family for Islam. It is a big sacrifice he tells them. He must have heard it from her, I don't remember telling him. By 5:00 I'm in the room alone. I am ready to go. She parts the curtain and looks in the room. She enters.

"I'm sorry Noor Mohammad, for this time. You've come a long way. God knows better these things," she assures me. "Next time we will be together."

"*Insha'Allah.*" I add.

I say my goodbyes. Shaking her hand I squeeze it softly. It's hard to let go but the doors are wide open so I can do no more.

Going out into the street I see the husband. I hesitate.

"I'm going now," I say as I approach him.

"Already?" he asks out of politeness, yet with a genuine look of surprise.

"Yes, I must get back to Peshawar. If it is alright with you, I will come back in ten days?"

"Five or six days is fine," he replies.

"Then I'll come next *Juma.*"

We shake hands. Even a brief hug. Is this strange or just normal in Pakistan? What is normal anyway? I don't even know anymore.

Don't know if I ever did.

Chapter 4
Kabuli Jan
(Questions)

Badshahi Mosque from Lahore Fort

April 1st (1988)
Lahore

I'm sitting in the back room of her house. She is squatting in the corner ironing clothes on a towel spread out on the floor. One of her husband's younger brothers, Iqbal, about 20 years old, comes in the room.

"*April fool*," he states.

"Yeah," I say, "it's me. I'm the April fool."

"*April fool.*" Nasreen laughs.

I look at her. "Do you know the meaning of that?"

"Yes.... Why not?"

God, I wonder how many common experiences we share? I can probably count them on my fingers. We are from two completely different cultural backgrounds, upbringings... but I seem to be falling pretty much on her side of the fence. I'm so comfortable in her culture. Something about it is so familiar, so easy to be with. Being with her allows me not only to be in, to live in Pathan society, but to live within it in a way I never imagined possible.

As my capacity for the language grows so does my involvement.

Until the nuances of a language are known one can never do more than scratch the surfaces of a people's culture in my opinion. You can only be an outsider, living in a make-believe world of your own concepts of what you want a people to be. Sometimes I wonder if that stage of innocence is not a better way to experience a culture? To become so involved in a culture definitely has its painful moments and revelations, and its many unfolding wonderments. Mine may only be a rental romance, but then aren't they all, anyway? Isn't this a rental world? Nothing is ever really ours, is it?

31

Every visit to Lahore, every time I see Nasreen, I become more Pathan, more Pakistani—firm emotional roots forming inside me. Slowly I dig up the roots I formed since first arriving in Afghanistan in 1975.

My American roots? In many ways they are an unfathomable distance away in my mind. This relationship is such a powerful transition period. To what, I do not know. I am being forged on an anvil of intense emotions of longing, fullness, desire and emptiness.

Also of course, it is a wild adventure. To get to the heart of a creature like Nasreen is so incredible. She thrills me with her simple, yet so sharp uneducated outlook on life. She is truly alive and vibrant, concerned with the fundamental aspects of living. She's not all wrapped up in phony fashions and outdoing her neighbors materially. God and family take preference. Work is something she was born into. She seems to handle it well. A mixture of self confidence and raw animal energy.

If only my Pashtu were stronger. Even simple conversations are slow and wearing. I can only digest so much Pashtu each week. My progress is good and I am happy with it, but the desire for full fluency is so strong. There is a saying... in Pashtu it is *"Saber trakha da, kho da mewah dera khoga da"*— "Patience is bitter, but its fruits are very sweet."

Can I wait? Maybe my progress is at just the right pace. Enough to get by, but not enough to get into trouble. More trouble, that is. Aren't I in trouble enough already? I can hardly breathe without thinking her name like a hidden *mantra* implanted in my heart by some hypnotizing tantalizing *guru*.

Is it right or is it wrong? The romance and love is overriding the pain, the wrong. What about this husband? Is this really only business as he makes it seem or will I end up on the wrong end of his gun barrel? Can she even relate to my love? She is so alien to me—her thoughts, her actions, her upbringing, her lifestyle. Well then, I am rather alien to myself. I must be to feel so totally in place with all of this. I am surprised at how natural it all seems.

Yet *Juma* to *Juma* I can't believe the bottom won't drop out of all of this. Where is the bottom? Is it only a case of my soul eventually falling through the hole in my heart? I never know what I will walk into when I round the corner on her dead end street, when I knock on her door. Is it just an imagined picture and the situation I am in love with? Or is it her? I just don't know. All I know is Nasreena.*

Is it a beautiful desert oasis that draws me with its sweet smelling flowers or a haunted, empty mirage? The vision draws me on. Am I the only one who has drawn it?

I arrive at her house. A girl I don't know lets me in. We pass behind the curtain which blocks the view of the inside garden courtyard from passersby on the street.

"Nasreena, your Kabuli Jan is here!" the girl shouts toward the back of the house. I chuckle at the girl's unknown play on languages and words. *"Kabuli*

---

* Adding an 'a' at the end of a person's name is a form of endearment.

Jan" is a term applying to people who are from Kabul, Afghanistan. As of yet I have not become so Pakistani that I've shed my Kabuli style turban. I think of another English meaning for the phrase *"Kabuli john"* with a sad chuckle inside.

I cross the yard and see her husband. We greet.

"I'm here to see Nasreen," I tell him.

"That's fine. Welcome."

"No problem?" I ask.

"No. Why?"

"She says she is your wife," I say.

"She's not my wife," he says.

What to believe? God knows I want to believe him, that they are only cousins, that they are not married. But inside I don't think she's the one who is lying.

Nasreen and I are in the back room just sitting together, looking at a small photo album I have brought from Peshawar. Pictures from Los Angeles, my family there and the house I used to live in. My house in Peshawar and some of my local music recording sessions. She sees a picture of me playing *rabab* taken in a recording session in Peshawar.

"Can you sing?" she asks.

"Sure," I tell her.

I hum a few lines of a song I have been writing for her.

"Shhh!" she shushes me, "They are reciting the Holy Qur'an outside on the veranda."

For the past 40 days since Baba's death an old woman has been reciting the *Qur'an Sharif* at the house. Singing is sacrilegious, there can't be any music in the house while the Holy Qur'an is being recited. But they work. I guess it goes under the category of necessity. Sin if you must, work is work.

She takes down a pile of assorted photos from a shelf over the door. We sit together pouring over them, laughing at the amusing ones, her explaining others. It so nice to just be doing something normal with her.

"You can take one of these old pictures," she offers, "but only one, or they will notice."

"Do you want a picture of me?" I ask.

"My husband would hit me if he saw it."

"Banchod."

"He is my husband."

"And the presents I bring you? Do you keep them?"

"He takes most of them. He is my husband. I must. Some I keep, others I hide," she tells me, smiling.

"How long have you been married?"

"Since I was small."

"How small? How many years ago?"

"Maybe 12 years," she offers hesitantly.

"Was it business, or a family marriage?"

33

"Not business," she insists. "He is my cousin."

"How old were you when you came to Lahore? To this house?"

"I was small. Maybe 14 years before."

"How long have you done this work?"

"Maybe a few years."

"How old are you, Nasreen?"

"Oh, I don't know. Leave it!" (in a largely illiterate country such as Pakistan it is not uncommon to run into people, maybe the majority, who do not know their own birth date or even their exact age.)

"I love you," I continue. "When I first met you I didn't know you were married. I wanted to marry you. I still do."

"What is this talk of marriage? Leave it!"

"But I love you. Yours isn't a proper marriage. What kind of husband can sit in one part of his house and be selling his own wife in another room?"

I've never proposed to anyone's wife before, especially with them sitting in the next room, but under the circumstances, why not try?

"My *niyat* (intention) with you in my heart is clean," I tell her. "Do you understand that?"

"Your *niyat* with me is clean." She repeats my words.

"I'm happy just to be with you, to see you, to try to talk. I don't care about the work you do. I care about you."

We lean back on the couch. I put my arm around her slender shoulders and pull her toward me. She lays her head on my shoulder. Her hair is soft and fragrant in my nose.

"I'm unlucky," she whimpers.

"Maybe sometimes, not all the time."

"No, I'm unlucky."

"Come with me. I'll take you out. We'll change your luck. I have enough for two," I say. I don't know if I can believe myself. Sometimes I've barely had enough for myself.

"I don't like this work Noor Mohammad. I am compelled." She looks at me sadly. "What can I do? I must."

I lift her face in my hands. Her dark luminous eyes are moist. I kiss her eyes. They taste the salt of tears. Oh, Nasreena! Do you know or guess how deeply I've dreamed you? You can't. I can't! What are you thinking? What are you feeling? What do you see when you gaze at yourself in the mirror? What do I see?

I want to get her to stop working even if it means I can't have her. I want to help her get clean. Does she want that? Is it just my concept, my love-distorted dream? Is it for the benefit of my conscience? This does infringe on most of my past morals. But as I told her, in my heart, in my intention, I feel clean. Doesn't Islam reaffirm that the intention is as important as the actual action?

Let **Allah** be the judge of true intentions.

It is difficult to change the patterns of our life. Even for me, brought up in a free society, at times it has been so difficult. And it hasn't been anything I have consciously tried to do, just natural progressions. But change is necessary for growth. And growth is necessary, isn't it?

Is it possible for her to conceive of such a thing? Maybe love is clouding my reason. Who am I to change her? Am I just another client? Is she just playing me along? Is it a game? Can I judge what is right anymore? What is wrong?

At times I despise this husband for the way he uses her and treats her. It kills me to see her act like it is all so perfectly normal. That's just how they play it. Is it my western side reacting? I want to plow into change and advance. At least take the chance. Maybe I haven't become as Asian as I think. She is so complacent as to where **Allah** has put her. It is something inherent in Islam. From earliest impressions Muslims learn to accept their fate. God knows best.

My Western upbringing played with me in another way. I'm not so complacent. Who is right? Is there a right? I just drive along as fast as I can go, my foot to the gas pedal. *Insh'Allah*, I can handle the curves. Can I even find a brake pedal to stop?

I do see something soft in her when we are alone. Is it professional coyness? No, I think it is real. My love is real, isn't it? I feel something for her that is more than just external. Outside her movements flow and she is so sleek, like a fox; smooth, easy, even slick. Yet she still maintains that certain demureness that makes Pakistani women so feminine.

Yet I still have so many unanswered questions. Do other men love her? Does she love another man? And what is it with this husband? Is he really her husband? Do other clients treat her so intimately, so kindly, so lovingly? Do they bring her presents? What do they tell her? Has she heard it all before? Does she have any special feeling for me, or does she think I am just some crazy foreigner?

Maybe I can win her if I am persistent. What would I do if I got her, anyway? What am I doing? I am hypnotized in her spell. I feel so much for her. I love her spirit so. I see something so pure in her, yet such a renegade. I love that renegade spirit yet with it runs a corruptness that pains my heart and soul.

Do I want this because it is so different from anything I have ever been involved in before or just because it is so damn impossible? That, I do not know. Now it is irrelevant. A risky, ridiculous, rental romance. Is it impossible? Most people would say so. My logic says so. But my heart is finding it difficult to hear the word impossible. I think of persistence. Persistence can push a blade of grass though a stone in the desert. Enough drops of water can make a hole in a rock. The Grand Canyon? How many drops did that take? How many can I spare?

One morning I arrive at her house at 9:00. Nargis, the girl who had been with my English friend on my first visit, lets me in. I don't see Nasreen. Then I notice the back room door is closed. Can she be working this early? Why not? It is business hours. God it can hurt, though I did know from the start that this is the way it is.

In a couple of minutes she comes out and crosses the yard to the bathroom to wash. I know the trip too damn well. Her customer comes out and leaves while she is still in the bathroom. He could be the man who sat next to me on the Flying Coach down from Peshawar or someone from the tea house earlier this morning. An ordinary anybody. At least he isn't hanging out at the house like me. An ordinary in and out customer (no bad pun intended here).

Finally she comes out of the bathroom and over to me, shyly smiling. She gives me her hand to shake. My heart feels cold and closed. She seems embarrassed that I arrived while she was working. I can't believe how easily she melts my heart, how quickly I open to her. Just to simply see her. Just by a touch. All other impressions are swept away. My anger, jealousy and frustration disappear in my love, in the glow of her smile.

What right do I have to be jealous?

Later, I'm sitting on a *charpoy* with Saira, a new girl. She's young, pretty and wearing a very stylish Punjabi-cut turquoise satin *shalwar kameez*. A filmy transparent white *dupatta* is draped over her shoulders. She's very friendly toward me. We sit and share a cigarette and some juicy sweet *gandari*. I see Nasreen work twice in one hour.

I keep an eye on my watch. The five minutes it takes for her to get it over with seems an eternity. I look at Saira. She warmly smiles at me as she licks the sweet sugar cane juice from her fingers with her pink tongue. I consider. I want to pull some reaction from Nasreen. Maybe if I choose to be with Saira this time it will draw some reaction from her. My body could, but my heart isn't cold enough for this method of attack.

It is her work. I know it isn't against me. It's against herself. How could I be so cold and uncaring as to punish her for it? I did know about it from the start yet that didn't stop me from falling so deeply into her. But knowing that it is just work doesn't make it any less painful. This relationship is difficult, but do I have a choice anymore? She's compelled to work, it's her caste. I am compelled to love her, it's my *qismet*. I can't forget her, can't get her off my mind. Don't know how I could replace her.

Saira looks in my eyes and softly sings a snippet of an Urdu song to me. Her golden nose ring and earrings glitter and jangle in the warm sunlight. Her eyes are dark with *surma*. Nasreen comes over occasionally, giving Saira the eye when she flirts too heavily with me. Is she jealous? I can only hope. She can't sit with me now like Saira. Saira is just sitting, waiting for a customer. Nasreen has work to do around the house; cleaning, washing, cooking, negotiating. Basically, she runs the establishment.

Nargis comes out of the back room and crosses the courtyard to the bathroom to wash. Saira hands me the fresh cigarette she has just lit. "I'll be right back," she smiles.

She goes into the back room with her customer, closing the curtain and the door. She comes out in a few minutes and goes to the bathroom to wash. The john comes out of the back room and leaves with his friend. Saira comes back to me and sits on the edge of the *charpoy*. I hand her back the cigarette she had given me which I have been smoking, the few last puffs remaining.

"Fast work," I laugh. "Fast, fast, finish... *Khuda hafiz.*"

She smiles and picks a fleck of lint off my shirt.

"Where are they?" she asks Nargis.

"They went."

"Fast, fast... *Khuda hafiz*," I repeat. They laugh.

Nargis tells Saira how I keep coming, but only for Nasreen.

"That is the decent way," Saira says. "One man, one woman. This is right."

I give a sad laugh, knowing the one-sidedness of that for me. Saira leans close to me and whispers, her breath moist and warm in my ear. "I was with my own boyfriend last night. We were watching Indian videos on the television. We didn't sleep all night." She shows me a hickey mark on her neck.

"Yeah, I noticed it," I say. We both laugh.

A *dola* (pimp) comes into the yard. A regular shifty, junky type.

"Who brought you?" he questions me. "Which *dola*? Give me some money!"

"I don't need a *dola*. I'm my own personal *dola*," I tell him. "You give me some money!"

The girls laugh.

At her house I spend much time sitting on the *charpoy* on the veranda between the back rooms and the garden courtyard. It is interesting to watch this unusual bordello go through its daily routines. Also I get to see Nasreen. Painfully it is sometimes to see her work. At least they're quick ones. But they are always an eternity to me. At times it doesn't seem strange that this is my girlfriend's house and her work, that I can sit here whilst she's in the back room with some other man and chat with her husband.

People here don't distinguish much between her profession and the entertainment field. Musicians, actors, dancing girls and prostitutes are all *dumaan,* a low caste—the performing arts. Not exactly looked up to in Islam, though a necessary part of life. I suppose I've just fallen into caste—a *rababi* and a *kanjra*.

The joy of watching her brush out her pretty, luxurious brown hair. I'm stealing her in every glance with my eyes. Talking and hanging out with the working girls at her house waiting for their turns. Playing with the children. Occasionally talking with a customer, a pimp, her husband, other family members. It has taken some time to become accepted as more than just a customer (am I?) though I have forced myself on them. I refuse to be treated as just another client. I refuse not to be friendly with everyone in the house. Just as I refuse not to love her.

Saira and I are talking in the back room. Four johns enter. Nasreen comes in the room to run the show followed by three other girls. Her hair is out, down and wavy. Her smile enticing, inviting.

"I'll take you," I joke with her.

"Please sit outside and wait, Noor Mohammada," she tells me.

She takes my cigarette from me as I pass. I brush her satin covered hip with my hand. I sit on the *charpoy* by the door. I mentally check off the girls as they come out of the room. Only two remaining. Then Nasreen comes out. It is always a relief to see the curtain close with her on this side. I do know both sides of it.

One girl goes out followed by her john to the front room. The other girl is doing her work in the back room. These are the only two rooms used for business. The other girls and the next two johns sit on the *charpoys* on the veranda with me. Their friends finish quickly as usual and they all leave. The other two were only waiting. It all feels so normal. What am I doing here? Maybe I should try something easy, like climbing *K2*?* It seems so foolish, so impossible. But then lovers aren't known for their sanity.

What can I say to her husband? "Do you love her?"

What kind of *Western* question is that?

More like "will you sell her?" Ah, now that's more *Eastern*.

Will he sell her? As Anwar Khan in Peshawar pointed out, for him she is a money making machine. I hate seeing her there. I want to take her out. Does she want it?

Am I ready? And then, when you pick a beautiful fragrant rose and remove it from the bed of thorns it grew in, even if you put it in the most fantastic of vases, give it the purest of waters, doesn't it eventually wither and die? Is that where we're at? I can't believe she enjoys her thorns. But is it a question of her enjoying or not? Is this just what I believe?

I don't know what I believe anymore.

I don't know what she believes.

"Are birds ever free of the chains of the sky-ways?"

Later, I'm in the back room again. Nargis is sleeping on the couch. Saira is on a *charpoy* just outside the door curled up and asleep under a diaphanous black *dupatta*. Her golden bangles, double tiered earrings and diamond nose stud are shining through in the golden warm afternoon sunlight. Another girl is asleep in the room with us, on a *charpoy*, a baby suckling at her breast. I'm sitting on the bed with Nasreen. She has just washed her hair and it is still slightly damp, dark and wavy. She's wearing cream-colored *shalwar kameez* with a thin gold stripe glistening through the weave. The room is warm and sultry, though the looseness of my *shalwar kameez* permits me to stay fairly comfortable.

Comfortable? Here I am sitting with my prostitute girlfriend in a room full of *whores. Whores?* They're just people and my friends. This is just their profession. Their lot in life. Sometimes life can be so strange. This feels so peaceful and relaxed, so normal.

"Noor Mohammad, can I have 100 rupees?" Nasreen asks.

"Is it for you, or your husband?" I ask, a little too loudly.

"Shhh!" She puts her slender finger to her lips, frowning. "It's for me. I need."

I take out my wallet and give her a 100 rupees. Then I notice how little

---

* *K2* - *the second-highest mountain on Earth, after Mount Everest (also see glossary)*

money is left in my wallet.

"Ummm. I'm not sure I have enough to get back to Peshawar now," I tell her.

"No problem," she says, and hands me back my 100 rupees.

"Will this help?" I hand her a 50 rupee note.

"Thank you," she says as she slips it into her bra.

"Nasreen," I say. She looks at me. "Do other people come for you as often as I do?"

"No. Why?"

"I'm glad," I sigh. She smiles.

"What if I stop coming?"

"Why do you talk like this? Have you found another girl you like?"

"No. But this is so very difficult for me. I love you too much. It is not the right way for me. For you. And besides, you don't love me anyway."

"I don't?" she asks seductively smiling.

"Would you care if I didn't come back again?"

"Yes. I would be sad. You are my friend now. I like you."

"Like and love are different."

"Love? What is love? How can somebody like me know what love is? How can you love somebody like me?"

"I don't know. I keep asking myself that same question. I just do. You say you like me? Why?"

"I don't know, I just do."

"Why? Because you like my business?"

"Don't talk like that. Leave that talk. People come here, they pay. We spend a little time with them, then they go. Sometimes we give them tea or water. Noor Mohammad, you stay all day. I give you lunch every time because I like you. You have to pay my husband sometimes. He is my husband. It is our family business. I am sorry for that. I am compelled. But I like you."

"I love you, my sweet friend."

I hold her hands in mine. She softly hums a Pashtu melody to me. I kiss her hands. We fall back on the bed and hold each other tightly. I stroke her moist hair. She fumbles with her bra, taking out a pack of Gold Leaf cigarettes. We laugh together.

"What else do you have hidden in there?" I laugh, playfully grabbing.

"Stop it, Noor Mohammada! We're not alone. They might wake up and see."

"So what?" I say as I light her cigarette.

"We are still in Pakistan. This isn't *Amerika*."

I take her hand and kiss it again, my lips lingering on her long slender fingertips. "Oh, Nasreena," I sigh, "I love you so much. I am going crazy for you!"

"Leave it, my friend. We can only be together this way."

"But I can't leave it. I want you so bad."

"You have me—now."

"I want you always."

"That cannot be. We must accept how God wants it."

"I cannot," I say, frustrated. "We can change it."

"No. We must accept."

I hold her closer, my lips lightly brushing her soft face.

Why can't I be so complacent and accept fate as she does? Why do I want her so? How did I become so consumed?

GT Road near Attock

Chapter 5
GT Road

In 1977 a red haired fellow came into Enshallah Imports, my Afghan import store in Los Angeles. His family lived around the corner. He had been drawn in by a black silk Peshawari turban that hung on the wall, glimpsed one night whilst peeking through my window, and a dream of going to Afghanistan and riding horses through Central Asia. I fed him *Kabuli pilau* and tales and pictures of Afghanistan as we drank dark Heineken and sweet black tea. We became fast friends and brothers in our dreams of Afghanistan.

In March of 1978 we met up again in Kabul. Partially planned, partially by chance (as if anything ever is). He had left the United States in November 1977 to go to a riding academy in England. I had flown into Afghanistan in February on one of my annual after-Christmas buying trips. He had told me he would try to be in Afghanistan at the beginning of the year. I told him to leave a message for me at the American Embassy, though I never happened to go there to pick it up. As it was we ran into each other on *Kuche e Murgha** one day as I was transporting newly purchased carpets back to my room with the aid of a ten-year-old boy, the servant from my friend's shop.

We journeyed through the snowy whiteness of the Hindu Kush via the Salang Pass to the fabled cities of Mazar-i-Sharif and Balkh. To Aqcha, where I helped him aquire his first Central asian saddle and accoutrements. From there my path lay southwest, over an icy and muddy rut of a road through Turkestan to another fabled city, fabulous Herat, in Khoristan near the Persian border—collecting carpets, marvelous sights and enchanted memories. He went east to Kunduz.

Our paths met again back in Kabul before I headed off, east this time, over the Khyber Pass to Peshawar. He headed west, back to Herat and on to Iran, Turkey and Europe.

Back in Los Angeles we still met in my shop and ate *pilau* and drank our dark Heineken and sweet black tea and talked of Afghanistan. He wanted to ride horses across Afghanistan, a dream that altered as Russian troops hunkered in for a prolonged decimating war of oppression and suppression in our beloved Afghanistan. Now we talked of the high, barren mountains of Northern Pakistan, the Karakorams. To ride horses through Hunza, even as far as riding down into Peshawar, a city we were told was now swarming with Afghan refugees and *mujahideen*....

"The city of Peshawar was coined the *'Paris of the Pathans'* back in the thirties by journalist Lowell Thomas. It was also known as "the city of a thousand and one sins" and "the gateway to Kabul, Bokhara and Central Asia." It derives its name from a Sanskrit word *Pushpapura*, meaning "city of flowers." The great Emperor Babar even mentioned the flowers of Peshawar in his memoirs when he marched through the historic Khyber Pass in 1526 to conquer the

---

* *Kuche e Murgha (Farsi) - Literally Chicken Street; a street in Shari Nau, Kabul, Afghanistan with many handicraft shops and restaurants/hotels for tourists.*

Indo-Pakistan subcontinent, founding the Mughal Empire.

Alexander's legions and the southern wing of his great army marched through in 327 B.C. and held up for 40 days in a fort at Pushkalavati (Lotus City) 17 miles northeast of Peshawar near present day Charsadda. The pass and valley have resounded to the tramp of marching feet as successive armies hurtled down this crossroads of history, pathway of commerce, migration, and invasion—Aryans, Scythians, Persians, Greeks, Bactrians, Kushans, Huns, Turks, Mongols and Mughals.

Peshawar is now, as always, very much a frontier town. The Land of the *Pathans*, it is a completely male dominated society. North and south of Peshawar spreads the vast tribal area where lives the largest tribal society in the world and the most well known, though much misrepresented.

Peshawar has seen the passage of 25 centuries. It is the journey's end, or at least a long halting place for those traveling up north or coming down from the Middle East or Central Asia. It is redolent with the smells of luscious fruits, roasted meats and tobacco smoke, placid and relaxed, yet pulsating with the rhythms of craftsmen's hammers and horses' hooves, darkened with tall houses, narrow cobbled lanes and intricately carved overhanging balconies."

It was September 1982 and we met again in Delhi, India. He was waiting for me in a small hotel built around the Qazi Wali Mosque in Pahar Ganj bazaar where I had sugessted he wait for me. I (true to form) arrived two weeks late. In our room we read from a small green book, *'Elementary Lessons in Islam,'* and began the process of teaching ourselves how to pray. We started growing into the fresh identities of our new names. He had taken the name Mirza (from the Urdu poet Mirza Asadullah Ghalib). I had been using Noor Mohammad off and on since becoming a Muslim in 1978 in Kabul. We practiced our first prayers shyly, away from all eyes but **Allah's**, on the roof of the mosque in the shadow of its scalloped white domes and many spired pink minarets. We listened to the *Azan* from our small bedroom window that looked down into the mosque as if it were a magical incantation, a beckoning.

By the end of September we crossed the border from Amritsar (Attari Road/Wagha) to Lahore and were soon in the far reached northern mountains of Gilgit Agency. At that time the Karakoram Highway wasn't yet completed to China though we went as far as one could get, to the small village of Passu in Gojal, Upper Hunza, at the foot of the 58 mile long Batura Glacier. Somehow, by naive determination it seems, we acquired two farm ponies and a piece of rope—and with a farmer named Mir Zamon (who had never been further than Gilgit) as our guide we set off to ride to Peshawar.

Of course we never made it. Mir Zamon went back to irrigating his fields barefoot after the second day. We camped in Karimabad, Hunza, to discover much to our dismay that one of our horses had a hole the size of a quarter (US) in his back. I rode our remaining horse to Gilgit alone, two long days in the saddle. Mirza went ahead by jeep to see if other horses could be had there.

Through a mutual friend we met the owner of a well known book store, Ghulam Mohammad Baig, a man of much local power and influence. Though Mr. Baig tried to help, it seemed we were just not destined to make the journey at this time. Winter snows were rapidly closing the mountain passes.

We flew down to Rawalpindi from Gilgit in one of PIA's Fokker planes through the Karakorams, flying not much higher than, indeed, sometimes lower than the snow covered mountain tops. Pindi to Peshawar by bus, settling in and becoming again involved with Afghans and Afghanistan. Old friends from Kabul, and new ones arriving in a steady stream as refugees trudged over the mountains from war torn Afghanistan. Our lives became more and more intrinsically involved in Peshawar and Pakistan and with our many Afghan friends on both sides of the border. I started making acquaintances and re-acquaintances in the music scene and buying handicrafts for select customers I still had in the United States.

I had originally gone to Afghanistan not so much to start an import business as to record music and learn to play local instruments. In Afghanistan I traveled everywhere with a small tape recorder, recording and playing with local musicians. Eventually, in Kabul I met a *rabab* player named Mir Mohammad, who played for Radio Afghanistan, and my heart was won over to the study of the *rabab*.

In Peshawar I wandered in Dabgari Bazaar where most of Peshawar's Pashtu musicians kept rooms; where they could meet, hang out and where customers could come when looking for a band to book for a function. Armed with my small tape recorder I wandered looking for *rababs* and *rabab* players.

It was there I met Shah Wali, a very well known Pashtu singer from Afghanistan, Amir Jan Herati, his *rabab* player, and became friends with the rest of his band—some of Peshawar's most accomplished session players. I met a young musician about 17 years old named Master Ali Haider and we became fast friends. He introduced me to many Peshawari musicians, including *rabab* players Ustad Baktiare and Mukhtiare Ustad.

By 1986 I was full-fledge bringing recording equipment to Peshawar with the dream of opening a Pashtu music recording studio. I set up my first small studio in a house I rented in *Koochie* Bazaar. Then in early 1987 I was recording in a room in the Amin Hotel on GT Road in Hashtnagri.

In March of 1987 Mirza and I were sitting in his room at the Amin Hotel. We were looking at a map of the Karakoram Highway, the famous Silk Route, just being completed over the Kunjarab Pass into Kashgar, China. We were talking of a trip—a horse trip to China.

We could ride north to Chitral from Peshawar along the Afghan border. Mirza had done this leg of the journey solo back in 1983. Then we would ride westward from Chitral over the Shandur Pass to Gilgit. We would ride up to GM Baig's shop in Gilgit, then north, via Hunza and the 16,000 foot Kunjarab Pass into China and on to Kashgar. It would be over 1500 miles, through some of the highest mountains in the world. We would be in the Hindu Kush, the Hindu Raj, the Karakoram and the Himalayan mountain ranges. It would be a monumental ride. This wouldn't be like our inexperienced try on farm ponies from Hunza in '82. We would prepare, we would be ready. This would be a real expedition!

1987 saw Mirza at his job working with Afghan *mujahideen* and me teaching English part-time at IRC (International Rescue Commission) to Afghans. It helped with my Farsi and Pashtu and secured my visa to stay in Pakistan. It was a time of many aid organizations in Peshawar, helping and living off the Afghan war; a time of many intrigues and bomb explosions in and around Peshawar.

We had moved from the Amin Hotel to Takhal, on the outskirts of Peshawar, where I built my recording studio. I was working with Master Ali Haider, who was coming up in the music scene, and other local and Afghan musicians.

Mirza went back to the U.S. in the end of '87. I stayed in Peshawar.

On January 2nd, 1988 I moved back into the old city of Peshawar, to the house of Bibi Ji in *Mohallah* Gari Saidan in Hashtnagri. Bibi Ji's husband had been a highly esteemed doctor in Peshawar, their family an old and respected family of *Sayids*. The doctor's ancestry was from Bukhara and Bibi Ji's roots were in Iran. A very serious and dour lady with a heart as large as her linage and grand old house, Bibi Ji warmly accepted me into her household as a part of her extended family.

All the while the dream of the horse trip never died. It grew and grew. Mirza had been making preparations in the United States with his wife to be, a photography student. By the beginning of '88 they had gotten some minimal sponsors, collected equipment and information and had done some radio and television publicity stories.

And me... I had stepped off a cliff in Lahore and was quickly being swept away by the river that is Asia—in the arms of a Pathan girl.

May, 21st, 1988, afternoon,
Lahore
Waiting for the Flying Coach to Pindi (Rawalpindi). *Ramazon* is over. Mirza and Shelly have arrived from the USA and it's time to get busy with this horse trip. Since February only one thought has occupied my mind—Nasreen.

Deep down a part of me doesn't even want to do this horse trip. Not if it means leaving her. Yet this is something I've dreamt for so long—before I ever guessed there would be a Nasreen.

Walking around the bus stands I see a lady squatting, holding a sleeping baby girl on her shoulder. A little boy is standing next to them, holding on to the woman's arm and kissing the baby's face and softly touching its eyes. Pakistan is a beautiful place I think fondly. I look away from them into the dust, dirt, traffic and noise and feel the heat of May in Lahore.

"*Oh Nasreena! Whyee*.*" I moan to myself. Life can be strange.

Many pretty girls around the bus stands. To glance at them, many are

---

*Whyee - Pashtu exclamation — "Oh my!"

desirable looking. I don't fear replacing Nasreen by looks, though. It is something else that has so captivated me with her. It's her spirit I want to get close to, her wildness, her simple, smooth slickness, her shy coyness that I've fallen in love with.

I enjoy the uneducated simplicity of her being. She has a certain strong, worldly, streetwise education, picked up in her house, in her business. It is something I like so much in her. Maybe uneducated, but definitely not dumb or dull. It's the very part of my education I value most. My nights on the rock and roll road, playing on the smokey spotlit stage—in the mountains, the deserts. Walking starry Topanga Canyon (outskirts of LA) nights with my Alsatian German Shepherd, Max. Wandering the beaches of California, Hawaii, Morocco and Southern India. Arriving in Herat, Afghanistan, from Meshad (Iran) in 1975, completely fresh and knowing so little about Asia. Drawn like a moth into a flame. I think of a Pashtu verse...

"It's good that your eyes are very small, because if they were ever big they would surely eat me."

Well, hers are big. I've been eaten. I'm being devoured.

In Peshawar I had bought her a watch for an *Eid* present. Walking home with it in my pocket I wondered if she would know how to use it. An amusing thought, to buy your girlfriend a watch and then not even know if she can tell time. Earlier I found out....

Second day of *Eid*
May 21, 1988
Lahore
We were alone together in the back room, sitting on the bed. She had jasmine blossoms, lily white and pearl pink, plaited into her long dark hair and in her ears in place of earrings. I breathed in her sweet fragrance as I gave her the *Eid* card I'd brought from Peshawar.

I read her the couplet by *Rahman Baba*, the famous Pashtoon mystic and poet, which I had painstakingly written on the card in Pashtu. I knew she couldn't read it but I wanted to do it. A friend in Peshawar had guessed that I had some involvement with a Pathan girl and had taught it to me...

*"Che po meena ki, Majnoon ghunday, sadiq vee
Che Layla, po darwaza ki, darbon neeshta."*
(When you are in love like Majnoon, all is right
When Layla is at the door, there is no guard.)

I gave her a *dupatta* for her mother. I had given her one like it before and she had asked if I would bring her one for her mother.

"Don't tell anyone," she said, putting her *henna* stained finger to her pouted lips. She slid a metal trunk out from under a *charpoy* and put the *dupatta* in it.

I gave her the watch, which I had carefully wrapped. She ripped the wrapping paper off and nonchalantly dropped it to the floor. She looked at the watch.

"Do you know how to tell time?" I asked.

"A little," was her answer.

I looked at the face of the watch. It was the most feminine one I could find, with the smallest band. Her wrists are so slim, and besides I didn't want to take any chances to see it on her husband. There were no numerals on the face, only tiny sparkling diamonds in their places. The time was 10:15. She looked at the watch.

"What time is it?" I asked.

"Leave it!" she pushed my shoulder and frowned.

"Is it for your husband?"

"No, it is for my sister,"

In Pakistan it is not unusual to give a gift received away to another. No embarrassment is attached. The way I grew up I got attached to seeing my gifts kept and used by the person I had given them to. Leave it! Constantly concepts and preconceptions are falling away.

"That's okay," I told her, "It is a gift from my heart to your heart. Do you understand that?" I said, checking my Pashtu.

"Yes. Thank you. And I have an *Eid* present for you also, Noor Moham-mad."

She tossed the *Eid* card on the shelf over the door. Then she got up on the bed and stood on her tiptoes. She got a small paper bag from the back of the shelf. I tickled the bottoms of her feet.

"Stop it!" she giggled, coming down and sitting next to me. She handed me the paper bag, smiling. "This is for you, Noor Mohammad. Please do not tell anyone I gave you any presents. Not Mama, nor the other girls. Especially not my husband!"

I reached into the bag and pulled out a slim black watch trimmed with gold.

"Our think is one think," she laughed. "For this watch water is no prob-lem. I saw you drop your watch when you took it off to make *wuzu*. This one you can leave on. My sister went with me to the bazaar to get it. She is my friend. Only she knows. Don't tell anyone else. They would hit me. They were upset I gave you the picture. They noticed it was gone."

"I'm sorry, I'd like to take my own picture of you. Like you are now. Natu-ral. In the other picture you had so much makeup. I'll bring a camera,"

"No! They would be upset."

"There won't be any trouble. They won't know. I'll bring a very small cam-era." I explained. She shrugged.

"Look in the bag, Noor Mohammada. There is something else."

I turned out the bag. A lapis lazuli silver ring fell out. She helped push it onto my little finger.

"A guest was here. Saira was with him. He was wearing this ring. I told Saira to try to get it from him, that I wanted to give it for you. It is like the blue stones you brought me from Peshawar. I knew it was your design."

"You are my design sweetheart. I like you. Nargis said you were waiting for me yesterday?"

"I wanted to see you on *Eid*. You said you would come on *Eid*. I was sad.

I thought you forgot. I am happy now to see you."

"Oh Nasreena, I love you so," I moaned, taking her sweet face in my hands. "Don't you know?"

"I know," she purred, closing her eyes and smiling sweetly. Then she scrunched up her face in frustration and confusion. "I don't know. I can't know anything. We are friends but we cannot love. It isn't possible. It's no good."

"I can't help it."

"I cannot love. My brain is messed up. My think is no good."

"Your work is no good. Why not leave it? You don't like it."

"I like it with you," she smiled seductively. Then she got up off the bed. "Come on. They will wonder what we are doing in here so long. They will knock. Let us go now. And remember, don't tell anyone about the gifts."

"Of course. I promise."

I hid them in my bag. She opened the curtain with a well-practiced flick of the wrist and we walked out into the bright sunlight on the veranda. I sat on a *charpoy* and she brought me lunch. Then it was time I must go. I was already two hours late in leaving to meet Mirza in Pindi as planned.

I stepped into the back room. She was standing there with some customers, discussing prices and which girls they wanted. She looked so pretty, so smooth, sleek and totally in charge. Her bright, dark eyes slay me.

"I need my bag and cap," I told her. "I must leave for Pindi to meet my brother. I am already late."

She handed me my things from the *charpoy* on which they were lying.

"Are you coming on *Juma*?" she queried.

"I'm not sure. Friday, Saturday or Sunday I will come, *Insha'Allah*."

She held her hand out to me. I took it. She melts me in her liquid smile and shining eyes, her silvery voice.

"Good bye," she said in English. "Bye, bye."

"Bye bye, cutie," I answered, also in English. Then, "*Wa aleikum asalaam.*"

I squeezed her hand, trying to suck her essence into me. It's hard to let her go—hard to separate. Finally, I let it slip away.

"*Pa makha day kha. Good bye.*" *

As I turned to walk out I hear one of the johns asking if I am an *Englaise* (English). No, she said, he is my friend from Peshawar.

How do I break her spell?

I went out and closed the metal front door. Walking down her dead end street, feeling the usual fullness and emptiness. I took a *rickshaw* to the Flying Coach stand and sat on the hard, brown, leather bench in the waiting room and tried to write. The bus was honking. Time to go.

June 7th
Peshawar

Twenty trips to Lahore. Twenty trips to see Nasreen. A time of contrasts and paradoxes. Of love of loving God and plunging headlong into living life in

---

* *Pa makha day kha (Pashtu) — goodbye, literally 'face the good.'*

Pakistan. A time of loving Nasreen beyond all reason, falling ever deeper into the well of her eyes, into her hypnotic mesmerizing spell. Painting both sides of the page.

I don't feel I am hurting anyone. It's not like she was married to some nice unsuspecting husband. Her husband is a snake-eyed pimp who sells her body. He eats her blood.

Am I hurting her? That, I would never want to do. Maybe it is me who is getting hurt? Why should I be afraid of hurting her? She is only a *kanjra*, isn't she? I just know that no matter who or what she is, I don't want to hurt her. It doesn't matter what she is, I love her.

Seeing to government ministers and other matters in Islamabad, Pindi and Peshawar in preparation for the horse expedition. Through all of it all I can think of is her. Luckily Mirza drags me along and we do get things accomplished. For so long we have talked of this trip, planned it, prepared and dreamed. Now that it has come so close to reality it is strange to have my mind off all the time on something else—on Nasreen. Is it? Who are we to say in which directions we go, and when? God knows better. Sometimes unplanned things hit us so very hard.

Just returned from Lahore and now I'm back in Lahore again. Always I give a prayer of thanks for another safe journey on GT Road.

Down on the morning bus from Peshawar, arriving mid-afternoon. I get a shave and a shine at a barber shop, pick up a big bag of fruit to give to the family and then go out to her house. I tell the *rickshaw* driver to stop where there is a stall selling flowers by a street side shrine—yellow marigold garlands hanging on a brick wall. I buy some. The vender wraps them in damp newspaper and string. I get to her house and she lets me in. I hand her the flowers. She takes them and I go in the back room to wait for her. She comes in.

"Where did you put the flowers?" I ask.

"Oh, they're outside. I don't like flowers in the house. They are messy, and then they die. They are in the yard with the other flowers. These are better in the house." she says, signifying a vase with plastic flowers.

She brings a pitcher of ice cold lemonade. The icy condensation is beading silvery sweat on the gleaming stainless steel pitcher. Even with the ceiling fan on droplets of warm perspiration roll down my back and chest under my loose shirt. I drink glass after glass as she pours.

At 4:30 I offer my *Asr* prayer in the back room right next to the bed where we have lain so many times. I turn my head over my right shoulder in the final *salaam* of the prayer and see her husband outside the door. He is finishing his prayers as well. At sunset I offer my *Maghrib* prayer in the yard next to him. Is it strange we can be together in that, yet at such opposite ends?

Yes, but no. I don't think so. This is an aspect that draws me ever deeper into Islam. No matter where we are in this world, we're all together with God. We may not be the same in God's eyes, that is for God to say, but we will all face the same God one day. Right now, I'm in Nasreen's house praying next to her husband. Is this a contradiction, or are there any contradictions? Nargis comes in the back room and sees I have folded the prayer rug and have put it on the bed. She quickly picks it up exclaiming, "*Toba...* the bed is dirty. We work on it."

"Yeah. Right." I answer her in English. "*Ah cha.*"

The girls move four *charpoys* into the center of the yard. They cover them with soft quilts and cushions. Her husband, one of his brothers, some friends and I eat our dinner there. A big bowl of buffalo stomach pieces sits before me swimming in spicy, greasy red gravy. Not my favorite dish though a Peshawari/Pathan delicacy. There's also a flat, straw basket piled with *roti.* She comes over and spoons more onto my plate.

"Eat Noor Mohammad. I cooked this specially for you."

"Thanks," I answer.

The women sit on *charpoys* on the veranda to eat. Later we all lounge on the padded *charpoys.* It's comfortable, a chance to be with the family. Strange family? The husband's wife is my lover and he encourages it. After all, it is his livelihood.

Saira, Nargis, a few of the other girls and some children are sitting with us; her mother, her sister and her sister's baby, Shahbo. Just being easy, talking, smoking and relaxing. In Pakistan it is so easy to just sit and be together. You don't always have to be doing something. Just being together is enough.

It's a warm, hazy evening. We're sitting in the cool, muggy breeze of an oversized swamp cooler watching a mottled, swollen yellow full-moon rising over the minaret-pierced skyline of Lahore. Flags are fluttering from the rooftops. Nasreen is sitting in front of me bouncing Shahbo on her lap. The pale moonlight is reflected in her sparkling eyes and lights her golden glittering earrings and nose ring with a warm rich glow. Her diamond teeth flash and the dim light accentuates the graceful movements of her slender arms and hands.

I hear the call to prayer wafting through the tepid night air from the neighborhood mosque. **Allah**-u-Akbar (God is Great). Her husband has gone somewhere with his mother and brother. She gives me a signal with her flashing eyes and an ever so slight flick of her head. We get up and go into the front room and sit on the bed.

"Well, do you want to do a program?" she asks.

"I don't just come for business, you know," I tell her. "I don't only come for your body."

"Why come?"

"To see you makes me glad. I wish you loved me. I wish you could come with me. I wish there were two Nasreens."

"There are two Nasreens. One is here," she says, placing her hand on her heart.

"That is the Nasreen I want. I want your heart, I want your soul. I want all of you, always. I'm unlucky. I found you. I fell in love with you but you are married. You don't understand my love."

"You have this Nasreen, Noor Mohammad," she says, taking my hand and holding it over her softly beating breast.

"Not like this. It isn't right."

"I'm compelled in this life, in this work. It is the work of my family, our caste. There is no other way for me. No other way for us."

"Nasreen, I want to have my own wife, just like you. I like your design. Can there ever be another?"

"Then you will forget Nasreen?"

"No, I won't forget you. How can I ever forget you? It is you I want! I cannot have you, yet I cannot forget you. I will always love you my dear sweet Nasreen."

"Don't love! Leave it! It's not possible. It's not right. Only *bizzness* I can do." *

"Is it only business with you? You don't have any love?"

"For you there is some love."

"You say there is some love. Where? I love you truly, with all my heart. Don't you know that?"

"I don't know what to know."

"Why not? Don't you understand my language?" (because she is uneducated some of the Pashtu words my educated mind has learned are not even in her vocabulary. I do try to learn the common words but it is hard to get all the inflections down. My Pashtu grammar is not the best).

"No, I understand your talk," she says defensively. "Your Pashtu is good Noor Mohammad. But what can I do? My brain is messed up."

"Just now messed up or all the time?"

"All the time."

"Yeah, my brain is messed up too. Messed up for you. I'm going crazy for you darling."

"Then?"

"Then? Then I love you dearest. Oh, Nasreena, my love! Can't you see?"

"Don't love me Noor Mohammad. You can't! We can't love!"

"Why? Is all you know business?"

"Leave it!"

"No, I won't leave it. You don't love. It is only business for you!"

"Only bizzness." She laughs. "It must be only bizzness."

"Is that what you think?"

"Don't think! Just give the money."

"Give the money?" I shout. "Is that all you know? Is that all you feel after all this time? You don't love! It's only business."

"So, then?"

"So then? So then call Saira to come in the room."

"Saira? Why Saira? What are you saying?"

"It is only business you say? Well, if that is all it is for you I'll do my business with Saira. Your family will still get their money."

"You say you come every time for me. What are you lying?"

"I come for your love. You tell me not to love. You say it is only business."

"You are my friend. I like bizzness with you."

---

* She uses the English word for business pronounced "bizzness."

"You like my presents! My money. Not me!"

She picks up a tea cup and saucer and throws them at me. They shatter on the wall behind my head, covering the bed with tiny shards. Oh God, finally a response from her. Thank you. I've tried so hard to catch her off guard, to see how she really feels, instead of mouthing the words I'm sure she is conditioned to reply.

She spins to the door, reaching up for the latch at its top. The golden sequins on her white *dupatta* send sparks from the bare light bulb across the room. I come up behind her, turn her around and hold her trembling arms. She halfheartedly tries to at scratch me. I hold her close to me. She struggles, then relaxes in my arms. I kiss her face. She finally, softly, returns my kisses. It is always such an accomplishment to get a kiss from her; she is such a prude.

"Nasreena, oh Nasreen, I love you so much. I do only come for you. I only want you to show me you care."

"Care? Why care?"

"Because I love you!" I insist.

"Don't love me! Don't care! It's no use. It isn't possible."

"Why? Why not?" I plead, shaking her by the shoulders. I can't take no for an answer. I thought I had just made a breakthrough but here we go in circles again. Her hair flies across her face.

"What can I do? I have a marriage. Change is not possible. This is my *qismet*, my fate."

"Now your *qismet* is my *qismet*. Your marriage is not a right marriage. He's not your husband. He is your pimp!" I shout, utterly frustrated. She closes her eyes tightly and screws up her pretty face. I hold her tighter. Her back is cool and damp in the stifling room.

"It is a marriage." she stubbornly insists.

"It's not! Why won't you see?" I can be stubborn too. I won't take no for an answer in this.

"Noor Mohammada, this is my life. This is my family, this is my place. You will go back to Peshawar. Your friends will find you a 'clean' girl and you will get married. You will forget Nasreen. Why can't *you* see?"

"No! I won't forget you. Oh, I want you so bad my flower."

"You have me."

"It's not right like this. And it isn't enough," I protest. "I want you always. Not just on rent for a few hours a week."

"You have me, Noor Mohammad," she again insists.

"No I don't! For that reason I am sad. I am unlucky. I found you but you keep telling me you are married."

"I am. What can I do? Don't think about it. For now I am your wife."

"It's not true. Not like this! You are my sweet friend, maybe my rental wife, but you are not my real wife."

"What in this mortal world is real, Noor Mohammad? We are here now, what more can we do?"

"I don't know what more I can do. I will try not to love you like this. It is too difficult for me. Too painful. You are my big problem."

"What problem?"

"I love you too much!"

"You are my sweet friend also," she repeats. "I don't like this work. That, I think you know. It's not my choice. But it is my life. It is God's choice. Change is too difficult. I don't know any other way. Maybe there is no other way! But with you I like."

I hold her close, kissing her again.

"Come next *Juma*, I'll be waiting," she whispers. "Now it is getting late. My husband and Mama will be returning. You should go now."

"I'll count the hours," I tell her, looking at my new watch. She laughs.

"Really, it's true," I assure her.

I never know how much she can believe me. Unfortunately, it feels so doomed. It is her soul I want to reach. I've gone beyond the satin of her clothes. I want to get beyond the silk of her skin, to touch her heart. If I touch it will it burn me? Already I'm burning in my love. What am I playing at? It sure seems serious to me. But then it's nothing, I guess, compared to those fellows who hijacked that plane in Karachi.*

Peshawar City — wedding street late one night

---

* Referring to the 1988 trial and sentencing taking place in Karachi of the high-jackers of Pan Am Flight 73 that occurred on September 5, 1986.

Chapter 6
Horses, Weddings and Rababs

*F*rom Lahore I had a new destination—I caught a night minivan to Sargodha. In Rawalpindi we had heard that the Pakistani Army had a horse breeding farm somewhere near Sargodha. My mission was to find it and see if there was any possibility of acquiring horses there. Up to this point we hadn't had any luck in the animal markets of Peshawar; nor Pindi, not to mention the famous animal market of Taxila. We had gone there with an Afghan friend from Kunduz who raised *buzkashi* horses but among hundreds of water buffalo, cows, sheep and goats all we found was one very young and green pony.

Arriving in Sargodha at 3:00 A.M. I walked the streets looking for a hotel. There was just ever so slight a tinge of cooling still night air before the dawn. I stopped at a cigarette/*paan* stall to buy a Gold Leaf cigarette. I gave the elderly proprietor a rupee. He took a thin strip of paper from a little tin can and held it over a small oil wick lamp, igniting it. Then he held it to my cigarette, lighting it as I pulled a drag. He pointed me toward what he said was a cheap hotel. As I turned to walk away he asked me if I were a Pathan. I answered his question by saying I was from Peshawar.

"I thought so," he said. "I can always tell a Pathan by the way he walks."

At the hotel I drank a cup of *chai* in the open-front restaurant. The manager woke a boy sleeping on a *charpoy* under a grease encrusted quilt that had once boasted a colorful floral pattern. The boy got up rubbing his sleep smeared eyes, his dusty black disheveled hair sticking out like so many pine needles, and picked up a small hand broom from the corner. He went upstairs to sweep out a room for me.

The plaster was cracking off the cement walls of the tiny room. There was a small bathroom with no door and no running water in the sink; an Asian squat toilet with a plastic *lota* next to it, a grimy cracked useless sink and a phosphorescent orange plastic bucket. An equally garish lime-green plastic scooper cup comprised the rest of the bathroom accessories. Water was supplied by a tap in the wall placed two feet above the soap slimed concrete floor. The only window was fixed permanently open with strong wire screen stretched tautly across it. From the cobwebbed ceiling hung an ancient electric propeller fan. The bed had a travel-stained striped sheet over the thin lumpy mattress and equally chunky pillow. The boy left me a small dirty many-times-used towel for my personal use.

After a few fatigued hours of sweaty sleep I rose and doused my body in water that retained only a slight coolness from the early dawn hours. I went down to the restaurant for a breakfast of *cholay, parattas* and *chai*. I was delightfully surprised when I was informed that the Army Remount Depot was just on the outskirts of town—no more than a ten minute *tonga* ride away.

At the gate of the Remount Depot a crisply uniformed guard nodded and returned my *salaam* from inside his guard booth. I walked through the stately military stud farm on a road lined with ancient gnarled trees. I came upon several gardeners tending flower beds and told them I was an American Muslim and asked if there was somebody to whom I could speak. They directed me to a barrack where some young soldiers lounged about in various stages of dress, smoking, off duty.

They didn't speak Pashtu nor English, so after tea and a cigarette one of them took me to a dispensary and left me there. One of the fellows there spoke some English. I explained to him that I was looking to buy horses and again asked if there was anybody on the base with whom I could talk. He pointed me across the field where three men sat at a long table and watched as various horses were put through their paces in the field in front of them. I declined the offer of another tea and started down the well-tended dirt road to the table.

The Major spoke excellent English, with British overtones, as many of Pakistan's favored upper class do (British educations). After I introduced myself and told him of my quest to purchase horses he said the man I needed to talk to was the base commander, Colonel Chugtai. As he was just now finishing testing these horses he would take me to the colonel's office.

We entered through an anteroom and sat in straight back wood and wicker chairs behind a massive glass topped oak desk. On the desk were a gleaming brass pen holder and an equally shiny brass holder containing a small Pakistani flag, glass balls and cubes of onyx (paper weights to keep papers from being blown about by the circulating air of the overhead fan) and *Eid* cards. On the wall behind the large padded leather armchair was a Pakistani Army calendar displaying tanks manuvering across a field. Next to it was a framed picture of *Quaid-i-Azam*, Mr. Jinnah (the founder of the State of Pakistan) and several pictures of horses and carriages.

The Major and I sat and chatted, discussing matters of mutual interest. An aged orderly brought us glasses of ice-cold lemon *sherbet*. Then he brought in a service of tea. Not the milk, water, sugar and tea, all-boiled-at-once variety available in the bazaars, but English style; on the tray was a white porcelain tea pot with the green insignia of the Government of Pakistan and china cups and saucers. In separate containers of cut glass were sugar and hot milk. The small, shiny, stainless teaspoons also had the insignia of the army on their handles.

Colonel Chugtai arrived and sat at his desk. The orderly brought him a glass of clear, icy, water on a plate; on top a small white napkin protected the water from dust. The Colonel drank the water first, intoning *Bismillah*, then he looked to the Major and I. The Major introduced me and then excused himself as he needed to shower and change for a previously arranged game of tennis.

Colonel Chugtai told me that it could be possible for us to buy horses from the military, though it wasn't common that they sold horses to the public. He said we would need to speak with a General Zaid at GHQ (General Headquarters) in Rawalpindi. In fact, he informed me, permission from GHQ was needed even to come on the base. We laughed over the fact that I had just walked in. No one had told me I couldn't.

Back in Peshawar plans were being made for the wedding of Mirza and Shelly—Peshawar style. Mirza and I went to the police barracks to find and hire the police band for the procession. He had seen them perform and really liked them and their mustachioed animated leader. My house was to be the groom's house but we needed a house for the bride. We turned to our dear friend Mohammad Arif. Mirza and I had met Arif in his little open-front calligraphy, rubber stamp and printing shop on Cinema Road just outside Kabuli Gate in 1982.

Arif and his old sidekick Anwar Khan Durrani still run the small print shop Arif took over after his father's death in 1976. Arif's father, M.M.Sharif, had been one of the foremost calligraphers in all of Pakistan. All of his sons are well established artists in their own right. Arif, the youngest son, remains in the shop, which still bears the sign board M. M. Sharif Artist.

Arif is a sweet, gentle, family man with a child's grin and quick laughter. He is a true citizen of Peshawar, a *Shari*, a local inhabitant of Peshawar originally migrating from the Punjab. His family speaks *Hindko*, a language close to Punjabi and the language of the citizens of Peshawar.

Anwar Khan, on the other hand, is a crusty old Pathan. His family's holdings are near Charsadda, though in the city they have a large mansion not far from the shop in Gulab Khanna, near Bajauri Gate. He had been a close friend of M. M. Sharif and Arif had inherited Anwar Khan along with the shop.

Anwar had spent his younger years in Hira Mandi, Lahore and in Ajmeri Gate, Delhi, an area with a similar repute—the 'red light' district. He has an incredibly vast repertoire of ribald Pashtu jokes and lore and a sense of humor to go with it. Every morning I am in Peshawar I sit with him and over tea, sometimes breakfast, always *nuswar*, we go over a list of Pashtu words and sentence structures I've jotted down the previous day, improving my Pashtu and learning words and meanings I could never glean from other more proper and sedate instructors.

Anwar and Arif had been among the first to encourage my initial visit to Lahore. Little did they guess what I would get into. They knew about my involvement with Nasreen, especially Anwar, who gave me much advice, albeit much of it jaded.

Arif volunteered his house as the bride's house, but more importantly his family as the bride's family and himself as the father of the bride. I was to be Mirza's father for the marriage. A *deg wallah* had to be arranged for cooking the rice necessary to feed the guests. Arif said not to worry as he would arrange everything.

"What is a *deg*?" asked Shelly curiously.

"A *deg* is a huge pot," Arif told her, "a cauldron, used at weddings and other festivities to cook the rice. One *deg* can cook approximately enough rice to feed fifty Peshawaris, or forty villagers, or thirty-five Afghans. Really!" He laughed and then proceeded with a story....

"One day a man went to his neighbor, who had a large deg and asked to borrow it. He didn't do the return after three weeks. The owner became too much worried. But then one day the man came back carrying the deg. He gave the deg back to the owner and he gave him a small deg too."

"'What is this?' the owner of the deg asked.

"'Well, the reason I have returned your deg so late is because it had a baby,' the crafty man said.

"The owner of the deg was too much happy."

Anwar chuckled and spit a small brown wad of *nuswar* on the floor. Arif went on, *"The next week the neighbor came again and asked if he could borrow the deg again. 'Of course,' said the owner of the deg.*

"But now the man never returned it. After a month the owner of the deg could not wait any longer. He went to the house of the man who had borrowed the deg. 'Why haven't you returned my deg yet? Did it have another baby?' he asked hopefully.

"'Oh, I didn't return your deg because it died,' the tricky fellow said.

"'Died! How could that be? It was only a deg! A pot! How could it die?' the owner cried.

"'You believed it had a baby and now you cannot believe that it is dead.' was his answer."

Imam Gul Sahib, another old friend we had met in 1982 when he ran a photography shop on Sikunder Pura in Hashtnagri, said he would marry Mirza and Shelly but she must first become a Muslim (before being married as one). Not really a rule of Islam, a religion tolerant of other religions of the Book with belief in one God, but it does seem to be a rule in Pakistan by my experience.*

One night in Haji Mahboob's medicos shop on Sikunder Pura, across from where Imam Gul Sahib's sons now run his shop, Shelly became a Muslim and Ayesha Sadiqqa.** Mr. (Haji) Mahboob explained the responsibilities of being a Muslim and the benefits. "Really, my dear sister, if you say the holy *Kalima* and truly accept Islam into your heart you will be saved from the fires of hell. Even your parents, who must surely burn in the hell's fire, will be saved from this evil fate. It is a most wonderful thing, the power of this *Kalima*. Really, I mean it."

"*La illaha, il **Allah**, Muhammadur rasulullah*," she repeated after Mr. Mahboob. (There is no God, but **Allah**, and Muhammad is the Messenger of **Allah**)

"Congratulations, dear sister. Now you are our sister. And remember, you must now learn your prayers and remember them five times a day, and learn to recite the Holy Qur'an, *Insha'Allah*."

We had come to Mahboob's shop that night with Shelly and left with Bibi Ayesha Sadiqqa.

---

* A Muslim man can marry "a woman of the Book" (meaning Christian or Jew—monotheistic religions with a revealed book) without converting. Muslim women cannot marry a Christian or Jewish man if he doesn't convert. 'Non-believing' women (ie; Hindu, Buddhist, etc.) must convert to marry a Muslim man.

** Ayesha Sadiqqa was the name of one of the Prophet's (PBUH) closest wives and the daughter of his close friend, companion and the first Caliph, Abu Bakr.

In Pindi, Mirza was visiting with Brigadier General Shafi, head of the Agha Khan Foundation, author of several books on the Silk Route and the Pakistani military, plus a friend of the Chinese Ambassador. We were hoping he could help us get permission from the Chinese to ride our horses across their border at Kunjarab, a touchy, newly-opened border which up to this point no individual travelers have been permitted to pass. Travelers from Pakistan have to switch over to Chinese buses at the top of the Kunjarab Pass and continue into China via these, the Pakistani vehicles returning back to Pakistan.

Mirza mentioned Sargodha, the Remount Depot and General Zaid. The next thing he knew Brigadier Shafi was on the phone to a Brigadier Yazdani who was head of the Rawalpindi Horse Racing Association and a close personal friend of General Zaid at GHQ, and that was that. We had our official permission to enter Remount Depot and maybe purchase the horses we needed for our trip.

As for the Chinese... they wouldn't gave us permission to enter China.

June 25th (1988)

The ride down to Sargodha from Pindi was long, hot and boring. I looked through the window of Brigadier Yazdani's cream-colored Mercedes at the hot dusty arid landscape, sweating and listening to the stories Mirza was pulling out of him about horses, the military and the *old days* immediately before and after the creation of Pakistan. As we drove along all I could think of was Nasreen. Her smile, her dark eyes and long jasmine-scented hair. Of when I would see her again.

In Sargodha the Brigadier dropped us off at the 200 rupee a night air-conditioned Sargodha Hotel (the rooms had massive *swamp-coolers* in them). We couldn't very well have the him drop us off in his Mercedes at a 30 rupee a night *musaffar khanna*. He went to stay at the Remount Depot officers' mess.

The next morning he picked us up and we officially drove into the Remount Depot. The tree lined paths, the low whitewashed buildings with their columns and arched verandas and uniformed guards with high turbans standing as stiff as their dress were all reminiscent of a bygone era; of a time when the British Raj ruled the Sub-continent and horses were the transportation of the military.

Colonel Chugtai arrived in a yellow and black glossy lacquered carriage with glistening brass fittings and a gorgeous gigantic flossy black horse, a footman riding behind on a brass step. He informed us that in a few hours there would be an auction. Eight horses would be auctioned to us and a few other select people. We could go first to look at the horses and choose the ones we wanted. Then at the auction the ones we had picked would go to us, no problem, but to make it legal they must be sold by auction.

Everybody on the base is extremely helpful, friendly and typically Pakistani. We get the four horses we want. Officially they are bought by Brigadier

Yazdani for approximately 6500 rupees each; foreigners cannot buy horses from Remount Depot. Their sires are French Percherons imported to Pakistan from Argentina and the dams are Pakistani country mares. These horses were bred to carry artillery into the high mountain regions on the border of India.

We name the biggest of our new horses Hercules. He is so tall we have to stand on our tiptoes to look over his back. His chest is as massive as a barrel. Mirza names our smallest horse, still bigger than most *tonga* horses, Shokot, after a favorite servant from the Amin Hotel, though in a short time he will be nicknamed *Baby Shaitan,* due to his feisty, belligerent nature. Ayesha names one, a flecked bay, Kodak, after the thousands of exposures of film given to her by Kodak Company for the trip. I name one, slightly smaller but the same white-gray color as Hercules, Horse, just because it seems rather simple in a simple way and I am a simple man.

It is deathly hot, muggy and dusty. We can feel the monsoon getting ready to break loose in the thick, gray, hanging air. When will it arrive to cool us off with its torrents of waters pouring down from the heavens? Wet inconvenience be damned, the welcomed rains will cool the land and lay the dust.

Deni (what the Brigadier's wife and daughter call him) takes us to a transport depot in Sargodha to see about booking a truck to take us and the horses back to Peshawar. He starts dealing with the depot *wallahs* in Urdu but once it is realized they are Pathan I take over the talking in Pashtu. Deni leaves for his stud farm to the south at Toba Tek Singh and we make preparations to leave at sunset for Peshawar.

The truck arrives at Remount Depot an hour before sunset and we load the horses with the assistance of the Major and some grooms. We pack the floor of the gaily painted truck with straw to keep the horses from sliding and to help cushion their legs from the sharp metal edges of the truck bed.

We stop at a roadside *chai khanna* just out of Sargodha as the sun sets, for *Maghrib* prayer. Mirza and Ayesha sit at a wobbly wooden table in front of the tea house and order plates of greasy meat qurma, bread and sliced raw onions for dinner. The driver, his mate, a friend along for the ride back to Peshawar and I make *wuzu* at a well behind the tea house. We pray in an area marked by stones on the hard packed dust.

As we again start driving, Mirza and Ayesha sit above the cab with the driver's mate. The idea is, if there is any problem they will yell down to me and I can translate it to the driver. No sooner do we utter *Bismillah* and leave the tea house than the driver's friend empties a cigarette into the palm of his hand and fills it with *charras*. The driver slaps a wobbly cassette of Punjabi music—wild and intensely pounding—into the tape player and we blaze down the narrow unmarked and unlit road into the hot dark night. At all the government road tax check points we yell out the truck's window, "Government horses."

In answer to queries regarding our origin and destination, we say, "Sargodha Remount Depot, going to Peshawar, Sherqi *Tanna* Police Lines." It sounds good and it is true. Even the occasional times I have to get down and show our papers it only proves our words and shows the registered owner of the horses to be one Brigadier General Yazdani. We never have to pay a rupee of tax.

About 9:00, after crossing a long, narrow, wooden bridge over the Jhelum River, we stop in a town called Khushab (literally meaning *'happy water'*). I overhear the driver saying something about changing a tire, but our main objective I assume is dinner. Up to this point we in the cab have been smoking *charras* cigarettes constantly and listening to the same Punjabi cassette.

As Mirza, Ayesha and I sit at a rickety wooden table on the dusty ground by the truck to order our food we notice the truck is beginning to be jacked up.

"Hey! What's going on?" Mirza asks me.

"Oh," I reply. "I heard the driver mentioning something about changing a tire while we ate, or was it eating while we changed a tire."

Mirza and I have already had our first confrontation, me being stuck between the driver and him. As always, stuck between East and West. Mirza wanted to know why we weren't heading directly north to GT Road, but rather were taking smaller, bumpier back roads. I explained to him that the driver had recommended cutting across this way to save many hours, as one of our objectives was to get to Peshawar in the cooler morning air. Also it would save much in petrol. If we went the longer route the driver had said he would have to charge us an extra 500 rupees for petrol plus we probably wouldn't reach Peshawar until about noon. Additionally we would avoid much government checking and delay and besides, the roads weren't much worse than GT Road.

Mirza argues with the driver through me and I happen to take the driver's side. By the time we are half-finished with our meal the entire truck is up on jacks and all four tires have been removed. The truck, with our four untrained horses in the back, is perched on uneven bricks and wobbly jacks.

"Noor! I thought you said they were only changing one tire," Mirza says, reasonably perturbed.

"That's what I thought too."

"Ask them what in God's blood they think they are doing. If those horses decide to shift or get frisky that whole bloody truck could come down!"

I go over and confer with the driver.

"The driver has just informed me," I tell Mirza as I return, "that he needs four new tires so he is changing them here before we head up into the Salt Range."

"Why didn't he get them changed in Sargodha when the truck was empty before we left? And what in God's name is the Salt Range?"

"In answer to your first question, because tires are cheaper in Khushab, of course, and in answer to your second, God only knows. The driver says wait and see, that we will be duly impressed."

"Impressed! In a good or bad way? So far I am not very impressed by your ignorant Pathan friend!"

Being unfamiliar with much of Pakistan south of GT Road, we hadn't heard of the Salt Range until now.

Shortly after leaving Khushab we are driving with the same Punjabi cassette wobbling in the tape deck (fortunately I happen to like Punjabi music) when ahead of us in the night sky I see some lights.

"What is that in the sky?" I ask the driver, craning my neck up to peer through the windscreen. Could it be stars, an airplane or a hallucination reflected in the glass?

The truth starts to dawn on me as the driver says, "Those are the lights of a truck. At the top of this pass is the Salt Range."

Impressed? Slightly. That will teach us to study maps more thoroughly. Up we go, painted truck, horses, Punjabi music and all!

We survive the pass, Mirza and Ayesha tugging their gloved hands raw on the horses' ropes to see that they stay upright and shouting down to me to tell the driver to take the turns more slowly and careful. At the top of the pass at a deserted intersection where a road branches out to Chakwal a lone donkey stands silhouetted in the moonlight.

"*Pakistani policeman*," our driver tells me deadpan.

The Salt Range is stark and barren, the moon is full and bright, the silvery moonlight giving sharp edges to angular rocks and withered trees. Its sandy empty reaches glow in the luminous lunar light. We follow the Indus River on its eastern bank up to Attock. We cross the bridge in the shadow of Akbar's fort and ride into the NWFP, the swollen orange globe of the sun rising behind us over the Punjab.

I see to it that the horses are safely stowed at the Peshawar police horse lines in Sherqi *Tanna* in *Cantt.* I go home to shower, shave, put on fresh clothes, then head over to the Flying Coach stand on GT Road across from the Firdoz Cinema. I take the noon bus to Lahore. The sleep I catch on the bus is half of what I need.

By 9:00 I'm asleep in my hotel room in Lahore. I awake at 3:00 in the morning. The sky has unleashed its pouring fury of the beginning cooling monsoon rain. Lightning flashing in the sky, pounding thunder, warm air and wet winds. The power goes out and the ceiling fan rolls to a gradual standstill as humid sweat streams down my body. I open the window, though the wind is blowing in torrents of rain. The floor is a puddle in the warm rain lashed night, a splash of moonlight dancing on it's surface.

I'm in her city again.

Lahore

I arrive at Nasreen's house at 9:00 in the morning. The streets are terribly flooded; I don't even know if the *rickshaw* can get me there. When I get down at her *chowk* I try to keep to the higher ground on the sides of the roads, stepping on bricks and the front steps of shops. I pass small Suzuki pickups and *rickshaws* stalled in the knee-deep tepid waters. Some laughing children float by the corner using a *charpoy* as a raft. Outside her house the street is a pond. I hike my pants up to my knees and wade to her front door.

Her husband's youngest brother, little Iqbal, lets me in. "Nasreena," he shouts. "your *Englaise* is here!"

I cross the brick yard. It is covered in a sheet of water. Overhead, huge white gray clouds billow in a sultry sky. The torrents of rain have momentarily subsided but it is still raining slow, large drops. I sit in the back room with her and a few other girls. The electricity is off. It is hot and muggy inside. Outside is cooler but still raining too hard for grownups.

She is dressed in a long *kameez* of filmy black voile with opaque red flowers sewed into it and black, shiny, silk *shalwar*. Her hair is in a long, thick plait with white jasmine blossoms worked into it. The scent of jasmine wafts to me. She is wearing a set of carnelian and silver Afghani earrings I had given her some weeks ago. She had put them in immediately when I gave them to her and has been wearing them ever since. She is also wearing the metallic silver nail polish I had given her. I am not so Pakistani that I don't enjoy seeing her keep the gifts I give her. The Pakistani people I know don't seem so attached to their gifts once they are given. She brings me tea.

"Nasreen, your Kabuli Jan has come," Nargis teases.

"I am not a Kabuli!" I tell her. And in English I add, "And I am not a john!"

"Nasreen, your lover is here," she corrects. She looks at me and sings a verse of Farsi poetry, slightly altered....

"*My lover's tongue is Pashtu, but I can't speak Pashtu,*
How sweet it would be if my lover's tongue was in my mouth."

Nasreen smiles shyly.

The rain stops and Nargis goes outside to recline on a *charpoy* on the veranda and apply her makeup in the patchy sunlight. She is dressed in flowing yellow satin with a black and golden *dupatta* falling around her shoulders. She is wearing her usual gold and diamond studded nose ring and large gold hoop earrings. She lazes like a contented cat.

"We have been having trouble with the police, Noor Mohammad," Nasreen tells me.

"You don't give them bribes?" I ask. Before, she had told me they give the police at the local *police tanna* 10,000 rupees a month in bribes.

"Our station is no problem, but some police are coming from other stations," she explains to me. "*Bizzness* is slow now. Sometimes only one or two customers a day. Some days none. I haven't worked all week."

"Little work? Oh, that's too bad. I'm so sorry," I tease. "Maybe your husband will have to get a job."

She slaps my shoulder. The sky is clearing, bright blue gashes in massive cotton clumped clouds. The electricity comes back on. The overhead fan slowly starts circulating the stifling damp air. The sweat cools on my body.

She tells the other girls to leave. Saira takes a cigarette from the pack I've left on the *charpoy.* She lights it with the cigarette I am smoking. She smiles and walks out of the room. Nasreen closes the curtain and the door also, latching it.

"What's that called?" I ask. "In English?" I had taught her how to say '*close the door'* several weeks ago.

"Leave it! I forgot," she says, annoyed, as she sits on the bed and takes the cigarette from my mouth.

"No, remember it! What kind of student are you?"

She closes her eyes and thinks for a brief moment.

"*Cloz dador,*" she says impatiently, slurring the words into one sound.

"Now, that's a good student."

I look in her eyes as she sits down in front of me. She returns my gaze, softly humming a Pashtu melody under her breath.

"What song is that?" I ask.

"Oh, it's a song I danced to in a movie," she answers casually.

"In a movie? You've danced in movies?" I say, surprised.

"Yes. I used to. In some I just had small parts. That song was from a movie in which I had a solo dance. It was called '*Ajrati Qatil*' (The Assassin)."

"I would like to see it sometime. I think you are so beautiful."

"What of me is beautiful?"

"All of you. Not just your body and face. Oh, that I like, for sure. But your heart and your soul I think are so beautiful. Your nature and personality. You are a beautiful woman." I try to convince her. She smiles sweetly. "I get so much pleasure from your smile."

She smiles again prettily and searches in my face.

"Oh Nasreen, darling, I want to find a wife just like you."

"Are you looking in Peshawar?" she asks.

"No, I can't look right now. All the time I am thinking about you. I don't know what to do. I don't want another. I want you!" I explain. "There is only room in my heart for you! You've changed my life. Do you know that?"

"No, I don't."

"Why not?"

"Because I cannot! How can I matter to you?"

"I don't know," I laugh, "but you do!"

"And then?" she smiles and rubs my leg.

"And then? Give me a hug," I say, using the word for hug I had just learned. I mispronounce it.

"Huh?" she looks at me strangely.

"Hug," I say, demonstrating. She corrects my pronunciation.

"Okay." I agree, hugging her, feeling the soft plait that runs down her back. I am intoxicated by the heady perfume of the flowers in her hair. I am in the *Shalimar Gardens*, a gentle breeze blows the richly scented air into my nose. Water fountains cast their pearls of shimmering light into the brilliant morning sunshine. Her hair sweetens and tickles my face. My brow is sweating in the heat of Lahore.

"I have so much to say to you and so little language," I say.

"Your Pashtu is good, Noor Mohammad. You are learning. What talk is this?" she replies.

"There is so much more I want to tell you."

"Leave it." she says, pulling me down on the bed with her.

"Soon we must leave the room. We can't stay in here too long alone, you know that. Come on, now, now...." she purrs....

Outside on the veranda, Nargis brings me *roti* and a plate of meat swimming in spicy red gravy and a glass of ice water. Nasreen brings me tea after I eat. She squats at the end of the *charpoy* I am sitting on and takes the half finished cigarette from my hands.

"Drink tea, Noor Mohammad! I'll smoke."

She plays with a baby. Her husband isn't home. She seems so much more free and relaxed when he is away. He doesn't seem as friendly to me lately, though he does remain cordial. After all, I am business.

"I must be going back to Peshawar now," I tell her. "My brother is getting married. I am going to be his father for the wedding. His wife has become Muslim."

"**Allah** *shoker, al-hamdu-lillah*," Nasreen says (thank God, all praise to **Allah**), "That is very good news."

"I wish you could come to Peshawar for the wedding but I know it isn't possible."

"No, it isn't. I'm sorry."

"So am I. Also we are busy in Peshawar training the horses for the trip we are planning to China."

"Will you come on *Juma*?" she asks.

"I'll come as soon as I am free. I come whenever I can."

"Will you bring your *rabab* the next time you come?"

"I will try."

"Don't try. Just bring it!"

"*Insha'Allah*."

I say goodbye to Nargis and another girl who is sitting on the *charpoy* with her. I walk to the door of the family room and say goodbye to Mama. She is still basically friendly to me. Whether she likes it or not, I refuse to just be a regular customer. She is getting to know my different ways. She seems to like my Muslim manners. Or is it my business she likes?

Nasreen walks with me to the front door. I hold her hand, squeezing it. I am reluctant to let her go. She smiles at me and I have to catch myself from swooning into her eyes. I draw myself out of her smile. It is time to leave.

"See you soon, *Insha'Allah*."

"*Insha'Allah*."

"*Khuda hafiz*."

THE WEDDING

Mirza was in my room tying his royal blue and golden striped antique Raj era turban for the umpteenth time. I watched the street from my third story window. All was quiet. We had told the guests to arrive at 8:00 and here it was almost five minutes til. Most of the chairs I had rented sat in the courtyard empty. What if nobody else showed up?

Suddenly I heard the pounding of drums and the sound of out of tune trumpets and clarinets as the police band came marching down Gari Saidan, nearing my house.

"Hurry up and get that rag tied on your head brother!" I told Mirza. "I'll go down and see that things are properly organized. The band is coming."

As I hurried down the stairs guests were already crowding on the lower steps. In the courtyard and on the veranda wedding pandemonium was breaking loose. I went to the front porch of the house to see that the musicians came in the right way and took their places in the center of the chairs set around the lower courtyard.

I ushered the band with their beating drums and screeching battered horns up the steps. I spied Gul Shir, Anwar Khan's young servant, arriving with the gaily caparisoned wedding horse. He started to bring the horse up the stairs and into the front entry of the house, much to the delight of the many children milling around in the confusion.

While I was explaining to Gul Shir over the din of the band as they swarmed past us to leave the horse with the horse-man waiting in the street the video *wallah* arrived. His camera was already running, the scene bathed in a white blaze of light by three blaring bulbs on a pole held by an old, white-bearded man. Inside, people and the performers were noisily gathering on the veranda. I arrived in time to direct the band down into the courtyard. The excited guests followed suit. Everybody seemed to arrive virtually at once. I turned around to see Mirza coming down the stairs.

At the moment this was an all men's affair. Bibi Ji, the owner of my house, who lived with her family on the ground floor, had left earlier with two of her daughters, Batool and Zenobia, and various other female relatives and Ayesha for Arif's house and the *mehndi* ceremony. The other women would be of Arif's family. We were actually having a condensed Peshawari wedding. The *mehndi (henna)* ceremony, the *bharat (parade to the bride's house)*, the *nikka (marriage ceremony)* and the *walima* (after marriage celebration) all took place on the same day. It was enough.

Usually, for up to a month before the actual ceremony, guests start coming to the houses and making preparations and music. The music is mostly the sound of drums. The action starts intensifying the week before the actual wedding. A day or two before the actual marriage ceremony the women will come to the bride's house for the *mehndi* celebration. *Mehndi,* called *nacraizi* in Pashtu, is *henna*—a dye that stains the skin iodine-orange and is used on the hands and feet as a decoration. It is also said to toughen the hands and feet and give a cooling effect in the hot weather. The men limit themselves to dipping the ends of their fingers into it or making a circle on the palms of their hands. In summer some men do the soles of their feet. The women paint all manners of intricate designs on their hands, especially at weddings and on both *Eids*.

On the eve of the *mehndi* celebration there is a procession through the neighborhood. The leaders carry trays decorated with flowers and laden with many lit candles. If the families involved in the marriage are of means this is followed with music, maybe dancing girls or boys, and a meal.

The day before the *nikka* ceremony (the actual marriage ceremony) there is a big gathering at the groom's house. A large hall is used, or a field or vacant lot, and *shamiyana* tents are erected. Everybody is fed and there is some musical entertainment. Nowadays, if a family can afford it they hire a disco band from Lahore. They usually have (trap) drums, a synthesizer, maybe an electric guitar and a distorting echo affected P.A. system. They always bring their own dancing girls (or boys).

There is rarely any mixing of the sexes at these functions. The men are fed and entertained on the ground floor and the women usually eat on an upper level or separate tent where they can watch the entertainment through windows or from balconies.

Then comes the actual day of the *nikka*. The guests of the groom's family meet at his house. There they are sometimes fed, the men and women of course being in separate areas. A band will come and sometimes even a horse, which in our case Mirza insisted on. Special white horses are available for hire as are all the wedding necessities. The band can be the police band with their brass instruments and drums and baton wielding leader, or the army band with bagpipes and of course drums, or a multitude of wedding bands available in the *Ghanta Ghar* area of the old city with *surnais*, old battered brass instruments, the inevitable percussion instruments and *hijra* dancers.

The band leads the entire entourage to the house of the bride. This parade is called a *bharat* (in Pashtu, *jaanj*). The groom, walking if no horse has been hired, is completely bedecked with garlands of flowers and decoratively folded crisp new rupee notes (*kanta*). Another garland (*serri*) is placed over his head; strings of tinsel and flowers fall over his face. The horse is similarly adorned, the appearance being closest to that of a decorated Christmas tree.

As they march through the streets they stop in prominent places and the men dance. The groom and his party are showered with rupee notes. This money becomes property of the band and each band comes complete with its own money changer who supplies the bundles of smaller rupee notes, and collectors to scramble and pick up the lose notes, chasing away the children who scamper after a few easily earned free rupees.

The women, as brightly dressed as the groom in shimmering sequins, glitter makeup and swinging golden ornaments, follow the procession sedately. No respectable woman dances in public.

At the house of the bride the *mullah* is waiting. The groom offers the girl so much in *haq mahar* (bride price) and so much in *naan nufkar* (daily living expenses). If the bride and groom are not of the same family, usually a house, or at least half a house, is signed over to the girl's name. The groom, his representatives and the witnesses sign the *nikka namma* (marriage certificate) which is then taken to the bride, her representatives and witnesses.

Until this point the bride and the groom have not seen each other. In many instances with more traditional marriages they have never even met. The bride is picked by female relatives of the groom, though this way of choosing (ending up with) a life's mate is slowly being replaced with more modern ways, or at least the boy is allowed to see a picture of the girl.

If all is satisfactorily agreed upon, and it usually is way before this point, the girl is asked if she accepts the groom's terms. She answers *'yes.'* There are two witnesses who are asked if they have heard. They answer *'no.'* This is repeated three times. After the bride has said three times that she accepts, the papers are signed and the *mullah* recites blessings over the entire proceedings. There is more food and another entertainment program which goes on late into the night. But in the early part of the celebrations the new wife climbs into a *dholey* (a freely swinging shoulder-carried palanquin covered in red cloth— the color of marriage) and is carried off to the house of her new husband. Many times these new husbands and wives are no more than mere children going to live at the house of the boy's parents, already relatives of the girl.

The next day is the *walima*, usually in the afternoon, at the house of the groom, to celebrate the consummation of the marriage (if the bride and groom are of age—otherwise it is just a formality). Everybody gathers and after much traditional waiting while the new husband and the new wife are each congratulated individually by members of their own sexes, another full meal is served.

In Islam and in Pakistan much merit is given in the feeding of people and these are not invitation only affairs. Any neighbor who wants to is freely welcomed to join in the meals, as is any poor man off the street. The music and parade usually draw again as many people as have been invited to the wedding. No problem: the more people fed, the more blessed the occasion.

The band was playing what sounded like two or three songs at once and Mirza was sitting on a chair in the middle of the courtyard, beaming. Guests were individually dancing and gesticulating around him, placing *kantas* around his neck and showering him with rupee notes. Children were scrambling under the blows of the band's money collectors, their illegally gained rupees clutched in their dirty little hands. I was talking with guests, talking with the video *wallah*, talking with Gul Shir about where to position the horse, in Pashtu, Urdu and Hindko. A representative came from Arif's house to tell me that Imam Gul Sahib had already arrived and *'what was taking us.'* It was 8:30.

Mirza was seated upon the white horse, both bedecked with flower and tinsel streamers, and was led through the twisting narrow streets of old Peshawar. Due to the decorations, neither of them could see. The band played before them and the guests surged around them. What women there were followed at the rear. We stopped in front of Faisal's restaurant in Hashtnagri, then in Jenda Bazaar, in Meena Bazaar, in Chowk Nasir Khan and at last just before Arif's street, in Shahbaz Quay.

At each stop the band would be led in a rousing song by their leader with his flying baton and waxed and twirled mustachios, and men would dance, rupee notes being showered over the dancers and the groom.

Then we proceeded around the corner and up *Mohallah* Noor Khan to Arif's house. If there had been room for me to be more surprised in all the noise and chaos, I would have been. The street leading up to Arif's house and his house were entirely covered in colored lights and festooned with tiny paper flags. As we approached on our left we caught a glimpse of the gigantic silver zinc washed *degs*, red embers glowing under them, the smell of cedar smoke filling the air. From here Arif took over and I only had to follow his directions. Too much was happening to be able to function normally.

We rode almost up to Arif's door and Mirza dismounted. For a brief second we saw Ayesha peeking at us from a small second story window over the doorway, something a more modest Peshawari bride would never have done. Arif's little daughter, Farkhar, brought us a silver bowl with heavily sweetened milk that was liberally laced with cardamom. First Mirza drank from it, then I followed. I put a 100 rupee note in Farkhar's hand as I had been instructed.

Arif then told us to go back down the street to his neighbor's house—that is where the men would be. The women were in Arif's house. We sat in a room and the *nikka namma* and city register were brought in and read to the entire gathering. We were informed what Mirza was promising for the hand of Bibi Ayesha Sadiqqa in marriage—50,000 rupees *haq mahar*, four Sargodha horses, $3000 a month *naan nufkar,* two golden rings and a partridge in a pear tree. Needless to say, nobody understood the last one, but we told them, tongue in cheek, that it was an old American custom.

Everyone *oooh'ed* and *aaah'ed* at the mention of 50,000 rupees and especially at the mention of $3000 a month. The papers, once filled out, were taken by Arif and the witnesses to his house to be read to Ayesha to see if she would accept the terms. Word came back that the terms were accepted and the marriage was official. Gul Sahib said a long string of *duas* (prayers) over the blessed union and the *pilau* was served.

After everyone had eaten, Mirza and I were led to Arif's house. We sat among all the women and children (relatives of the bride and from my house) and pictures were taken as we were assaulted by the sounds of Pakistani disco music which blared from a boom box. Pictures were taken of the bride and groom feeding each other sweets, looking at each other's reflections in a mirror (traditionally the first time they see each other), repeating a short *ayat* (verse) from the *Qur'an*, of him looking at her while holding back her red and golden *zarri* (veil) and of them sitting with each guest individually.

Ayesha was entirely made up, something very rare for her, with lipstick, rouge, mascara and various colors of eye blush, and her hands covered with patterns of *mehndi.* Every female relative had wanted a hand in decorating the bride so she ended up looking more like a garish caricature than herself. Her clothing was golden embroidered *zarri* as was her veil and she was wearing golden shoes (something she and I had quite a difficult time finding in the bazaar for her large American size feet). Her golden jewelry was borrowed from Arif's daughter. From her knees to the floor was a huge *kanta* with many colors of tinsel, plastic beads, mirrors and crisp rupee notes.

It was time for the bride and groom to go. Bibi, Arif's wife, lit a candle and led Ayesha to the *dholey* while a Qur'an wrapped in red velvet was held over her head. Her large Western frame had trouble fitting into the tiny *dholey,* which was more intended to accommodate smaller teenaged Pakistani brides. The two *dholey wallahs*, not accustomed to such tall and weighty girls, had trouble enough just getting the *dholey,* in the hot Peshawar night, down to Shahbaz Quay. There a car was waiting to take the couple to an air-conditioned room reserved at the Amin Hotel.

I went back to Arif's and eventually walked back to my house in Hashtna-gri, exhausted.

Mirza and Ayesha went to Swat for their honeymoon.

I took my *rabab* and headed to Lahore.

Sitting in the back room at Nasreen's house I tuned the *rabab*. Its mother-of-pearl inlaid neck flashed with iridescence from the sunlight coming in through the doorway. Some of the children came in and squirmed around in the after-noon Lahore heat. Several of the girls congregated on a *charpoy*. I played a few short melodies, striking the strings hard and fast, then more finely tuned the freshly stretched strings. Nasreen came in and sat down.

"Do you want to hear the song I wrote for you?" I asked. "I am recording it in Peshawar but it is not quite ready yet. I will bring it for you soon."

"Sure. I would like. Play it."

I began the intro on the *rabab*. Some of the girls started swaying their heads to the music. The song had just come to me one night walking in Jenda Bazaar (Peshawar) as I listened to the sound of my footsteps and the water rushing in the gutters. It was practically written by the time I arrived home and I picked up my *rabab,* playing the melody.

I looked in her smiling eyes and sang the words....

"I try to tell you how I feel,
that my love for you is real.
Do you know just what I mean?
Or is it only an empty dream?

"Just one look was all it took,
to see what you could mean to me.
Now I'm wondering what to do,
zama zera tata pata shoo
(my heart is stuck on you).
Nasreena, janana, janana, Nasreena....

"It's a game I've never played,
I don't even know the way.
But I know I could love you,
if you would love me too ...
I see you come, I see you go,
it's hard for me darling don't you know?
You say Noora, can't you see?
Even love is never really free.
Nasreena, janana, yarana, Nasreena ....

"Dreamed a dream into existence,
now I want to take you there.
Need to learn just what to say,
what to say to Nasreena.

68

Nasreena, janana, janana, yarana ....

"When I see you sitting there,
can you guess what's in my stare?
Is it my choice, is it my flaw?
Che zama zera tuh khawkha da
(that my heart likes you).
Janana, yarana, janana, Nasreena ....

"Is it a game so cut and dry,
that I shouldn't even try?
Is it some joke, I just don't know,
all I know is Nasreena.
Nasreena, Nasreena, Nasreena, janana ....

"I pay the way, we talk a while,
you give me your sweetest smile.
Can you guess, just what I see,
or are you only my fantasy?
Counting days now, one by one,
until I see Nasreen again.
How I fell, I'll never know,
now all I know, is Nasreena.
Janana, Nasreena, Nasreena, yarana
Nasssss.......... reeeeena...." *

During the song nothing in the room existed except for the music and her endless eyes. Then the children shuffled and demanded I play another. Some of the girls nudged Nasreen and chided her that the song was for her. It wasn't an accident her name was in it seventeen times, I wanted her to understand some of it. I knew none of my audience spoke much more English than that.

Thinking back, it does appear quite an exotic scene. At the time it just seemed like my life. Surreal, but also becoming oh so normal. What is normal anyway? My Western past is like a distant dream—not unreal enough to be completely forgotten, yet, not real enough to be part of my present. Not now.

Well, on I go. Each visit is a roller coaster of feelings and emotions. Taking me where? Up and down, down and up, sideways, back and forth. Which way does it go? Back to where it began? Can we ever go back?

It's up to her, it's up to me.

It's up to God.

My/our fate is with **Allah**.

---

* The song 'Nasreena' can be heard on the net at:
www.youtube.com/watch?v=TfHz4jX7nZ8
Recorded in Peshawar—Noor Mohammad Khan with Master Ali Haider: *tabla*

A musical program in Peshawar (Abdul Sattar: tabla)

Recording in Amin Hotel, Peshawar City

Chapter 7
Training, Trucking and Malaria

Photo by Ayesha S.

August 1988
Peshawar

Did you ever attempt to plan a 1000 mile horse ride through the mountains of Central Asia in the midst of Peshawar's summer heat with four heavy-breed untrained Pakistani Army horses?

Firstly all the horse tack that we had purchased from well known horse outfitters and leather workers Shamas Din and sons, in Rawalpindi, was inadequate. It all had to be reworked, enlarged and strengthened back in Peshawar.

Nothing against the respected sons of Shamas Din, but their knowledge of outfitting a horse expedition basically amounted to making picnic baskets for afternoon excursions into the Margala Hills around Islamabad for embassy *wallahs* and making saddles which are saddle-soaped and polished by servants after an afternoon's outing. They were used to thinner Punjabi and Arab horses and smaller country ponies. Nothing fit our massive beasts. The pack saddle kept slipping from left to right. Just the constant strains of training four to five hours a day tore stitching and leather fittings. No, it would never do.

To our good fortune we found Abdul Hamid in his tiny stall on Katchery Road, near Chowk Yadgar, in Peshawar. Abdul's father had made accouterments for the military and police back in the days of the Raj, when horses and good strong tack were still deemed important in such matters. These are the days of Bedford trucks and Vespa *rickshaws*, Japanese Flying Coaches and F-16s. Shock absorbers and carburetors are more important than bridles and bits. As horse business is a slowly dwindling trade nowadays Abdul Hamid and his brother mostly sell and repair gear for *tongas* and sell rope and plastic sheeting.

They worked wonders with a leather stitching needle and strips of heavy water buffalo leather. All our fastening straps had to be fortified and enlarged.

71

We made daily trips to their shop as stitching tore out in training. We never once entered their shop that the shop boy, Abdul Hamid's son, didn't disappear down the street, reappearing after several minutes with ice cold frosty bottles of Coca Cola for each of us, much appreciated after a hot sweltering day of training.

Ayesha and I needed boots so we went to Khoristan Afghan Refugee Camp on the Charsadda Road near the Khazana Sugar Mill. There an Afghan Turkoman cobbler named Haji Arif lived. He had made Mirza a pair of *buzkashi* boots in '87 and we had rough buffalo leather boots made to match.

Training wasn't made any easier by the fact that by 10:00 the temperature soared to 110-120 degrees. After morning prayer I would walk over to the Amin Hotel where Mirza and Ayesha were staying, loath to give up the luxury of their air-conditioned room for the more primitive comforts of life back at Bibi Ji's house. The three of us would cram our long American bodies into a *rickshaw* and ride out to Sherqi *Tanna*. The horses would be saddled and taken along the noisy truck and *rickshaw* cluttered Khyber Road to the uncompleted army stadium. There they were put through their paces.

The first day it only amounted to getting them used to having saddles on their backs and running them on a lunge line. Soon we were riding them in formation; turning around obstacles, up and down piles of dirt and gravel, next to water buffaloes and finally alongside speeding screeching trucks.

By 9:00 or 10:00 we were back at the police lines bathing them at the side of a large concrete trough with a water tap at one end that doubled as the barrack's bathtub. As we doused our horses, scooping water with an old tin can, policemen would wash down in their underwear, standing on flat stones or bricks on the muddy ground. By noon we were too hot, sweat soaked and dirty to do anything but go home and shower under cold water. Some days I would sleep a few hours in Mirza and Ayesha's air-conditioned room before going home.

By the end of July we were ready to leave. We had decided due to the extremely hot season to bypass the ride through the hot lower altitudes of Tribal Territory. We would truck the horses up to Dir, at the foot of the Lowari Pass and what we hoped would be high enough ground to be relatively cooler.

I was ready to go to Lahore to see Nasreen.

To say goodbye.

I arrived off the night Flying Coach at 6:30 in the morning. I had breakfast, and showered and got a shave at my usual *hammam*. I was at her house by 8:00 and spent the entire day. I saw her work several times. Too many for me. Once is too much. But the joy of being with her made me able to bear the pain. What could I do? A part inside has become immune. What part of you has to be stomped on, to die, in order to become immune to that? I tried to be detached so it wouldn't be too painful.

I was sitting with a customer on the veranda. He told me he has been coming a year for her. "She's a good girl," he told me nonchalantly, gesturing toward her with his eyes.

"Yeah, I know," I gave a sad inner sigh.

I was happy at least to see he didn't seem to get any special treatment at all. Not even tea! He left quickly. Am I just special because I am a foreigner and a Muslim, as seems the case in so much of Pakistan, or is it something else? Maybe I'm just an amusement for her? There does seem to be more there than that or is it just my wishful imagination? I love her so much. I don't think Pakistani men could seriously love somebody like her as I do. People seem to have different feelings, different concepts here.

Some months ago the Herald Magazine ran a story about a man and a woman who had had an affair. She had met him at the shop where he worked. There she visited him often and eventually they ran away together to another city where they had lived for over a year as husband and wife. Even though neither of them was married (to anybody else) their families searched them out. Finally the police caught up with them. Running away together is an offense under the Hadood Act, a Pakistani Islamic anti-vice law. What they had done was improper and illegal. There is very little looseness in Pakistan between the sexes. The newspaper interviewed the man in jail. The woman was incarcerated in a separate woman's prison. When asked if he would marry her when they were released he replied, "Of course not! She is a woman of loose character!"

With this kind of attitude prevailing how could Nasreen ever believe I could want her as a wife? If I were she, would I believe me? Probably not. Is my love something she needs or wants? Or is it only my fantasy?

It's not that women are inferior here (though sometimes they are treated that way just as in any society), just different. They take their pride in serving their families. Women have one set of functions and men another.

How seriously do I love her? Is it just a temporary girlfriend I want? Maybe it is just an infatuation. After all, she is a beautiful Pathan woman. What other chances do I have to experience a relationship with a Pakistani woman? At least I haven't deflowered somebody's daughter, nor am I sleeping with some unsuspecting husband's wife.

My sight has gone so beyond the sex, though. It is deeper that I have fallen. Visions of Nasreen only tangle up my mind—longing, intense love, sadness, gladness, fullness, emptiness, frustration at not being able to fully express myself in her language. Until this my Pashtu has only been needed to handle the basic necessities of life. Now my needs have grown. I want to convince her of my sincerity. To convince myself.

As I lounge on a *charpoy* in the yard I watch her move around the house doing housework. Even as she performs these simple, basic chores I find myself totally mesmerized by her graceful, sleek motions. She squats across the yard from me washing tea cups at the house's only water tap in front of the bathroom. The milky runoff of a spilled cup flows into a puddle....

The clouds are reflected in the Kabul River on a crystal clear spring morning, now a long time past. A young rabab player and his ustad squat on the stone wall at the side of the river. A rabab wrapped in a purple velvet bag is between them. Smells of freshly baked naan and the odor of horses permeate the air. The sweet aroma of charras wafts across the river to them. The ustad hums a short haunting melody. The young man smiles in the warm sunshine. Suddenly the roar of jets and rapid bursts of machine gun fire shatters the idyllic peace. Orange, blazing fire and billowing black inky smoke fill the air. Children are crying....

I'm tied to Nasreen and we're chained to a charpoy in a fort somewhere in Tribal Territory. Her husband paces in front of us carrying a machine gun. He has a beard and his eyes are hollow and crazy....

"Come with me!" I say in English as I come out of my daydream.

"What?" she says. She must have come and sat next to me to smoke a cigarette while I lay dozing. "What?" she says again, giving me an impatient, frustrated, sweet smile and a playful slap on my arm.

"Oh, I said *'come with me,'*" I tell her in Pashtu.

"Where?"

"To the room," I laugh.

It is quiet and slow around the house at the moment. It's the late afternoon. We get up to walk the short distance to the back room. We leave the door open, sitting on the couch where we can't be seen from the yard.

"Come with me," I tell her again.

"We're here," she answers.

"No. Away from here."

"Where?"

"Oh, Peshawar, Srinigar... America. Any place you like in the world."

"Leave it! Don't talk that! I can't leave here. It isn't possible for me."

"Oh Nasreen, I want you so bad. I love you so much my darling."

"Don't talk of love with me. You have me now. *Baas!*"

"No, I don't have you. You don't have love for me. For you it is only business."

"*Bizzness?* Yes, it is *bizzness.* It must be. But, for you, Noor Mohammada, there is also some love. But love isn't important. This is my life. This is my *qismet.* I cannot leave this life. As you have your life in Peshawar. You cannot leave your life!"

"With you I can leave everything."

"It is too difficult. You are only talking."

"I'm not. But if you think so, at least leave your work then. I'd be happy even for that."

"Why?"

"It's not good for you."

"We could not meet like this then," she smiles, taking my hand.

"If you are happy in your heart, then my heart will be happy my love. It hurts my heart to see you work. I know you know in your heart it's not right for you. It's not good."

"It is good for you to see me work, Noor Mohammad. Then you know me. Don't love me."

"I must. I'm compelled."

"Why is this work bad?"

"I think you know in your heart. I know your heart is clean." She closes her eyes as I speak. "It's not just bad for your body and health. It's bad for your soul."

"If I did not do this work we would not have met," she says squeezing my hand.

"*Ah cha*," I say, not able to refute the point. "Strangers are always coming. You can get sick or die."

"I am sick," she tells me. "I have fever." She takes my hand and places it on her smooth flat tummy under her *kameez*. It is a bit warm. I put my lips to her forehead and kiss her. Her hair is soft and fragrant on my lips and nose.

"No," I say. "This is only little sick. I mean big sick. AIDS. Do you know about AIDS?"

"No. What is that?"

"It is big sick. You can get it from this work. There is no cure. When you get it you die."

"Then Nasreen dies," she shrugs. "Who doesn't die? It is all by **Allah's** wish."

"Why not leave it?"

"When I die, then I will leave it. No?" she smiles.

"Oh Nasreena. You are such a problem for me." I say in English. She understands her name and the word problem.

"What problem? Don't think! Leave it," she says with a note of finality.

"I love you so much."

"Thank you."

"But you are here. You are just public property. I want to help you. But you won't let me. I have no control in this. And now I am going away on this horse trip."

"So then, don't go."

"I must go. My friends and I planned this for so long. From before I met you. Still, if you said you would leave this house with me I wouldn't go on this trip. But now, if I stayed, you'd still be in this house working. You would still be with your husband."

"Do you want me to go with you?" she smiles enticingly.

"More than anything. It is my dream."

"Sleep?" she puzzles. In what I've learned of Pashtu so far, the same word can be used for dream and sleep.

"No, dream," I say. "You know, sometimes when you are sleeping you see a story."

"Oh, I am your dream," she carefully repeats.

I wonder if that has any meaning in Pashtu. I take her hand I am holding and softly kiss it. She lightly kisses me. Then she moves her face away from mine as I try to catch her lips with mine.

"More," I say.

"No more kiss," she says, moving away.

"Oh Nasreena, you prude," I say in English.

"It's dirty."

"No it's not! Our lips aren't dirty."

"We say the name of **Allah** with them."

"I know. That must mean they aren't dirty. Why don't you love me?"

"I love you some. It's dangerous for me. From my family."

"Well, you'll be safe now. I am going away on horses, maybe to China. I won't see you for a long time."

"Can you bring my (real) mother a red tea pot from China?"

"*Insha'Allah*. It will be difficult to come see you while we are on this horse trip, but somehow I will manage it, *Insha'Allah*."

"*Insha'Allah*."

"Can you give me one thing before I leave?"

"What is that? Haven't I already given you it?"

"No. I want to take your picture."

"No. They will be mad at me."

"They won't even know. I brought the small camera like I said I would. You look so pretty now, so natural. If I can't have you at least let have your picture to carry with me."

"Okay, but you must hurry. It is dangerous if they know."

"They won't"

"Hurry," she urges as I set up the camera and take a few snaps.

"Put it away," she says. "We'd better go out. We've been inside too long. They will start to wonder."

Before she can move to open the door I take her and hold her in my arms. I kiss her forehead and embrace her tightly, not wanting to ever let her go. But I must. At the front door I have another brief moment of privacy with her in the few feet of space between the metal front door and the curtain. I hug her again, trying to soak her into me.

"Goodbye, my love. I will come and see you again as soon as I am able, though it will be very difficult. I will be thinking of you constantly. Will you be thinking of me?"

"What can I do? I am a very busy woman. I will be remembering you on *Jumas*. Will you remember to bring my mother a red tea pot from China?"

"I will try, if we can even get in to China. I don't know when I will be able to come here again."

"I won't see you next week?"

"Don't you understand? I am going on a long horse trip into empty, deserted places."

"Yes, I understand. I am here when you come."

"*Insha'Allah*."

"Yes, *Insha'Allah*. Now go! *Khuda hafiz*."

"Okay, goodbye. *Waleikum asalaam*."

DIR

We arrived in Dir the last day of September by truck from Peshawar. We unloaded our horses and all of the gear at the hotel Mirza and I had always stayed at in the past. Only now it wasn't a hotel anymore. It was closed, though it did house the *GTS* bus office. The *"in charge"* in the office said the hotel belonged to the *Nawab* and was being looked after by his cousin, the Second Nawab. A boy was sent to see if we could have permission to stay overnight. We planned to head up the Lowari Pass in the morning.

Permission granted, we and all of our gear were stowed in a second floor room. The horses were staked in the corner of the yard behind where the *GTS* buses parked, right under the hotel's veranda. In the untended yard the paths were overgrown and the fountain was silent. The sky wasn't. That night rain poured down in a deluge. Crashing thunder deafened us and every few seconds the drenched horses were illuminated by brilliant flashes of lightning.

Ayesha and I went to a restaurant near the hotel to eat and get some skewers of kebab to take back to Mirza. At first we thought the water in the dented aluminum pitcher was some kind of *sherbet*. We then realized it was just full of mud. I asked the waiter to bring us some clean water. The water he brought was the same as what he had just thrown away. It was the same water coming from the tap in our hotel room bathroom. All the water in Dir comes from the river and at present the river was choked with rushing mud.

We drank, figuring it was the only water anybody had here so they all must drink it. Besides, later in the trip we would probably be drinking dirtier water than this. After drinking we did have second thoughts when a rough-and-tumble bearded turbaned Afghan *mujahid* sat across from us, looked into his pitcher, turned up his nose in disgust and tossed the entire contents of the pitcher out on the floor.

In the morning the ground was so soggy we thought it would be best to wait one more day before heading up the pass. Also we discovered the iron *moogays* we had made in Peshawar were a bit on the weak side. After one night's use two of them had broken. Likewise we noticed Kodak had already thrown a shoe. Off to a good start.

Shouldering my seven millimeter parachute rifle, I headed up the street to the bazaar to see if I could find a blacksmith. Everywhere were streams of water and puddles of mud. It felt good wearing a rifle in the Dir bazaar even though most men carried machine guns. As said in Pashtu, 'neeshta na khedee' (something is better than nothing).

I found a blacksmith who had a heavy enough iron-rod stock to suit our needs. I sat drinking tea with him while I watched a teenage boy in grimy, greasy clothes pump up the forge with a hand bellows and heat the bars to a glowing orange-red. Then the blacksmith pounded them on his time-beaten anvil into the proper specifications according to my instructions.

When I returned carrying my six newly made still warm *moogays*, I checked on the horses before going up to our room. They were standing in the mud munching on stalks of green corn we had brought up on the top of the truck coming from Peshawar. Hercules had pulled off the bumper of the bus he was tied to. But that didn't occupy my attention for long. It was Horse. He was lying on his side in the mud. Now, I don't claim to know much about horses, but this didn't seem right to me. I didn't think he would normally be resting in such a position on the filthy, wet, muddy earth.

I entered the room and called Mirza out onto the porch for a look. Knowing more about horses than I, he was instantly alarmed.

"We must get him up," he said. "If we can't get him up he will die!"

"I thought that was with camels?" I asked.

"Maybe. But also with horses. Maybe he's just got a twist in his intestines. All that dry barley he ate on top of the corn could have given him colic. If he can get up it may straighten out."

But as much as we tried we could not get Horse to stand.

"He will die," Mirza informed me. "We must shoot him and put him out of his misery!"

"Shoot him! Where? In the head or the heart? I've never shot a horse before."

"Neither have I! But I will do it. It is my responsibility. Keep trying to get him up. I'll go get the gun."

While Mirza was up in the room Horse rolled in the mud. I thought he was trying to get up but just couldn't. Maybe he sensed how near his end was. Mirza arrived with the gun. It was starting to rain again; clouds and thunder rolled off the mountainsides.

"I'm here, Noor," he told me, "with death in my hands. This really sucks, but we can't let him lie in the mud and die in pain."

"I think he was just trying to stand."

"Okay, let's try again. You pull on his halter, I'll push from behind."

After some concerted effort Horse finally rose. We both breathed a sigh of relief. We were soaked with rain and it washed mud down Horse's filthy flanks.

"Let's get inside Noor. When the rain slows down we will wake Ayesha from her nap to shoe Kodak."

It took all three of us to shoe Kodak. At least at the start it did. Ayesha held his halter and tried to distract him by rubbing his nose. I held up his right rear foot, trying to keep it still and Mirza trimmed his oversized hoof. We were working on the end of the veranda, out of the mud.

Suddenly Ayesha swayed and fell over. Kodak kicked out his hind legs and lunged forward, running down the cement porch. I ran after him, catching him at the other end and led him back by his lead rope. Mirza had dropped his tools and was bending over Ayesha.

"What happened?" I asked.

"I think she fainted," he told me.

She started coming around.

"Ayesha darling," Mirza said, "are you okay? What happened?"

"I don't know," she said. "I guess I just passed out. I feel sick. And oh, so very weak."

She started to get up but she was swaying, wobbly on her feet. She lay back down on the cement walkway. I tied Kodak's lead rope to one of the chipped teal-green posts of the balcony.

"Here, Noor," Mirza said, "get on her other side and we'll help her up the stairs. Maybe she'll feel better if she can lie down for a while. Noor, I didn't tell you earlier because we just weren't sure, but now we are fairly certain—Ayesha is pregnant. We figured she could ride at least to Chitral after going through all of this preparation work, and then maybe fly back to Peshawar and then America from there. You and I would take the horses on."

"A curious development, to say the least."

"Well, maybe that is all that is wrong with her. Maybe after a little rest she will be able to ride. She has been feeling a bit ill in Peshawar. But never yet this much."

But it didn't seem like she was getting any better. The rest of the afternoon Ayesha swooned in and out of consciousness, her brow drenched in a cold clammy sweat, her body burning in fever or shivering with cold.

Mirza and I shod Kodak, tying his lead rope securely to the balcony post. The Second *Nawab* arrived and wasn't happy to see Kodak tied on his veranda, nor the pile of horse manure under his feet. That night the heavens released their fury of waters again. I sat on the porch smoking and watching the surrounding mountains revealed in silvery bursts of lightning. The old hotel and the very mountains themselves seemed ready to tumble down in the rumbling roar of the thunder.

The next morning, August 3rd, was Ayesha's twenty-first birthday. She wasn't any better. At one point when she regained consciousness for a few moments Mirza gave her a gift he had purchased in the back alleys of Ander Sher off the gold bazaar in Peshawar. It was a piece of raw rock with a rough ruby protruding from it, intended as a memento of the Karakoram Highway, but now it seemed she wouldn't be riding on it with us.

Mirza asked me to see if I could arrange transportation to the local hospital. We were fortunate for modern times. In the past, under the rule of the *Nawab,* there was no hospital for the people of Dir, though he did keep an extensive hospital for his dogs.

The Second *Nawab* donated his jeep and we drove across the boulder-strewn riverbed and up the hill to the hospital. With each jarring bounce Ayesha grabbed her head, trying to control her nauseating headache.

When it was explained that Ayesha was a foreign woman we were ushered into a cold, bare, cement-floored room with a hard, wooden bench to wait. Outside on the concrete veranda local women covered in full *burqas* squatted on the ground waiting with snotty-nosed babies.

In Dir, as in most of the Frontier the tradition of *purdah* is still strong. Men bring their ailing womenfolk to the hospital/clinic where they sit outside while the men go in to talk to the doctor. If the doctor has a question about the ailment that the husbands or brothers can't answer, he will send them out to ask the woman and relay the information back to him. The doctor will never examine them directly. Better to be ill with their family honor intact than risk dishonor from inappropriate contact.

After a brief wait we were ushered into the doctor's office ahead of the other patients in the examination room, and those who had been waiting all morning on the veranda. Most had either walked up the hill themselves or had been carried if they were incapable of walking. Motor transport is not a luxury of the masses in Dir. Rain was coming down intermittently. After a diminutive interview, the doctor said he thought it was malaria and wanted Ayesha to go further up the hill to the lab for a blood test.

Our jeep wouldn't start. While we waited in the doctor's office Ayesha became violently cold, shaking and shivering. We asked an orderly for a blanket. After several minutes he returned to inform us that after searching the entire premises not one could be found. By this time Mirza and I had wrapped her in our own.

As we sat, the doctor's desk started shaking.

"Noor, are you tapping your feet and rattling the desk?" Mirza asked.

"No, I thought you were doing it."

I went outside to see the mountains shaking under us. Great! I thought. What else? Now an earthquake. After a few moments of not knowing which way it would go, the mountains and the building stopped their trembling and all was back to normal.

The jeep started and we drove to the lab. The electricity was out. The technician came out with a tray holding needles, syringes, cotton and a small bottle of Detthol (antiseptic) to draw blood. While we waited an aged orderly brewed us tea and we sat on the veranda to drank with the technician. He explained he was waiting for the power to come back on so he could have enough light to see through his microscope.

We couldn't wait any longer as we had our horses to attend to so we suggested he bring the microscope out on the porch to use the available sunlight. After looking through his microscope he confirmed malaria and we drove back down to the hospital. The doctor gave Ayesha an injection and some pills and suggested we get her to Peshawar and Lady Reading Hospital as soon as possible.

What to do with the horses? They are a lot of work for one person. Also it seemed that in this season the only available food was barley, which didn't sit well with them, especially Horse. The manager at the *GTS* office told me the truck depots were mostly on the road below the hotel along the river. I went to see if it I could hire a truck to take me and our animals back to Peshawar. I would try to hire a Suzuki for Mirza and Ayesha.

As I was walking to find the transport office I was informed that water from the intense rains was washing over the roads in several places this side of Timagura and that no small vehicles could get through. Along the road behind the hotel trucks were parked. Drivers sat around, repairing, washing or smoking and chatting. On one side the road dropped down to the swirling muddy river. The other side steeply sloped up to the backs of the buildings fronting the main bazaar, propped up with rough hewn wooden supporting posts. Obviously building permits were unknown in this part of the world, though somehow buildings kept standing year after year. Was it just strong faith keeping everything upright? *

I talked to some drivers about our needs and was escorted to a steep ladder stairway which led up to a crate-wood shack clinging to the hill side like a matchbox supported by matchsticks. Inside, nearly fifteen men were seated. Many by their rough, unshaven-faces and greasy clothes looked like truck drivers. There were two telephones and several large dog-eared ledger books. The man who had accompanied me explained my requirements to one of the agents and shortly afterward I found myself making arrangements with a driver and his mate. They would meet us at the hotel in one hour.

On the way back to the hotel I talked to several drivers along the road. All agreed that smaller vehicles could not cross the overflowing river banks between Dir and Timagura. "If someone agrees to take you," I was told, "you will be stuck at the rivers and will have to wait or cross in a truck and then get a car up to the next flood."

I discussed the situation with Mirza and we decided we would all go in the truck; at least it would be high enough to get through the flood waters flowing over the road. Ayesha and he could sit in the front seat with the driver while the mate and I would sit in the open box compartment above the cab.

A boy at the hotel said even though the wheat threshing season hadn't begun yet he knew where he could procure some sacks of *boose* to pad the truck floor. He returned in some 45 minutes with news that he had failed. We were all packed and the truck was arriving. We needed something to pad the hard metal floor. Behind the hotel were small trees. It was time for them to meet our axe. When the truck arrived we covered the floor with freshly cut sprays from the trees.

We arrived in Peshawar at midnight and I had the truck drive up to the front of Lady Reading Hospital. There we dropped Mirza and Ayesha off and then proceeded to Sherqi Tanna. I woke up Akbar Ali, the police inspector in charge of the Peshawar Police Horse Lines. He and a few of his men helped me unload the horses. We stowed the gear in the storeroom. I took my rifle and the shotgun over my shoulder and got a *rickshaw* home to Hashtnagri.

In the morning I visited Ayesha in the women's ward at the hospital. The brick walled cement-floored room had 40 steel cots with thin mattresses. The beds, due to the overcrowded conditions of the hospital, were filled with two women per bed side by side, head to foot. Because of the hot season most of them were getting glucose drips. As we sat visiting with Ayesha, next to her

---

* There is a popular story in Pakistan about a Chinese delegation that came to observe the country. When they got back to China people asked them about Pakistan and they answered that they now believed in God. People asked "why?" and they answered "We saw how the Pakistani Government is and there must be a God for Pakistan to exist!"

head were the blue tattooed feet of a young *Koochie* woman.

Ayesha recovered enough to fly back to the (United) States after two weeks. Deni (Brigadier Yazdani) graciously consented to letting us winter the horses at his stud farm in Toba Tek Singh, down in the Punjab about 100 miles southeast of Sargodha, a grueling twenty-four-hour truck journey.

Then Mirza flew back to the States to be with his Ayesha. Because of her extended high fever and general weakness from malaria she lost the baby.

Such is the will of **Allah**.

And me? I'm waiting for the Flying Coach to leave for Lahore.
That also must be the will of **Allah**.

Inside Badshahi Mosque, Lahore

Chapter 8
Religion and Decision

*"To **Allah** belongs the East and the West.*
*Whichever way you turn, there is the face of **Allah**."*
Al Qur'an

There are two facets of religion—an inner and an outer. Heart and soul—spirit and social. I feel rather esoteric at times on an inner level, though my heart's devotion is to Islam. God is God. I know it is easier to fool myself than God. God? With God, there is no fooling.

How close is God? Show me the distance between us all. On the outside I love the trappings of Islam. The brotherhood and unity brought through communal prayers and one strong ideology is unbeatable. It is my chosen way to worship that Great Power which most people call God. For me it is so full time and concrete. It fills my social religious needs.

Only God can fill my heart. I didn't become a Muslim because I wanted to change my life, but in it a gradual/quick change is constantly taking place. To be myself is what I want to be. To be me. But Islam fits quite nicely into me. I fit into Islam nicely.

Lately it seems even more I have fallen into the Pathan culture, and in the Pathan culture, *al-hamdu-lillah*, Islam is strong, an underlying force. Thank God and pray as much as you can. Sin as much as needs must. **Allah** is all understanding and merciful. Thank God, for man isn't. Didn't Martin Luther (1483-1546) say something like, "Sin strongly, but believe more strongly"?

Change? I think it is easier for someone from a culturally diverse, loose, egocentric society like I grew up in—a so-called "advanced society" to change. At least in the West we are brought up with the idea (is it to our advantage?) that if we want to we can change anything. However, actually we can only rearrange. We can change nothing. God changes.

Nasreen—I don't know. Maybe she has too much Asian acceptance of fate to even conceive of change. Whatever will be will be. She seems happy enough with her family, in her place, if not with her work. But I can't forget her head, gentle and soft on my shoulder; her telling me she is unlucky, that she is compelled by life and circumstances. Is it life and life only?

Is my vision a vision of pure insanity? How much of it can really be? What if she asks me to take her away right now? It is almost beyond my imagination. Like having a gun. One day you might just have to shoot somebody—maybe yourself—in the head. I'd better make sure I am prepared to take her away before I ask. Hell, I'm sure enough to try. Play the cards as they come. She is dealing. **Allah** has already arranged the deck. I'm ready to play. I've already been dealt a full hand. If she decided to come with me it could surely complicate my life. But then, I don't care!

Well, there is no need to ponder if un-poured milk will spill.

Waiting for a tonga, with horse gear, near my house in Gari Saidan

Loading the horses into a truck at Sargodha Remont Depot

Photos by Ayesha S.

Chapter 9
A Goodbye Visit

May 1989
Peshawar City

Mirza and Ayesha have returned from the U.S.A.

Another grueling, dusty, 24 hour truck trek across Pakistan ferrying the horses back to Peshawar from Toba Tek Singh. We have a servant, I have a companion, Habibullah, a farmer and relative of my neighbor Musa Khan. From our experience last year we've realized that at times just three pairs of hands are not enough. Also, I wanted a Pashtu speaking friend along. And now we're ready to leave Peshawar on horseback once again. If I can get myself away from Lahore. I feel so at place there in her house. So right in my heart that it's hard to relate to getting into any trouble with it.

Any more trouble than I am already in, that is. But anything is possible. I have survived 44 trips up and down GT Road, *al-hamdu-lillah*. But in recent months there have been police troubles at her house. Some days there has been absolutely no business or only a few privately brought customers. I've been carrying two extra 500 rupee notes in my wallet. Would a bribe get me out of a dilemma?

Several times upon arriving I'm told I have to leave right away due to the police. Twice they are at the front door when I arrive. The alibi is I'm just the brother's friend from Peshawar. Still I have to leave, but at least the police don't arrest me. This month she has stopped working. Or so she says.

There has usually been at least one girl there to do the work and Nas does the negotiating. She comes out of the room, crosses the courtyard and hands her husband or Mama the money. Then the other girl goes in the room. I've seen it from both sides of the curtain. I'm glad it's not her behind the closed door. Several times she tells me the customer wanted her and left when he discovered she wasn't working. I haven't seen her work in a month. If it's true I'm happy for her, but I'm only there one day a week.

Nargis is still the reigning champ and fastest worker. No one is in the room with her for longer than five minutes. Her record is two minutes. When the customer came out of the room I looked closely at his clothes. It didn't seem he'd had enough time to take his pants off and put them back on. Of course, it's hard to really blame the fellow. With the lack of exposure to the opposite sex, just sitting alone with one of these "loose" ladies, a cigarette held to the lips, a hand on the leg is enough to arouse. That is enough sexual fantasy in Pakistan. Life is simple. So are the fantasies.

I still want her so bad it hurts. I wouldn't have been ready to leave on this trip without a final visit to say goodbye and to bring this thing to some sort of resolution. I want to make her, to keep her, my friend. Is such a thing possible or conceivable in Pakistan (for me)? I don't know. Highly unusual for sure. I know it's unacceptable. So what? Whether she is my lover or not, I love her. I want to keep a special friendship. Am I only dreaming?

I arrive at 9:30 in the morning. She answers the door; it always thrills me when I see her face at the door. The house is quiet. Her husband is away and Mama is asleep on a *charpoy* on the veranda. I relax on a *charpoy* in the back room waiting, dozing under the fan. Twice I open my eyes to see her turning away from the doorway after having peeked into the room. Then I open my eyes and she's in the room with me, standing over me smiling with a cup of tea.

"Tea?" she asks in English as she sits on the *charpoy*. "You were sleeping?" she continues in Pashtu.

"I was, but now I'm awake. I saw you at the doorway before as you walked away.... "

"Twice," we say in unison, laughing.

She takes a pack of Gold Leaf cigarettes from her bra. We laugh again. It always strikes me funny that she carries them like that.

"You know I'm going on a long horse trip," I begin.

"Yes, I remember you telling me. You said you were going to China." She looks down, fidgeting with her cigarette on the table top.

"I told you we weren't going there. Remember? The *banchod* Chinese Embassy wouldn't give us permission to ride the horses into China."

"Oh yeah. The Chinese dog eaters," she says, shaking her head and tugging her ear lobes (*toba*).

"Yeah—you know I'll be gone three or four months. I won't be able to come see you. I'll be remembering you all the time. I do now,"

She's running her slender silver-tipped fingernail around the brim of the tea cup.

"Will you remember me?" I ask. "What do you think?"

"Don't think."

"What are you feeling?"

"Don't feel. Leave it!"

"No, tell me!" I press.

"I don't know! How can I feel?" she demands.

"You must feel or you are dead," I say as I look at her.

She runs her fingers through her wavy hair, wiping her brow. "It's hot in here," she smiles seductively.

"Well, that's some feeling." We laugh together. She looks out onto the veranda, then shuts the door.

"Noor Mohammada, come on, lie with me, then you are going. Now it is possible," she purrs as she stretches out on the bed next to me.

"I thought you weren't working? I'm happy just to see you, darling, just to be with you."

"I am not working. But now, with you, I like. I want. It is our last time, then you are going," she says softly as she curls up along side me, her lithe form long and warm as she sighs sweetly into my ear.

I sink down on top of her holding her body tightly to mine, melting into our own heat. All things are right for a limited eternity. But at the back of my mind

I know I came here today for something more, something definite. She almost drives those thoughts from my mind. I lie on the bed thinking. Listening to our breathing and the clop-clop rhythm of the overhead fan. Now at least there is a glimmer in her eyes as she lies next to me. I hold her slender form tightly in my arms and breathe in her sweet breath.

"Nasreena," I start in again, "tell me the truth. What are you thinking about me? Will you miss me?"

"What choice do I have, Noor Mohammada? You cannot love me anyway. Someone like me? Come on, now you speak truth!"

"I do!"

"Don't!"

"Why? Why?"

"Because it can't be... but I will think of you... at least *Juma* to *Juma*."

"God knows if you'll be remembering me. I'll be remembering you all the time."

"Don't think it. It's impossible. There is too much difference between us. I cannot change my life, my family," she says as she wiggles out from under me. "We've had some love. That is something. Love is different. It is not important. This is my family, this is my life Noor Mohammad. It's not your life. I've been here since I was a small child. How can I change?"

"If you want to, you can," my Western mind says so very easily.

"No I can't!" she says, looking down at the bed sheets, bunching them up in her hand.

"But I love you!" I plead, bending to place my face between her face and the bed, "Nasreena, look at me!"

She turns away. "Don't love me, leave it!" she says.

"I can't."

"You can if you want," she retorts.

"I don't want to. You make me happy. Still, I'm sad."

"Sad? Why sad?" she asks, seemingly concerned.

"You don't know?" I laugh painfully. "Because I love you so much but can't have you. It's been very difficult loving you like this. But loving you makes me happy. I'm compelled. I'm happy just to know you, to see you."

"This love is not important love. People's loves come and go. This is where I am. You'll go back to Peshawar and find a nice, clean (decent) girl to marry. You could not marry me. What would your friends say and think? You will forget me."

"I can't forget you Nasreen. I don't care what anyone else thinks. You are the only one important to me."

"That, God knows better," she says and abruptly stands. "We must go out now. I need to open the door before Mama wakes up or my husband comes home."

"Nasreen, I must go back to Peshawar tomorrow," I say, exasperated. "I'm not free now. I've been busy helping get the horses and equipment ready for this trip. When I've been free I've come here to see you. How can I stay away? My heart is here, with you. We'll be leaving for the mountains in a few days. I'll miss you so very much."

I raise and take her face in my hands, running my fingers through her silky soft hair. Her cheeks are warm and smooth. I kiss her forehead lightly. She closes her eyes and smiles. She seems content. I am. She puts her arms around my neck. I brush her lips with mine.

"No kiss. It's dirty," she protests, trying to move her face away from mine.

"Our lips aren't dirty," I say, holding her face and kissing her again. She relaxes and softly kisses me back, her arms tight around my neck. I lower my hands from her face. We look into each other's eyes and lock hands. Then our fingers loosen and we slip apart.

It is nice to be in the garden lounging on a *charpoy* in the afternoon shade. As we sit quietly talking her husband comes home. He knocks at the iron door. She gets up to answer it. The iron front door's hinges squeal as she opens it. Mama wakes up. Nasreen brings me lunch and tea. A pimp comes with a customer. She goes into the front room to negotiate. Then she comes out with the money and gives it to her husband. Nargis goes into the front room, closing the door.

Nasreen tells me to go into the back room. Her husband is sitting there on a *charpoy*. We greet, shaking hands. I sit across from him.

"Do you want to do a *program* with Nargis?" he asks. "She's a good girl. You can have 100 rupees off her price. You know Nasreen has stopped working, don't you?"

"Yeah. If it's true talk, I'm happy."

"It's completely true."

"*Insha'Allah.*"

"Nargis is working," he pursues.

"No, I don't want to do it with Nargis! Thanks anyway"

"You don't like her?"

"Of course I like her. She's a friend. But I haven't been coming here just for that. I come here to see Nasreen. I think you understand."

"Yes, I understand. You are in love with her, aren't you?"

"I think you know that."

"So then, why don't you marry her?" he says.

What? I'm stunned, caught off guard. Here we go again. Two stories by two people. Now I want to play it out. He seems more the liar than Nasreen, though. She comes in the room and sits beside me. "What's going on?" she asks.

"Isn't she your wife?" I continue on with him, motioning at her with my eyes. Now that all three of us are in the room together I'll press it to my advantage.

"No, she's my cousin," he answers. "My mother is her mother's sister."

"She says she's your wife," I say, looking at her. She returns the stare. Her dark eyes seem to be agreeing with me. I shift my gaze to him as he continues, "She's lying. She's not my wife. Why don't you marry her and take her to Amerika?"

"I would love to take her there to visit, but I live in the *Sarhad* (Frontier Province). Understand?"

"Nasreena," he says, switching to faster Pashtu, "he says he is in love with you. That he wants to marry you and take you to Amerika. What do you think? Do you want to go?"

I'm not sure if he's joking or not. She smiles sadly and lowers her head.

"He says he's not your husband," I repeat to her, "just your cousin. What do you say?"

"He's lying," she answers me. "If he said it was night that would not make it night. He is my husband. He is also my cousin. Our family would never allow it." She looks me sadly in the eyes. I find it hard not to believe in her eyes.

"I'm confused," I confess.

"Why?" he chuckles.

"My mind is burning in this."

"Really, you should marry her. She's not my wife. She's the liar. I'm not married. I only took her to the bed, like all the girls. For me one is not enough," he boasts.

"*Ah cha,*" I tell him, starting to think more Asian. "How much bride price do you want?"

"Five *lakh* rupees," he states blatantly.

That is a ridiculously high bride price. Nobody pays 500,000 rupees, roughly $24,000, for a bride. Yet, I consider, mentally counting on my fingers. Could anything be too much—too much for Nasreen?

"He's lying," she insists, breaking my thought. "He's a fraud, a cheat."

He's a pimp and a first class scum. And my lover's husband.

"Well, you know what you want," he says to me as he looks at his watch. "I have to go now. I'm late. I'm leaving for Karachi tonight. I must get my car ready. If you want her, remember, five *lakh!*" He stands up, straightens his *shalwar kameez* and leaves the room.

"Noor Mohammada," she looks at me sweetly, brushing up against my shoulder.

"Nasreena darling, let's get married," I tell her.

"Leave it! Don't talk that. You know it can't happen!" she snaps, a look of irritation creeping into her face. "He's a liar, I said. We are married. Besides, where will you get the money? Five *lakh* is very much. It's all impossible."

"None of that matters. I'll get the money somehow. If I have to steal it I'll get it. Even if he is your husband, that doesn't matter. By his talk he has given you divorce. Listen to me," I say, grabbing her shoulder, "I speak truth!"

She dismisses my words and turns.

"We have to go now. Mama will want me to cook dinner," she says as she stands up. "We've been in here too long and she will want to know what our loud talk is about."

She tries to leave but I grab her arm, pulling her back down on the *charpoy*.

"Don't go yet. We still have much talk to do."

"No, I must go," she insists, slipping free from my grasp leaving me with no answers and a funny feeling inside.

I follow her out onto the veranda.

"Come tomorrow, we can talk then," she tells me.

"No. I want a little more private talk with you now!"

She looks at me for a few moments. I won't give in.

"Okay, then. Let's go into the front room. But it must be fast."

"Don't worry. What I have to say won't even take five minutes," I laugh sardonically.

I sit in the front room in an upholstered over-stuffed arm chair. She goes out and returns with two lit cigarettes. She sits next to me, putting a cigarette to my lips.

"Okay already, talk," she says impatiently, inhaling on her cigarette.

I take a drag on mine and say, "Nasreen, I want to sleep with you."

"Are you not satisfied with me now (today), Noor Mohammad?"

"No, I mean tonight."

"What talk is this? You know I cannot work at night."

"I didn't say work. I said sleep. What time is he leaving for Karachi? I'll come back. Who else needs to know? You run this house anyway."

She closes her pretty eyes and thinks. Realization and a smile dawns on her face.

"He'll be leaving about 10:00," she says. She then continues quickly and quietly, "Look, you come about midnight. You'll know he's gone if the car is not there. Everyone else should be asleep by then. Then I will leave the street door to this room unlatched. I will be waiting. Now go."

She rises, dropping her cigarette butt on the brick floor. I step on it as I stand, crushing it out with my sandal. I toss mine out onto the bricks in the yard. It rolls across the bricks lodging in a crack. I go to the front door. She walks with me. We say goodbye and I leave.

At midnight I'm quietly walking down her dark, empty street—no car in front of the house. Good. I'm not exactly sure of his position but he does carry a pistol. I test the door. It's locked.

I hear the bolt slide. The door cracks and I slip inside. I hope it is her in the room. It seems like I feel I can never fully trust her. Sometimes it's hard.

It is her. I kiss her but after a moment she turns her lips away so my lips are on her warm cheek. I kiss her behind her ears. Her hair smells of jasmine and cigarette smoke. She turns out the light as we lay down on the bed together. She lights a cigarette and I can see her face dimly illuminated in the orange glow as we talk.

Finally alone with my Nasreen—*nazbeen* (pet)—at night. We finish the cigarette and merge into the darkness of the room. It's the first time we have ever spent a night together. I'm in Pathan heaven. Though, as usual with Nasreen, it is only temporary. At 5 A.M. we're too merged in the closeness of our bodies to wake from the sound of his car pulling up out in the street. We stir, to awake instantly to the sound of the metal yard door being pounded upon.

"*Nasreena, war kalo ka!*" he yells (open the door). "I'm home. Let me in."

We untangle our bodies and get out of the bed.

"Go, Noor Mohammada. Come back at 10:00. Now hurry, get out of here! Goodbye." She motions me to the front *behtak* door as she glides out of the room. She goes out to open the courtyard door. In the noise of the metal door opening and him coming into the yard I slip out and down the street.

Close escape. Do I need this movie? Can I stop it?

In Pakki Thatti Chowk I find a *rickshaw* and wake the driver, who is sleeping curled up on the back seat wrapped in his blanket like a shroud.

"You want to go?" I ask.

"Where, Khan *sahib*?"

"Hira Mandi," I tell him.

He looks at me sleepily and strangely. "25 rupees, Khan *sahib*. It's late."

"It's early, friend," I say, glancing at my watch as I climb in. "Prayer time. Let's go!"

He drops me in Hira Mandi. I go to a *hammam* to take a shower, then to a mosque for morning prayer. Breakfast of *puri, cholay, chai* and a Gold Leaf cigarette. I use the toilets around the side of the Badshahi Mosque. Later I sit in an archway of the mosque overlooking the morning bustle and buzz of Lahore and the *Minar* of Pakistan.* The majesty of the mosque never ceases to amaze me. I kill more time aimlessly strolling the bazaars. In Hira Mandi a pimp I vaguely recognize approaches me.

"Are you going to Nasreen's house?" he asks, joining me as I amble.

"Later," I say.

"Good. I'll go with you."

"No you won't. It's my own house. I go alone."

At 10:15 I'm back at her house. I pay Mama to spend an hour alone together with her. We're lying in the back room on the bed with the door locked when her husband knocks. She gets up and lets him in. He hasn't seen me yet today. He says hello and asks how I am. It's okay now, this time I've paid to be with her.

"I thought you were leaving for Karachi last night?" I ask him nonchalantly.

"I did. But I came back early this morning, before prayer time. There was a problem with the car."

"Well, I hope it isn't too big a problem."

"No it's not."

"*Insha'Allah.*"

He puts his pistol in the small suitcase she keeps her jewelry in, then leaves the room. She locks the door again.

"Nasreen darling, I must leave," I tell her, not letting go of her body. "In a few days we are leaving on the horse trip. It will be very difficult to come and see

---

* *Minar-e-Pakistan is a tall minaret in Iqbal Park Lahore on the northeast side of the Badshahi Mosque, built in commemoration of the Lahore Resolution. It is constructed on the site where on March 23, 1940, seven years before the formation of Pakistan, the Muslim League passed the Lahore Resolution (Qarardad-e-Lahore) demanding the creation of Pakistan. This was the first official declaration to establish a separate homeland for the Muslims living in the subcontinent.*

you, but I will, *Insha'Allah*. I will come whenever I am able, from wherever I am."

"*Insha'Allah*. Will you bring my mother a red teapot like we talked?" she asks seductively.

"I will try. I will look for one in Gilgit." I look her in the eyes. "And then?"

"And then? God knows better. I don't know. Mama may decide."

"Why don't you decide?"

"It's not for me to decide. I am only a (young) girl. You understand Pakistan, Noor Mohammad. The family, the personal clan is important. What the elders say is important."

"Five *lakh* is a lot for me to raise."

"Five *lakh! Banchod!* He's crazy. It's for Mama to decide."

"God knows better. I must go. Will you give me one last good-bye kiss? A farewell kiss. A sweet memory?"

I hold her head. Her lips are warm soft and moist. Finally we stand. I can't let her go. I kiss her forehead. The cigarette we're sharing falls to the floor. I don't care if it burns the house down. I'm already burning. I tell myself I must and I let her go.

"When will you come to see me again? On *Juma*?" she asks so innocently.

"*Juma!* I wish. Next *Juma* I will be on a horse somewhere in the mountains, missing you. I will try to come see you when we reach Chitral, but that may not be for a few weeks. It's hard for me to go, but I must. I'm committed. Goodbye my sweet friend, goodbye my love, my heart's problem."

She scrunches up her pretty face, "Forget this problem talk. Try to understand, God is kind."

"Yes, *Insha'Allah*. Now I must go. I love you so much. I can't forget you. Still, when I think of you my heart weeps."

"Noor Mohammada, I was here doing this before we ever met. Because of it we met. Don't worry. May you journey safely now. What has happened with us, God knows. What will happen, that also is known to God. Be well, Noor Mohammad Khana. Travel safe. *Khuda hafiz.*"

"*Khuda hafiz.*" I hold her at the doorway, trying to soak her essence into my body and soul. Into my heart.

And then I'm gone. Walking down her dead-end street. Feeling full. Full of emptiness. Her sweet goodbye echoes in my mind, in my heart.

Where do we go from here?

Lahore — Gateway from Hazoori Bagh (gardens in front of
Badshahi Mosque and Shahi Fort) to Shahi Mohallah (Hira Mandi)

Peshawar, from my window in Gari Saidan

Cooking rice in degs for a wedding in Gari Saidan,
Peshawar City

Back street between Gari Saidan
and Takiya Saigaan

Gari Saidan — Bibi Ji's house in
background

Qasim Ali Khan Mosque
Mez Garan, Peshawar City

Jenda Bazaar, off Karim Pura
(near my house)

Wedding *jaanj* (*barrat* or parade) — the groom is so hidden under his flower *kanta* (garland) and *seri* that he and his horse have to be led through the streets.

Badshahi Mosque, Lahore

The Badshahi Mosque (Emperor's or King's Mosque) is the congregational mosque built by the Emperor Aurangzeb (Alamgir), grandson of Akbar, in 1673-4, to the south of Lahore Fort. It has one of the largest open courtyards of any mosque in the Islamic world, capable of accommodating over 55,000 worshippers.

The architecture and design of the Badshahi Mosque is closely related to the Jama Masjid in Delhi, India, which was built in 1648 by Aurangzeb's father and predecessor, Emperor Shah Jahan, also the builder of the Taj Mahal.

96

Wazir Khan Mosque, Lahore

(Top photo) In the courtyard of Wazir Khan Mosque is the grave of Syed Muhammad Ishaq, known as Miran Badshah, a divine from Iran who settled in Lahore during the time of the Tughluq Dynasty (14th century). The tomb predates the mosque.

The Wazir Khan Mosque has been described as *"a mole on the cheek of Lahore,"* a mark of beauty on the Subcontinent. It was built in seven years (1634-1635 A.D.) during the reign of the Mughal Emperor Shah Jahan. It was built by Shaikh Ilm-ud-din Ansari, a native of Chiniot who rose to be the court physician to Shah Jahan and later the Governor of Lahore. He was commonly known as Wazir Khan.

With Khan Baba (Anwar Khan Durani), Cinema Road, Peshawar City

Charekobaan Bazaar, near Sabzi Mandi (the vegetable bazaar), Peshawar City

Mez Garan (the Copper Bazaar), Peshawar City (near Qissa Khanni Bazaar)

see all photographs in color at:
http://www.pbase.com/noorkhan/00journalphotos

G T Road, Hashtnagri, Peshawar City

'The Boys from Sargodha' *Photo by Ayesha S.*

Abdul Wahab and son (with ice cola, for us) working on our equipment

Chapter 10
We Leave Peshawar

Jumaraat (Thursday), *Mazdigar time* (mid-afternoon)
Suba Sarhad (Frontier Province)
June 1st, 1989
Tangi, second day out

Looking across the dusty tobacco fields in Tangi. A mud walled Pathan fort, women passing by, white *chaddars* blowing in the wind. Horse *tongas* with clanging bells rattle by. It's great to be in the North West Frontier Province. A burst of staccato machine gun fire peppers the air. A wedding no doubt, or a *sunat*. Yet it does remind me how hopelessly out-gunned we could be if it came down to it.

Yesterday we rode out of Sherqi *Tanna* where the horses had been staying in Peshawar, riding to Charsadda in the height of the summer heat. Stayed at the Charsadda police *tanna*—at least the horses did. We stayed at the Venus Hotel in Bacha Khan Chowk.

We barged our way into the *tanna* in a haze of dust and jangling bells, causing confusion with the policemen on afternoon duty. They didn't know how to cope with armed foreigners from Peshawar riding Pakistani Army heavy breed horses—equestrian behemoths in Pakistan. Fortunately for us, as the dust and confusion of the spectacle of our arrival settled down, the second in command of the *tanna* showed up.

Yousaf Ali Khan, whose family lives behind Inspector Akbar Ali at the Sherqi Tanna police horse lines told us that we could tether the horses out on the side of the building next to some crumbling old stables. While Habibullah wiped the sweat and grit off the horses we unloaded all our gear into the *tanna's mal khanna*. Our personal saddlebags were loaded onto the back of a *tonga* out in front of the *tanna* gates and Mirza and Ayesha left for the hotel. Habibullah and I stayed to arrange dinner and breakfast for the horses.

"I thought we had 'official' letters to guarantee us official accommodations?" I joked with Habibullah.

"The horses are Army, huh?"

"Yeah, they're official. We're not. We're just their servants."

Habibullah left with a policeman to bring 100 pounds of fresh corn stalks. I walked to the hotel in time to take Ayesha across the *chowk* to a *hammam* to take showers. The hotel's only facility was a small room on the roof with a toilet and a water tap.

Hammams are public bath houses which in Pakistan are usually combined with a barber shop, and of course are only for men. You can tell them by the multitude of towels hanging out to dry in front over the dusty street. You enter the florescent bright and mirrored barber shop where you get a towel and soap if you need it (included) and shampoo (at an additional price). The bathing rooms are usually small cubicles with a bucket and a scooper-cup. Generally there are two taps, slightly higher than the bucket, for hot and cold water.

We got some curious looks from the barbers and the all-male clientele of the *hammam* but people were too discreet to say anything if they suspected. In Pakistan a woman never goes to a *hammam*. Of course Ayesha was dressed in men's clothing and a turban covered her long hair, but that in itself was as unusual as her going to a *hammam*. After riding horses for seven hours in above 100 degree heat breathing diesel and eating dust it is difficult to stand on traditions.*

When we awoke early at 4:00 the next morning the hotel was locked with no one to unlock it to be found. We had anticipated this eventuality and prepaid our bill the evening before. We crawled out a downstairs window. The normally busy and noisy *chowk* was completely deserted except for a few stray dogs.

Saddlebags hoisted on our shoulders, we walked down the deserted street toward the *tanna*. Habibullah had gone ahead to give the horses breakfast and brush them. Our first morning out and we're not the happiest of campers; grumbling about bad beds, bad hotels, the lack of *tongas* when you need them and the weight of our saddlebags.

"I thought you said the horses were supposed to be carrying these things?" I called over my shoulder to Mirza in the silent dark morning street.

"Have I told you to go to *hell* yet today, Noor?" he answered.

We drank a quick pot of *chai* in a dark, dilapidated tea house across from the *tanna* while the horses finished eating. We found a sleeping policeman inside the tanna to unlock the *mal khanna*. We carried all the gear outside, piling it on a broken brick wall next to the horses.

Finally the horses were almost ready. Watered, fed, brushed and saddled. Mirza, Ayesha and Habibullah did the final touches, adjusting the pack saddle on Horse. I had a smoke with the policeman on duty who was watching us as he finished his night watch. He gave me a small *tanka* (piece) of *charras* for the way.

Hot and dusty road, murder getting to Tangi....

Stopped to adjust the pack saddle in a graveyard just outside Charsadda. As usual men and an assortment of boys gathered around. Two of the men assisted me to lead Hercules, Shokot and Kodak to a well where water was being pumped by an electric corkscrew pump into an irrigation trough. We gave them a drink while Mirza and Ayesha tried to properly distribute and tie down the load on Horse.

When I arrived back a table and some rickety folding chairs had materialized. A few older grey beards were sitting, younger men and boys standing around us in a circle. Morning *parattas* and *chai*. It was 8 A.M. before Charsadda was behind us.

We rode for several hours and stopped in front of a huge lavish deserted looking estate next to a building of the Pakistan Tobacco Corporation. We

---

* *It would have been too dangerous for her to do this horse trip dressed as a woman. In Pakistan, a woman just doesn't go on a journey like this! Besides, it would have attracted too much attention. From a distance we appeared as four men.*

dismounted and led our horses down a long tree lined drive. My right hand was starting to ache. Yesterday after a lunch of *pakoras* and *chai* at Nagoman on the Kabul River Habibullah had taken a bus on to Charsadda to make advance arrangements for our arrival (to no avail). Until then he had been walking and leading Horse by a stout, blue lead rope tied to his halter as we hadn't brought his bit. After Nagoman I started ponying him, holding the lead over my right side. He was resistant and the constant jerking and tugging must have pulled something inside my wrist.

Two *chowkidars* appeared from a small shack on the side of the mansion with chairs and a small table. They brought a plastic pitcher with *gor sherbet* and a jagged chunk of ice so large it stuck out of the top of the pitcher like an iceberg. "We are poor and simple men," they explained. "This is poor man's drink."

No problem. The weather was hot. The drink was cold. Besides, I liked the cooling effect and taste of *gor sherbet*. I'm a simple man myself. *'Sada khund kavee'*—simplicity gives enjoyment.

The house was closed, the residents in Islamabad. When we departed my left my hand was aching, an intensely throbbing pain. Mirza wrapped it tightly with my turban. He had to help me on to my horse.

Just outside of Sherpao we stopped. I felt as though I would pass out from the pain of my hand. Some locals informed us we've stopped outside a hospital. It was a one story cement building with a few rooms and a veranda in front with a broken down wooden bench against the wall. Dry dirt clod flowerbeds separated the dry front yard from the dusty dirt drive. The leaves of the rose bushes looked gray with dust in the hot sunlight.

We went in. The doctor was sitting in an almost bare room. Behind him was a cabinet with some boxes and jars of pills and medicines, a desk and a few unraveling wicker backed chairs.

I couldn't move or straighten my hand.

He wrapped a bandage around it and gave me a package of aspirin. He wrote me a prescription for muscle relaxants, a cream and some sort of vitamin syrup.

"You should be able to fill it in Tangi," he said. *"Insha'Allah."*

We drank water from a tap on the side of the dry flowerbed outside. The excess water running off was instantly swallowed up by the silty, thirsty earth.

We continued riding.

By noon the horses were miserably hot, sweaty and tired. So were we. The temperature was somewhere between 105 and 115 degrees. We were hoping Habibullah had done better with our arrangements today than he had yesterday in Charsadda. I tried to impress on him to insist using our government *firman* but I realized I didn't know the proper word for "insist" in Pashtu. I told him to "ask strongly."

At 1:30, as we ride into Tangi, we see Habibullah sitting in the shade by the side of the road. He stands and takes Horse's lead rope, leading us to the Tangi Community House. Now this is the way to do it. Water running in flowerbeds alongside a fenced, grassy field. Awaiting us are shade, rooms with overhead fans, *charpoys* and food. A cartload of 60 small bundles of fresh green clover arrives for the horses.

Maybe early to say, but the trip seems to be getting into gear. It is hard work. Hot and slow. Sometimes I hate being such a spectacle. I've grown accustomed to being able to blend in fairly unnoticed in the Frontier. It's rather hard to arrive unnoticed with four loaded and hungry horses, bells a jangle. But my main problem isn't being incognito. My main problem is still Nasreen.

My visit last week with her is still etched in my mind. I'm completely enthralled by her. Enticed. So damned compelled. But if I really love her, how can I leave her there for another four or five months? She's a prisoner, but she doesn't even care. How can I leave her there doing that?

And yet I do.

It burns into me knowing where she is. I tell her I'll take her out but I just don't act. How can she believe me? Can I believe me? What am I doing? What should I do? And what will happen if I do it? People say "Don't." My heart says, "Do."

Is she just joking with me? Playing some game? Or is it me who is playing a game? I don't know. Is she my door to an entirely new and wild future? Or my gateway to hell? She says how does she know I won't leave her for someone else if I fall in love again? Is it me who can't escape the upbringing of my tribe and culture? How far will it go? How far can it go?

June 2nd, *Juma* (Friday)
Rest day at Tangi
I'm a liaison officer. Hanging out with the locals. Talking. Smoking. Handling supplies and arrangements. Clarifying the purpose of our strange equestrian quest to curious villagers. Why would we want to ride horses when motor vehicles are available? —a reasonable question. Explaining our needs (mainly the horses' needs) and improving my language skills with every step.

Off to *Juma* prayer with Boztan Ali, the community center *chowkidar*. Leaving the mosque I sight a Hindu dome poking over the rooftops. We wander through the narrow back lanes of Tangi to find the old Hindu temple.

Later I return with Ayesha so she can photograph it.

June 3rd
Tangi to Takht-i-Bhai along the Upper Swat Canal (*"forbidden Tribal Territory"* as stated in Mirza's travel *rutter*).

Rode all morning until noon in sweltering heat along the Swat Canal. On our right was a 15 foot slope down to a gully lined with trees. Beyond, fields led off to small, rolling hills. On our left the cool, blue waters of the canal, about 40 feet wide. The road was hot and dusty. No time to stop.

Here we discovered that Kodak and Hercules were deathly afraid of camels. As we passed some calmly grazing on brush on the other side of the line of trees Ayesha and I had to hang on to our reins with all of our strength to keep the horses from bolting.

Halfway to Takht-i-Bhai we stopped at a place with some small open shops under thatched roofs supported by poles for cold bottles of *Shazan*. I got a shave from a barber who had his chair set up under a tree, a cracked and weather stained mirror hanging from a nail in the tree. Ayesha hovered around us taking photos.

As we rode on Ayesha was ponying Horse. Horse to show his independence decided to head down the embankment to eat the short grass on the other side. Kodak refused to do anything except get his neck entangled with Horse's lead rope. Ayesha kicked his sides (lovingly) and screamed at him trying to get him to follow Horse down the embankment to assist in pulling him back to the road. In her stubbornness she refused to let go of Horse's lead rope. No stupid, belligerent animal was going to get the better of her. She was pulled off, hit the ground and rolled down the embankment in the powdery dirt.

Mirza and I turned around and jumped off our mounts. Mirza threw me his reins and ran to his Ayesha. She was lying on the ground, the breath knocked out of her. Luckily nothing was broken but her pride. Mirza took the end of his turban and wiped the grit off her sweaty brow.

Mirza's turn to pony our inexperienced pack animal.

Arrived in Takht-i-Bhai at 2:00 in the afternoon. Dead tired and feeling well cooked. Our clothes were crusted white with sweat salt. Trusty Habibullah had again procured the community center for us. This time even air-conditioned.

Exhausted!

Settled the horses and lugged all our gear inside. Ate a pile of famous Takht-i-Bhai *chappli kebab,* greasy and wrapped in newspaper all blackened with grease soaked through and fresh naan which somebody had brought from the bazaar.

Mirza talked to the *chairman* (the head of the community center) while Habibullah and I went to locate grass for the horses. The community leader and some men offered to take us in a car to see the famous Buddhist ruins of Takht-i-Bhai but we ended up crashed out on the floor in the cool refreshment of the carpeted and air-conditioned room.

June 4th

Up at 3:00

Habibullah watered and fed the horses while we packed the gear and carried it out. He was still brushing the horses while we started saddling them. We got Horse's pack saddle as right as we could.

Off at 5:30. More traffic, dust and heat. Arrived in Dargai half past noon.

Here trusty Habibullah hadn't found us a place to stay. After arguing with a rude chief engineer at the *WAPDA* enclave to no avail we ended up as guests of the Political Agent. We stayed in the courthouse at the Frontier Levy road check post at the foot of the Malakand Pass.

Ayesha and I went to the Dargai bazaar to find food for the horses. The Political Agent lent us a jeep and driver for our errand. He also sent a *Kalashnikov*-toting bodyguard along. Nothing to find in the way of green grass for our spoiled army brats. Finally we located *boose* at the Dargai *tonga* stand. On the way back we picked up a sack of *atta*. Habibullah mixed it on the ground, pouring water over it right in front of our boys. They weren't impressed. They didn't seem to conceive of such a mess of dry weeds as food, being used to high-class fresh army feed. It was the first time they'd eaten such a dry concoction. They weren't pleased.

We sat in the garden of the Political Agent looking across the fields at the Malakand Mountains as the sun set behind our backs. Tomorrow morning we would ride up the pass. (In the late 1880s the British fought their way up the Malakand Pass, building piquets on the surrounding mountain tops to provide cover for their forces. The Pathan tribes of the area fought them every inch of the way. Here the young Winston Churchill, reporting for the London Daily Telegraph, covered the Pathan uprising and operations of the Malakand Field Force as a war correspondent in 1897.) Now, colorfully decorated trucks and buses daily plying every one of Pakistan's roadways fight their way up the pass.

Our *sepoy* driver filled a cigarette and Habibullah and I smoked with him. We taught each other the names of the different flowers in the garden in Pashtu and English. A firefly appeared in the dusk's gloaming. *"Or orakay,"* an interesting word to know in Pashtu. Just because it's a firefly.

We slept on *charpoys* in the Political Agent's court room. Mirza slept on a table under the *punkah* fan to try to keep the fleas and mosquitoes off of him. All our gear, saddles, bridles, saddlebags and blankets, horse grooming gear, boots and guns were stacked along the wall.

June 5th

Woke early. We wanted to get up the Malakand Pass before the real heat started in. A glass of water for breakfast. Didn't want to spend the time waiting for tea. Left at 5 A.M. It was already getting light but the sun had some time yet before it blazed over the mountains. The Levy post was right at the actual start of the pass. Within a few minutes of leaving its gate we were ascending the pass. On one curve a truck passed so close to me it scraped Hercules' saddlebag. I looked over my shoulder to see if it had left any paint on the bag.

We climbed and wound our way up the pass for three long hours vying with trucks and buses for our small piece of road. As we neared the top of the pass old, deserted, stone British piquets like broken teeth, watched over the road. We passed the many colored and tattered flags of a *zirarat* on our left* and under the stone walls of Malakand Fort, continuing over the top of the pass and into the small town of Malakand at 8:30.

Tying the horses at a tea house we had a breakfast of *chai*, melons and biscuits, sitting at a table in the area in front of the establishment where the horses were. Habibullah, who had been leading Horse up the pass on foot went ahead to Piran to find Mirza's friend Daoud Shah and advise him we would be arriving shortly. Mirza had informed Daoud of our approximate arrival date by post from Peshawar. They had met in 1983 when Mirza was riding solo to Chitral and had been attacked by Afghan refugees along the road who thought

---

* *The shrine of Hazrat Sikandar Shah Baba, known as Spin Shaheed (White Martyr)*

he was a spy. Not being able to converse in any local language hadn't helped his predicament. Luckily Daoud spoke English and was able to explain to the Afghans in Pashtu that Mirza was a Muslim convert on a horse journey, not a spy. He invited Mirza to stay with his family with typical Pathan hospitality. Now, six years later he was returning—en masse.

Riding downhill to Piran the horses' shoes slipped and slid on the smooth worn pavement throwing small stones and sparks as they went. We reached the crossing leading to Rangmahalla and Piran where Habibullah was waiting at the roadside, lighting up a *duc cigarette* (per my earlier private instructions), as he pointed the way to Piran. I lagged behind letting Mirza and Ayesha lead the way down the dirt road. I reached down and took the smoking cigarette Habibullah offered me. Mirza seemed somewhat perturbed at my behavior, but this is Agency and I can't seem to feel like a foreigner. Smoking, along with praying, just seem normal parts of daily life here.

We settled in at the fort of Rafiq and Daoud Shah. Their father Haji Sahib is the *Khan* of the village of Piran. The rest of Haji Sahib's sons are living and working in Qatar on the Persian Gulf. Behind the main house was their silk weaving factory with its 20 imported, shiny, Japanese looms.

Mirza and Ayesha slept in the guest room of the main house. Habibullah and I slept down the road on *charpoys* in the yard of their huge new walled fort, under the trees with the horses tethered along the wall. Horse bells and starlight. Horse's back was swollen around the withers, probably due to the rubbing of his pack saddle on the long ascent.

June 6th

Ayesha and I go to Peshawar by bus, taking just over two hours. We spend the early part of the day running around the bazaars attending to horse equipment. Searching out *numdas* (heavy felt) for additional pack saddle padding, extra blankets to go under the other horses' saddles, some tins of Russian tuna for those times when other food isn't available and French's Mustard for Mirza. Mustn't forget Horse's bit, which we had left stored in my house.

In the afternoon Ayesha goes to Lady Reading Hospital to have her legs checked, the main reason she had accompanied me to Peshawar. They have been red, burning and puffy since our second day out and. I go to the PIA office in Saddar to book a seat to Lahore for me.

In the evening I have an arrangement to meet with an Indian friend, an aid-worker, to have dinner. I go home to shower and change my clothes. Her driver drops her in Hashtnagri Chowk at 8:30. We walk to Chowk Yadgar for dinner in a small private booth at the Qaddafi Restaurant. After dinner we walk the twisty cobbled streets of the old city, intoxicated by its colorful and ancient mystique.

Her father is Indian, her mother European. She isn't East, nor is she West; like me, a hybrid. It's very easy for us to talk. She is one of the few people who knows the entire story about Nasreen. She is as far from me in one direction as Nasreen is in the other. For some reason I can more easily see myself with someone like Nasreen. Is that my misfortune?

She gives me a beautiful Afghani tassel for Hercules. I give her an outrageously cut and filigree silver, gold and carnelian Turkoman bracelet. It looks good on her smooth wrist. I have its twin in the bottom of my saddlebag, stashed for Ayesha's twenty-second birthday somewhere down the road in August.

Next morning....

I go to the Special Branch office to have my visa extension, which I had received the previous week, stamped for validity. Then out to the Peshawar airport to catch the 11:15 flight to Lahore.

I'm at Nasreen's house by 12:15.

It's hot in Lahore. I sit in the back room with her and Nargis. They are lying on the bed like two colorful and indolent sleek, patterned cats. Nasreen is in an orange satin *kameez* with snaps. Nargis hands her a *duc* cigarette. She puts her fingers to her lips, telling me not to tell. She takes a puff. We spend a lot of time together just talking and holding hands.

She brings me spicy, red, chicken qurma for lunch. It's so nice to be with her. It's so hard to be in love with her.

I tell her I love her. I do. I hate to think of her staying there for the next four months, though it seems to mean nothing to her. It digs deep inside me, yet I can't stop loving her. In her arms I forget the past. I forget America. I forget who I was before I was here. I also forget most of the important things I want to tell her. She tells me that when I come back I have to talk to her husband, that I should offer him two *lakh* rupees for her. We go to the door leading to the street and kiss and hug in the dark between the metal door and the curtain separating it from the courtyard.

"I'll come back as soon as I can, understand?" I tell her.

"Yes," she answers me. I brush her lips with mine and kiss her forehead.

"*Salaam aleikum.*"

"*Khuda hafiz.*"

And then I'm walking away, down her dead-end street again. It's 9:30 in the evening. I catch the 10:30 Flying Coach back to Peshawar. By 6:30 in the morning I'm in Peshawar. I'm used to the eight hour jostle on GT Road. I'm still always happy to get home and lay my body out flat on my bed for a bit.

Ayesha and I finish getting the supplies we need. As to her legs, the doctors at the hospital say maybe it is the riding, maybe it's the heat, maybe her boots are too tight, maybe an allergy to the horse. Basically they don't know. They prescribe some kind of ointment and some tablets, plus a vitamin syrup.

We bus back to Piran.

Sleeping again out under the trees and stars on *charpoys* in Haji Sahib's walled fort compound with Habibullah and the horses. Lying back and smoking, looking at the twinkling stars and chatting in Pashtu. The ever-present accompaniment of the horse bells.

It's all so familiar. It's easy to just drift away, forget the English, forget the past. What was there before Nasreen and Pashtu? Before the Northwest Frontier Province? A memory of Kabul stirs as the sound of *rabab* wafts across the still night air from a neighbor's radio.

One day in her sweet arms in Lahore. The next in Malakand Agency... in a Pathan fort... under the stars with the four horses and Habibullah.

Rocks, bus and 35 feet of snow near the top of the Lowari Pass

Decorated Pakistani truck

Lower Swat Canal near Mandani

109

Lowari Top (10,500 ft.)

The horses staked out just below Lowari Top

Chapter 11
Dir and Goat Pizza

Juma, June 16th
Written in Deputy Commissioner's guest house, Panakot (outside of Dir)....

While in Piran Horse's withers had gone from swollen to a hard, discolored sore, to an open wound. Mirza and Habibullah had been treating it with some sort of antiseptic wash (tumeric based) that colored the skin around it henna-orange and a white boric acid powder to keep down the puffiness and to ward off flies. These wonderful potions they had acquired at the Batkhela animal husbandry dispensary. We started giving him shots of tetracycline from our own store of animal medicines. I dipped the end of his tail in the orange wash—a festive flair.

We left Piran on the morning of the 10th. Most of our mountain gear we stowed at Haji Sahib's fort and ponied Horse bareback hoping his unencumbered back would heal by the time we reached Chitral. Just outside Batkhela we stopped at the dispensary where they gave Horse an injection of oxytetracycline and washed him and powdered him as we had been doing.

In the late afternoon coming up the mountain toward the town of Talash we are overtaken by a wind and rain storm. With thunder and lightning cracking at our backs and blowing gusts of leaves and blasts of rain around our heads we unroll our plastic army ponchos and start to don them. I fumble with mine. "I hate this damn Western crap!" I bitch to no one in particular.

"Noor, have I told you to go to hell yet today," Mirza shouts, maybe not half in jest over the roar of the wind.

The storm is short lived though, *al-hamdu-lillah*. I don't want to get drenched so early in the story. We ride down the main (and only) street of Talash and see Habibullah sitting in front of a tea house cum restaurant. Written on the wall in Urdu behind him is *'Noor Habib Hotel.'* Fitting coincidence.

He tells us to take the horses down a small rock-strewn alley next to the tea house. In back is a dirt courtyard where we stake them and a *kutcha* mud building with a veranda and two rooms. One is a storeroom for the restaurant and the other has four *charpoys* and a rustic wooden table on the hard packed dirt floor. This is the hotel. The light is a lantern.

We pull the cots outside to sleep on the porch. Two Frontier Levies drop by and inform us they are there to guard us. The last foreigner who stayed here a week ago came through on a bicycle. At night some locals stole his money and his bike. Of course he wasn't a Muslim, nor was he armed, nor did the bicycle have Pakistani Army brands on it, but the local police don't want to take any chances this time.

In the morning Habibullah and I feed the horses at 4:00 A.M. We brush and saddle them and Habibullah helps Mirza and Ayesha with the pack saddle while I smoke with our two guards inside the room. Another point against me with Mirza. He's feeling I want to be with the locals more than I do with them. A nearby resident tells us there is an old Hindu temple/fortress up in the hills just outside town. When it was built? Nobody knows. He wants to take us there.

We ride through Talash and cut west down a narrow lane following this man into a graveyard. We cross and continue up a narrow trail until the animals can't go any further. We tie them to some trees and one of the Levies stays with them. I shoulder my rifle, Mirza his shotgun, and we continue with the remaining Levy and the local as a guide.

Feeling sick. I've had a cold the last few days, probably from sleeping in the air-conditioned Flying Coach when I last went to hot Lahore. Mirza gloats and says that it serves me right. I lay on the hill under the crumbling towers and walls of the ruins and doze in the quiet sunlit mountain air. Feeling very little like a tourist or sight-seer. It feels I've seen enough old rocks around the world to last a lifetime.

On to Timagura....

Riding through the town of Timagura feels endless in the heat and dust. Crowds of honking buses, noisy tractors and people. A pack of young boys walking home from school follow us and throw rocks at the horses' feet which they think is quite funny. I scream at them in Pashtu which they also think is rather amusing.

In the late afternoon of the 11th we arrive at the District Commissioner's Guest House, which is on a hill overlooking the Panjkora River and the town of Timagura. Very modern accommodations with carpeted, air-conditioned rooms, real beds (4 inch-Molty Foam mattress) with sheets and real bathrooms. Outside the rooms there is a veranda with potted flowers, a delightfully cool green manicured lawn and well-tended flower beds, a brick wall separating the lawn from the cliffs that fall off to the river several hundred feet below.

Habibullah and I share a room, Mirza and Ayesha another. The *chowkidar* is a Pakistani Christian named William Bill. He boils the drinking water, serving it chilled in old Johnny Walker bottles. I spill gun oil on the carpet while cleaning my pistol. Sorry Billy Bill.

He doesn't want to serve Habibullah, our *"servant"* along with us in the dining room. I say I'll eat with Habibullah outside. We all end up eating outside on the lawn. The meals are a mixture of Pakistani and Western food. Habibullah doesn't care for the non-Pakistani parts of the meal. Neither do I but we're hungry. Personally I'd rather be eating buffalo stomach in Lahore. Ah, hem....

We write rude comments in the dining room's guest book. Most of the other comments are by American DEA agents who have stayed there to observe the progress American money is doing towards the eradication of poppy cultivation. Ah, hem....

The morning of the 12th as the sun is starting to rise I come out on the porch to see Mirza standing over by the brick wall watching the river and wispy clouds turn from orange, pink and purple to blue over the slowly clearing mountains. I walk up to him in the calm quiet of birds and river.

"Noor, we need to talk," he tells me.

"Okay," I answer, though I don't usually like to hear English this early in the morning, lately. We both continue to gaze at the mountains.

"Noor, we have a problem. It seems like you hardly want to be friends with Ayesha and I anymore. That you don't want to be with us. You rarely even talk to us. You mostly hang out with Habibullah or locals. And you're smoking far too much *charras*. Do you want to be on this trip or not?"

"I'm torn. Of course I want to be on this trip. We've planned it for so long. But it's so hard for me now, you know, with Nasreen there in Lahore. I want so to concentrate on trying to get her out of there. It's dangerous for her there."

"What do you care? I don't recall her asking you to get her out of there."

"I love her, damn it. How can I not care? I've got to try. Because of that, at times this trip seems such a drag. I talk to Habibullah because it helps develop my Pashtu and although he's uneducated he's Pathan and I can relate to the way he thinks. I smoke to help me forget that she's there and I'm here. That she's her and I'm me."

"You've just got to become more of the team. It's becoming you and Habibullah—Ayesha and I. It's not good. Not for us. Not for the trip."

"*Ah cha, yaar.* You're right. I will try. *Insha'Allah.*"

The morning of June 13th we leave Timagura for Warai. Habibullah goes ahead on the bus to make arrangements in Warai. On the road about 10:00 we see Habibullah in a pickup. He tells us there is nothing in Warai for the horses to eat. He's going back to Batkhela to bring green grass.

The day is hot. We stop by the banks of the Panjkora River to relax and cool off. Our mounts stand in some shade under a line of trees and munch the weeds. Ayesha and I wade in the swiftly flowing icy water. Mirza picks gold flakes out of the wet sand with the point of his knife and we try to decide if they're gold or not. Wishing for something to smoke.

Some young Pathans come by and ask if I smoke.

"Sometimes," I answer guardedly. They fill a cigarette.

"Now is a good sometime," I laugh.

One of them goes up the hill to the other side of the road, returning with a full pot of tea and tea cups. Two little girls come down to the side of the river wrapped in raggedy *chaddars* to wash their family dishes and pots. Sand is their soap. The air is fresh.

The hotel in Warai is just an unfinished room over a cinder-block tea house. The floor is gravel, the walls facing the road on two sides are completely open. The animals are staked out in the dirt of the alleyway next to the hotel restaurant. A massive crowd of men and boys gather around. A very rowdy feeling. We carry all our gear up a rough hewn wooden ladder to our quarters on the roof. An exhausting affair. Habibullah hasn't arrived. Ayesha and I take the horses to a creek to water them. There is a field with short short grass. Some boys say they will bring green grass for them to eat.

"See, this isn't so bad," I tell Ayesha.

They return carrying armfuls of *bhang* (cannabis). The animals won't eat it. Considering Shokot's wild temperament we're probably lucky. Just after dusk Habibullah pulls up with a truck full of fresh grass. He hadn't been able to procure any in Batkhela so he had gone to Swat. I'm sick; a fever, body aches and pains.

A ten-year-old renegade kid attaches himself to us. He brings us a plate of kebabs from somewhere in the bazaar. He says he works as a *cleaner* (conductor) on his father's Suzuki pickup truck. He has six other older brothers. We sit around discussing if we want to bring him along as Habibullah's assistant. He smokes cigarettes and uses *nuswar*. He even smokes *charras*. Habibullah talks some reason into us. To have this urchin along with us would be insanity.

The crowds of onlookers have advanced up the ladder and gather around the open sides of our room, blocking the light and air circulation. Reasoning with them in Pashtu only helps as long as Habibullah and I are talking. Once we sit down again the human wall of staring eyes and gaping mouths closes in.

Finally it's Ayesha's turn to blow up. She calmly asks Mirza for his riding crop. She asks me to tell them in Pashtu to leave. They don't. Then she gets up. They laugh. All hell breaks loose. She attacks the crowd with a vengeance, lashing out with the crop and screaming in the little Pashtu she knows, mixed with English.

The men are surprised to be attacked by a crop-wielding, turban-wearing, Pashtu swearing woman. They scatter, scampering down the ladder. Many jump to escape her flaying lashes. With about five of them still climbing down she shoves it away from the roof and they crash down over the heads of the others. Everywhere is pandemonium, but we do finish our dinner in relative peace.

After eating Habib, Mirza and I go down to settle in the animals for the night. My job is explaining to wounded ego, macho, machine-gun wielding Pathans that after a hard day's riding in such hot weather one sometimes loses one's temper and it's really nothing to get upset over anyway, really, and after all, she is *only a woman*. "Travel madness" has reared its ugly head.

Mirza and I sleep wearing our chambered pistols.

I'm still sick in the morning. We decide that Habibullah will take my place riding and I'll take the sack of horse gear ahead in a Suzuki to Panakot to make arrangements. Habibullah informs us that though he had told us he had ridden before, he had never done it in a chair (saddle). Ah yes, these small interesting Pakistani differences keep arising.

And now we're staying at the beautiful guest house built by the Nawab of Dir for his British visitors. When Dir became a part of the newly forming country of Pakistan in 1947 the guest house was seized by the government and is now the property of the Deputy Commissioner of Dir; large rooms with carpets and fireplaces, private baths with bathtubs and hot water heaters; a huge separate cookhouse and a dining room with polished oak table, chairs and a china cabinet; concrete walls three feet thick to guard against the extremes of weather.

Habibullah gathers wood and chops it. He and Ayesha prepare dinner while Mirza and I attend to the horses out back. We eat on fine china and a white table cloth. The *chowkidar* and his mate put up with us begrudgingly. It seems that we've disturbed their solitude.

In front is a long, wide veranda with plants in brightly-painted red terracotta pots. There are big, wooden chairs with softly padded cushions. The lawn is on two levels and the flower beds are well tended. The roses are in bloom. The lower lawn has two cannon, one British built and the other a perfect Pakistani copy. They're trained on the road leading down out of the Lowari Pass. They are well oiled and seem in fine working order.

Habibullah shows up with a sack of straw to mix with the flour I have already procured. Last week we were complaining about having to give this to the horses. Now they're learning to be happy with whatever they can get. So are we. We're all hungry. It's Juma and Ayesha and Mirza are off with the *D.C.* to meet with the *Nawab* in his castle.

Habibullah and I stay around smoking and sleeping. I'm still sick and he's Pakistani. Sometimes it takes something to slow the western mind down. Habibullah does it naturally! We listen to some Khayal Mohammad and Farzana tapes I've brought with me on Mirza's small cassette player.

"Noor Mohammad, what are you thinking?" Habibullah asks me, seeing me sitting on the bed staring off at the ceiling.

"Oh, nothing Habibullah."

"Noor Mohammad, your people never just sit idly, but then truly, you are different from any other I've met."

"Well, Habibullah, you're right. Actually I'm thinking of my girlfriend in Lahore. I miss her too much."

"It is definitely strange. How did you ever become close with a Pathan girl? Pathan families are very closed with their women. Especially a young, pretty girl."

"They live in Lahore, you know. Lahore is much looser than Peshawar."

"Maybe for Punjabi people. They have no respect and honor, the dogs. But even for Pathan people living in Lahore—that you could meet a daughter is very strange."

"I've known her father, actually her uncle, for a very long time, since I was doing business in Kabul. Then I was in Lahore and I ran into his oldest son. He told me they were now living in Lahore so he brought me to their house to see his father. I didn't see her, of course, or any of the women on the first visit. But then one time I was there and a girl brought us tea. I looked in her large dark eyes and since that moment I've been trapped in those eyes, in her spell. And now they treat me like family. They are very free with me." (In case I actually do marry Nasreen it would never do to let it get out under what circumstances we originally met, nor her family's business. Habibullah would never understand or approve no matter how much he likes me. I would lose honor with him.)

"Very typical Pathan story, your catching a sight of her like that. But usually there would be no more. It is unusual they are so free with you concerning their women. Was the son also your friend in Afghanistan?"

"Not really. He was away at school most of the time when I was there. Now he is my enemy. He has been engaged to her since they were children.

He treats her like a dog. Now he is my very big enemy."

"Ah! Even a more typical Pathan story. It was the family's mistake letting you two see each other in the first place. They still let you meet her?"

"Uh-huh. And sometimes we are alone. They have a big house in Lahore."

"Then it's a dangerous story, also."

"*Che po meena ki, Majnoon ghunday, sadiq vee—Che Layla po darwaza ki, darbon neeshta.*" I quoted a favorite poem by the 17th century Pashtun poet Rahman Baba.*

"Maybe, but these stories often end in death."

"Habibullah, my brother, life always ends in death. When, that is for **Allah** to decide."

"Yes. *Insha'Allah* the black eyes will not decide yours, Noor Mohammad Khan."

"That, God knows better. I can't stop loving her. It is my *qismet.*"

"Yes, it is fate. You are really more like a Pathan than an *Englaise*"

"Yes, it is fate."

I lay back and close my eyes. Habibullah goes out to see to the horses.

Thinking of Nasreen much today. Why do I feel so happy when I'm with her, so incomplete without her? Not quite sure how I'll pull off getting from Chitral to Lahore, but I've got to see her before riding into the mountains. To spend another night with her. And so I dream on in my fever.

Horse's back isn't any better. In fact it's worse. We're still treating it with the orange washes and the white boric acid powder. We're out of tetracycline.

When Mirza and Ayesha returned from their visit with the *D.C.* she related this story to me — After visiting the Nawab's grandson at his palace, the *D.C.* took them to visit a family friend. This house was nothing like the sturdy buildings of the Nawab. It was a typical rudimentary subsistence dwelling, but the family was so much more welcoming and kind than the cold treatment we had been recieving at the guesthouse. Sweet tea kept flowing and flowing, spicy snacks were set before them, everyone was curious about their story. Then she made the mistake of mentioning she was cold. Up jumped their host, going into the back family section of the house. He soon returned with what she knew was one of the only sweaters in his house, offering her to take it. She had to think fast to find a graceful way to decline because she couldn't stand thinking that one family member would be cold up in these mountains this winter. This generosity to complete strangers from a family with nothing extra to spare reminded her why she loved the people of Pakistan so much.

Ah cha. This is Pakistan! *Zendabad!*

June 23
Written in Bumburet, Kafiristan (Kalash)

We left Panakot shortly after dawn and rode up the Lowari Pass. The mountains above us were covered in snow. To our sides were pine forests and icy valleys. Nearing the top we crossed places where the glaciers had been cut

---

* *'When you are in love, like Majnoon, When Layla is at the door, there is no guard'*

back to allow the frail road to proceed. Packed ice towered 35 feet above us. Water ran from under the glacial ice creating frigid rivers across the road, though the crystal clear water just covered the horses' ankles, cold pebbles at their feet. Crews were cutting ice into blocks with axes and loading it into the backs of Suzuki pickups to take down to Dir to use in stores and restaurants.

We arrived at 3:00 P.M. at an altitude of 10,000 feet—500 feet below the summit of the pass. There were two small stone huts with a canvas tent between them that served as tea houses. Also there was a small leveled plot of land where another was about to be constructed. We staked the animals on the hillside above. Habibullah hadn't arrived yet. A few fellows came up with an axe and some wooden stakes. Our iron *moogays* were with Habibullah. They made us impromptu *moogays* with the wood and their axe.

We off-loaded all of the gear, piling it on some large rocks and on the short grass. We opened our "horse hospital" and tended to Horse's withers. They didn't appear to be getting any better even though since Piran he had been walking along with no weight on his back. The few locals helped us carry our baggage into the tent. This constant lugging before dawn or after spending all day in the saddle has becomeg familiar and old.

Habibullah drove by in the back of a jeep as we were sitting in one of the huts eating a meal of goat meat and melted goat cheese with *naan*. Goat pizza! I ran out to hail him. Amid confusion the vehicle stopped for a few brief seconds to permit Habibullah to jump out. He forgot the bag of vegetables on the backseat he was bringing for our meal.

After the heavenly diversion of a meal Ayesha and I passed out from sheer exhaustion on the straw-matted floor of the tent. When evening came we brought the horses down and staked them out on the small leveled plot next to the tent we would be sleeping in. Here we could keep our eyes on them and hear the constant jangle of the bells around their necks. Shokot escaped three times during the night.

In the morning we started late after tea and *parattas*. It was already getting light. We walked our horses up the hillside behind the huts over the short, green turf and many-colored tiny wild flowers. In and out of gullies, the horses' hooves slipped and scraped on the granite stones.

We reached the top (10,500 feet) at 8:00 A.M. and headed on down into the Valley of Chitral. Forty-two switchbacks and two and a half hours later we were down the major part of the pass and in Chitral Valley. We stopped in a village called Ashrit around noon for lunch. Tea and biscuits. Nothing else was available.

We rode on and on. It seemed a long way to Drosh.

Drosh
Arrived at 5:00 P.M.
Staying at the Drosh Hotel, right on the road coming into town. They gave us buckets of hot water to wash in and a decent (though greasy) meal. Amazing what will pass as a suitable hotel sometimes. It's all a matter of perspec-

tive. The horses didn't fare so well. Habibullah got a pile of old bread from the hotel restaurant and mixed it with water for their dinner. They're definitely learning to eat what they can get, a lesson we've already learned.

Picking our way along the precarious road to Kalash

Resting in Kalash (no saddlebags)   *Photos by Ayesha S.*

118

Chapter 12
Kafiristan

June 20th we "rest" in Drosh.

Mirza and Habibullah go to Chitral to talk to the *D.C.,* get permission to enter Kalash and check on horse food. Ayesha and I spend hours looking for anything for the horses to eat in Drosh. We walk through the fields trying to locate where wheat has been threshed so we can get some *boose.* We comb the bazaars for flour, barley, anything! Never thought we'd be so happy to find a sack of barley. The flies in the barren lot behind the hotel where the horses are staked are loathsome. The stench of their old bread and barley shit is nauseating.

The next morning we leave Drosh. Horse's withers are bad. Coming down the Lowari Pass Shokot's withers have started developing the same type of hard lump that Horse started with. Mirza rides Hercules, Ayesha on Kodak, Habibullah and I walk leading Horse and Shokot.

We stop at an animal husbandry hospital on the outskirts of Drosh to see what can be done for the horses. The dispenser washes their wounds with the same orange wash we've been using, powders them with the same white mixture and has a boy bring out a bottle of oxytetracycline. There is only one shot left in the bottle. The rubber seal has already been punctured but he plunges the dark green fluid into Horse's neck.

The boy goes to the bazaar to bring more medicine. We have tea with the dispenser on the veranda. The liquid in the fresh bottle is a pale translucent amber color. He gives Shokot a shot. Mirza and Ayesha leave Drosh ponying Horse and Shokot. Habibullah and I remain to get supplies and hire a jeep to take us to Ayun. It's enjoyable doing business in the bazaar with Habibullah. He does the bulk of the talking. No one realizes I'm foreign. Just a couple of simple Pathans from down country. It's nice not being the show for a change, just to relax in a part of it.

Habibullah and I hire a jeep to take us and the gear to Ayun. He will find another vehicle there, *Insh'Allah,* to take him on to Kafiristan. I plan to meet Mirza and Ayesha at an old suspension bridge that spans the river. We pass them on the road. An hour later I get off before where the bridge, built in 1927, crosses the muddy, rushing Kunar/Chitral River.

Beyond the bridge the road becomes dusty dirt on the west bank leading on to Ayun. It saves the distance of first riding to Chitral before backtracking to Ayun. Mirza had obtained our passes to enter Kafiristan when he went to Chitral with Habibullah. My job is to wait at the bridge to help them cross the four horses over. I sit on a grassy hillside overlooking the river with stream-lets of clear cool water gurgling through the short grass around me and tumbling down the rocky banks to join the swirling river. I smoke a cigarette and idly watch some grazing sheep.

Mirza, Ayesha and the horses arrive shortly after noon. Before crossing they join me on the grass for lunch—a can of sardines, crackers and water. Mirza wants to take pictures documenting our crossing of the suspension bridge but it is not to be. Before we can shoot anything a soldier comes up to us and tells us that it is illegal to photograph the bridge. He is an older fellow, approaching middle age and a potbelly, who could probably only be posted in such a useless post as guarding some *stupid* bridge (In all fairness we are right on the war sensitive Afghanistan border).

We show him our letters from Islamabad, first the English one to duly impress, then the Urdu one so he can read it. He's rude. He doesn't seem to be able to read Urdu very well anyway.

"We don't give a *shit* about your stupid bridge, anyway," I tell him. "We just want pictures of our horses crossing it. What importance can it have? It's an antique. That is why we want the pictures."

Mirza and I discuss shooting him but wisely decide just to head on. We still have a long, hot ride to Kafiristan and besides, bullets are costly.

After crossing the bridge I lead Horse. He is becoming lethargic and needs to be coaxed along. The bank of the river is rocky and 40 feet below us. The water is impossible to get to. In half an hour I decide to try to cadge a ride on the next jeep passing by to get into the valley of Kafiristan before the horses do to make sure all arrangements are satisfactory.

Kafiristan (Kalash) is the home of the Kafir Kalash—primitive pagan tribes known as the Wearers of the Black Robes. Their origin is cloaked in controversy. Legend says that five soldiers from the legions of Alexander the Great settled there and are the progenitors of the Kalash.

They live in three valleys in small villages built on the hillsides near the banks of the Kalash River and its tiny tributaries in houses of rough hewn logs, double storied because of the steepness of the slopes. The lower portions are usually for animals and fodder storage for the long harsh winters. They practice a religion of nature worship. It is the only area in Pakistan or Afghanistan that hasn't been converted to Islam, though that is slowly changing with the times. Across the mountains in Afghanistan the *Kafirs* were converted in the 1890s by Amir Abdur Rahman, the '*Iron Amir*' of Kabul and *Kafiristan* (land of unbelievers) became *Nuristan* (land of light).

Fifteen minutes after walking on ahead of Mirza and Ayesha a jeep passes. It slows for me and I climb in. On the front seat sit two men along with the driver. The older of them, with a bushy, brown, wavy beard and wearing a camel color *pakul* cap, asks me if I have heard of Rambur Valley. He tells me he is the headman of the village of Rambur. I vaguely remember him, but to my good fortune he doesn't recognize me. When he had last seen me two years ago I was speaking Farsi and English, not Pashtu, and wearing a turban, not a white *topi* (cap). We had fought because I had defecated down by the river which I hadn't known at the time was their *Kafir* 'holy place.' He had wanted me to wash in the river to 'purify' myself to rectify the situation but I wasn't going to bathe in that icy water. I had told him the hell with him and his foolish *Kafir* superstitions. I promptly left and walked the 10 miles back to Bumburet!

We drive past the Kafiristan turnoff, a steep dirt road leading up and west into the narrow valley of Kafiristan. The jeep stops short of Ayun and I walk the remaining distance. Habibullah isn't anywhere to be seen. I assume he has caught a jeep into Kafiristan and that everything will be prepared for our arrival.

I sit at a rough wooden table set on the side of the wide dusty street with some chairs around it and a tattered canvas overhang to shield customers from the sun and drink mango *sherbet* with delightfully cold, dirty, shredded snow ice, most likely from the Lowari Top.

Ayun is dead as it was on my last visit in 1987. It reminds me of a semi-deserted western ghost town. It is getting late in the day, almost 3:00 P.M. and there aren't even any jeeps waiting around to go to Kafiristan. Not feeling too patient, I decide to start walking the distance. If a jeep comes there is only one road and I'll be on it.

I head back down the road I had come into town on and make a sharp right turn up the dry, rocky, mountain pathway that leads to the Kafir valleys, winding back and forth up the mountain until I am high above the silvery Kalash River twisting through the valley below me on its way to join the Chitral River. At my feet is a steep incline of jumbled rocks and scree tumbling chaotically down to green golden fields of wheat nurtured on the life-giving crystal waters of the river, ripening in the warm summer winds. Good news, I think. Wheat is ripe and ready for the thresher. There will be *boose* available for the horses if we need it, though still I am dreaming of fields of tall green grass in Kafiristan.

At its highest section the road precariously carves into the mountain side, leads through stone cliffs, rock completely overhanging the way. Virtually two miles of rock tunnel. I had been in this rocky tunnel two years before. Then I rode standing on the back bumper of a cargo jeep with two Pathan traders. We had to duck our heads in order to keep them from being chopped off by the sharp rocks overhead. The northern side of the road drops vertically straight off hundreds of feet down to the rushing Kalash River. High up on the opposite mountainside is what appears to be an even more precariously perched narrow road. In reality it is an aqueduct bringing water down to Ayun from higher up where the Kalash River comes out of Afghanistan.

The way is long and I speed up my pace. I want to arrive before the horses to make sure Habibullah has gotten things together. I don't mind walking, in fact, I rather like it as long as I'm not carrying anything. Presently I'm only carrying my pistol and its weight bumps against my hip but it's a feeling I've gotten used to. A heavy, reassuring feeling. In a metallic way.

All the way into Kafiristan only two jeeps pass. One is full of tourists and they don't stop to pick me up. I must look too Pakistani. The other is completely piled with Pakistanis. They really know how to load a jeep in these parts. Two fellows are perched on the hood and a double layer of passengers hang off the rear bumper. I shout to them as they grind dust and gears past me, asking if there is any room, but obviously there isn't and they don't bother breaking their momentum for me.

It takes me three and a half hours to cover the distance between Ayun and Bumburet. I cross a small bridge over the river and walk past the Pakistani government check post at Dobash. I imagine I seem too local for them to bother with me. Even Pakistanis from other parts of Pakistan need to get a permit from the *D.C.* in Chitral to come here, and they need to sign in at Dobash too. The same happened the last time I passed this way, though at that time I was covered under the guise of a turban. Afghan Mujahideen don't need any permit. I guess with my white Peshawari cap and pistol I look too Pathan to bother with. And everybody knows a Pathan's pistol is his permit. What is the point of my entry permit?

I chuckle to myself thinking of a story told me by Anwar Khan in Peshawar about a policeman who asked a notorious *badmash* to show him his pistol permit. The badmash drew his pistol and shot the policeman in the leg. "Do you want to see another page now?" he asked the stunned policeman.

The first hotel to appear as I walk into Bumburet is the Benazir Hotel where I had stayed my last time in the valley. Thirsty, I don't even mind paying eight rupees for a *Shazan* (four rupees at most in Peshawar). I know it is difficult to bring anything up here as it all has to come by jeep from Chitral. It's hard enough getting anything up to Chitral. The *Shazan* is ice cold, having been submerged in a metal basket with other soft drink bottles in the cold irrigation channel across the road from the hotel. Dusk is falling as I trudge on up the road. I pass a few more small hotels. At one there is a familiar face sitting at a table under a veranda directly off the road.

I sit down with a Pathan in his early 30s from Tangi whom we had met on top of the Lowari Pass who had lived many years in England. He is just finishing filling a cigarette. A pot of *chai* arrives as I ask him if he has any news of Habibullah. As we drink tea the *chowkidar* from the government rest house comes down the road looking for me.

In Chitral Mirza had obtained permission from the *D.C.* to stay at the guest house in Bumburet but there is a slight problem. The guest house is under repairs. There is no electricity (the upper end of Bumburet Valley has electricity supplied by a small water-powered generator built by some Swiss people), no running water, no bathroom... nothing! He says Habibullah left all of our gear there but has gone down to the Kalash Hotel to see about making some other kind of arrangements.

As we talk we hear the sound of the horses' bells like an audio mirage growing in the gloaming. A Kalashi boy comes running up the road heralding the approach of our little caravan. I see Mirza and Ayesha. The sun has just set. The fragrant air is calm, quiet, fresh—nothing else is.

As they come up the road and into sight, sweat stained and worn out, the *chowkidar* is just finishing telling me the news of the guest house and of Habibullah. Just then Habibullah comes down the road. There is only one road running through Bumburet and the Kalash Hotel is further up the road, the guest house further still. After the guest house the rough dirt road becomes two trails, one leading south and up the mountain to the valley of Birir and the other following the Kalash River into Afghanistan.

We meet in confusion all at once. Horse looks bad. Almost dead. He is covered in sweat, especially his head, neck and withers. His large eyes are closed and tears are staining his cheeks. Do horses cry? His legs are wobbling. He's barely able to walk. I can see that Mirza and Ayesha are exhausted from the long day's journey plus the mental and emotional strain of getting Horse this far. As we lead the horses up the road I explain to Mirza and Ayesha an English version of what the *chowkidar* has just completed telling me. At the same time Habibullah is telling me (in Pashtu, of course) what is happening with the Kalash Hotel.

He says there are two small rooms but he neglected to make any reservations because he was afraid to give them an advance on the rooms and find out we still wanted to camp out at the guest house. He still hasn't quite to come to terms with the fact that even though we are Americans and therefore "infinitely rich" and seemingly spending so much money on a horse trip of no apparent value, we still count and watch our every rupee, which I'm sure to him seems to be miserly fastidiousness.

"I know that hotel," Mirza says. "I stayed there for a bit with my horse in 83. There's a huge grassy field right in front of it. A good place to tie the horses."

"*Noor Mohammada, selor Punjabian, samon sara, woose hotel la zee. Road banday ma ohleeda,*" Habibullah informs me.

"Habibullah says that four Punjabis are on the road with packs, going toward the hotel just now," I tell the others.

Just then Horse collapses in the road. He won't get up. Mirza, who has been leading him hands me his lead rope. I pull and Mirza whips his behind with his crop. "Get up you bloody bugger! Get up!" he screams.

"Quit it you guys!" Ayesha yells, "Can't you see he can't go on any more."

Habibullah doesn't say anything. He obviously can't understand our actions and motives. He thought we should have taken the horses over the Lowari Pass in a truck. He just looked at me blankly when I explained to him that wasn't the point of the trip and besides after Chitral there would be mountains and passes much worse than the Lowari. If they couldn't make it over the Lowari, they'd never make it beyond Chitral.

"We've got to get him up," Mirza shouts, "or he'll die right here. He can't spend the night here in the road. The hotel is less then a mile away. We've got to get him there."

Finally Horse gets up and stumbles on.

"*Noor Mohammada, zer makkhi lar shah. Haghwi Punjabian akhairi kambray ba akhlee, ou beir munga ba suh oku?*" Habibullah tells me calmly in his low gravelly voice.

"Habibullah's right," I tell Mirza. "I'd better go ahead to the hotel quickly before those Punjabis get there and take the last two rooms. I'll ride Herc."

I swing onto Hercules' massive back and head up the road. Behind me I can still hear the other horses' bells as our weary caravan struggles up the road in the rapidly darkening dusk. Hercules can sense the urgency of our flight and gallops up the road under me. We pass the four Punjabis and jump the small stream that crosses the path leading to the hotel.

The Kalash Hotel faces east, back down Bumburet Valley. The two-story, wooden building looks out over a large, semicircular grassy field. The north side is bordered by the road, the south is ringed by a rock strewn ravine in which 30 feet below the Kalash River rushes noisily by. As I ride up to the hotel I can see some long haired tourists upstairs on the porch. I can smell the familiar sweet scent of *charras* in the air. Some Pakistanis and Kalashis standing around the front of the hotel watch in surprise as I gallop up. I dismount and quickly tie Hercules to one of the poles holding up the porch.

A short man approaches me followed by two others. He's wearing a Nuristani (*pakul*) cap over his greasy black hair that hangs down behind his ears grimy with dirt. His pocked complexion also has an unwashed pallor and he looks at me through close-set, small, piercing black eyes.

Abdul Khaliq is the proprietor of the Kalash Hotel. I explain our situation to him. By the time we hear the horse bells approaching the hotel hasty preparations have been made. Several fellows go off to cut and fetch fresh green cornstalks for the horses' dinner. The sound of the bells waxes louder and our footsore little caravan appears in the twilight.

"What's happening, Noor?" Mirza asks me wearily.

"Look, come, we'll unload the horses here in front of the hotel. Then we can stake them over there." I point with my hand in the darkness to the edge of the field bordering the river ravine. "I've already arranged for some men to bring down some cornstalks from the fields."

As we talk I am still finalizing arrangements with the hotel's jeep driver to drive Habibullah up to the guest house to get the rest of our gear. We leave the other three horses tied to the porch supports and take Horse down to the field under a tree. He collapses and is breathing very hard, lying flat on the short turf. After a time he lifts his head and then rises to urinate. Mirza walks him around. His abdomen is completely swollen. He alternately lies, rolls and gets up on wobbly legs. When he rises Mirza walks him gently until he falls again. We cover him with our blankets.

Ayesha and I unload the other horses in the light of the bare light bulbs hanging on the porch. Habibullah I send off in the jeep to collect our gear from the guest house. We need the *moogays* to stake the horses securely for the night, plus we want the animal tranquilizers for Horse.

At a quarter to midnight I'm squatting outside the cookhouse talking and smoking with the cook, an Afghan from up the valley in Nuristan. Ayesha and Habibullah are asleep in their respective rooms. Mirza is lying in the field next to Horse, propped up by his saddle and covered with a blanket. I hear him call out to me. I go down and join him next to Horse.

"Horse just had some really bad convulsions," he says.

"Do you think he'll make it?" I ask.

"I don't know Noor. God, I wish now that I knew more about horse medicine. This is all my fault for not knowing more. I brought Horse into this and I don't know enough to get him out."

"It's nobody's fault. These things happen. It is the way God wills it."

Horse gets up and we gently lead him as he walks himself. Then he starts to topple again. He's falling against Herc and Herc can't get away because he's at the end of the rope he is staked to.

"Pull him Noor!" Mirza says hurriedly, pushing him with his shoulder to try to keep him from crashing against Herc. Mirza pulls out the razor sharp knife he wears on a sheath around his neck and with one quick swipe slices through the thick rope, freeing Hercules. Horse hits the grass. He's lying on his side and kicking violently. The cook comes down and squats beside us.

"You should cut a hole in his stomach to let the air out," he tells me in Pashtu. I translate this grisly information to Mirza.

"I've never heard of that," he tells me. "I'm afraid it will kill him. I still think he can make it if he can just make it through the night."

But he can't. He stops kicking and holds his head back stiffly. Low, raspy breaths come from deep down in his throat. It's his death rattle. His eyes are already glazing.

"Cut his throat now," the cook tells me. "*Halal* him and then at least the Muslim people up the hill can eat him."

I tell Mirza what the cook has said but he can't hear. We both feel that some miracle will pull him through and he'll be recovering in the morning. But it is not to be. It's too late. He's dead.

HE'S DEAD

"He's dead," Mirza said in English.

"He's dead," the cook and I echoed in Pashtu.

"I can't believe he's dead," Mirza said, dazed.

"You should have *halaled* him," the cook went on, "then the Muslim people could have eaten him. Well, no matter, it's not a waste. The Kafir people don't care about *halal*, the eaters of filth. They will eat him anyway."

That I didn't bother to translate.

We covered Horse with our plastic tarp and a rain poncho. A beautiful, silvery full moon was rising over the mountains heralded by a pearly glow rimming the hill tops. A few silver-lined clouds highlighted the star-studded sky. The moon and starlight reflected diamonds in the ripples of the stream as it splashed over white stones below us down the moss-covered rock-strewn river banks. Horse's body was laying on the greensward, half-a-ton of lifeless, stiffening meat. Life had fled him as the sun had fled the day's sky. The night was still, quiet and peaceful. It was seven minutes after midnight. Mirza and I watched the silent moon rising, neither speaking....

After a time we went upstairs and quietly entered Ayesha's room. She was asleep, exhausted on a *charpoy*, still in her travel-stained clothing. On the other *charpoy* our equipment was piled, atop our rifles and Ayesha's pistol and turban lay perched. At first she couldn't comprehend, or wouldn't believe that Horse had died. Then she began to softly weep.

I left them alone in the room with their sadness shared and sat at the

125

table on the porch alone in the night and filled a cigarette. As I smoked I looked down on the moonlight bathed field. Over by the tree near the edge of the ravine was the covered lump that had been Horse. Wrapped in my blanket I gazed at the crystal bright moon in the sky, shivered and thought of sitting on a *charpoy* cozily with Nasreen on a warm night in Lahore (sweating).

Mirza and Ayesha emerged from the room and we went down to the field so she could see Horse. She petted his soft, cold nose. Only the wind in the leaves and the crickets spoke in the velvet mountain night. The three of us went back to the porch and sat silently at the table until 3:00 A.M., each in our own private thoughts. I went to my room, an eight by eight cubical with the floor covered with colorful quilts to get a bit of sleep. No need to wake Habibullah I reasoned. He could wait until morning for the bad news.

At 5:30 I awoke and went outside. Horse was still laying there, an olive green covered mass on the emerald dewdrop sparkling grass. His body was completely bloated. Last night had really happened. I hadn't dreamt it.

The other horses were standing oblivious in the quiet morning air. Mirza and I had moved them in the night to the other side of the field. They didn't seem to notice their dead comrade as they calmly munched corn stalks. As I stood quietly looking at the pile of cold stiffening meat that was our traveling companion the hotel owner, Abdul Khaliq, came and stood beside me.

"So sorry about your horse," he said shallowly.

"Yeah, so are we," I said, already taking a dislike to the shifty little man. "God knows better."

"What do you want to do?" he started in. "We can't leave him here. It's not good for the hotel. And the local people are superstitious about such things. Yes, we must do something about him right away."

Already some local children were gathering around looking.

"We can get some men and a jeep to haul him away and bury him in the mountains," Abdul Khaliq continued.

"What's going on Noor?" Mirza asked as he joined us blearly-eyed by Horse's side, his blue turban wrapped haphazardly around his head.

"Well, Abdul Khaliq here says he can get a jeep and some men to haul Horse away and bury him in the mountains," I informed him. "We can't leave him here."

"Yeah, we must bury him," he agreed. Turning to Abdul Khaliq he asked, "How much will it cost?"

Abdul Khaliq thought for a moment. He squinted and scanned us with his crafty eyes. "The jeep will be 1000 rupees. And then we must give the men each something for their work."

"You can't get a jeep for less then that?" I asked. It seemed rather dear.

"I don't think so, my brothers. We can't bury him near here. He will have to be taken a long way up into the hills."

"God's blood, it does seem expensive," Mirza said. "But he was our mate. We brought him all the way here to die. We have to bury him."

By now Habibullah and Ayesha had joined our grim little circle and I explained what was happening to Habibullah in Pashtu while Mirza explained to

Ayesha in English. Abdul Khaliq stood by and looked at Horse with his crooked grin. Ayesha agreed that the expensive price no matter, Horse must be buried at all costs, what else was there to do? After the events of the previous day we were all in a state of slightly shocked stupor to say the least. Habibullah just stood there silently as I told him. He understood enough to know that, as it wasn't his money, what he thought was of no real consequence anyway.

"Okay. I will go see about arranging the jeep," Abdul Khaliq said as he walked off grinning.

"*Hagha khor ghod Kafir, ohgura. War-rawan day po ohkhanday, dah da hagha da mor kus ohghaim. Sta po makh banday ghool okama, banchoda!*" Habibullah said under his breath.

"What was that, Habibullah?" Ayesha asked.

"Oh, he said," I took the liberty of answering for him, "Look at that no good *Kafir*. He's smiling as he walks away!"

"Are you sure that's all he said, Noor Mohammad?" she asked, having picked up quite a smattering of Pashtu herself. "I thought I heard some other words I recognized. I think I heard some of them when you were speaking with the truck drivers." she teased.

"Ayesha, my dear, do you doubt my linguistic abilities? Sister, I speak truth! Now let's go back to the hotel and have some breakfast."

We sat at the table on the porch outside our rooms and ate in silence a breakfast of *chai*, greasy *parattas* and greasier fried eggs. None of us could think any further into the trip than the present: what should be done with the lifeless carcass of Horse and what to do with the three remaining horses that morning? As we ate, Abdul Khaliq came up on the porch and stood by the table. "I can't arrange a jeep," he started in suspiciously.

"What do you mean?" Mirza jumped in. "We have to do something about our horse."

"Yes, for sure, brother. But my jeep is gone and there isn't another available just now." He hesitated briefly and with a badly hidden smirk on his face he continued, "Look, my friends, here is the only solution for you. We need to do something quickly, yes? I can get some men who can cut him into pieces. Then they can carry the pieces up to the mountains in baskets and bury him. It's the only way I can arrange."

Ayesha naturally freaked at the idea of cutting up Horse. Mirza and I looked at each other in bewilderment. Habibullah sat and went on drinking his tea as we were talking in English and he hadn't understood a word of what was going on.

"Look, Abdul Khaliq," Mirza said, "let us discuss this among ourselves. Then we will tell you."

"Okay, talk friends, but decide. We must do something quickly," he said, leaving us alone on the porch.

As we were all in an emotional and physical state of shock we decided there wasn't really anything else we could do. We were stuck in Kafiristan and our horse lay dead on Abdul Khaliq's lawn. The greedy *Kafir*, Abdul Khaliq, played on the emotional attachment he knew Westerners have for animals.

Had we been Pathan we would have just said, "So what, he's dead in your field, Kafir. It's your problem now."

We decided Habibullah and Ayesha would take the horses across the road and up the hill to a rock walled corral to bathe them. Lord knows they needed it; they hadn't had a good washing since down country—and we didn't want them to witness what was going to happen to their dead companion, though in afterthought I think it was more to satisfy us than any of the horses' needs. For sure we didn't want Ayesha there to witness the macabre scene that would be unfolding in Abdul Khaliq's field.

Five men arrived with baskets, axes and large butcher knives. They wanted to chop him up down by the river where there was water available, plus out of sight of the inhabitants of the hotel. Too heavy for them alone, Mirza, Habibullah, Abdul Khaliq and I helped drag his stiff, lifeless form to the edge of the ravine. We rolled him over the edge and his big, bloated body rolled and crashed down on the rocks of the river bank below. We heard the sickening crunch of the bones in his legs snapping. Just a heavy, cold piece of spoiling meat now, though just yesterday he had been Horse. Well, that's life... and death. One day we all become just dead meat, don't we?

They took out their knives to skin him. They were only visible if one stood on the side of the ravine and looked down but the thudding blows of their axes could be heard in the hotel, the cold thuds of butchers chopping through meat, gristle and bone. Mirza and I walked down the road to look for grass to buy to feed the remaining horses. Or maybe a field of green grass to rent? Before we left I walked over to the edge of the ravine to see the butchers' progress. Just as I arrived at the edge they were chopping off Horse's head. Big, beautiful Horse, his large, sweet dead eyes. Now just meat. Rather grotesque but we are so far away from the world we had come from.

As we walked down the road a "hippyish" looking moustached fellow with longish hair approached us. He was a Pakistani artist from Lahore. We introduced ourselves and had a bit of a chat. Even though Mohammad Bugi is a Muslim from Lahore, he has been working wholeheartedly on preserving the Kalash arts and culture. He was just then in the process of putting on the first art workshop and show in the long history of Kalash. He had seen us riding in yesterday. He told us of the Frontier Hotel just down the road. It was run by a Muslim and there was room for us. We wanted to get away from the Kalash Hotel and its _Kafir_ owner Abdul Khaliq. We wanted to forget what had happened there.

When we went back to the Kalash Hotel to fetch our little caravan Horse's white skin was laying stretched out on the ground next to the rivulet by the path leading to the hotel, not a good omen.

Now I'm sitting on the porch of the Frontier Hotel. The horses are with Habibullah grazing in a field of grass behind the hotel. The field isn't completely horizontal but it should keep the horses in green grass for at least a week. The hotel proprietor, Shukar Ali, helped us negotiate with a *Kafir* farmer, Ditullah Khan. It was confusing, the languages flying, but accomplished in the end. Ditullah Khan talking to Shukar Ali in Kalashi, Mirza talking to me in English and Shukar Ali and I bringing it together in Pashtu.

Ditullah Khan and his wife are *Kafir*. *Kafir* men wear the same clothes as Muslim men; usually *shalwar kameez*, waistcoat and woolen *pakul* caps, though their women dress differently than their Muslim sisters. They wear black, coarse cotton, ankle-length dresses with red, orange and yellow embroidery and caps with similarly-styled embroidery plus a mixture of red and bright phosphorescent colored plastic beads, cowrie shells and coins. They never go veiled. They also wear a profusion of red bead and cowrie shelled necklaces. Many make a paste of burnt goat horn (called *puru*) and decorate their faces with black dots and patterns. It appears to be made from mud.

Ditullah Khan's daughter, about 17, also confuses me. She dresses in Muslim clothing but Shukar Ali tells me it isn't unusual in Kafiristan for individual family members to become Muslim, thus making *Kafirs* and Muslims in the same family. Some girls choose to become Muslim in order to avoid the obnoxious attentions of Pakistani men tourists, who credit the *Kafir* women with a very loose reputation (though I find many Pakistani men think that about any woman who is not veiled or in the house).

As I sit here and write Ditullah Khan's daughter is sitting on the hillside opposite the porch watching me. She smiles coyly every time I look her way. Is she just curious and friendly or is she making eyes at me? Are the Pakistani stories true or have I just become too Pakistani to be able to rightly judge anymore?

Dead Horse in Abdul Khaliq's field

129

Chitral (from *'chetr'*, basically translated as *'field'* in the local language, Khowar) with snow-covered Tirich Mir, at 25,230 ft. (7,690 m) the highest peak in the Hindu Kush, in the background. It overlooks Chitral town and can be seen from the main bazaar. It can also be seen from Afghanistan. The mountain was first climbed in 1950 by a Norwegian expedition. According to a local legend, it is impossible to climb because of all the jinns, demons, witches and fairies who inhabit it.

The word Tirich Mir has its origin in the Wakhi language. In Wakhi *'trich'* means shadow or darkness and *'mir'* means king, so Tirich Mir means 'king of darkness.' It got this name because it casts long shadows on the Wakhan side of its face.

Phandar and the Ghizar River looking west towards the Shandur Pass

Chapter 13
Side Trips

Aziz's yard in Turi Khuz (village of Brep is in the distance)

June 24th, morning
Bumburet
"Well guys, looks like this horse trip is over," Mirza said.

We were sitting at a round wooden table on the second floor porch outside our room at the Frontier Hotel, looking down the narrow idle peaceful Kalash Valley. The mountains were covered in lush green pine. The fields of wheat and maize, green and golden, rippled in the gentle summer breezes. We could hear the sound of the river rushing through its rocky bed to join the muddy Chitral River somewhere beyond Ayun. Habibullah was up in Ditullah Khan's field behind the hotel watching the horses, slowly rotating the places of their *moogays* to keep them in grass and making sure none broke away to make for the neighboring field of ripe corn separated from our field by only a low wall of loosely piled stones.

"What do you mean? We haven't even gotten to Chitral. For me, for reasons we all know, I could end it in Chitral. I would like to ride as far as Gilgit, to ride up to Mr. Baig's shop, especially after he listened to our dreams and tried so hard to help us back in '82 when we were trying to get horses to ride to Peshawar. I've never ridden to Chitral before, so for me even this has been something. But with Nasreen on my mind, even though this trip is so great, it's hard not to be thinking of her and Lahore."

"Yeah, I know you'd be happy if it were over, Noor."

"In some ways, but not here, not like this. Besides, you've already ridden once to Chitral. This can't satisfy you."

"No, it doesn't. This is one of the worst moments in my life. I've always figured the trip would start after we've left Chitral, once we've headed our faces into the high mountains. To leave the city of Chitral behind us to the south and head into the real mountains toward Mastuj and beyond to the Boraghil Pass. Heading into range upon range of high desolate peaks that we've never set eyes upon before. Every day a new terrain to cross. New vistas. Never going back."

"Yes, that sounds good to me too, even though I know there are quicker and easier ways to get to Lahore."

"I know we could finish it now, Noor, and next week you'd be happy on the Flying Coach on your way to see Nasreena."

"In some ways. But I did also want to do this trip. We planned it together, only then Nasreen dropped into my life."

"I've given my life's blood to get here. Yet we've only gotten as far as Kafiristan and Horse is dead. How can we go on without a baggage animal? I brought him here to die in this barren place. If I had known more about veterinary medicine he might be alive today. There's the three of us and Habibullah. Horse is gone. Poor Horse. I led him here to his death. I should have known better."

"Don't blame yourself. It wasn't your fault. All things come to pass as *Allah* wills it. Besides, chances are it was that bad shot of discolored oxytetracycline that backward country dispenser gave Horse that killed him. What could you do? What could any of us do? What can any man do against the will of *Allah*?"

"Still, I feel that it's my fault. Horse is dead. You'd rather be with Nasreena in Lahore. Bibi Ayesha is only along because I go. I worry about taking her into unforeseen danger. And Habibullah thinks I'm some kind of nut. Hell, you said yourself that even he thought we should have taken the horses over the Lowari Pass in a truck. And now Shokot's withers are getting hard like Horse's did. I don't want to kill another animal. I don't want to endanger my wife. From now on we'll be needing our high terrain gear plus all the extra food supplies we can carry. We barely got by before. What now?"

"We could get some donkeys."

"DONKEYS! NO! NEVER!"

"Don't give up so easily *yaar*. We could take turns walking. I like walking, as long as I don't have to carry anything heavier than my pistol and an extra clip. It wouldn't hurt my pride to not be mounted. I'm not really a horseman by choice so much as by chance."

"I don't mind walking part time either," Ayesha, who had been sitting silently by listening all this time, added. "My back hurts after all day in the saddle. Also, on foot is better for taking pictures. Don't think you're going to quit on us like that. I'm not just doing this for you."

"Look Mirza, you're the horseman. We know your feelings on walking." (he liked to quote a Tuareg saying, "Walking is only for getting from the bedroll to the saddle.") "Ayesha and I can take turns on foot. Kodak and Herc can take turns with the baggage. You can ride."

"I can't ask you two to do that. We're in this together," he said.

"You aren't asking us, we're telling you," Ayesha responded. "We've all sacrificed for this trip. Quit being so melodramatic."

"Isn't the idea to get the rest of us to Gilgit?" I said, trying to ease the mounting tension. "We can even make Habibullah carry his own clothes and bedroll in the Russian backpack. He's had it dead easy up to now anyway. When he 'signed on' didn't he boast that he was a strong Pathan farmer who could walk anywhere and carry anything?"

"And we may not need to carry so much food for the horses. People say after Mastuj it's all fields of green grass," Mirza added.

"Yeah and no rocks! Don't believe it. I think we need to go up north to scout the road; to see what food is available for the horses, to see if the road north out of Mastuj exists, if the rivers are cross-able, the passes passable. I can leave this afternoon for Chitral. Tomorrow morning I'll find a jeep heading north, *Insha'Allah.* I'll instruct Habibullah to go to Chitral while I'm gone to check on animals. Maybe we can still get another pack horse."

"Knowing that ignorant rustic, Habibullah, he'll probably come back and tell me he wants to buy a donkey," Mirza bemoaned sarcastically.

"That's okay. You wouldn't understand him anyway. And besides, I'll teach you how to say, 'I'll throw donkeys on your mother' in Pashtu. It's a common slur."

"Good, Noor. I knew I could count on you for the really delicate cultural maneuvers. So you want to leave today?"

"Yeah, why not? Let's find out what lies ahead of us before we make any major decisions regarding the trip."

"How can we be sure you won't run away to Lahore?"

"Wah! Busted. Oh well, I tried.... Well, what do you think?"

"I think you're right, Noor Mohammad, for once."

"*Shokriya meribani yaar.* Bundle of thanks."

"And I can go too," Ayesha jumped in. "I can bring my camera and take pictures."

"I don't believe it. You're just coming to check on me."

"I should have thought of sending her with you myself. Maybe I should handcuff you to her with a chain."

"If you did I would only rattle it at you when I got back. And then I'd be off to Lahore anyway."

"Noor Mohammad, have I told you to go to hell lately?"

June 25th, evening

Couldn't leave yesterday. Busy making arrangements for Mirza and Habibullah. And patching up their differences. I had heard Mirza shrilly screaming at the top of his lungs in the field behind the hotel. I arrived on the scene to find him almost ready to hit Habibullah over the head with our small hand-held sledge hammer.

"Don't do it *yaar!*" I yelled. "Anyway, you'd probably only succeed in breaking the hammer's head."

He threw the hammer down and picked up a shovel.

"What is going on?" I asked Habibullah.

"I'm not sure," he answered. "Something about cleaning up the horse shit in the field. Let that *banchod kafir* do it when we leave. He charged enough for his field. He didn't even throw his daughter into the deal."

"Habibullah says you want him to clean up the field?"

"I want him to shovel this shit out of here so the horses aren't standing in it. It is really bad for their feet," he explained. "And besides, the flies bother them."

"That sounds logical to me," I agreed.

"It is," he assured me. "Tell Habibullah if it is below his stupid Pathan pride to shovel shit, I'll do it."

"And he can go down to the hotel and add his thumb print to your journal." (about the level of Habibullah's writing ability to help with that chore) When I outlined the reasons behind Mirza's actions to Habibullah he agreed it was a good idea.

This afternoon Ayesha and I sat for two hours under some trees by the stream across the road from the Benazir Hotel waiting for a jeep to come by that could take us to Chitral, or even Ayun. Finally one did come by with room for two more people to squeeze in.

After close to two and a half hours of dust and bouncing over rocks and ditches we arrived in Chitral and were situated in a room in the Tirich Mir Hotel. We went to the bazaar to eat at one of the now numerous Afghani restaurants. Kebabs, fresh hot *naan* and green tea for dinner. Nice change. Not much meat available in Kalash, nor *naan*.

June 26th

Turi Khuz, north of Mastuj

This morning walking in the Chitral bazaar we saw *Subedar* Mohammad Ali, the in charge at the government check post (at Dobash) on the road leading into Kafiristan. He had met Ayesha and Mirza when they stopped at the check post on their way into the valley. She told him Horse was dead.

"So sorry, my dear," he said. Being a practical, curious policeman from Ayun and having an intimate knowledge of the *Kafir* people, he asked, "How did you dispose of him?"

She told him the story.

"How much did Abdul Khaliq," he said the name with some contempt, "charge you for that work?"

"1000 rupees," she answered.

"1000 rupees!" He shook his head incredulously and tsk'ed his tongue. "That is too much! To butcher an entire water buffalo costs only 250 to 400 rupees at the most. Abdul Khaliq is not a good man. There are many complaints against him."

"What could we do? We weren't in any position to bargain. It's over."

"I'll look into it," he said. "I'll see what I can do, if I can help. You are travelers and you are our Muslim brothers and sister. *Kafir* people are very bad people. Is there any service for me, anything I can do for you?"

"Thank you," we said.

"No, what can I do for you? Where are you going now? Will you have a tea with me?"

"No really. Thank you, Ji. So kind of you but we just now finished tea. We're just going to post some letters and then we need to find a jeep heading toward Mastuj so we can go and scout our road."

"Then follow me," he insisted. "We will go to the post office and then I will take you to where the jeeps going to Mastuj load up."

He led the way, helped us weigh our letters and attach the practically gum-less stamps. How typically Pakistani I thought as I watched the government uniformed *Subedar* lick and place the stamps on the card I was sending to Nasreen in Lahore. After we had sent off our mail Mohammad Ali led us between some buildings off the main bazaar of Chitral to a dirt parking area where several jeeps were in the process of being loaded or worked on.

"This is where you will find a jeep going north if any are going today, *Insha'Allah*," he told us. "I'll check on brother Mirza. I'll see what can be done with that *Kafir* rascal, Abdul Khaliq. Good luck to you. I hope to see you when you get back, *Insha'Allah. Khuda hafiz.*"

At 10:30 we left in a jeep going to Mastuj. Ayesha was crammed in the front seat with the driver and two other passengers. I was in back with seven other riders, half a dozen wooden doors and eight five-gallon tins of *ghee.* On the way one of the tins broke open as some of us passengers in the back had to stand on them, splattering us with *ghee* and making the floor slippery. Dust sticks quite nicely to your clothes when they are spotted in liquid butter.

The scenery was spectacular when I could open my eyes through the grit. High rock mountains rose to snowy peaks on either side of us. The stony Yarkhun River gorge sometimes dropped more than 1000 feet at the side of the road. It was bumpy and uncomfortable standing on the *ghee* slippery floor, hanging on to the side rails with knuckles white. After eight hours we reached Mastuj. The last 30 kilometers I counted down every kilometer on the white painted rocks that serve as milestones. We arrived in Mastuj at 6:30. Not much there. A few stores and a small ramshackle hotel with a tea house in front of it. The fields around Mastuj did seem to have grass though.

Aziz, our driver, said if we wanted to we could stay with him in his village about 16 kilometers further on up the road. The following day he was driving on to Brep to deliver his cargo. First, we needed to go to the petrol station where he filled his vehicle with a hand pump from petrol stored in rusty 50 gallon drums. On the way he told us he had gone to college in Peshawar and had become an advocate but then he had bought the jeep and came back north to work as a driver. A more free life in the mountains.

At 7:30 we arrive in Chapali. Aziz and his mate, Nadir Khan, who is also his cousin and brother-in-law, unload the doors at a roadside store. Aziz informs us we still have to walk a couple more kilometers across the river and up the adjacent mountain to his village, Turi Khuz.

Ayesha and I are squatting in the dirt road in front of the jeep. We're contemplating the vanishing purple-orange pellucid twilight and our exhaustion. We're ready to sleep right there on the gravel. It's been a long journey from Bumburet where we woke in the morning. It is dark before we start on the trail with Aziz, Nadir Khan and two others. Aziz is carrying a long, chrome flashlight and a motorcycle tire around his neck. Nadir Khan is carrying a sack on his back and a watermelon in his hands.

We go down a pathway and over a narrow swaying rope suspension bridge that spans the Yarkhun/Mastuj River. We have to go slowly to avoid falling through some of the broken planks of the bridge. Then we continue up the path and along a long water canal clinging to the side of the mountain.

When the way gets extremely difficult Aziz points with a beam of light from his flashlight. In places we have to walk in the cold water, crouching, almost crawling so we don't bump our heads on the overhanging rocks. The stone retaining wall on which we're walking, made of loosely piled slabs of slate, moves under our feet. In one spot where the sharp rocks over our heads become extremely low, I step back onto the shale side. The flat rock moves from under my feet and tumbles down the side into the blackness, crashing into the unseen river speeding somewhere below us.

"*Kala kala da say keygee. Khudai molik day,*" Aziz says.

"Yeah, I bet," I laugh.

"What was that he said?" Ayesha asks me, trying to glean as much Pashtu as possible.

"Oh, he said, 'Sometimes these things happen. God is boss.'" I tell her.

We come onto a rocky inclined stretch lit by silver starlight. Uphill. After close on two hours of walking in the murky night Aziz tells us it's just another 15 minutes. As we cross this stony plain our other three companions leave us one by one, heading off into the dark to their own homes.

In the dark, hanging on to the mountainside we had almost forgotten our fatigue, as one tends to do in times of extreme exertion. Now that we don't have to worry about plunging into the black hole of the cold swirling unseen river if we take one wrong step we again agree that we can just lay down and sleep right where we are on the rocks.

Finally we gain our goal. We enter a wooden gate in a stone wall into a yard, then head up onto a porch and into the guestroom. The night is cold and our blankets are wrapped around our chilled sweaty bodies.

The guestroom is rough hewn wood, stone and mud—plush and comfortably covered in colorful carpets, quilts and pillows. At the moment, the one thing we can truly appreciate is a soft, flat place to lie down. We're fully spent. Aziz disappears and we lie back on the cushions and quilts dozing into easier times.

Aziz reappears with a pitcher of ice cold clear mountain water. He leaves again and returns with our dinner. Two large plates, each with a double layer of husky *chapatti* with a thick, slightly-fermented milk-like cheese in the middle swimming in melted *ghee*. This is better than wearing it, I think. There are glasses of sour buttermilk. Out the open window, in the darkness of the black night we can hear women's high pitched voices whispering and giggling. We're almost too tired to eat after ten grueling hours in the jeep and our little nocturnal stroll, but we do.

After the meal Aziz piles the brightly flower-patterned quilts over the felt rugs to serve as our beds. We sleep under more warm, cozy quilts. For we who would have been satisfied to sleep under the stars on the rocks the cushions are as soft clouds. *Al-hamdu-lillah!*

Thanks to God!

June 27th

Brep

Spent the morning sitting at a small table in Aziz's garden of tall grass and apple and mulberry trees ringed by a low rock wall. We gazed northwest across the wide bolder strewn river bed at a patch of green vegetation Aziz informed us was Brep. Seemed very remote, even looking at the name on charts when we were in Kafiristan. We looked at our maps, again discussing the route north to Brep and beyond. Aziz's uncle and cousin came by, adding many varied opinions concerning our road ahead.

One of the fattest chickens, if such an adjective could be used for the scrawny birds running around the yard, was killed for our lunch. We ate politely, though sparingly, so there would still be some chicken left when we passed the bowl to the remaining three men. Then Aziz was ready to leave for Brep to deliver his goods. He said a shopkeeper along the way, another of his relatives, had been over the Darkot Pass a few years back. We would stop to talk to him. As we crossed the stony plain we had so wearily traversed last night separating Aziz's village of scattered houses and the neighboring sparse hamlet he told us the story of their ongoing warring....

In the 1920s there was a British Political Agent in Chitral named Mr. Smyth. His servant was a man from the other village. Fighting in Afghanistan for the British he was wounded and lost his arm. He went to Mr. Smyth and demanded some sort of compensation. Smyth asked him what he wanted and he said he wanted the entire township in which his family lived.

Smyth didn't know or, care about the people residing there. By simply signing a piece of paper he effectively gave the entire area to the man. But there were two families involved. There was a meeting in Chitral over the issue. Aziz's grandfather, representing his side, argued with Smyth. "Don't you know that other families live in the village?" he demanded.

"So?" was Smyth's flippant response. "What do I care? It is inconsequential! They are nothing." A very demeaning attitude in general.

They argued and Aziz's grandad got so upset that he picked up the bread and threw it in Smyth's face. Smyth branded him rebel and *badmash* and banished him from returning to Chitral. When the servant died he didn't leave any children so all his properties reverted back to the *Mether* of Chitral. But his relatives still claimed it as their own. Since that time the fields between the two families' holdings became a rocky no man's land as the two families continued to feud over it.

The people in this far flung place are poor and don't have many guns so they usually battle only with stones. Sometimes they do set up some gun posts and take some shots. Then the police come up from Chitral and arrest some of the shooters and take them to Buni, the administrative center for Northern Chitral. There, each side fills out a list of the chief offenders and five or six from each side are taken to jail in Chitral where they spend a week or so.

It is war on a rather primitive scale. Last year the enemy stole the millstones from Aziz's tribe's mill. As we walked on a stony path lined with thin stunted poplars he told us that two weeks before their adversary had lain in wait along this road and ambushed two fellows from Aziz's side, beating them up with sticks. Ayesha and I felt our pistols at our sides. No ignorant rustics would dare shake a stick at us.

But the opposition is weak, Aziz said. Some are slaves and they don't have much heart to fight. Others have come over to Aziz's side and lately some of the enemy tribe have made a compromise with Aziz's tribe.

So that explains why Aziz's dog's name is named Mr. Smyth!

Aziz told us we were the first foreigners to visit the village since before the days of Mr. Smyth. As the tree lined ambush path ended we started along the irrigation channel we had followed last night in the dark, only this time we could see the churning, frothing river 40 feet below our precarious path.

Aziz said the villagers had made this channel a few years back. Before that they had used a trail going up and down the mountainside. The wobbly stones forming the outer side of the channel didn't seem the greatest of roads but in the places where we could see the remnants of the old pathway we realized our way was indeed an improvement.

He told us that back then there wasn't even a bridge. One had to swim the Yarkhun River holding onto a rope stretched between both sides so as to not be swept away. When we got back to Chapali and the jeep I glanced at my watch. The journey had taken us one and a half hours in the daylight!

Aziz took the canvas cover off his jeep and jacked up the rear end. Then he picked up a large stone and pounded a steel plate into place where one of the leafs of the spring had fallen out. We were ready to go. We drove up to Brep. If I had thought the road to Mastuj was bad, the road to Brep (if it could be called one) was worse. It was mostly comprised of rocks and boulders that we had to negotiate over ever so slowly. Everywhere we looked were rocks. It looked as if it had been rained upon by a shower of stones. Raw pieces of chaos. When God made the world this must be where He dumped the extra rock and debris.

We stopped at Aziz's relative's shop. Ayesha sat on the one short stool, I on a sack of barley. He told us it had been three years since he'd been up to the Darkot Pass. He said yaks and mountain ponies can cross it usually. We showed him a picture of our horses so he could comprehend their enormous stature. He tsk'ed his tongue and shook his head, "They are VERY big...." he said, "maybe they breaking the ice."

We drove up another steep, rutted, dirt path of a road off the main track to the Brep Government School. The headmaster had been up to the Boraghil Pass on the Russian border last October polling for Benazir. They had ponied from Lasht to the Boraghil Pass. He said several of the bridges were gone on the way from Brep to Lasht. The rivers would be deep now with the melted snows of June.

We drove back down the hill, onto the main road to visit another relation of Aziz's who was married to a girl in Lasht. We parked the jeep on the roadside and started up a narrow pathway through rolling, steeply rising, verdant meadows following a small, lively, skipping stream. The trail was made up of smooth stones, the icy waters dancing back and forth among them. The sun was just setting at our backs, painting the glowing snow covered mountain peaks so many shades of crimson and orange in a darkening azure sky. At last we came on a seemingly deserted house. On the veranda was a *charpoy* stacked high with quilts and rugs. We spread a colorfully diamond patterned *kileem* on the hard dry mud veranda and piled some of the quilts against the wall to rest upon.

After a short wait a young man about 19 came down from somewhere behind the house along with a younger boy maybe 12. They brought with them a metal glass and a metal *lota* of icy water. Then the young man took about a dozen walnuts out of his pocket and placed them on a metal plate. He began to crack them with his large rough hands. So this is dinner in Brep we wondered?

The boy disappeared and shortly reappeared from behind the guest house on which veranda we were sitting with a platter of something that appeared to be *pilau*. When it was placed in front of us we realized it was a platter of crumbled *chapatties* fried in *ghee*. We washed it down with a thermos of hot salted tea.

Our host told us that he went to school in Chitral and that his break was coming next month. Then he planned to go up to Lasht to visit his wife and her family. We could go with him he said. He knew the way and places we could stay. There are no hotels after Mastuj. And he said he could arrange food for the horses. Again we showed pictures of our behemoths and he didn't seem so positive, but didn't say anything. As to the missing bridges, they were still missing. He said the rivers could be crossed by ropes strung over them. This time of year the water is nine to ten feet deep. I guessed the horses wouldn't be able to cross over on the ropes. Could they swim?

Our hosts brought *charpoys* from inside the guest house, placed them in the grassy, stone-walled yard and put felt rugs and quilts on them. Ayesha and I slept out in the cold, fresh air. After all, it was summer and there were no clouds in the sky. Aziz went back down the mountain to sleep in his jeep. He said it wasn't safe to just leave it alone.

June 28th
Written in Buni (really the 'boonies!')
Slept under the stars, the towering granite snowy daggered peaks of the Hindu Raj and piles of heavy quilts. Woke to the sound of gurgling waters of the

small, playful stream we had followed up to last night's lodging place. Icy crystal dew sparkled on morning emerald grass. The air was brisk.

After a breakfast of *parattas* (more bread) and salt tea we went back down the mountainside to the road and the shop of another of Aziz's family members. We sat around for two hours waiting for a vehicle to take us south, back toward Chitral. Aziz wanted to spend the day in Brep. Just quiet nature and tall mountains looking down on us; rock, sand and open fresh air. Too damn quiet for me. I really felt like a city boy. I wanted a jeep, a *Shazan*. I wanted to be in Lahore. My feelings for Nasreen were still pulling me apart. So peaceful and still here, yet my desire to be with her raged.

Finally a vehicle comes along the apology of a road we are waiting on, but it is only going as far as Buni, 35 kilometers below Mastuj. We wanted to meet the *A.C.* in Buni (no *D.C.* in Buni) and check out the guest house, plus ask about the supposed guest house in Reshan—between Buni and Chitral. Besides, it isn't like there is an abundance of traffic on the road.

Just below Mastuj a policeman stops the jeep. He peers at Ayesha and I.

"Are you foreigners?" he asks.

"Yes, *taqriban* (approximately)," I tell him.

"Then you have to sign in the book," he tells us.

"No we don't!" I say.

"Did you sign in when coming through before?"

"No."

"Okay, then you can go," he says, waving us on.

"What do I know of writing?" I tell our driver. "I am just a simple man." He laughs.

We come to a bridge crossing 60 feet above the gray swirling river. The other side is luxuriant with trees and planted fields. Our side of the road is rock, gravel and dirt. We cross over and drive up a hill on a lane lined with straight poplar trees, lush bushes and stone walls. It ends at an intersection branching perpendicular left and right. Welcome to downtown Buni.

We're quite amazed. It is the biggest town we've seen since leaving Chitral. There are a few restaurants, tea houses and stores. Vegetables are available. We see a shop with a heap of watermelons piled in front. We walk a couple hundred feet to the residence of the *A.C.* It has a deserted look with round holes in the plaster walls, as if they had been beaten in with a sledge hammer. Many of the windows are boarded up glassless.

On entering the tree studded grassy yard a *chowkidar* asks us what we want. We tell him we would like to see the *A.C.* He goes into the house and presently comes out with a young police officer in a clean pressed gray uniform and a neat sharply trimmed short dark beard. He asks me in Pashtu what he can do for us. I tell him we are American Muslims and that we would like to see the *A.C.* He tells us to come inside to sit. I fish in my vest pocket for our government *firman* from Islamabad and hand it to him. He looks at it and says, "Very interesting. I thought you were Afghan refugees." He leaves the room.

We sit on heavy upholstered couches in our dusty, dirty, ragged travel-stained clothes, our turbans wrapped windblown and wrinkled around our grimy faces. I haven't had a shave in days. The police guard re-enters the room and politely ushers us into the *A.C.'s* personal guest room.

Khalid Mahsood, the *A.C.*, is from Multan. Despite our ragtag appearance he is very pleasant and cordial. I think he is happy to see new faces up here. Some glimmer of intelligence, if not showing through our grimy outward appearance, must shine through in our English, proof that we, leaving our appearances aside, are definitely foreign.

He tells us that two days ago the local people took out a procession against the government over water rights and stoned his residence. That explains the holes in the walls and lack of glass in the windows. "At least it was a change from the normal," he laughs. "Really quite exciting."

He says the guest house isn't quite completed. Also there is no electricity as it stops above Chitral. There are two rooms, though one is permanently occupied by the extra *A.C.*, the other is empty. There is also a guest house in Reshan we can stay in. He has a brief discussion with the policeman, Fazal, his personal guard. They agree grass can be provided for our horses at both guest houses. We should call before leaving from Chitral. His telephone number is Buni Exchange—number one. Easy enough to remember. He says we can stay here tonight if we wish. We tell him our friends and horses are anxiously waiting for us in Bumburet and we want to hurry back with the information we have collected.

Fazal and a driver take us down the road in the *A.C.'s* jeep to a mud restaurant-cum tea house built on the down banked side of the road. Its roof is level with the road. It's a long smoky room with an arched ceiling, lined with *charpoys;* greasy quilts on them. At one end are two large brass *samovars.*

From 3:00 to 6:30 we drink tea and doze. No vehicles come that are going south toward Chitral. Finally we walk back towards Buni. As we are crossing the bridge a jeep comes in the opposite direction. The driver asks me where we are headed. He informs us he is leaving for Chitral, *Insha'Allah*, at 4:00 tomorrow morning. He is just off to get petrol and to load the goods he will be transporting. We tell him we are staying at the *A.C.'s* guest house and will be waiting for him in the morning.

We arrive at the *A.C.'s* house at dusk, but the *chowkidar* says he has gone to the guest house to see the extra *A.C.* We start down the road to the guest house but on the way the *A.C.* drives by. When we inform him of our situation he tells us to go on to the guest house to get settled and he will send the jeep for us for dinner.

Fragrant fluffy Basmati rice, *bindi*, garlic flavored *dal,* salad, *chutney* with fresh mint and sweet *qawah* with cardamon. A veritable feast in a wilderness of bread. Later Fazal drives us back to the guest house. We feel spoiled, it feels nice. *Al-Hamdu-Lillah.*

It's cold tonight but we are sleeping in real beds, in a real room, with clean, warm, woolen blankets over us... if still only freezing water to wash with and kerosene lantern light to write by.

June 29th

Bumburet

Hard to crawl out of soft beds from under warm blankets at 3:45 in the cold morning. Our jeep arrived within 15 minutes of schedule with horn blaring and engine revving. We left Buni by 4:30 and arrived in Chitral by 9:30.

I got a shave and we had an early lunch of kebab and *aash* at an Afghan restaurant. Then, after bottles of *Shazan,* we walked out of town to the fort of the Chitral Scouts. We wanted to talk to them about the possibility of staying with them in Chitral. They said we would need to speak to the commanding officer, but he wasn't there. He was in Drosh. We would have to get his permission to stay.

We headed to the *chowk* where the jeeps leave for Ayun and Kafiristan. After a short wait we were lucky to get one going directly to Bumburet. We even paid ten rupees extra apiece to sit in the front seat in more relative comfort than the back. We were gone only four days if time here can be counted in such increments here.

Now somebody needs to go back to Piran to get the rest of our gear. I decide that it will be me. I can also go to Peshawar to develop the film shot up until now, drop off the story of our progress to The Frontier Post (newspaper) and pick up supplies. I'm perfect for the job, not to mention the logical choice. Seeing that Shokot's withers are still somewhat swollen and that he can use the rest who can begrudge me a short trip down to Lahore also? Begrudged or not, practical or not, logical or not, I have let it be known I am not going on in the trip without a quick trip to Lahore to see Nasreen again.

I had wanted a hot bath when I got back from the north but it was not to be. If I would be leaving, as it seemed, for at least six days, then I would need to go with Habibullah to find some grain and *boose* to make the animals' field of grass stretch out. We caught a jeep to Chitral where we spent over an hour searching the bazaar for grain, a replacement horse and some *charras,* before we found a mill back along a stream leading down to the river and behind some donkey camps. We managed to buy a 25 kilo sack of flour.

In the bazaar we picked up another smaller sack of vegetables, rice and other assorted supplies. I gave Habibullah money for cloth and he ordered a new *shalwar kameez* suit from a tailor for *Eid ul Qurban* which is coming up soon. Another jeep back to Ayun. On the way into Chitral we had seen a thresher and people threshing wheat in a field just below Ayun. They were still at it.

We left our flour and other supplies at the one restaurant in Ayun and walked back down the hill to where the thresher was. Written on it's back was *"da ghanum dushmanm"* (the enemy of the wheat). We negotiated for two gunny sacks full and we sewed up the tops with straw to keep the *boose* in. We carried the bags balanced on our heads back up the hill and into Ayun. Habibullah's stout farmer's neck proved to be stronger than mine. A jeep full of tourists passed us as we came up the hill, the bulging sacks on our heads.

142

They took a picture of the two ragged Pathans carrying their over-stuffed burdens up the hill in the dust of their wheels. It must look oh so terribly romantic. My neck didn't think so!

The sun was getting low and there were no passengers in Ayun, hence no drivers who were planning to go into Kafiristan. We hired a private jeep for us and our four sacks.

Now Habibullah is making dinner as I try to push the pen across the page and try to keep up to date. Should be looking more forward toward sleep but today's exertion and the excitement of leaving tomorrow to see Nasreen has got me wired....

June 30th, *Juma*
Still in Bumburet.
Rest day.
Thinking of Nasreen.
Thinking of a bucket of hot water for a bath.
Habibullah and I get something to smoke at Benazir Hotel.
No more thinking.
Time pass (passing time).

July 2nd
Peshawar
The morning of the 1st I got a ride to Ayun. Then after a short wait another for Chitral. There I went to the office of *PIA* but there were no plane tickets available for Peshawar. Even my government letter didn't help me obtain one. If by chance the good weather held out it would still be several days before I could secure a plane ticket I was informed.

At noon I left in an Afghan "Mercedes" Flying Coach (bus) direct to Peshawar. We stopped for tea at the Drosh Hotel. They had already heard the news of Horse dying from a local driver. News travels fast on the Frontier. I filled them in on details.

At the bottom of the Lowari Pass, on the Chitral side just before Ashrit, before heading up the endless switchbacks of the pass, we stopped at the government check post. I gave the Levies manning the post the news and had to stay for tea, holding up the entire bus. None of the passengers seemed to mind though and besides, the driver was also having tea with us.

At 9:30 we stopped for dinner in Talash at the Noor Habib Hotel. Reunion with all the hotel *wallahs* and local Levies. We reached Peshawar half past midnight.

Spent today taking care of horse trip business and some personal business... like getting a ticket for tomorrow morning's flight to Lahore.

Lahore tonga stand

Court yard of Wazir Khan Mosque, Lahore

Chapter 14
LAHORE BREAKS
(the Lahore Movie Continues)

Monday morning, July 3rd

11:20 flight to Lahore

Arrive at Nasreen's house at 1:00. Nobody is home except one old lady who only speaks Punjabi. She says Nasreen is at Nargis's house. She doesn't know what time she will be back—today, tonight or tomorrow. My Punjabi is fairly nonexistent though I can understand somewhat. I can't get her to comprehend I've just come all the way from Kafiristan to see Nasreen. I tell her I will come back at 3:00.

I go to a small circular park in the center of a traffic roundabout and sit in the shade of a tree smoking Gold Leaf cigarettes. Luckily the weather is mild, for this time of year. As the plane landed at Lahore airport they said it was 32 degrees centigrade (only 90 F).

At 2:45 I decide to go to the mosque for afternoon prayer before going back to her house. As I walk down the street Anwar and little Iqbal (two of her brother-in-laws) drive by in a car with some women in the back seat. They pull over to get some water from a public roadside drinking tap. Anwar says to come over after prayer, he is sure Nasreen will be home soon. I go to the mosque to pray.

Again I knock at their door.

"Who's there?" little Iqbal asks from behind the steel door.

"Noor Mohammad." I say.

I hear him telling the people inside that it's me as he opens the door. I cross the yard and sit in the back room. In about 15 minutes I see Nasreen come into the yard. Little Iqbal tells her I am there. She comes into the room, all smiles, looking surprised and happy to see me. She asks me for 50 rupees to pay the *rickshaw wallah*. It's really quiet. When she comes back she reclines on the *charpoy* and smokes. She seems to be brooding.

"*Sta da sturgu bala akhlama, janana, zama,*" I hum a line from a Pashtu song (*I'll take the tragedy from your eyes, my dearest*).

"Why do you sing that, Noor Mohammad?" she asks.

"I don't know. You just seemed to be thinking about something—some sadness," I tell her.

"I'm not."

"Then what's the problem?"

"There isn't any problem... for me."

"Well then, what are you thinking about?"

"Nothing."

"There must be something on your mind. I can see it by your expression."

"Well, maybe. Three of our girls from the other house were arrested the other day. So was Malang Iqbal (her husband's 20 year old brother)."

She brings me an Urdu newspaper. She turns to the back page of the eight page paper and shows me the pictures. There is my buddy Iqbal. Strange folk I know.

"I was once in jail in Rawalpindi for two months," I tell her. "I was framed and acquitted."

"I was in jail once also, for one and a half months in Karachi a few years ago," she recalls. "Pakistani jail is no good!"

"No jail is good. Not even the jail you are in now."

She looks back at me. "It's no good, why?"

"What do you think?"

"How else could we meet?"

One good outcome is there is no business coming to the house now. The pimps have the word not to bring anyone out here or they are told to leave at the door. There are many family visitors from Peshawar. I relax on the couch and doze between her comings and goings. At 9:00 she comes in the room and sits next to me. "Well, what do you want to do?" she asks.

"What do I want to do? I think you know. I'd like to sleep with you."

"I'll go ask Mama," she answers. I'm surprised. She comes back. "She says it's okay. You can stay."

Now I really am surprised.

"I'll bring you some dinner. Then I have to help serve the guests."

After dinner she comes back and tells me to go into the front room to wait for her. She has to help get the guests settled on the *charpoys* clustered in the yard in front of the gigantic swamp cooler and pedestal fans. She comes in a little after 11:00. Well, here we are, in the *behtak* again. She lights a cigarette, inhales and hands it to me. "*Light off kum (turn off the light)*?" she asks.

"Mixed languages," I say (English/Pashtu).

"Sometimes," she smiles.

"Yeah, I know. How come it's okay for us to be sleeping together now?" I ask. The only other time I've been able to spend a night with her is when she let me sneak in the *behtak* door when her husband was away before the start of the horse trip.

"Because Akbar is in jail," she smiles, "in Malakand."

"What's he in jail for?"

"I don't know."

"What's he in jail for?" I repeat. "Come on, you must know."

"He shot a guy—with his gun."

"Did he kill him?"

"Maybe."

Great, I think. I'm lying in bed with this girl I'm hopelessly in love with, a Pathan madame and cocotte whose husband is in jail for shooting someone in Malakand. Many and strange are the workings of **Allah**.

Who knows? What is next?

146

It's great to wake up and watch the morning sunlight sneaking into the room through the curtained doorway lighting her calmly slumbering face. Before going to sleep we had opened the wooden door to provide fresh air for the ceiling fan to circulate. Nargis brings me *chai* and The Jang (an Urdu newspaper). She hands me a lit cigarette.

Nasreen stretches and yawns next to me, our legs still entwined. She takes the cigarette from my hand. I slowly read the headlines in the paper, trying to understand the Urdu (Urdu is written in more or less the same script as Pashtu). She falls asleep and I take the cigarette from her hand and finish it.

I leave at 11:00.

At noon I'm on the Flying Coach leaving Lahore for Peshawar. At 6:00 the bus reaches Pindi. There they tell us it is not going on to Peshawar. The clerk in the bus office says another bus will be coming in half an hour. Another clerk says there isn't another bus coming but there might be one in one and a half hours, *Insha'Allah*. They give me and some other Pathans and Afghans our 40 rupees back (the fare for the remaining distance). We still have a three hour journey before us. We pile into two taxis and go to the mini-wagon stand behind the Moti Mahal Cinema.

We arrive in Peshawar at 10:00 P.M.

July 6th

The Mingora bus horn is screaming. We make our way through the crowds of people waiting for their buses and grimy ratty dressed urchins selling fruit, cigarettes, chewing gum and soft drinks. Conductors are shouting at us, "*Chairta zee, chairta zeeeee?*" (Where are you going?)

"Piran," I say.

We are pointed in the direction of one of the bright, gaudily decorated buses with horns blasting and revving engine roaring. She quickly follows behind me, her blue *burqa* blowing and flowing over her graceful body in the still breeze of her movements. We climb in and make our way to two vacant seats near the front, stepping over bags, crates, chickens and children.

She slides into the seat first, wrapping her steel-blue *burqa* around her as she sits next to the window. I sit next, shielding her from the aisle and the rest of the bus. Over the windscreen, cut out in colorful plastic overlays are words written in flowing Arabic calligraphy. On the right is **Allah**, on the left the name of the Holy Prophet Muhammad (PBUH), in the center *Masha'Allah*. The entire ceiling is decorated in like manner with abstract flowers and patterns, layer upon layer of colorful and intricately cut and placed plastic.

As the vehicle slams its rough gears and lunges forward I lean over and raise the window several inches. She faces the window and lifts the front of the *burqa* over her face so the warm breeze blowing in can cool her sweat covered brow. I can see the reflection of her golden nose ring and dark eyes in the glass. Through our small crack of ventilation pours the dust of the road. She pulls the edge of her *burqa* up with her slim delicate fingers to cover her nose and mouth. For a few moments my eyes are filled with grit. I curse my evil fate as I clear my stinging eyes with the tail of my powder blue silk turban. In front of us an old man sits wearing a ragged, threadbare, dirty green turban. He turns his white bearded, smiling face in our direction. Both his pale blue eyes are whitened by heavy cataracts. How strong is my faith, I wonder?

The bus stops in Nowsherra and through the bus window I buy two glasses of cold *sherbet* from a grubby faced boy with a grease encrusted white cap carrying a bucket with a large, jagged block of ice floating in the dusty cold liquid. We take on more passengers and luggage, making use of every spare inch of space. The conductor couldn't be more clever in utilizing the space than a Swiss watchmaker.

An old man holding a small girl, her short straight cropped hair orange with *henna* and her large, deep brown eyes made darker by a liberal usage of *surma* squeeze in next to us, pressing us closer to the side of the bus. I look at the little Pathan girl in her begrimed, yet still brightly colored floral patterned dress and cap with beaded and silver amulets jangling and smile. She smiles back as the old man wipes some dusty snot running down her face with the end of his frayed turban.

Before heading up the Malakand Pass we pull over for afternoon prayer. The women and children remain in the hot and stuffy vehicle. The men wash, filling plastic *lotas* from a truck tire rubber bucket pulled up from a stone walled well. We pray at a roadside area marked by a square of stones on the dry and hard packed earth. The driver begins blasting the horn as the last stragglers climb back in. The gears crunch and we begin twisting and climbing the pass. Approximately half way up there is a sound that appears to be a loud backfire toward the rear of the bus.

But something is wrong. It's too loud. It is followed by an even louder blast and a whoosh of hellish orange flame and flesh-searing heat. Satan has breathed his life exterminating breath into the bus. The concussion causes the driver to hit the rock wall on the left side of the road. His head is reduced to a ragged, bloody mass of flesh as it perforates the blood-splattered windscreen. The bus careens across the road, pitching over the short rock retaining wall and plummeting off 500 feet of sheer cliff, engulfed in a ball of ghastly licking fire and black billowing diesel smoke. I quickly look to my side in the all-encompassing heat to see if she is...

All I see is the wall of my room in Hashtnagri. I've fallen asleep in the afternoon heat only to wake, my face covered in sweat. The electricity is off (load shedding—the insufficient power is rationed in intervals) and my ceiling fan has stopped circulating the air. It's late. I must leave if I'm to go to Piran, as needs must.

I leave Peshawar at 3:00 P.M. from Haji Camp bus stand on the Mingora bus for Piran. Walking through the parked buses with horns blaring, diesel and dust swirling in the stifling heat of July, an atmosphere that would have made even Lucifer envious, a vaguely familiar feeling stirs as if something from some half-forgotten dream.

I reach Daoud Shah's home in Piran at 5:30. I go down to the fort where Habibullah and I and the horses had stayed and where we had left our high mountain gear. Too much damn *samon* (baggage).

We have dinner in the guest room of their house and watch *"Commando"* on their video player. I can't keep my attention on it. Thinking heavily about Nasreen, about our visit the other night.

July 7th

Awake at 5:00 A.M. with a gnawing feeling. I've got to go back to Lahore. I need to see her one more time. I hope the gang in Bumburet won't kill me. I know I'll deserve it but then love is blind, isn't it? I'm surely finding out.

I give Rafiq (Daoud's older brother) some cock and bull story about something very important in Peshawar I forgot to do. He gives me a ride to Batkhela. The Levy watching the road is his friend. He stops a minivan and they make room for me. It takes two and a half hours to reach Peshawar. It's my 14th time over the Malakand Pass. I arrive at 9:30 and take a *rickshaw* to the *PIA* office in Saddar. All I can get is a "chance" seat ticket (standby) on the flight to Lahore. I have to go to the airport to see if there are any available seats. At 11:15 I get the last "chance" seat on the 11:20 flight to Lahore. As we land they announce that it's 37 degrees centigrade in Lahore. That's body temperature (98.6 F).

Arrive at her house at 1:00 and drop off my bag. Then walk to a barber shop near the mosque for a shave and over to the mosque for afternoon prayer. Back at the house Nargis works once and a new girl I have never seen before works three times. She actually seems to enjoy her work. One time she is in the back room with a customer for close to ten minutes. Anwar and Nargis both tell Nasreen to knock.

Knock! Knock! "Hey, hurry up, it's one time, isn't it!"

I laugh. The *johns* are usually gone by the time the girl finishes cleaning and comes out of the bathroom. I spend the day and night. I just sort of plop myself down there, but then she always says no problem that I stay.

She comes in the room I'm in when she isn't busy, holding a small baby.
"Whose is that?" I ask.
"Mine," she smiles.
"And who else's?"
"Just mine."
"Yeah?"
"Sure. Do you want to marry me, Noor Mohammad?"
"Of course, you know I do! I keep telling you."
"When Akbar (her husband) gets out of jail you need to talk to him. You will have to give him some money. He can get another wife. He doesn't care."
"What about you? Do you want to come with me?"
"Sure. Why not?"
Can I believe her? Is she joking? Am I?
"What do you want to do tonight?" she asks.
"I'd like to stay."
"Then stay. There are plenty of *charpoys* in the yard."

149

"I want to stay with you—together. I came all the way back from Malakand on the hope that we could spend another night together. My friends and horses are waiting for me in Kafiristan and I'm already late. They will probably be very upset. After the other night I just had to come back. After Chitral who knows when will be the next time we can be together?"

"Okay. I'll check with Mama. My husband doesn't like me working at night. When he comes back we won't be able to sleep together."

At 9:30 she comes back in to tell me guests have arrived from Peshawar. She has to make food for them and help them get situated for the night, as usual. I ask her for a glass of cold water and a cigarette. She brings a pitcher of ice water, two cigarettes and matches. I think I know what I want, but she knows what I need. I keep looking out into the yard and at the door of the *behtak* hoping I don't see her go in there with some unknown man and shut the door. She has told me the truth. Tonight it is actually relatives from Peshawar.

At 11:30 I finish the last cigarette. By midnight everything is quiet in the yard. I need to cross it to go to the toilet, plus I wonder if she hasn't fallen asleep herself on one of the *charpoys.* The yard is crowded with sleeping people. I see her adjusting the sheet covering one of the children. She comes into the room with me and we sit on the bed. She takes a cigarette out and I open a box of matches to light it for her. But she drops it on the bed along with a small piece of *charras*.

"You're going to fill it?" I ask, pleasantly surprised.

"You do," she says.

She goes over to her suitcase (many Pakistanis use suitcases and metal trunks in place of closets) and sprays on some perfume. We smoke, lock the door and turn off the light. Our lovemaking seems easier and more relaxed. More sensual. Not so Pakistani professional. At 3:00 A.M. she opens the door and we cross the yard to go to the bathroom to wash. The yard is full of sleeping forms on *charpoys.* The fans are blowing air. It's hot. We sleep with the door open, the curtain drawn.

Again to wake, to see her face, her straight, slender nose and golden bejeweled nose ring. To feel her softly breathing and smell her hair, scented with perfume and the smell of cigarettes. She yawns and stretches like a cat, the small round bells plaited into her dark hair softly tinkling.

At 7:00 she brings me hot sesame *roti, cholay* and a cup of sweet milky tea for breakfast. She clears the plates she brings me another cup of tea and a lit cigarette. She throws a *chaddar* over her shoulders and hair and leaves for the bazaar to bring something for the guests.

"Hurry a little," I call after her. "I have to leave for the airport by a quarter after eight."

She returns at 8:00, comes in the room and sits with me.

"One more smoke," I say, "and then I must go."

She takes the freshly lit cigarette from her lips and holds it to mine, leaving it there. Then she lights another for herself. When we finish smoking I say goodbye. We stand behind the door so nobody in the yard can see us. I give her a kiss and a hug.

"When I rejoin my friends we will be riding from Chitral to Gilgit, through really big desolate mountains. I don't know how long it will take to get there. Until we reach Gilgit there will be no way of getting here. Do you understand?" I ask, my hands encircling her smoothly covered satin hips.

"Yes, I understand."

"But as soon as we get to Gilgit, for sure darling, I'll come to see you even though from Gilgit it will also be very difficult to get to Lahore. Now I must go. Goodbye."

"Goodbye. *Khuda hafiz.*"

"*Insha'Allah.*"

At 9:10 I fly back to Peshawar. At 4:00 P.M. I leave Peshawar by bus. Over the Malakand Pass again, arriving at Daoud Shah's house at 6:30.

It's July 8th.

Malakond Pass

❖ ❖ ❖

THE MAD BUS FROM HELL
(Batkhela via Dir to Chitral)

July 9th, Chitral
Tirich Mir Hotel

Samaan. Too much *samaan*. Two large, heavy panniers, at least 35 kilos each; the wooden frame for the pack saddle, the big canvas satchel of sleeping bags and cooking gear, my saddlebag with the added weight of our extra horse shoes—all 12 pairs.

Rafiq's driver gave me a ride down to the bus stand in Batkhela. After some searching around for the most direct means of transportation we got everything loaded onto the roof of a colorfully painted and designed "Super Delux" bus heading to Dir. Only the decorations were 'super delux.'

At Timagura I got out to check on the situation of the baggage on the roof. The roof was covered, legs and bags hanging off the sides. The two panniers were perched over the sides strapped to the edge of the roof rack by their thick buffalo-leather straps. Inside, the bus was equally jammed full. Chickens, goats, crates, old men with axes, babies, etc... the little boy sitting on his white-bearded grandfather's lap across the narrow isle from me puked on my leg. The only thing worse, I felt, would be if they were speaking English.

When we arrived in Dir the bus conductor and another fellow helped me carry all of the gear over to the office where I could get a pickup going over the Lowari Pass to Chitral. I sat on a *charpoy* in front of the office with the office clerk and a Suzuki driver, smoking a *duc* cigarette. The Suzuki driver had been in Bumburet yesterday. He knew our news.

I walked over to the main (and only) *chowk* to buy some *charras* from a small cigarette shop on the corner I knew. The proprietor was sitting with a friend and filling a cigarette as I walked up. I bought five rupees worth. He reached into a large plastic bag and pulled out a large chunk, biting off approximately five rupee's worth. I also bought a ten-pack of Wills cigarettes and a *Rooh Afza* to drink. By then the pickup was honking down the street, but we weren't to leave Dir yet.

We all crowded in; saddlebags and assorted baggage in the middle on the floor between the two rows of narrow metal benches on either side of the pickup bed, people and feet piling on top. Up the street we drove and stopped in front of a store, loading in sacks of sugar.

We sat in the brilliant, eye-squinting sunlight trying to pack in the last remaining inch. If I had thought the conductor in the bus had been skillful in his craft, here was a master. Well, I guess all it took was waiting on our patience until the proper combination of baggage and people came along. Eventually we passengers persuaded the driver to start, much to the conductor's chagrin at having to depart Dir with still two or three vacant inches.

At last we pulled out of Dir at 1:00 P.M. and headed up the Lowari. We stopped at the two tea houses just below the top at 3:15. After tea I spent the remaining time of our stop squatting atop a rock on the side of the road by the pickup. I filled a cigarette and smoked it, trying to be somewhat discreet. The ride down was uncomfortable to say the least, packed into the back of the pickup on my narrow perch. I closed my eyes, trying to imagine being alone with Nasreen at night. Occasionally it took me away. I hated so to come back, though, after all, I was in the back of a pickup truck zigzagging down the Lowari Pass. At the check post before Ashrit I didn't bother getting out to sign in the foreigner's registration book or to chat with the Levies.

Arrived in Chitral Town at 6:30. After dropping off the other passengers the driver took me and my well-trampled and dusty bags to the Tirich Mir Hotel. The sun was setting, the snowy peak of Tirich Mir glowing a rich shade of purple-pink in a streaked azure sky. Just time to settle the baggage in the entry of the hotel and have the manager save me a room. I made *wuzu* at the water tap on the side of the lawn and walked down the gravel road to the mosque as the *Maghrib Azan* sounded.

A silvery half-moon was going down over the pale pastel domes and spires of the Chitral Shahi Mosque. As I turned my head to the right side in the first of the ritual ending *salaams* of every prayer I could see the purple-tinted hills, the mountains and the river. The moon was setting through pastel, scalloped arches. As the air darkened the moon tipped the distant mountain peaks with a dim, mysterious glow.*

Out for *Shazan* and kebabs. Alone and missing Nasreen; though hungry, I don't seem to relish the food as if she had brought it to me. Even the tea had no taste for me now. Isn't even poison nectar from the hands of the beloved?

Body smashed from today's journey. I much prefer the morning PIA flight from Peshawar to Lahore. Now that is my idea of traveling, or roughing it on a reclining seat in an air-conditioned flying coach on GT Road.

I think I left some of my vertebrae in the Suzuki.

---

* *At the end of prayer first the head is turned over the right shoulder and "salaamu'aleikum" is said, and then looking over left shoulder, it is said again.*

Shahi Mosque in Chitral (the Royal Mosque) was constructed in 1924 by Mehtar Sir Shuja ul Mulk. Skilled craftsmen were brought from India, hence the resemblance to Mughal architecture. The tomb of Mehtar Shuja ul Mulk is situated in one corner of the mosque.

N.M.Khan 1986

Chapter 15
Chitral

July 18th
Written in Reshan guest house, north of Chitral, bekar (crummy) place, under repairs....

Left Tirich Mir Hotel at 7:00 A.M. on the 10th after arranging to stow most of the gear there until we reach Chitral with the horses. Rode to Ayun in a jeep carrying ice. Actually the floor in back was piled with snow for cooling in refrigerators and stores in Ayun. Soon after starting we stopped to load on four five-gallon tins of *ghee*, four crates of tomatoes and more passengers. On the road to Ayun we passed a jeep coming toward Chitral. Shah Ji, a relative of Bibi Ji (my landlady in Peshawar) was in the back. As we passed each other he stood up excitedly and shouted, *"Noor Mohammad... Mirza... Bumburet... jeldi!* (hurry)"

Okay, I know I'm late. I was so surprised to see Shah Ji up here I didn't say anything to him as we passed in the middle of nowhere except *"salaam aleikum."* In Ayun I got a ride quickly to Kafiristan.

Reached Bumburet at 10:30 July 10th,
"Well, it's about time you arrived *banchod*!"
"Wa aleikum asalaam, bro."
"Noor, where have you been? And where's the gear?"
"The gear is stowed in Chitral at the Tirich Mir Hotel. As to where I've been, I don't think you need many guesses."
"Damn your eyes, you jerk. I was just getting ready to go to Lahore to look for you. We figured you were probably in jail or something."
"Well, the something is more right. There was just something I had to take care of in Lahore before coming back up here."
"Did you?"
"Yes and no. I'm still in the middle of a conversation with her, as usual."
"So, what will you do?"
"What can I do? I'll go back to Lahore when we get to Gilgit, that's for certain, *Insha'Allah*. Maybe I'll stay."
"Noor, have I told you to go to hell lately?"
"Maybe I'll go there also."
"Well, do you want to hear the developments here or do you even care about this trip anymore?"
"Of course I care. I came back, didn't I? Why, what's new up here, besides electricity, and intelligence?"
"Those men who disposed of Horse—they were butchers! The bloody *Kafirs* ate Horse! That *banchod* Abdul Khaliq, treacherous *Kafir* dog, sold him for meat."
"Toba."

155

"*Toba shit! Subedar* Mohammad Ali has been here. He says he will demand our money back from that son of a dog. If he doesn't get it, he says he will drag him to Chitral in chains."

"What has been done as yet?"

"Nothing."

"That's what I thought you'd say. What news of the prices and availability of horses in Chitral?"

"Not many horses for sale. Most of them have been taken to Afghanistan for the *jihad*. What horses there are we can't afford."

"There must be an easier way to get back to Lahore."

"For you there is, *banchod*. I'll send you back in a box."

"Promises, promises...."

CHITRAL

July 12th

We leave Kafiristan for Chitral. Back on the horses again.

We stop at the government check post (at Dobash) and have tea with *Subedar* Mohammad Ali. I've still never signed into their "foreigner registration book." We try our marksmanship firing our pistols at rock outcroppings over the road and across the ravine from us. The *subedar* hands Ayesha his Kalashnikov to try her hand. Habibullah, who was waiting for a jeep at Benazir Hotel when we rode out of Bumburet passes us on the road while we are negotiating the rock covered sections and cliffs.

When we arrive in Ayun at noon Habibullah is still there waiting for a jeep to take him the remaining distance to Chitral. We climb up a wobbly wooden ladder to sit upstairs in Ayun's only restaurant to eat kebabs. We head out for Chitral. Habibullah is still waiting for a vehicle. His mission is to go to the *A.C.'s* residence in Chitral and inform him we are on our way and should be arriving sometime around sunset.

Outside Ayun Ayesha sees what seems to her to be a great path across some ridges. Always one for a shortcut, she gets bored with the jeepable road quiet easily, she convinces us to take it. Mirza and I agree that shortcuts make for long delays but as usual she can be stubborn. As we near the top of the first ridge Habibullah passes in a jeep down below us on the road. He yells that the path we are on is *kharab* (no good).

"And you know (you ignorant farmer)," I yell back to him crossly.

We're committed and in no mood to turn back. I just want to get to Chitral. The sooner we're in Chitral, the sooner we're in Gilgit. The sooner we're in Gilgit the sooner I'm in Lahore. And anyway, we're supposed to be the horsemen here.

"*Teek da* (it's okay)," Ayesha yells back to him.

But it's not so okay. We end up walking the horses down a loose rock trail and over large, granite boulders and stones. The horses' shoes slip and throw up sparks. Finally back on the hot, dusty trail to Chitral we see small, rectangular holes about eight feet up on the rocky side of the road. Looking inside we discover human bones. Old graves of who knows who, most likely broken open when they bulldozed the road.

It's hot and dry, except for our sweat. We stop around 3 P.M. at a place where we can follow a scree covered pathway down 100 feet to the muddy Chitral River. We fill the canteens with the silt-laced icy, cold water, filtering it through our turban tails, as we slake our thirst. It's so full of dirt it clogs the thin turban material every few gulps. It's difficult to suck the water out of the opening. Ayesha and I soak our turbans in the cold water: instant air-conditioning— for a few minutes.

A new Pajaro jeep drives by and stops a short distance from us. A Pakistani fellow with a neatly trimmed beard and clean pressed, cream colored *shalwar kameez* emerges and hails me. "Can you come here?"

"Why?" I shout back, not wanting to be bothered.

"The American Consul wants to talk to you."

"What's he want to talk to me about? I don't know him and I don't have anything to say to him!"

"Is your name Mirza?"

"*Ah cha*... just a minute."

Mirza comes up from the river. He knows the consul from when he worked in Peshawar in 1987. He just wants to say hello and wish us good luck.

We continue hot and exhausted. We stop and lay down against the rocks at the side of the road; the gravel strewn road is our bed, the stones our cushions. We doze for half an hour in the shade of the horses. They are exhausted also. They stand next to us and nod. No need to tie them. We're too tired to even worry about it. They are too beat to wander.

Herc pulls on his lead rope, tugging my hand. I hear his bell and wake up groggy, thinking I'm in bed with Nasreen, that it is her moving my hand. The last time I slept with her she had bells plaited in her hair. Here the only perfume I smell is the scent of horse sweat and dusty earth. Too bad. I'm lying on the hard Chitral/Ayun road, not in her soft bed.

On the way into Chitral we ride through three Afghan refugee camps. Talk about the proverbial *"being between-a-rock-and-a-hard-place."* Nothing green. On our right the camp/village of mud and stone shanties and drab, dusty, olive green tents donated by UNICEF slopes down over the rocky, gray-brown ground to the swirling gray-brown river. On our left the same dismal structures slope up the stoney vegetation-less hillside, ending in the naked granite peaks.

Afghan women in bright, gaily-patterned clothing can be glimpsed behind the mud walls of the compounds, and going back and forth from the wells. Groups of children are sitting or playing; the girls' clothing an imitation of the women, the boys' an imitation of the men. A few grey beards can be seen sitting in front of the shacks. The younger men, who in other more peaceful times would be working, are walking on the road or loitering about in front of the scarce, poorly-provisioned shops. Many come up to us curiously to engage us in conversation. Due to our appearance; turbans, horses and weapons we appear as *mujahideen, so* they usually begin in Farsi. I let them know we are not Afghans. I refuse to answer in Farsi. I'm hot, tired and impatient and besides, my fluency and desire to speak Farsi since I met Nasreen has greatly waned.

We reach Chitral at 6:30 and stop for a cold, pink *Rooh Afza* at the first drink stall we see. On the road going up the hill to the *A.C.'s* residence we stop at another stand for cold bottles of *Shazan*. The blistering, dusty road has left us fairly dehydrated. We ride past the *D.C.'s* office and residence, arriving at Irfan Ali's house (the *A.C.*) at 7:00 P.M. After unloading the horses and piling all our gear on his front veranda we lead the animals out of the grassy, tree covered yard and back down the hill, past the *D.C.'s* residence, to Irfan's stables.

July 13th

Today Irfan's driver takes us in his jeep to the first Afghan refugee camp out of Chitral on the road back toward Ayun. We've been told there is an Afghani *nal bandi* (farrier) there who has a small shop. The only *nal bandi* in Chitral has gone up to the Shandur Pass for the polo match—on the 23rd of this month the Chitral and Gilgit polo teams will be meeting midway, on top of the pass, for their annual polo match though it seems up here annual means every year, or so. They haven't had a match on Shandur Top in several years, though it is a long time tradition. The highest polo game in the world.

We find white bearded and turbaned Mullah Mohammad at his shop. Mullah is maybe 65 or 70 years old. His beard is sharply trimmed, his body wiry and spry. In the hard life of Central Asia physical weakness and infirmity usually die. Old men are quite competent for physical work.

He is from Panshir and doesn't speak much Pashtu. I have to dig into my memory to speak Farsi with him. Besides the basics, mine is sorely lacking. To our good fortune Irfan's driver speaks it fairly well. When mine fails I tell the driver in Pashtu and he tells Mullah Mohammad in Farsi. Slowly I remember.

Mullah's son, a man in his 40s is also sitting in front of the shop. In general I don't care for most of the men hanging around his shop (though you really can't blame them for their loitering, having lost their country and being exiled in a country too poor to even support its own people).

At the time I don't feel like chitchatting, as they would like. I've got the responsibility of our horses and the trip on my mind. Any extra time in my mind dwells on Nasreen. Besides, I feel if they don't have work in Pakistan plenty of *mujahideen* are needed in Afghanistan. Obviously I'm not taking into consideration individual circumstances, but at present I can't even have compassion for myself.

Mullah Mohammad had a farrier shop in his native Panshir. There being less horses here he now runs a sundry supply shop for the camp. He does have a crate of cold iron horse shoes and he still does the occasional shoeing job. He gathers his tools into a cloth sack. When he reaches into his crate of cold shoes we laugh and tell him we won't be needing them; we've brought our own from Peshawar. His horse shoes would fit inside of Shokot's shoes, and Shokot is the smallest of our beasts.

July 14th, *Eid ul Qurban*
Luey Akhtar* Mubarak Shah—Eid Qurban Mubarak!
Mirza and I go with Irfan Ali and his friend from Lahore down to the Shahi Mosque in his jeep at 7:00 A.M. for the *Eid* prayer. We're late, though it hasn't started yet. We find places in the lines near the rear of the mosque.

Afterward we have to rush out as Irfan has to get his buddy to the airfield to catch the flight to Peshawar. As we hurriedly make our way through the crowd I meet somebody who looks familiar, though I don't quite recognize him at first. He tells me his name is Jamshid and that I had met in Lahore at Nasreen's house about nine months back. He is from Nowsherra and works at the Habib Bank in Chitral. I tell him I'll come meet him there tomorrow.

Irfan's pal makes his flight and we drive back up to Irfan's house. It being *Eid* and he being the *A.C.* he has many guests to receive. His chief servant and cook, Mr. Hazrat, along with two other servants, set close to 30 chairs in a large circle around the yard. As guests arrive in small groups the servants bring pitchers of iced *sherbets* and squashes.

It's a strange *Eid* in Chitral. *Qurban* means sacrifice. It is the *Eid* of Sacrifice marking the end of the *Haj* when an animal is supposed to be sacrificed by anybody who can afford it. It is in remembrance of when Ibrahim (Abraham) was ordered by God to sacrifice his son Ishmael.**

Though it is *Eid ul Qurban* we have no meat for lunch. Being such an important holiday every shop in the entire bazaar is closed, including butchers. Irfan sent money to his family in the Punjab to do the sarcifice there. And of all the many guests, not a one brings any meat. The bringing of gifts of meat, a bit of the *Eid* sacrifice, and of giving a portion of it to the poor is traditional in Islam. It made us feel even more that although we are still in Pakistan, click by click, we are slowly riding away from the Pakistan we know.

July 15th
I go to the Habib Bank. We are about ready to leave Chitral but I want to find and talk with Jamshid before I go. It's the second day of *Eid* and it is closed, along with the rest of the bazaar so we can't get the supplies we need to leave, nor do I meet Jamshid.

July 16th
I go back to the bank at 11:00 A.M. They had been open half day but had closed at 10:00 (I'm running on Pakistani time so I'm late). I do find a *chowkidar* at the bank who knows approximately where Jamshid lives. We walk up a hill covered in row after row of ramshackle mud and stone dwellings. We ask as we go from children playing on the dirt path in which house Jamshid stays. After several queries we find him. He and I walk into town chatting. Most of the bazaar is still closed.

---

* *Pashtu—literally the Big Eid, Eid ul Adha*
** *The Qur'an states that it was Ishmael (Ismail) that Abraham was called to sacrifice, though the Bible states it was Ishak (Issac).*

When Jamshid and I had met in Lahore we had conversed in a mixture of Pashtu and his bank *wallah's* English. Now, for ease we just use Pashtu. We meet Ayesha in the bazaar and the three of us walk up a back path towards Irfan's house. To cross a stream we have to take off our sandals and hike up our pants past our knees. The water is brisk. We pass shacks, walking right through their front yards and continue up the hill, coming out behind Irfan's house. Ayesha goes in.

I take Jamshid down to see the horses. He says he has an arrangement to meet some friends but he will meet me back at Irfan's at 4:00 P.M. so we can talk about Lahore and other topics of mutual interest. Ayesha, Habibullah and I go to the bazaar to get supplies. We'd like to leave by tomorrow, the 17th, *Insha'Allah*. We're lucky to find enough open stores to get the goods we need. I wait in Irfan's yard for Jamshid. Mirza and Ayesha go to the polo field with Irfan. Habibullah is waiting in town for a sack of flour for the horses.

Jamshid arrives at 4:30 and we walk down the grassy, rocky hill. Again we cross the stream and sit by its side in some grass to talk. He says he thinks it's great I marry Nasreen. It's nice to be talking to a Pakistani, a Pathan, who has a different point of view than other Pakistanis I have talked to or know. He's known her family for five years, yet when I had met him at their house he was just there a short time like all the other customers. He says he is in love with Nargis. He is of the same tribe as Nasreen's family, *Kaka Khel*. He tells me he will be glad to come to Lahore to help me get her from the family. He doesn't like her husband. He says that the husband smokes heroin but I think he's just talking. I've never seen him appear to be on heroin, plus Pakistanis are always quick to spread bad gossip concerning one another, not that her husband is any saint. They are also quick to offer help in things they cannot really do. That part is just innocent Pakistani, big-hearted politeness.

If she wants to, I'm ready. I worry about her there and AIDS—her and jail. I'm still thinking of her all the time. Right now what can I do? I'm involved here too. Is she just playing with me? If only she would give me some indication to drop everything and just go for it. Something serious.

At night we go for a jeep ride with Irfan past the airfield along the Garam Shishma road. The dirt road is rocky and furrowed. There is lightning in the clouded sky. The river is foaming frothy silver grey in the Eid moonlight on our right side in the dark.

We come home and finish packing. I get to sleep after midnight. Habibullah is already snoring. I hear Mirza and Ayesha in the other room arguing over the packing of the pack saddle. Too much *samaan*.

❖ ❖ ❖

On the road north of Chitral

❖ ❖ ❖

Monument near Samnabad, Lahore—The Chauburji (four minars) Gateway is all that remains of an extensive garden known to have existed in Mughal times. An inscription on the gateway records that the garden was established here in 1646, in the reign of Shah Jahan, by a lady described as Sahib-e-Zebinda Begum-e-Dauran, or *"the elegant lady of the age."* The lady referred to is probably Jahan Ara Begum, the eldest and favourite daughter of Shah Jahan, who was known to have built gardens at Lahore, but then bestowed it upon Miyan Bai, most likely a high-ranking attendant.
(my landmark in finding Nasreen's house)

The Karakorams near Passu, Gojal, Upper Hunza (8,500 ft.). The mountain on the left is Tupopdan (6016 m-20,032 ft.), "The Sun Drenched Mountain." It is also called the Passu Cones or Passu Cathedral for its many spires.

Suspension bridge over the Yarkhun River to the village of
Turi Khuz, north of Mastuj (pg. 136)

see all photographs in color at:
http://www.pbase.com/noorkhan/00journalphotos

Photo by Ayesha S.

Following the makeshift pathway (an irrigation ditch) to Turi Khuz (pg. 136)

Dir Bazaar, NWFP

Habibullah cooking in Teru

"On your marks... *darzoo!*" — leaving Chitral

Photo by Ayesha S.

Mountains, clouds and rainbows on the Shandur Top at 12,200 ft.,
Buni Zom (21,495 ft.) in background

"In the back of beyond" — Teru, Northern Areas

Kalashi houses (Kafiristan)

Maroi, north of Chitral — before saddling up

Near Buni, between Chitral and Mastuj — roadside rest

❖ ❖ ❖

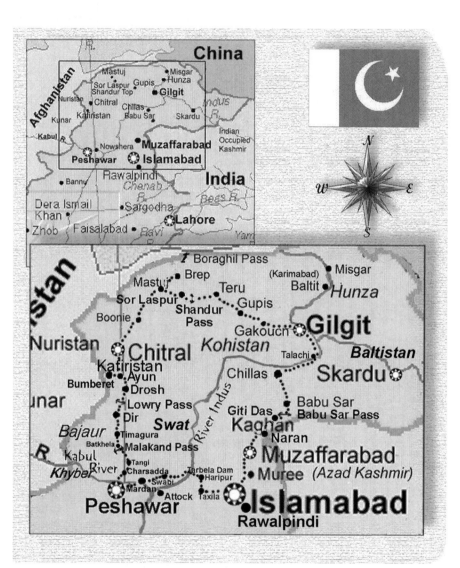

Trip Map: the dotted line is our basic route

❖ ❖ ❖

Chapter 16
On the Road Again

July 17th

Wake at 3:00 A.M.

Not on the road until 6:30. It's the first time Hercules is our pack horse. Need time to walk him up and down the road in front of Irfan's house to get the pack saddle properly adjusted on his broad body.

Just outside Chitral it starts a heavy drizzle. We ride through rain and mountains for the first half of the day. The Chitral (Yarkhun) River is churning brown and frothy below on our left. The way leads up and down, sometimes rising many hundreds of feet over the river, sometimes dropping to within 20 feet of the raging, rampaging water. In places the road is carved right out of the side of the stone cliffs, the loose sheets of raw rock completely overhanging our path (pg 161).

Mirza and Ayesha are riding Shokot and Kodak respectively and I'm walking, leading Hercules and the baggage. Habibullah is also walking, carrying his pack on his back. He is very frisky in the rain. With the new haircut he got in Chitral and his new *pakul* cap he looks like a little boy. It's 28 km to Maroi. I walk the first 20 km.

About eight km out of Maroi Ayesha and Habibullah get on a passing jeep to take them the rest of the distance. I ride stupid Kodak. He doesn't want to respond to my gentle kicks in the ribs or tugs on his reins. He won't do anything. It's a chore to keep him going forward. So this is what Ayesha has been complaining about, and I thought it was just her being stubborn.

It's the first time in the trip Mirza and I have ridden alone together. About six km out of Maroi we switch mounts and I ride Shokot. On our left the rocks drop sharply to the river far below us. Mirza rides Kodak. He wants to teach Kodak some travel pointers, as he says bluntly, "To kick out his lungs." Gently, of course.

We reach Maroi at 5:30 and set up at the mud tea house along the side of the road where our compatriots are waiting for us. There is a room next to it that serves as a roadside mosque with one small window in the thick mud walls and fragrant soft straw on the floor.

After unloading and settling the horses I pray *Maghrib* prayer in the mosque. Aziz, the jeep driver who had taken Ayesha and I to Brep, and his mate, Nadir, stop for prayer. We have tea with them. They are surprised we are so late in getting out of Chitral. I explain how we needed to let Shokot rest in Kafiristan because of his bad back and that we were further delayed by *Eid*. Mirza understands a few words and makes some comment about Lahore but they fail to understand it.

For dinner we go down the hill with a villager to his house. He tells us he had been in the military. His guest room is comfortable and plush with carpets, cushions and pillows—especially after 11 wet, muddy hours in the saddle.

He says it's impossible for us to go near the Boraghil Pass or the Russian border without permission from the Pakistani government. After a wonderful dinner of fat succulent chicken, curried vegetables, rice, salad, bread and tea he leads us back in the dark up the hill to the tea house that is our hotel.

We don't get to sleep until after 11:00.

This morning we woke late at 4:45. We sat on the veranda and watched the road as we finished our breakfast of *chai* and maize *parattas*. The aroma of wood smoke hung heavily about us.

"Look, we don't even know if we can make it past Mastuj without another pack animal but let's check to see about getting permission," Mirza suggested. "Besides, if I go back to Chitral, I will get that other breastplate we left at Irfan Ali's house."

"It wouldn't hurt to try," said I. "We can see how the horses do up to Mastuj. I just think without animals to carry additional food the horses won't have enough to eat. Especially after the Boraghil. Of course we could always come back down the Darkot Pass to Yasin, that is if our behemoths don't break through the ice. Now as far as getting past Brep to Lasht, well... do you think we can get the horses to swim nine to ten foot icy streams? I know I've seen it in movies but I'd like to see you get Shokot to jump on in. What do you think, Habibullah?" I said in English, turning to Habibullah and taking his plastic bag of *nuswar* from his hand.

"Yes," he answered, in his gravely English, grinning, not having understood a word of what I had said except for his name.

"Ah, that's what I like, agreeable partners," I added, making a small round ball of the brown snuff from Habibullah's bag and wedging it behind my lip.

"God, I don't know if the horses can make it either," Mirza replied, "but I sure would like to ride into Misgar from the back side."

"We could always head to Sor Laspur from Mastuj and up the Shandur," I continued, "it would put us there just in time for the polo match, *Insha'Allah*. We could see how the horses and money holds out to Gilgit. Then either head on to Baltistan or go back up past Hunza to Misgar and back to Chitral."

"If we can't get permission," Ayesha said, "then the Shandur is our only option."

"And if we approached the Boraghil from the back side no one would expect us," Mirza pointed out.

"Permission? Nobody told us you needed permission from that side," I agreed. "Oh, by the way, Habibullah was telling me he was somewhat surprised he had to walk so far today. And his back is sore from his pack."

"Tell him that's how Horse started out. If it continues we'll get a dispenser in Mastuj to give him a shot," said Mirza with mock compassion.

"Yeah, I will. I told him from here on there will be much walking. But maybe we could work his backpack onto the pack saddle. One thing is for sure, no matter which way we go from here, we won't see *metalled* road again until we leave Gilgit. Here's your ride *yaar*, you'd better go."

The jeep that had been loading started honking. It was ready to leave for Chitral. A few other fellows who had been waiting got up to get in. Mirza and

Ayesha went into the room and kissed goodbye, away from inquisitive eyes. Sometimes a bit of privacy is nice.

At 6:30 Mirza left for Chitral. Gone is our leader, our resident horseman. I couldn't go. It's not in my job description to talk to government *wallahs*. After all, aren't I the cultural expert, advisor and native liaison officer? Didn't I sign on to talk to the "natives"? It surely wasn't for my talent with horses. We definitely need someone to talk now. Finding English speakers is getting scarce. And who would fight with government guest house *chowkidars* (though, in that Mirza is quite proficient)?

We're ready by 8:15. The animals are saddled, loaded and ready to go. I settle the hotel/restaurant bill and have a smoke. We get our rifles, the last item every day, and start walking to where the horses are. I see that little *Shaitan,* Shokot, bucking across the field while the other two stand patiently by. Habibullah chases him back to our direction and Ayesha and I catch him. We push his saddle, which has fallen around his belly, back up and remove the saddlebags. He's broken his reins by tripping over them as he ran.

We have to dig deeply into the pack saddle completely disarranging one of the panniers to find the leather sewing kit. By the time the damage is repaired and another tea (and cigarette) it's 10:30.

Ready to roll.

Habib is leading Kodak (whom he calls Kalikk), today's pack horse. Ayesha and I are both riding and walking leisurely, the distance between Maroi and Reshan being only 22 *clicks*. Slowly we head on, bit by bit, up and up. Always rugged mountains towering ahead of us, above us. The river far below us on our right. The sky today brilliant deep crystal cerulean with billowy, white, massive cotton puffs of clouds resting on the snow covered peaks rising high over us.

Though we offer, Habibullah doesn't want to ride. He has had enough of riding in a *chair* (saddle) the day he took my place between Warai and Dir. We stop by the roadside and he goes down into a stone-walled, small, grassy orchard with a sparkling little brook gurgling alongside to collect apricots. So peacefully idyllic—I am reminded of pleasant roadside stops years ago in Indian Kashmir, a time when it was possible to go down and doze in the grass, lulled by the water's gentle, sweet, song, as my companion and I were traveling by foot and we didn't have to concern ourselves with three pranksterish, overgrown horses.

Habibullah returns with a load of apricots, carrying them in his *jolay* (the front skirt of his long *kameez).* We eat them, squatting by the side of the road and cracking open the *"apricot bones"*—as Habibullah informs me the stones are called in Pashtu—on the rocks by the side of the road. The horses decide they also like the fruit. They slobber all over my clothes as they gobble all offered to them.

Further down we stop for half an hour at a place where up a four-foot embankment on the side of the road is a field of long, green grass and succulent clover, sloping up to the ever present mountains. We let the horses eat, the edge of the field being at their neck level, while we squat in the shade of a tree across the way. Habibullah takes our small hand sickle and goes into the field cutting clumps of luscious verdant grass and placing little piles in front of each horse. Shokot decides to start down the road back to Maroi. Habibullah chases him down.

We ride on to Reshan, not having any idea what to expect there. Ayesha says the guest house was pointed out to her when we had passed by in Aziz's jeep. I must have blinked as we passed Reshan; all I remembered was seeing one restaurant as we approached and then shortly after a signboard saying Reshan in Urdu with a red slash through it. We reach the restaurant at 4:30 and ride on through town until we come to a bridge.

"We must have missed the rest house," Ayesha says. "I do remember it was definitely before this bridge."

We turn around.

"I thought she knew where the guest house is," Habibullah grumbles. "Why didn't you ask where it was?"

"She told me she knew," I answer him.

"She knows everything!" he snaps.

"Why didn't you ask, Habibullah, if you were so worried? You speak the language. I thought she knew."

"You thought she knew!" Habibullah repeats sardonically.

"Shut up, Habibullah!" I answer impatiently.

We're all feeling testy and tired today although we've only been on the road seven hours. Add two hours to repair Shokot's mischievousness. Maybe it is also the increased altitude. Though we've been steadily climbing since leaving Chitral (3700 ft.) we still must not be much over 6000 or 7000 feet.

Nothing is ready for us at the guest house. No one even knows about our coming, contrary to what Ayesha and I had been told in Buni. I lose it with the *chowkidar*. He wants me to call the *A.C.* in Buni! I stomp up to the Reshan bazaar, pulling him with me. He says there is a telephone there. A small group of locals follow us. Ayesha, Habibullah and the horses wait on the grass in front. I tell them to unload while I'm gone.

"What if we can't stay here?" Habibullah asks.

"Don't say, 'what if we can't,'" I tell him, making sure I say it loud enough so everyone can hear and know my intentions.

We get to the one shop with a phone. Fortunately I memorized the *A.C.'s* phone number—Buni, number 1. We can't ring an operator. It's 5:20, the exchange closes at 5:00. Funny, something in Pakistan that is on time.

I do manage to get in a fairly heated argument with the locals. It is centered mainly on the shopkeeper with the telephone who seems to be someone of some authority. He also seems to be someone with some intelligence, something becoming a rarity it seems. I shout in Pashtu for comprehension, occasionally throwing in some English for added weight and to remind the locals that though I may look like a filthy, begrimed, Afghan refugee, I am in actuality a filthy, begrimed, *Englaise sahib*.

"But guest house under repair," says the melancholy faced *chowkidar*.

172

"I don't care if it's under repair," I yell. "I'm sure we've stayed in worse places."

He says something to the shopkeeper in the local language, Kowar, which I can't understand.

"This man says the key for the guest house is at his house," the shopkeeper tells me. "a long way away."

"I don't care. I've got my own key here," I say, placing my hand on the butt of my pistol. There must be a key available and this should raise it. If not, I imagine it won't be too hard to blow the lock off.

"Look, we're staying at the guest house, as the *A.C.* said we could," I continue. "If you have any complaints you can call him in Buni. For that matter you can call the *D.C.* in Chitral or the Minister of Tourism in Islamabad. Who is he anyway?" I poke my finger into the chest of the *chowkidar.* "The guest house is nothing, just some empty rooms!"

"This *chowkidar* is a poor, illiterate man," the shopkeeper tells me. "Anyway, do you have some *chit* from the *A.C.?*"

"I don't need it! We have a letter from Islamabad. It's with my friends back at the guest house. You know Islamabad? It's the Capitol of Pakistan! Pakistan! You've heard of Pakistan? But how will he read it?" I say, looking at the *chowkidar* again, "It's not in pictures, you know!"

We send off for the key and the *chowkidar* and I walk back to the guest house, followed by our crowd of onlookers. I've cooled off, letting all that steam out and we speak together easily. After all, a job like his must be difficult to find in these parts and we've just ridden in out of nowhere looking for all the world like Afghan bandits. He didn't want to make a mistake, to lose his job. And I didn't really want to blow the locks off his door, anyway.

Habib and Ayesha have all the gear piled high on the lawn. The horse blankets and saddlebags are spread out on the ground to dry off the sweat. The animals are staked by a shallow, small, clear stream flowing next to the guest house, standing on the short green grass. They've just finished brushing them. Some men arrive with straw, corn and flour Habibullah has arranged and we feed them, ignoring the people standing around gawking. I tell Ayesha and Habibullah the story of the missing key, having to tell it twice, once in each of their languages.

The key arrives and they start to carry gear into the furniture-less guest house. The sun has set and darkness is rapidly approaching. I walk down the road to the eating establishment we saw riding into town to see if I can procure some food. On the way I stop to help some locals push a tractor stuck in a stream running across the road. How can I not? I can use a boost in my community image, anyway. I am able to acquire meat *qorma*, big thick *chapatties,* some raw onions and tomatoes.

By the time I reach the guest house it's pitch dark. We eat on a blanket spread out on the lawn by the light of a kerosine lantern. I discover to my dismay the chunks of black-looking meat are liver—an animal part I do not particularly care for. Ayesha and Habibullah gobble it down. I eat a bit, mostly sopping up the hot *qorma* sauce with pieces of *chapatti.* At 9:30 they spread their sleeping bags on a plastic tarp on the lawn under a tree and go to sleep.

Now I'm inside the room with the pack saddle and saddlebags. As there is no furniture I'm sitting on the floor and writing by the light of a kerosine lantern. The *chowkidar* is silently squatting, watching me as I hurriedly scribble, as if I were performing some sort of magic rite. It's after midnight.

Today I've actually had some periods in which I haven't thought of Nasreen. They've lasted half an hour or so. Progress? Thank you God for small wonders amid great wonders.

July 19th, 5:00 A.M.
Reshan

After tossing and turning in my blanket on the hard cement floor, I fell asleep about 2:00 A.M. Bad night. Bad dreams. Thinking about Nasreen. Tomorrow will be only two weeks since I last saw her, yet as always, it seems so long. It has been so many miles. Miss her so. Want to just hang out, to be with her again. Don't know if we can spend a night together, if it will even be possible when I get back to Lahore. I guess it depends on how long her husband is in jail. Though I do need to start talking to him if I'm going to buy her out of there.

Traveling by horse is so great; the places we are going into, the places we have been, so wild, so remote, though it is tiring work much of the time. Definitely not the "horse holiday" some journalist met back in Peshawar had called it.

Thinking of quitting this trip after Gilgit. I can teach Ayesha all the basic Pashtu she needs to deal with Habibullah. She's already picking it up splendidly. It's not the hard work and difficulties that are the reason.

It's Nasreen, as usual. I keep thinking of her in that house. If she's working, anybody that wants to can have her if they have the money. It makes every day a hell. The wear and tear on her body, on her heart and soul. And now the idea of AIDS is there and it makes it so much worse. Sure, if she had it I could get it, but more than that I'm thinking of her. What would I do if she got it? I can't turn off my love for her. I'd still want her. Definitely a complication. Sometimes I can think maybe she's not working, like before I left on this trip, but it's so hard to trust her there. And I know she has to do whatever her husband says; he definitely cares for money more than he cares for her.

I can think maybe the police are hassling the house like so many times before and there won't be any business. But then I worry about her going to jail. That also would complicate my life. I don't know how I would go about getting her out of jail, but how can I love her like this and not try?

I try to have faith in God, but sometimes it's hard, isn't it? Aren't God's ways sometimes seemingly cruel? Look at Afghanistan and countless other places of conflict. The sufferings of innocent people in this world. Am I leaving her on a rope hanging over a chasm? "Just hang on, Nasreen honey, I'll get you off just as soon as I finish my horse trip."

But how can I leave after Gilgit? There's Mirza and Ayesha, my two best *ghora* friends—and Habibullah. Sure, I can teach Ayesha the basic Pashtu she requires, but what about in those emergencies that always crop up on a trip of

174

this magnitude? Can I desert them?

We could sell the horses in Gilgit.

I do need to go to the U.S. at the end of the year and there's yet a lot of talking to do in Lahore. Maybe I can get her a visa and take her to the U.S? But that takes time. I won't have the time if I get back in September or October. I don't want to leave her in that house any longer than necessary.

Well it's 5:30, time to hit the road,

Reality....

July 20th

Buni

Reached Buni yesterday after seven hours on the road from Reshan. I rode Shokot, Ayesha rode Kodak and Herc was *"samaan dapara."*

Rugged mountains and monstrous ravines. Rocks are beginning seriously everywhere we look, from the small ones on the road to cottage-sized boulders that have tumbled down from the lofty heights to choke the gullies. The rapidly churning river most of the day is several hundred feet below us, its rushing roar muted to a consistent drone. We eat apricots and drink water out of the ditches flowing at the side of the way.

"I hope it's been boiled," I tell Ayesha, scooping the cold water up with our shinny stainless cup.

"Can you imagine those *"water-boilers"* in Peshawar drinking this?" she jokes.

"I know Habibullah can't," I say. He looks at me on hearing his name. "Can you, Habibee?" I ask him in English.

"What did you say?" he asks in Pashtu.

I don't bother explaining to him that *"water-boiler"* is a term coined by us and a few other friends in Peshawar for the foreign community in University Town who dare not drink the water without it being boiled or purified to kill foreign bacteria. I know the concept is too foreign in itself to imply humor to Habibullah. Some things just do not hold up in the translation from East to West.

"Good fresh natural water," I say to him, "cold and sweet."

"Ow kena! **Allah** *shoker, al-hamdu-lillah,"* he answers. (It sure is! Thank God, praise God.)

We arrive at the tea house where Ayesha and I had waited almost a month ago. There isn't any decent place to tie the horses so I ask them to bring our tea outside. We squat on the rocky hillside across the road and hold the saucers in our left hands, lifting the cups with our right, reins between our knees. We try not to spill any when the horses tug at the reins.

The last few hours the animals have been showing signs of altitude tiredness or stubbornness. After I pay and we start to leave the tea house Ayesha freaks out with Kodak. He won't go straight like she wants him to (not an entirely unusual occurrence with Kodak). He pulls hard to the side, a nasty, annoying habit I've noticed when I've ridden him. Well, she can be more stubborn than any cantankerous horse can be and she won't have any of it.

175

She starts lashing out with her knotted rope quirt, screaming at him and kicking him in the sides to get him to go straight. This only succeeds in getting him to turn in circles, which in turn succeeds to get Ayesha only more flustered. Kodak backs towards the edge of the road and I fear if he goes any further they will both crash off the roadside and through tea house roof. She beats him and he rears and kicks up more dust, an impasse of stubbornness. Finally they reach an uneasy status-quo. I lead off, telling Habibullah to pull Hercules hard behind, hoping by seeing us go Kodak will start to follow, and he does.

We cross the bridge and ride up the hill into Buni. We arrive at the *A.C.'s* house at 3:30 but it is locked. No one home. We rest under a tree in his grassy yard. The gardener comes and tells us the *A.C.* went to Multan for *Eid* and still hasn't returned. His guard, Faiz, is also away at his home.

"Far away." the gardener tells us as he points west over the mountains. Ishmael, the extra *A.C.* has also gone to Chitral.

We ride to the guest house and not without a little bit of trouble succeed in fighting our way in (it all seems so routine). Finally the keys are produced by one of the workmen helping with the repairs in the cookhouse. We stake out the animals under some huge apple trees in a field of short, green grass in front of the guest house. There's no horse food around, of course. What's new? Habibullah and I walk back to the bazaar to look for food. We can only find a bag of stinking *orbashie* (barley).

We make ourselves at home in the room, the saddlebags piled in a heap in the center. The saddles, horse blankets and other tack are spread out on the veranda. Ayesha and Habibullah are cooking dinner in the kitchen with the aid of light from two kerosine lanterns. Since Kafiristan we've discovered Habibullah can work wonders with rice, some onions and a few potatoes (when we can get them), a bit of *ghee*, red pepper and tomato powder.

At sunset I go out and make *wuzu* in a small ditch of clear running water bordering the field; the water in the guest house isn't running. I pray *Maghrib* on the lawn next to the horses. As I pray Ishmael, the extra *A.C.*, returns from Chitral. I see him as I come in the front gate of the guest house after prayer. He looks flustered. "You have to leave first thing in the morning," he tells me brusquely. "You can't stay here. And you can't keep those animals there."

Not the right way to speak to me lately. "Look, talk to your boss," I say. "Who are you anyway? You're only the extra *A.C!* I don't even talk to anyone under *A.C.s.* No peons or extra *A.C.s,* for that matter! If you don't like it you can call your boss the *A.C.* or the *D.C.* in Chitral or the *A.C.* there or Islamabad. After that, I think you'll be the only one leaving in the morning."

I walk past him into the kitchen....

Still can't find decent horse food. Habibullah and I do manage to get a 20 kilo sack of flour from a Pathan baker in the bazaar, but after walking all through Buni we can't find a thresher started yet. Habibullah takes a jeep back to Maroi where the wheat fields are already being harvested. We've out ridden the season.

Mirza arrives back before Habibullah. Irfan in Chitral said there'd be no problem for us to ride to the Boraghil (pass) or anywhere we wanted but it had to be cleared with the *D.C.'s* office. The *D.C.* says we can't go anywhere within 30 miles of the Russian border. With the way the horse food scene is shaping up (or down) maybe it's just as well. It doesn't look like we could get them over the northern route alive.

I'm giving Ayesha a crash course in "horse expedition Pashtu." Mirza is not a "language man." I'm thinking about Nasreen so much. Worrying about AIDS, about jail. Isn't that how the mind works? You leave the house and then you start thinking you forgot to turn the stove off. The mind just picks a course and makes a problem. Oh, they may be there also, but they sure get magnified when you're so far away and can't do anything about them. The mind can take you anywhere. Don't know if I will go on past Gilgit.

The original idea was to ride to Kashgar until the Chinese decided not to be kind enough to even consider our request for permission to take our little expedition into China via the Khunjarab Pass. Now where are we going? Back to Peshawar? To Gilgit, for sure. *Insha'Allah.* After seven years to finally ride up to G.M. Baig's shop in Gilgit.

❖ ❖ ❖

July 24th
Written on the Shandur Top (catching up on writing)
We left Buni and rode along the old Mastuj Road on the east side of the river, mostly climbing through green lofty Alpine meadows and cold, gushing streams. A beautiful day. Clear, deep, endless, blue skies and white cascading clouds. We passed through two small villages, Meragram and Sonoghur, cling-ing to the side of the mountain.

The river running in its rocky gorge almost 1000 feet below us gave us helicopter aerial views. Finally our road disintegrated in a loose track of shale switchbacks which we followed down to the riverbed. As we crossed a bridge and started up the opposite mountainside it started to rain in large, singular drops, barely wetting the dry, stony ground as it soaked into the thirsty dust.

Traveling 10 hours we finally reached Sarghoz, our destination. The altim-eter, which we started using since our altitude started escalating read 7500 feet. On our right side large slabs of rock and boulders led up to the mountain peaks. On our left, next to the river several hundred feet below us, a green and settled hamlet was opening up out of the river valley—a handful of houses.

When Ayesha and I had journeyed north from Chitral to Brep last month, the two people sitting in the front seat with Ayesha were an Ismaili *peer* named appropriately enough Peer Sahib and his wife, with apparently no name. Peer Sahib is the local teacher in Sarghoz. When he and his wife got out of the jeep amid the rocks over Sarghoz, he had offered his hospitality to us when we should pass this way on our trip.

And now here we all were....

❖ ❖ ❖

North of Chitral, near Mastuj

❖ ❖ ❖

Chapter 17

Guests of the Peer Sahib

*W*e led the horses down the rocky slope to a shale-strewn, grassy dell that turned out to be Peer Sahib's front yard when we inquired from a pack of grubby-faced children who came forth to receive us. They didn't speak Pashtu, but the few that went to school spoke Urdu, so Habibullah spoke with them. Peer Sahib would be here shortly they informed us.

We tied our horses to the overhanging branches of a tremendous oak tree and sat on the soft cool grass. The children quickly brought us a pitcher of lemon *sherbet*. After some time Peer Sahib arrived. He was a wiry man with dark, curly hair and thick, black plastic rimmed glasses. He seemed put off we had actually taken him up on his offer of hospitality, a sentiment we weren't very used to in Pakistan.

Things were a bit strange. We argued as to where to put the animals. It seemed when Ayesha and Peer Sahib were walking near his house and talking in English he told her it was okay to tie them anywhere we wanted. There was a spot she liked on the side of the house with tall green grass, so after unloading she and Mirza hammered the *moogays* in there and led the horses over to tie them. We sat under the tree and relaxed while our tired beasts grazed greedily on the tall lush grass.

Later, when Habibullah and Ayesha went with Peer Sahib and some of his men into the fields to cut clover for the horses, Habibullah overheard them talking. They were upset. They didn't want the horses where we had tied them, so close to the house. They thought they would mess up the place. On returning Habibullah told me this development and I relayed the information to Ayesha and Mirza. She was adamant that Peer Sahib had told her any place we wanted would be fine and Habibullah was adamant Peer Sahib and his minions were upset and wanted them moved. As usual I was in the middle of this cultural and linguistic impasse.

A table was placed under the oak tree and dinner was brought. I was late coming to table and the dinner brought was small. I thought Mirza and Habibullah had hidden most of the food, leaving me only a few morsels, as a joke. Peer Sahib and his family did not appear to be poor people, but then who knows? It was Sarghoz. Near the oak tree, at the side of the lawn, was a mud and stone guest house with two rooms and a covered veranda. The rooms had thick felt rugs and piles of thick quilts. We stacked all of our gear on the veranda. Strangely enough its use for the night was never offered us.

"I think you will be more comfortable outside," Peer Sahib told us, his beady eyes buggy behind his thick glasses.

"I think I'd be more comfortable sleeping with your daughter, *banchod*," I jokingly whispered to Habibullah.

"The weather is fine," he said as his children cleared off the table. "Sleep well. Good night."

They went inside. At least he was polite enough to leave us a lantern. We slept outside. Mirza and Ayesha spread the pack saddle tarp on the lawn and laid their sleeping bags over it. Habibullah and I spread the plastic ponchos on the ground in front of the guest house porch, grumbling.

"What kind of people are these?" Habibullah complained.

"Not Pathans. Maybe not even Pakistani or Muslim," I ventured.* "We've traveled far, my brother. We're among strange folk. Let us take some blankets from inside. I feel suffocation in the sleeping bags."

"Good idea, Noor Mohammad. In my bag I feel like I'm in my death shroud."

We laid our sleeping gear on the plastic and covered ourselves with heavy quilts. I wondered if they had any of their own inhabitants. Shortly after lying down it started to rain.

"Forget this," I said to Habibullah.

"*Ow kena!* (for sure)," he answered.

We picked up our bedding and went into the tenant-less guest house. Mirza and Ayesha shifted their sleeping place to the relative dryness of the veranda.

The gray misty morning light cracks over the tops of where the rocky, snow-capped mountain peaks of yesterday should be appearing. Last night's rain lay heaped in masses of mist about the hillsides. Habibullah and I walk into the fields to cut clover for the horses. It's cold, wet and drizzly—the tall grass and rain dampening our baggy clothing and the blankets in which we are wrapped.

As the sky gets lighter we can only see a couple of hundred feet up the mountain sides, our vision being obscured by lowering cloud layers. As we come back, laden with heavy wet grass over our backs, the skies release their burden in a steadily increasing downpour. By then Mirza is awake. We move the horses into a covered cow pen.

Peer Sahib brings breakfast and we eat in the guest house which we have taken over in the rain. One fried egg each, some *roti* and a small plate of goat cheese. Around 8 A.M. the rain stops and the clouds lift, swept up the valley in damp gusts of wind. Peer Sahib tells us if we saddle up our horses they will be a lot warmer. We don't know if he is trying to be helpful or if he just wants us out. We're more used to people giving us more food than we can eat and not wanting us to leave.

We pack, saddle and load the horses in record time (one hour) and we're out. *Khuda hafiz*, Peer Sahib. Just out of Sarghoz, before we start up a rough trail that will bring us back to the main road, we ford the stream and come to a small shop.

"Habibullah," I say, "go and ask the shopkeeper if he has any *charras*."

"No," he answers belligerently. "This isn't the Frontier. These people aren't Pathan. You can't trust them. I won't ask them for anything."

I stomp past Habibullah and up to the front porch of the shop.

"*Asalaam aleikum*," I say to the shopkeeper.

"*Wa aleikum asalaam*," he answers guardedly. So far so good. "What do you need?"

---

* Many *Sunnis* consider *Ismailis* non-Muslim.

"I'm looking for a small piece of *charras*," I tell him. "In Buni people told me I would be able to find it in shops on the road to Mastuj, but as yet I haven't found any."

"No. I don't have any here either," he answers, looking at me askance. "Say, you aren't Afghani, are you?"

"No. My friends and I are American Muslims. We live in Peshawar. We're on our way to Gilgit."

"To Gilgit, by horse?" he asks, incredulous.

"*Insha'Allah.*"

"And that one?" he asks, signifying Habibullah.

"Oh, he is just a loafer," I say loud enough for Habibullah to hear me and laugh. "No, he's a Pathan, from near Utmanzai. He is my brother."

"You have a long, hard trip ahead of you. I wish you luck," he says. "I don't have any *charras* to sell but here is a small piece you can take with you." He reaches into his vest pocket and hands me a small, gummy, brown ball. I thank him and we say our goodbyes. As I walk past Habibullah I say, "So what do you think now? I've got a little piece and I'm not going to let you smoke any of it, you stupid farmer! Next time don't be so stubborn."

Four more kilometers on the road and we cross the Mastuj bridge and start heading south east, climbing steadily. No more road signs, no more apricot trees—rocks, mountains and big sky, the river somewhere far below us. The mountains continue before us rising beyond the river, new ones appearing ahead of us like giants raising from sleep, our path blocked by mighty walls against which our feeble wanderings seem in vain.

We stop to rest on a hillside where there is some short grass for the horses to pull up and munch. The sky has cleared and is a rich lapis blue with opalescent cotton-puff clouds. I decide to share my gleamed refreshment with my brother Habibullah after all. Then we continue on, the road still climbing up and up.

Mirza and I are riding, Habibullah and Ayesha are somewhere behind us, leading Herc. As my eyes take in the natural beauty of our surroundings and my mind plays with the logistics of the rugged terrain we are riding into, my mind is churning a myriad of emotional feelings.

"You know I've started teaching Ayesha a rush course of Pashtu." I say.

"Yeah, I know. You can't leave us, Noor. We started this together. I know Ayesha is picking up Pashtu remarkably fast, but she won't be able to handle every unexpected situation that can arise in a trip of this scale. We need you to talk, Noor. This is what we've talked about and planned for so long. Isn't this great? Look what we're doing! Look what we're seeing!"

"It is definitely great. But for me there is also a hollow feeling. What can I say? My heart isn't into it. I don't have that burning desire."

"Damn your burning desire."

"Inside my heart is burning. I can't stop thinking about Nasreen, I can't stop worrying about her."

"Nasreen! Even though she has never left Lahore, never put her foot in a stirrup, she has been riding with us every step of this trip. She's a plague on me, a black widow spider stealing the very life from you. How long will this go on?"

"I don't know. I'm sorry. My desire is to pull her away from her corrupt family and life."

"Did she ever say she wanted that?"

"I've seen it in her eyes, felt it in her talk. She can be so sweet and gentle. We've had some intimate moments."

"Noor, you romanticist, you foolish romanticist. I can't tie you to this trip."

"I know. I'll stay as far as Gilgit. We've got to ride up to Baig's shop together. After there, we'll see. We could sell the horses in Gilgit or you, Ayesha and Habibullah can continue on. Maybe I can hire a translator in Gilgit to go on with you."

"You know what the chances of that working out would be?"

"Well, we will talk about it in Gilgit. For sure I am going to go to Lahore from Gilgit even if I can't get on a flight; it will only take a day or so to go by road, *Insha'Allah.*

"Noor, we wanted to ride away from Peshawar, from the world. But you keep bringing Peshawar, Lahore, Nasreen, all that back into it."

"I can't ride away from all that, I'm too involved. It's my life, too. I can't ride away from my heart. And besides, now that we can't go to China aren't we riding back to Peshawar anyway? It's just a matter of time. And anyway, it's not as if we're completely incommunicado with the world. Most of our route is jeep-able. Besides, don't lie to me, you need me to bring you French's mustard and tins of Russian tuna from Abdullah Jan's in Peshawar." *

"Noor, have I told you to go to hell lately? Let's let Ayesha and Habibullah catch up to us. There's a local coming up behind them. We'll discuss this later, in Gilgit."

As the four of us trudge up the steep mountain road the local keeps up with us, slightly behind. He doesn't speak Pashtu, I assume. He doesn't speak English, I know.

"Speak to him in Urdu," I tell Habibullah. "He probably speaks it."

"He probably doesn't," he answers me negatively.

"You don't know unless you try. Talk with him! Ask him about Harchin and Sor Laspur. Find out if there are any stores."

"No," Habibullah answers belligerently.

"What's your problem, Habibullah? Try to talk with him."

"He's just a local villager. He doesn't know anything."

"Like you, you stupid, backward Pathan," I say, losing my patience. "Why don't you ask him if his donkey mounted your mother, *banchod*? I'll try."

I ride back and try speaking to the fellow in Urdu. To my surprise he speaks Pashtu. He tells me there is a store in Harchin, approximately four kilometers, or miles, ahead. In Sor Laspur there are stores and hotels. It's a big village. We've heard the same from others.

---

* Abdullah Jan's—one of the few stores in Peshawar (Saddar Bazaar, Arbab Rd.) where imported foods could be had. We called it "Long and Narrow" because the shop was amazingly "long and narrow." Mirza had a liking for Russian canned tuna and French's Mustard.

Chapter 18
This Table Is the Store!
(Harchin and Sor Laspur)

I'm several hundred yards in the lead. The road levels off and I'm riding amid stone and mud walls and a double row of stunted poplars. Two boys are squatting on a stone wall on the side of the road.

"Is this Harchin?" I ask in Urdu.

They repeat the word "Harchin" and point onwards. They don't even speak Urdu. Most likely the closest school is in Mastuj, a half day's walk and farther than they've probably ever been.

I come to a place where there are a few stone dwellings to the left on the hill above the track I am riding on. To my right is a small stream flowing through short green turf and a handful of trees. There is a table set up on the side of the road with some packs of cigarettes, a few packages of biscuits, boxes of matches, toffees and a plastic bag of green *nuswar*. I ask how much further to Harchin and the boys behind the table say "this is it." I ask where the store is and again they answer, "this is it."

Welcome to Harchin....

By now the rest of us have arrived. We tie the horses to some trees on the grass. On negotiation a boy from the store brings us a pot of salted tea and four cups from one of the dwellings on the hillside.

Ayesha has the unenviable position of being in charge of our finances, hence in charge of being frugal. This position has earned her the loving nickname "Baby Hitler." She only permits us one package of stale biscuits, split four ways. She reasons they are overpriced, but then Harchin is a long way from anywhere. Mirza and Ayesha get in a scrap over money.

"I'm starving," he complains, "and my wife is too cheap to buy us two boxes of biscuits."

"I'm only trying to save money so we can finish *your damn trip*," she fumes. "You want to have enough money to make it back to Peshawar, don't you?"

"Not if I starve before I get there," he answers.

"Oh! I don't understand you! You won't starve. Do what you like, you big baby." She gets up in a huff and starts walking down the road out of town.

The air is thick. Hercules tears a huge chunk of bark off of the tree he's tied to. An old man has just come up whom the trees seem to belong to and begins to yell at us about despoiling his trees. Luckily I can turn the tables on the shop *wallahs* who told us we could tie the horses there in the first place.

Here the hamlets are set in patches of green and golden brown wheat and ripening corn fields rippling in the winds, nestled 1500 feet below us on our right. The road drops off in a broken shale slide ending in several hundred feet of scree. The river, fields and scattered stone houses are below on our west, sloping up to the 20,000 foot jagged snow covered peaks of the Buni Zom range towering overhead. On our immediate left stones rise directly into craggy mountains of raw rock and ice. We ride on, going higher and higher, leaving

Harchin and its table behind and below.

At a curve in the road when Ayesha is leading Herc, pulling him along, a jeep rounds the bend speeding towards them. She can't take Herc to the right, the drop is considerable and the edge is small. She tries to wedge him up the tiny space between the road and the rocks on the left. In the dust the fully loaded vehicle almost clears the loaded horse. But at the last moment it catches the pack saddle, tearing it open along the seam. It would take anti-aircraft fire to tear through our heavy duty American canvas but the seams are vulnerable. Mirza jumps off Shokot and throws me his reins.

I know he's not concerned over Ayesha. That she is okay is apparent. Nor is he concerned over the pack. It is his sword, the "Mirza Sword," custom made for him by a renowned American knife and sword maker, that recieves his worry. His sword belt had been torn and needed mending so it was riding in the top of the right pannier. The end of its scabbard is sticking out of the torn pack saddle.

With the dust still swirling I see him unbuckle the remaining top buckle of the pannier and take out the scabbard. Then he apprehensively slides the sword out of the scabbard. From where I sit atop Kodak I can see the blade in the glare of the bright mountain sunlight. Its usual shiny razor edged point is missing. It's chipped!

He goes over to the side of the road and faces the drop and encircling mountains and looks at his sword—his alter ego. I can feel his anguish from where I sit. I know Ayesha can too. Habibullah, I'm not so sure what he thinks of Mirza's attachment to his big shiny knife. He puts it back in the scabbard and Ayesha and I help him tie the pack so nothing will fall out.

"We'll fix it in Sor Laspur," Ayesha says reassuringly.

There is not much else to say. I know his thoughts are not on the repair of our pack saddle just at this moment.

"I bet a new point can be ground on it. Only a small piece is chipped off the end," I interject, trying to lighten things up a bit. I get on Kodak and start on down the road, knowing he doesn't want to talk.

A jeep comes along in the direction in which we are headed and we send Habibullah ahead to Sor Laspur to check on arrangements for our stay and horse food. There is a lot of traffic on the road due to the proximity of the polo match, maybe a few jeeps an hour. It is scheduled to start in two days. It is even rumored Benazir (Bhutto)* will be flying in by helicopter.

I'm riding 100 yards ahead of Mirza and Ayesha enjoying the spectacular view; though hot, tired, dusty, sore and day dreaming of Nasreen, wondering when the spur of the mountain side will open into a valley that will be Sor Laspur. I hear, or sense, a commotion behind me. I turn to see Shokot rearing on the road's rocky left embankment. He bucks a second time and the back of his head connects with the front of Mirza's, proving once again a horse's huge skull is stronger than a frail human head. Mirza goes down.

I turn Kodak and quickly ride back. Hercules and Shokot are standing on the side of the road, reins hanging loosely. Ayesha is squatting on the side of

---

* Ed note: in 1989, Benazir Bhutto was Prime Minister of Pakistan.

the road over Mirza. His face is covered in dust and blood. His glasses, broken by the impact of Shokot's head, have cut him deeply under the right eye. It looks bad. Ayesha tries to help him but almost passes out from the sight of all the blood.

I pick out pieces of glass, trying to clean the wound with water from the canteen and his grimy handkerchief. Then I make a bandage from the handkerchief and tie it in place with a bit of turban tail (always a useful item).

At 5:30 another verdant valley starts to unfold among the rocky peaks before us. I ask a man on the road how far it is to Sor Laspur and he points to the valley and says the wonderful word "there." *Al-hamdu-lillah*, we have gained our goal. According to the altimeter we're at 9,800 feet. We've climbed 2,500 feet! The grand hotel we've been told about in Sor Laspur is a dirt-floored room that serves in the day as a tea house next to a similarly floored store measuring six feet by six. Habibullah has arranged a place down the hill to stake the horses. I go with him to settle them once they are unloaded.

We get in a big row while mixing flour, corn and *boose* next to a stream. Ayesha comes down and insists we have rice with our dinner as we hadn't had much to eat at Peer Sahib's nor had we had lunch. Habibullah says he has already checked and only *tanda* (squash) is available. She says the hotel *wallah* said we could use his kitchen to cook our own rice. For some reason Habibullah says stubbornly it isn't possible and Ayesha insists stubbornly that we can do it. I'm not sure of the provocation, maybe just exhaustion, or altitude, or a language mix-up, but neither of them will budge an inch. I'm in the middle, trying to sort out the English words, the English ideas and concepts into Pashtu and into Pakistan (i.e; Habibullah's brain). Not always an easy task. The proverbial square peg in a round hole. I'm exhausted also. Result—I take my open hand and hit the *boose,* spraying it over Habibullah and into the steam. "*Ohdayghiam khor ghod!* Do it yourself!" I stomp off.

The pack saddles we store in the shop. After the table in Harchin it seems a big shop and fully-stocked; rice, sugar, tea, cigarettes, *ghee*, biscuits, toffees, pant draw-strings (an important item here) and other essential sundries. The tea house next to the store has enough room for four cots.

A restaurant up the road ends up cooking our meal for us. They say it will be ready at 9:30. We supply the rice. We sit down to a huge platter of steaming white fluffy rice, a generous bowl of *sag* and *chapatties.* So much food, a veritable feast. Ayesha looks at Habibullah and asks sarcastically, "*Tanda chairta dai?*" (where's the squash?)

At 5:30 in the morning there is a terrific pounding on the doors of the room we are sleeping in. The double wooden gateways are swung fully open, letting the glaring first light of the morning into the dark, windowless room. The *chai wallahs* start clearing out the cots and sweeping the floor for the morning rush.

And there is. Fully loaded jeeps arrive taking passengers up to the Shandur for the polo game scheduled to start in one day. While Habib and I feed the animals an old man and a large, grizzled, middle-aged fellow offer us some *charras*. We buy a small bag of unpressed pollen. It's green and looks like

185

nuswar.

We spend the morning mending breast plates, the pack saddle and Mirza's sword belt. Habibullah looks for grain for the horses and tennis shoes to walk in. Lately he has been complaining about the discomfort of trekking such long distances in his *chappals*. The other day he cut off a huge chunk of skin hanging dirty and loose from between his big and second toes. It had been a blister. Now he is also entertaining thoughts of leaving the expedition after Gilgit. Things and circumstances are becoming too strange for him. Maybe we are?

We have a serious talk with him.

We make him promise if we pay for new shoes he will stay on with the expedition. We don't want to invest in new footwear for him if he is only going to use it to walk into Gilgit and then ride the bus back to his village. Gilgit can't be more than 150 miles away over the Shandur Top and the Hindu Raj and Karakoram Mountains. Why doesn't he like the expensive hiking boots we borrowed from our *mujahid* friend Mahsood in Peshawar? He's a Pathan farmer. He can walk to Gilgit barefoot!

Seeds of dissension are sprouting.

The plan is Mirza and I will ride Shokot and Hercules up the Shandur, which we are at the foot of, and Kodak will carry the baggage. Ayesha and Habibullah will go to the top by jeep and take enough gear to set up camp.

We stock up on supplies from the store. At 1:30 a vehicle finally comes along with a little extra room for Ayesha and Habibullah to squeeze in with their sack of tents, *moogays*, tarp and tools.

Mirza and I saddle up. We leave slightly after 3:00, clearing with the police check post as we ride out of Sor Laspur towards the top of the world. I light up a *duc* cigarette as we start up the hill out of town. Up and up we ride. We can see our road carved into the mountainside above us zigzagging in a gigantic "Z."

We take turns leading Kodak. Carrying the baggage is a job he excels at. When you're on his back it's like having a faulty steering linkage but with the pack saddle he follows along no problem. I'm happy to be riding Herc. After Shokot and Kodak it's like having power-glide. I recall when I first started out on this trip atop these huge behemoths it was all so new. Now, here I am riding up the legendary Shandur Pass, a *duc* cigarette in one hand, Kodak's lead rope in the other, maneuvering between rocky cliffs and drops, dust and diesel-spewing jeeps passing in the fresh, high, mountain air.

We continue up and up, stopping every twenty minutes or so to let the horses breathe and rest. Growing between the cracks of the rocks on the side of the road and up the mountain sides are countless minuscule, wild, high-mountain flowers in brilliant tiny splashes of white, purple, blue and pink.

Sometimes a jeep (or a group of several) going up or down the pass for the polo match is a problem, a bit of a hassle. Especially when vehicles meet going in opposite directions. Barely enough room to squeeze the horses by. We stop at an ice cold stream at 7:00 P.M. to don our warmer thermal-knit shirts, pee, drink water and eat some *jawbreaker* (dry roasted chick-peas). I have a smoke. The altimeter reads just over 12,000 feet.

Another half mile and we ride up and through an outcropping of rock onto a grassy meadow surrounded by snow covered mountaintops. Behind us the world drops off from 12,600 feet. Across the misty chasm that is the valley of Sor Laspur rises the 21,495 foot peak of Buni Zom which we have been watching grow larger and larger in our sight since midday yesterday, leading us on to Sor Laspur. Before us is a lake mirroring the azure and wispy orange shades of the gloaming as we ride eastward across the short green turf. The feeling of having made it over the pass from a world of towering rocks over the spotted vegetation of the valley of Sor Laspur far below us to this is purely exhilarating. But we can only appreciate and enjoy it as we ride onward. The sun has set. It is too late to stop. The evening is darkening and the cold wind is laced with rain.

We follow the dirt trail skirting the lake. We can see some lights flickering on the facing hillside upon which we gaze with gladdened eyes. A tent city. We pass the water and ride past the polo field. The rain is now coming down in sheets, the biting wind blowing it in our faces. Ayesha and Habibullah appear out of the darkness. Habibullah takes Kodak's lead rope and they lead us to our tents. It's after 8:00 P.M. We unload the horses in the rain, wind and dark.

With some labor we have everything situated in our two small tents with the pack saddlebags and saddles under a tarp stretched between the two tents. Mirza asks me to ask Habibullah if he has seen the horse brushing kit, a zippered canvas bag the size of a loaf of bread. In the darkness, altitude, exhaustion and confusion Habibullah thinks we want him to brush the horses right there and then. We get into a verbal tussle. "Just shut up," I tell him. He answers me back "shut-up" and stomps off into the rain and darkness. The altitude is taking its toll.

We give the animals some of the grain Habibullah got in Sor Laspur—a mixture of flour, wheat, corn and wheat kernels—though we couldn't get it milled in Sor Laspur as the water-powered mill operator had already gone to Shandur Top for the polo match. We sit in an improvised tent restaurant, one of many constructed for the polo match, and eat substantial plates of goat meat *qorma*, rice and *chapatties*, followed by steamy hot tea. We're hungry.

Habibullah and I sleep in the larger of our two tents. With the saddlebags piled on one side there is just enough room for us to stretch out in our sleeping bags. For Habibullah, that is. I'm too tall. I have to bend my legs to completely fit in.

Woke this morning to frigid dampness. I check on the horses. They're shivering—stomping their feet to try to stay warm. All we had to cover them with last night were our plastic ponchos. We worry about them freezing to death. A far cry from the start of the trip when our concern was for them dying of heat prostration.

We find an industrious trader set up in a makeshift tent selling, among other supplies, blankets for the cold. We purchase extras for the horses and Mirza and I sit in the tent sewing them into horse blankets. Ayesha and Habibullah go to the polo grounds to watch some commencement matches between Gilgit and Chitral. Gilgit wins both.

While we sew in the tent the wind whips the loose canvas. We feel a low shaking rumble. Looking out the tent flap the mountains are rolling to a stop. An earthquake. It's getting rainier and rainier, the clouds progressively coming lower and lower down the jagged peaks that ring us in.

And now I'm freezing and wet in a tent, perched at 12,000 feet on the Shandur Top. Luckily, this is only the middle of summer.

Isn't it fun?

A break near the crest of the Shandur Pass coming up from
Sor Laspur, at approximately 12,000 ft.
I dedicate this photo to the photographer, my brother, Mirza. It was an incredible day.

Ed note: The first time a polo tournament took place at the Shandur Top was in 1936. A British Political Agent, Major Cobb, who was fond of playing polo under a full moon, had the polo ground on Shandur named "Moony Polo Ground." It is smaller in width and breadth than the conventional field, being 60yd wide and 220yd long. Also alien to a modern western player would be the 2ft high stone wall which surrounds the ground and could prove rather dangerous in the event of a fall.

Ready to go up the Shandur Pass at Sor Laspur (9,800 ft.)

Habibullah and I dining out at a "restaurant" on Shandur Top

Camped on Shandur Top

Leaving Shandur Top, facing east

Photo by Ayesha S.

190

Chapter 19
Polo at the Top of the World

July 25th
Still on Shandur Top
Weather is getting worse and worse. Raining consistently. Now the clouds have almost reached our camping area, blocking out all the surrounding peaks. Cold veils are slowly rolling down the mountainside behind our tiny encampment, already obscuring tents not 100 yards above us. Mists are rising like smoke from the valley where Sor Laspur lies.

Awake at 4:45 to look out at the weather. I don't need to go outside to know I am cold and wet. Condensation forming in the tent has dampened the sleeping bags along with everything else. The end of mine is exceptionally wet as my feet come right to the zippered doorway and the rain-laden wind during the night has found its way in under the badly closing zipper. I do need to check on the horses to make sure they haven't frozen to death. Everything is wet and dirty, or well on its way to becoming so.

After seeing the animals have survived the night, I walk down along the rocks at the edge of the lake to "use the facilities." Oh so cold, yet so beautiful. As I look across the silvery, mirrored lake's surface to the arrowhead peak of our mountain mascot Buni Zom behind Sor Laspur misty clouds steam out of the now invisible valley. A pale rainbow arches it's way over the frosty surface of Shandur Lake. Gusts of wind lash at my aching face trying to pull my turban and blanket from my head. I think of an old African saying once translated by Dick Burton,*

"The face of water is beautiful... but it is not nice to sleep on."

Alone with myself. Well, not exactly alone....

As usual, Nasreen is with me (not to mention three horses, etcetera, etcetera). This morning really strong thoughts of her, of her family and business, of her life, of mine. In all this natural beauty still I am reminded that it really does cut deep.

This trip is great, though at the moment in a wet tent at 12,000 feet in an icy driving rain at 6:30 A.M. with three freezing horses stomping the ground outside my tent it does kinda' suck. I try to remember the magically beautiful silver lake rainbow vision I witnesssed only brief moments ago, but it seems I keep remembering waking up in a warm bed with her soft body next to mine. I try to remember it's hellishly hot right now in Lahore. It's hard to hold the pen in my freezing fingers.

After the intimacy we shared the last two times we were together it's hard to think of her in that place. Available for anybody who wants her. No protection for AIDS. What if she got that? It's too late for me to turn off my love. Not sure exactly how strongly I can talk, to express my feelings in Pashtu. Our sex seems to have softened her up, it is a part of her I feel I do want to break into,

---

* Noted 19th century British explorer and linguist, Sir Richard Francis Burton

something I haven't thought about for a long time, but it can be a way to the heart. Or is that only another Western male concept that has no place here in Asia?

I love the raw adventure and beauty of this trip, no doubt. To continue on, just getting wilder and wilder, always riding on to some new, unbeknown mountain vista or hamlet, some newly unfolding adventure (or problem). But now I'm doing it out of obligation. How would I rather be judged? As the chap who rode a horse from Peshawar, through Pakistan and back to Peshawar, or as somebody who gave Nasreen a chance instead of leaving her hanging there after she said she told me she wants out?

Does she really even want a chance or is she only playing with me? What about my friends, my partners in this trip? Can I desert them? Can she leave her family or stop her work? Is it asking too much? Will her family permit it? Would they ever give her up? Is she serious?

Noisy questions rattle my mind in the quiet solitude of the endless eternal mountains.

July 28th
Written in Teru, 10,500 feet
Before the big polo match Mirza and I took the horses down by the polo ground to graze figuring the movement would help keep them warm. On the edge of the field was a dead horse. He had died in the previous day's preliminary games, his heart burst from the altitude and exertion. They just dragged him to the side and there he lay. Shokot ran away. Hercules followed him. We had to follow them a mile along the side of the lake to get them back. Habibullah and I searched restaurants trying to buy a sack of flour for the horses to eat with the bundle of straw we had acquired from the army who had trucked it in for the polo teams.

Benazir (Bhutto) arrived at the match with three helicopters. They appeared through the mist coming up out of the valley of Sor Laspur. The clouds and rain broke for her. She and a gaggle of journalists paraded before an honor guard of the kilted, bagpipe regiment of the Chitral Scouts in a white *chaddar* and gave a speech before the start of the big match, the crowd of several hundred huddling in their blankets in the rocks-cum-grandstands lining the field. The journalists surrounded her like so many moths around a flame, blocking our view.

With the opening ceremony concluded, the match began. A local band played traditional screeching polo music, pounding on their large, primitive drums and blowing with bulging cheeks on their *surnais*. The "stands" were so close to the pitch that we could feel the thundering of the mounts from where we squatted. This wasn't your typical gentlemen's polo, mind you. Yes, there were men on horseback with long mallets smacking a white ball around, but that is all this event had in common with countryclub polo. No starched white Jodhpurs topped by black helmets; instead there were army olive or Chitral Scout blue pants, windswept hair or a *pakool* cap. The riders and mounts saw no problem with riding off the field and into the bystanders.

192

Gilgit won. Benazir flew away (in her helicopter). The weather closed in and rain pelted us again. Tents started coming down. Jeeps began ferrying people back down the mountains towards Chitral (to the west) and Gilgit (to the east). By sunset very little remained of what had been organized for the match—a few canvas top restaurants, some remaining military to pack official tents and the last stragglers, including us. The stone shepherd huts, of course, were still there on the side of the mountain, which from several hundred yards down hill were hard to distinguish from the rocks. They and the empty field had been here before any of us had disturbed these mountain tops and now they remained.

The morning of the 26th there was so little left on Shandur Top it seemed like the tournament had been a figment of our imaginations. The lake and snow clad mountains were still there with their icy watery runoff. And the bad weather. The clouds, without any pretense, had finally made it down to our level and wandered freely around the remnants of our small camp. We packed and left the Shandur to the shepherds and their sheepy droves, the rains and the winds.

We followed a crystal clear stream not two feet wide, the bed below its icy clear surface composed of so many smooth, multicolored stones and pebbles sparkling in the golden sunlight; the beginning of the Ghizar River which we will continue to follow until we reach Gilgit. We rode through a defile and down into dew-sparkling emerald green pristine meadows. We seemed to have left the clouds and bad weather behind us on the Shandur Top. The sky broke into the purest, deepest blue with occasional massive downy, billowing clouds. Just below the Shandur we came to a meadow where men were harvesting peat, cutting it into square blocks to carry away on donkeys. When dry it burns, or I should say smolders, and is used for cooking and warmth due to the absence of firewood at these altitudes.

Still the omnipresent snow covered rocky mountain crags towered several thousand feet above us. We rode out of the high meadowland and down a crumbling hill into another meadow surrounded by high pinnacles of raw rock and ice. The stream was getting larger, still crystal clear, with smaller tributaries joining through the soft, thick, boggy, verdant grass. No longer could we jump across, the young river was widening.

We reached a deserted place, on our military survey maps listed as Burbolango Shal, though there were no road signs proclaiming it. By our altimeter we were at 11,000 feet. We found a good spot and decided to camp early. We washed clothes, horses and ourselves in the very cold stream. We could only keep our hands in the water a few moments before having to pull them out to rest them, burning and stinging from the cold. Besides us and our three horses several cows and five ponies were also grazing in our field.

My emotions were mixed. We'd only been on the road four hours and stopping would put us a day behind. The moment of the now was beautiful and all that, but unfortunately I was counting the days one by one until I could get back to Lahore. We all sorely needed the wash. Even though it was cold, the lack of rain was greatly appreciated and I could not argue with the grandeur, beauty and solitude of our surroundings.

We unloaded all the *samaan* into a big ring on the ground, each person using their saddlebag as a couch. We didn't even bother to erect the tents. We ate dinner by the light of our tiny campfire and slept content by star light, our horses nickering to their wild neighbors.

The next morning we rode out of the valley of Burbolango Shal along the stream which was now a river, treading down a long rocky switchback, over a rickety wooden bridge and into the hamlet of Barsat. As we rode through the valley, sparsely dotted with houses and fields of wheat, barley and clover, we amazingly enough found a small hotel (restaurant).

We tied the horses along the road and went inside. A man walked in with four small trout on a string which we bought for our lunch. The hotel *wallah* brought bunches of clover for the horses. The meal was superb, considering the circumstances—*sag* cooked in *dal*, salad, *chapatties, chai* and the fish.

Still following the river we rode up and down the steep, rocky grades, bringing us out onto new levels of high meadows. At 4:00 in the afternoon we struggled up the steepest grade we'd encountered all day, taking us far above the river. At the top the road opened onto a polo ground. We were in the village of Teru, country untainted by civilization in the back of beyond.

And here we are, resting and doing odds and ends, trying to keep the horses and ourselves fed. Staying at the government inspection bungalow. It's *Juma* and I'm trying not to think of Nasreen, with small success.

I pray my *Juma* prayer alone on the corner of the inspection bungalow veranda. We're in the heart of *Ismaili* country and there aren't any mosques.*

July 29th
Phandar, 9,800 feet

Last night the *chowkidar* (in Teru) asked Mirza if he had any medicine. It's a common question in these remote parts, and we are the great white *sahibs*. He said his stomach was upset and he has trouble sleeping. Mirza usually gives people aspirin or vitamin C for these ailments and any other complaints and has me instruct them to chew them (I do when they are pesky).

This *chowkidar* had incurred Mirza's dislike. When we had first arrived he hadn't wanted to confer even one of the two rooms to us. In one, he told us, an engineer was staying who should be back by evening. The other room was reserved and the official occupants would be arriving before dark.

We surrendered the engineer's room, though we insisted on taking the other room, telling the inhospitable *chowkidar* if the actual occupants did arrive we would relinquish it and spread our sleeping bags on the cement veranda. They never showed, nor did the mythical engineer. Mirza and Ayesha used the two beds in his room to sleep in. The entire bungalow was empty though the *chowkidar* would have had us ride on knowing there was no other place to stay within riding distance and we would be forced to camp out on the hard, cold rocks.

---

* *Ismailis pray in a "jamatkhana" and non-Ismailis are not allowed in; see glossary*

So being especially endeared to Mirza, instead of giving him the usual vitamin C prescription he gave him two of his precious supply of light blue vitamin 'V' (Valium).

"Take both of these before you go to sleep," he had me tell him, "and we'll see you in the morning."

Up until now we hadn't once had to pay for our accommodations but this *Ismaili chowkidar* showed us a list of tariffs for non-official use of the inspection bungalow—80 rupees per room per night! No doubt the fellow would oversleep in the morning and there would be nobody to pay.

Ayesha and Habibullah didn't know what medication Mirza had given the *chowkidar,* though he and I were quite surprised in the morning when the *chowkidar* showed up as we were saddling up and demanded the money for our stay. He had probably kept the pills for some future time when he really was sick.

We rode out of Teru at 7:00 in the morning through jagged rock gorges; shades of puce and orange, thousands of feet of crumbling rock slides and smooth stone glistening in the morning sunlight. We followed the river, by now quite wide, to a place with a rustic, swinging bridge which two locals passing by told me was called Gologh Muli.

After the bridge was an exquisite shimmering lake with red flowers floating on its surface surrounded by lush grasses. Trout were jumping in the air, breaking the mountain's mirrored reflections in concentric sparkling ripples and diamonds. An incredibly gorgeous natural park. The horses stood and pulled at the sweet scented grass with their muzzles. Mirza was determined to catch some fish, but no matter how hard he and Ayesha tried, none bit the line he threw in. Habibullah and I sat on the green sward, resting.

We arrive in the village of Phandar at 1:00 P.M., a tiny village with a few small shops There's a restaurant with a few jeeps and tractors parked in front. We order tea and buy a loaf of stale *double roti.* Mirza cuts open a can of sardines with his knife and slices an onion for our lunch. Then we ride on several *clicks* up a grade rising over green fields and the river to the inspection bungalow. It rains.

Usual problems with the *chowkidar*, having to fight our way in. At the end of the precipice which the inspection bungalow is on is a round cement helicopter landing pad. It is for the Agha Khan's helicopter. We have entered *Agha Khan territory* big time. As we rode through the last group of switchbacks into the valley of Phandar we saw high up on the mountainside across from us written in large white stones the epitaph, *"WELCOME OUR HIZAR IMAM."* This is for the benefit of welcoming his highness the Agha Khan (the head of the *Ismaili* sect of Islam).* Not the last of these we see before reaching Gilgit.

There is a helicopter waiting on the pad to fly some Ismaili upper echelon to Gilgit, some 40 minutes away as the chopper flies. We talk with the pilots who are Sunnis from Islamabad. Up to now the *chowkidar* hasn't let us into the inspection bungalow, which is quite a nice-looking long wooden building with an enclosed veranda running along the front. We've unloaded our gear onto the

---

Hizar = present, Imam = spiritual leader

195

veranda so it won't get any wetter. The horses are staked out on the side of the building at the edge of a steep drop to a clear crystal blue pond.

The inspection bungalow is situated slightly back from the road. On the road is a small store and tea house with a yellow tent in front of it. The *chowkidar* insists we can stay in the tent, which is the non-official hotel run by the store. He says our official *chit* from Islamabad doesn't mean anything here. This is Gilgit Agency and he takes orders from the government in Gilgit, not from Islamabad. Threatening to beat him up hasn't helped. Doesn't he notice we wear the keys to all inspection bungalows on our hips?

Finally the *Ismaili* bigwigs make their appearance and successfully intercede for us. I wasn't planning to threaten him with a gun until they had flown off to Gilgit, anyway. It isn't the kind of publicity we really need preceding us. The rain starts to pelt down and the pilots warm their engines as heavy clouds roll down the surrounding mountainsides. They need to get off while they can still see the surrounding towering rocky walls. As they bank, flying east and up through the walls of mountains the clouds close in. We move into our carpeted rooms.

At twilight the errant thunderstorm has stopped, leaving smoky clouds in the evening twilight. Mirza, Habib and I climb the hill behind the inspection bungalow to look for grass. We are lucky to procure two *maunds* of slightly-dried grass from a farmer. Habibullah shows us how to twist lengths of grass into rope. Mirza ties his bunch with his turban and we carry it down on our backs.

We watch the sun set gloriously behind the emerald fields and purple blue mountains, setting the sky ablaze in shades of azure, crimson, pink and tangerine. The river, now choked with mud washed down from the rain storm, turns from deep sky-blue to mud-brown before our eyes, It's a stunning view but I'm still wanting to get to Gilgit and Lahore. To see Nasreen. To hold her in my arms. Still can't get her out of my mind.

August 1st
Gupis
Left Phandar at 9:00 A.M. Riding through more and more desolate country. Four hours of rocky switchbacks taking us high above the river and bringing us right down to its now roaring side.

At one place we come to a tiny store with some men sitting on its front porch (the cement front porch serves as a counter). We buy toffees and a pack of cheap cigarettes. They have a sack of rice and our supplies are running low. As I tell the shopkeeper we want to buy some Habibullah butts in biliously saying the rice is no good, that we will find better in Pingal, the next town on our map. We argue over the possibility of this next town being any better provisioned. I'm feeling too tired to argue and Habibullah wins.

At 1:00 P.M. we ride through our first stunted fields of the day. On the mountainside we again see the cryptic inscription, "*WELCOME OUR HIZAR IMAM.*" We're down to 8,500 feet. I reach down from Hercules' back and pick a tiny wilted ear of corn from a stalk over a stone wall. It tastes fresh and succulent as we ride into the desolate, deserted town.

Maybe I speak too suddenly to call Pingal a town—or deserted. It probably was of more importance at a time when the only transportation in these parts was by animal or foot. But in this age of motorized jeep travel Pingal has been bypassed, though its meager fields and few stone and mud structures still stand on either side of the road leading to Gilgit.

A group of children follows us into town. A handful of men and boys greet us. There is a store and a one-room school house, though both seem closed. At the other end of town is another store, also closed at the time of our arrival. The rest of the town consists of two ancient-looking stone and mud, crumbling structures. We ask where the government guest house listed on our map is. The men point to the two decaying buildings before us. I ask where the *chowki-dar* is and I'm answered with laughter....

The guest house has been deserted since the British left Pakistan in 1947. We bust the lock with a stone and push open the door of the least decrepit looking building and sweep out the dust and dirt with a dried sage bush cut from outside. A decent night's resting place—better than sleeping outside on the rocks. We arrange with a man to bring firewood for the hearth and with another who says he can bring grass for the horses.

I go to the store to see if they have rice. We have enough for our dinner, but after seeing the state of Pingal I would like nothing better than to prove to Habibullah how foolish he was (let alone us for listening to him in the first place) for suggesting to wait to buy our supplies. None in the store, maybe some in the other store but the shopkeeper isn't in the town. No one knows when he will be back.

Habibullah and I try to light the backpackers deluxe kerosine stove Mirza and Ayesha have brought from the United States. This is the first time we've tried it on the trip. Habibullah knows little about modern things and I'm not in any point or mood in my life to put up with them. But we are hungry, so we give it a go. We only succeed in getting the pressure, after pumping it up and lighting it, to spew burning kerosine all over the dry, wooden floor. Habibullah insists he can still get it started and I yell that the gas canister, which is surrounded in orange and blue licking flames, will blow up. Finally Habibullah gives up and we stomp the fire out. The wood arrives and we cook in the fireplace of a small cookhouse to the side of the guest house. We spread our sleeping bags side by side on the dirt floor. The guest house's one resident, a bat, flies over our heads during the night.

In the morning the jagged, barren mountain tops can be seen through flat elongated breaking white-gray clouds like layered slabs of slate. We leave at 7:00 and ride into more desolation. Huge cliffs of broken granite. Everywhere is rock, occasional tiny hamlets and small yellow-green fields. Still following the Ghizar River. It's flowing swollen and fast with long islands of rocks and trees in its center.

We stop by a group of 20 to 30 men and boys working on a water channel for an electric generator, one of many Agha Khan Foundation's rural betterment projects. They invite us to stop for tea with them, brewed in two immense pots.

197

Habibullah stays on the road and holds Kodak's reins. A boy takes him a cup of tea and a piece of local homemade bread (*mastaki*). Later Habibullah informs me that he ate the bread (at this point I don't think any of us would not eat something given to us) but most of the salt tea he tossed out when nobody was looking.* Too strange for him.

At noon we ride down a hill and into a rocky gorge where the Balti River flows out of Kohistan into the Ghizar, the Balti's clear blue water quickly mixing with the muddy water of the Ghizar. At this place last week the flimsy wood bridge broke with a tractor and trailer on it. The tires of the upside down trailer can still be seen sticking out of the water.

The bridge, a swinging affair, is the most rickety we've crossed to date. A rope is hung across it to regulate the traffic to make sure nothing too heavy crosses it until it is repaired. A man comes out from an army tent pitched in some rocks on the other side. Fortunately Herc isn't deemed too heavy and the fellow unties the rope for us to pass.

The stones on the other side end in a lovely blue-green pool of water at the river's edge with stunted trees lining it. The mountains rise steeply, their lofty peaks lost in misty wisps of cotton sharded clouds. After this place the road rises in a steep "Z" switchback. We're surrounded by high, jagged walls. The inhabitants of the tent, a young soldier, an unshaven grizzly middle-aged man (the one who had untied the rope to let us pass) and a dirty-clothed teenaged boy, are sitting out in front brewing tea over a small fire.

All we have for our lunch is a few handfuls of dry roasted chick peas and an onion. Ayesha asks me to tell Habibullah to go over to the tent and ask in Urdu if they have some *chapatties* we can have, but he won't do it. He says it is not the way of Pathan people. It is better to starve than to ask strangers for food. Especially these strangers in this strange, remote land.

Instead of arguing with him, a part of me understands his point, even if my stomach doesn't. I decide to go ask them myself. I'm supposed to be more logical than Pathan. I explain our situation as best I can, though with my Urdu I can't answer all the questions they ask. I point to our little group and say the one with the black hair speaks Urdu.

They come talk with Habibullah, bringing *mastaki* and a tray of tea with sugar. The sun breaks it's way through blue tears in the clouds. Habib and I doze on the rocks in the sun as light drops of misty rain fall on us. The horses stand in a circle and eat the remainder of the grass we've carried from Pingal. Mirza and Ayesha try casting their line into the pool for fish with no luck, as usual. Mirza is becoming fairly obsessed with the idea of catching a fish to eat. A fun obsession without any luck.

We leave at 1:00 and ride up the steep switchback. I've walked since morning and now it's my turn to ride. After about half an hour I turn around and see Habibullah pulling Kodak and Ayesha on Shokot. No Mirza. Ayesha says he is walking. Mirza walking is about as unusual as me not wanting to be with Nasreen in Lahore. Ayesha explains that she is feeling sick in the stomach. I

---

* In these mountainous areas it is very difficult to get sugar, but salt is available, so it is used in the preparation of tea; as in Tibet, Kashmir, Baltistan, etc.

ride back to look for him. I find him slowly ambling along, his turban wrapped around his face with just his blue eyes showing, the long turban tail blowing in the strong wind, sword and gun dangling at his waist.

"Get on Herc *yaar*," I tell him. "I walk faster than you."

I insist, he mounts and on we go. It starts to rain.

I catch up to Ayesha and walk along with her, leading Shokot by the reins as she slouches down in the saddle. Finally a jeep comes along and we put her and Habibullah on it to Gupis.

We come to a place, Jandroot, where the river becomes a lake (in 1980 there were extremely heavy rains and a mud slide, bringing down rocks and mud which destroyed two villages and created this lake—Khalti Lake). There is rain and a pale rainbow over the lake. Across are mud thatched houses of the relocated villages and green and yellow-brown fields, the sunlight breaking through the clouds and shining on them. The light on the rain against the backdrop of the mountains becomes a mist. It appears as if the mountain ranges we are riding into end into nothing. We see the first store we've seen all day, but all they sell to eat are toffees (for fast food).

We ride on and on, the steep grades ending in fields and occasional houses. We've reached the outskirts of Gupis. It seems to take forever to ride through to the main town, maybe five *clicks*. We ride across a wooden bridge painted in white and red stripes over lush green banks, white rocks and foamy rushing water, past a well kept fort and into the center of town.

Two small hotels and a street of shops, most of which are closed, is the Gupis bazaar. It is only 6:30 and there is still plenty of light. It is amazing to see a hotel with *charpoys* and tables out in front; jeep travelers sitting and drinking tea. We see our first electric lines since leaving Chitral.

Ayesha and Habibullah are standing in front of one of the few open stores buying supplies. The shopkeepers are Pathan, as many of the shopkeepers here are. In front of the shop is a smashed tractor, the same which plunged off the bridge we had crossed earlier in the day Ayesha tells us. They say the government guest house/inspection bungalow is just up the road. Just before the guest house, at the Civil Hospital, the road is blocked with a commotion of people and jeeps. There has been some trouble in Gupis today.

We try to get our tired horses through a virtual mob. The people eventually squeeze next to the jeeps to permit us passage. A man who appears to be in shock is carried by on a cot. I see other cots on the hospital lawn with red-brown blood spots on the white cross-lattices. Ayesha informs us there had been a *firing* (shooting) in Gupis earlier. Eight people had been wounded and one killed. Gupis is a peaceful community. This is unusual.

Kohistanis had come down out of the mountains and kidnapped an 11 year old girl. This has been the second such kidnapping in two years and people were protesting at the courthouse. The *A.C.* was listening to their grievances when the Frontier Constabulary opened fire on them. This much I gather from Ayesha and Habibullah as we ride through the pandemonium. Well, that helps explain the coldness of people on the road. The Kohistanis ride out of Kohistan through the same pass from which the Balti River flows, and with our turbans, horses and arms, we appeared not a little unlike Kohistani bandits.

Everything is disrupted here. Officials flown in from Gilgit by helicopter are staying in the couple rooms available in the guest house. We are staying in the *chowkidar's* room. He and Habibullah are sleeping in the room of the kitchen boy. We rode 25 miles today in nine hours.

August 5th
Gupis

Accommodation struggle. Some nights we've slept in the guest house when there has been a room available. Other nights we've slept outside on the lawn. We've been here five days and now Mirza and I are staying in the kitchen boy's room behind the guest house. The town is still disrupted.

The story of what this disruption is all about is....

Two years ago the Kohistani badmash Shakra rode into Gupis and kidnapped a marriageable girl, taking her back with him into the mountains of Kohistan. Word was sent down to Gupis that she had become Shakra's wife. The girl's family was naturally upset and complained to the government in Gilgit. The politicos in Gilgit waited, but Shakra seldom came out of Kohistan so it was difficult apprehending him. The girl's family kept up their complaints. Shakra's men continued their plundering raids on the Indus Highway. The government in Islamabad finally began to complain. The Indus Highway is Pakistani domain, even if what happened in Gupis could be shuffled under the table as an unimportant complaint from some backwater Ismaili mountain town.

The DSP in Gilgit decided to send a raiding party of 50 policemen into Kohistan. In a shoot-out at Shakra's fort they captured him and brought him down to Gilgit. The girl was returned to her family in Gupis. Shakra spent six months in jail in Gilgit. Then a bribe of 50,000 rupees was paid and Shakra was allowed to go free. He returned to Kohistan and mustered his forces. Two weeks ago they rode into Gupis and surrounded the house of the girl. They fired at it and fire-bombed it. In the melee, they kidnapped an 11 year-old girl and rode back to Kohistan. Word was sent down that the girl would remain in Kohistan with Shakra until he got his wife back.

The peaceful citizens of Gupis were upset. They protested, holding demonstrations and meetings. The largest of these took place on the day we rode into town. Half the town was gathered outside of the *A.C.'s* residence voicing their opinions when the firing occurred. The Frontier Constabulary, who have a post across the river came over in case the gathering should get unruly. It seems they were the ones who got out of control. They are all Pathans from NWFP, strong Sunni Muslims and *"natural"* enemies of these "*heretic Ismailis.*" For some reason, though the order to fire was never given, and even when it is they are first supposed to fire over the heads of protesters, they fired point-blank into the crowd. The result was what greeted us our first day in town.

Now the people are again holding marches and protests, appealing to Gilgit to do something and the Pathans of the Frontier Constabulary are sitting in their fort across the river. These are the problems of Gupis. We have our usual problems. To find food for our horses and to keep a roof over our heads and equipment. Also Shokot's back is bad again.

The *chowkidar*, Mohammad Raza (an *Ismaili*) and the cook, Ali Dad, are very nice to us, as are some *Ismaili* engineers in an office down the road. They have an animal doctor who they sent over to look at Shokot. He is very kind and concerned, but it seems his forté is cows, goats and chickens.

The kitchen boy is *Sunni* Pathan from Swat. Many of the shopkeepers in the bazaar are Pathans from Bajaur. They close their shops in the hard snow bound winters and go back to their homes in the barren dry rocky mountains of Bajaur Agency. Maybe one day I'll be able to visit Bajaur. I hear it is beautiful in the spring time.

There is even a mosque in Gupis.

The first day here Habibullah and I searched the bazaar for something for the horses to eat. Anything. Grass, corn, even a sack of barley. Most of the shops were still closed. We were able to locate a small sack of maize with a promise of more to come. I got into a fight with Habibullah. He said there was no way to find anybody in town to sell us the quantity of grass we required. So sure he was. Finally we sent him down to the polo field with the animals for a little exercise and to graze on the short turf, and to get him away from me. Mirza and I went to one of the two restaurants in town and talked with people. A boy was dispatched up the hill to bring a farmer people said may have some fields of grass he can spare.

As we finished our tea the boy returned with Nadir Khan, a small, wiry farmer with a bushy, black beard flecked with gray, wearing coarse *shalwar kameez* and a tan colored, wool *pakul* cap. To our good fortune (and the horses') he had unharvested green clover and grass he could spare.

We now have an arrangement with him to supply two fresh *maunds* per day. It arrives, one *maund* on his back, half on the back of his 12-year-old son, the remaining on the back of his eight-year-old son who is so small he looks like a walking green haystack.

We have spent many hours and meals at the house of Mir Iqbal, the Chairman of Gupis, just down the road from the inspection bungalow. His brother is a teacher from Yasin who is addicted to opium. His addiction started when he had an exceedingly bad toothache and somebody gave him a small piece of opium to ease the pain until he could get to Gilgit to see a doctor. He is an extremely bright fellow in a position of little prospect and unfortunately, he discovered opium was also an excellent way to ease that pain too. He says he can find me some *charras*. I don't want to touch opium! I could get into that and never get out. One dream is enough for me.

We are so close to Gilgit, but how do we ride Shokot there with his back in the condition it is?

The other night Mirza, Ayesha and I went for dinner to the house of a young Pathan from Peshawar who has a cloth shop in Peshawar and one here. Mirza feels he has been getting a little too friendly with Ayesha, to the point of concern. So going into his house, with how many of his personal friends we knew not, we had our pistols in our pockets and chambered. We must be ready for any eventuality out here. Very different from a city mentality—all alone, who can we call on for help besides our guns (and, of course, **Allah**)?

We went to the west end of the town to look at one man's horse on the possibility of trading him for Shokot. The man was a polo player, and Shokot, being the smaller of our horses, would be a good choice for polo, but he needs to rest his withers for a month or so, not carry a rider or a pack saddle through the mountains.

We were ushered through the gate in the mud walls of this fellow's property. First he showed us his gardens. Then he showed us his house, though we did not enter it. He showed us his guest house, where we sat on the porch and tea was brought. While we were drinking tea a boy came out carrying a pistol and a shotgun to display his guns. We could hear his macho stallion snorting and whinnying out behind the house.

I thought of an old joke of Arif's—*A man brought his friend to his house. He started showing off his house and possessions. "This is my garden. And this is my guest room. These are my couches and these are my pillows. And this is my television," he proudly told his guest. "This is my kitchen and this is my refrigerator."*

Then they went into the bedroom. "This is my bedroom and this is my bed," he said, but when he looked toward the bed he saw his wife in the bed with a man. He quickly continued, "That is my wife and that is me in bed with my wife."

The trade didn't work out. In fact we never even saw his horse. Nor did we see his wife in bed with him, nor anybody!

Looking west from Teru—the back of beyond.

"Main street" — Pingal

"Guest house" — Pingal

Roadblock in the Hindu Kush
(near Gupis)

Bolough Muli, Northern Areas
(near Shandur)

see all photographs in color at:
http://www.pbase.com/noorkhan/00journalphotos

The road out of Gupis (towards Gilgit)

Chapter 20
Roadblocks

Yesterday evening we had a serious discussion with Mister Habibullah.

He is having reservations about going on with the trip. He doesn't understand the purpose of it. Why we should want to expose ourselves and these horses to this danger and depredation is beyond him. Seemingly there is no reason to this madness. *(Remember, he thought we should have taken the horses over the Lowari Pass in a truck!)*

He couldn't understand why we had waited so long in Kafiristan. He told me he had thought it was a two or three day journey from Chitral to Gilgit. He must have been listening to accounts of people who had made the trip by jeep. He said the way we are dealing with the animals was not to his liking. He didn't realize he would be walking so much, though we had made it perfectly clear to him in Peshawar the idea must not have really sunk into his brain. And all this for a paltry 50 rupees a day! Why, he could be earning 100 a day in his village driving a tractor and he would be close by his wife and children.

Open rebellion and dissension. He doesn't know if he wants to continue with us even though he had given us his word when he "signed on" with us in Peshawar. Things change.

Naturally Mirza was upset with him. He has the thought of me leaving hanging over his head and now maybe Habibullah won't last past Gilgit. That is, if we can even get Shokot and this trip any further then Gilgit, technically only a three days ride from here.

The conversation was left rather up in the air and not on the best of terms as the three of us walked off to Mir Iqbal's house to get away from the inspection bungalow and Habibullah. Before leaving I asked Habibullah if he would have dinner waiting for us when we returned. His answer was noncommittal. On the road walking the short distance to Mir Iqbal's I told Mirza if the food wasn't cooked when we got back, I would personally throw Habibullah's clothes out on the road. My patience is frayed.

August 5th
Gupis
This morning we piled Ayesha, Habibullah and most of our gear into a packed jeep bound for Gilgit at 6:45 in a steady downpour. She will check with the *D.C.* there on the possibility of buying or trading Shokot for another horse. In this country a woman's sweet countenance can work wonders with officials. Definitely more than a couple of grungy *Afghani cowboys*. Habibullah will go back to his village for a few days visit to see his family. Mirza and I will ride Hercules and Kodak and pony Shokot (bareback) to Gilgit, *Insha'Allah*.

It kept raining today so we stayed. Tomorrow we go no matter what, *Insha'Allah!* The next town is Ghakoch. Going bored crazy today. A little piece of *charras* found its way to me via Nawroz, the kitchen boy. Much harder to locate this side of Sor Laspur. Nawroz and I sat in front of his tiny stone hut and smoked, looking up at the towering mountains ringing us in on all sides.

August 7th

Gupis

Yesterday the weather was fine and clear. We left for Ghakoch. Even Shokot's back looked somewhat better in the clear, bright sunlight. Outside Gupis we rode across a long, narrow suspension bridge with a small stone building overlooking us from the opposite end. Two meager roundish windows facing us made it appear as a ghoulish, stone, jack-o-lantern skull. By the last 20 feet Hercules was staggering back and forth like a drunken sailor with the swaying of the bridge.

At noon we stopped by a broken stone and cement bridge crossing a small but swift tributary of the Ghizar River. We ate our lunch of *mastaki*, raw onions, biscuits and an apple. We drank cold, if slightly muddy water from the river. It was fresh though—even the mud.

After our meal and a brief rest we continued under the bridge and through the rushing water of the stream. Coming back onto the graveled road again we went up a hill. Rounding a bend we saw a line of jeeps parked, blocking the road. Ahead of the traffic jam a bulldozer was clearing the broken rubble of a landslide. People standing by their vehicles told us the way was gone and there was no passing. Maybe for jeeps we thought, but not for equestrian travelers. We rode past the jeeps and up to the top of the incline where the bulldozer was clearing the pile of dirt, rocks and boulders from the road in a cloud of dry choking dust.

The tails of our turbans were pulled tightly over our noses and mouths as we halted at the edge of the loose mountain of crumbling scree. Peering ahead through the particle filled air to where the path should be all we could see was the Ghizar River swirling madly hundreds of feet below. The road was completely gone. Not even a track. The entire mountainside where the Gupis-Gilgit Road had once been had fallen into the river. Army engineers were clinging to the hillside and drilling holes with an air drill to plant explosives. Some space had to be blasted from the precipitous mountain to accommodate a new road.

I sat on Hercules' high back and held the reins of the other horses. Mirza got down to talk to the head engineer in charge of repairs. This was one of those times where we wanted to establish our foreign identity as quickly as possible. Sometimes I have a hard time convincing people I'm truly a foreigner. Small rocks and debris were still showering down off the mountainside throwing up a cloud of dust.

The chief engineer told us it would be three or four days, *Insha'Allah*, before they could blast another road. I couldn't believe it, but looking at the magnitude of their task, I had to. Then what? I wanted to get to Gilgit! We both did! Mirza's beloved Ayesha was in Gilgit expecting us and I, of course, wanted to get to Gilgit so I could go to Lahore to see Nasreen. There must be some way around this obstacle?

We went back down the road to where a local had set up a tent tea house and several small tables and chairs surrounded by a low stone wall. We tied the horses to rocks across the road in succulent green foot-high grass. We

206

took our rifles from the *bookies* and sat down, ordering *chai*. I spoke with various locals, drivers and Pathan traders, who all knew the area better than we. There was an old trail, the old road, across the river from us. Most of it was carved out of the bare rock 40 to 50 feet above the river. Sticks were driven into the face of the cliff and flat stones were piled over these to create a road. The overhanging rock made this trail a virtual rock tunnel. From the distance where we sat it seemed only four or five feet high. We could duck, but to get Shokot, Hercules or Kodak to crawl on their knees on this pathway seemed rather unlikely. We could see a few shepherds on this trail with their goats and this only helped to reaffirm our fears. It was a haphazard trail for local midgets.

With the help of three Pathan traders we were drinking tea with I negotiated with the tea house *wallah* on the possibility of feeding our beasts if we camped there and waited for the new road. He said up the rocky hill from the tea house he had fields of grass. It sounded good until the greedy entrepreneur said he wanted 200 rupees per day, per horse, for the grass. We laughed in his face and called him several names I won't elucidate here. We got up to pay for our tea. Our Pathan friends apologized for the greed of this local. They paid for our tea and biscuits.

As we started walking out the *chai wallah*, who was sitting on a bench near the front entrance, asked us about paying for the grass the horses had eaten while we were drinking tea. On the side of the road where they had been tied there were three circles of short grass in the taller grass. Neatly trimmed by their teeth and delineated by the length of the short lead ropes.

"How much?" I asked.

The greedy *chai wallah* thought for a fleeting moment, his crafty eyes shifting, and then said, "100 rupees."

"100 rupees?" I laughed. "We've been paying 100 rupees for two *maunds* of grass back in Gupis. Are you joking?"

"This isn't Gupis," he replied.

Mirza, who had gleaned some of our conversation, asked me, "Is he saying he wants 100 rupees for that 15 minute measly horse snack?"

"You got it, *yaar*."

It was the proverbial straw (grass) that broke the camel's back. Shokot's bad back and the road block separating him from his beloved Ayesha had piled up on Mirza. Now we would have to go back to Gupis to wait it out due to this man's greed. A place we had been so anxious to leave. And now this last outrage. We had figured 10 rupees per horse would have been more than generous. We should have been riding into Ghakoch about now.

Mirza flew into a rage. He stomped the few feet of distance to stand squarely in front of the *chai wallah*. Then, with his gloved hand, he slapped the man's face and spit on the dirt floor at his feet. I just stood there watching and grinning. I put some *nuswar* into my mouth. Mirza took his 18-inch sawed-off shotgun and pointed the double barrels right up the *chai wallah's* face, holding it from the hip. He said some things in English which I won't repeat here (being the gentleman that I am) and the two of us turned and walked out of the tea house, got on our horses and rode away back toward Gupis.

45 minutes down the road we came to a bridge crossing the river. On the other side, where the path led up into the mountains, was a store. We crossed over to see if we could get any information about the old pathway, maybe take a look at it. We both were still determined to get to Gilgit if it was at all humanly possible.

As we talked to the men sitting around on the front veranda of the store we noticed a posse of men coming down the road on foot from the direction of the road block. They were looking at us and waving to bring our horses back across the narrow bridge presumably to talk to them. The way on our side of the river was impossible for us to negotiate so we decided to go back for a chat. Or should we just play Frontier Constabulary and start blasting? It definitely would have been more exciting, but I guess we want to live to the end of this movie? We decided to ride back to settle with the irate *chai wallah* as the posse informed us he was planning to go back to Gupis and lodge a complaint with the *A.C.* 45 minutes back to the road block tea house, but damn if we would give in to his greedy demands. 10 rupees per horse was fair; we gave him 15. In Gupis we were getting almost a *maund* for 45 rupees. Still he wanted more, but too bad. If he goes to the *A.C.* now, the *A.C.* will definitely agree we have been more than just.

Riding back to Gupis the sun was settling low over the mountains lining the western sky with a majestic cerulean horizon. We were still two hours from Gupis. We came to a place where on a large boulder overlooking the road scrawled in irregular Urdu characters were white letters spelling "*Talidass.*" There was a field with short grass and many stones in it, partially flooded with water. Bordering the field, behind stone walls with low trees peeking over, was a house and orchard. A young man, Dil Jan, came from out of the gate. This was his field and we could definitely spend the night. We staked the animals, pounding the *moogays* into the rocky ground with a round stone (Ayesha and Habibullah had carried our hammer to Gilgit along with most of our other gear). Dil Jan brought us a tray with coarse, homemade corn *chapatties* resembling pancakes, apricots and rice. As we finished our dinner he came back with a pot of tea. We chatted and drank.

There was so little dry ground that we tethered the horses on short lead ropes. We piled the equipment to one side, laid the plastic ponchos on the wet ground and made our beds within a few feet of Hercules' massive feet. They were hungry. The entire night they chomped the short grass and stomped at the ground. Several times one or another of them worked their *moogay* free and started to wander. We have found they have become such a team they won't really wander far, but not wanting to take any chances in this dark and wet place, several times in the cold night we had to get up to pound in the *moogays* again with the aid of a flashlight and a stone. Under the short grass were so many large rocks it was not an easy task.

I wanted to be on my way to Gilgit so bad (and Lahore) I was in a black mood and would barely speak to Mirza. In the morning Dil Jan brought us tea and bread. Then we saddled up and rode back to the inspection bungalow in Gupis. A helicopter had flown in bringing officials from Gilgit.

Again we are staying behind the inspection bungalow in Nawroz's small room. Went up into the fields and found Nadir Khan and his children cutting and bundling grass for the oncoming winter. There was a light rain falling casting rainbows in the mist. We arranged with him to continue supplying us with two *maunds* a day. He says he can manage to keep it up for a few more days, then he will need to keep the rest for his own animal's winter feed.

Went into the bazaar and ate lunch at the Charinzar Hotel, run by Pathans from Dir (here the word hotel, as in most of the subcontinent, constitutes restaurant). Two stone and mud constructed rooms. A front room with several rough hewn board tables and benches and a back smoke-filled room with two benches and an open hearth fire place. We had turnips.

The turnips are as plain and beaten as the women here in Gupis.

August 11th
7:00 A.M.
Not in Lahore. Not even in Gilgit. Still languishing in Gupis.

August 15th
Writen in Gilgit (at last)
As I was jotting down that last entry, Ali Dad (the inspection bungalow cook) came in to inform me that the inspection bungalow's jeep had come in from Gilgit late last night. Four more had arrived early in the morning. The road was open. We gave the horses the last of the grass, packed, saddled and left by 10:00. We rode directly to the road block. We saw our friend Dil Jan on the way as we passed Talidass.

They were still working on the road. It had been open the previous night for a little while to let the five-days buildup of jeeps pass, but again it wasn't passable for vehicles. There was enough room for our horses to carefully squeeze, slip and pick their way down the narrow rock-strewn path. Once across we felt safe enough to take the time to stop for a lunch of dry crackers, raw onions, some biscuits and river water.

At Ghakoch the inspection bungalow was under repairs. The only room available was the VIP suite. I went off with a Pathan from Mardan, who lives summers in Gupis, to find a local farmer to supply us with grass. We carried it back wrapped in our *chaddars*, slung over our backs. Mirza, with the aid of our *firman* from Islamabad, a letter from the engineer's office in Gupis and his gumption, had secured us permission to use the VIP suite for the night.

During the night the lawn where the horses were staked flooded. There were three 15-foot, black, muddy circles in the emerald green lawn, the centers being the *moogays*, the circumference described by the length of the lead ropes. It looked like a helicopter had tried to land upside down on the lawn and had bounced three times. The inspection bungalow staff thoughtfully didn't pay it any attention. It had been dry when we had staked them there.

We rode out at 9:00 A.M. after a breakfast of sour dough *parattas* and *chai*. Before the town of Singal we came to a restaurant situated before a bridge.

From a loud speaker on the roof the *Qawali* music of Aziz Mian was playing loud and scratchy *"Nabi Ya Nabi"* (a favorite of ours from our early days in Peshawar). We staked the horses on a small patch of land in front and gave them the last of the grass we had carried from Ghakoch. We ate *chapatties*, tasteless *dal* and meat bones.

The bridge was an open-railed affair with corrugated metal strips for vehicle tires to ride over. The horses were spooked by the sound of their feet scraping the corrugated iron. If they fell it wouldn't have been good. We went up the river bank to an old, dilapidated wooden bridge instead, crossing over one at a time. I watched carefully as Herc's feet bent the weathered wooden planks under us.

Past Singal we came to another wooden strip bridge. We found a place where the river looked fordable. Leading, I plunged Herc in. It was deeper than it looked, in the middle we almost got swept away. Herc stumbled forward. The water filled my boots, rifle *bookie* and the bottom half of my saddle bag as Herc swam forward finally finding his footing on some underwater rocks. We got ourselves through and up the rocky bank.

Next we had to lead our mounts down a steep gully, across rocks, a small rushing side stream and up a steep bank. Kodak stumbled as I tried to guide him up the bank by his lead rope. I pulled, bracing my feet against a twisted tree and he managed to get back on his feet.

At another metal bridge we rode up the river to an old rickety swaying wooden bridge. The edges of the floor were rotted and broken. We had to carefully ride the horses down the middle, watching their steps under us. Hercules swayed back and forth under me. Drunk again! At the far end was an 18-inch gap between the bridge and land. A piece of metal attached to the freely swinging bridge was rubbing the rocks making a screeching, grating noise Herc didn't like. Difficult to get him to cross. I gazed through the gap into the river 40 feet below as I nudged him over to land.

At 7:00 we rode into Gulapur, but the only hotel was just a small tea house. They told us there was a good hotel in Beyachee about a mile further on. Also, we were informed grass would be available there.

A long, toilsome mile later we rode over a stream crossing the road. It was 7:45. We saw a stone building, its crumbling front broken in, a canvas tent for a roof. A tractor was parked in front next to the pile of stones that was the wall. The light emanating from the Coleman lantern inside looked warm and inviting in the dark exhausting night.

The proprietor, Malang, a Pathan from Batkhela, led us and the horses out back to a stone walled corral. We bought a *maund* of grass from an old local man. Half we gave them for dinner and the other half we piled on the roof of the overhang at the back of the corral for the morning. The next day was *Ashura*.*

---

* *Ashura, the 10th of Muharram—the day commemorating of the martyrdom of Imam Hussain-the son of Hazrat Ali, the son-in-law and cousin of the Prophet Mohammad (PBUH) by Yazd, the Umayyad Caliph, on the plain of Karbala.*

Sunni Muslims commemorate the occasion by gatherings and discourses. Shia Muslims celebrate it a bit more flamboyantly, with parades in which they beat their bare chests with their hands and whip their bare backs with many razor-sharp steel blades fastened with small chains to wooden handles. To this bloody display of self flagellation Sunnis violently object, saying it is sacrilegious and un-Islamic. In all of Pakistan, especially divided Gilgit Agency, it is a time of flaring sectarian feelings and sometimes violence. The Ismailis do not observe the 10th of *Muharram* in the same impassioned way as other Shia.

Malang warned us to watch out on the road for Shias. It rained from 6:00 to 7:00. We left at 7:30. It was our last day to Gilgit. Knowing such a big town with so many luxuries was ahead of us, not to mention Ayesha and (for me) the Rawalpindi bus stand, was alluring. Neither rain, Sunnis, nor Shias could keep us when our goal was finally so close.

Since Gupis the vistas had been getting more grandiose. So vast, with seemingly endless mountains to pass through. Areas where the road hung high and precarious over the river. Since Ghakoch we'd been following the Gilgit River. It still seemed to be the Ghizar River, though somewhere around Ghakoch the name, according to our maps, had changed.

We stopped near a village called Hanzil on our map and perched on a huge rock in a field to eat our lunch—*parattas* bought the previous morning in Ghakoch, onions, a box of biscuits and stream water. We rode on and on wondering when the mountain panoramas would open up into the valley of Gilgit? Finally between two ranges we saw a long, sloping, green valley. Gilgit!

It took us another hour to reach the outskirts of town and an hour or more to ride into town. We arrived in Gilgit at 3:30. We saw Ayesha on the road. She handed each of us a *samosa* from a greasy, brown paper bag.

It was the 13th of August (10th of *Muharram*) and we were just ahead of the *Muharram* procession. The police had machine guns set up on rooftops overlooking the street. They (police) stopped us for carrying guns. "Ordinance 144" was in effect making it illegal to carry arms except by special permit, but judging by our circumstances and that we were Sunni, and American, they permitted us to go on to the hotel with our guns. We rode on in single file through the long main bazaar of Gilgit, tired, dirty, and glad to be in civilization.

And now we're staying right on the river at the River View Inn.

The first morning Mirza and I went to a *hammam*. It had been a week since either of us had shaved and longer since a proper bath. Cleaned up, we went to visit our old friend Ghulam Mohammad Baig at his book stall, feeling proud we had finally made it to Gilgit from Peshawar by horse.

And I'm still dreaming of Nasreen. I want to see her.
Tomorrow I leave for Peshawar, *Insha'Allah.*

211

August 18th, 10 P.M.
Lahore
A strange world we live in. Well, a strange world I'm living in. That much I am aware of....

Left Gilgit on the 16th. Had a 2:00 P.M. minivan booked to Rawalpindi but I got into a fight with the driver and the booking clerk over the money for the extra luggage. I was taking the two pack saddle panniers with all of our high-mountain gear back to Peshawar. They had told me it would be 60 rupees extra, but after we had loaded it on the roof they said it would be an additional 100 rupees. My fare was 35 rupees. Looking back, I can tell myself the reason was principle, but maybe the fact that I am living in a Pakistani frame of mind and on the razor's edge greatly attributed to the disagreement. The clerk pushed me and I shoved him against the van. The driver and I shouted obscenities at each other.

"I will never take you now, you *kafir*," he shouted.

"You call me a *kafir!* And you are a *Muslim?* If you are a Muslim, maybe it is better not to be one. But I am. **Allah** is my witness. **Allah** is Great. Now I would not go with you. You are truly a *kafir* and a *kafir* driver can only drive one to Hell!" Always good to blow off a bit of steam.

Fortunately for me there were two friendly drivers whom I had been chatting with earlier. They said to wait and go with them. One was scheduled to leave at 4:00 P.M., but his van was full. His friend was leaving at 4:30 and he had one available seat in his van. I had really wanted to leave at 2:00 but sometimes these things happen.

As the vehicles were loading four foreigners arrived. One was a girl dressed colorfully Pakistani in brown flower print *shalwar kameez* and an orange *dupatta*. She was tall and her hair was tied in a loose bun behind her head, tawny wisps floating down her long slender neck. I was in the row of seats behind the driver sitting beside two male Chinese tourists. In back of me were four Lahoris loudly chatting away in Punjabi. They held up departure when they disappeared to pray *Asr* prayer. To their rear were the foreigners. I could hear French and a drawling English accent.

We left Gilgit at 5:00. At sunset the Lahoris got the driver to stop for *Maghrib* prayer. I went with them down a steep rocky slope to the river (Indus) to make *wuzu*. We prayed in the dirt at the side of the road. At 8:00 we drove through Chilas. The Lahoris informed me that the people of Chilas, though it was not a large town, were such strong Muslims that there wasn't a single cinema in the town. Guess I won't catch a movie.

At 9:00 we came to a fort that was the police check post. We were told this was a dangerous area full of *dacoits*. We would have to wait for a bus coming back to bring more police to accompany us as escorts.

While waiting, I went with the Lahoris inside the fort to pray *Isha* prayer in a tiny, packed-mud-floor mosque. Standing out in front waiting with the drivers they joked with me that I should chat up the foreign girls to get them to befriend me. They were serious. Their implication was to get the girls to lay (have sex) with me. Many Pakistani men think you can just ask a Western girl, "Come on, let's do it," and it won't upset them or be impolite.

The cops explained that about two hours from where we were there was a road block.

"Oh no," I shuddered inside, *"not another road block!"*

They told us we should spend the night safely in their fort; in the morning we could go to the road block and cross over by foot in an hour or two and then catch a vehicle to Pindi. I should even be able to hire porters to carry the heavy pack saddle panniers over the rocks and mud.

It was a beautiful night, the silver full moon bathing the majestic mountainous lunar landscape in a magical light. A balmy breeze gently caressed my face. I went and stood by the bus for a bit of quiet. The tall girl came up to me and asked me in Pashtu if I spoke English. She wanted to know if I could explain to her what was happening as she couldn't understand it all in Pashtu.

Switching to English we talked. She thought I was a Pathan. What's new? The drivers looked at me and winked. One track minds I thought, but understandable here. This culture unfortunately does that. The mind always wants what it can't have.

Finally the bus with the other police arrived. With their rifles pointing out the van windows, two came in each vehicle with us. They only accompanied us for half an hour to the next police check post. There, while the foreigners signed the foreigner registration book, I chatted with the drivers and the police. I heard a driver say I'm a Pakistani. I didn't know if they were joking or not, but no one asked me to sign the book.

At 10:30 we stopped at a seemingly closed restaurant. They opened and cooked *keema* for us. I sat on a *charpoy* with a thin mat on it with the drivers. They were telling me how much they wanted to bed the foreign girls. I told them it just doesn't work like that. It must be a two-sided affair.

The English girl came up and they moved to let her sit next to me. Her hair was out of the bun now, slightly disheveled and half way down her back. She told me her mother was American, her father an English professor who spent most of his time in some remote part of Asia or another. Though she was only 19, she had deeply experienced many parts of Asia with her parents. She lived in Peshawar, in U (University) Town, but hated it and *"water-boilers."* She loved Peshawar and Pakistan. She worked teaching Afghan and Pathan women English in Gul Bahar. She spoke some Farsi and a bit of Pashtu.

After dinner we drove another half an hour. There it was in full glory in the moon light—the road block; about 40 or 50 feet high, big chunks of rocks and mud for several hundred feet, then more road, another slide and more roadway going around a curve. We were told after the bend was an even larger slide. The drivers told us if we were to go to the other side we would have to sleep there on the road as no buses would be leaving until morning. The English girl wanted to cross, as did I (to get to Lahore as soon as possible). Feeling impatient. Her friends wanted to stay and sleep in the van. She said she didn't want to cross over to sleep alone. I definitely wanted to cross and told her I would be happy to accompany her. It was nice having fresh company, fresh female company at that.

The drivers gave us half our fares back and the *cleaner* (conductor) from the other van who had helped me load the panniers in Gilgit helped me carry them over the road blocks. Scrambling over the huge boulders with a 60 pound pannier over my shoulders was like trying to walk on Jupiter. My legs felt like lead, but we made it.

The entire scene was brilliantly lit by the silver glow of the moon peeking over the remote mountain tops, the huge angular rocks, the short stretches of remaining road and the towering Karakoram peaks looking down on us tiny mortals from all sides. The night was silent except for the wind rustling our loose clothing and our labored breathing. At the end of the road block waited a long line of parked cars, buses and trucks.

My new companion informed me she didn't have a sleeping bag. Her pack was filled with more important items: fur hats from Kashgar, a velvet coat, books, embroidered shawls and other necessities. At least she had her white *chaddar* and orange *dupatta*. I had my blanket and Habibullah's sleeping bag was in the panniers.

"Let's find a place with some *priv-iss-see*," she said.

We made our bed between a Toyota car and a Flying Coach bus, laying Habibullah's bag on a part of the road that was least pocked. The head and feet of the bag didn't unzip, so we were a bit crowded on those ends. We used my blanket as a cover and rolled up her chaddar for a pillow. We lay there listening to the brooding silence of the eternal mountains and the gentle, caressing wind. Before we got to sleep the French girl came over and made a bed on the other side of the Toyota. On her way over the road block just now the driver from our van had propositioned her. 500 rupees, right there, on the rocks!

We slept from 3:00 to 5:00.

At 5:30 I found a van driver who was getting ready to drive back down the Karakoram Highway to Besham. We could have the front two seats. We pulled away from the road block at 5:45.

At 9:30 we reached Besham, drank some *Shazans,* and were in a battered van bound for Mingora by 9:50 via Khwazakhela (the only way) over the Shangla Pass. It was a beautiful road, climbing through incredibly lush, grassy, forested mountains. I was nostalgically reminded of sun-filled travels in the Vale of Kashmir, then rudely brought back to the present by the bumpy road, wishing of all this grass for our horses.

We took unannounced turns dozing, our heads bouncing on each other's shoulders and the seat as the dilapidated van trundled us along. We arrived in Mingora by 1:00 P.M., had a cold *sherbet* at the bus stand and were on another van bound for Peshawar by 1:30. The driver was a maniac, teasing us with close calls, but close calls are common fare on the highways (roads) of Pakistan and by the Grace of ***Allah*** we lived to tell of it.

My new friend got down at Rizalpur to visit friends and I was back in Haji Camp, Peshawar, by 5:00. I visited Arif and told him of the progress of our trip and got what mail had come for us at his shop.

I came home to Nejma's sister's wedding (Nejma is an adopted daughter of Bibi Ji. Her parents live in the neighborhood and have many children. They are poor so Bibi Ji adopted Nejma, a common practice here.)

As our house is the largest in the neighborhood, many local functions are held here. The women use the second floor rooftop (patio) where my room is located. Except for coming in and going out, during a wedding I usually respectfully keep my doors closed and stay to myself. Some girls knocked at my door and shoved a huge platter of rice and other wedding goodies at me. I wasn't hungry enough to eat all that was on the platter, but I was tired enough to sleep through all the noise.

The next morning is *Juma*.
At 11:15 I'm on PIA flight 315 to Lahore.

Beeyachai, the last night stay before Gilgit

Lahore Flying Coach bus stands

Chapter 21
Quick Visits To Lahore
(and Back To Gilgit)

August 19th

Chohan Hotel, Lahore

Spent yesterday *(Juma)* at her house from 1:00 P.M. to 9:00 P.M. At 1:45 I went out to the neighborhood mosque to pray my *Juma* prayer. When I arrived back Nasreen opened the door to let me in. When we were alone she said I could spend the night but she was acting and talking strangely, hard to tell if she was joking or not. Later, she said I couldn't stay the night, but could come back tomorrow.

At 8:00 all the lights in the house went out, a blown main switch. Nasreen came in the back room where I was waiting. The fan was off. The night was hot and muggy. We lay on the bed smoking cigarettes in the sultry, still darkness. We held hands and kicked our feet together at the end of the bed, rubbing ankles and trying to pin each other's feet down. I rubbed her back under her *kameez*. Her damp skin felt cool and smooth to my touch. She asked me to promise to bring her a bomb the next time I came from Peshawar.

"Who do you want to blow up?" I asked.

"I have somebody," she smiled coyly.

Now it's afternoon and I'm waiting at the Chohan Hotel. She told me to come at 5:00, that today I would be able to spend the night. I hope she is telling the truth. I feel so doomed with her, yet I just can't stop loving her. When she talks about plans for our future together, what we will do, where we will go, I feel so good inside. When I think about it logically, I can't believe she isn't just playing with me.

August 21st

Peshawar City

Back from Lahore just after midnight. Ten hours in the Flying Coach. Life going too fast. No time to write it down now. Barely enough time to live it. Looking at Nasreen's picture on my mantle in Hashtnagri. "Whyee," I sigh. "Oh Nasreen, why are you such a problem to me? Why do I love you so damn much? Damn!"

August 23rd, 12:15 P.M.

Lahore Airport

So, what's new?

Caught the 11:00 P.M. Flying Coach from Peshawar last night back to Lahore. Arrived at 8:00 A.M. Got to her house at 9:00.

I just had to come back to see her again before leaving for Gilgit. I wanted to apologize for the last time I was there, I was so upset at her. Several times in the middle of the night I was just ready to leave, just tell her to shut the iron yard gate behind me and say goodbye. But each time, just looking at her sleeping face in the dim yellow light of the room, looking at her body there softly breathing on the bed next to me, I just melted. Her attitude had been so callous. The only affection I had felt from her was when she came in the room when the power was out. And then she had asked me a most dangerous request: to bring her a bomb. She didn't even seem to care if I stayed or left.

Today she seemed to listen seriously to my apology. She looked so pretty and fresh in a yellow *shalwar kameez* and pearl beads plaited in her jasmine cigarette scented hair. I want to be able to see her always. To know she's close, that she isn't working.

She tells me so many lies. I never know where it really stands with her. I know one *lakh* isn't much money to give her family for her, not when I consider the amount of money she makes them and her expertise at running the household. But at what price do you judge health and happiness? And then is that even a consideration with these people? What is she telling me? Is she just having fun with my weak Pashtu? Before I left her house I asked her if I were too much of a problem for her. Is simple business easier?

"Yes," she answered.

"If you want me to stop this marriage talk, I will. At least I'll try."

"No," she answered. "When you come back we'll talk. You'll have to talk to my husband and to Mama."

TO GILGIT

August 24th
Gilgit
Trying to keep track of it all. A few minutes to write it down here, a few minutes there. Will the memories go up in a haze of *Gold Leaf* smoke?

Arrived back in Gilgit at 11:30 this morning. After the half hour flight from Lahore to Pindi yesterday and my head full of Lahore and Nasreen I wasn't in the best of tempers. In the parking lot of the Pindi Airport a taxi driver told me the short ride to the Gilgit bus stand would be 100 rupees. I impatiently shoved him aside. "You *fucker!*" I snapped under my breath, not caring if he understood any English or not; it was more an aside to myself.

"I *fuck* you!" he shouted back, squaring off as if to fight. There was a curb and a planter behind him. I threw my bag down.

"Come on, *khore ghod,*" I cursed as I pushed him back over the cement curb and he landed on his butt in the soft mud of the planter of flowers much to the amusement of the other drivers standing about.

The bus stand was in the parking lot of the Masriq Hotel behind Raja Bazaar. All of the drivers were Pathans. The two drivers I knew from my trip down came in from Gilgit. Nice to see friends.

I left for Gilgit at 4:30. Two minivans and two new Pathan driver friends. The trip was long and there were too many stops for tea. The music varied between one Pashtu cassette and one Urdu cassette until 1:30 A.M. when we stopped at Besham. There our driver, Akram Khan, bought a new cassette. Twelve more hours of Gulnar Begum. Luckily it was one of my favorite Gulnar Begum cassettes.

I got about 45 minutes of nodding sleep. Akram Khan told me if I fell asleep I would have to sit in a back seat as he wanted someone to talk with to help him stay awake. At dawn we stopped with a few other minivans and trucks in an incredible rocky gorge. We used the icy, clear water running across the road for *wuzu*. We all prayed right there on the road, the ragged, jagged rocks and crystal clear mountain tops towering above us, the dull murmur of the river far below us. **Allahu** *Akbar!* God is great!

About an hour out of Gilgit we were following a pickup truck loaded down with cages of chickens. I asked Akram how much a chicken costs in Gilgit.

"70 rupees." he answered,

Very expensive from the down country price of not more than 35 rupees. Just then a chicken fell out of one of the cages and onto the road. He stopped the van and we got out. He picked up the chicken and I slipped the knife I carry around my neck out of its sheath . Akram cut its throat, *halaling* it right there on the side of the road.

"I thought you said chickens are expensive up here? That one was free!" I told him. We laughed and got back in the van, putting it on the floor at our feet.

At one of the government checkpoints, I foolishly wasted time signing the book with the rest of the foreigners. After that I didn't bother. At the final check-point, Akram and I sat in the front seat chatting with the police while the foreigners signed in. They didn't notice I wasn't a Pathan. Or maybe it was I who didn't notice? There are lots of foreign tourists up here, but I'm falling so deep into Pakistan, I'm barely a part of that world. And, of course, I don't see many foreigners at my usual hangouts in Peshawar or Lahore.

Near Mastuj

Coming down into Kaghan Valley
from Babu Sar Top

Nanga Parbat, taken from Talachi

Nanga Parbat *is the ninth highest mountain on Earth (8,126 m-26,660 ft). Nanga Parbat translates to "Naked Mountain" in English; "parbat" deriving from the Sanskrit word "parvat" meaning mountain, rock, and "nanga," an Urdu word meaning naked. Known as the "Killer Mountain," Nanga Parbat was one of the deadliest of the "eight-thousanders" for climbers in the first half of the twentieth century; since that time it has been less so, though still an extremely serious climb. It is an immense, dramatic peak that rises far above its surrounding terrain. It was first climbed on July 3, 1953, by Austrian climber Hermann Buhl.*

220

Chapter 22
Back To the Horse Movie

August 30th
Talachi
Now we're in Talachi. Haven't had any time to write since I got back from Lahore. We've crossed the confluence of the Gilgit and the Indus Rivers. On horseback, that is. I crossed the junction twice last week on my way to and from Lahore. Leaving the Karakoram Mountains and heading into the Himalayas, in the shadows of Nanga Parbat and Rakaposhi. Resting for a day. I'll try to write down some of what has happened since arriving back in Gilgit....

Arrived back to find Mirza and Ayesha at a table on the front lawn of the hotel being interviewed by some *CID wallah** from Islamabad; dressed in Western clothing, styled hair, Ray-Ban sunglasses and a cop attitude. He implied we were being watched, that our movements were known, so we should watch our steps as we go traipsing about the mountains looking like a bunch of Afghani or Kohistani bandits.

I had my own problems at the office of the Gilgit Special Branch. The fellow in charge was somewhat vexed over the fact I had never signed in at his office when I had arrived in Gilgit. He said my visa extension from Peshawar wasn't stamped properly and some other such crap. Mirza and I said we would sort it out at the Gilgit *DSP's* office, with whom he and Bibi Ayesha had become rather friendly. The Special Branch *wallah* decided he was arresting me and sending me to the *DSP's* office so as we left a policeman was sent along with us. I imagine it meant I was officially under arrest.

"You can go back," I told the policeman following behind us.

"You," he said, pointing at me, with probably the only English he knew, "*arrest.*"

"Arrest?" I laughed. "Just what I need. A good rest!"

As we were crossing the narrow wooden bridge spanning the Gilgit River from the Gilgit main bazaar to the sparser east side of the river where the government quarters were located, Amjad Ali Jan, the *DSP*, drove by in his jeep. He stopped, holding up traffic, to say hello and see what we were up to. We told him we were on our way to his office to clear up some things to do with our visas and that I was under arrest. He laughed and told us to hop in the back so he could drive us. With his bodyguard crouching in the back of the small jeep, his Kalashnikov cradled between his knees, there wasn't room for the policeman escorting us. It was only then that Amjad Ali Jan even noticed him. Well, he could just trot along beside us or go on back to the office of the Special Branch.

After we got to his office and after tea and cakes we explained the problem; that the chief of Special Branch wasn't satisfied with my visa extension from Peshawar, or maybe he was just upset I had not registered with his office

---

* *Crimes Investigation Department*

221

upon arriving in Gilgit. It had been *Muharram* and the office had been closed most of the time, and I had been busy with the horses.

As it seems so many times in Pakistan, the *DSP* shared no liking for the Special Branch chief, and to our good luck, the *DSP* is a much higher authority in Gilgit, plus our friend. After another pot of tea, he personally called the Special Branch on the telephone and gave the chief a sound tongue lashing. Then he said his driver would take us down to the office so my passport could be properly stamped.

The chief of Special Branch squirmed, ate his pride and stamped my passport. Ha! We walked out triumphantly, I with my newly "validated" passport in my pocket.

One other news item I discovered upon returning to Gilgit; our trusty Pathan servant and brother, Habibullah, had never returned from down country. He must have decided enough was enough and that he didn't want to argue and debate the point.

Now it was just the three of us and the three horses.

On the morning of the 27th we left Gilgit. As we rode out of town we stopped at the Gilgit Hotel for breakfast and to say goodbye to the proprietor of the handicraft shop in front of the restaurant—an old friend and local competition of our friend G.M. Baig.

He informed us that the previous morning Mr. Baig, his wife and two of his children had left on the *PIA* flight to Rawalpindi. The plane was missing and hadn't been heard from since their last communication from somewhere near the Babu Sar Top. It was thought the plane and all 54 passengers went down somewhere in the vicinity of Nanga Parbat. As I look at the icy vastness of that monstrous piece of rock and ice I shudder to think of Baig and the rest of the plane's passengers frozen somewhere on its wastes, buried under tons of eternal snow or at the bottom of some high frozen lake.

We were riding Herc and Kodak. Shokot was carrying a light pack consisting of only a saddlebag as his withers were still sore with a lump reminiscent of Horse. We had tried again to trade him in Gilgit, but it just didn't work out and besides, we all feel a camaraderie with the little devil. The six of us have made it this far and we wanted to get him back to Peshawar with us, even if we have to pony him all the way. About an hour out of Gilgit Shokot's pack slipped off and we stopped in a grass field with a small murmuring brook to resew it.

In the afternoon we came to the junction leading down and over the river and off through the barren, dry mountains to Baltistan and high Ladakh. We stopped under some cliffs inches off the roadside to eat our smorgasbord of *parattas, pakoras*, carrots and raw onions dipped in French's Mustard (imported by me from Abdullah Jan's shop in Peshawar*), dried apricots, mulberries and roasted *channa*.

The sky was a beautiful cloud patched luminous blue. It was starting to rain sporadic, large drops. I decided to cadge a ride in a jeep with two Kohistani

---

* Abdullah Jan's—*see footnote bottom of page 182*

222

fellows going to Pari Bungala, our night's destination, to make arrangements and let Mirza and Ayesha ride Herc and Kodak. To our left, the road dropped off at least 500 feet to the gray Gilgit River. As we were driving some wild birds flew low across the road in front of us. "Let's try to get a free, fresh poultry dinner," our driver shouted as he stopped the vehicle in the middle of the road. We all drew our guns and jumped out but we were too late as the birds quickly hid among the rocks of the hillside above us.

We pulled into Pari Bungala just before dusk, where my friends dropped me off at a restaurant and store, pretty much all that consisted of Pari Bungala on the road. The guest house where we planned to stay, with the permission of the Commissioner of Gilgit, was up the road from the restaurant.

The driver of the jeep told me he would return in an hour with fresh grass for the horses. For free! I told him we would gladly pay as we would need about a *maund* for the night and next morning. He said it was no problem though he would never take money for it. We were travelers and, besides, his foreign Muslim brothers. It seemed too good to be true. Since leaving Chitral I had become rather used to at least paying for grass, if not having to fight for it.

After an obligatory tea and chat with locals a boy led me up the road and down a rutted, dirt side-track to the government guest house. It was full, more than full. There had been an earthquake at Skardu and even in the surrounding yard there were Balti refugees staying in makeshift tattered tents. The sun had set and the light was leaving quickly. I went back to the restaurant to see if quick last-minute arrangements could be made. A familiar scene in the half dark.

Usually the horses' food is the most difficult part. As I arrived back though, true to his word, my friend was just unloading a jeep-full of fresh grass. Back before Gilgit, I had become more accustomed to people saying they would bring us something and then not showing up half the time. Of course the other half helped us get through to Gilgit in relatively good shape. I again tried to give him money for the grass but again he said I was a traveler, a guest to his country and a brother Muslim and he wouldn't hear of it. Muslims are very hospitable to travelers. The Holy Prophet *(PBUH)* said it is a very good deed to help wayfarers.

Our lodging was a spare room at the restaurant (or was it a hotel?) in the adjoining building facing the dirt parking area and the road. There was a small open shack 100 meters or so down the way where the horses could be tied for the night. It had been used for animals so there was also a hard dried-mud feeding bin built into the wall. So even the animals would be covered. Good, it was starting to rain more steadily. Several men helped me carry the grass to the shack. Then I sat back against the wall, leaning on a colorful round bolster on the raised, carpeted platform of the open fronted restaurant waiting for Mirza and Ayesha to ride up.

The sound of the horses' bells appeared first in the quiet evening, finally followed by their physical manifestation. We unloaded in front of our room and the gear was carried up the several steps to the floor level. The foundation was solid earth and the floor was small pieces of granite gravel. There was ample space and four *charpoys*. On one were piles of colorful, flower-patterned new quilts and pillows freshly covered with embroidered pillow cases.

"Nice room," I told Mirza. "Kinda reminds me of a giant cat box."

Ayesha took up my position against the restaurant's wall. I ordered dinner and then Mirza and I led the horses over to their shack. Mirza could have relaxed as locals led the horses for us, but he couldn't rest until he checked out their accommodations himself.

We got back, ate dinner right where we were, leaning on large bolsters on the carpeted platform. We sat wrapped in our blankets watching the rain come down in the night and chatted with locals. They were Kohistanis from somewhere along the road. An actual resident of Pari Bungala insisted on paying for our dinner. He said it was his duty to have us eat and stay at his house but because his wife was away at some relatives' down the road it would be better to stay where we were.

"And, by the ways, you no pay for the room. Okay?"

Sayid Jan had gone to Kashmir with thousands of Pathans and other Kohistanis in the late '50s for *Jihad,* where he had lost his leg. As he lay back on the carpets relaxing, drinking *qawah* and telling us stories, he stretched out and removed his plastic leg from the knee down.

He told us about the time a few years back when two or three thousand Kohistanis decided to attack the *Shias* in Gilgit. Their *mullahs* had told them the *"kafir" Shias* in Gilgit had been kicking a football in the bazaar with the names of Hazrat Umar, Usman (Uthman) and Abu Bakr—the first three Caliphs of Islam whom the Shias reject. Of course the people living in the mountains of Kohistan couldn't stand for that and they gained momentum village by village, as they marched on Gilgit. *"Dahzoo, dahzoo!* I shoot one *Shia*," he told us. "Then I see another. *Dahzoo! Dahzoo!"* Now we see why everyone in Gilgit had warned us the Kohistanis were so dangerous. They are dangerous to the *Shias* of Gilgit. Once they knew we were foreign *and Sunni*, no problem.

The rain continued throughout night and was still falling in the morning. We could only see a couple of hundred feet up the mountains surrounding us. Mirza and I decided we must do something about Shokot's back. When we had fed the horses before dawn we noticed the swelling on his withers was worse. He couldn't even manage the light pack he had carried from Gilgit.

"Remember when I lanced the boil on Baqi Makoo's leg right in his shop in Murad Market after he had come back from Afghanistan that time?" Mirza asked me. "Soon after he was able to walk good as new. We need to lance Shokot's back."

After breakfast us doctors got to work. We led Shokot to a large tree by the side of the road where Mirza twitched him, wrapping a rope around his lower jaw and twisting it with the aid of a stick for leverage. The idea was to cause him enough harmless pain in his jaw that he wouldn't feel the large caliber needle I was going to be digging into his back. Half an hour ensued of jabbing and pushing pus out into rags. It was gross, but *horse vacations* in Northern Pakistan aren't always a bed of roses. We covered the wound with white powdery boric acid and strapped a towel on him with a girth. The next morning his back looked better.

We needed to go on, rain or shine, and it looked like we were going to get some of each. We had breakfast and saddled up. Shokot was still carrying an almost empty saddle bag and his saddle, rigged to sit back so nothing would be on his wound except the towel bandaging.

The next spot on our map was Juglote, about 25 clicks away. We were approaching the Chilas high desert (Diamar Desert), a massive expanse of high mountain plains and crumbling rocks bereft of any vegetation. To our right towered the ending teeth of the Karakorams, in places advancing right to the roadside. On our left, the rocks and sandy brown dry earth sloped down to the Gilgit River, winding through the rocky ravine. About a mile away the Indus River could be seen winding out of the mountains, the rocky borders of Baltistan.

We arrived in Juglote early, around 4:00 P.M. Riding into town trees were planted on both sides of the road and for a mile or so we rode through very British style Pakistani Army barracks. We were close to the border of *Maqbuza* (occupied) Kashmir. I had been there before in 1980, on the other side, journeying from Srinigar to Ladakh. I had passed a freezing night sleeping in the cab of a truck just outside Dras, only a few miles from the disputed border, waiting for the dawn and the army to open the pass (Zoji La). Beautiful, but cold.

After the barracks we were surprised to ride into a bazaar that seemed to be transplanted directly out of *Suba Sarhad (NWFP)*. On either side of the road were small provision shops, tea houses and restaurants, a hotel and even a few barber shop/*hammams*. The hotel's courtyard-cum-parking-lot was too full of oily water and old rusting trucks to decently accommodate the horses. There was no government guest house in Juglote. A young Pathan tea house boy from Mardan, an instant friend who latched on to us, led us across the road to a restaurant where we could comfortably stay. Next to it was a grassy, stone-fenced meadow filled with trees belonging to *WAPDA*. We were able to secure its use after walking up the hill behind it to haggle with the old man who was the guardian of *WAPDA's* transformer in Juglote.

Outside, next to the restaurant was a raised earth platform with a small rail around its carpet-covered top. At the front, pointing southwesterly to the Holy City of Makkah, was a prayer niche, colorfully decorated with child-like painted flowers, arabesques and calligraphic inscriptions. I offered my night prayer there along with a bus load of Chinese *Hajis* returning on their long journey home to Kashgar from *Haj*.

Buses heading up the highway stopped for one last cup of tea before plowing on to Gilgit. It had been three long days since we had left Gilgit, yet it wasn't much over a couple of hours in a truck or bus. They kept straggling in until 3:00 A.M., sitting on the *charpoys* not occupied by us and our equipment.

Supplied with grease-grimed, smoky smelling quilts, dark and once flower patterned, and hard, heavy, flat pillows whose cases seemed to have seen one too many dirty heads, we bedded down in the corner of the restaurant. It meant not having to unpack our sleeping bags, and better yet, it meant not having to pack the sleeping gear in the morning. Personally, I am always more than glad to trade sleeping in one of those plastic coffins (bags) for a *charpoy* and quilt, even a sagging *charpoy* and a time-worn quilt.

As the buses pulled up the music would come up and the remaining empty *charpoys* would fill with people, sipping pots of tea, sitting at low rickety wooden tables. I had a smoke with some bus drivers I knew from the highway.

The morning came soon enough. After breakfast, paid for, as was our dinner, by a local barber named Malang, we were not going to be permitted to leave without accepting free hot baths and shaves from our benefactor. Malang owned the *hammam* next to the restaurant. In the corner of the barber shop was the old, rusted iron water boiler. In another corner was piled dozens of old snow shoes recently discarded by the Army, which Malang was burning to provide the hot water for our baths.

We've crossed the confluence of the Gilgit River and the Indus coming out of its high springs somewhere on the border of Ladakh and Tibet. This was also the junction of the Hindu Kush, the Karakorams and the Himalayas— three of the world's mightiest mountain ranges. We could see the rock and ice sides of Nanga Parbat ahead of us as we rode into Talachi.

August 31st
Talachi
The guest house in Talachi is quite large—made of stone and old, smoothly-worn wood' its stone fenced grounds are covered in tall grass gently swaying in the wind. Nobody has stayed here in quite some time. Very nice, though dusty. It took a while to locate the *chowkidar* and talk him into unlocking the doors for us. He lives in an outbuilding in back with his family.

Looking over the stone wall, wind ruffles my *shalwar kameez* and the dark brown blanket wrapped around me. Southeast I see the mighty, icy massif of Nanga Parbat, "the killer mountain," towering 26,660 feet and guarding the start of the mighty Himalayas. To the northeast 25,552 foot Rakaposhi towers in the distance from its home in the Karakorams.* We're spending the day here, giving the horses a chance to graze on the tall grass and get ready to attempt crossing the Babu Sar Pass.

Spent a lot of the day sitting in front of the tea house across the road from the guest house, drinking tea, watching the brightly-patterned painted trucks that ply the Karakoram Highway and thinking of Nasreen. A man came up to the road from somewhere behind the tea house with a basket of crystals from the mountains. Ayesha and I bought some raw garnets, some almost an inch around, and long, black crystals of tourmaline.

---

* *Rakaposhi is also known as Dumani ("Mother of Mist").*

September 3rd

Government Guest House, Chilas

We leave Talachi September 1st, Nanga Parbat facing us on our left (southeast). We ride over high sand dunes. We can't help wondering aloud about the fate of *PIA* flight 303 and of our old friend Ghulam Mohammad Baig.*

It takes only seven hours to reach Julipur. I walk most of the way, far ahead of my companions, out of range of their voices and the sounds of the horse bells. Indeed, out of sight. I walk alone with my thoughts among the sandy, rocky plain and the mountains, just the sound of the wind in my clothes. The silence of wind and rocks. I see nothing living at all, except living rock. I take out my pistol and try to shoot one. No one hears me.

I would not have noticed Julipur from the other indistinguishable half dozen house hamlets if not for the small Urdu sign on the side of a dirt track leading down from the road. The map says there is a guest house there, or once had been. I can see a handful of houses behind stone walled fields and a building that seems like it must be the guest house. We get off the horses and let them drink from a ditch. Of the children who follow us down the lane we ask where the *chowkidar* of the guest house is. One little boy comes up to us, saying "I am the *chowkidar!*"

"This will be easy," I tell Mirza. "If he doesn't want to open the guest house for us we can spank him."

When I ask where the keys are he clarifies that it is his father who is actually the *chowkidar* and he will be in from the fields shortly. Someone has already gone to fetch him. Eventually Mir Agha arrives with the keys. There is nothing; no furniture in the guest house, no shops in the village, no hotel or restaurant. In front of the guest house there is another small building. We look in a window in the door. There is a *charpoy*, some clothes hanging on hooks on the walls and a shiny tin storage box with the name "H. OMAR" painted on it.

Mir Agha brings us *parattas* and tea from his house. He comes back with a *charpoy* and our dinner, also from his house; *chapatties, sag,* raw scallions and tomatoes. He laughs as he and I shake the dust out of the *charpoy*. Mirza and Ayesha spread their bedding on the cement back porch. I'm going to sleep on the *charpoy* on the lawn.

The horses are tied to trees in front of the guest house, munching on the long grass. The mountain falls away from us for a few hundred feet tumbling over rocks and small scrubby trees to the Indus, the roar of the river is ever present in the clear air. There are thousands of small, pale white, almost transparent flies. "No See Me's," Mirza says the British called them. They are eating the hair off our horses' bellies, drinking their blood. When we take our hands to brush them away, our hands come away covered with blood.

We go to sleep shortly after 9:00. I lay on my *charpoy*, covered with a soft, heavy quilt, listening to the river and watching the stars in the Himalayan night sky. The horses' bells jingle as they try to swipe the "No See Me's" from their bellies with their feet. I wake up about 10:00. Some little animal, maybe a rat, is crawling over my quilt. I swish it off. Mirza wakes. We're both bitten, and

---

* Pakistan Airlines Fokker flight 303 was never found.

the deserted, imposing, lonely feeling of the place is ominous.

We discuss if we're safe or not. We have our pistols ready. Mirza takes his sword and a flashlight to check on the animals. He says he thought he saw two lights coming around the building before. It would be easy to do away with us down here by the river and nobody would ever know. The price of our horses and gear could go a long way up here. I have gotten into the habit of telling people the horses are on loan from the army. After the trip they are going to the police at Sherqi Tanna in Peshawar. Their army brands make it a fairly convincing story. It gives the impression the army may come looking for their horses if they should ever happen to disappear, if not for us.

Mirza goes back to his bed of horse blankets and sleeping bags on the veranda. He has his sword and pistol near by. I lay down with my holster and chambered pistol on my stomach where I can sleep with my hand on it. Shortly I see a flickering, yellow light slowly advancing around the building. Then I see a man carrying a dim lantern and a flashlight. He comes across the grass. As he approaches my *charpoy* I shine a flashlight in his eyes, my hand on my gun.

"Who are you?" we ask each other in unison.

Hiyat Omar is a soldier. He lives in the front building. He is from Chakwal. He has just returned from his work, driving a bulldozer at the Tatta Landslides. The landslides here are recurring and have names. There are even road signs informing you when you are entering one and leaving it. When the snows melt, even after it rains heavily, the mountains start their age-old advance down toward the river.

Hiyat Omar is checking if everything is all right. He comes back bringing me another quilt. As he covers me with it, I smell a familiar, sweet scent; I see the half-finished cigarette in his hand. "*Charras hey?*" I ask (it's *charras?*).

"*Ou jee* (yes sir)," he answers.

We share a laugh and smoke.

Mirza doesn't seem to wake up. Or maybe he has ascertained there is no problem and has drifted back to an easier sleep. Good night.

In the morning Hiyat Omar gives me a small piece of *charras* for the road. Mir Agha wants us to sign the guest house official register. It is a new register and we are the first names to be signed in. The date listed that it was put in the guest house is 1982. We are the first guests in seven years. I joke with Mir Agha that this is the "grand opening" celebration; for us.

This is Pakistan. We're riding through deserted terrain, nothing but mountains, rocks, and wind—the widening Indus gorge; a soldier gives me some *duc*. At one of the landslides a road worker from Swat gives me a package of fresh, green *nuswar*. Luxury of luxuries. *Pakistan zendabad!*

September 2nd we ride only 12 clicks, arriving in Guner Farm at noon.

It's late to push on to Chilas. We ask at a shop where the guest house is and are directed up a dirt road. Another packed guest house. This time it is 20 folks from Hunza—a search party for the missing *PIA* flight. We can set up a camp in the yard. They also have tents pitched on the lawn. On the hillside behind the guest house are tiered, narrow fields of grass surrounded by low, stone walls. The Hunzaites arrange with the local farmer to let us tie our horses in one of the fields for the night. We want to go into town after dark to find a restaurant. It is just the one row of shops along the road. "Nothing is open," our Ismaili friends tell us. And besides, "The dogs will eat you!"

"If we don't find a restaurant we might eat them," I grumble.

But they are right; nothing is open in the bazaar. Only barking dogs are about. We arrive back at the guest house in time to eat dinner with the search party. The 23 odd of us sit in the yard on large cloths spread over the lawn.

We crawl into our sleeping bags under the great open sky.

"I hate camping," I complain as Mirza and Ayesha crawl into their sleeping bags. A Pashtu song is in my head,

"Tuh ka po khar, ka po jungle, ki ohsee,
Guli zama, da zera po tul, ki ohsee...."
(If you live, in the city, or in the forest,
My darling, flower, you will live always in my heart)
Well, it wouldn't be so bad if only....

This morning, September 3rd, we lead the horses down from the guest house. Shokot's back has been getting better since doctor Mirza and I performed our surgery. We figure with Shokot completely unencumbered, Mirza and Ayesha can readily push on to Chilas. They leave me at the roadside with Shokot's saddlebags and saddle. Also feeling extremely unsociable today, slightly sick and weak. A covered Suzuki pickup pulls up to see if I need a ride. I pile my luggage on the roof and hop in the back. One of my fellow passengers asks me in Pashtu if the people on the horses are Englaise.

"Yes," I answer, "and Musselmen (Muslim) also!"

"*Al-hamdu-lillah!*" several people answer my statement.

We chat for a bit, holding on to the sides of the pickup bed, our knuckles white as we grip tightly, the road bending this way and that.

And now I'm sitting on my bed with fresh, clean blankets, looking out the window to the massive mountains to the north, the mountains we have just come through. This is my idea of camping. The guest house is up a steep newly paved road at the beginning of the Chilas bazaar. A graded gravel parking lot and watered flower beds line the raised, wide, cement verandas. The building is cement and plaster with rich dark brown wooden window frames and doors, laid out in the shape of a large letter L, with three rooms on our side of the "L." On the other side are another four rooms, a dining room and a carpeted mosque/prayer room.

Before coming up the hill to the guest house I had met Shir Dil Khan, the chief engineer at the *WAPDA* office, the man I needed to give us permission to stay at the guest house. He is a *Sunni* from a good family in Gilgit. He knows the DSP. As we sat around drinking tea and smoking Gold Leaf cigarettes with some friends from his office he called the government farm and ordered grass for our horses: only 15 rupees per *maund*. At what time were my friends expected he asked? A jeep would deliver the grass to the guest house. Definitely my idea of getting horse food. Am I just day dreaming? Shir Dil even arranged for a man to drive me and the bags up to the guest house in his jeep.

Ready to head up the Babu Sar Top. In many ways I'd like this trip to go on forever. But then I want it over. I've got to some way get something settled in Lahore. These monthly visits are driving me crazy. I'm driving me crazy.

A rest just before the summit of Babu Sar Pass (13,300 ft)

Chapter 23
Babu Sar and the Road to Kashmir

Babu Sar Top, looking down into Kaghan Valley

September 5th

Chilas, down to 3000 ft.

Sometimes I get so tired of relating in English words and ideas. Just want to be with Nasreen. Not having to relate in English. Not being drawn into the past, just forgetting it and just being plain Noor Mohammad, once from Kabul, now from Peshawar. Is it possible? Sitting on a *charpoy* in a yard full of Pathan people—the life I had in America seems as a dream to me here.

Mirza is sick today so we're still resting, building up energy for the ride over the Babu Sar Pass and through Kaghan to Azad Kashmir. The horses are staked out in a rocky field behind the guest house. There is a small, gurgling brook running close by and grass is still coming by jeep at 15 rupees a *maund*. The *maunds* are a bit light, but at that price, unlimited supply, telephone ordering and delivery, no complaints.

September 17th

Written in Balakot, NWFP. The last entry, September 5th seems a long long time ago. Haven't had time to write in last 12 days. Some catch up....

We were prepared to leave Chilas on the 6th but Ayesha and I were sick in the night. My knee was inexplicably sore and had been getting progressively worse all day. I woke in the middle of the night with my knees drawn up to my waist, in excruciating pain. Almost paralyzed. High fever. Maybe a spider bite? Ayesha had personal stomach problems.

The air in Chilas was stale, hot and dry. The people were great: had the *moogays* fixed by an iron monger in the bazaar who wouldn't take any money. While buying small assorted sundries in the bazaar it was hard to get shop-

231

keepers to accept our money. Everybody wanted to aid the foreign Muslim horseback wayfarers. "It is our duty," we were told. "God has sent you as strangers to our city so we may be allowed the privilege of helping you."

September 7th we rode out of Chilas.

Right out of town the way doubled back through a copse of cannabis higher than my horse. I could have picked it without reaching down if I had felt so inclined. The road leading up the mountain was dry and barren, as were the surrounding mountains. Then we doubled back toward the canyon leading to the Babu Sar. At the entrance to the canyon a beautiful, old British-era brick bridge stood over the small, rock-strewn river. The approaches connecting it with land had washed away many storm-swollen years before.

We followed the river up the canyon. The landscape was becoming greener with scattered rocky fields and forested mountainsides of tall Alpine trees. The air was getting fresher and cooler. We stopped at a small roadside restaurant for lunch, the only business we passed all day. It was built into the hillside, the back wall of brown-gray rock the same colors as the stone and mud man-made walls. They were pulling fish out of the river and frying them in a blackened, grease-encrusted pan over a smoky fire. Fresh greasy fried fish, corn *chapatties* and smoky green tea.

I didn't eat much. I still wasn't feeling so well, still a bit hung over from my strange ailment in Chilas. I'm also beginning to feel more and more like the Habibullah of the trip. My thinking isn't in gear with my companions. I am more into sitting and chatting with locals and praying with them in their rustic mosques. It is my job to deal with locals, to arrange food and accommodations. We are in the backwoods of Central Asia. Even if I hadn't been into it, relating personally is an important part of life here. Everything is done on the personal, human level. You don't just check-in, pay your bill in the morning and leave. Hanging out is there. Mirza is dedicated to the journey, he is an equestrian explorer. Knowing that I only go on in order to get back to Lahore and Nasreen makes things rough at times.

On the road we began running into armed bands of men, half a dozen or so at a time, one or two carrying Kalashnikovs and the rest carrying old Enfield rifles, British or Pakistani made, or shotguns. From what I could gather someone had shot and killed somebody down the canyon that morning. This was local justice. These bands of bearded, baggy-clothed men were heading down the mountain to kill the offender. Judge and jury. Why waste money and time on corrupt government courts?

I was feeling feverish. When a loaded jeep drove by on its way up towards Babu Sar I asked if I could get a ride. Ayesha took over on Herc. The mountains were green with pine forest; the sky deepest blue with clean, billowing clouds rolling overhead; the air fresh and fragrant. The road had at least as many rocks as the river bed. After two and a half bone-jarring hours to cover nine miles they all seemed embedded in my back.

The town of Babu Sar was at 9,300 feet, green, pine-scented and cold.

Feeling a bit out of sorts. Mirza, Ayesha and I had a big blow up as they arrived. They had asked me to come down the road to meet them with a lantern if they hadn't arrived by dusk.

In trying to locate the *chowkidar* for the guest house, I met Abdul Rahim and Abdul Majid, whom Mirza later dubbed "*The Babusar Brothers.*" Their main family house is in Chilas. They also have a house in Babu Sar where they spend the summer engaged in harvesting timber, which eventually makes its way down to Naguman on the Charsadda Road and on to the Peshawar lumber mills.

We found the *chowkidar* and made arrangements to stay at the guest house. Green grass was available in a field between the guest house and the river. The Babusar Brothers, the *chowkidar* and myself cut enough to feed the three horses, carrying it back to the front porch of the guest house. As the sun set I went with the Babusar Brothers to the mosque to pray Maghrib prayer, after which I could take the one lantern from the mosque down the road to meet my friends they told me.

The open-top *wuzu* stalls were made from large, flat pieces of gray slate. A small, gurgling brook channeled through so one could wash in the fresh, though chilly, mountain water. The mosque itself was made from rough-hewn pine logs, with fragrant dry golden straw covering the packed earthen floor. After the prayer I started down the road with the lantern in the quickly diminishing light. I heard the sound of the horse bells coming up the road.

"Noor! Is that you with the light?" I heard both Mirza and Ayesha yelling sharply. Clearly they were travel tired and altitude affected. Weren't we all?

"Where the hell were you, Noor!" Mirza shouted when he saw me. "We're dying trying to get these horses up the road in the dark and where are you? On your butt, drinking tea and probably smoking dope with the natives! Damn your selfish eyes!"

"The sun has just gone down," I explained. "I was in the mosque for Maghrib prayer. Then I got the lantern and started down the road."

"Oh great! You were praying," Mirza raged.

"What if we had missed the road to the guest house in the dark?" Ayesha fumed. "Couldn't you have skipped prayer this time?"

"The only lantern I could locate was in the mosque," I answered, yelling as we trudged to the guest house where grass and rooms were waiting. "You know, there isn't a Big Five sporting goods store up here to get another light like in the San Fernando Valley. And I couldn't very well take the only lantern from the mosque until after prayer. You won't have to worry about me for very much longer, anyway. As soon as we get over the pass and down the mountain far enough for me to find a bus, I'm leaving. You can make your own arrangements from now on. You don't like my style. I don't need this *crap*. I'll be sitting on a *charpoy* with Nasreen in Lahore smoking Gold Leafs and drinking *Shazan* and you great adventurers can take care of ignorant *chowkidars* and locating *boose* yourselves! Maybe I'll take Habibullah to Lahore with me also!"

Amid our frayed nerves we unloaded our gear into the guest house. The horses were in an old outbuilding. Two friendly, curious policemen came down to the guest house to see if we needed any help and chat. Nothing much out of the ordinary must ever happen up here.

The police and I walked up to the road and the small log cabin bazaar of Babu Sar to see what could be found for dinner at the one small restaurant there. Mirza and Ayesha stayed in the guest house with the lantern. I was happy to be walking in the crisp clear starry night with two Pakistani policemen who didn't speak English, away for the time being from my two travel-weary compatriots. The Babusar Brothers, who as it turned out spoke a little English, stayed with them in the guest house.

The restaurant was an open-fronted log building. The bazaar was all closed except for it. Inside, a handful of men were sitting around drinking tea in the firelight. The only food available was *dal* and *chapatties*. I left alone into the dark night carrying a hot metal bowl of smoky-tasting *dal* covered with the *chapatties*.

The batteries in the small flashlight I was carrying soon gave up the ghost. There was no moon and in the dim starlight I crossed the grassy fields stumbling over rocks and logs. It seemed like I'd gone too far and I hoped to see some light from the lantern-lit guest house. Soon I was almost to the river, hearing it tumbling over its rocky bed. Hell, I've lost the way, I thought. I'll have to back track. As I headed back, trying to guess when to cut to the right to get near the guest house, I saw a light bouncing across the fields. My policemen friends suspected I might get lost in the dark and were on their way to see if I had made it back safely. The three of us walked back to the guest house.

Mirza and Ayesha were too tired to even be excited over the prospect of eating *dal!*

❖   ❖   ❖

THE ROAD TO KASHMIR

We left Babu Sar on the morning of the 9th, riding through beautiful pine forests. *Gujars* were moving their flocks down the mountain toward Chilas for approaching winter. We passed them as we rode on up toward the Babu Sar Top.*

The British had heard of a passageway leading into Kashmir through the Kaghan Valley, but for many years its discovery eluded them; not so many years back it was the only way to Rawalpindi from Gilgit, Gupis and Yasin. At 13,690 feet, it will be the highest pass yet we've crossed on this trip. We zigzagged back and forth up the mountain. No more trees the last couple thousand feet. At the top were large shale orange-ish brown cairns reminiscent of Ladakh and Tibet. Looked like the top of the world. It was... for us!

Kaghan Valley stretched out at our feet, the thin silver ribbon of the Kun-

---

* In 1890 the British built this new shorter track across Babusar, directly connecting Gilgit and British India. Before this the only route to Gilgit had been the difficult track from Srinagar over the Burzil Pass (13,410 feet), following the Astore river. The Babusar road was the main route from Rawalpindi to Gilgit from 1947 until 1978, when the KKH was opened.

har River winding down and away below us. In every direction were layer upon layer of mountain ridges. To the immediate northeast, one snow covered peak rose a thousand feet above us. The only other things above our lofty perch were the magnificent clouds whipping over our heads in the biting wind. To the east were the peaks of Kashmir, covered in white snow, glowing orange in the lowering sunlight. To the northwest huddled the many layers of gray brown mountains we had just come through, leading back down to Chilas and then up again into the wilds of Kohistan beyond.

We ate a can of Russian tuna, onions, *parattas*, crackers and water for a late lunch—quite the feast. Shot some photos and video. Two policemen came walking over the mountain, also headed down into the Kaghan Valley, a lonely beat. I interviewed them for the video camera. Flecks of snow were blowing down on us in the wind. The cold stung as the sun sunk into Kohistan.

We told the cops we were headed to Giti Das where the Babusar Brothers had given us a letter of introduction to somebody named Haji Batool. There were several clusters of stone huts a few clicks down the trail, the whole of Giti Das. Haji Batool's was pointed out to us. Then our visitors wished us a safe journey and headed down the trail, to spend the night in Basel before heading on to Naran.

We headed off the pass at 4:00, Gupis, Gilgit, Chilas and Kohistan faded out of our sight as we journeyed into the Kaghan Valley, once again back in the North West Frontier Province. As we approached the stone huts of Giti Das we rode through a dirty, stone-age gaggle of ragtag children. They followed us shouting and laughing.

"*Aram sara oka!*" I yelled at them. ("Cool it"—literally "do with peace.") Amazingly it quieted them down.

Several men came up to us as we rode into the middle of the sparse stone settlement and produced our raggedy, hand-scribbled letter of introduction. A man with a bushy black beard clutching a Kalashnikov and squatting on a rock who appeared to be Haji Batool read the letter.

Quick words of Kohistani were uttered and we were shown to an empty stone hut. We unloaded and unsaddled. The men helped us shove everything through the three-foot high stone doorway. In the center, at its highest, our room was maybe five feet high. Two teenage boys helped me lead the horses down to the beginnings of the Kunhar River to water them. It seemed water would be the only dinner for them as all of the grass had been nibbled to the quick on this summer grazing ground.

September 18th
Written in Muzaffarabad....
Woke this morning in Gari Habibullah and now we're in Muzaffarabad, Azad Kashmir. The Emperor Jehangir (A.D. 1605-1627) and his beloved Empress Noor Jehan on their way to Kashmir—where they liked to travel each spring—passed through Gari Habibullah. The Empress once suffered a headache there and she bathed her eyes in the icy waters of the Kunhar River. It cured her headache. Not being so magically endowed, I took two aspirins when

I woke up this morning.

But that is all another story. Now let me continue with this one. Where was I? Oh yeah, in a stone hut at 12,000 feet in Giti Das, just under the Babu Sar Top....

In the center of our cave-like accommodation our Kohistani hosts kindled a fire in a shallow pit ringed with stones. The low dark windowless room immediately filled with smoke. I went outside to pray *Maghrib* prayer on the earthen roof of the hut across from ours, just barely a foot higher than the hard earth path running in front of our door. The water in the plastic *lota* I used for making *wuzu* was freezing cold.

The horses were staked next to our little dwelling on equally hard, dry, barren earth with not even a single blade of grass to munch. They were restless and stomping for the dinner that wouldn't arrive. They had come a long hard high way and were not used to ending their day without anything at all to eat but there was nothing we could do for it.

In the smoky hovel we drank tea and ate with Haji Batool, our bearded machine gunned benefactor, whom Mirza had tagged as Ali Oop (for his caveman-like appearance) and two other bearded herders. Dinner was a cup of hot salted goat's milk and corn *chapatties* tasting of wood fire. Over and over again they warned us not to go outside during the night. They told us to pile our saddles in the low doorway and hang something over it. They explained they would be busy packing during the night and there would be many ferocious dogs about.

When they left us alone we doused the fire with water and went to sleep. It was 8:15. We were exhausted, there was no light and it was frigid. Besides, what else was there to do in Giti Das? We didn't have a restaurant or cinema guide.

We could hear the horses stomping the hard earth next to our hut. They were hungry and cold. We lay against the wall with one open sleeping bag below us and another, plus our personal blankets over us. Small rocks in the hard floor poked into our backs. During the night a rat ran back and forth behind our heads, dancing dusty patterns on our sooty tangled hair. All night long we could hear the barking of dogs and bleating sheep.

Woke at 5:00 in the morning to more dogs, sheep and shouting. I got up and shook the dirt from my hair. I crawled to the blanket-draped doorway so I wouldn't bump my head on the low, uneven ceiling, parted the blanket and looked outside. Most of the camp had moved out, heading back over the mountains to Chilas for the winter season. The last flock of sheep was being led up the stony mountainside by the remaining men and dogs. They slowly faded into the distance and Giti Das was empty and quiet. Closed! Nobody said a word of goodbye. Thank you for your stone age hospitality, Ali Oop!

I went outside to pray and shiver. Our animals were still stomping. They looked at me with a what-is-going-on look. By the time I was done praying Mirza and Ayesha were up. We saddled up with hands freezing, the icy buckles burning into our fingers like ice fire. The horses, especially Herc, were shivering and looking around for the breakfast that wasn't.

Mirza shot some documentary video while I stood, wrapped in my blanket, holding the horses. Ayesha took photos with my little Rollei 35 camera; her Nikon, much to her chagrin, had broken the day before on the Babu Sar Top. At 6:30 we rode out of Giti Das, down stony hills, the high birthplace of the Kunhar River and Kaghan Valley. We followed the clear stream rushing over its white granite slabs of stone, riding on earth covered in short verdant tufts of emerald green.

The granite hills on the west already rising 1000 feet above us glowed golden-brown-orange in the pristine rising morning sunlight. The hills to the east on the other side of the river were lower and more rounded, covered with short grass brilliant in the crystal light. The white boulders shone, multicolored, smooth wet stones in the riverbed glistened and sparkled as the light danced on its bejeweled surface. In the distance rose the snowy peaks of Kashmir still tinged with purple as daylight liquidly replaced early morning glow. Clouds sallied by white, clean and billowing like so much cotton fluff in a deep turquoise sky. The horses were listless with hunger, fatigue and the high altitude. So were we. The warm sunshine and the chill fresh air kept us on as we led them eventually to something to eat.

We fell in with a band of armed Kohistanis from Chilas, still up in the high passes with their flocks. Three were carrying older Pakistani rifles; one a long blue barreled shotgun and two fellows sported Kalashnikovs. Some walked along with Mirza and Ayesha and I trailed behind chatting as I rode surrounded by my own personal bodyguard.

Our road skirted the mirror surfaced Lulusar Lake as it twisted along, never more than 30 feet above its mirrored face. The nearly vertical brown and black cliffs on its western bank, the steep mountain side behind with patches of green, the azure sky and silvery clouds reflected brilliantly before our eyes on its surface. One couldn't tell where the earth ended and the water began. The lake before us vanished around the bend of the valley.*

Our Kohistani friends began taking pot shots at birds and stones. The next town marked on our map was Basel, the destination of our fellow wayfarers. We could see it a quarter of a kilometer off, down the road. We passed an old, white-bearded man dressed in wonderfully raggedy and colorfully patched clothes perched on a rock wall overlooking the road, the keeper of the stone *zirarat* down by the river.**

We had arrived....

Basel was just a handful of deserted, roof-less stone huts and animal pens. The Kohistanis said with winter coming, the town, no more than an upper pasture supply station, had closed. Soon it would be covered in snow. Next

---

* *Lulusar Lake (11,000 ft/3,353m) is the main source of the Kunhar River, running down the length of the Kaghan Valley. Lulusar marks the historic place where 55 participants of the 1857 War of Independence, known as "The Mutiny" by the British (all is in the eyes of the beholder), were arrested.*
** *Keepers of zirarats (shrines), usually a malang, will traditionally wear a long jacket/robe made of many colored patches.*

spring after the snows melted the black stone huts would remain to become shops for another summer.

Why were they going to Basel? Why, to pass the time, what else?

We left them sitting on a low rock wall in the town playing with their guns and chatting and led our animals into a field of short grass reaching out into a loop of the river. We hoped the horses could pull up some of the half-inch tufts for a snack and to distract them from their hunger.

It was lunch time. In a very un-Islamic and un-Pakistani way we did not share our one remaining can of Russian tuna with some rustics who would probably think we were crazy for eating fish from a can anyway. Besides, we didn't even have enough *mastaki* left over from the rounded loaf given us by the Babusar Brothers for ourselves. Behind us along the river the *zirarat*, festooned with many brightly-colored flags, stood in the sunlight on the other side of the stony meadow. Orange, red, green, white and black, the flags fluttered and whipped in the crisp wind. There was also an old British guest house cum fort between the *zirarat* and the river, its high stone walls crumbled with age and neglect.

"It's been a long time since any Brits rode over this pass on their way to Gilgit or Chitral." Mirza mused aloud.

We decided to push on to Burawai. We had heard there were stores and hotels (restaurants) there and a government guest house. We followed the river, our road rising high above it. Down below us tents of nomads dotted the green hillside alongside the riverbed. We could see the wisps of blue/white smoke and the colorful dresses of the *Koochie* women. The nomads were no longer Kohistanis headed down the west side of the Babu Sar to Chilas and Kohistan. Now we were riding among Afghan *Koochies* and Kashmiri *Gujars* heading down the Kaghan Valley to the warmer plains of the Hazara and the Punjab.

Our way descended over rocks toward the river through rolling grassy downs. At a place there were some horses alongside the road. Off toward the riverbed were several tents. Sitting on an orange, black, red and white diagonal diamond-patterned Afghan *kileem* rug in front of a new, white, four-door Pajaro land cruiser was a *Koochie* family; two men, half a dozen women and some children.

The two men came up to us, the first Afghans we'd seen since leaving Chitral. They thought we were traveling merchants and they poked around our saddlebags wanting to know what it was we had to sell. They couldn't see the reason why we had nothing to sale. On the contrary, we wanted to buy grass.

They informed us there was a shop around the next bend in the road where we could possibly get it. Unfortunately, the next bend meant heading way up the mountain again and then down, around and over its spurs. Over an hour later the shop was there, made of stones and adobe. In front, three Afghans and a *Gujar* were standing about. One of the Afghans had a shotgun slung over his shoulder. No grass was available. Practically the only food stuff they had was dry *dal,* and very little of that. We were told Burawai was close, just around the next bend.

"Just under the snow over there," they said, pointing at a peak ahead of us. We could reach it by nightfall, *Insh'Allah*. Horse food would be available there. All things would be available there, we were told.

There was talk regarding our firearms. One of the Afghans, looking at Mirza's pistol, asked him if it was any good. In response, Mirza pulled it out and fired a round over the roof of the store. The Afghan leveled his shotgun and fired at a boulder across the road. We decided to move on.

We'd come to know the meaning of "just around the bend'" here. Distances are measured on a grander scale in the mountains. The horses were ready to push for it. They seemed to sense our aim was to get them food. We crossed over the spur of the mountain. Mirza and Ayesha were riding. I walked way in advance, leading alone with my own thoughts. As the road started to level out they passed me. I strolled along leisurely tired, letting them ride now in the advance. The road was lined with low piled stone walls. I walked along with several children goat herders, carrying their smallest charges on their shoulders. The mountains were covered in pine trees, their tops starting to glow golden in the sinking sunlight.

Finally the way dropped and crossed an arched wooden bridge high over the river. My legs were as rubber coming up the grade on the other side of the bridge, having walked over seven hours since I had stopped riding at noon. Another half kilometer and I was in Burawai. The guest house was at the start of the town—a dozen shops, a few tents and a small stone mosque.

Mirza and Ayesha were inside the stone walled courtyard of the guest house, already unloading in the midst of a mob of 20 or so ragged *Koochies,* a very picturesque lot with sloppy, billowing turbans, bushy beards and sweeping moustaches. Rifles or machine guns were slung over their backs and their chests were crisscrossed with bandoliers filled with shiny brass cartridges. I came into the yard out of breath and was instantly surrounded, everybody talking at once.

"Noor, what are they saying?" Mirza shouted as he unbuckled his saddle. "Find out where the *chowkidar* of the rest house is and if they know where we can get any food for the horses!"

The *chowkidar* showed up and I made arrangements where to put our animals, our gear and our tired, hungry bodies. This went on while I was in animated conversation with the *Koochies* over the price of grass and where to find it. I ended up going with a local fellow back down the road and over the bridge that I had crossed coming into town. We then headed up a path into fields between stone walls and dwellings. We came to a house where women were stacking golden grass on the roof.

The local and I negotiated with an old wrinkled woman. She was speaking *Hindko*, though a different accent than Peshawari *Hindko*. We settled on six bundles weighing about 15 pounds apiece, tied with rope made of twisted grass. My new friend insisted on carrying four of the bundles and I carried two. As we crossed the bridge some young boys joined us walking into town. One of them took one of the bundles for me. I was too damn tired to be macho.

Burawai....

Good little mountain staging town at 10,000 feet. In another month it will shut down with winter, buried under the coming snows. Lying back on a carpeted platform in one of the few smoky little log eateries, we have thick, greasy goat *qurma* and heavy *chapatties*—nomad prime rib. Our souls rejoice in the relative civilization of it all. Our stomachs rejoice in the feast of hearty meat. The next day the horses relax down by the river. Mirza tries to bring his journal notes up to date. I hang out, talking with *Koochies*. Ayesha shoots endless rolls of film.

The following morning, the 12th, I leave by jeep for Naran. There is barely enough room among the other passengers and luggage to get in the two saddlebags I'm carrying to Naran so Mirza and Ayesha can ride lighter and quickly. Passing *Koochies* and *Gujars* on the narrow curvy road, I can now easily relate seeing them beat their animals to the side of the road and out of the way of our jeep. Seeing them struggle to re-adjust their packs in the clouds of our jeep's dust. All too familiar!

After three hours we pull up to a small hotel with an Urdu sign proclaiming "Pak View Hotel." Myself and the saddlebags are covered in mica-filled powdery, silvery dust. The hotel *wallah* shows me to a small room with a gravel floor, three *charpoys* and piles of travel-stained quilts and pillows. A couple of locals sit in the room with me and we chat in Pashtu. Tea is brought and some cigarettes are filled. Nice place. I like it already, all the amenities. And I'm too tired and relaxed to relocate myself and the saddlebags anywhere else. There is a good grassy place on the side of the hotel next to a stream for the horses. They all need a wash. So do we. There is even a *hammam* right down the road.

Mirza and Ayesha arrive at 3:30. They are, of course, tired. I order them food and help get the horses situated. They retire to their *charpoys* and I retire to the shop of one of my newly made friends.

The following morning we bathe the horses and follow with a trip to the *hammam* ourselves. We then ride out to visit a *Koochie* family Mirza and Ayesha had met as they were riding into Naran the previous day. They are camped just off the road on the river about two kilometers outside the village of Naran....

Ghulam and his family originally were from around Gardez in Paktia Province, Afghanistan. Before the war, in the snow-bound months they used to winter in Banu, across the border in Pakistan. But nine years ago, when the war with the Soviets intensified along the border, they had stopped going back to Afghanistan. The last three years they have been hiring a truck or a bus to carry the women, children and baggage when they migrate. Ghulam, his brother and his son go over the mountains with their flock of 200 sheep. The upper mountain tracks are too tiring for the whole family and by keeping the animals off the roads they avoid paying the Pakistani taxes. In the summer they pasture in the high meadows east of the Babu Sar and for several months during the winter they camp outside Haripur, near Tarbella Dam.

We spent the afternoon with them chatting and drinking tea, our horses grazing near their tents. Because the entire family lives under a single open-air tent, *purdah* is impractical, we were able to sit with the women of the family, young and old alike. Lovely clear weather. Unforrtunately not enough time nor energy to visit Lake Saiful Maluk, a days excursion away.

The next night we sleep in a beautiful pine wood resort hotel in Kaghan, a day ride further down the valley. The hotel is great and deserted and we have an indoor place to keep the horses. The hotel owner supplies us with inexpensive grass.

The following day is *Juma*. I wake up in an extra foul mood to still be away from Nasreen. I used to spend every *Juma* in Lahore with her. I'm lost in Pashtu Pathan thoughts and I won't even speak with Mirza and Ayesha. I ride on out of earshot as they discuss their favorite American TV shows. I can't bear to be brought back to that kind of world. Not right now.

Kaghan is so beautiful... when I can see it through my thoughts.

We finally come to a village named Pahris—not much there (not even a Hilton). We stay in the Sarhad Hotel, overlooking the road. Downstairs is a restaurant. There is a little old man with a white beard and turban standing on one of the tables praying. He has grass up the way at his house he will sell us.

We struggle to get all our gear up the narrow stairway and into a large room upstairs. We stake the horses down in a field of trees on the other side of the road. I come up the stairs after the animals are secure, the hotel manager is scooping up *charras* and tobacco from his open palm into an empty cigarette skin as we talk. It seems a decent hotel to me.

In the morning Mirza takes a bus to Pindi/Islamabad. Off on some official work to see about getting our photos taken with Benazir (Bhutto). He takes all the extra *samaan* back to Peshawar to deposit in my house so we will be able to travel as light as possible for the final haul. It's time to start riding Shokot again.

Ayesha and I fall into the morning horse routine. After they are saddled and ready we leave them tied to trees on the side of the road and go back to settle the bill with the hotel manager and get our rifles. I have a smoke with him and I'm in better spirits than I've been all week. When we get back to the horses we find Kodak has succeeded in getting twisted up in his own rope, falling off the side of the road and becoming completely entangled in barbed wire. Not without a little bit of work do we get him back on the road and ready to leave.

The way loops up and up over green rolling spurs, the river always running in the crease of the valley below us. Many contours of sloping mountains in our sight. Finally, in the early afternoon, we ride down the last eight clicks into Balakot. It's the biggest town we've seen in quite some time—real bazaar, real cement buildings, actual streets. Even three *chappli kebab* restaurants.

We stay in the fancy, multicolored, cement-slab Taj Mahal Hotel. Our room is upstairs on the second floor. It has two foam-slab beds, a ceiling fan and a bathroom. We hang the saddle blankets on the railing of the front porch and soak the feed bags in the bucket in the bathroom. They stink ripely of fermenting grain. Right next to the hotel is its number one attraction for us, a field of tall grass. We can tie our horses in it and there is nobody to complain. We see Ghulam, the *Koochie* from Paktia, and his brother in the bazaar.

On the 17th we leave at 11:00 A.M. for Gari Habibullah. Before leaving Balakot Ayesha fills the canteens from the sink faucet and I drink water from a water cooler. Signs of civilization. We stop on the road for lunch at a deserted shack, eating *chappli kebabs* wrapped in grease soaked newspaper, which we've brought from Balakot. Herc lays down and starts acting really lethargic. He rolls limply on his side and won't get up. We take off his saddle bag and saddle. He lays and rolls in the grass, his eyes glazing, covered in sweat. We douse him with cool water.

After two and a half hours I put my saddle on Shokot and ride him ponying a languid Hercules alongside. Two kilometers before arriving in Gari Habibullah we see our first *tonga*. We take the turnoff for Muzaffarabad and find a hotel right off the road near the end of town. Behind the hotel short grass covered banks lead down to the river. I walk back into town with a *tonga* driver to get grain for the horses. I end up getting the *tonga wallah's* special—*channa* and rice husks.

In the morning we bathe the horses in the river. *Pakoras, seekh kebab* and *barfi* for breakfast. We leave at 11:00 A.M. for Muzaffarabad. I'm riding Shokot. About five *clicks* out of Gari Habibullah we come to a gateway over the road. Written across it in Urdu letters are the words *Azad Kashmir* (Free Kashmir) and *Khush Almadee* (Welcome). We've reached the border—Bararkot. A policeman tells me I need to sign the arrivals book in the border post which is up some cement steps.

I stop at the bottom of the stairs. Several men are standing about, also some uniformed policemen. I tell (ask) them to bring me the book so I can sign it without having to dismount. They insist I come up the stairs and inside to sign. I'm in no mood to dicker around. I kick my heels into Shokot's flanks and angrily lead him up the cement stairs. Hercules, whose lead rope I am holding, follows closely at my side. We stop at the top. Hercules releases a massive river of piss down their steps to sounds of onlookers' laughter. I get off Shokot and hand the reins to the guard standing closest to me. I hear an official-looking man in clean white *shalwar kameez* say something about "go back to Pakistan." I figure I had better relax and start making friends.

There is some problem about bringing our guns into Azad Kashmir. I point out our arms licenses are "all Pakistan" licenses. The guard points to the back of the sign I have just ridden under that said "Welcome to Azad Kashmir." The side we are on now says "Welcome to Pakistan."

"This is Azad Kashmir," the official says, pointing back the way we have come. "that is Pakistan!"

"Let me see what kind of money you have in your wallet. Is it Pakistani or is it Kashmiri? And besides, we have this letter from the Minister of Tourism, telling all government officials to help us. You are a Muslim, aren't you?" I produce the letter from *PTDC* which by now has become a letter from the Minister of Tourism (indirectly it is).

"Well," says the official, "it does include Azad Kashmir in the list of areas

242

you plan to visit. Why don't you and your friend," he gestures at Ayesha, who is still standing down on the road with her powder blue turban and baggy, wrinkled clothes looking for all the world like an Afghan tribesman, "come with me to my quarters for a cup of tea? It's just over there."

I sign in the book and some policemen take the horses on the side of the building to tie them in the grass. We stay for tea and biscuits and to meet some of the more important locals. We refuse an invitation for lunch. We've already gotten a late enough start from Gari Habibullah and we want to get into Muzaffarabad early enough to get settled. We have no idea where we will stay in Muzaffarabad, but we do know it is a bigger city than we've been used to and bigger cities can mean bigger problems as far as hotels with horse accommodations.

After Bararkot, our road starts rising higher and higher with embankments of long fragrant tufts of grass overhanging the road. As the way nears its peak we come to a small shop with an old ice cooler out front. The shopkeeper hands up icy Gold Frost mango juice in waxen boxes with straws and we drink, still sitting on the backs of our mounts. Then over the pass and seven clicks down the mountain is Muzaffarabad. It looks big and appears bigger and bigger as more of it unfolds before our eyes. The white road markers tell us we are only 135 kilometers from Srinigar. We see our first *rickshaw*.

We enter town from the northwest, by the bus stands. It seems so smoky, noisy and dirty. So much traffic. We've been in the mountains for such a peacefully long time. Confusion on finding a hotel, riding the horses among the cars and honking buses and vans. Crowds of people gather around. We must be quite a sight. It has all become so normal for us.

Down an unpaved alleyway beside the river I find a Pathan scrapmetal dealer amid piles of crushed scrap-metal and welding shops. It all appears so industrial. There is a hotel up the hill between the alley and the road. We stake the horses on the hillside; not the most ideal pasture but better than some. Certainly better than Giti Das.

The hotel doesn't have a bathroom but it is better than Giti Das also; there is plenty of open space on the hillside where the horses are staked. Further into town better hotels are obviously available, but nightfall is approaching and we worry about finding some place that can accommodate the horses. And here we can take them down to the river for water.

The gear has to be unloaded and I still have to find them their dinner. I find a fellow down the street who takes me to a shop and unlocks the door. From a 50 kilo gunny sack he sells me 16 kilos of wheat kernels. I carry it back to the hotel in a dusty sack over my back. By the time I get back and we dole out dinner into individual feed bags it is dark.

And then it is time to see about our own food. In front of the hotel is an open fronted restaurant. *Keema*, *palak aloo*, *cholay*, mint and yogurt *chutney* and hot, *tandoor* cooked *roti*. So many things. A veritable feast! After dinner we walk over a bridge and up the twisting, windy streets to City *Tanna* to meet the Police *SHO* Razzak. We talk in his office, drink icy cold bottles of Sprite and leave a message for Mirza. We had agreed on leaving word at the police *tanna*

243

as to our whereabouts. He sends one of his older officers back with us in a *rickshaw* to make sure our accommodations are suitable.

September 20th

Muzaffarabad

Yesterday morning, when I woke up and looked at the horses I thought to myself, "We've got to find a better place for the horses." There was a small shop near the hotel that had ice cold *Shazans*. We each drank two. Ayesha and I that is. The animals were content with the river water.

Later, while "going to the bathroom" behind a bush next to Shokot, I thought, "We should also find a place with a toilet." Taking a crap on a rocky hillside behind a bush was workable in desolate mountain areas, but in the city a bathroom wouldn't be bad. We looked at a few other hotels nearby with equally lousy horse space or less, and still no bathrooms. I called the police to see if Razzak knew of some better place where we could keep the horses. He sent the man from last night and another officer in uniform. We talked. There was a pudgy, unshaven fellow with a stubbly, shaved head who had been lurking about. He hadn't said a word to us. Razzak's man introduced us to him.

"He's a very important man around here. From a very respectable family. He owns this building and most of the buildings on this street," Razzak's man explained. And that is how we met Mohammad Nawaz. He had some men bring three bundles of grass for the horses and said he would see if we could bring our animals to his house to stay.

I sat in our hotel room, surrounded by horse gear, looking out the open door at the city of Muzaffarabad layered on the hillsides across the river. A veranda overlooked the hill we were on and was the only access to the room, but being no stairs, the only way was to vault the four feet up onto it. The horses were chewing on their grass and swatting flies with their tails on the hillside sloping down from our porch to the river beyond. A fellow came and chatted for a while. He asked if I smoke.

"Sometimes," I answered, always being noncommittal and guarded.

He came back in 15 minutes with a large chunk of *charras* and a half packet of Wills cigarettes. He insisted on buying us lunch. The restaurant sent it down to the room. More *chai* and cigarettes. Later in the afternoon Mohammad Nawaz returned. He told us it was no problem; we could come along with our animals to his house. By the time we had all our gear loaded into the jeep he brought it was evening. We walked the horses across the edge of town through the dusk and dark to his house.

Mirza arrived at 11:00 P.M.

Today we found a farrier to put the new one-kilo horse shoes on Hercules which Mirza had Qayum make specially in Peshawar. Now, as we approach metaled roads again, Hercules is wearing his shoes into shiny steel wafers far too quickly. It's not as easy a maneuver for me in Urdu as in Pashtu or Farsi, but the job gets done. Shokot and Kodak can wait until Islamabad. But I can't.

Tomorrow I'm out of here.

Off to Lahore....

Chapter 24
Crystal Or Glass?

"One Moment in Annihilation's Waste,
One moment, of the Well of Life to taste,
The Stars are setting, and the Caravan
Starts for the dawn of Nothing. Oh make haste!"
Omar Khayam

September 21st
Back in the Punjab; Lahore; 10:45 P.M.

I've been wanting to see her so badly, but now I've got to mix my dreams with reality. Plus, the clumsiness of matching my sluggish faltering Pashtu with her family, with her smooth, slick tongue. She says my Pashtu is good but there is so much more I want to tell her. She's such a sweet liar.

Accompanied Mirza, Ayesha and the horses to the bridge leading out of Muzaffarabad. Then I went back to the bus stands and boarded a colorful, though dusty and decrepit bus for Rawalpindi. From there Flying Coach (almost five hours) to Lahore.

By God, Lahore is alive and buzzing on a *Jumaraat* (Thursday) night. The streets are the sights and sounds of a parade, Ali Baba gone wild. Compared to the clear air of the mountains, the air holds a dusty tepid heat. And tomorrow is *Juma*....

Arrived at 9:30 wishing my Pashtu was strong enough or I was brave enough to drop in so late at her house unexpected. What is she doing? It's hard to believe I'm in the same city as her again. Just a 15 minute *rickshaw* ride away from seeing her. No mountains or roadblocks between us.

Went out for an ice cold *Rooh Afza* and milk, rice and kebabs from a favorite street cart vender. A pack of Gold Leaf cigarettes and a traveler-sized single usage packet of shampoo. I'll have a shower and shave tomorrow morning in my usual *hammam* on the corner near the bus stands. There is anything one could want in Lahore, and definitely everything that I want.

Sultry Lahore night. Swarms of people wildly pounding drums. Dark, swarthy, shirt-less Punjabis dancing with sweaty glistening heaving chests. Pennants and flags, garishly decorated *tongas* and horse carts filled with women and girls in colorful flowing *shalwar kameez*, filmy *dupattas* wispily draped over their shoulders, dark hair and liquid eyes, golden jewelry jangling. Restaurants, pushcart vendors, traffic of every sort—cars, bicycles, design painted carts, *rickshaws* and buses, people walking everywhere. So much raw life. Such a contrast from the serenity of mountains and tiny, solitary hamlets wrapped in so much silence of the north.

My senses are overwhelmed. And tomorrow I will see her, *Insha'Allah.*

September 22nd

Lahore

Woke up in time to go to the mosque for morning prayer. My appetite is never very good in Lahore. For breakfast I had a cup of tea and a Gold Leaf cigarette waiting for the *hammam* to open. Walked to Delhi Gate and into the walled old city, through Moti Bazaar and past Wazir Khan Mosque to the Badshahi Mosque near Shahi Mohallah (Hira Mandi). Always enjoy to stroll around in Badshahi Mosque. Just killing time, waiting to go out to her house. I don't want to arrive too early. Walked over to Anarkali Bazaar and then back to the hotel.

After dropping four rolls of film from the trip off in a camera shop for developing near my hotel I caught a mini-van out to Samnabad. It was 9:30 by the time I arrived. Nasreen met me at the door. "*Salaam aleikum,* Noor Mohammad. You've come. Go in the back room and wait for me. I'm just going to the bazaar to get a few things. I'm coming back soon. Do you want me to bring you a *Shazan*?"

"No thanks, I just want you," I said.

"I'll bring you a *Shazan*. That much I can give you."

"Okay. Don't be long."

"How long has it been since you've seen me, Noor Mohammad? You can't wait another half hour?"

"I've waited this long. I'm always waiting. I can't wait another minute"

"That is what life is about. We're all waiting for something. Waiting to die."

"Okay. But don't die until I can see you again."

"*Insha'Allah*," she laughed.

She returned and came into the back room where I was sitting. She handed me a icy bottle of *Shazan*. I gave her a few of the tourmaline crystals I had purchased in Talachi, in the shadows of Nanga Parbat. "These are very special," I told her. "Some people say they have very special power."

"What are they?" she asked, fingering the long dark crystals with her long dark fingers.

"They are crystals."

She held them up to the light, looking at them curiously. "They are glass," she pronounced.

"No, they are crystals. A kind of *jewel*," I insisted.

She looked at them some more. "No. They are glass," she stubbornly insisted. She took one slender crystal and held it against the table top, pressing it firmly. It shattered. "See, I told you. They're glass," she said, convinced.

I looked at the fragmented crystal and at her, myself now partially convinced. "Maybe you are right. Maybe they are glass," I shrugged. After all, glass is a form of crystal, isn't it? What are all my perceptions, my school education worth anyway? Sometimes it seems she knows so much more. It's so much easier.

The rest of the morning I sat around relaxing and playing with her and her sister-in-law's children. I ate lunch in the sun on a *charpoy* in the yard, watching her come in and out of the back room, negotiating with pimps and johns for the other girls. A very busy afternoon for the house.

I wanted to spend the night but she said she was too tired. "Some of the girls and I stayed up all last night watching videos at our other house in Iqbal Town," she explained.

"Are you sure it was the other girls you were up with all last night?" I asked, feeling snooty. "Or maybe you have someone coming to see you tonight?"

"You don't trust me, Noor Mohammad? You know, besides my husband, you are the only one I sleep with."

"I'd like to believe you, Nasreen, so much. Something is better than nothing. But it is hard."

"Cut out this kind of talk! Come tomorrow afternoon at 5:00. I'll okay it with Mama so you can spend the night."

I went back to the hotel. I hadn't planned to be alone that night. I took a Valium early and went to sleep. I needed to catch up on my rest anyway, though I find my mind has trouble letting my body sleep lately.

The next day I lazed about dozing off the Valium running in my bloodstream. At 5:00 I picked up my photos and caught a mini-van/bus out to Samnabad. I arrived at her door at 5:15. Fazi, the servant, answered the door. He didn't seem to want to let me in. "Nasreen isn't here."

"She told me to come at 5:00. Where is she?" I demanded.

"One minute," he said, leaving me standing in the street as he went back inside. Then he came back and let me in, telling me to go in the back room. Nasreen was sleeping on the bed. Her knees were raised and her flowered *kameez* was pulled up so that her flat, wheat-brown tummy was exposed to the wind from the overhead fan. I quietly sat down across from her on the couch to wait. I watched her peacefully sleeping and breathing and was content.

At 5:30 a Punjabi servant woman came in and pulled Nasreen's *kameez* down, covering her stomach, then woke her and left the room. Nasreen looked at me, stretched like a cat and smiled. She rolled over and spit off the side of the bed onto the brick floor. Then she picked a pack of Gold Leaf cigarettes off the bed and slid two out of the red and gold box, lighting them and reaching her hand out to offer me one.

At 10:00 in the evening I was in the family room with Anwar smoking and showing him the pictures I had picked up earlier at the camera shop. Nasreen was sitting watching TV. She had seen the photos earlier. Akbar came in to look at the snaps. Seeing my gun in the pictures, he was interested in it. He wanted to see it. We had Nasreen get it from the other room where she had locked it in her personal suitcase along with my passport and money when I had arrived. We compared each other's gun licenses. Mine had a special endorsement allowing me to carry 500 rounds of ammunition, his the usual 50. We sat around and watched an Indian movie video.

At 11:30 Nasreen and I retired to the other room. She locked the door. I let her sleep. For a long time I laid next to her in the low light just watching her sleep, my lips to hers, feeling her breath, the rise and fall of her breasts. It was enough.

At 8:00 in the morning somebody knocked on the door yelling, "Nasreena!" Time to wake up. At 9:00 she left the room to bring me breakfast. She told me Mama wanted me to buy them a house in her name in Lahore, then she and I could go to Peshawar.

Later in the afternoon she said Mama wanted money for her, two *lakh* rupees. She brought me out on the veranda and sat me on a *charpoy* across from Mama, just finished from her bath. Nasreen sat on the *charpoy* behind her combing out Mama's long, wet hair. With facial expressions and dark eyes coaxing, she edged me on to talk.

Mama said she wanted three *lakh* rupees but Nasreen kept saying two *lakh*. Finally Nasreen finished combing and plaiting Mama's hair. She looked at me and said, "Okay, it's settled. Do you want to say anything else?" She took me by the hand and led me back into the room.

"Settled?" I ask. "What's settled? Is it two *lakh* or three? She kept saying three and you were saying two."

"It's two," she said impatiently, "Now what more talk is there?"

"Then I'll see about arranging the money and I'll be back as soon as possible."

"How soon?" she asked, looking at me seductively.

"I need to meet my friends in Muree and ride with them down to Islamabad," I told her. "Then I'll be back, *Insha'Allah*."

I would have been more excited, but something didn't quite feel right, like they were just playing with me. Also, just coming off this horse trip, I was somewhat perplexed as to how to initiate getting the money.

I left her house at 3:00 and arrived in Pindi at 10:00 P.M. Took a taxi out to the Muree bus stand and waded through the confusion until I found a bus. The commotion inside the bus was only worse than outside. I decided to take a cab back to the Pakeeza Hotel on College Road to spend the night. What would I do arriving in Muree after midnight, anyway?

I caught a mini-van at 6:30 in the morning, arrived in Muree and had a breakfast of *puri, halwa, cholay* and *chai*. Then I went to the police station to check on my friends' whereabouts. I found they had been through last night but had ridden on. My Urdu was too weak so they enlisted the aid of some little Pathan girls to translate for me. Leaving the station the girls wanted to know if the police had arrested me.

I took a minibus back toward Islamabad. At 10:00 I yelled for the driver to stop. We weren't anywhere near anywhere but ahead of us on the road I saw Mirza, Ayesha and the horses. I clambered down, got my boots from my saddle bag and sat on the ground by the roadside pulling them on. I got on Hercules and we headed down the mountain towards Islamabad.

Arrived at 4:00 P.M., ending up near one of the main market places, Appara Market, at the tourist camp. Ugh! Camping again! Sleeping in the tents. There was plenty of space and tall green grass for the horses. Right across the field from our camp was the sparkling white minaretted Appara Mosque.

We enjoyed the restaurants in Appara Market. I particularly enjoyed the luxury of waking to the sweet sound of *Azan*, washing and praying at the mosque in congregation and afterwards having a cup of tea and a Gold Leaf cigarette at a *chai* stall. The *chai* stall I went to was always playing the Qawali music of Aziz Mian. This lull lasted a few days....

While at the Tourist Camp, Mirza brought a *nal bandi* to do Kodak's and Shokot's shoes but I wasn't there. I had gone the night before back to Lahore to see Nasreen. I wanted to tell her how this would be a great sacrifice for me but it was worth it for her, if she was serious.

Mirza had told me one morning in Islamabad that Arif, in Peshawar, had said he would not let "a woman like that near his wife and children," and "If Noor Mohammad did this, he would just be like a common *bazaari*." Arif means a lot to me, he is my family. He is an honest, serious Muslim without being preachy, he has always accepted me for what I am. I love Nasreen and enjoy being around her when I can, but it feels as if she is just playing a game with me.

September 28th
Back in Lahore
Nasreen and I sat next to each other on the upholstered chairs just inside the doorway of the *behtak*. She had pulled me into the room right upon arrival. Mama came in and sat cross-legged on the bed across from us. The lady is always so sweet, so happy to see me. Like some fat venomous spider.

"I would never sell Nasreen," she explained. Her huge gold hoop earrings shook with her head and shone in the sunlight filtering in through the open doorway. "She is my son's wife, my younger sister's daughter, one of our clan, of our own caste."

"I just thought that Nasreen would want a clean Muslim life. That you would want it for her."

"We are good Muslims. This is our *qismet*, this is our *zot*," she told me. "I did this work, so did my mother," she laughed, putting her hand on her forehead, "and her's too. Nasreen was born into this caste."

Nasreen looked at me with a modest gaze and large lowered lovely eyes smiling and lit a cigarette. She took my hand. "I'm going to completely stop working."

"I bet."

"No, really, Noor Mohammad."

"If it is true, then I am glad for you. I can still come to visit, can't I?"

"Yeah, I like. And you said you would bring your *bhabi* to meet me."

"I will, once we get the horses back to Peshawar."

September 29th
Islamabad
Feeling lighter. Still loving her but much more accepting of the situation. I guess I needed her to beg me to take her out or at least coax me a little more seriously. *Qismet.*

The morning after I arrived back we left the tourist camp and rode through the wide avenues of Islamabad out to the base of the Margala Hills and the newly finished Saudi inspired (and funded) Shah Faisal Mosque, gleaming pure white and golden against a clear blue sky. We then cut across dirt back roads and fields riding through a few villages, edging our way southward toward GT Road. We reached it by the early afternoon. A late lunch at a tea house, the horses munching on grass growing under a small grove of trees. Colorful beflagged and bejangled trucks and buses rushed by in clouds of swirling dust, horns blaring and screeching their staccato melodies.

Two hours heading into the sunset and the North West Frontier we came to a small line of shops called Parcha Town. At the far end was a restaurant-cum-tea house decorated with colored Christmas lights and tattered, faded paper flags. Grass to tie the horses in. *Charpoys* to sleep on. Food. *Baas.*

I smoked with some truck drivers and the waiter. After the buses and the few trucks there left he went up the road to Margala and brought back some friends with a boom box, the latest Urdu and Punjabi cassettes from Karachi and Lahore and a large piece of *charras*. Cigarette after cigarette, tea and music all night long. Mirza and Ayesha pulled a *charpoy* over to a dark side of the porch and fell asleep under their sleeping bags.

I needed the sleep less then I needed the company, the music and the smoke. I walked to a little mosque in a field next to the tea house for morning prayer. As the night's final stars were setting over the mountains of the North West Frontier, I sat down at a rickety little wooden table to *parattas* and *chai*. Mirza came up to me. "What is this place Noor, the disco tea house?"

"*Ah cha,*" I nodded.

We laughed. I poured him a cup of tea and he sat down.

We rode on to the top of the Margala Pass where the road stop of Margala sits—just a few shops and a restaurant looking out on the road and down on the Punjab. On the rocky hillside beside Margala stood the granite obelisk built in 1868 in remembrance of John Nickleson.* There was a welding shop and we needed to get two of the *moogays* fixed.

From Margala we rode down to Taxila, heading north to Haripur. We stopped at the Taxila Museum, a very famous Buddhist site but I was far from the mood of thinking about or looking at aged Buddhas and stuppa ruins.** We slept on carpeted platforms at a tea house in Jaulian at the entrance to one of the ruin

---

* *Brigadier-General John Nickleson (December 11,1822-September 23,1857) was a Victorian-era military officer known for his role in British India. He was instrumental in the settlement of the Northwest Frontier and played a legendary part in the "Indian Mutiny," leading the storming of Delhi, where he died of his wounds.*

** *Taxila is an important archaeological site dating back to the ancient Indian period. It contains the ruins of the Gandharan city of Takshashila (also Takkasila or Taxila), an important Vedic/Hindu and Buddhist center of learning (6th century BCE - 5th century CE). Historically, Taxila lay at the crossroads of three major trade routes — the royal highway from Palaliputra; the northwestern route through Bactria, Kapisa, and Pulkalavati (Peshawar); and the route from Kashmir and Central Asia, via Srinigar, Mansehra and the Haripur Valley across the Khunjerab pass to the Silk Road. Its elevation above sea level is 549 meters.*

sites. A local and I rode Shokot and Hercules through a thinly running, sandy river bed which fell into a narrow lane between tall, yellowing reeds leading to a farm by a graveyard. A farmer and his sons were cutting cane in the gloaming. They sold me four bundles for 40 rupees. A good price, I thought, as it was already getting dark and where else was I going to go? Later, sitting around smoking and drinking tea with locals in the open air tea house the matter came up that I had paid money to the farmer. One of the men sitting with us counted 40 rupees out of his pocket and handed it to me. "Here, please take your money," he said. "You are our guests. He must have been a very poor man. That is why he asked for money. I am so sorry."

In the morning, after a quick look around at the ruins we rode the remaining 20 kilometers to Haripur. We found a hotel, but the horses had to be staked out on the oil-stained dirt of the *GTS* Bus stand across the street. No room for animals at the hotel. After getting settled I went over to see the horses. The fellow running the restaurant at the bus stand said he had a friend living nearby who had a much better place to keep them, a "big Khan" with a big house with an animal paddock in front. There was only one stallion there. He said we should move our mounts there. Better and safer. Sure, good luck for the horses.

The next day we met our horses' benefactor, Shariyar Khan, a nephew of Ayub Khan, the military ruler/dictator of Pakistan from 1958 to 1969. Ensuing conversation, plus a race between Shariyar on his stallion and Mirza on Shokot, led Shariyar to decide to buy our horses. He told us he was making a riding farm in Raihana, near Haripur. We knew that Akbar Ali at the Peshawar Police Horse Lines barely had enough funding to feed his own animals. We met Shariyar in the hotel restaurant and over dinner signed papers. He gave us 1500 rupees earnest money. We said we would call him when we reached Peshawar in a few days so he could collect them with a truck. Deal done.

In the morning we headed out for Tarbela. After a few hours we rode into what we were told were the Ganghar Hills, though we couldn't locate them on our maps. I had just finished saying "at least we don't have any more mountains to ride through." So much for what I say. We rode north, up and up through graveyards with black slate tombstones intricately engraved with petroglyphs.

Seven hours and 30 kilometers after leaving Haripur we rode into the little village of Sirikot. The local *chai wallah* didn't want us to stay in his tea house. Instead we bought *chai* and *pakoras* from a little wizened old man making them by the roadside. We ate, resting and relaxing for a few brief moments, deciding if we were going to tear up the town or try to push on to Ghazi, 15 to 20 clicks off. A young local fellow named Khorshid offered the use of his uncle's house, who was away in Karachi. The tall grass in the courtyard even needed mowing. Our three always-hungry beasts were the perfect mowers. A farmer brought a bundle of fresh corn stalks for them but he said he didn't have enough to sell. He was just bringing a gift. Later Shokot's back leg broke through a wooden well cover, taking three of us to pull his scraped leg up.

In the morning, outside Sirikot we came across a small shimmering *zirarat* all done in colored tile and mirror relief mosaics (a style commonly seen in the Sindh) tucked in a graveyard. Tattered flags fluttered from crooked poles. Every surface inside, including the coffin on its raised platform, shimmered with mirrors. LANDA BABA was inscribed over the doorway in Arabic.*

We reached Ghazi a little past noon. We ate lunch and continued our slow trudge heading due north on the approaches of Tarbela Dam. At the guard house (after the guards got over the initial surprise of just seeing us) our papers were checked and we were given a *chit* upon which was written in Urdu, permission to cross the Tarbela Dam—for three American Muslims, three horses and three pistols.

Riding up to the Tarbela was like riding up to a structure of ancient Egypt. The dam is a massive edifice of rocks and earth piled up, cut from the surrounding mountains in which it is nestled. It is the largest land filled dam in the world. Cascading colors of rainbow foam billowed hundreds of feet to the base of the gigantic cement spillways. Before crossing onto the top of the dam there was another guard house where we showed our permission *chit,* then we crossed the top of Tarbela Damn.

Twenty-eight more clicks to Topi. We arrived two hours after sunset. Back in *Suba Sarhad.* We stayed at the bus stand restaurant, sleeping outside on *charpoys* under quilts among the trucks, buses and horses.

The next morning was a short 18 kilometer ride to Swabi. We decided to spend the night. Feeling hot, sweaty and sick. Blood in my urine. It was the color of *Rooh Afza* (pink) and lemon *sherbet.* A decent hotel, four charpoys in a room upstairs from a restaurant and a courtyard out back to keep the animals. I paid 100 rupees for corn stalks and we ended up with more then they could eat.

Rested and dosed on Mirza's antibiotics, my urine normally colored, we left in the morning for Mardan. A long ride. In the afternoon we rode up a side road to the Ashoka Rock Edicts.** Mirza and Ayesha videoed the old rock until their battery died while I watched our mounts and chatted with locals. Then they fended off the locals while I climbed up behind the rock for a smoke. We rode on into the sunset. My urine was again as red as the swollen setting sun. It took us 12 hours to cover the total 46 clicks to Mardan, riding through town after dark to the *tonga* stand. Finally the horses were settled in front of the Mardan Police Tanna behind a low wall with a crowd of approximately 100 onlookers. Two young fellows helped me carry corn stalks back from the bazaar. In talking I discovered, much to our mutual amusement, that all three of our names were Noor Mohammad.

After the horses were fed and tucked in we took a *tonga* across town to a *musaffar khanna.* It was upstairs from a courtyard surrounded by shops, all of

---

* *Landa Baba — Syed Suleman Shah (born in Sirikot around 1800), was the son of Syed Hussain Shah and descended from Hazrat Ali Murtaza of the Mashwani Sadaat tribe from Afghanistan. He was a Pashtun sufi saint, scholar, mystic and poet.*

** *Ashoka ruled the Morian Empire, whose capital was in Patna, India. He ascended the throne about 273 B.C. After a battle in Kalinga, now the state of Orissa in Northeast India, in which he killed 100,000 people, he renounced aggressive warfare and adopted Buddhism. He decided to rule by nonviolence, ecology and conservation. All religions were tolerated in his realm. Rocks and columns were set up throughout the domain on which were inscribed descriptions of his life and policies.*

them closed at this late hour. The room left something to be desired, though it did have *charpoys*. The communal bathroom down the veranda left more to be desired. The *chowkidar* gave us a candle for light.

The next day we switched to a "real" hotel. Ayesha and I spent most of the day lazing about crashed out on the beds. Mirza went out to video the monument that honors The Guides, who were massacred in Kabul with the British Mission in 1879.* We all needed the rest. All that remained was to get back to Peshawar.

In the morning I walked with Mirza and Ayesha to the outskirts of town and set them on the road to the Kabul River ferry crossing to Pabbay (locally pronounced Pabbo). Then I caught a bus to Peshawar carrying a saddlebag stuffed with the remaining gear not needed. I dozed and awoke in Peshawar. I took a *rickshaw* to the entrance of Gari Saidan, off Sikunder Pura, and put the bag in my house, resting for half an hour. Batool, Bibi Ji's daughter, brought me a cup of tea. Then I was back out to Haji Camp for a bus to Pabbo.

There were no hotels in Pabbo and the restaurants closed at night. Where to stay? It's too close to Peshawar to need hotels. But we did. My partners would be lucky to arrive by dark and it would be very inconvenient, not to mention dangerous, to ride the last 20 clicks to Peshawar at night. I found the Pabbay Police Tanna down a long, quiet rutted dirt road. When I explained our situation they said it would be no problem for us to stay there with our horses. They didn't need to see any papers from Islamabad. I took a *tonga* out of town to where the road to the ferry crossing leaves GT Road. I walked down the road a little, but found walking rather difficult. I limped back to GT Road and squatted down to wait. *Maghrib Azan* was just starting.

It was getting dark and the gang still hadn't shown. What if they had taken some shortcut and come out on GT Road in some other place? I started walking back to Pabbo, peering through the darkness and dust of speeding traffic. At a lull in the sounds of engines, tires and horns I heard the horse bells, then I saw their silhouettes across the road in the bare lights of the shops. We were right before the road to the *tanna*. We had a room in the *tanna* and plenty of space for the animals under the trees in front.

I went with some of the policemen on the side of the jail for a smoke. Later, sitting in the room, they showed me a recent article in the Urdu Jang newspaper about a police chase and shoot-out on GT Road. I was sitting with the men who chased down the Kalashnikov firing car of heroin smugglers and filled them and their car full of machine gun fire. The *charras* we smoked had

---

* ***The Queen's Own Corps of Guides*** *was a regiment of Britain's Indian Army. It was a unit with a formidable reputation for excellence, innovation, individual initiative, endurance, daring and toughness in battle. The brainchild of Sir Henry Lawrence, the Corps had modest beginnings. When it was raised in Peshawar by Lt. Harry Lumsden in December 1846, it comprised just one troop of cavalry and two companies of infantry. However, it soon grew a fair deal in size and whatever it lacked in quantity, it never lacked in quality. It maintained the quirky "cavalry and infantry combined in the same regiment" format for many years. The Corps of Guides was always part of the crack Frontier Force brigade. They were famous for being the first unit in the Indian or British Armies to dress in khaki. They were soon followed by the other Frontier Force regiments. The Guides were comprised of British officers, plus Muslims, Sikhs and Hindus. They were headquartered in Mardan.*

come from that car.

In the morning I took the remaining saddlebag to Peshawar on a bus. I could walk, just slightly better than I could ride at this point. I rested a little, then took a *rickshaw* out beyond Haji Camp. They hadn't arrived yet. I started walking east on GT Road. I put a wad of *nuswar* in my mouth to take my concentration off the pain in my gut. Then I saw them. They were watering the horses off the side of the road at a shallow pool under some trees.

The three of us rode the final eight clicks into Peshawar City. As we came to the corner of Hashtnagri, I saw Ghulab Sayid, my neighbor, standing in front of the Royal Hotel (where he sells chickens). He was smoking a *duc* cigarette. I rode up to him and he handed me the cigarette to finish. Good to be home.

We rode past the Hashtnagri Police Tanna and tied the horses up in a small cobblestone lane next to Haji Mahboob's medicos shop on Sikunder Pura. Tea and *samosas* with Mr. Mahboob as promised before we had left. Locals who had safely arrived back home. Then up Sikunder Pura to Katchery Road to Abdul Hamid's shop, who had patiently enlarged and fitted all our saddles and tack and oversaw the construction of the pack saddle. A short visit. Ice cold bottles of Coke arrived, as usual, and were drunk.

Our little parade continued through Chowk Yadgar to Qissa Khanni Bazaar, riding among horse carts and *tongas*, buses and *rickshaws*, donkeys, cars, bicycles and pedestrians. No amount of traffic, commotion or noise could bother our horses now. Down to Kabuli Gate and Arif's shop. Cold Shazans with Arif and Mukhtiare, also promised and well deserved.

We rode out to Sherqi Tanna. Akbar Ali and the boys at the police lines were so happy and surprised to see us. The horses had finally come to familiar settings.

❖　❖　❖

Ferry at Pabbay, Kabul River, looking west

Confluence of Indus and Gilgit Rivers, near Bunji, where three mighty mountain ranges also meet — to the west the Hindu Kush; north the Karakoram; and east the Himalayas.

Indus River near Bunji, between Gilgit and Chillas

Master Ali Haider and friends, Dabgari Bazaar

see all photographs in color at:
http://www.pbase.com/noorkhan/00journalphotos

At my front door in Peshawar

Back street near my house

Buying grass in Gupis   On the road, Azad Kashmir

Photo by Ayesha S.

Photo by Ayesha S.

Chowk Yadgar, Peshawar City — Arriving back home after 5 months on the road, one of the minarets of Mahabat Khan Mosque can be seen in the background.

"Photo op" between Phandar and Pingal

Barain, Swat

My family at Bibi Ji's house, including Bunny the cat

Akbar's Fort at Attock

Photo by Ayesha S.

On the road near Muzzafarabad, Azad Kashmir

Stone hut where we stayed at Giti Das, just below the Babu Sar Top

Photo by Ayesha S.

On the road near Chilas

The Taj Mahal Hotel, Balakot

Karakoram Hwy, south of Gilgit

Dancers in Hira Mandi

Photos by Ayesha S.

Chapter 25
The Trip Is Over
(Shootout in Samnabad)

The yard in Samnabad

October/November 1989
Peshawar
The trip is over.

A week after riding back into Sherqi Tanna we met Shariyar Khan in the restaurant of the Amin Hotel on GT Road. We drove with him in his cream-colored Mercedes into the bowels of old Hashtnagri. We parked as close as possible to the entrance of Mohallah Gari Saidan and brought him up to my quarters to discuss which of the equipment he would purchase. Most of it was upstairs on the very top floor in our friend Abdul Haq's room above mine, which we had acquisitioned being that he was out of country.

Mirza wanted to keep his saddle, I wasn't attached, Ayesha never said. The pack saddle and tools we kept. The rifle *bookies* I kept to store the rifles in my house. The two saddles and all of the remaining tack and horse medicines went to Shariyar.

It was amusing, yet so typical, that although he was from such an important prominent and rich family he still had to try to get some concession on just a few thousand rupees of already very discounted tack. The horses there was no bargaining on. We had agreed cheaply enough in Haripur at 7000 rupees apiece, basically only 500 rupees over the price we had purchased them for from the Army. We didn't want to sell them to *tonga wallahs* and a possible life of drudgery. Our friends in Peshawar congratulated us on our profit. Good business, they all said. We gave Shariyar a 500 rupee concession on the tack and his pride and honor left the bargaining table intact. His two men carried the gear out to his Mercedes.

Then we drove down to Hashtnagri Chowk where we had arranged to

263

meet his cousin who was waiting with the truck. They followed us to Sherqi Tanna.

They had their ideas about how to load the horses. We never listened. We didn't need any ideas. We had done it six times before. The policemen assisted us. We redistributed the insufficient straw they had picked up before bringing the truck to the *tanna* to keep the animals from slipping. Mirza and Ayesha led them from the stable to the makeshift loading ramp constructed from the wooden slats of the tailgate of the truck and some bricks that were laying nearby.

Herc was first and he was a bit hesitant. I pulled on his lead rope while Mirza booted his butt and he jumped up the ramp into the truck. I shuffled my sandaled feet to avoid meeting with Herc's one kilo horse shoes as I tied his head into place on the left side of the truck. Then Kodak got in as effortlessly as walking to his dinner, on the right side. His usual position.

It took a little shouting and kicking to finally squeeze Shokot between the fat rumps of Hercules and Kodak in the narrow Bedford truck, but it was quickly enough accomplished. Then they were secured and ready. The truck men put the brightly painted, patterned, wooden horizontal slats back in place over the metal tailgate, completing the bright garish picture of a lion killing a deer, and the truck pulled out.

It was difficult trying to talk to Shariyar. We were still hot and tired from the loading. Our thoughts were far away in the towering northern mountains, the sounds of horse hooves, icy rushing waters and jangling trail bells, as we watched the swaying butts of our travel companions one last time, sticking over the wooden tailgate slats as the truck pulled away.

Then they were gone.

And then a few minutes later so was Shariyar Khan in his cream-colored Mercedes; and then my mind drifted back to Lahore. That night Ayesha and I took the 11:00 P.M. Flying Coach to Lahore.

It was a secret trip. None of our friends could know I was taking Ayesha to Lahore to experience Hira Mandi. Even Mirza did not approve of our trip and if Anwar or Arif knew we were going they would surely suspect I was taking her to meet Nasreen, not something Arif really wanted for his "daughter."

We arrived in Lahore at 7:00 A.M., got off the bus across from the Bad-shahi Mosque and had a breakfast of *puri, halwa, cholay* and *chai* at a street-side stall in Hira Mandi. After, we strolled and Ayesha took photos; Hira Mandi waking in the morning, the Badshahi Mosque, Wazir Khan Mosque, Sunari Mosque. We did a little shopping for cloth Ayesha was looking for.

At 10:00 we went out to Samnabad. Knocking at the metal door, Nasreen's husband's brother, Anwar, answered. We entered the yard. Nasreen came out of the family room. Though she had asked me to bring my *bhabi* (sister-in-law) she, as everyone else, seemed surprised I actually had.

She took Ayesha into the family room with her. I sat on one of the *char-poys* on the veranda. Fazi, the family servant, was dispatched to the corner store for some bottles of soft drinks. He returned shortly with two icy cold dripping bottles, a Coke and a Shazan. The Shazan was for me. Nasreen knew my preference for the mango flavored drink. The Coke was for Ayesha, as anybody in their right mind would rightfully drink Coca-Cola.

Akbar came out. We greeted.

"So you brought your *bhabi*?"

"Yeah, I said I would as soon as our horse trip was over. She's going back to America soon."

"And she became a Muslim?"

"Yeah, when they got married in Peshawar, before the start of the trip."

"That is great talk. *Allahu Akbar*—God is great."

"Yes. Truly, God is great," I echoed.

Something I love with Pakistan, with Muslims, is that Islam is always alive and deep. Always there. In any situation. Here I am, talking to a pimp who has been selling me his wife for the past two years and yet we can talk about the beauty of Islam and the greatness of God. *Allah Akbar*—God *is* great!

Mama came out and said her hellos. So nice and smiling, as if to be saying "oh, so nice to see you, my dear sweet Muslim boy." (the fat whore monger—*sta da kus oghaim*) It's nice to see you too mother. She and Akbar left the house for their other place in Iqbal Town.

A girl I had never seen before, heavily made up and wearing bright violet colored satin *shalwar kameez* brought Ayesha lunch. I wasn't hungry. The doorbell rang and Fazi let a pimp and a john into the yard and escorted them into the *behtak*. Nasreen went into the *behtak* with the other girl, then came out while the john and the other girl went into the back room and closed the door. The pimp waited in the *behtak*. Nasreen came up to me.

"Your *bhabi* doesn't know what work we do in this house, does she?" she asked.

"Of course she does. What did you think?"

"*Toba!* Why did you tell her?"

"Don't worry. It's no problem for her. She's American. She has a free open mind."

"Well today is slow. He's the only one who's been here. Come on, let's go in the family room. I'll show you my new baby."

I followed her into the family room where Ayesha was sitting with Anwar's new wife, a small Punjabi girl who didn't look any older than 15. A small baby, just a few months old was lying on the bed. "Do you like my baby?" Nasreen asked me.

"Your baby? Yours and who else's?" I replied.

"Yours, Noor Mohammad."

"Mine? I wish. Last time I was here you didn't seem very big."

"Are you sure?" she smiled.

"Well, I did look rather closely."

"*Chup shah*! (shut-up)," she reacted, putting her finger to her lips and crinkling up her pretty nose. "Well actually, he belongs to a girl in our other house. But I'm going to take care of him."

She took a ring off her long, slim, finger and tried to hand it to Ayesha.

"Thank you," Ayesha politely said. (In Pakistan a "thank you" generally implies "no thank you.")

"Tell her to take it," Nasreen told me.

"Take it," I told Ayesha, "she insists."

"Thank you," Ayesha said again, this time accepting the ring.

Nasreen then proceeded to give Ayesha some beaded earrings and a beaded necklace. She took the anklets off her own slim ankles and put them on Ayesha. She wanted to give Ayesha some shoes. They had boxes and boxes of them piled in a storage area on the veranda; left over stock from when they had a store, "Anwar's Ladies Shoes," before it had become "Anwar Video."

The other girl came back into the room and she and Nasreen emptied one box after another, trying to find a pair big enough to fit on Ayesha's large American sized feet. At last they found some slippers. Then they generously applied lipstick to Ayesha's lips, something she rarely did herself. They gave her a *dupatta* to wrap around her shoulders while she was visiting.

Ayesha took out her camera and handed it to me. We took some photos inside, then Nasreen suggested we move outside into the sunlight of the garden. We hung out. No other customers came. Very relaxed.

At 5:00 P.M. I told her we had to go to visit my friends in Gulbarg and then we planned to go to Hira Mandi so Ayesha could take photographs there. Nasreen and Anwar were really surprised I would take her to Shahi Mohallah. She's American, she doesn't have those sort of taboos, I reminded them.

"You don't want to spend the night with us?" Nasreen joked with me.

"Sure," I answered her quietly to the side. "I'll see you later."

She smiled at me.

"No. I would like to, but I need to get Ayesha back to Peshawar by tomorrow morning so our friends won't become suspicious."

Goodbyes....

Then we left for Gulbarg.

In Pakistan there is a small group of rich elite. Most have adopted more Occidental styles in furnishings and in interpreting *purdah*. My friend Nadeema is a prominent journalist in her own right; her husband a leading industrialist. They are friends of a dear mutual friend in Peshawar. Their beautiful, plush, spacious white two-story air-conditioned home is full of gorgeous European and Oriental style furniture, carpets and objects d'art.

We ate a wonderful delicately spiced dinner with her, her husband and their 18 year old daughter, all together, from impeccable china and silver place settings, sitting at a hand carved oak table and in similarly carved oak chairs. Served by servants. Not quite the same as sitting around on *charpoys* at Nasreen's house eating *bindi* (okra) and buffalo tail. Strange contrasts. Interestingly, I feel more comfortable at Nasreen's. Hmm....

I told them Ayesha wanted to photograph Hira Mandi. They are liberal people and I knew that Nadeema had connections in Hira Mandi with some well-known performers. Unfortunately, at such short notice, nothing could be arranged. Also, in this season, many of the performers were out of Lahore.

However she said later two of their servants would take us there in a car. One, a fellow from Abbottabad, Ghulam, spoke Pashtu which made it easier for me. The other, Ishaq, spoke mostly Urdu. My Urdu isn't much better than basic survival, with a smattering of jokes, poetry and cursing thrown in.

On our way to Hira Mandi, we stopped at the Shrine of Data Baba.* Ayesha had never seen it. It was after 10:00 but the action doesn't start in Hira Mandi until after 11:00. Ayesha could look around and take photographs of the shrine while we offered our night prayers in the shrine's mosque.

Ayesha was a little bewildered in the thick, dusty hot Lahore night air and the scores of ragtag beggars, cripples and deformed humans we had to wade through to reach the entrance of the shrine. It's very meritorious to give alms on the way into or out of a shrine and these types of unfortunates always congregate thickly in these places. (God must be keeping closer tabs around such places)

Inside, the rich smoke of hundreds of incense sticks sweetly wafted through the air. People were clustered around the marble lace-screened room where the tomb of the saint rested. The tomb was completely swathed in a green satin coverlet, edged with gold fringe and decorated in gold embroidered Arabic script praising **Allah**, the Prophet Muhammad (PBUH) and the saint resting in the tomb. Worshipers were looking in or kissing the fine, white carved-marble lacework, many with their palms raised skyward in front of them in supplication, offering their personal *duas* (prayers). Many others were singing in unison a song of the saint's poetry in Urdu. The walls of this room, where they weren't carved into fine lace filigree screen, were inlaid with Arabic Islamic inscriptions or verses of the saint's works in Persian, in bright shades of blue, green and red.

We left Ayesha to ponder the mystical religious significance of it all in a religion that frowns upon saint worship and to take photographs, also frowned upon in strict Islam. Actually, Data Baba Shrine has always reminded me of an Islamic version of a Sikh *gurdwara* or a Hindu shrine. Of course, Lahore is right across the border from Amritsar and seems a smaller (Islamic) version of Delhi. After all, Lahore has been a part of the Punjab for centuries innumerable, a part

---

* *Data Baba Durbar is one of the oldest Muslim shrines in the subcontinent. It houses the remains of Syed Abul Hassan Ali Ibn Usman of Hajvery, more commonly known as Data Gunj Baksh, meaning Bestower of Spiritual Treasures, one of the most important religious leaders who brought Islam to the subcontinent. Born in the Ghazni area around A.D.1009, his lineage traces to Hazrat Imam Hassan, son of Hazrat Ali. He visited Turkistan, Syria, Iraq and Iran and studied with various well-known religious scholars before settling in Lahore. Here he built a mosque and began to preach to the common people.*

He wrote both poetry and prose in Persian. His most famous work has remained the standard text on Sufism for centuries. Thousands of people still visit his tomb every year. It has a been a practice of Sufi saints coming to the Indian subcontinent to first visit the Shrine of "Data Baba." Hazrat Khwaja Muinuddin Chishti first came to Lahore to pay his respects at Data Ganj Bakhsh upon his arrival in the subcontinent. From there he was directed to settle in Ajmer Sharif (1192) to commence his spiritual mission in India. The shrine was originally built by the Ghaznavi king Sultan Zakiruddin Ibrahim in the late 11th Century and has been expanded several times since.

of the Islamic Republic of Pakistan for merely 42 years.

My two companions and I wandered to the newly completed and enlarged mosque of the shrine. Congregational prayer was over, though people were offering their prayers. Here and there people were also lying sleeping on the cool marble floors or the slightly softer *daris*. We completed our prayers and went back to the shrine area to find Ayesha.

We retrieved our shoes at the door with the aid of the attendant and the heavy, frayed, old piece of cardboard with a number scrawled on it that he had given us when we had left them. We gave him a *rupee* and made our way out through the pressing crowd and noise into the bustle of the Lahore night. People were lined up to receive the free food from the shrine's kitchens. Finding our way to the car we waded through a chaotic mass of people, cars, bicycles, *rickshaws*, *tongas* and horse carts crammed with passengers, high loaded camel carts and freely wandering water buffaloes. The vehicles' drivers made known their presence by generous (as in constant) usage of their horns and bells.

Behind us, on our right, lines of people were receiving their meal of *chapatties* and yellow runny *dal* from the shrine's several food lines. The kitchens are always serving free food to the needy. Many of life's unfortunates live their entire lives around such a complex. Free from the basic worries and problems of life, I sometimes wonder if it is they who are the unfortunates, or I.

We found our car and drove the short distance to Hira Mandi. Whatever you're doing in Pakistan, Islam isn't far. Even Hira Mandi is in the shadow of Badshahi Mosque's minarets.

We cruised around Hira Mandi until we could find an empty space to wedge our Toyota into. We walked up and down the main dancing street. Although it was past 11:00, there was very little going on. I was rather surprised at the lack of activity, a contrast from the two nights my English friend and I had spent there back in January 1988. Was it less than two years ago? So much has happened. A lifetime. Not all of the pastel-colored curtained doorways with music emanating from them that I remembered so vividly. Where were the sounds of *harmonium, sitar,* throbbing pulsing *tabla* and jangling *ghungrughan*, the girls sitting up on the balconies smiling down on passersby? The crowds of milling men were still there, as were the money changers selling crisp new one, five and ten rupee notes to shower the dancers. So were the squads of policemen patrolling with their antiquated Chinese rifles slung over their shoulders, their officers with 30 or 32 bore pistols on their hips, still looking for mischief, still looking for bribes. Dancing is legal in Hira Mandi and most other things are available, if one knows how to go about finding it.

But this night it seemed quiet. There were far less rooms than before and most of them were quiet. Many had been converted into billiard rooms. Pakistan is changing. We finally found a room with two girls who agreed to have their pictures taken whilst they danced as long as we promised to toss a minimum of 200 rupees on them. We changed 300 rupees. The music started: *tabla, harmonium* and tambourine. The girls began to dance both at once, then individually. They shook and ground their ample buttocks and hips, covered in

268

long, satin *kameez* and brocaded *shalwar*, ankles heavy with the shiny jangling *ghungrughan*. Their thick makeup bright, colorful and garish. The lead dancer was dressed in white and her partner was wearing a deep pink. She mostly sat on the couch next to me.

Ghulam, Ishaq and I took turns showering them with rupee notes. Ayesha photographed to her heart's content. Our 300 rupees didn't last long and then our wallets shed their remaining 10 and 50 rupee notes. Finally, Ayesha had her photos and we had used enough money for that kind of entertainment. The dancing didn't seem all that inspired, anyway. Neither were we.

We left Hira Mandi and Ghulam and Ishaq dropped us at the Flying Coach stand. Shortly after midnight we were on a Flying Coach, Peshawar bound.

Arriving in Peshawar at 9:00 A.M. I went to Arif and Anwar's for morning tea. I had arranged to meet Master Ali Haider at Sherbaz Khan Music Studio in Dabgari Bazaar at 10:00 A.M. Master and I have been close friends since 1982, when he was still, as he describes himself, without moustaches. He is now composer and band leader with Gulzar Alam who has become in recent years one of the more popular Pashtu male vocalists.

I walked in during a break while they were waiting for the power to come back on (load shedding*). Master, Gulzar and Farzana, a popular Pashtu female singer originally from Afghanistan, were going over the words to the intro of the song to be recorded next. It was hot and stuffy in the studio with no fans. Most of the other musicians were standing around outside in the cooler air.

After greetings, I sat next to Master and Farzana.

"Noor Mohammad, do you see Farzana?" Master said to me. Farzana giggled.

"Yes, I see her," I answered. Then looking at her, "I haven't seen you in a while. How are you?"

"I'm fine, **Allah** *shoker, al-hamdu-llilah.* How are you, Noor Mohammad? Yes, a long time. Do you still want to marry a Pathan girl? You know Sartaj, the song writer, don't you? He's in the engineering room. He said that he wants to speak to you."

I hadn't seen Sartaj in some time. I had met him years before at Shah Wali's place in Dabgari.** Sartaj told me he knew a girl in Mardan who would be perfect for me to marry. I thought I would check it out. It looked like it would never work out with Nasreen and something about Mardan rang a chord. I realized I wouldn't find a replacement for Nasreen by sitting in my house in Peshawar. Still hoped to one day re-experience that initial spark that captured me when I first met Nasreen and looked into her dark mesmerizing eyes. Am I a dreamer? How else could I break her spell? I do like the Mardani (Hashtnagar) dialect of Pashtu, and so... on the following *Juma* I went out to Sartaj's house for lunch. I met his two children and his younger brother, in his early

---

* In Pakistan, due to a shortage of electrical production, during high usage periods, such as the heat of midday, electrical service is cut off to predetermined localities at predetermined times.

** Shah Wali, a well-known Afghan singer living in Peshawar.

20's, though I didn't meet his wife or mother. Women are for cooking the meat, not to meet. His father was married to a second wife and living with her. He also had a family with her, yet still married to Sartaj's mother, though he hadn't lived with them in years. We arranged to go to Mardan the next day to talk to the family. *Insh'Allah* to meet the girl.

I arrived at his house at 9:00 as planned and we took a *rickshaw* out to Haji Camp to catch a minivan to Mardan. In the Mardan bazaar we shopped for groceries to take with us out to where they lived about eight miles outside of town. Nothing fancy, we were in Mardan, N.W.F.P. The essentials are a luxury. We bought spinach, potatoes, tomatoes, fresh green coriander and mint, some cucumbers and a few kilos of beef, which the butcher separated from the flies and chopped into pieces for us on his age-worn tree stump cutting block, wrapping the pieces in newspaper and shoving them into plastic bags. We put all of our purchases into a canvas sack and hired a Datsun (pickup) to take us out of Mardan and to the village where the girl lived.

On the way out Sartaj, who didn't want people to know I was a foreigner, told the driver I was a Pathan who went to school in America and had grown up there. That would explain flaws in my Pashtu. In an area such as this, this kind of behavior wasn't unusual. People are naturally suspicions. I've been here long enough to know. So am I. I had my 30 bore pistol in my pocket.

After innumerable rutted, dirt roads we came to a walled *kutcha* house in a rural area. The house was to our right; to our left was a smaller *kutcha* building. People came out of the house to meet us and a tall, thin man in cream colored *shalwar kameez* came out of the small building and escorted me inside, then left. Sartaj took care of the groceries while I sat in the mud room and waited.

It was a country doctor's office. There was his desk and a chair, a few more seats on one side of the room and a rickety wooden bench on the other. Behind the desk was a cabinet, its dusty shelves lined with boxes and bottles of tablets, rolls of gauze and medical tape, bottles of vitamin tonic syrup and cough medicine and green boxes of glucose. Along the wall, behind the bench, another cabinet was stuffed with ampules for pain, insulin, more injectable vitamins and boxes of disposable syringes. A framed picture of *Mr. Jinnah*, it's dusty glass cracked in one corner and an old calendar with a colorful calligraphic *"Bismillah"* in Arabic hung on the wall. A small green and white Pakistani flag stood in a brass holder on the desk along with the red flag of Khan Abdul Wali Khan's Awami Party.

Sartaj came in with the tall man. He had a neatly trimmed mustache and his clothes were freshly ironed. This was his clinic. He was also Sartaj's cousin, or like a cousin—related on his mother's side, or wife's side, or something or other. The girl in question lived in his house. Her father was like the doctor's brother, the girl like his niece or sister....

In talking he said she was 18, wheat color, slender, not too highly educated but very smart. And, of course pure Pathan. Sounded perfect, but could I see her?

While we discussed, tea and biscuits were brought. I met some locals who wandered in and other relatives of the girl. Her father wasn't there; he was in Peshawar, a problem in a telephone-less existence. The catch was, I couldn't meet the girl face-to-face without her father being there.

Lunch was brought in typical Pathan village hospitality; large platters of rice, chicken *qorma*, *seekh kebab* laying in a plate like sausages swimming in tasty spicy gravy, scrambled curried eggs, curried cauliflower and curried scalloped potatoes. A salad of sliced cucumber, tomato, onion, fresh coriander and mint and bowls of yoghurt/cumin *chutney* accompanied piles of flat, hot, freshly-cooked *roti*. After lunch sweet *qawah,* richly laced with cardamom, was served.

I'd had village hospitality in so many situations. Now I didn't care. I just wanted to see this slender, wheat-colored, Pathan girl; wanted to see if she could break the spell. After all, hadn't I stumbled on (or fell into) Nasreen by spending two days in Lahore? Looking for treasure or poison. Sometimes they can be the same.

Sartaj said he would come see me in Peshawar after talking to the girl's father.... He didn't come.

Back in Peshawar there was still cleaning up to do from the horse trip. Remaining items had to be packed into the two metal trunks to be stored away in Abdul Haq's room. Items not needed had to be given or thrown away. We had to pay final bills to the police for the horses' last week stay in Peshawar. Video footage was shot of Inspector Akbar Ali and his police crew at ease at the Sherqi Tanna police horse lines.

Mirza and I made a trip out to Dara to film cottage arms factories, RPGs and boxes of hand grenades, pistols, machine guns, anti-aircraft guns and the like.* We wanted video showing us shopping for and buying the weapons for our trip, something we had neglected in the hot weather and rush of preparation before we had set out. While there I traded Mirza and Ayesha's pistols for a 32-bore Spanish Llama pistol I had seen previously in the shop of our old friend, arms dealer Atlas Khan. They weren't remaining in Pakistan and couldn't secure permission to export their pistols out of the country.

"Ah, this will fit nicely in my vest pocket," I mused. I had been carrying my 30-bore on my hip for five months and had become used to its weight but I wanted something a little more discreet for city use. Also, I had become Pakistani enough during the trip that now I could definitely appreciate the quality of foreign-made goods. With some items the novelty of buying Pakistani doesn't quite make it. Not when your life depends on it. Even my Pakistani 30 bore SpainStar pistol has a foreign made barrel. Now, also I had the Pakistani pride of owning a foreign weapon.

---

* Dara Adam Khel on the road to Kohat, southwest of Peshawar right after the Kohat Pass, has been supplying arms to the entire tribal belt for the last 100 years. The people are basically Afridi, respected for their toughness and courage. Village gunsmiths are highly proficient in the manufacture of popular firearms, including the Kalashnikov assault rifle. Arms, ammunition, opium and charras are readily available in the local bazaar.

◆ **Ed note; "Son of a Lion (2007)" is an excellent movie filmed in and around Dara Adam Khel (by Australian filmmaker Benjamin Gilmour). This author highly recommends it to have a glimpse into life in Tribal Territories....**

We filmed Mirza test firing his pistol to sell it. We filmed me going through cases of locally made and Russian hand grenades. Also the occasional Stinger missile, some assorted rocket launchers and me panning an RPG for the camera. I did not fire it though, on the principle that they wanted an outrageous amount per rocket. Highly understandable due to its popularity nowadays in the Pakistani tribal household arsenal and the demand on the Afghan battlefield, a very sale-able item.

We also managed to video Atlas Khan pounding on the head of a large tank shell with a hammer and me firing several rounds from a Russian Dashtaka anti-aircraft gun into the mountainside, jokingly discussing the merits of its ability to scare off snow leopards in the mountainous wilds.

There were brigadiers, officials, police and friends to say thanks to, and in Mirza and Ayesha's case, goodbyes to in Islamabad, Rawalpindi and Peshawar.

In Peshawar, we were buying and packing Russian military gear for shipment back to the USA—uniforms, medals, hats, belts, dead soldier I.D. papers and books, maps, tools, plastic chemical warfare suits, mine detectors and field radios from friends in the Afghan resistance for our business "Dead Red Imports." Good business at the time, selling to military re-enactors and collectors. We had gotten in the business the previous year and basically financed the trip with it.

Mirza and Ayesha went to Islamabad to make last minute corrections and verifications on their tickets that couldn't properly be done in Peshawar. All was done by the end of October, their tickets were set—the trip was over. The three of us took the day bus down to Lahore. The next day we went to the Lahore airport. Their tickets included Lahore-Karachi, then to Bangkok, Seoul, Tokyo and Los Angeles. After they cleared security and immigration I headed outside.

My ticket had only one stop: Samnabad!

Outside the airport I saw a Pathan *rickshaw* driver I knew from previous landings in Lahore. As we discussed the current price of petrol and the fare he took me out to Samnabad. As usual, I got out indiscriminately in Pakki Thatti Chowk, not too far from her house. The driver said there used to be a Pathan "house of ill repute" down the street. I told him I knew, it was right near my friend's house, *toba*. I didn't know if he could guess I was off to that house. That it was my girlfriend's house and she and her family ran it.

It was a warm, slow, quiet day at Nasreen's house.

She and I took Adel, the baby who had been there the time I had brought Ayesha, to the bazaar. He slept most of the time on her shoulder. We were shopping for a tea set. She liked one that was a somewhat art nouveau/psychedelic pattern, but it was made from a hard plastic and I didn't like it. We decided on the one I liked more, a slightly more traditional pattern made of china.

At home I sat around smoking Gold Leaf cigarettes while Nasreen, Yasmin (Akbar's 17-year-old sister) and Anwar's wife prepared dinner on the *cholla* in the yard. She told me to go into the back room where she brought me dinner—a deep plate of pieces of beef and *bindi* cooked in tomatoes, chilies and grease served with a flat basket of *roti* covered with a cloth and a pitcher of ice water.

She put Adel to sleep on the *charpoy* in the corner under an insect canopy, arranging a large kitchen knife under his pillow. "So he won't be afraid while he sleeps," she explained. She threw a small chunk of *charras* on the table. "After you eat, fill a cigarette. I'll come back with tea." She returned with sweet milky tea. We shared the cigarette. She smiled and produced more *charras* from her pack of cigarettes. "Here, make another. I'll be right back," she said, taking the dirty plates with her as she left.

She came back in pulling the curtain shut. She shut and locked the door. We lay back on the bed and smoked the cigarette, looking at the cobwebs on the gold foil covered ceiling. The gold foil, which she had covered the walls and ceiling of the room with before I had left on the horse trip was starting to fray and small tatters were blowing in the warm air circulated by the ceiling fan. Although it was almost November and 8:00 in the evening it was still hot in Lahore.

A still hot summer night in Lahore.

Nasreen's house.

Anwar is here, as is his wife. Also Yasmin and Fazi (the servant).

After 10:00 we open the door of the room we are in. Nasreen goes out to use the bathroom. I see seven or eight, dark Punjabi-looking fellows in white, loose Punjabi-cut clothing in the yard. Some pimp bringing johns I assume. I pass them as I cross the yard to the bathroom. I hear them talking to Anwar and Fazi in Punjabi in the middle of the yard. When I come out Nasreen tells me to sit in the family room to watch TV. I can hear them talking to Anwar and Fazi in Punjabi. The words are unclear, but not the tone. It is definitely antagonistic.

I place myself in a chair facing the TV and the doorway looking out into the yard. I can't understand much of what is being said as they are speaking very quick Punjabi, but it doesn't take much vocabulary to tell that an argument is ensuing. Pakistani police, I think. I know the type. Better for me to try to stay put and be a Pathan—a Pakistani, at this point. It would be more difficult explaining my presence as a foreigner in this house. A couple of them come into the room I am sitting in. Anwar follows.

"Do you speak Urdu Khan Sahib?" they ask me politely.

"No. Very little. You don't speak Pashtu?" I return.

They return to Anwar, and Punjabi, not so politely. Nasreen enters the room, a crumpled, cream-colored shawl over her head for a *chaddar*.

"What work do you do?" they demand of Anwar.

"I have a video store on Ranjah Road, right down the street from here."

"What work do you do here? In this house?"

"This is our guest from Peshawar," Nasreen shouts, quickly looking from me to them, eyes flashing. "This is none of his business. Come outside to discuss." They leave the room.

In a minute I hear Anwar's voice raised at a high, emotional pitch. Sounds of a scuffle. Yes, it seems the style of the Pakistani police.*

Suddenly, I see Nasreen shoved by one of these slimy, greasy, dark white-suited Punjabi thugs. She flies across the doorway of the room that is my field of vision. I don't care if it's cops or not. I jump up from my chair and rush into the yard to defend my Jesse James. She's already picked up a two-by-four and is swinging it.

"They're Punjabi pimps," she yells to me, "not police. Get Akbar's gun! You know the place!"

I rush into the back room and search behind the mirror for the tiny key. I know where she keeps it as I've kept my own gun and passport in the suitcase where she stores her jewelry, money and Akbar's gun. I find the key and hastily unlock the suitcase, take out Akbar's black, 30 bore Chinese pistol and pull back the bolt. I glance down and see a shiny brass and copper cartridge. Knowing Akbar, and Pathans, I assume the clip is full, and let the bolt snap back, chambering a round.

I rush recklessly into the yard. Anwar and Fazi have somehow beaten them back to the doorway with the help of Nasreen swinging her two-by-four and Yasmin, who is wielding a length of pipe. Anwar's little wife is hiding, nowhere to be seen. Fazi picks up a clay water jug, smashing it over the shoulders and back of an assailant. It shatters and clatters to the ground, dousing him with water.

"Go! You pimps! You sister lovers!" I scream in Urdu. That much Urdu I do know. I fire two rounds into the air. The large 30 bore cartridges slam into the thick, quiet, Lahore night air. My Urdu is weak, but this they understand quite clearly. Now they don't hesitate to flee out the door and into the street. Nasreen and Yasmin swing their weapons as we chase them to their cars.

"Go man!" I fire another round.

They're scrambling into their two small, white Toyotas.

Nasreen and Yasmin's blows are raining on their shoulders and the closing car doors. Such soft feminine ladies, yet as hard as the rocks of *Puktoonistan*.

The cars take off. Yasmin takes one last bash at a fleeing trunk. The dust is settling in the light of the dim streetlights on this warm Lahore evening. Night sounds are returning after the crashing, thunderous discharge of Akbar's pistol.

"You should go now," Nasreen tells me when we re-enter the house. "You don't need to get any more involved in this."

---

* I've experienced it before when Mirza and I were beaten by Pakistani narcotic officers and falsely imprisoned in the infamous Rawalpindi Prison in 1983 on false heroin charges— manufacturing, transporting and possession! Two months later we were out of jail, though it took another two months of trial before the High Court proved the narcotic police had framed us and we were fully acquitted and permitted to stay in Pakistan.

"I am involved. I was involved the first time I looked in your eyes, *yaara*."

"No, go! They were Punjabi pimps, the sister fuckers. The sons of pigs. I throw donkeys on their mothers," she says so sweetly. "They weren't police," she continues. "We were lucky they didn't have Kalashnikovs."

"I know," I tell her. "I thought of that when I opened the fire. After I said *Bismillah*. Look, they could come back."

"They won't. We scared them."

"What if they get guns and come back?"

"Anwar, or I, can fire the pistol also. I am a Pukhtun woman!"

"No! I'll stay here until Akbar comes back with the car. Then I'll go. I don't need to be back in Peshawar until morning."

"Thank you," she says with a smile.

At midnight Akbar, Iqbal and Mama return. The pimps haven't. I make my way to the Flying Coach stands and back to Peshawar.

Gear from horse trip assembled on my rooftop in Gari Saidan. Pack saddle is in back (left of tent) and saddles and saddle bags are on the wall behind.

Sunset view from my roof, Gari Saidan

Chapter 26
Leaving Again

Wakht tereeghee (time passing)
Mid November, 1989
Lahore

After killing some early morning time walking around Hira Mandi and the narrow dimly lit back alleys of old Lahore, my blanket wrapped around me to ward off the early morning chill, I find myself in Anarkali Bazaar. From there I take a *rickshaw* out to Samnabad. Get to Nasreen's house at 10:30.

I sit on a *charpoy* in the yard with Anwar and some girls. I don't see Nas around. The door to the back room is closed. Not a reassuring sight for me. Of course, it could always be another girl in there working or somebody sleeping late. In a few minutes, Nasreen comes out and crosses the yard to the bathroom. My mind jumps to wonder what she was doing in there. No one else comes out.

I hang out with the family all day long. Nasreen works the most I have ever seen. Five trips. One time she was finished and standing at the door not three minutes after she went in and closed it. Akbar and I, who were sitting just outside the door on the veranda, looked at her and said "record time." She coyly smiled and took a cigarette from my hand. What am I having to become? It is so bizarre. Is this what she wants? Me to be more like the others, more casual and uncaring about her work? I laugh with them. It hurts so much. I have to laugh to keep from dying.

Business slows down by 4:00. Nasreen and I sit around in the back room and smoke weak *duc* cigarettes with Javid, Akbar's sister's husband. Akbar and Mama aren't around. In the evening I am in the family room with most of the family. Nasreen finishes up some house work and takes a bath, changing into soft, cotton, pastel-brown and green intricately flowered *shalwar kameez*.

We eat rice Nasreen and Yasmeen have cooked over the *cholla* in the yard. Yasmeen gets friendly with me for the first time. She wants me to bring her a skirt from America. She gives me a bottle of hair oil. Akbar, Iqbal and Mama come home. Nasreen tells me to go into the other room to wait.

At 11:00 she comes in with Adel. We lay on the bed with Adel and a Punjabi girl, talking and playing with the baby. Iqbal comes in to hold Adel and chat with me. Then just Nas and I and the baby. Then she goes out. Just me and the baby. I pat him and hold his pacifier to his mouth to keep him from crying. Finally, after midnight, she comes in, shuts and locks the door. We lay there until Adel falls asleep. I fill a cigarette and she has a few hits with me.

"I think, after today, you don't need any more sex," I tell her. She smiles a shamefaced smile. "Let's just sleep."

I hold her and stroke her to sleep. Before dawn I wake her, running my hands under her silky satin *kameez*, savoring her smooth warm skin. We cuddle and fall back to sleep to the sound of the morning *Azan*. I miss the morning prayer, but my logic tells me I need *ghuzal* (to shower) first anyway. I wake at 7:00 and just smoke a cigarette and watch her sleep until 8:00. We never make love, but that doesn't matter to me. We do have some feeling, serious talk. How seriously can she take me? At 10:00 I go out to do some shopping I need to do in Lahore. I am back by noon, then I get my bag and say goodbye.

She likes her family and her life, or so she says. And in the next breath she says she is compelled into this life. What to believe? When I leave, after seeing me to the door, she goes back into the front *behtak* to negotiate with some johns. How did I ever wrench my heart so deeply? I also am compelled.

Back in Peshawar, I see my Indian friend in the gold bazaar at an Afghan friend's shop. She is looking through piles of silver, gold, lapis and carnelian Turkoman jewelry. We drink sweet green tea—I end up buying a multicolored rhinestone covered *surma-dani* from the pile of treasure—and go to eat at the Qazzaffi Hotel in Chowk Yadgar. After we wander the darkened quiet twisted streets of the old city.

November 22nd
Busy buying Soviet military gear for "Dead Red Imports" in the USA. Monday I went to Islamabad to plead my case for a more secure visa situation. Same old answer... We'll take care of it when you get back. Come in with the girl you're going to marry." Should I say there was only one girl in Pakistan I could think of, but her husband's mother won't let me marry her.

From Islamabad I caught the 3:00 P.M. flight down to Lahore. Out at Nasreen's until 10:00. We smoked a lot and talked a lot, but there were always people coming in the room sitting around with us. Finally I paid Javid 500 rupees to let her and me go into the back room and lock the door for an hour alone together. We lay on the bed, hugged and talked.

"I know I paid to be with you," I say. "I know I can do whatever I want. But I just want to be with you, to talk to you."

"What talk?"

"I want to tell you more about the sickness AIDS. It is in Pakistan also. And very dangerous. This work is very dangerous for you."

"I don't like working, Noor Mohammad, but I must. I am forced to. I don't get pleasure from it."

"Never any pleasure?"

"Well, I did enjoy those couple nights with you," she blushed.

"I don't care about sleeping with you. Oh sure, I really enjoy it. But we're not talking about that now. I would rather see you stop working and be safe from disease. It doesn't matter if you enjoy or not, if you want to or not. You can still get AIDS if you work. Maybe when I come back from America we can spend another night together, with or without the sex."

"Yeah, I would like. You can stay a couple of nights."

"*Insha'Allah.* Do you ever think of me when I'm away?" I asked.

"Yeah. I think of you on *Jumas*," she laughed.

Then it was time to go, I said goodbye in English.

"See you tomorrow," she replied in English, just only it as a form of goodbye.

278

"I wish I could," I told her. "Well, I have to go now, I must. *Khuda hafiz*."

I walked to the door of the family room and said goodbye to the family. She saw me across the yard to the door. I hugged her in the doorway, behind the curtain. I looked at her, standing in the dark gateway... and then I walked away from her again.

Took the night Flying Coach back to Peshawar. I had missed my 6:00 flight. Arrived off the bus just before dawn. Went to an early morning *hammam* for a hot bath and the mosque for morning prayer. At home I changed my clothes, had a smoke and walked down to Arif's shop to have breakfast and chat with Anwar Khan. Then it was time to go to Shinwari Market and finish packing boxes of Soviet gear going to the USA.

I was still thinking about my last conversations with Nasreen. I had told her as much as I could about AIDS, trying to convince her of its danger. But I had forgotten to tell her to go ask a doctor about it. Am I naive or is it love (haha)? Or just insanity? I felt a doctor would be able to explain it to her better in Urdu than I in my faulty Pashtu. Feeling that pull dragging me back one more time to Lahore. I went to the PIA office in Saddar where they refunded my unused Lahore-Peshawar ticket from the previous night. I bought a Peshawar-Lahore-Islamabad ticket. Why am I so crazy?

One night when Shakeel and I returned to his shop in Chowk Nasir Khan after *Isha* prayer at the mosque he showed me the cover of an Indian movie magazine I had brought him the last time I had come from India. "Noor Moham-mad, how much did this magazine cost you?" he asked.

I wasn't sure. I looked for the price on the cover and quickly converted the Indian rupees in my head to Pakistani rupees. "Eight rupees," I said. "Why?"

"Because I told you before you went to India I would pay you for the magazine," he said. "I never did. I know you are not hungry for the money, Noor Mohammad, but you must take it." He reached into his pocket and took out a 10-rupee note.

"No, the magazine is a gift."

"No, you must take it. I must complete what I say."

"Okay, I'll take it. It's somebody's *khiriat*," I told him (money for charity)

Walking home through Meena Bazaar and Shaheen Bazaar I usually would give a rupee each to two *burqa* covered beggar ladies who usually sat a hundred yards down the bazaar from each other. They had been in the same spot for years. I couldn't divide the 10 rupee note. I really would have liked to give it to someone special. As I approached the junction at Kalan Bazaar where they sat, I heard singing. An old blind beggar was slowly coming up the street, cane in hand. I handed him the note.

"**Allah** Akbar, al-hamdu-lillah, **Allah** shoker, **Allah** Akbar!" he said, strok-ing his ash-white beard with his hands (God is great, praise to God, thank God, God is Great!).

In three days the boxes were all sent off to America. At 11:20 I was on Flight 315 to Lahore, then at her house from 1:00 to 5:00. I tried to drive the danger of AIDS into her head. She gave me *chai*, we shared Gold Leaf cigarettes and she told me again that she was going to stop working.

"I'm telling you this because I love you," I said.

"You love me," she repeated.

"Yes, you know that, even though you don't love me."

"I don't love you?"

"No, unfortunately, for you it's just business."

"Just *bizzness?* You see other people coming here, Noor Mohammad. They just come and go. Nobody stays like you do, except our family. I bring you food. I bring you tea. We've gone outside together and we sleep together. It isn't only bizzness with you."

"I hope so. I'd like to be able to still see you at least as a friend. You can be married to Akbar and you can run the business. But be careful for your health, my love."

"I am going to just run the business. I'm tired from working. Akbar has got some new, young girls. Maybe next time you come you will like one of them?"

"I don't think so. Look how long I have been coming for you. Only to see you, dear. I can't forget you. It's impossible!"

"Impossible?" she smiled mischievously.

I had to catch the plane to Islamabad at 6:00. From there I would Flying Coach it back to Peshawar. There was no more delaying. The next day I had to finish some last minute business. I was meeting Anwar for lunch, my Indian friend at 4:00 and my traditional arrival/departure dinner at Arif's at 7:00. A busy, full, last day schedule. Always hard saying good-byes. In the night a friend would drive me back to Islamabad and in the morning, as the sun rose blood red and swollen over the Punjab, I would be in a silver tube headed for the United States.

Chapter 27
Sai Chai

Wat Phra Kaew — The Temple of the Emerald Buddha

I had stayed in the USA until January 1990, then back in
Pakistan until September 1990, then back to USA. Now we pick up...

November 1990
Metro Hotel, Bangkok

Waiting for Beer.
Better clean Sai Chai's long black hairs out of the bathtub.
Drinking a cold one while the girl cleans my room. Feeling somewhat
upset with Beer, a Thai girl I had met on my way to the States in September. I
had called her from Los Angeles to tell her when I would be arriving in Bangkok,
but then she wasn't at the airport. I called her house, but they said she was
out, that she had gone to Chiang Mai for a couple of days. I was sad after the
fun time we had spent together. Felt like seeing a familiar face.

Checked into the hotel after midnight. I called down to the desk.
"Yes sir?"
"Can you arrange a girl for me?"
"Yes sir. You please wait half hour? I send boy in taxi for girl."
"No problem, but I don't want old or fat!"
"You no worry. We bring you nice *lay-dee*," he laughed good naturedly.
In Thailand the sex scene is very different from anything I have ever imag-
ined—not a seedy feeling as is usually associated with the profession. It is
really more like dating, but with the sex guaranteed. I guess it's how you look
at it, but it does seem to me that in dating you see a woman you like, be it

physically or emotionally and you want to get with her. You go out to eat, to a show, a holiday. You buy her some flowers, some jewelry, a dress. If you are a normal, healthy male you would like some chemistry to happen; to eventually sleep with her.

In Thailand you can sleep with the girl first. Cut the formalities. You're going to pay for it anyway. Putting your money down on the table and going to bed first seems very sensible. If you like that part, carry on from there. It saves time, energy and money. There doesn't seem to be a sleazy connotation here.

The time old question, "Do you want a girl?" comes across as casual and clean as if you were being asked if you want a cup of tea. People don't look at working girls all that askance. They are escorts—in the dating business. They aren't really loose woman, they are just earning their livelihood and fulfilling a much needed service. Obviously there are bad girls in this profession as in anything, but many are nice girls who are just in the business of sex and companionship. It's hard for a poor girl to earn a living in Thailand.

Is that only my male tourist take on it?

The hotel boy brings a girl with long, straight, glossy-black Chinese hair, bangs and a very short tight pink dress. She smiles shyly and sweetly as she enters the room. The boy politely stands at the door. "900 *baht* you give me sir please, for *lay-dee*. One hundred more for taxi please. Okay."

I give him the money and he shuts the door. The girl locks it from the inside and smiles at me....

I meet Sai Chai. She says she's 18 but she looks so much younger in bed I feel obscene. She undresses and preens in front of the mirror, watching herself as if watching a Madona music video. Her body is long, lithe and fresh. Her skin glows the color of warm amber. She hangs her dress on a hanger, presses it neatly several times with her hands and places it in the closet. She has a small golden Buddha, encased in a clear plastic and gold case, pinned inside her bra. She hangs my shirt in the closet. Folds my pants and places them on the end of the other bed. Then she lies at the end of my bed and slithers up my body like a burning serpent....

We wake late, shower and order coffee.

As I finish shaving she removes her towel and wipes my face, leading me back to the bed. When we do finally go outside, it's to eat spicy street food; then she wants to shop for shoes. The second day we're together she tells me,

"You pay man too much. I speak for you my boss. You only pay 600 *baht*. I speak you true. I know. I rrove you."

She's still shopping for shoes. I start to burn out. I mean, how many pairs of shoes can one look at?

"This one too tight... this one too big... this one color no goood."

"Come on Sai Chai, make up your mind!"

"Aw you nooo know. This no goood. I know."

The ones she buys she only wears a short while before she complains, "These shoose no goood. They bite me."

My mind is starting to fray around the edges.

Then Beer calls.

She confirms she was in Chiang Mai, her hometown. Her sister was ill. She sounds a bit unemotional, but maybe it's just the Buddhist in her. Buddhists are great. They let people be. I love Pakistan, though people there just don't believe in letting one be. It's just not in the culture. Practically anything goes here. It's a very easy environment, but sometimes I miss the Pakistani warmth and emotional attachments.

Beer comes to me in the afternoon, giving me her silly smile and swinging a mock punch at my arm as she enters the room. She had come to Bangkok from Chiang Mai when she was 18. She had a boyfriend there and a baby girl. The boyfriend is gone, the baby is with her mother. She had come to Bangkok like so many others in her trade to earn money for her baby and her family so they could have a better life, or even just a life.

"You hardly look any older," I joke with her. She was 19 when I had last seen her in September and now she is 20. "Happy birthday."

"Thank you very much. But why you speak to me 'happy birthday' now? You speak me before on telephone."

"Yes, but this time I get to see your pretty face when I speak you."

"Thank you, sweet mouth." She wraps a towel around herself and goes into the bathroom to take a shower. Thai girls are so clean. Beer takes lots of showers. If she drops a cigarette ash on the bed she picks it up in the end of her fingernail and flicks it into the ashtray. Far cry from Nas, cigarette ashes anywhere, on bed or carpet. Spitting on the floor. A dirty rag under the bed.

Beer makes me stand at the door before going out, buttoning my shirt sleeve cuffs and picking lint from my pants. She is energetic, dancing, bouncing to the TV's music videos as she comes across the room. Her creamy light almond skin is so very smooth, so warm. She feels good to hold. She stays up until to 2:00 in the morning reading cheap Thai romance novels, smoking Krong Thip cigarettes, her soft leg crooked over mine while I watch Thai music videos and doze. We sleep with the AC on full blast, naked with double blankets.

When I was first with her, one night I jokingly locked her in the bathroom.

"Okay. You sleep alone!" she yelled out. She knew the key. I immediately liked her sense of humor. I also immediately opened the door.

Sight seeing in Bangkok
The Temple of the Emerald Buddha and Wat Pho.* A fantastic mosaic of myriad multicolored glazed tiles, mirrors... golden spires pointing toward the blue sky glistening in the hot moist Asian sunlight. Hundreds of temple bells

---

* Wat Pho it is the largest Wat (temple) in Bangkok and is technically the oldest too as it was built around 200 years before Bangkok became Thailand's capital in 1768. However, today the Wat bears virtually no resemblance to that originally constructed, as it was almost entirely rebuilt by Rama I when the capital was moved to Bangkok. It holds dual honors of having Thailand's largest reclining Buddha image and the most number of Buddha images in Thailand.

lazily chiming in the warm winds. Thousands of Buddhas, all sizes; a 150 foot long golden reclining Buddha, gigantic feet, the soles gorgeously inlaid in mother of pearl. Beautiful to look at but compared to the Taj Mahal or Badshahi Mosque like a Disney-inspired Fantasyland dream to Heaven.

Beer takes me to a "sex show" in Patpang....

Patpang, off Suriwongse Road, in the heart of the business district of central Bangkok, is the main night spot of a wickedly wild city. The most notorious night-life probably in all of Asia, though clubs and discos of the same sort are scattered all over the city. The two main streets of Patpang are lined with clubs and bars offering everything from bikini clad go-go dancers on raised stages with bars built around them to Thai kick boxing; massage parlors and hair cutting salons where you can get more than just a haircut or massage; and restaurants where you can find more than just a meal.

The clubs' flashing neon signs accompany music blaring out the doors and sexy female hawkers in short short minis or bikinis enticingly calling the visitor in. There are also clubs with male hosts to entertain one if female entertainment isn't one's fare. In the middle of the street are the tables of entrepreneurs selling Thai handicrafts, jewelry, knock-off designer jeans, bootleg cassettes, cassette players, watches, toys and more.

The club Beer takes me to is in a dark, quiet back alley with an unassuming front. We pay our cover charge at a high window and enter through a large, heavy, wooden door; 300 baht for me, 50 for Beer. A girl leads us to a table. Inside is a mixed clientele of Occidental and Oriental, from seedy to straight-laced. There's a bar behind us and a stage in front, mirrors behind both. At the front of the stage, on either side, are chrome poles extending to the ceiling for girls to hold on to as they dance and gyrate.

The lights are down as we come in and two girls in G-strings are painting a third girl's naked body with phosphorescent paint under black lights. After the painting is finished she does a solo dance, undulating to an old Eagle's tune. Then the lights come up and a boy and girl begin a slow sensual dance to classical music. As they dance they disrobe each other and begin to having sex. It is slow and erotic, nothing about it really obscene; an x-rated ballet. But Beer is too embarrassed to watch. She may be a "lady of the night" as she had once apologetically referred to herself in a letter to me, but in matters such as this she is still shy.

After the "love" act, the entertainment gets more creative. A girl shoots darts out of her private parts while another girl holds balloons for her to pop. Three girls insert cigarettes into themselves, puffing smoke out in rhythm to music. A girl squats over a large piece of paper, twisting to the beat with a pen in her privates. When the song is finished she lifts up the paper. She has written, "Hello, welcome to Patpang, thank you."

The lights are lowered again and three girls dance with sparklers inserted between their legs. With the lights come back on a girl stands and shoots ping-pong balls from within herself into a glass between her feet. Then a girl comes on stage with a string hanging from between her legs. She slowly pulls on the string, pulling out a razor blade tied to it. There is still more string coming out of her, but she stops to pick up some paper to cut it into a doily to prove that the blade is sharp. Then she continues to pull about 10 feet of string from her and every foot another blade. A girl comes out with a banana and lays on the stage with her legs spread facing the audience. She slowly inserts the banana. A girl stands on the dance floor and catches the banana as it shoots toward her. Much of the show is more comical than hard-core sexy. People chuckle. Even Beer watches.

I go to the bathroom. The men's room, the women's room and the dressing room are all one and the same. While I stand at the urinal, an attendant comes up behind me and starts giving me a back massage. After I wash my hands she hands me a small towel to dry them on. I give her 10 *baht*. As we walk out of the club there is a warm light drizzle falling in the tepid Bangkok night air. A fellow follows us to our taxi, holding an umbrella over our heads. Beer reaches into my pocket and gives him 10 *baht*.

On the way home we see a fruit vender from the taxi window.

"Let's get a banana," I say.

"Then you can eat it," she jokes.

This time, when we get out of bed in the morning there is a slight trace of red on the sheet.

"Uh oh," she says.

"What problem?" I ask.

"My *menn* (menses) come. I cannot leave the house for three days now. Mamasan will not permit. Now I can only do housework."

"Why? It doesn't matter. We don't have to do anything."

"No. Cannot! It's not clean."

I call Miss Sai Chai. (What's a fellow on holiday gonna do?)

She knocks and lets herself in, locking the door behind her. She leaves her shoes by the door. I'm lying on the bed, a towel wrapped around my waist, reading a book. She sits on the bed and takes the book out of my hands. "Aw you. What is this? No goood! English. I don't know? I kizz you."

Her skin is smooth and smells of sweet jasmine perfume.

Today she's wearing tight jeans and a white lace transparent blouse. She looks very Chinese with her long, glossy, black bangs cut straight across her eyebrows and her dark brown almond-shaped eyes. She hangs the blouse in the closet and folds her jeans three or four times to get them exactly the way she likes. She arranges them on one side of the bed, then the other side. Then she places them on the chair. She prances into the bathroom and turns on the water.

She comes out of the shower and tears the sheets off the other bed in the room, drying her hair with them. She takes a bottle of talc out of her purse and stands in front of the mirror powdering her sleek body. White powder rains on the top of the dresser and dusts the red carpet. She leaves her towel lying on the floor. It doesn't matter to her as she messes up the room,

"It's okay. *Lay-dee* will clean room," she says as she pulls off my towel, also throwing it on the floor. "This no goood. I know. *Lay-dee* will clean. No problem."

We go out for dinner, eating spicy foods at street stalls. After, she's still shopping for shoes. She takes me to a hotel to visit her friend. Many very young girls in very short miniskirts sitting around in the hallways and coming in and out of the rooms.

"This no for tourist," she tells me. "This for Thai boy. Thai boy come and *fuck* girl for 150 *baht*. These *lay-dees* stay inside, no outside going, no walking the street. No staying the *oltel* (hotel) with men. No... boys just coming, *fucking*, then going. These young *lay-dees*, no *olwn* (old) girls. This Thai *stie* (style). You want make rove with one these *lay-dees*? I fix. No problem."

The next afternoon we're out shopping for shoes again. We're hitting the modern, air-conditioned, department type stores. After maybe my thousandth pair I blow it with her. "I've had enough, you *bimbo!* They're all the same! Make up your *fucking* mind! Let's go home."

I grab her by the arm and lead her out to the street, flag down a taxi and throw her in. Back to the hotel.

She takes a long hot bath. She doesn't like to sleep with the AC on. It gets warm and sticky in the room. I awake at night and she's entwined around my body like some smooth heated vine. She wakes and twists her body in the bed, cracking her back and neck. She throws her arms about, snapping her shoulders and wrists. She says things I can't understand.

"Is that English or Thai?" I ask. She looks at me, strangely upset.

"Aww you. I speak man. I know. You nooo English."

She says something else I can't understand. I look at her quizzically. She looks back at me, equally puzzled.

"I don't know?" she queries.

End of November 1990
Beer is back. She's still asleep next to me. Tonight we go to the airport. I leave for Pakistan.

Chapter 28
Return To Pakistan

January 1st, 1991
Peshawar City
My recent life has been relatively sanitary, until the end of November 1990, that is. Three months in America and a month in Thailand. Then I went into the bathroom of PIA flight #576 from Bangkok to Karachi. It appeared that the last time it was cleaned was several flights ago. Maybe I should have been forewarned I was headed back to Pakistan when I arrived at the Bangkok airport at 10:00 P.M. to discover the flight had been delayed until 5:00 A.M. Obviously the extra time hadn't been spent in cleaning the airplane's facilities.

And then Karachi Airport.

I guess I had also forgotten about flies. Even with the mass of humanity and open food stalls and market places of Thailand, there just weren't all the flies. Maybe they just lacked the audacity of Pakistani flies? Or were they just welcoming me home as they crawled on (caressed) my face and hands as I sat in the outside waiting lounge at Karachi International?

The dirt and the flies aside (or included), it was good to be home.

Of course, I had missed my connecting flight to Peshawar due to leaving Bangkok more than seven hours late. I put my luggage in a safe place (I hoped) and walked over to the airport mosque. Inside was gorgeous with Arabic inscriptions and multi-colored mirror mosaics, though as with so many mosques (in Pakistan), it was still under construction. Maybe because of the multitude of mosques always being built, the slow pace of construction, or both. Always another cup of tea. It was already a beautiful mosque anyway, complete or not.

It was good to be home.

I walked to some stalls just outside the terminal and bought a Gold Leaf cigarette from a *paan wallah* and had *samosas* and *chai*.

The *rickshaw wallah* at the Peshawar Airport I didn't know, though he had good friends in my neighborhood and knew many of the same people I knew. He invited me to his house, anytime, and gave me his address in Saddar Bazaar, telling me, in typically Pakistani fashion, that if he could be of any service at all I should not hesitate to call on him.

It was good to be home.

I walked up the stairs in my house. Neighbors helped carry my luggage from the *rickshaw* to my door. I was without any keys to my room. I had lost them months ago in an airplane between Bangkok and L.A. Coming up to my floor I heard coughing coming from Zora's old room. It had been empty when I had left for America. The door opened and I was greeted by a black, grinning face and bloodshot yellowed eyes shrouded in a thin, cotton blanket.

"*Asalaamo' aleikum,* brother Noor Mohammad. Welcome home. By God, much time you have been gone," he said in Peshawari accented Pashtu.

"*Waleikum asalaam.* Who are you?" I answered, never having seen him before.

"I am Iqbal and my family and I now live here in Bibi Ji's house. We have big houses in Mohallah Takia Saigan, but for a little time they are in the *grew*.* Now we are living in this room. We are your neighbors. And you are my Muslim brother. Is there any service I can do for you? I'll have my wife clean your room for you, it must be very dusty being closed for so long. Just a moment, I will bring you some tea."

"Well Iqbal, first I need to get into my room."

"Yes. Of course my brother. You have the keys, yes?" he rasped, coughing and hacking up phlegm, spitting it on the porch.

"No, I don't. That's the problem. I lost them in an airplane."

"No problem. I have some tools. We can open it. *Insha'Allah.*"

Iqbal went into his quarters and returned with a hammer and a large, bent screwdriver. Three of his children followed him. As we proceeded to break off the two padlocks holding the door his children swarmed around us on the step like dirty-faced flies swarming on sweet, spilled tea. Finally we succeeded in busting off the locks without splintering too much of the ancient wooden frame. Iqbal helped carry my luggage inside, then he backed to the door. Standing outside on the step, he poked his black head back into the room and asked, "Noor Mohammad brother, do you want to smoke some *powder*?"

"No Iqbal. I don't smoke heroin."

"Do you want to smoke some *charras*? If you can give me 10 rupees I can just now bring some."

"No thanks, Iqbal. I've been away and I haven't smoked in a while. I don't want to start yet. I have things to do and friends to see."

"Okay brother, it is as you wish. If you want it, tell me, I can get it. Number one quality, also. No problem."

"Okay Iqbal, I'll see you later. Now I have some things to attend to."

"Yes. See you later. Oh, one more thing brother Noor Mohammad."

"What's that?"

"Can I borrow 10 rupees from you?" he asked, stroking my chin with his black fingers. "I will give it back later."

Ah cha.... Good to be home.

In the middle of December dear Arif arranged for me to meet a girl, the daughter of a *naan bai* (bread baker) friend of his who lived in Swat. Arif had been with him years ago in Gujranwala, where he had been on some family matter. I knew nothing about this fellow except that he was Arif's friend, his daughter was beautiful (they said) and they lived in Mingora—about four to five hours by bus from Peshawar. Arif said give it a try. That was enough for me.

Arif had arranged that I would meet this man on the 16th in Mingora at 3:00 P.M. in front of the Dapo mosque—a mosque I had never heard of before. Arif said the fellow had seen me before at his shop and he would recognize me.

He gave me the instructions on a slip of paper in Urdu. The man's name was Molik and we would go to his house and have tea and I could look at the

---

* Grew - A form of Pakistani mortgage (in Pashtu - grana). Basically, somebody who needs a house will loan you money in exchange for staying in your house until you can repay them.

girl. He wasn't sure if I'd be allowed to speak to her or not, but it wouldn't hurt to look. Maybe there would be something there. If I liked her then I could send a delegation from Arif's family to question her. I already had a bus ticket to go to Lahore for the night of the 15th, but I turned it in. To find a serious replacement for Nasreen was becoming important for my sanity it seemed.

The morning of the meeting I woke up to chilly weather and rain. I had a cold and wanted to stay in my warm bed in Peshawar, but I wrapped myself in my blanket and walked down to the bus station. Had a steamy *chai* and caught a bus for Mingora.

Arriving in Mingora early, I visited with some friends I hadn't seen since I had gotten back from America. They told me how to find the Dapo mosque. Mingora is a small town so it wasn't far from their shop. It was raining off and on, more on than off.

At 2:45 I walked over to the Dapo mosque. I stood by the front steps. Rain was pouring down, soaking the outside of my blanket, making the inside cold and damp. The sky was dark with cloud. I stood there on the unpaved street watching the raindrops splash patterns across the mud. *Asr* prayer came and went. Nobody showed. I didn't go inside for the prayer. I didn't want to miss my "girl" connection, nor did I feel like taking off my socks and washing my face, arms and feet in cold water, or any water at all at the moment. I'd been standing in the rain for over an hour. My pistol hung hard and heavy cold in my pocket (I was waiting to meet someone I didn't know in front of a mosque in the Northwest Frontier. Caution is a sign of sanity, isn't it?).

By 4:45 nobody had shown up and I was cold, sick and angry. The rain was getting heavier. I was close to the bus stand so I caught a bus to Peshawar, not even going back to say goodbye to my friends.

Wife search, try number one—failure!

Subsequently, Iqbal and his wife said they would find me a girl to marry. One day I came home and went into my room. There was a knock on my door. It was Iqbal. He said some relatives of a girl had come and they wanted to see me. Could they come in?

Two girls in their mid-teens and another about 12 came into the room. One spoke to me in Pashtu. She told me she was the sister of the girl I was to meet. The other young lady was her cousin, the little one just a friend. She asked me some generally personal questions about my life and my plans in Pakistan, looked at some photo albums of my life in Pakistan and my family in America and chatted and giggled with her cousin in *Hindko*.

Iqbal stuck his head back in the room and invited us all over for tea. When we entered there were two women in their forties sitting cross-legged on a *charpoy* swaddled in their *chaddars*. After tea the older of the two ladies came to my room along with the two teenage girls. The girl who spoke Pashtu said the woman was her mother, the mother of the girl who was up on the marriage block. Or was it I on the block? Both of us, I presumed.

I tried talking to her in Pashtu. Iqbal had said they were Pathan. She answered through the Pashtu speaking girl. They were speaking *Hindko*. We carried on our conversation in a mixture of *Hindko* and Pashtu, using the girl as our translator. It's funny I thought, if these people are Pathan why isn't the mother speaking Pashtu? The girl told me her father was Pathan and her mother was *Shari* (Peshawari). Well, that would explain why the mother was speaking *Hindko*. She asked me questions about my life, my family, why I had become a Muslim, my plans, my property, my savings, etc. She looked at my photo albums. While we were talking Iqbal's children brought us cups of sweet, hot tea.

She told me her husband had died several years ago. They live in a small rented house in Gul Bahar with her older brother. The daughter being offered for marriage was training to be a teacher and she assured me she spoke Pashtu, Urdu and a little English, besides, of course, *Hindko*. She said they would come back in two days with the girl—then I would be able to see her.

I was busy making final arrangements with Khawja Asadullah, from whom I had purchased my house in June of last year, to finally take possession of it. It was overdue. He had been waiting for the new house he was building to be finished.

In two days, I arrived back at my house at the pre-described meeting time. As I was fumbling with the lock on my door, Iqbal came out of his room and informed me my guests had arrived and were sitting inside. He sent one of his children downstairs to get Bibi Ji. The woman, the girl's mother, had another lady sitting on the *charpoy* with her. She was about 30 years old, wearing a thin, white *chaddar* and glasses. It was her oldest daughter, also a teacher. She started gently interrogating me in Peshawari-accented Pashtu. Her sister still hadn't come. She told me her uncle wanted to meet me before I could see the girl. Besides these two ladies, Iqbal was there. So was his wife, Bibi Ji and a younger sister had also come along with the cousin.

Iqbal's children were swarming in and out of the room. Everybody was there except the girl. It was starting to annoy me that except when people were addressing me the conversation was in *Hindko*, a language very close to Punjabi and a language I only understood minimally. It annoyed me that I couldn't really even converse with the mother without one of the daughters translating. And now I had to meet the girl's uncle, be interviewed by him, before I could even see the girl.

I thought of Nasreen's house, of how all the conversation among family members was in Pashtu, a language that was beginning to feel like my own. Also I was appreciating the free way in which I met Nasreen. I didn't have to go through all of this family scrutiny, endless repeated questions and the need for various family member approval. Of course, it was an entirely different circumstance. Nasreen and I met and had our "wedding night consummation" all within the space of an hour. Maybe not the most respectable way to meet a girl, I admit, but definitely practical. I instantly knew I liked everything about her physically. As far as her ideas and feelings, well that would have to take some time. I had to learn her language.

At the time we met my Pashtu was limited to dealing with *rickshaw wallahs* and shop keepers. When I think back, it seems strange that first meeting I wasn't even comfortable enough in Pashtu to ask her name. I learned to talk to her word by word, line by line.

No, it would never do to have a houseful of relatives jabbering in *Hindko*, even if to me they spoke Pashtu. I was getting fed up, I missed Nasreen. I told them I felt if I couldn't see and meet a girl sooner than this, then she was too traditional for me. How would I bring her to America to meet and visit my family? How could she even go to America where she would have to talk to strange men in shops, etc.? I told them thank you. I also really wanted to marry into a family that spoke Pashtu in the house.

It was the end of December and I still hadn't seen Nasreen since returning from America. I wanted my Pashtu to be stronger, to have some practice before I saw her, having gotten rusty in the four months I had been away. Also, I was trying to prove to myself I wasn't so attached and that I could be in Pakistan and still stay away from her. How does one fool one's own heart?

I had been busy looking for a building for my music studio and for a girl I could marry. I still hadn't found a suitable building, nor had I even seen one girl.

December 30th I flew down to Lahore. It was great to see Nasreen again. Beer had been a pleasant distraction in Thailand. We had spent 10 fun days and nights together, we had spoken to each other several times by telephone while I was in America and had even written each other. Then I saw her quite a few times on returning to Thailand, plus Sai Chai, who was a further distraction, to say the least. But seeing Nasreen brought me back to my true heart's desire in an instant.

Thai girls are really sweet, they can really show you a good time, make you feel so comfortable, but still Nasreen, for some reason, really plugs me into the live wire. I'm trying to keep it more casual, a friend and a lover. It seems to be more the way she wants it.

I wanted to spend the night with her on New Year's Eve but she told me guests were coming from Peshawar. Really? So we were together the night before. Since we had started spending nights together, before the start of the horse trip, it had always been in the hot season. Now it was nice cuddling under a heavy quilt instead of sweating under a fan. I woke early and watched her face in the quickening morning light, feeling her warm body softly breathing next to mine. She woke at 8:00, coughing. She rolled over to the side of the bed and spit onto the brick floor. I laughed, trying to imagine Beer doing such a thing.

She went outside to the bathroom, returning with a steamy cup of *chai* for me. She lit a cigarette and snuggled down next to me under the covers. I held her tightly, not wanting my time with her to ever end, as if I could ever hold her by holding her in my arms. At 9:00 I left to do some personal errands. I returned at noon.

As I came to her corner I saw her going toward the bazaar. A flowered *chaddar* flowing over her thick dark hair. She smiled at me with her large lumi-

291

nous eyes, sparkling diamond stars in the dark night of her hair.

"Where are you going?"

"To the bazaar. Come with me," she answered.

We wandered in the bazaar, her buying small odds and ends. In one shop she wanted to buy a box made of clear plexiglass. Inside were small, badly made models of a bride and groom standing six inches high. Western style, the bride in a white wedding gown and the groom in a black tux and bow tie. Around them were flowers made of shiny colored tinsel. The groom's arm was broken and dangled from the material of his tiny jacket.

"It's really cute," she said. "Let's buy it for the house."

"It's ugly, in my opinion. And besides, the groom's arm is broken. If you look inside his pocket his wallet is probably broken, also."

Putting it down she turned her attention to clothing hanging on the wall. "Buy me a new suit, Noor Mohammad. The red one. For *Nevee Kal* (New Year). I like it."

"Umm, that's a good idea. Is that one Lahori design?"

"It's my design."

"Okay. You're my design."

"*Shhh!* People will hear."

"So?"

"It's impolite talk."

She asked the shopkeeper how much the red suit cost.

"400 rupees, ma'am."

"400 rupees!" she gasped. "Don't give me that! We'll give you 300 rupees."

"300 rupees is my cost, madame," he replied. "I don't make any profit. Give me 350, okay."

"Give him 320 rupees," she told me.

I counted the money out of my wallet. He folded the suit and placed it in a plastic bag. She took 20 rupees from my change and bought herself a bottle of red nail polish.

"Just keep all the change," I told her. "You'll get it anyway."

"*Chup ka* (shut up—quiet)!" she said, slapping my arm.

Back at the house I spend the rest of the afternoon lounging on a *charpoy* in the yard. There are three other girls sitting around waiting for work. They are all dressed up, made up and available, but I'm not here for them. My eyes are only for Nasreen. Without makeup and in rags she would look beautiful to me.

When she isn't busy around the house she sits with me to talk or share a cigarette. Iqbal enters and sits by me. It's dinner time. One of the girls brings us a bowl of food and a flat basket of *roti*. The meat is small cylindrical pieces. Nasreen comes over and laughs.

"Have you ever eaten that before?" she asks.

"What is it, buffalo tail?"

"Yeah. Is it tasty, or not?"

"Not bad, though it is a bit stringy."

"After you eat you can help me cut up some more. Our guests are coming from Peshawar later."

After we eat a girl brings us tea. She squats on the ground in front of us and picks up my pack of cigarettes. She hands one to Iqbal, one to me and takes one for herself. She lights a match, first holding it to my cigarette, then to Iqbal's. The filter on her cigarette is quickly coated red from her heavy red lipstick. Her eyes are black with surma and her eyelids made up a lustrous pearly blue-green. She's wearing shocking pink *shalwar kameez* and her black shimmering hair hangs halfway down her slim, satin covered back. Iqbal looks at her.

"Her name is Shameen, Noor Mohammad," he says. She smiles at me. Her golden earrings and nose ring jangle and glitter in the slowly softening evening light.

"Is she beautiful?" he asks. She smiles seductively.

"Yes she is," I answer.

"Do you want to go in the back room with her?" he asks. "Don't worry about her," he says, gesturing across the yard at Nasreen. She looks back and cuts him with her smile.

"No. Nasreen is my friend. I come to be here with her."

She comes over to us carrying a big flat aluminum bowl and a large, wooden-handled knife. Shameen gets up and walks away, taking the empty tea cups. Nasreen lays the bowl down on the *charpoy* and squats on the *charpoy* next to it, pushing Iqbal away.

"*Zah* (go)!" she shoos him off.

In the bowl is more raw buffalo tail. She picks up a hand-held, woven straw fan and tells me to fan the meat to keep the flies off. She holds the knife, facing upwards, between her toes and starts cutting the tail into small sections, tossing them into an empty bowl. I look at her slender feet holding the crude knife and her red, cracked toenail polish. Blood drips down the wooden handle onto her toes.

"I want to spend the night with you again tonight," I say.

"It's not possible. I told you yesterday. Wasn't last night enough?"

"Every night for my entire life wouldn't be enough! But last night was good. Thanks."

"It's not my choice. I must do as my husband wants."

"Yeah, I know. You are like a slave."

"What can I do? The back room is empty. After I finish cutting this meat we can go in there and spend some time together alone. Then you must go. You can't stay here tonight."

We go in the back room.

"Do you have any *charras* left?" she asks.

"No, we smoked all mine last night."

"Wait just a minute. I'll go and ask Iqbal." She comes back and throws a small chunk of *charras* on the bed, then turns her back to me and pulls the curtain shut over the doorway. She shuts and locks the door. "*Light off kum* (shall I turn off the light)?" she asks.

293

"Not so soon. Wait a moment."

"No. Look."

She takes two candles off the shelf and lights them, fixing the bottoms on top of a metal trunk with molten wax. "*Woose light off kum* (now shall I turn the light off)?"

"Okay, off *ka* (turn it off)." *

She lies on the bed next to me. I finish filling the cigarette and lay down, burying my face in her hair, smelling her perfume.

"A smell is coming," I tell her.

She jumps up and makes a funny face, crinkling her pretty nose.

"Not a bad smell," I laugh and pull her back down next to me. "A nice one. The scent of your perfume."

As we smoke the cigarette she asks if I will bring some candy like I had brought once or twice before from Peshawar.

"Sure," I answer casually, engrossed in playing with strands of her hair.

"Did you understand what I said?" she asks.

"Yeah," I say.

"What did I say then?" she asks, checking.

"You asked me to bring that candy I brought a couple times before. The candy I got in front of the Peshawar Flying Coach stand. The one with dried fruit and nuts, coconut and almonds covered in white sugar. Yes I understand, and I will remember, *Insha'Allah*." She laughs.

"And what do you want for you, my darling?" I ask.

"Buy me some gold," she answers, taking a brass bangle from her slender wrist. "I want gold bangles. This is my size."

"Okay, I will price them and see if I can afford them."

"You can."

"I don't know. I've spent all of my money on you. Besides, I feel funny buying gold for another man's wife."

"But you don't feel funny sleeping with me?"

"He made the decision to sell you. If not, we never would have met. Now I'm compelled. But if I bought you that much gold, I'd like to know that you can keep it. That he won't sell it. To be able to see it on you."

I reach into my bag and pull out a tiny bottle of Kahlua, feeling like an outlaw. I had gotten it on the plane when coming back from the USA.

"What is that?" she asks.

"It's a good taste. A kind of *sharab* (alcohol). I don't think you've ever tasted it."

"*Sharab!... Toba.*"

"It's just a little bit, for the taste," I say. "Try it, you'll like it."

We take sips from the little bottle. She crinkles up her nose.

"Good taste?"

"Maybe."

"*Toba*," we both say in unison.

---

* In modern usage, a mix of English and Pashtu is sometimes used, mostly by people living in major cities where English would tend to be used more.

The candles have burnt down to dripping, molten pools on the lid of the metal trunk. It is time for me to go.

"Are you coming back next week?" she asks.

"I don't think so. Maybe in two or three weeks. Why?"

"Oh, just because you used to come every week."

"That was when I thought there was a chance I could marry you. That you would come with me. But that seems impossible now. My friends are looking for a wife for me. But until now I haven't seen anyone I want to marry like you."

"How many times did you do *it* while you in America?" she changes the subject.

"What?"

"You know."

"How many times? I didn't. But maybe in Thailand."

"Maybe you'll marry a girl from Thailand?"

"If I can't marry you, who knows what I will do?"

"Your friends will find a decent girl for you to marry in Peshawar."

"Maybe.... Well, I don't want to, but I must go now." I hug her. I take her head in my hands and kiss her lips. I lower my hands brushing her sleek flanks before coming to rest on her hips.

"Happy New Year, my darling," I say. "*Insha'Allah.*"

"Happy New Year to you, Noor Mohammada," she answers. "It's cold, put on your sweater."

"Thanks mother," I say. She playfully hits my shoulder. I kiss her again. "Okay, goodbye."

"*Khuda hafiz,*" she says, always so sweetly.

In the *rickshaw* to the Flying Coach stand I take half of a blue 10-grain Valium and smoke a Gold Leaf. It's 10:30. An hour and a half from 1991. I'll be alone on the Flying Coach to welcome in the new year. My new year's celebration was last night, anyway. Tonight I plan to be asleep at midnight.

I buy a ticket for the 11:00 bus and take the other half of the Valium. I wake once in Gujranwala, chai and a cigarette; stop again in Rawalpindi, then in Nowshera. Finally I open my eyes in front of the Firdoze Cinema. I'm in Peshawar. It's 1991. Happy New Year!

Mid-January

Still in Peshawar

Haven't gone back to Lahore yet. Haven't found a place for a music studio yet. Besides talk, I haven't seen a girl yet. Shopping for gold bangles for Nasreen. Around 2000 rupees each. Thinking of when I am next going to Lahore. Nothing has changed. I think about it all the time still. It's so easy to just hop on a Flying Coach and be in Lahore—only eight bone jarring hours away.

My old student, Shahnaz, invited me over to her house the other evening. When I had taught her and her sister English at my dear friend Professor Soofi's house it had been mostly a chaperoned affair. Even when I had gone to her house it was always with Soofi. Now it was nice, though so unusual in Peshawar, to be invited by her to come over to her house alone. We drank tea in her room and talked, then we watched a Pashtu drama on TV* with her younger brothers, sisters and a servant girl. She said to call her in a few days as she had a friend working in her office (she works for an American aid organization) who wanted to meet me (about marriage). She had been trying to arrange it, though as yet I hadn't met her.

Shahnaz was looking very pretty in a collegiate sort of way. She had just come from work. I suppose her English is fairly good by now and I am honored and glad she only speaks Pashtu with me, albeit educated Pashtu, with a smattering of English words thrown in. Fortunately, I went to school in America so I understand the English.

She's pretty, yet so tame. Could I be with a secretary or a school teacher after being around someone as wild as Nasreen? I guess anything is possible, but isn't Nasreen more what I'm used to? Looser, like the rock and roll women I used to hang out with when I played in bands or my first wife and the hippy commune background she came from. Maybe I can find a singer?

Anwar Khan says he has a girl relative who is a Pashtu news reader (newscaster) for the television and radio station in Islamabad. I told Mr. Mahboob this and he disapprovingly shook his head. "I don't like it. Really, Noor Mohammad, all these women are just as prostitutes. Don't you feel it?"

Well, Mr. Mahboob, let me explain about Nasreen, Beer and Sai Chai's hair in the bathtub.

It's strange meeting someone knowing it is for the sole consideration of marriage. Being around Nasreen's family and around Shahnaz's makes me more certain than ever that I want relatives who speak Pashtu. *Insha'Allah.* It feels comfortable. I like the sound.

January 27th

Saw Nasreen again on the 23rd. I had held out just over three weeks this time. So proud of myself. Such constraint. For what?

I went down to Islamabad to get my gun license extended. On the way, at one of the numerous police check posts on GT Road crossing the Sarhad to the Punjab the police frisked everybody in the bus. They found my pistol. Showing the green, passport-size book that is my "All Pakistan" arms license was enough. It didn't matter it had expired several weeks earlier. In Islamabad they extended the licence for five years. It seemed ludicrous to have a five year arms licence, yet my three month tourist visa will expire in another month.

I went over to General Yazdani's house but he was out. I visited with his daughter for an hour. My American upbringing brought me up to her level of "caste" and conversation, though emotionally I felt of a much different caste. Actors, musicians, dancing girls and prostitutes are all of the same caste basically, and it's not the same caste as a general's pretty daughter!

The Brigadier came home and we had tea and a chat. There didn't seem

---

* *Khapuna—"footprints" to give this a time frame for the few who would know.*

as much to talk about with Deni without Mirza there. My interests lay more in the direction of dancing girls, music, Pashtu poetry and *malangs*, instead of horse racing and breeding, military campaigns and politics.

Then I caught the Flying Coach from Committee Chowk to Lahore. Spent the next day with Nasreen. We went to the bazaar shopping. I bought her another tea set. Then we went back to her house and spent a few hours alone together....

It was a slow quiet day in Lahore. We smoked and laid together for a long time, her falling asleep in my arms. When we awoke she asked me for a cigarette. I lit it and we shared it back and forth. Finishing the cigarette, she picked my wallet off the bed and looked inside it. The largest bill was a 500 rupee note. "Don't ask me for *pinzo sow rupee*," I said, mispronouncing the word for 500 *rupees*.

"Okay, I'll ask for *pinzo sowa*," she smiled, correcting my pronunciation.

"Okay, you can take it all. Just leave me enough for the bus back to Peshawar, and cigarettes and tea on the way."

"I'm getting married," she suddenly blurted out of nowhere.

"With who?" I askd.

"With a guy with a beard."

"With an old man?" I laughed.

"No, not an old man. But a guy with a short beard."

"When did you meet him?"

"When you were in *Amerika*."

"How much money is he paying your family?"

"It's not for money. It's secret talk. Don't tell anyone."

"You're joking me."

"It's not a joke. I'm leaving soon. If you don't come back quickly they will tell you 'Nasreen has gone.'"

"You're just saying that so I will come back quickly. I'll be moving into my new house in Peshawar next week. I'll have a lot to do. I wasn't planning to come back for at least a couple of weeks."

"Well, you'd better hurry or I will be gone."

"You're just trying to get me to come back sooner. I guess you need the money?"

"No, I'm telling you the truth. Soon I'll be gone. I'm even making a passport, look."

She went to her suitcase and produced three passport sized photos, holding them out for me to see. For some reason I just couldn't believe her. Sometimes we get so locked into something, we think things will always remain the same, never changing.

"Don't give me that. Hand me that other cigarette I filled earlier. Let's smoke it. Cut out the nonsense Nasreen."

We smoked and I pulled her closer to me. Half an hour later she told me, "We should go outside, we've been in the room a long time."

"Okay, but give me a kiss first," I replied.

She held her lips to mine stiffly, but didn't do anything. "I'm waiting," I said.

She laughed and relaxed moistly into my lips. As I can talk more and more freely with her it seems to get more relaxed. More friendly. Better? Unfortunately, it makes me want her even more.

A week after my last visit with Nasreen, my new place in Karimpura Bazaar was finally empty. I finished packing my belongings in my room in Hashtnagri. Raheel, Bibi Ji's son, and his wife came one day and we swept out the entire new house. Actually, Raheel and I discussed what basic fix-up work was needed and moved a few heavy items and removed the higher up cobwebs (some rooms are two stories tall) with a brush attached to a long bamboo pole while his wife swept the enclosed roof, the two patios and all four levels. She never said a word of objection even though she did the majority of the work. It all seemed so completely normal.

That same night we had scheduled a wagon to come just after *Maghrib* prayer to carry my belongings to the new house. We had figured after *Maghrib* the bazaars would be less crowded and, therefore, a more advantageous time to move. It is a long distance from Shaheen Bazaar, the closest place a horse and wagon can park, to my door.

As I finished praying in my local mosque, I heard the rolling peals of thunder and could see the beginning flashes of lightning. As I covered the short distance home, I felt the first large drops of rain splashing on my shoulders.

The wagon wasn't waiting at the entrance to my *mohallah*. Because of the rain, I didn't really care. It would be difficult enough carrying my household belongings and all the heavy boxes of recording gear down my stairs and out to the street, not to mention the walk from Shaheen Bazaar to my new house without the added complication of rain and mud. Raheel came up to my room shortly after I returned home. It was pouring now, the sky flashing with lightning, thunder rumbling over the jumbled cluttered rooftops of old Peshawar.

"Noor Mohammad, it has become raining," he told me.

"*Ah cha,* Raheel? Where is the wagon?" I asked.

"That lazy *rayda* (wagon) *wallah. Banchod!* He doesn't coming. Maybe he think rain has become too much? Shall we go and fetch him?" he asked in return.

"No Raheel, I don't think so. The mud will be too much problem. And besides, I don't want to get all my things wet."

"You're right."

"So Raheel, what are you doing tonight, now?"

"Noor Mohammad, I nothing any doing. Shall we arrange the *charras* program?"

"I don't have any Raheel, do you?"

"No I don't, but maybe I can arrange some from the black man. I will go and see." In a few minutes Raheel came back into my room. "Do you have 10 rupees, boss? Iqbal says he can bring some. Tomorrow I am getting 300 rupees pay back. Then I can personal purchasing and back you but today any personal money I have no."

"Okay, here's 10 rupees," I handed him a 10 rupee note, then I counted out another three rupees. "I know we need four Red and White cigarettes and four Rangers." *

"Okay boss. Ranger—danger."

Within a few minutes Raheel returned, a tray in hand; two cups of milky tea and a bowl of sugar, the cigarettes and a small ball of *gorda* (raw *charras)* rolled in a piece of thin, brown wax-paper bag. He poured tea. He then proceeded to press the *gorda* in the palm of his hand, adding water to get it to the consistency of chewing gum, then sticking it on a match stick and heating it, then kneading it more between his two palms. After he had turned the sticky *charras* pollen into a dark and gummy piece, he emptied the tobacco out of several cigarettes, rolling them between his two fingers. He again heated the freshly pressed *charras* with a match and crumbled it into the tobacco. He then scooped up the mixture of granulated *charras* and tobacco cupped in the palm of his hand into the empty cigarette skins and used a wooden match stick to tap down the ends.

We drank tea and talked.

Raheel seems to have it in the back of his head that I am some kind of spy or American CIA agent. He is always bringing me "top secret" confidential tidbits of news and info about the war in Afghanistan or Pakistani politics.

"May I tell you the fresh news or not, Noor Mohammad?"

"What news, Raheel?"

"Anyhow, I have some news for you and in your favor. China have find the AIDS medicine which kill the germ in 30 second. Really."

"Really? I haven't heard this yet."

"No, this is the secret government news. Nobody is know this yet. Oh yes. The Afghan Resistance delegation and USSR Vice President met in Islamabad and both agree in favor of Hekmatyar ** government and also agree to (give) back the POW and Soviet Union Vice President went to asked Najeeb *** to exchange the POW and don't stop the war because they afraid of Islamic Block with Soviet Union new Islamic states. But Pakistan is still working with Afghan *Mujahideen*."

"*Ah cha.*"

"Today I heard that Afghan *Mujahideen* attack with missile and launcher radar. Both side loss much bodies."

"*Ah cha?*"

"Oh yes. Pakistan and Afghan Resistance agree to exchange soldiers with Soviet Union, but Najeeb is refused because the meeting of Najeeb with Vice President of Soviet Union is still confidential because Professor Rabbani **** and Vice President of Soviet Union has decided to (give) back Soviet Union soldiers so Afghan *Mujahideen* backed (gave back) some Russian soldiers,

---

*   *Ranger — a cheaper and stronger, filterless cigarette that Raheel smoked*
**   *Gulbuddin Hekmatyar — an Afghan mujahideen leader, the Amir of Hizbi Islami*
***   *Najeeb — the present President of the Communist regime in Kabul*
**** *Prof. Burhanuddin Rabbani — an Afghan mujahideen leader, the Amir of Jamiyat Islami*

about 50 persons, but Russia still giving large quantity of arms to Najeeb. Two trucks of arms has caught by our force with POW of USSR. Most are belong from USSR new Muslim states."

"*Ah cha?*"

"And more news. Some *Amerikans* are still prisoner with Afghan *Mujahideen*. One is died and two are sick."

"That is too bad."

By now Raheel was filling his third cigarette.

"What are you doing?" I asked incredulous. "Why are you making so many?"

"These are Stinger Missiles boss. We are getting ready for the launch. This is brain attack."

"Raheel, I think your brain was already attacked."

"Oh yes. Four Afghan *Mujahideen* commanders is killed on the Jamrud Road. Someone first attacked with launcher rockets, then with *Kalashnikovs*. They were going to border. These were VIP for Afghan *Mujahideen*."

"Yeah?"

"The Afghan *Mujahideen* striked in Peshawar near Jinnah Park. Our police used tear gas and stopped the *Mujahideen* and beat them. Many are arrested. Then our Pakistan general Asif Nawaz went the Rome for to met Zahir Shah* for make new Afghan government from Pakistan the delegation of Afghan Resistance, namely Gulbuddin Hekmatyar also going with Pakistan delegation to Bonn and Zahir Shah will be also be met and Najeeb is agree to go to Bonn."

"Light it, Raheel."

"Just a moment, Noor Mohammad, I have news. To Najeeb the USSR Vice President has conveyed for Zahir Shah our General Asif Nawaz has conveyed. Now USSR is giving arms by the side of Russia. This conference will be failed. This is my think."

"Okay, let's light the joint, you've filled enough."

"Right boss. Give me some the matches. Today I come to your room some times ago, but door was locked. You anywhere out go, I think. I bring my new baby for your look. She is well and healthy and other baby is still excited and happy, but doing jealous with her." Raheel took a deep hit on the cigarette. Orange glowing embers fell from the end onto the bed. Our hands hit as we both reached to brush them off onto the floor at the same time. We both laughed. The embers exploded on the brick floor like splays of streaking rockets.

"Noor Mohammad, I think between you and me is tellypathy systems working perfectly exact. Mine talk will be explain to you and I hope you will be do me favor."

"What is that, Raheel?"

"I hope you will be do me favor of U.S. visa. When I writed you when in *Amerika* for this purpose I hoped you be reply as soon but, you no any reply any so soon. And please, if there is any mistake in my speak, you will be

---

* *Zahir Shah — Last King of Afghanistan (until 1972); now living in exile in Italy*

ignored."

"Don't worry. Just light the cigarette."

"Okay boss," he said, putting the third cigarette in his pocket, he continued, "This one I am taking for later, when you be sit in night office with friends in Chowk Nasir Khan."

"No problem."

"Noor Mohammad, do you know about *made in Pakistan*?"

"What is *made in Pakistan*?"

"You see, the scientists of Russia, *Amerika*, India, Japan and Pakistan became together. And the scientists from the Russia made the most strongest needle in the world. Now they said, 'Let each country take it and do something to it.'

"The Japan scientists took it and said, *'It needs a hole.'* They drilled it. The Amerikan scientists said, *'It needs a point.'* They sharpened it. The Indians said, *'It need the polish,'* they do polish it. Then they give it to the Pakistani scientists. The next day the Pakistani scientists bring back the needle. The other scientists say, *'What is this, you banchod Pakistanis have done nothing'*. But the Pakistani scientists are too much smart. They say look, and they give the other scientists a look (magnifying) glass. And the scientists look up surprised. On side of needle is wrote *'Made in Pakistan'* ."

"*Ah cha*. Thanks Raheel, see you tomorrow."

"One more talk, boss. Can you do the help for me of 50 rupees?"

"No. I told you I would not loan you any more money until you pay me back all the previous money you borrowed."

"Just this time, boss, I have some personal money problem. I hope you will be pray for me for money. And *dollar* money, not *rupee!*"

"*Insha'Allah.*"

"Then give me the permission boss, I will become go. If rain doesn't tomorrow I will be ordered *rayda* driver to here."

"You don't have any personal work to do tomorrow?"

"Noor Mohammad, I no any personal work having. If I burn, I no work!"

"Good. Then I'll see you tomorrow."

"Insha'Allah."

The next day with the aid of two Afghan *samaan wallahs* (baggage carriers) hired from the front steps of the Hashtnagri mosque we shifted all of my assorted possessions over to the new house.

Raheel informally became my contractor. Not a wise decision, but I was too distracted by life in Lahore with Nasreen to bother about thinking wisely or sanely. Besides, though I had done household repairs when I lived in the United States, everything was completely different here in Pakistan.

"We need a *woodpecker*," Raheel told me.

"Why on earth do we need a *woodpecker*?" I asked him.

"To make the door on the fourth floor you want and the windows."

I started to laugh, realizing in Pashtu the word for *carpenter* and the word for *woodpecker* was the same.

We walked to a lumber mill and asked if there were any woodpeckers available.... The carpenter we acquired was a young Afghan refugee from Kunduz named Bashir. The three of us walked back to my house and we showed him the work I wanted done. Originally, being from a country where work like this was done with power tools, I had expected it would take two or three days at most. I couldn't believe my ears when he said it would take him 10 days. Finally, he said if he brought an assistant, he could get it done in seven days, *Insha'Allah*.

We walked back to the lumber mill and the three of us chose logs, picking the few best suited to our purposes. Then, on a gigantic, antiquated, electric band-saw, standing deep in fresh fragrant sawdust, two antiquated men with bushy white beards dusted with sawdust milled the logs down to rough planks close to our requirements.

The next morning Bashir showed up at my door with his assistant, a dirty, raggy-clothed 10-year-old urchin with a smile bigger than his grimy cap. Their tools were slung over their backs in dusty, patched cloth sacks. The lumber was being carried by a donkey. I paid the donkey *wallah* 10 rupees and he turned his animal and was gone, switching the donkey's behind with a twig switch and clucking his tongue loudly.

Bashir set up on the third floor patio and began fashioning the boards to the proper sizes with rough planes. His assistant began to notch the ends of boards with an axe. Maybe my grandfather watched his father work with wood in a like manner.

Raheel worked on replacing faulty electrical switches and rewiring tube lights and ceiling fans. He fixed the kitchen drain pipe and had a water storage tank (*hammam*) made in Jungy Mohallah. I began painting, starting on the fourth floor. Every day on my way home from the bazaar I bought one or two new potted plants and began to make the third floor patio into a potted garden.

The month of *Ramazon* was rapidly approaching.

THE END?

March 1991

Third week of *Ramazon*

Leaving for Lahore. Will I see Nasreen? I don't know. She was telling the truth. She's gone! I'm going to her house to see if by some chance she has returned.

How did it happen? How did I flunk my biggest Pashtu test? It was just a simple conversation. She told me she was getting married, that she was running away. Damn, and I didn't believe her. I thought if I couldn't have her, at least she would always remain a prisoner in that house for me. I treated her casually and just wanted to party. And she was sharing her big secret with me. When I was leaving she even said, "Come soon."

We could have at least talked some more. I could have wished her luck and a happy life. But I waited too long. I didn't go right back.

And now she's gone!

I hadn't seen her in three weeks. I was at the Flying Coach stand in Pindi just about to get on a Lahore bound bus. I had been in Islamabad at the Ministry of Interior to see about having my visa extended. As I walked toward the Lahore coach on my other side I heard another conductor shouting, "Peshawar, Peshawar, Peshawar!" I figured I would go back and then see Nasreen on the following Monday. They had told me to come back to Islamabad on Sunday. (The longer I could go between visits, the better I could tell myself I was doing, though the attachment wasn't really getting any less. I was just getting more hardened to the pain of separation.)

Sunday was a repeat performance of the previous Wednesday in the Ministry of Interior. In the foyer at the reception desk, I got my *chit* giving me permission to go to the office of the visa section officer. Before the elevators, one of the security guards asked to look in my small leather hand wallet. He asked me if I had any camera or knives.

"Yes," I told him, "I do have a small camera in my bag. No, I don't mind leaving it at the reception desk."

Again, as he didn't frisk me, nor did he ask me if I had any pistol in my pocket, I found myself walking through the hallways of the Ministry of Interior with my loaded 32-bore Llama pistol in my pocket. Fortunately, for the government, I was not an assassin.

I was hoping for at least a year residence visa but all I was given was another paltry three-month tourist visa. I was told by the head visa officer when my marriage arrangements were made and I came into his office with my Pakistani bride, or bride to be, then we would discuss a more lasting visa. Hmm....

Arrived in Lahore about 10:00 P.M. on a Sunday night, two weeks before the beginning of Ramazon. Monday morning I went out to her house. As I approached her door that conversation we had had several weeks before started playing in my head.

"I'm getting married," she had said. "It's secret talk. I'm running away."

A premonition began to well up from my heart. When Anwar answered the door, the feeling only got stronger. He told me to go in the back room. Nothing unusual about that, but inside it didn't feel right. Something seemed different; I could sense she wasn't there.

While I waited, I surveyed the room. On the shelf that ran the length of the back wall I noticed something different about the family photos. Two eight by tens, one of her when she was about 15 years old and another of her and Saira taken several years ago were missing from their frames. They were her favorite pictures, ones she might have taken if she left.

Anwar came in the room and sat down. "Nasreen isn't here," he informed me.

"When will she be back?" I asked. It was possible she had only gone to the bazaar, I hoped.

"I don't know," he answered.

A pit in my stomach. "She has run away then," I stated.

"No," he quickly denied. "She's gone to Mardan to visit her mother."

"So then when will she be back?"

"I'm not sure. Maybe next week. She just left the other day."

"No, you're lying. She ran away. I know it. I can feel it."

"No really, she went to see her mother. She'll be back in a week or so," he said. "Do you want to do it with another girl? We have some beautiful girls here."

"No thanks. You know I only come for Nasreen, to be with her, just even to see her. I've been coming to see only her for the last three years. You know that. There are always other beautiful girls here, there are beautiful girls many places. My heart likes Nasreen."

"Well, come back in a week or so. She will be back by then."

I left hoping maybe Anwar had been telling me the truth and I would come back next week and she would be there and everything would be the same. Was I just being self centered? In my heart of hearts, I was burning. My heart told me she was gone. *Nothing would ever be the same.* Life has a habit of doing things like that, doesn't it? Well, God knows better. I would hope. Hope for what? That Nasreen didn't get out of her prison?

I would come back next week.

Counting days, one by one.

The next week I came back, but she hadn't. I sat in the back room with Iqbal. "She is still at her mother's in Mardan, Noor Mohammad. But she will be back before *Ramazon*."

"*Ramazon* is coming in a week, Malang, my friend. No, I don't think she will be back. I really think she has run away."

"No, she will be back, Noor Mohammad. I tell you, you will see her again."

"If God wills. I will come back a day or two before the start of *Ramazon*."

As I was walking down the street on my way to Pakki Thatti Chowk to get a *rickshaw* I saw my friend Jalil who worked at their house. In fact, he had been the one who had brought me back to the house the second time in the beginning of 1988 when I didn't even know her name.

"Jalil, my friend, do you know anything about Nasreen? Is she really in Mardan like the family tells me?" I quizzed him. "I think she ran away. She told me she was going to the last time I saw her. She said she was going to run away with a guy with a beard."

"You are right, Noor Mohammad Khan. She ran away with a guy with a short, little beard. A young and handsome fellow from Bajaur," he told me, commiserating with me. "I know you really loved her a lot. I remember when I first brought you here from Hira Mandi, back when you used to wear a turban."

"Yeah, we've known each other a long time, Jalil. How long have you been associated with their family?"

"I've been with them since I was young. Yes, I've known Nasreen since she was young. She was very beautiful then."

"She still is beautiful. But now she's gone. I guess at least it's better she isn't in that house. I just wish it were with me."

"Yes, she did all the work. She ran the business."

"Jalil, will you call me if she comes back, or if you hear anything at all about her?" I said, reaching into my pocket for a scrap of paper and a pen. "Here, take my phone number in Peshawar."

"Okay, you've been my friend for a long time. If I hear anything I will call you. Oh, and by the way, when you come next time from Peshawar, can you bring me a silver ring with a stone in it like you gave to Fazi? And a pair of good, Peshawari leather sandals, size eight?"

"Okay. Call me first thing if she returns."

Back in Peshawar, my mind was hanging on by a thread, and a slim one at that. Why hadn't I believed her? Why hadn't I gone back sooner? At least I could have talked to her more. She trusted me, shared with me such a big, important secret. And what did I do? Nothing! I asked her to light another cigarette and roll over to lay with me. If she was going and happy I could have wished her well, a good life, given her my address and told her if she ever needed me, she could contact me. I could have given her one last goodbye kiss on the forehead. Or I could have tried to talk her into going with me. My Pashtu has greatly improved since the times I used to ask her to marry me with star struck eyes.

It's like I came back and just found her dead. Gone! Right now my life seems bleak. Everywhere in this huge house I look I see she isn't. Back thinking. Sorry I let other's opinions influence me. I let my mind and logic override my heart. I told her I didn't want to marry her. I accepted it. She was ready to escape and I never offered her a plan.

Even when she warned me, what did I do? Nothing! I didn't even come back. At the last minute I could have said, "Come on, honey, don't go with some new guy, come with me. We'll make a nikka namma. I'll rent a car and wait in Pakki Thatti with two plane tickets for Peshawar. We can go to America, or any place you want to." What did I say? "You're lying to me. Cut out the nonsense. Let's get stoned." So shallow, so stupid.

I can cope with her being gone, especially if she's okay and happy. But if she is somewhere working, I've got to find her. But I think she's gone from me. I burn inside when I think I didn't believe her, I didn't go back. Does she realize how I feel? I've been so casual with her since I've been back and last year also. Just having a good time, enjoying her, "getting my money's worth," as a friend advised. What a fool! I let her down, let myself down, by acting so casual. By accepting her work and my friends' preconceived concepts. I thought I had a good thing. I could wait while I looked for a wife. I could pass time with Nasreen and the waiting wouldn't be so difficult. I used her. But my heart never stopped loving and wanting her from that very first look.

Now I've just come back from Lahore. Feeling very melancholy and lonely remembering visits to Lahore the previous three *Ramazons*. Only then, it was worth the effort. Having *Iftari* at her house. Dinner in the yard on *charpoys*, listening to the _taravi_ prayers sounding over the loudspeakers from the neighborhood mosque. Being with her. The journey back to Peshawar, our conversations fresh in my mind and the feel of her body fresh in my arms. Having _Sehri_ on GT Road usually somewhere near Gujranwala or Jhelum. Smoking one last Gold Leaf cigarette for the day, one last cup of _chai_, then on the road again.

Back in Lahore again. Anwar let me in. She hadn't come back and the family finally admitted to me they did not know where she was or if she would return. We sat on _charpoys_ in the yard and talked. Anwar asked me what I knew, what she had told me the last time I had seen her. I told him the little I knew.

"We don't know what kind of person took her. She could be anywhere, with anyone," he said. It wasn't what I needed to hear. I've heard too many tales of agents (pimps) coming from the Gulf States and finding girls in Lahore or Mingora to take back to the Gulf to use as prostitutes or to sell to rich _Sheikhs_. Maybe she ran away with somebody she loves and offered her a good chance to escape, or maybe she ran away with some slick operator and she would find herself in a worse situation than she had run away from?

Anwar told me a few details Jalil hadn't told me. How she had told them she was going to the doctor for a drip,* and then when she hadn't returned after a few hours, Yasmin went to the doctor's to find Nasreen had never even shown up there.

How could she have gone with me? With my weak language and notoriety, how could I have hidden her? Akbar came home and he joined in our conversation.

"Have you tried to find her?" I asked him.

He looked at me and said, "No, the _kus_ is gone. I'll find another girl."

The liar. I can't believe he hasn't tried to find her. She ran his business, she was his livelihood, the cynosure of the house. You're the _kus,_ Akbar, you _banchod_.

"Why don't you do it with Nargis?" he smiled like the snake he is, "She is more sexy than Nasreen was. She will make you forget all about Nasreen."

After all this time you still haven't got the point, I thought. Well, neither did I, I suppose. _Maghrib Azan_ came and we had _Iftar_. Oh how I missed having Nasreen bring me a small plate of salt and dates, a sweating pitcher of iced lemon _sherbet_.

Akbar and I did the first round of prayers on the house's two prayer rugs. Whenever I pray by his side I can't help but wonder if his prayers can do him any good. Well, they can't hurt, I guess. Dinner was served. Akbar went into the family room with Mama and Yasmin to watch television. Anwar, Jalil, two of the girls—Shameen and Noreen—and I sat around, talking and smoking _charras_.

Anwar, always the businessman, tried to get me to go for a time with Shameen into the back room. She looked pretty enough made up in her color-

---

* _In the long, hot weather many people, especially women, get glucose I.V. drips to replenish their energy and hydration._

ful turquoise satin *shalwar kameez* and glittering, golden ornaments, but that wasn't why I was there. Nobody came for business. The last couple times I've been there since Nasreen has left their business has been really down.

And now she's gone. To better or to worse, I guess I'll never know. There must be some way to find her, but how? Does she want to be found? Definitely not by them. Probably not by me, either. But I feel I must have one more chance to talk to her. What good can it do if she doesn't want to come with me? Well, I can try, make one final effort. At least I can say a final goodbye. Where can she be? Jalil did say she had gone with a Bajauri, but then can Jalil be sure?

Let's see, Bajaur. Isn't Dir in Bajaur? Or near it? Everybody there has machine guns. All of a sudden my pistols seem awfully small.

A cool drink in Bajaur Agency

307

Dir, NWFP

Takhal Studio (I used custom made quilts for soundroom walls)

Chapter 29
Stuck On Song Three
(The Road To Dubai)

"Jahnanna tuh, khoshala ohsay, ka ma pa tol omar da gham vee terr
ba she na, layla.... ru ru keda qadamuna, layla."   Pashtu song
(Darling, have a happy life, even if my entire life I will be in sadness)

May 1991
I must still be sane. I still wash. I shave. I try to eat. At least once every couple of days....

Can't find Nasreen. I peer into every car and *rickshaw* ridiculously trying to look closely at every covered woman. I gaze under the eye screen of every *burqa* for maybe a flash of her eyes, a glance of slim ankles or wrists. I'm not sure what I can do but I know if I see her, I've got to talk to her. I have my gun ready in my pocket in case someone doesn't want me to. What will I do?

I feel so empty. Life feels so empty. She must be out of Pakistan. How could I feel so hollow in the same country as her?

About Dubai....
She once said she wanted to go to Dubai. And Anwar (her brother-in-law) had mentioned she could be anywhere. Could she have met some slick operator from Dubai who talked her into going with him to the Emirates? He would know the tricks on how to get her a passport, visa and how to get her out of the country. She had shown me those passport pictures. I don't think she could have done it on her own.

May 2nd
After repeated badgering, I finally got a *nikka namma* from Anwar Khan, just in case I need it in Dubai. If I find her and she wants to get out, I can always go to the police and show them the *nikka namma* and say she is my wife and was abducted from Pakistan.

I want to go to Dubai, Sharja and Abu Dhabi. I guess I'll just take her picture, get a taxi driver and start looking. I won't do anything crazy there. Not any crazier than going there in the first place. Unless I find her, that is, and then only if she wants to come with me. Then I will do anything I have to.

Booked a ticket for May 15th to Dubai at Qazi's (Shahkeel's friend) travel agency. Returning to Peshawar on May 27th. At present it seems I don't know in the near future what country I'll be sleeping in, what woman (if any) I'll be sleeping with, what language I'll be speaking. Don't even know where I'll get money. Starting to live on credit cards. A very nice, secure feeling.

My neighbor's son is getting married. For the past week people have been coming over. Women have been playing drums at all hours. Now their relatives from Karachi are staying in my second floor *behtak*. One night I heard sounds of girls laughing at about 8:00. At first I thought the voices were coming from my guests downstairs, but the voices seemed to be coming from the third floor porch just outside my bedroom, or above. I stuck my head out of one of the opened double wooden doors.

"Good morning, sir!" I heard a girl's high-pitched, giggly voice say in gracefully accented English above me. A small, wooden window in my neighbor's brick wall overlooking my patio at the fourth floor level which is always closed was open. Two girls had their heads sticking out the little opening. Their golden jewelry sparkled against their black hair and in the dark night like stars in an Indian miniature painting.

"Morning, it isn't," I answered.

"Good afternoon then, sir," the one in front said.

"Well, that's closer. What are you doing there?" I asked.

"What are you doing?" she countered. They both laughed.

"This happens to be my house. I live here. And this patio that you're looking down on is right off my bedroom. Who are you, anyway?"

"This is our Auntie's house. We are here for our cousin's marriage. We are guests. This is also my cousin," she said, motioning with her head at the other girl. "She can't really speak much English. She wants us to talk in Pashtu so she can understand the conversation."

"Okay, let's talk in Pashtu then," I said.

"But English is better. Our Auntie doesn't understand English," they giggled. "Do you live in this big house all alone?" she continued. "Don't you get lonely?"

"No, now you are here. Why should I be lonely? Where do you live?"

"I don't live in the city. I live in a big old house out on Kohat Road. Your porch is so dark, how can you see anything?"

"Not very well," I said, reaching inside and flipping on the light switch. "Now, is that better?"

The girl who didn't speak English put her head back inside.

"You speak English good. Where did you learn it?"

"Oh, I go to an English medium school. I have just passed the matric." *

She was cute and graceful. A chance meeting. Too shy to know how far to push it. We carried on our conversation. In the morning I pinned a note to the arched shutters on my fourth floor bedroom window directly across from the window where my nocturnal visitors had been. I assumed, or hoped, the auntie couldn't read English. "Come to the window at 8:00 tonight," it read. What do I have to lose? Arranged meetings just don't seem to make it for me. Might as well give this a pull.

Still thinking of Nasreen.... Of Dubai....

---

* *Matric (matriculation) is a term that refers to the final examinations of 9th and 10th grades. It results in the issuance of SSC (Secondary School Certificate) or TSC (Technical School Certificate). After the SSC or TSC, students proceeded for 11th year of education at college.*

How will I find her if she's in some harem? Shoot my way in and out? With what? I can't take my guns with me!

There goes the phone. Another call for my neighbor. Lately I think they have given out my number to more people than I have. They get more calls than I do. Yesterday they even asked if they could put an extension in their house. It would be so convenient for me. They could answer the phone for me when I wasn't home. So thoughtful. The important calls I get are from America. Who in their house speaks English?

Another neighbor, an elderly, white-bearded *Mohmand* and his two sons want to rent out my bottom floor for 200 rupees a month. They don't seem to want to take no for an answer. I told them as a foreigner I wasn't allowed to rent to Pakistanis. That worked. And the neighbor in the house next to mine wants to connect to my Sui Gas connection. Remembering Nasreen's family, lately they don't seem so lecherous.

May 6th
Plans....

Tell Dubai police she is my wife and she ran away. I've got the *nikka namma* to prove it. What if I go to the police with the *nikka namma* and try to have them find her? What if they do and she wants to be there? Likes what she's doing? I don't want to mess up things for her if she's happy. I just want to see her. To talk to her. Can I sign a *talaq namma* and release her from the supposed marriage?

I was informed the police could probably tell the fingerprint wasn't hers (unlettered people in Pakistan use their fingerprints as signatures). My friend's brother, a fingerprint expert at the police academy in Islamabad, told me if you put a slightly smaller fingerprint over the first print, no one in the world could tell whose it was. Done. Who knows what I am getting into? But seems I can only get out by going through.

May 10th
Juma

Woke up this morning missing her, as usual.

Went down to Dabgari at 10:00 A.M. to Gulzar's. Met Master (Ali Haider) and went to his cousin's wedding, for rice and congratulations. Then we went back to Master's house in Shardon and sat around in the *behtak* listening to two new Gulzar cassettes, newly released, recorded in each of Peshawar's two existing studios. We compared the sound.

I told Gulzar the entire story of Nasreen.

"Pakistanis are, how you say, very narrow-minded," he said when I told him fears of my social standing in Peshawar had greatly affected my relationship with Nasreen. "I am a singer," he continued. "If there is anything I can do, just ask. I understand this kind of love. Don't be shy with us."

Gulzar went home to be with his family. Master and I walked through

Kabiristan,* past ruined Mughal brick walls and tombs and the green lawns and flowering bushes of Wazir Bagh** to Farzana's house. We were on a diplomatic mission. Master was supposed to record a new cassette with her, but she didn't want to work with him because some people had spread a rumor that he had said he had taken certain liberties with her.

Farzana's mother met us at the door, welcoming us with a firm handshake. Farzana entered the room and said hellos, also shaking our hands. We sat in the *behtak* with her, her father and her mother with a suckling child at her breast, spitting *nuswar* over her shoulder onto the brick floor. Her younger brother sat with us and a younger sister brought *chai*. Farzana may be one of the current top, young, female Pashtu singers, but she still lives with her family—a normal family life.

Master explained how it was that the rumors were spread by some *bekar* musicians who were jealous he was recording with her. When we left Farzana and her mother both saw us to the door. They each shook our hands again. Her mother kissed Master's forehead. He had known them since he was a young boy. He confided in me Farzana's mother was a "little bit crazy."

Qazi says I don't need a visa for Dubai (UAE). United Arab Emirates Travels in Saddar Bazaar says I do. They say it only takes one day to get at the embassy in Islamabad so I take the *GTS* bus to Pindi, then a taxi to Islamabad, out past the massive fortress of the new U.S. Embassy and past the Chinese Embassy, to the UAE Embassy. There the *banchod* embassy *wallah* says it takes 15 days for the visa and I need a letter from my embassy in Peshawar.

"Look, it's an American passport," I tell him. "I'm not a Pakistani! I'm just going for a 10 day look and you want me to wait 15 days for the visa? Are you afraid I won't come back? Why would I want to stay on that pile of sand, anyway?"

Why do I stay in Pakistan?

They tell me if I only want to go for such a short time my travel agent or a hotel can arrange the visa for me. I try to call Qazi from the Appara Market Public Call Office, under the mosque. He hadn't told me that. I'm blowing it. I waste 80 rupees on the damn phone and all I accomplish is getting the girl in Qazi's office to call me back. Qazi isn't there.

Not maintaining so well. I should be on Valium but they only depress me. I don't need any more of that. Can't sleep at night. Keep waking up thinking of

---

* *Kabiristan — a large cemetery in the southeast of Peshawar. Kabiristan is the word for graveyard, literally meaning "land of graves."*
** *Wazir Bagh — A well-kept park on the southern outskirts of the city; the last famous surviving historic garden of Peshawar. Begun in 1802 by Fateh Khan, it postdates the Mughal period by several decades but emulates many of the qualities of late Mughal gardens. This park was constructed when Prince Shah Mahmood Durrani sent his forces under the command of Sardar Fateh Mohammad Khan Barkzai (aka Wazir) against his brother Shah Shuja, who was the ruler of Peshawar at that time. Sardar Fateh toppled Shuja's rule and laid the foundation of this garden beside his residence in the south of Peshawar. It has been frequently and heavily restored.*

her. Can barely eat. Losing weight. Nothing else has any meaning. Hating myself for how I ended up treating her. How I took her so for granted. Trying to hang on to my sanity. Or what is left of it. There must be some, only I can't see it. My insides feel like they are shriveling up and dying. Can't think straight. All I know is that I can't snap out of it. Feel like I'm going to kill someone. Who? Myself? Smoking, coughing and crying. What's going on here?

Qazi sends me to another travel agent in Shoba Bazaar for visa information. It turns out to be an old friend, Hafez Sheikh, whom I had bought tickets from in the past. He had moved his office from Saddar when I was in America and I hadn't known where his new office was. He says I need to stay in a $100 a night hotel to have my visa arranged or pay an agent in Karachi 2500 rupees. Someone would meet me in the Dubai airport with the visa. I'd have to book a ticket via Karachi because there was someone at Karachi immigrations who would let me leave for Dubai without a visa for 500 rupees.

He gives me a small tourist booklet from the Emirates with a map. Wish I had taken Nas there. It looks so clean and modern compared to Pakistan. I can use the change, if I can ever get there. But it looks so big. How will I ever find her there? How will I even start looking?

My friend living in the next *mohallah* says he has a friend in Dubai we can call about arranging a visa. The roller-coaster is starting to pick up speed.

With the time spent in devising a way to get a visa for Dubai my permission to remain in Pakistan was expiring. I went to the Peshawar Passport Office but they wouldn't extend it. They told me that Special Branch would, though I knew they wouldn't. I told the fellow there I was only waiting for a visa to go to Dubai, that I had my ticket, but just a slight delay. He said I was here as a tourist and there was nothing he could do.

"I came here to live because I am a Muslim and this is your Islam?" We were talking in Pashtu. "Thank you, brother," I now said in English.

"Are you an Afghan or an *Englaise*?" he asked.

"I'm a Muslim, a human. I was born in America."

"Show me your passport."

He thumbed through its travel-worn pages filled with visas and stamps, mostly from Pakistan, India and Thailand, and some colorful assorted stickers on the last pages I had applied myself.

"When you have a date on your ticket for Dubai bring it in here and I will write you an extension up to that date," he told me.

Pakistan is great, but not great to be stuck in. Maybe that is a reason so many Pakistanis seem to want out. Like 20 year old Ali Bashir in a Hashtnagri cassette shop who had never kissed a girl. That part sucks. He had to dance with boys and maybe kiss them too. Who knows what else? But that isn't Islam, that is a culture.

I was so stupid not to ask her where she was going. She showed me the passport photos. I just couldn't believe her. One minute I want to go to the Emirates to look for her, the next minute I'm thinking about just going to Bangkok to spend time with Beer. I could use a relaxing visit. None of this police paranoia. I wouldn't even mind a few days with Sai Chai. I'd even go shoe shopping with her. I don't even have a bathtub here.

I've never disliked Pakistan for the things other foreigners dislike it for. Those are the things I like. The comforts of home. Now I'm learning to hate it as only a Pakistani can. A lover's hate.

One morning I arrived at Gulzar's in Dabgari to be informed that Sherbaz Music Studio had just burned down; my competition burnt to the ground. Finished. There were jokes about me striking the match. We had a tea and waited for Master to arrive. Then a few of us walked down to where the studio had been. A total loss, just a charred pile of Peshawari rubble. Bad luck for Sherbaz, but a golden chance for me, everyone said. Only I'm too bent on looking for Nasreen to think seriously about anything else.

My old neighbor from Hashtnagri came over and told me there was a wedding disco party at Bibi Ji's house. Peshawari musicians and two Pathan dancing girls. Did I want to go? Why not. I could use the distraction from my mental torment.

One of the girls was about 17. The other was younger, an apprentice (and/or sister), maybe 14 or 15. The older one was attractive, similar to Nas when she was younger, lots of makeup and the same flashy eyes. The musicians were friends of mine. The tabla player, Wali Dad, plays on many recording sessions. At midnight they were leaving to go play at another wedding party in Dabgari Bazaar. They invited us along. On the way out to the car, my friend told me to go up to the dancer and talk to her. I had told him I liked her look while we were watching her dance.

"What do I say?" I asked him. "I've never done this in Pashtu before."

"Ask her her name. And where she lives."

"*Salaam aleikum*," I said as I walked up along side of her. "What is your name? Where do you live?"

From the way she looked at me, I realized in any language it was a pretty lame opening. And there were guys pulling at her from every side. Everybody trying to grab her attention. Bangles jangling, her father pulled her into the back seat of the car. We piled into the back of a Pajero jeep with the musicians and raced through the streets of Peshawar. It was a balmy May night. Heat lightning streaked a cloud-laced sky.

At the second party, when only a few of us had scrambled out of the Pajero, the driver gassed it. The Pajero lunged forward. Wali Dad tumbled out landing head-first on the gravely street. He got up dazed and bleeding. We wrapped a rag around his bloody head. Inside, the musicians sat me next to the dancing girl. She asked me to hold a small hand mirror for her as she tried to comb out her dark bangs. Men swarmed around her like flies.

At this Peshawari wedding, not atypical, were about 200 obnoxious, young, female-hungry men smothering the two young dancing girls. I felt sorry for them. The dancer I was sitting next to seemed to enjoy it though. She did a spectacular routine with a glass of water balanced on her head. While she danced the younger, overly made-up girl sat not far from me as guys tried to kiss her or sit her on their laps.

"Look at that," I told my friend, over the din of the music. "Do they not even respect their own young sisters... *banchods!* I think hell for women will be filled with young Pakistani men like this."

When the older girl wasn't dancing so many men were pulling on her and talking to her. I thought she might think I was some rustic *muhajir* sitting next to her so I said to her in English, "When you're free, I'd like to talk to you."

"Talk to me in Pashtu, man!" she said to me (in Pashtu).

I repeated it in Pashtu.

We chatted through the clatter. She lives in Dal Garan, behind the copper bazaar. Her father's name is Meru. He's the one to talk to if I want to visit.

A wildly exotic scene on the rooftop patio; lightning flashing across the cloud-strewn Peshawar night; a girl with glittering, golden ornaments on her nose, ears and arms, silken tassels in her hair, dancing balancing a glass of water on her head. If I come back from Dubai alone, maybe I'll look her up. My musician friends are trying to hold me here and they realize it will take a woman. It's funny. After all the stupid fear, now I can tell most people the truth about Nasreen and it's not a problem. And if it is, I don't care.

But she's gone.

May 13th

Wasted a second trip to the UAE Embassy in Islamabad, as their stupid Pakistani clerk had told me to do, I had gotten a letter of introduction from the American Consulate in Peshawar explaining they had no objection to me going to the Emirates. It was the first time I had been to the U.S. Consulate since I had lived in Takhal in 1987.

The UAE consular, after saying *Masha'Allah* when he heard I was a Muslim, basically told me to have my *"kafir"* consulate in Peshawar arrange the visa through their embassy in Dubai. *Banchods.* If that doesn't work, I'll buy a visa for 2500 rupees in Karachi.

Master, Gulzar and Wali Khamoosh (an Afghan businessman and poet who had just written the songs for a new Farzana/Majubeen Qazilbash duet cassette) arranged a meeting for me with a Peshawari pimp they knew. It's funny, but with all of my so called low-caste musician and *charrasi* friends, I can't seem to locate any kind of girl, anywhere.

When I met him at Gulzar's place in Dabgari, Bacha Khan (the pimp) said he would find me a girl that would make me forget Nasreen. Can he even guess? Can *I* even guess what it will take to forget her? They just seem to think I am looking for someone to bed. They don't really get the full drift of my mind, of my desire.

Sick of the male attitude here. They are afraid to let their wives talk to other men. Why? Is it because they don't satisfy their own wives? It's frowned upon to divorce, but the men can marry a second wife or go to a prostitute or look for a girlfriend. Hypocritical? Where will I find another Nasreen? Does it

315

have to be in a brothel? The Brits intermarried. But then it was mostly with the lower classes, wasn't it?

Well, up your upper class asses.

May 15th

She didn't leave me. She just left the cage where even I had decided to keep her.

Now I'm booked to leave on May 29, PIA 222, Peshawar to Dubai. Talked to my neighbor's friend in Dubai. Her husband will come to meet me at the airport and say I am visiting them and leave his passport for security. The only way to get a visa is to have a sponsor. Of course, you can buy a sponsor for 3000 rupees in Pakistan.

Met Bacha Khan at a tea house on a side street next to the Firdoze Cinema. After icy cold mango shakes, we went by *rickshaw* to a house outside Yakatoot Gate. Walking along the hard, mud-banked canal we passed a woman and a girl wearing *burqas*. He spoke with them briefly. We proceeded to the house and sat around waiting. Then we helped two other men load *charpoys* and other furniture on to a Suzuki pickup. They were moving. The woman and the girl had gone in advance of the furniture.

The Suzuki left and Bacha Khan and I caught another *rickshaw* out past Sherqi Tanna and the new army stadium where we had trained the horses, to a part of the outskirts of Peshawar I didn't really know. I saw written on a mud wall in sloppy white washed dripping Urdu letters the name of the neighborhood, "Khalilabad."

There was the house and the girl and her mother. Bacha Khan told them about me and briefly about Nasreen. He told me to show them her picture. The girl looked like she recognized Nasreen, but when she spoke with her mother, it was only that she reminded her of someone she knew.

They all agreed that Nasreen and her family were "eating my money." The men arrived with the furniture and Bacha Khan and the mother went out to talk with them. The girl and I were left in the room and told to keep quiet. We sat on the one *charpoy* in the room. She was wearing a thin dupatta, loosely thrown around her shoulders and over her hair. Her many colored glass bangles clinked when she moved her wrists. She was pretty and seemed to have a decent personality. She even had a nose ring, a cosmetic feature I appreciate greatly. She looked about 18 years old. She held my hand and said, "So, Nasreen ran away from you?"

"She just ran away," I clarified. "She told me and I didn't believe her."

"Do you like me?" she asked coyly, casting her dark, *surma*-rimmed eyes down and squeezing my hand tighter. "Aren't I nicer than that Lahore *wallah*?" Her yellow, satin shalwar-covered thigh pressed warmly against mine.

Bacha Khan and the mother came back in the room.

"Do you want to stay?"

I guess I was overdue for some female company. I was excited just sitting next to her, just knowing that I could have her. Well, why not give it a try. I might just be able to like this girl.

"Okay, I'll stay," I answered.

The girl looked at me and smiled through heavy dark seductive eyelashes.

"How many times?" Bacha Khan asked. "One or two times?"

I felt funny with the girl sitting right there, as if we were bargaining for meat. She didn't seem to give it a second thought, after all it is only *bizzness.*

"I don't care how many times. Or no times. I'd like to be with her at least an hour. Any less time wouldn't be enjoyable for me."

"Fifteen hundred rupees for one hour," the mother said, "and 500 rupees for one time. What do you want?"

"Nasreen *ate my money?*" I laughed. "Her mother only wanted 1500 rupees from me to spend the entire night. And usually I spent the previous day and the day after with her also. I ate there and she even gave me free nights occasionally. If that is *eating my money,* then eat!"

"For the entire night it is 3000 to 4000 rupees," Bacha Khan said.

"For that I went to Lahore, spent two nights with Nasreen and still had enough money left to take her Eid shopping and buy her two suits and a tea set."

This isn't Lahore, they said....

And the girl wasn't Nasreen, I thought.

Pass....

Bacha Khan asked me to give the mother 200 rupees. Then when I was leaving at the gate, he asked me for 200 rupees more, for himself. I thought... and you are Wali Khamoosh's friend? Now, I know what pimps are really like. Nasreen's people weren't pimps like you.

He said he would meet me at *Maghrib* time (sunset) *at Ghanta Ghar* (the clock tower) just down the street from my house.

He never showed.

Maybe he realized I was nuts?

May 21st

Went to Majubeen's recording session. It was at Mohammad Wali's studio, upstairs from his tape shop on Cinema Road, across from Arif's shop. It was small, crowded and hot. There was a tremendous wind, rain and hail storm. It took out the electricity. They were stuck on the fourth song.

I left Majubeen sleeping under her *dupatta* on the studio floor and went across the street for a cup of *chai* with Anwar. Then I caught a *rickshaw* to Saddar to go to Gulzar Alam and Master Ali Haider's recording session. Their electricity was also out. Some of the band were standing out in the street in the rain cooled air. Gulzar and Master were sitting inside with candles for light. They were stuck on the third song. Gulzar said he would put up 100,000 rupees for my studio. So even if I don't find her in the Emirates, I can still get speakers, a playback amp and a cassette mastering deck in Dubai.

Missing her so. I've had wild sex with other women but I was satisfied just to lie in bed next to her watching her and feeling her breathe. The smell of her hair. I'd trade all of the sex in the world for one of her hugs. I wasn't planning for it to develop into anything like this when I met her, but then what can we plan anyway?

An accident? An accidental fatal attraction?

Was she really as corrupt as people said? Or was it just their thinking that was corrupt?

Was it the airplanes that killed King Kong?

Or love? What is love?

This culture corrupts....

In the USA maybe there are no morals or a lack of them, but there is a certain honesty. Here, so much of the morals are false. Little children can stay up until 2:00 or 3:00 A.M. at weddings watching dancing girls, disco dancers or transvestites dance while being showered with rupee notes by lecherous reviling men. But when the boys are old enough to like the opposite sex, the girls are old enough to be separated from the boys. The womenfolk watch the same dancing and carrying on from upstairs windows and balconies.

Only the "morally loose" dancers can associate with men like that in public. And the boys can hug and kiss each other and it's okay if they bugger one another but for God's sake, don't talk to the girls. If you want to have a casual fling with a lady you have to be brave enough to face the police in Hira Mandi, or more dangerous, a non-corrupt girl's father or brothers. It is very easy to get shot in such a situation.

And Hira Mandi isn't as easy as it once was. Many of the dancing establishments are now billiard rooms. The rest of the scene is getting sleazy feeling. Nas was so safe for me. So relaxed for me. Like being in my own house—with my own family.

Thinking of running an ad in the Jang Newspaper matrimonial section. People tell me such an ad would draw prostitutes. What do I care? It seems I like that type, anyway. At least I won't get shot looking. I need to start improving my Urdu. It is too basic. Even my Pashtu isn't fast or slick enough to pick up Pathan girls in the bazaar (*toba*). You do have to be more cautious in Meena Bazaar than on the Boardwalk at Venice Beach (Los Angeles).

Mr. Mahboob was walking in crowded Meena Bazaar and he happened to see an Afghan refugee quickly grope at a Peshawari lady. Mr. Mahboob knocked the Afghan to the ground. Then he pulled out his pistol and began to pistol whip the offender. A policeman arriving on the scene told Mahboob, "Give me your pistol."

"I am a Pathan," Mahboob told the cop. "The only part of my pistol I will give you is the bullet!"

Then the officer told Mahboob he would take the culprit to the police station. "No you won't, bugger," Mahboob told him. "You will just take him around the corner and take some bribe from him. We cannot have these people coming here and molesting our sisters. I will take him to the station myself."

I still can't find a place to make my studio, but right now I'm too centered on Nas to go about anything else with any sense. People are starting to say my studio is coming with *Sharia Law* or with elections. As in... when? *

I went to Lahore with a friend from my neighborhood who was visiting from the United States. We went out to Nas's house. I thought maybe with his more fluent Pashtu he might catch some talk at her house that I had missed.

Maybe it was because I was with somebody new, but they opened the *behtak* door and had us sit in there. I felt like a pimp bringing a john, which was kind of what we were acting at anyway. I explained that my friend lived in America with his wife, but he was visiting Pakistan without his wife and he was looking for a girl (note; remember, in this environment that means five minutes to half an hour at most).

I spoke with Akbar. He said they didn't have any news about her. They had no idea where she was, in Pakistan, or out... and they hadn't even tried to find her. Yeah, I bet! As Anwar Khan once said, she was Akbar's money-making machine. Hard to believe he wouldn't try to find her for financial reasons if not just for revenge and punishment.

I asked him for a cigarette. He apologetically offered me a Gold Flake cigarette. It's okay, I said. No problem. Ha, I thought, "When Nasreen was here you always smoked Gold Leaf, banchod! Now you smoke a cheaper brand." We waited in the room. Finally Khelda, Akbar's sister entered the room, shook our hands quickly and left the room. She hadn't even spoken to me. She seemed embarrassed and shy. I cannot recall ever once before seeing her so quiet.

Akbar came back in the room.

"Where are the girls?" I asked.

"That was her," was his answer. "We only have one here today."

"Her! That was Khelda, your sister!"

"No it isn't. She is a new girl that looks just like Khelda."

Did I hallucinate that it was Khelda? Or if she runs away, will the next girl look like your own mother, Akbar? *Banchod!*

My friend explained that he was used to America where you could have such a better selection and under much better circumstances. Not just a few minute quickie. But it was Lahore, not New York. We went in the evening to Hira Mandi. The few dancing rooms remaining open hadn't started by 11:30. We left. We were ready to go back to Peshawar.

Between Lahore and Gujranwala we encountered two and a half hours of road blocks, a combination of accidents and police checking. One of the many joys of living in a country with a single, two-lane, pockmarked road spanning it and living with constant government surveillance. My friend and I got in an argument with the driver over the air conditioner. The driver wanted to save petrol and turned it off. It was a hot, summer, Punjab night. Luckily, I dozed for a while on five mg. of vitamin 'V' (Valium)—I thought I had forgotten to bring any but found one of those dear little highway helpers in my wallet.

At 5:30 A.M. we stopped for prayer and tea at Jhelum. Three quarters of us

---

* When General Zia ul Haq took power in 1976, he said the military rule was only temporary and that there would be elections in 90 days. They still haven't come. Nor has Sharia (Islamic) Law. The government is always saying it is coming.

piled out of the bus. Two Afghans sitting in front of us slept. I figured we'd have to reclaim our leg room once we were back in the bus. I was one of the last ones to get in. The Afghans were still sleeping with their seat backs upright. I was surprised. "No wonder they haven't been able to even get Jalalabad in 12 years. They couldn't even wake up to lean the seats back!" A little Anwar Khan humor. There were chuckles from people around me.

May 22nd
Rainy in Peshawar. And slightly cool.
I feel like moving back with those "terrible" *Shias* in "dirty" Kutchi *Mohallah*. I met my old neighbor Shireen Gul's daughter there at a party shortly before I moved. She is really nice. She and her mother came up on my porch several times to talk with me. But they are proud *Sayids* (from Gari Saidan—Street of the *Sayids*). What chance does a poor, white convert like me stand? They can't marry outside *Sayid* families. But can they really prove they are *Sayids*? There are so many *Sayids* in Pakistan. *Sayids* are related to the Prophet Muhammad (PBUH), down from His grandsons Imam Hassan and Imam Hussain, sons of His daughter Fatima Zahra and son-in-law (and nephew) Ali ibn Abi Talib (Hazrat Ali).
Couldn't I be one, too? *Sayid* Noor Mohammad?
Who, and where, are the high and mighty friends I thought I had in Pakistan that I thought I'd lose by association with Nasreen and her family?

Arif and I were standing in the back of his shop as he set type for rubber stamps. Anwar Khan was at the desk taking an order from an Afghan from Jalalabad. I was listening to the Afghan's simple talk and thinking, "oh, there are people stupider than Pakistanis." But there was something about his face, so relaxed. He was with his young son who also had the same simple, relaxed demeanor. I started laughing.
"What?" asked Arif.
"That farmer from Jalalabad really sounded so simple and stupid," I told him, "but his face looked happy and relaxed. So who is smart? I'm not happy, nor relaxed." Arif laughed his boyish laugh and gave me a bear hug.
Outside the shop on Cinema Road two boys were riding by on bicycles in the middle of the road. A *rickshaw* had to veer to the left to avoid a bus which was blindly charging down the road, its driver talking to somebody behind him, his hand on the horn. The *rickshaw* hit the larger of the cyclists, knocking him into the smaller boy, who fell over. The *rickshaw* turned around and the driver yelled at the larger boy, slapping him upside the head. He then drove away. By then the smaller boy was up. The bigger boy turned and hit the smaller one. How Pakistani, I thought. The smaller boy probably went home and hit his sister.

320

May 23rd

Got an exit visa. I used to be so sad at the time when that was stamped in my passport. Especially when Nasreen was here. Now I'm actually happy. Things change. Six days to go until Dubai.

Waiting for the passport office to open I was sitting in a tea house nearby drinking a pot of milk *chai*. They put a new Gulzar and Farzana cassette on the player. Just a few weeks back I had been sitting in the room with Gulzar and Farzana as they recorded the song I was listening to. It still feels so like home to me here. The studio feels so close. If I can just keep these people, this country, the loss of Nasreen, the lack of female company and mostly myself from driving me completely crazy.

Now I can understand the various mentals (crazies) walking around in the bazaars. If I had no money to live the way I live, to go to Dubai on a whim, I'd be standing at Kabuli Gate making sounds like a bird, or something similar (as one local mental does). It has never felt so close. More likely I'd be yelling "Pakistan, sta da mor kus oghaim" (sorry—no translation here) and taking swings at *rickshaws. Insha'Allah*, Dubai will be a turning point. But which way will it turn?

I asked the man in the passport office (I skipped Special Branch as they don't want to do *shit* for me lately) about a permanent residence visa. It is difficult because I don't have an official service (job) here, nor am I stealing aid money and bribing officals. He said when I come back from Dubai I should talk to him. He could arrange it. "Some money will be spent along the way," he said. Good. Someone to pay off for a visa. Just what I have been looking for.

All you get for free is talk and tea. You have to pay off some family for a daughter to marry, if they'll take your white money, that is. Or pay some *taxi's* mother, husband or brother for a session. They don't mind taking your money. Is this a country of pimps? Benazir's people call Nawaz Sharif a "king of pimps" and IJI (Nawaz's party) calls Benazir other nasty names. Muslim brotherhood? Maybe PPP stands for *"prostitutes, pimps and police"* and not *"permanently pregnant prime minister"* as some people say?

May 25th

Since November in Thailand, I haven't spoken with another "Westerner." Maybe that is why I'm going crazy? Only stupid Pakistanis and Afghans to talk to. Arif and I decided the only one stupider is me. I'm the one who doesn't have to be here! But that's something I have to work out with Pakistan. Her going left me stranded in an ocean that I didn't realize I couldn't float in, because I was floating on her. I have had a handful of women I have been able to see, to talk to: the ladies in Nasreen's house in Lahore, some singers and dancers in Peshawar and the women in Bibi Ji's house. Oh, and my ex-English student in Gul Bahar and some of Arif's family since Mirza and Ayesha's wedding. I guess in that, I have been fairly lucky.

I saw Qazi in Chowk (Nasir Khan). He was upset I had re-booked my ticket with the travel agent he had sent me to for information, my old friend Hafez Sheikh.

"You told me I didn't need a visa," I told Qazi. "You just booked my ticket. Then, at the last minute, I had to make two trips to Islamabad. For nothing. Wasted 600 rupees! Had to cancel my ticket, extend my visa. And Sheikh sold me the ticket for 400 rupees less."

"But Noor Mohammad, I didn't know you didn't need a visa. You are an American."

"So, what does that make me, God? All you wanted to do was sell a ticket to make the commission!" Shakeel sat back, listening to a cassette of old Noor Jehan recordings, smoking a cigarette and letting me blow off steam on Qazi.

May 26th

Such lovely girls in Meena Bazaar; their slender, *chaddar*-covered shapes and dark, *surma*-rimmed eyes. But it's like being in a candy store where you can't eat the candy. What is the point? Men don't know *shit* about women here. Is that why they seem to like boys better? Nobody I know knows how to find the kind of woman I want. Or any woman, for that matter. They only marry when their families arrange it.

Talked by phone to Parvez in Sharja. My friend's friend turned out to be living in Abu Dhabi, quite a way from Dubai, so they connected me with Parvez, a relative in Sharja, near Dubai. I sent him my passport info and ticket ten days ago but they never received it. Today I faxed it.

Looking forward to Dubai. I'm really looking forward, as long as it isn't America, to being somewhere modern, clean, neat, where things work and people are hopefully more honest. Somewhere not so overcrowded where people won't be walking over each other in the bazaar. Now I know and understand Pakistan well enough to be happy to be leaving it. At least knowing I won't be stuck in the USA. Need to call or write Mirza. Someone should know where I am. Where I'm going in case I disappear. Who knows what can happen? I can hardly wait.

One of the regular beggars came by Arif's shop asking for money. Neither Arif nor Anwar had any change. "Do you have a five or 10 rupee note for this man?" they asked me.

I looked at the man. "What is wrong with you?" I lashed out. "Do your feet not work? Do your hands not work? Are you blind?" (Something I had overheard Mr. Mahboob telling an Afghan beggar.)

"I'll buy him a pack of Red and Whites (cigarettes)," I told Arif. "Then he can sell them one by one, as I see some poor people doing in the bazaars."

"If you did that, Noor Mohammad," Arif answered, "then tomorrow he would buy two packs with his profit. And the next day he would buy four packs. And soon he'll have a business, he'll get a cart. And then he'll want a store, and then a woman. And then he will be crazy like you, Noor Mohammad. Now he is happy. He has been coming here for years like this. Leave him alone."

We laughed. I gave the fellow 10 rupees.

I want to see her again. If only to say, "I love you" and "goodbye." It feels so incomplete, so torn apart. No real goodbye. Why? Cause I didn't believe what she was clearly telling me.

My house is so great, only so empty. I need furnishing, but I want a Pakistani girl to do it. I decorate like a foreigner. It's okay for a few rooms, but it is just too complicated, precise and cluttered. Like my mind. I want some Pakistani girl to fill it with plastic flowers and tinsel, "Home Sweet Home" signs, plaster cats, clocks, pictures of white babies, highways and modern buildings in Karachi or Switzerland and other goodies available in Meena Bazaar.

May 29th

Spoke with Parvez in Sharja. He said the fax transmission was so unclear my information was illegible. He said if I send it again to use another fax machine. That was the only *stinking* working machine I could locate in Peshawar—at the International Telephone Call Exchange. There is another at Grindleys bank, but it isn't working (they said). My Pak visa is expired. My exit visa says I must leave by May 31st. It took two weeks to get this flight booking.

❊　　❊　　❊

A Letter to a Friend

ᛈᚾᚵ

May 29, 1991
Peshawar City

Dear Mirza Jan,

I'm off! I've just got to go to the Emirates. I've wasted too damn long sitting on my butt doing nothing. She left in mid-February and I'm still here in stinking Pakistan. The pressure on my mind is great. I'm so sad. I hope going to Dubai will bring some relief, some closure. Just to be doing something.

I don't know why I'm so possessed by her. I know it isn't healthy, it never was. It just was. It just is. If I find her, I'll try anything to get her. I have such dear friends here. It's just that they are mostly all male. I miss the female side. Nasreen made life for me in Pakistan balanced. Now I'm out of balance. Way out! Out of balance and out of control.

And it's not just like I can go to Lahore and find any lady. It wasn't like that. Nasreen was so special to me. I woke up the day she left and I realized how I took her for granted. How much she meant to me.

Arif's brother asked me the other day, "Where is Nasreen?"

"What do you mean, where is she?" I answered. "I don't know."

"That is the point," he said. "In Pakistan we marry for life."

"Well, maybe you marry for life, but that doesn't stop you from drooling over girls like Nasreen." Lately I'm sick to death of Pakistani men and their attitudes toward women and sex.

Got to finish this note. Need to find a 24-hour phone number for PIA. Still having problems about my visa for the Emirates. I need to call PIA. I need to call Sharja. I need to call the airport. I will write you, or call you from there. Insha'Allah. If I get there. And if I don't get into something too intense, too quickly. At least you'll know where I went.

Yours in haste,

Khuda hafiz, *Noor*

❊　　❊　　❊

"Zama da khakhkhuli makh dedan, dumra ahsaan kho neh dee"
(To have a sight of my beautiful face, it's not so easy....)
Pashtu song

May 30th
6:00 A.M.
Just got through to PIA. Last night there was no answer from the Peshawar telephone operator. I was trying to find a 24-hour number for PIA. There isn't. Finally got some *stupid ass* clerk at the airport's international counter. The fact that my Urdu is so weak didn't help matters, but one would think the person answering the phone at the international counter would speak English. He was about as helpful as everyone else lately. He said no problem, I could fly the day after tomorrow. I told him it took me two weeks to get this reservation. He said I could get a chance seat. *Standby!*

This sucks. Pakistan sucks! What am I even doing? Maybe she was just the kind of woman who could be glimpsed, or touched, but never held. And here I am trying to catch her? Chasing shadows in the sun. Might as well try to catch the wind.

June 2nd
Peshawar still.
Now it looks like June 5th for Dubai, *Insha'Allah.*

Big ammo depot in Nowsherra just blew up. Was it just four years ago Ojrie Camp (another ammo dump) in Pindi went up, spraying Pindi with missiles and bombs for over an hour? Does that say something about these peoples' *donkey brains?* Two major munition dumps, both in heavily populated urban areas. It makes one feel if God is merciful and kind (and He is) then Pakistan won't get *the bomb.* If they don't blow up the world in the name of God, somebody is bound to drop one in the warehouse and take out Pindi to Peshawar with it!

There is such a friendliness here, but also sometimes such backward stupidity. Under-educated people can really treat each other as animals; older or bigger beating or picking on the smaller. The bigger the stick, the smaller the brain. Sometimes it can make one sick. People get lazy. They say God will take care of it, make it right. Nothing gets done. That is why it is so dirty here and nothing works. God does take care of things. But does this mean we should quit trying? Look at Afghanistan, Iran and Iraq. We cannot change the wind, but we can adjust the sails.

I've come to the conclusion women are the smarter half here (everywhere). That is why Badir Munir is still only a stupid actor with fake blood on his face and Musarrat Shaheen, although her butt may be getting fatter, is also directing films. Nas ran their house. Now the business is completely down. Akbar just knows how to sit on his tail and put the money in his pocket. *Banchod!* Maybe Benazir wasn't such a bad choice to govern? She couldn't have been any more corrupt than the others. But the men could never let her be. *This is Pakistan.* At least her husband isn't president! *

I thought I had my visa arranged through Karachi but the agent there, after reading my information, said he could only make arrangements for Pakistani passports, not for foreigners. My Pakistani visa is expired as of May 15th, but I have it taken care of, *Insha'Allah.* I don't want to push it, though. After many different phone calls to Dubai, Sharja, PIA, the U.S. Consulate, the UAE Consulate and Hafez, things are relatively set in Dubai with Parvez. I spoke with him again and re-faxed him my information. He'll also book me a room. Thirty dollars a night. Hafez said $50 would even be cheap in the Emirates. Flight PK 222, June 5th, 9:00 A.M., Peshawar to Dubai. *Insha'Allah!*

Now it's June 3rd

Talking with Khorshid, my neighbor Arshad's cousin, about traditional Pathan wives, he said he could be sitting downstairs reading, with a glass of water right next to him on the table, and all he had to do was say water. His wife would come downstairs from whatever she was doing, hand him the water, say not a word, and then go back to what she was doing. Not bad, if you're looking for an efficient servant.

He also confided in me that in the four years they have been married they have never made love with the lights on. Hmmm? It has to be his fault, though. I mean, if she listens to orders so well why doesn't he just say, "Turn on the light. Now come here, let me show you what I want."

The first time I slept with Nasreen it was secret. No one was supposed to know I was there so we slept in the dark. The second time we also slept in the dark. After that we always slept with a light on, or the last time she lit candles. When it comes down to it, it seems we were a lot more intimate than most men seem to be with their own spouses.

Khorshid also told me he was in love with his cousin but one of his other cousins was married to her and they lived right under his nose. Arranged relationships. It isn't the kind I want now. People think I'm being too picky, but I only want to marry someone I can love and want to be with. A lover for my life and nothing more. Otherwise, I feel it would be living a lie. I don't want to be desiring other women because my wife doesn't turn out to be exactly what I wanted. It wouldn't be fair to her either. I don't have a family to pass her off on (that she can live with).

---

* Ed note: Asif Ali Zardari, known as Mr. 10% for his business profiteering practices, was elected President of Pakistan on September 6, 2008, after Benazir's assassination in December of 2007.

June 4th

Peshawar

I've never worked so hard to get somewhere before. In comparison, getting out of Pindi Prison or to Gilgit by horse seems easy. I have a one month tourist visa waiting for me with Parvez at the Dubai airport. I have a Pakistani exit visa, saying basically "tomorrow, get out!" My ticket is confirmed. Wali Khamoosh is coming at 7:15 in the morning to drive me to the airport, *Insha'Allah*. Tomorrow night, who knows—at least I'll be in Dubai. *Insha'Allah*.

When I get back from Dubai I should be ready to live again, *Insha'Allah*. (If I'm not with her who knows what I'll be ready for?) There will be nothing left to wait for. God, I'm sick of sitting and crying, but it hasn't left yet. I'm getting used to the pain, though hopefully, when I get back, I'll be able to find a wife and try to forget Nasreen. I'm starting to say that as easy as Pakistanis do. Is it possible to move on? Lately, it is hard to see beyond her haunting memories.

Needless to say I'm confused on this Pakistani woman/relationship thing. So many men in general don't seem to be satisfied by their wives. At least on a sex/love level, that is. They seem happy enough with them as maids, servants, mothers of their children, family members. I think it is because they have an idea that a wife can't be sexy, that it is a juxtaposition. I think it is findable. Or as people say, "someone can be trained." The right someone, that is. Nasreen changed in the time I knew her. Oh, she didn't become an inventive sex partner but then I didn't need that kind of excitement from her.

Problem....

It seems whenever somebody is supposed to do something for you or help you, then their mother or wife is sick, or somebody has died. It is usually true, with diet, dirt and the backward medical beliefs and services here. Wali Khamoosh just called to say a friend's relative had died. He has to go to Swat first thing in the morning. He told me not to think of Nasreen. Easy words. Sometimes I think these people don't think love and sex can go together. I hear them talking about women as if they were just a possession. And the wives, children and mom are safely at home. You don't marry a girl who smokes Gold Leaf cigarettes and swings a two-by-four at Punjabi pimps.

People tell me when I have the studio going I will be able to find women. But they also said that about when I moved into my own house. Next I'll need a Porsche! I'm keeping my eyes open for pretty beggar girls. Girls without family attachments.

Maybe Kipling was right? Maybe East and West can never truly meet? Well, I will try again. It was nice trying, for all the pain and trouble. Why can't I imagine being with someone straight-laced? Not now. Maybe I was around her too long? Maybe I'm just growing up in Pakistan?

Is this my Pakistan teenage rebellion?

❖   ❖   ❖

Sharja Tower with the King Faisal Mosque behind, Sharja (UAE)

Chapter 30
Dubai
(Laywanay Keegum*)

❖ ❖ ❖

June 5th
Sharja, UAE

Made it! Now what to do? It is modern and spread out here. There are 700,000 women in UAE. Technically, I need to look at 35,000 per day. I don't have an idea in the world how to go about finding her. My heart is sad, freaked, mashed. Now that I am actually here, I realize what an impossible task I've set.

Well, I hear Al Ain in the south is smaller and there are many Pathans working there. Maybe a good chance to look there. But then I don't even know if she is in the UAE.

Parvez, my Pakistani visa benefactor, has lived here for 20 years. He says without her address it will be difficult, with a capital "D," to find her. The hotel he booked for me is good: AC, TV, phone, fridge, "real" bathroom, two "real" beds and "real" furniture. Pakistan is another world away. I hate it, I love it. That makes sense, doesn't it? All this makes sense, doesn't it?

Parvez also informs me, as far as he knows, you can ask at the hotels for girls, but you won't find anyone on the streets. But I just can't imagine her working in a hotel. The foreigner circuit? She can't speak English, only Pashtu, Urdu and Punjabi—of course there are enough Pathans and Punjabis here. I don't think she could please a Westerner. Now how would your average Pathan go about finding a Pathan girl here?

Parvez says why don't I have a girl up to my room. It is perfect. And Lord knows, I'm ready. But I can't. Not just yet. Maybe I am lonely for female company, but I'm not ready to side track my purpose for coming here. That definitely wasn't it!

It's a strange feeling. It used to be, whenever I left Pakistan I was sad to be back in the modern world, but not now (maybe it's the fact that this is still a Muslim country I am in now). When I lost Nasreen I lost so much of the joy of being in Pakistan. But I had that joy before I met her. So where did it go? How could *she* take it? Without even knowing. And now I'm trying to recapture it. Now it seems not a day goes by I don't curse the stupidity of Pakistanis or the obnoxiousness and backwardness of the country; my own stupidity....

Yet not a day goes by that I still don't love Pakistan with all my heart!

Nothing has changed except my perceptions. But we are all creatures of our own perceptions, are we not?

There are so many pretty girls in Pakistan, only how to go about meeting them without a "blood" mother, sisters or aunts? Pakistan still makes me happy in so many ways, only it is so lonely for me there without Nasreen. Life is lonely without her, not just Pakistan.

NOTE — Laywanay keegum (Pashtu) — "I'm becoming crazy." — The following segment is the closest I've ever been to insanity... looking back sweetly.

329

Coming here from Peshawar I was the only non-Pakistani I saw in the plane. Most of the passengers were uneducated Pathan laborers or drivers. I filled out no less than 15 UAE entry forms. Many of them made an "x" for their signatures. One tried to rub the ballpoint pen on his thumb to make a thumb print on the form. Maybe he didn't even know how to sign his name, but he had figured out how to get his thumbprint on the paper. It was refreshing.

Kept thinking of her. What would it have been like flying out of Pakistan with her sitting next to me in the plane? I'm so confused. Why can't I just let her go? Why can't I stop thinking of her? I can only see her face. Her image won't go away. Won't leave me. I'm so sad. I've never been so deeply down, sad, for so long. I've never felt so without hope. Desperately trying to get some joy back in my life. I can't go on like this. It's killing me. I'm killing me. I'm sane enough to realize that, yet there is no way I can pull myself out of it. Maybe I'm pulling myself through it? Or maybe just shoving myself deeper in?

Not feeling so sure about finding her here even if she should happen to be here, and even if I did find her, why wouldn't she just want to stay here and work if that is what she is doing? Didn't I tell her I only wanted to live in backward Peshawar? Why should she want that? Then maybe she really did just get married to some guy who realized what a jewel she was.

Now I can't imagine being with anyone more tame. It was her mixture of hardness, yet soft. Most women like that I have seen are also hard and masculine. Nas was hardcore, yet so softly feminine. So coy. People can't seem to understand. I can't seem to understand. Why am I searching for a needle in a haystack? Why don't I just find another girl like everyone says?

I never imagined meeting anyone like her. I don't know what was wrong with me. Why didn't I realize what she really meant to me? I can't stop berating myself for my stupidity. I am trying to recover, but it seems each time I make a little step forward, I end up two or three steps backward. Well, at least now I'm out of Pakistan and moving in the only direction I can think of. God, I hope I can clear my heart of this blackness. I can't continue in this sadness and darkness. I know it is stupid. It is ridiculous. But it is.

In the immigration line in Dubai International Airport I saw a Thai girl, or was she Chinese? Her light almond China complexion and dark glossy hair very pretty, but oh, I'm still so into Pathan girls. But maybe for me there can't be, won't be, another Nasreen. If the dryness and dullness go on for me much longer in Pakistan, maybe I'll go look for a girl in Thailand. The girls there are nice, clean, eat spicy food, sexy, and are not American.

My world has crumbled, but somehow I've got to repair it. Pakistani people can't seem to understand why I am so upset over just a *taxi* girl. What do they know? Most can't understand what she meant to me. What I saw when I looked into her eyes. Did I just make it up? The very first time I looked into her dark, captivating eyes I sank into her heart and still I can't find a way out.

I've never loved anyone so madly, and yet I used her. Oh, I was nice to her. We had a good time together, but I guess I didn't want her bad enough or true enough. I accepted what she was and where she was and I just let her stay there. At least I figured I could always see her there. That she would never leave. That she could never leave. That is what my friends and people told me. And I listened. She fooled us all. I was the fool. She told me and I never believed her. I went back too late. I just let her slip away without a word, without a whisper.

Dubai....

Nice. Modern. Clean. Big, well-paved streets, nice new cars. Tall glass buildings. Traffic all goes in straight lines and is so ordered. No horns or animals in the streets. No horses. No people crowding over you. People of all kinds and dress in the mosques, on the streets.

I went to the mosque across the wide, grass and tree divided avenue from my hotel for *Asr* prayer. I figured it would be a good place to meet a pimp. Why not? Centrally air-conditioned, soft plush wall to wall carpet, beautiful Qur'ans and *raihals* (carved wooden holders to keep the Qur'ans off the floor while one reads them). Fresh boxes of Kleenex placed about. The works. All conveniences. In Pakistan, sad but true, it would all be run down, broken or stolen. I was wearing the stone-ground jeans and short sleeve casual shirt I had arrived in. (I had been advised by my Pakistani friends to arrive in the Emirates not looking like a Pakistani to facilitate my easy entry into the country. Okay.)

As I looked down the prayer line there were people in all varieties of dress: jeans, slacks, *shalwar kameez,* Western suits and *thobes* (Arab robes). Nobody came up to me and said, "Hello mister—hello Englaise" in some stupid, minuscule, donkey-brained voice. Even this morning, on my own street in Peshawar as I was walking out to get a *rickshaw* for the airport wearing my Western garb and carrying a bag over my shoulder, I heard some kid say, "Hello Englaise." It is something I do not care for. Especially on my own street.

Pakistani people are warm, more accurately hot and affectionate (at least man to man, woman to woman in public). But children can be loud, impolite and obnoxious. It is a pleasure, coming from Pakistan, to be able to walk down the street here in any clothing you want and not have children drive you crazy (as if, at this point, I need any help).

I don't know what is wrong with me. I've never felt so negative before. I could always find the positive in things. And fairly quickly, at that. I couldn't get myself mired down in the muck of depression. And now I don't know how to get out of it, to get positive. I'm just sad, lonely and crying all the time. I can't think of anything for long, except her. The things I've loved, I hate. They don't make me happy anymore. Afghanistan and Pakistan. I'm sick of the backwardness and one sided-ness of the people. *Rabab*—I can't even play it lately. It pains to even touch it. The feeling is gone. She even took the music from my heart. I almost tossed it off my roof the other night, but I guess I am sane enough to realize that is too drastic. Felt like tossing myself off!

One day the music will come back, along with life, *Insha'Allah.* Along with all of it. Will she? That I don't know, can't say. I don't want to think about it yet.

Still walking around looking at every woman, hoping I'll see her. Looking in the back of every car. The same as I've been doing in Pakistan the last four months. The difference is, in Pakistan I kept my hand in my pocket on my gun in case I saw her walking or driving with someone who didn't want her to talk to me. Here, I don't have a gun. I'm a stranger here.

If only I knew she was all right. Parvez says if she was sold to a *sheikh* then I'd never find her. There are no laws about that here. She could be sold to some fat *sheikh* (or some thin one) and just be a slave to him, wishing she was even back in Lahore, or she could be happy with some Pathan who can give her more than I could have ever given her. And then, she could be turning tricks with Pathan laborers in Al Ain. My mind is playing all sorts of possibilities. Maybe she is right here, near me, or maybe she is in Pakistan.

I sit here writing in my journal. What is the point of it? It's all dated material. It all changes. It all goes in circles. Somebody should know what happened to me if I disappear off the face of this earth, I suppose. As if anyone will care.

I just keep spiraling down and down. Can't seem to get it in check. I can't even think of other women. I can only think of finding her or to find a girl like her. But what is the point of having someone like that? Who is she going to talk to in Pakistan? All my friends whose wives I can't even meet? What's the point? She's gone. I don't think I'll ever see her again in this life. Pakistan is still there, but I can't seem to get that back either.

Walking aimlessly around Sharja looking in restaurants. Really feeling hungry inside, but not able to sit and eat. Nothing looks appetizing. It's so modern here. Huge buildings. Big cars going by so fast on wide roads with a center divider of well manicured grass. It looks like the Wilshire Blvd Miracle Mile in Los Angeles, with mosques. The beautiful Arab style mosque (simpler and plainer than mosques of the subcontinent) across the street from my hotel even has ice-water drinking fountains. Spacious glass-fronted stores when you walk down the streets. Not the crowded, cluttered, open-fronted bazaar shops of Pakistan. No crowds of people, exhaust, noise and dust in the streets. So far I've seen one beggar here, an old blind man with a little boy. They were in the ultra modern, ultra fancy, air-conditioned shopping center, "The Souq," where Parvez's shop is. They were wearing clean white clothes. Of course, one can't compare the beggars of the Emirates with the beggars of Pakistan. Here, money oozes out of the sand.

Don't know what I'm doing. I wander, hoping I may see her on the street, in a shop, or she may go by in a car. I won't see her in my room, unless I find her.

Things change. I remember fearing if I married Nasreen she might have wanted me to take her to America. Oh no, I could never do that! I live in Pakistan. Now I want a girl who would be willing to leave Pakistan.

Ordered lasagna and salad from the hotel restaurant. Exotic foods. But when it arrived at my door, after a few bites, my appetite left. Food has no taste. Nothing has any taste. Watching Arabic music videos on TV. I push the food into my mouth and down my throat, thinking of the calories and nourishment my body must need.

The other day, before leaving Pakistan, a friend was telling me about when he had visited his brother in the UAE in 1983. "There are lots of restrictions there," he said.

"Like what?" I asked.

"The police are always checking your papers," he said. Probably nothing that applies to me. He's Pakistani.

"Also," he said, "there are public bathrooms and restaurants and shops all have bathrooms. They restrict you from going to the toilet on the street."

"It is Pakistan and India and other under-developed countries that use the streets for bathrooms," I laughed. "Most of the so called civilized world uses bathrooms."

An American friend in Peshawar once told me hanging out in Chowk Nasir Khan with Shakeel and friends, or in Dabgari with my musician friends, or at Nasreen's was my slumming. Maybe living in Pakistan is slumming. Even the most modern there is isn't really.

Am I upset? I'm just upset with myself, hence with everything. I thought my life was so full, but I was fooling myself. With Nasreen there I didn't notice the emptiness. Now even Pakistan for me seems empty. Where can I go that won't feel that way? I'm empty. Everywhere I look I see her eyes.

There is so much sand here. Empty lots are sand instead of dirt. And you can smell the sea brine in the air. This evening a pleasant, warm sea breeze is blowing, yet I'm alone. In Pakistan, it's true, you can go anywhere and feel like you are at home, with friends/family (albeit, sometimes a little pushy ones), but here, now, it's nice for me to be a stranger. To be alone. Lately, even with my friends in Pakistan, I've felt alone.

Note: *Please realize, at this point I am off the deep end. I am even shy to write this, but trying to be true to events happening at this point, I feel I should include the actual place my mind is in.*

June 6th

Nice hotel room, good bed, good AC, but I keep waking up during the night feeling so alone and miserable. Missing Nasreen. Wake up upset. Upset with myself. I feel I want to be somewhere where women are treated and looked at more normally. Speaking from a purely Western concept now. Here a foreign woman can walk down the street, even in shorts (*toba*) and people (men) hardly even look at her. In Pakistan they would drool and drive her crazy. I watch Pakistani men look at women (including Pakistani girls) with this hungry, starving deranged look. I'm getting it. Hell, I've got it. It's not healthy, it's not normal.

Hafez suggested I look for a wife in Egypt. He said Egyptian women are beautiful. Does that show my chances of finding someone in Pakistan? Their opinion of my marrying a Pakistani girl? They don't seem to want me taking one of their girls and changing her. Well, that's okay. I'll find someone they don't want. A *kanjri*, or a beggar, or something. Let them sit on their asses in

Pakistan. I'll take her around the world with me.

Is that why so many Pakistanis want to settle abroad? Pakistan is a nice place to visit, but to be stuck there like so many visa-less Pakistanis would be lousy. At least I can leave it when I want to! Pakistanis return when their daughters are of school age. They are afraid their daughters will get free ideas and then they will never consent to being married slaves to some jerky cousin their parents have picked for them who has only kissed boys. Are they afraid their daughters will learn the joys of a free and even life? *Toba.*

It's okay for their sons to bed a white woman, marry her, get a green card, enjoy themselves outside the country and then divorce her and come home to marry the Pakistani girl their parents have picked for them. The "white" marriage doesn't count. I guess it's the way God wants it? Isn't that why girls have maidenheads and boys don't? No accountability for men.

But us "white" people aren't allowed a second chance. People say if I divorced my first wife how can they know I won't do the same to a Pakistani wife. I'm tired of double standards but this world is full of them. I'm sick of only hanging out with men. It doesn't feel natural to me. I'm tired of men who think any woman who goes out of her house is a *whore*. Without Nasreen there, I find myself growing tired of the dirt and inefficiency. The bigoted concepts

Talked to the Pakistan Embassy in Dubai today. I'm ready to go back and sell my house. *Idiots.* They told me to get a letter from the U.S. Embassy stating they have no objections to me getting a visa to go back to Pakistan. When I called the Americans they said they never heard of such a thing.

Maybe God wants me out of Pakistan? Maybe God doesn't want me in this world anymore? I don't know what to do. I don't seem to have any desires left anymore except to find her. For what purpose? I'm not sure. I imagine I'm so sick of Pakistan because I am sick of everything. I've just been in some dark limbo haze existence for months now. There doesn't seem to be much of a future, yet. My whole past, my whole life, was, is Nasreen. Can that be true?

Oh, I do remember somewhere once, looking for and arguing with some rustic farmer over a *maund* of grass. Something about having to get from Gupis to Gilgit or Lahore or somewhere. Nothing is quite clear anymore. Except her flashing eyes and slashing smile. That is the jail I've put myself in. How do I get out? Where do I get the key?

Am I crazy? I still want to marry a Pathan girl. But not a straight-laced one. Thai ladies are nice. I can't stay on one decision for more than a few moments. Maybe I should look for a black woman? A black Arab? (God, it sounds as if I'm talking about horses, not a life partner.)

I went into the hotel's restaurant to eat. Ordered a pizza, something I hadn't eaten in a long time. While I was eating, this really gorgeous black lady came in. Very African looking, but with notably Arab features. She had a black shawl over her hair, like many women use here. Her eyes were large and inky black. Her sensuous lips were made up bright red. Her skin the color of clear dark milky chocolate. I couldn't stop looking at her. My Pakistani nature was telling me, so pretty and sitting in a restaurant alone, she must be a *taxi*. Every time she glanced at me, I embarrassingly looked away. Not sure how to react to local women. She was speaking to the waiter in Arabic. She was so pretty, exotic, dark... but I'm here looking for Nasreen.

Everything is so big and spread out here. I'll definitely be lucky if I can ever find her here, if she is even here? I did find her twice before, but then this isn't Samnabad, this isn't even Lahore. Does luck come in threes? Maybe luck is to not find her?

Today Parvez drove me over to Dubai. It's even bigger than Sharja. More of a downtown shopping area and large modern buildings. Cloth shops, electric appliance and camera stores. I looked for recording gear but it was mostly the home-user variety they were selling.

Then he dropped me off in front of my hotel just as *Maghrib Azan* started. Went to pray. The luxuriousness of the mosque never ceases to amaze me. And just out the front door of my hotel. Well, it isn't Peshawar. I do have to go down an elevator and cross a wide, modern, four-lane road with it's grassy divider and fast moving traffic. Western style though, without horns blasting.

Hard to keep my mind off Nasreen. Asking God to please let me find her, even if it is to only have her say, "Get lost." Just to know what happened to her. I'm not doing so well. I've been beating myself up, cursing Pakistan, though I know it is because my perceptions are so distorted.

What I want to do with my life now changes daily, at least. It's been so long since I've imagined a future without her. I figured one day I would either be with her or at least I would be able to continue seeing her. We never want to realize things can change. Sometimes big time and permanently. Not always to our liking or consent. The times that were won't come back again. Now, I don't know what I want. Sometimes I feel like such the uneducated Pathan. Is that my love for the place? The lure? The simple life? Do I need to mix with a higher class in Pakistan to find the somewhat semi-liberal girl I am looking for? Or maybe just stay down in the corrupt to find what I really like? But it isn't corrupt I want, is it? It's liberal. Free in spirit. It just seems these characteristics go hand-in-hand with the word "corrupt" in Pakistan. Maybe I just mix in the wrong circles? Maybe I should get a job in Dubai or Bangkok?

I was thinking of getting a girl for tonight—my birthday. According to Pakistani people, it's so easy to do. But it isn't really. At least not what I want. I don't feel like it. It is still her my heart wants.

People always told me she was taking advantage of me. In her way, maybe she was. But wasn't it really me taking advantage of her? It was okay to keep her there in her cage if I could keep seeing her? Oh, in my naive way I tried to get her to leave, but I wasn't forceful enough nor did I speak her language fluently enough. Or maybe she just plain didn't want to go with me? How will I ever know? I was waiting for her to say, "Okay, let's go."

What did I do? I asked her with star struck eyes, "Do you want to marry me? Do you want to go?" I should have been more definite, more forceful. I should have said, "Come on. Here are the tickets. Let's go!"

I just gave up and accepted that she would be there for me. What was I waiting for? Time doesn't wait. Neither did she!

10:30 P.M.

Room service just brought me a mushroom, tomato and ham omelette—sans ham. Yes, unbelievably enough, they seem to serve pig meat here.* And dishes with wine sauce also, though contrary to Pakistani opinion, they don't serve *sharab* or girls in the hotels. At least, not in this hotel. Maybe I just don't know how to find it here. I did talk to the desk clerk, an Indian Muslim from Kerela. I told him I was looking for my Pathan girlfriend who had been kidnapped. He gave me the names of six hotels in Dubai where he had heard ladies were available.

Room service also brought a *tabouleh* salad earlier, a big stack of *pita* bread, a plate of olives and pickles and fries with ketchup. Hard to get the food down. I don't have the patience to eat alone. I can barely swallow. At least now I can keep it down, if I can get it there. Before, I couldn't even manage to do that much. I've got to gain back some weight. This irregular eating is getting to me. Wearing my old jeans with a belt here I can realize how much weight I've lost. Not good. Must be at least 30 pounds gone. Actually I'm trying to recover from losing 105 pounds all at once (her approximate weight). I won't be able to gain that one back by eating.

June 7th

Sharja

I can't spend the rest of my days searching for a girl that I don't even know will care or not. She's gone. I hope she's happy. There is nothing I can do for her if she has made the wrong decision. We have to live with our decisions. We can't rectify them. Is Saddam glad he invaded Kuwait? Or will General Zia ever fly with a crate of mangos again? **

I wish I could speak Arabic. I do okay here with Pashtu and the Urdu I know because there are so many Pakistanis and Indians. But it would be nice to be able to talk to the locals in their own language. You can't really get into a non-English speaking people (even if they speak English) without speaking their native tongue. That's my feeling. It is my experience. But then, maybe it is better not to get so into it? Where did it get me?

Today, after *Juma* prayer, I went into Dubai and started asking in hotels. Also talking to Pathans on the street. I still love the company of Pathans and the feeling of speaking in Pashtu (which maybe proves I'm nuts, haha!).

I went to one of the hotels recommended by the clerk in my hotel. It was mostly staffed with Filipino girls. I talked with the manager, a short, portly fellow, in the lobby. The rooms are 200 Dirhams ($60) a night. Two hundred and fifty Dirhams for "other services." Mine is just 130 a night. Of course the room service only brings me meals, towels, and makes the bed. Thinking of Thailand

---

* *Pork and pork related products are un-Islamic, Haram (sin). Big no no!*

** *Referring to a mysterious crate of mangos supposedly taken aboard General Zia ul Haq's ill-fated flight out of Bahawalpur in which he and many of his top generals, including the chairman of the Pakistani Joint Chiefs of Staff, the American Ambassador and the head of the U.S. military aid mission to Pakistan were all killed when the plane exploded on take-off on August 17, 1988*

this does seem slightly costly. I'll save my money and myself to do what I came here for. To look for Nas. I didn't come for that. Going up to hotel clerks and random people on the street is somewhat embarrassing but I've got to do something. I didn't come here to sightsee.

After *Maghrib* prayer, walking by a taxi stand, I heard some fellows speaking Pashtu. I asked for a hotel I was looking for. They told me about an area called Overlaunch where there are houses with Pathan girls. But they are only open in the day they say. Ah, this is sounding a little more Pakistani.

Pathans here are really surprised when this *ghora* (I'm still wearing jeans and a short-sleeve, print shirt much of the time) comes up to them and starts rattling off in Pashtu. At first they can't relate to me so well, maybe the way I'm dressed. Then they think I am an Afghan. I give them the old story. How I am originally from America, I became a Muslim in Afghanistan, live in Peshawar, etcetera. Then I get into telling them my purpose, that I'm looking for a Pathan *taxi* girlfriend of mine and do they know any brothels. Needless to say they haven't met many American Muslim converts like this one. I don't know what they think. I can't care. They all say they are sorry for me, that love is a big thing. I say this is harder than finding grass in Pingal! (remember back there by Gupis?)

Looking for a share taxi to take me back to Sharja I overheard two Pakistanis asking a taxi driver where to get a share taxi. They were also going to Sharja. I started to follow them. I approached them and asked if they spoke Pashtu. No, just Urdu and some English. We shared a taxi back to Sharja. One was a policeman from some town another half hour further away than Sharja. I told them what I was doing here, but neither my Urdu nor their English was strong enough for them to really comprehend the insane quest I was on. Our driver looked like a Pathan, though they had been carrying on the conversation with him in Urdu. The policeman asked the driver if he spoke Pashtu. The driver and I chatted the remainder of the ride to Sharja.

After dropping our two friends off the driver came up to my room with me. He was from Bara, just outside Peshawar. He had been here eight years. I showed him some pictures of Nasreen. He said he thought he had seen her in a house in Overlaunch after Ramazon. Sure, I thought, he's feeding me a line.

"Does she have a false tooth here?" he said, pointing to the right side of his mouth.

I smiled, thinking maybe he had really seen her.

"Tomorrow I'll pick you up, brother," he told me. "We can drive out to Overlaunch. There are lots of houses there. I'm not sure if the house I saw her in is still open or not. We can see.

"Then, you did it with her."

"No, it was my friend."

"Don't worry. It's her work. I'm used to it. I've lived with it for four years."

"No, my brother. Not that I don't do that sort of thing. I don't save any money here. I spend all of my money drinking and screwing. *Toba.*" But not her. But I will try to help you find her. I'll pick you up tomorrow at 9:00. Be in the lobby."

I won't set my hopes too high. Maybe he just made a lucky guess. I don't want to think about it, but maybe? I'll see. It's a chance. It's all a chance. It's time to start looking.

❖   ❖   ❖

THE SEARCH IS ON

June 8th

At 9:00 this morning, Islam, my taxi driver friend from yesterday, picked me up and we drove to Overlaunch in the outskirts of Dubai. The area reminded me of Samnabad with sand. Narrow sandy lanes with old rugs thrown over the sand to facilitate walking. Homes behind high walls with metal gates, bright violet and pale yellow bougainvillea creeping over the walls. The main roads were *metaled* and quiet, with cars parked orderly along the sides.

We went to the house he says he saw her in. I half expected her to answer the door. But there was a heavy chain and padlock on the door. They must have moved, something Islam had mentioned last night.

Went to two other houses, but nobody was at home. Islam said they all live somewhere else and come to work in the day. We must have been too early. Walking back through the sandy maze to where we had parked the taxi, we saw a stoutish Pathan lady. Her loose floral, cotton, printed *shalwar kameez* and large gold hoop earrings instantly reminded me of Akbar's mother in Lahore. She walked with the loose, free gait of a madame. We went with her to her house. There was a girl with her whose name also turned out to be Nasreen. I showed them a picture of my Nasreen but they said they didn't know her. A Pathan fellow selling cloth door to door stopped by. We showed him the picture but he also said he had not seen her.

Islam swears he saw her. The fat madame says she will ask around. Islam says girls here get a lot of business. Six to ten times a day. If she was tired of life in Lahore, maybe this isn't what she wanted. But I don't think she would or could go back there now.

I could leave Pakistan after this but there is the fear she could show up there. Islam says he will drive me to Abu Dhabi where there are lots of girls and he has a friend there who can help me.

June 9th

Sharja

Woke up this morning out of it. I can't keep on waking like this. How much longer can this empty feeling go on? I have no peace of mind, heart or soul. Maybe I'll leave Pakistan. How can I leave without seeing her? How can I leave my friends? My life? Do I leave that, also? What is possible at this point?

I'm afraid to lose it, but I can't feel any help from that side now. I have been trying but I can't feel anything. Is it me not giving it a chance? This isn't fair. Life isn't fair. And if life isn't fair, do I want to keep playing? I don't want to play a game if the rules aren't fair. Well, I'll make my own rules. Can I any more? Maybe I'm not being fair? After all, it is all my own fault. Maybe at first my Pashtu was too weak. I could have tried and didn't. I thought I was a good Muslim (in my way) but who cared? God is in our hearts, not in mosques, *mullahs* or in people.

I didn't listen to my heart. I listened to all that so-called wise advice. I wanted to keep being respected. Where is it all now? Gone! I don't even respect myself. I'm honestly a little scared. I've never been down for such a long period in my life. And I'm still slipping. I need to see, to feel some future. But all I still know is Nasreena.

Maybe I should go to America, immerse myself in the property business Mirza and I started last year and let it beat a future into me? Or find me a nice Pakistani girl to marry (how?) and then beat her because she isn't Nasreen? I need to get a perspective on what is real and what is not.

Somewhere I remember the story of the man who asked God to show him the path of his life. God showed him a beach and along it were two sets of footprints. "The beach is your life," God told him, "and the footprints are you and I walking the journey of your life together."

The man looked down the beach and noticed in one place there was only one set of footprints. "Look," he said, pointing out the spot to God. "In that place there is only one set of prints. And that was the most difficult time in my life. Why did you desert me there, God?"

And God answered, "I never deserted you. In that place, I was carrying you."

Ah cha. Glad I'm being carried me right now.

Shireen Khan, another Pathan taxi driver (a Waziri from Dera Ismail Khan) whom I met yesterday, picked me up in the morning to go to the Pakistani Embassy in Dubai. They didn't want to give me a visa because I had just left Pakistan. The visa officer asked why I wanted to go back. It was hard to keep from laughing — *"Who the hell knows?"*

Luckily, I told him I want to go back because I am a Muslim and I have a house in Peshawar, etcetera. He shook my hand and then said, *"salaam aleikum,"* then said he would ask his superiors and I should come back tomorrow for my passport.

Last night I gave Shireen a picture of Nasreen to show around to his fellow drivers. He says a driver he knows thinks he saw her in a house in Overlaunch. Second supposed sighting there.

Walking in the bazaar, I peer into every shop, especially cloth and jewelry shops, on the off chance I happen to see her. It's better than looking at the ground. Today I walked into a shop where the shopkeeper looked like an Afghan friend of mine in Peshawar. When he looked at me, a foreigner coming into his shop (I was wearing my Western clothes for the benefit of the embassy *wallahs*), he said, "Yes, my frend. Hello. Cum in dee shop. It is your shop, cheap and best!"

I didn't feel like beating around the bush so began firing questions at him in Pashtu. His mouth dropped open. He called several Afghan shopkeepers over from neighboring shops. "I thought he was a tourist," he told them, "and called him into the shop. But listen to him, he speaks good Pashtu."

They were Kabulis. I told them my mission. It feels good to finally be telling people the truth about her, not caring what their judgments may be. One of them said he knew a Pathan girl from Mardan whose name was Nasreen who had also worked in films and on TV, but she had been here a long time. When he saw Nasreen's picture he was sure it wasn't her. Shall I look her up? Will any Pathan Nasreen from Mardan do? I don't think so.

I went to the Royal Shiraz Hotel, from the list given me by my hotel clerk. The desk clerk there, a Filipino lady, said lately the police had been arresting girls coming to the hotels. She told me the name of the station they hold them and that they hold them three or four months, then deport them. Maybe she could end up back in Pakistan? What could she do there? Where could she go? Or maybe if I find her in jail here, I can get her out with my *nikka namma*?

At the Bank of Oman in Dubai, where I went to get a credit card cash advance, I was invited to come behind the counter to take care of my business. The clerk asked me why I had so many Pakistani stamps in my passport. He happened to be from Peshawar so we spoke in Pashtu. He said he had relatives who grew up and were educated in the United States.

"They speak Pashtu with the same accent as you," he informed me. Him I didn't tell the exact purpose of my mission.

I've already met several Pathan taxi drivers who have offered to take me home for dinner, though none of them have sisters. At least not here.

Shireen has a friend who thinks he saw Nasreen in Karachi. He is a big rig truck driver. Shireen offered for me to stay with this truck driver friend so I don't have to waste so much money on my hotel and food.

Shireen also says he knows of a Pathan girl in Tank, near Waziristan, whose mother died when she was young and she was brought up in an English hospital. He said she is ready for marriage (must be at least 13 then?) and he will give me the address. I wonder if she spits on the floor? Shireen said Nasreen is making me crazy. I wonder why he would ever think that?

Right now I'm enjoying my air-conditioned room, my phone and TV, my "real" bed and "real" bathroom, room service, "exotic" hotel food and the privacy of the hotel. But if I want to stay a full month, and my purpose is finding Nasreen, not just resting in a modern hotel, I may take up Shireen's buddy's offer of lodging. Thirty-five dollars a night for 30 days is too much for me now. I've been checking, but there isn't anything cheaper.

June 10th

Islam arrived at 9:00 in the morning. We drove over to Dubai, to the house in Overlaunch with the fat madame. She told us she had asked around about Nas, but no leads. Maybe true, but she has that same sweet, venomous smile as Akbar's mother. Maybe they're hiding her from anyone looking for her from Pakistan?

Then we drove to Abu Dhabi. Two hours west through the desert on the Arabian coast. Wide, smoothly-*metaled* super-highway. Two lanes on each side and a paved shoulder. A center division of sand. Arabic and English adver-tising billboards, the posts supporting them piled high in drifts of sand. The desert camel brown, the ocean and sky a brilliant blue.

On the outskirts of town we picked up Islam's pal and drove with him into Abu Dhabi. Big, clean city with wide, new streets and ultra-modern buildings of steel and glass. Went to a square downtown in front of several high-rise, blue-glass office buildings, stood in their shade in the hot dry desert air and talked with two pimps, a Pathan and a Punjabi. A slight dry, gritty desert breeze ruffled our loose clothing.

When shown her picture, the Pathan said he hasn't seen her in Abu Dhabi. When the Punjabi saw her picture he said he had seen her in a house in Overlaunch. He gave us a phone number and told us to speak with Sabor.

Later this afternoon, when we returned to Dubai, I called the number in Overlaunch. Sabor wasn't there. A woman was speaking in Urdu so I handed the phone to Islam. He told her we had been there before and wanted to know if a girl named Nasreen was there. The woman said everybody from the house had left for Pakistan four days ago and would be gone a month. But I don't think she would go back to Pakistan like that. I'll call again tomorrow to ask how long Nasreen has been at their house. Nasreen seems to be a very common name, especially in her profession. I'll tell the lady I saw her there in January. If she says she was there in January, then it's another Nasreen. I was with her in Lahore in January.

What is wrong with me? I guess just being able to ask myself the ques-tion shows there is still a ribbon of sanity left.

The mosques here are rather simple appearing on the outside, usually just a minaret or two and a dome. In Pakistan they are like lace, up to 10 fancy spired minarets, lots of domes of various designs and decorations. But inside, half the time, the water isn't running for *wuzu*, the power cuts off in the middle of prayer in the heat of summer and the beads of sweat roll down your body as the overhead fans coast to a stop. The paint is chipped. The P.A. sputters and cracks. Like the people; fancy show and talk on the outside, but physical capability is lacking. The heart is there, but the physical ability isn't. Well, the Emirates are rich and Pakistan is poor. I can't blame the country for being poor. I know, I can say it is the fault of the people being lazy. But I am sure the people here are as lazy, if not more so. Only here, the money just oozes up from under their feet.

Islam told me, if I don't find Nasreen, then I should go directly back to Pakistan and get married quickly. Those words fall so quickly off Pakistani men's mouths, as easily as *Kalima*. A man can be lying to you and saying *Kalima* at the same time, "*La ilaha, ill Allah....* I swear to you, brother, I speak truth."

I think I'd rather just hang out with *kanjris*. At least they are honest and you know where you stand. What does it all matter anyway?

Back on to Thailand. It was nice. Being with Beer was nice enough. She's a bouncy little chick. But I'm not sure she would swing a two-by-four to beat off a contingent of attacking Punjab pimps. She'd probably grind up lion whiskers and poison them slowly. Much more Thai style. Maybe I'll just dust off my Thai dictionary and tell Beer to put on a short skirt and meet me at the airport.

I feel like leaving Pakistan (and at present, I'm not even there). But before leaving, maybe I ought to pop off a few rounds into Akbar's head. I can file off the Llama's serial numbers outside (the inside one as well) and dump it in the Samnabad canal after. Or maybe he's already paid his dues—not losing his love, definitely he didn't love her, but losing his business.

I once heard it said, "You need to kill somebody in the world in order to make room for yourself." Maybe here is my chance to make some room? But then it's really too late for all that now, isn't it?

June 11th

Today I realized it may be difficult getting a ticket back to Pakistan when my visa expires, which will be around *Eid* day. Too many Pakistanis may be trying to get home for the *Eid* holiday. If it is planned just right one could celebrate one *Eid* here in the Emirates, then fly home and have a second one in Pakistan. This is because *Eid* is declared at the first sighting of the new moon and the government of Pakistan usually sights the new moon a day later than the Arabs. I guess their eyes, or glasses, aren't as strong? Or something about longitude? *

Parvez has a friend who works in the PIA office. While I was at his shop he called PIA for me. As we waited for the return call it was time for *Asr* prayer. Parvez grabbed a prayer cloth big enough for two and we walked between the crowded piled rows of brass and mother of pearl inlaid intricately carved wooden furniture; gleaming silver, brass and copper filigreed vases, urns and water pipes; and rolled Pakistani/Persian rugs. We offered our prayers on the marble walkway surrounding the upper level of shops. We faced a cement, latticed wall with an arched opening in it looking out on a lazy, calm, glassy blue, watery inlet of the Arabian Gulf. When we came back in the shop, Abdul Aziz, Parvez's helper, an Indian Muslim from Kerela, informed us that the fellow from PIA had already called back. I have a seat booked on a flight leaving the night of June 23rd. That should be enough time here. I really can't afford much more.

Also, it will give me one *Eid* here on the 23rd, another in Peshawar on the 24th, and a third one in Lahore on the 25th. The Punjab invariably declares *Eid* a day after the NWFP. With all these different *Eids* dependent on the moon sightings, one would think we were living on a planet with more than one moon.

I want to go to Nasreen's house in Lahore on *Eid*. Can't think of anything else to do. Who knows? Could she be there? Shireen says she could have gone back to Pakistan to make a new visa. Who knows? I feel it's a very slim chance she would be back in Lahore at that house. It is all such a slim chance.

---

* *Actually the coming Eid, Eid ul-Adha (the Big Eid or Eid ul-Qurban—the Eid of sacrifice—is celebrated at the end of the Haj period, 2 1/2 months after Eid ul-Fitr) is not determined by the new moon sighting but on the day after the day of Arafat (in Saudi Arabia), the last day of the Haj, but for some reason this is also debated, being celebrated on day or another in different countries, and there are 2 or 3 in Pakistan (?)*

Earlier today when I went to the Pakistani Embassy to pick up my passport I was wearing *shalwar kameez*. Had gotten sick of the "Western clothes." The visa clerk shook my hand, congratulated me on my clothes, then shook my hand rigorously again. Repeatedly, Pakistan, for all its faults, shows me why I love it so. They gave me a three-month visa, gratis. The Emirates are filthy rich and yet they charge dearly for their visas. Pakistan is dirt poor and give their visas (at least to Americans) freely.* I'm glad I didn't have to ask the *ferangis* at the American Embassy for any help.

WAZIRIS IN THE DESERT
(Waziri taxi camp, somewhere in the desert outside Dubai)

June 13th

Still haven't found Nasreen. Still can't get her off my damn mind. Maybe I need a lobotomy. I do have Valium, but they only serve to depress me more and I'm not keen on sleeping as waking up is such a drag.

But I have found my own tribe of Waziris. They are *Mehsoods* from Dera Ismail Khan mostly. It saves me money, especially on hotel and taxis. How it happened is... well it just sort of happened. Doesn't it all happen that way?

Yesterday Shireen picked me up in the morning. I was planning to move to a hotel in Dubai. The Dubai hotel was the same cost as mine, 120 *dirhams* a night (approximately $30 U.S.), but there is more action in Dubai. More shops, bazaars, restaurants, hotels and people on the streets. A better place for my search.

I am starting to get used to this, though it is rather strange and awkward to walk up to the desk in a hotel and start asking about her. Sometimes they don't quite get my meaning, or they want to play dumb and tell me there are no girls from Pakistan staying in their hotel. Then I have to get more specific, telling them she wouldn't necessarily be staying in the hotel, that she is a working girl. I show them her picture, but no one admits to having seen her.

Shireen didn't want me staying alone or spending money on hotel and food. When he saw my 1000 *dirham* checkout bill, that cinched it. And here I am staying with Shireen's friend, Ahsanullah, a truck driver (and not a painted overheating Bedford truck that can only carry four oversized horses or water buffaloes, but a real truck, a Mercedes 50 ton container truck) and a load of Waziri *Mehsood* taxi drivers.

I'm even starting to pick up the Waziri dialect of Pashtu, similar to Kandahari or Ghazniwali from Afghanistan. No one I know here except Parvez and Abdul Aziz speaks any English. It's fine, it's how I like it. And living with Pathans I can't spend any money. It is the Pukhtun, or Pakistani way. The Islamic love and respect of guests. The Prophet Muhammad (PBUH) emphasized the importance of honoring guests and travellers. It is ingrained the culture.

---

* Ed note: As of February 2014 the visa costs $160.

If staying with Pathan taxi drivers can't help me in my search, what chance do I have on my own? Last night we drove to Overlaunch. Driving at night it's just cool enough to turn off the car's air-conditioning and roll down the windows.

Still no luck. Maybe she is back in Pakistan or hidden somewhere here? If so, then I don't know how I will ever find her. Occasionally I find myself thinking there are other fish in the sea, but I can't seem to keep that thought for very long.

I'm staying about 10 minutes outside Dubai near the airport, an area called Sonapur (literally City of Gold—a Pakistani/Indian driver/laborer's en- clave). Reminiscent of Palm Springs, California: sand, sage brush and dry heat. You park in front on the road and walk on a sandy path through a metal gate between a row of two low, one-story, stucco buildings. Six one room apartments in a row on our side and a dozen in the building on the other side. Each apartment has a glass window, but the blinds are constantly drawn to keep out the scorching desert heat. The constantly running air-conditioners drone and drip away. Our side of the camp is all Waziri Pathans. The other side is occupied by Punjabi Sikh drivers.

Now is afternoon siesta time—after lunch and prayer. Lunch was a big bowl of greasy meat *qorma* and large flat *roti* from a local restaurant. Good taste and not costing two to eight dollars per meal and not eaten alone. But that type of food does bring back memories of sitting on a *charpoy* in Lahore eating lunch at Nasreen's. I can't get rid of the memories.

It's hard to believe I used to be able to hop on the bus and go down to Lahore (only eight bone jarring hours on GT Road) to spend the night with her, eat food like this and only hear Pashtu language. Just the luxury of sitting in a room with her. It used to cost me under 100 rupees to take the Flying Coach to Lahore. I've spent 30,000 rupees so far just getting here and I don't even know that she is here. But half the Pathans in Dubai must know about Noor Moham- mad Khan, the crazy American Muslim and his missing Pathan Lahori girl friend, Nasreen.

I have no desire for another woman, but I do have my eyes open. I need to find a cure. Is there one? Is that it? Can I find it? It has to be some deep magic to break the spell of Nasreen. My Waziri friends tell me I need to have some *peer* make me a *taviz* to break the spell. I know what kind of *taviz* I need. Could the *peer* be Beer? I did enjoy spending time with her in Thailand, but I really can't see it as anything permanent. She was fun but that was just some tem- porary relief. Then I came back to Pakistan and saw Nasreen again and "just a look, was all it took."

June 15th
I'm with Nasreen. She's wearing a blue striped dress that comes slightly above her knees and it's raining like in an Indian movie song. Her hair is wet, streaming down her face. I hear her talking. It's English.... I'm in a dream. It's 1:30 in the morning and I'm sleeping in a room with three snoring Waziris. Good morning!

Tor Mohammad, a policeman in Sharja, is a friend of Ahsanullah's from

Derra Ismail Khan. He lives in the Pakistani slum area of Sharja, behind a rickety, corrugated metal gate, one of several cinder block rooms. A step down with a six foot high ceiling. Of course there is an air-conditioner—everyone here has one—but everything else about it is Pakistani. Crowded and primitive, yet Pakistani cozy. He shares the room with two others.

We eat dinner at 10:30. Ah! A change of diet I think, but too soon. Same Pathan food. Since I've been with these Waziris, I've eaten the same meal three times a day. At least I'm used to Pathan food and even like it. Not complaining, just noting. And the price is right. So is the companionship.

Maybe we've found Nasreen, but I can't count on it. I won't. Not until I see her face in life. I see it all the time in my mind. The other night we gave her picture to one of Ahsanullah's friends and villagers from Dera Ismail Khan, a taxi driver who lives in Overlaunch named Manu Khan. Last night, before going to Tor Mohammad's, Ahsanullah spoke with Manu Khan on the phone. Maybe he has some information. *Insha'Allah.* Have to wait until 8:00 tonight when we go to his house.

Last night after dinner when we got back to Ahsanullah's; Ahsanullah, Tor Mohammad and another driver decided to go to a hotel where they said there were all types of girls: Egyptian, Filipino, Palestinian, Indian and even English, though here English usually means anyone from west of Turkey with light eyes and hair. Usually a girl from Yugoslavia, Hungary or Poland. They wanted me to go too. They said if I "did it" with some girl I'd be all right. I didn't want to go. Especially if there is a chance that I'll find Nasreen. What is wrong with them? I love them and relate to them so well, but on the subject of women, we just can't seem to mesh.

Ahsanullah has two wives living with his family in Dera Ismail Khan and he just answered an ad in a Karachi newspaper's matrimonial section from a Pakistani teacher living in Abu Dhabi who wants to get married. He's looking for another wife! And last night he went off to screw some *hooker* in a Dubai hotel. I don't think they know what love is. Or maybe it is me who is wrong? I'm the one who is crying and dying. They're laughing and *enjoying.*

On that level, I don't relate so well. They've got wives and they don't seem to care. A wife is like a TV to them. Just leave it at home for a year or so. Rent another. Get a new model. If you can afford it, a TV in every room. No problem. Their relatives are at home to kill their wives if they should happen to look at another man. I knew Nas was with other men, yet my heart was with her. Maybe that was my weakness?

Ahsanullah and Tor Mohammad haven't come in yet and the other three here are talking at full tilt—just chit-chatting. My head hurts from their shouting. It doesn't help that it's difficult for me to understand their Waziri dialect, especially at the rapid pace in which they are speaking. I'm going outside to smoke a Gold Leaf from one of the packs I brought for her in the event I found her. The sun hasn't fully come up yet and the air is still ever-so-slightly cool. The AC is even off. I haven't been able to sleep since I woke from my dreams.

I don't like to sleep anymore. I hate waking. Every time I wake, I remember she is gone.

Yesterday, when Ahsanullah was praying, Tor Mohammad came in the room and started talking to him. Maybe they take God, and prayer, as lightly as their women? Being a rather new Muslim I would never think of talking to someone while they were praying. Just being a convert, what do I know anyway?

Now that I am staying with other people I can't cry as much as before in my private room. The latrines are in a separate building out back. I cry when I'm squatting on the porcelain Asian squat toilet. I can't seem to stop. I just need to let out some emotion. There is so much sadness and pain bottled up inside me, I can't even believe this is true. And then, what is really true anyway, except our own perceptions? I loved my life in Pakistan, but lately it feels like a dream, a stupid backward dream. The dream is over and I'm alone in the desert with a bunch of Waziris hiding my tears in the toilet so they don't think I am any crazier than I am. Mirza is in America taking care of our investment properties trying to get the business off the ground. I know he can use my help, but I am afraid of what I would do if I were there. I'd probably burn them all down—with the tenants inside. All I can conceive of doing is running around the Emirates looking for Nasreen. I haven't seen any tourist sights yet, but then there aren't many tourists out in Overlaunch, not any sightseers.

Maybe some news from America would pull me back in some from this insanity. Of course, even thinking that shows me how crazy I must be. Even so, I hope there is some mail waiting for me when I get back to Pakistan. I haven't received any mail in the last few months. If there isn't any, I'm going to blow up the *GPO*.

June 15th, 5:00 P.M.
Palms Springs Desert—Waziri Taxi Camp—Sonapur, Dubai
"I can see the bats," he said (once upon a time). Don't you see them? I know if you look hard enough you will see them also. And in Pakistan, too. Just have another hit of Sui Gas,* sit back and enjoy. Don't worry, you're not insane. Insanity is fun. This isn't. Is it?

Can a low flying bat give you rabies if it flies into your face when you're walking in Karimpura Bazaar at night? What! You can't see them here in the desert? You will see them yet. I know you will. Just put your gas pedal to the floor and take another whiff. And when you get there, maybe you will.... **

Tomorrow is the last day to leave for *Haj* by air. You could have made it by car if you left last week. Probably last month if you left by camel. But I can't go to *Haj* right now. I'm busy in Dubai. My mind won't let me rest.

For me it is very strange but since I left Pakistan I haven't missed it once. In fact, last night when we were going to Tor Mohammad's, in the area of Sharja

---

* *Pakistan natural gas, from Sui, Balouchistan*
** *Written with Hunter Thompson in mind*

that is mostly Pakistani, it was the first time since I've been here that I've heard jerk drivers honking their stupid horns (a constant occurrence in Pakistan). The neighborhood is mostly immigrant (or is it ignorant?) workers. Of course, all my friends here are Pakistani.

As for the Arabs, they haven't changed. They used to raid and capture their slaves to work for them. Now they are oil rich. They can afford to hire their slaves. A Pakistani policeman here gets 5000 *dirhams* a month (as opposed to the 1000 rupees—145 dirhams—a policeman earns in Pakistan). An Arab cop earns 20,000 a month. And there is a special branch of Arab cops to oversee the Pakistani cops to make sure they don't take bribes.

On *Juma* the international phone rates drop substantially. Even the rate to the United States drops to five dirhams a minute. But the rate to Pakistan remains seven and a half dirhams a minute. I asked Parvez why this was and he answered they had caught Pakistanis drilling holes in coins and using the same coin over and over, pulling them out with a string. They also caught a Pakistani using coins made of ice. A certain pay phone showed much usage on the computer but there was never any money in the box, only rust. They had a man watch the phone and he caught a Pakistani using coin replicas he had made from ice. Is that true? It figures. I wonder if they froze the evidence?

I'm dying here. I'm going crazy. Why doesn't God hear me? I pray five times a day and I can't even get a skinny, over-used Pathan *kanjri*? Is it fair? Does fairness even matter in any of it?

I recall a story Arif told me before I left Pakistan....

There was a Hindu begger and a Muslim begger sitting next to each other for 10 years. The Muslim was saying "Rahman" (an Arabic name of God, meaning "the Merciful") over and over again. The Hindu was repeating "Ram Ram" (a Hindu name for God). In 10 years the Muslim never once made a mistake in his pronunciation, but after all that time the Hindu got mixed up and said "Rahman" one time instead of "Ram Ram."

"YES?" God answered the Hindu.

The Muslim looked up in surprise, "What is this? In 10 years you never answered me, but this bloody Hindu only one time calls your name and you answer. Why?"

God answered, "You already have faith in me, but this Hindu doesn't. If I don't answer him, what would he think? You, I don't need to answer."

Is that my answer?

It is nice to have faith, but how long can it hold out?

June 16th

I went with Tor Mohammad and another cab driver last night to Over-launch to talk with Manu Khan but the Nasreen he found was the same one I had found last week. Maybe she isn't here, if all these taxi *wallahs* can't find her. Or maybe she has been sold to some *sheikh*? Or maybe she is in Pakistan? There are so many maybes. The only question that isn't a maybe is if I am crazy or not.

When we left Manu Khan's house we still hadn't prayed our evening prayer. Walking around the corner to the car we passed a dark, quiet mosque sitting behind high, white cement walls. Tor Mohammad tested the gate and found it open. We went inside, across the sandy courtyard and made *wuzu* by the light of the street lights. Inside we turned on some lights and in peaceful solitude the three of us individually offered our prayers. The serenity even took me away from my crazed search... for a brief while.

Tor Mohammad told me about his escapade last night: He made love to an Indian girl (though those weren't exactly the words he used). It cost him 200 dirhams for the girl and another 200 for the room. He was only with the girl 15 minutes and the rest of the night he slept in the room with Ahsanullah, who apparently was just along for the ride according to their account. It didn't really seem to matter to him. Fifteen minutes was as long as he needed the girl for anyway. It seems like much money for such a short time, but then I'm not earning 5000 dirhams a month. Only I just keep thinking what his family in Pakistan could have done with 2700 rupees, a lot of money in Pakistan, though it isn't my business to judge. How much did I spend to get here, anyhow?

June 17th

Still with the *Mehsood*s. Every morning at 4:30 somebody knocks on our door to wake us for prayer. Then the tube lights come on.

It is hard for me to fall asleep, to turn my mind off. It just churns out of control. Usually I doze off an hour or two after midnight. After I get up (I'm usually one of the first), make *wuzu* and pray it is really difficult to get back to sleep. At least in the hotel I was getting more rest, sleeping in until 6:30 or 7:00. But then I was missing morning prayer. Which do I need more, sleep or prayer? Might as well at least give God a chance. It does say in the morning Azan, *"Al-salatu khayru min an-nawm" (Prayer is better than sleep),* doesn't it?

Last night I went into Dubai alone. It's nice at night, exciting and modern, and completely crowded with immigrant Indian and Pakistani workers. Restaurants, cloth shops, electronics shops, modern air-conditioned bazaars, a little bit of everything. One can really feel at a crossroads of the Subcontinent, Africa and the Arabian peninsula here.

I got back at 10:00. Ghulam Ali, one of the taxi drivers who lives with Ahsanullah, had stayed behind to wait for me, to take me to the *tablighee* center for dinner. Shir Mohammad, another of Ahsanullah's roommates wanted to introduce me to his father who had arrived from Iran on his way to Oman on a *tabligh* mission with several dozen other Pakistani *tablighees* (lucky me).

As we were rather late, most of them had already eaten but Ahsanullah, Ghulam Ali, Shir Mohammad and father and several others ate with me. God, I didn't want to hear any *tablighee* talk. I guess it was God's mercy, at least, that I arrived late enough so I didn't have to eat with everyone.

In Dubai I had filled myself with wonderful, multicolored, ice cold, mixed fruit juice drinks. Dinner was big plates of goat meat and bread. All they seem to eat is meat. I would tell them it isn't healthy to eat all that meat, but they all seem healthier than I am. When I finally couldn't eat anymore they pushed another huge plate piled high with meat and bones at me.

"The Prophet, peace be upon Him, said..." I told them, "to leave one third of the stomach empty. It is a *sunnah* I believe, and it is good for health." No one could disagree with me. It is a well-known fact. I heard some say that I was really a good Muslim—and I didn't have to eat any more meat. Then we adjourned to another room where we sat with more people and ate fruit from large platters—bananas, grapes, mangos and oranges.

Most of my companions had beards and turbans. They were all very surprised when they found out I wasn't a real Pathan or a Muslim by birth, but a convert. Before that I had hardly received any attention, except the normal attention due a guest. All of a sudden I was fair preaching game.

One fellow sitting next to me, one of the younger ones (the older ones were more mellow and polite), started drilling a lot of *religious* talk into me. I quoted something I had heard in Peshawar from Mr. Mahboob, "The Prophet, may peace be upon Him, said, 'When a man is eating, don't disturb him. He is even excused from answering *salaam aleikum* and the answering phrases to the *Azan*.'" (When the *Azan (Adhan)* is being called, it is *sunnah* to silently repeat the words.)

He was trying to practice his theological rap in the little broken English he knew but it was so bad I refused to speak to him in anything but Pashtu.

"Speak Pashtu," his friends told him. "He speaks Pashtu really well."

He wouldn't let up. I looked at everyone sitting across from us and said, "You all know better than I. I am only a convert, but isn't it a *sunnah* not to speak with someone when they are eating?"

All agreed with me again and told him to shut up, but he just wouldn't stop. Sometimes it seems that some of these one-sided, religious fundamentalists don't even know the fundamentals of their religion.

"We're going," Ahsanullah said. "You can stay here tonight and talk with your friend."

"No, I have to go with you," I said. "I have some important work to do at your house (dreaming of Nasreen)."

"When are you going on a 40 day *tabligh* mission?" Shir Mohammad asked me.

"When I find Nasreen and we're married and we have our first son, then you can ask me again. Maybe we'll name him Shir."

"Come with me to that hotel," Tor Mohammad nudged me as we walked out to the car. "Then you will be all right."

"Do you think 10 minutes with some unknown *kanjri* will make me forget her?" I told him *(I like to know my whores)*. "A month with Reema (my fave Pakistani film star of the day) and I'd still be thinking of her."

And that voice in my head, that voice in my heart, keeps screaming, "God, you screwed up! Why were you so blinking stupid?" It won't stop. If I can only find her, have one more chance to talk to her. Maybe she won't give a damn. I only want the chance. To know if she is all right. If she is happy. Am I delusional?

And then, maybe she really is in Dir, north of Peshawar. But what do I do there? Dir isn't Peshawar, nor is it Lahore, nor is it Dubai. And a 32 bore, or a 30 bore for that matter, isn't a Kalashnikov.

June 17th, afternoon
Sonapur, outside Dubai,
Just back from Dubai. The mosques in Dubai are nice, modern and impressive. Keeping up on my prayers, but my faith is low. Does it matter? As my dear friend Anwar Khan always says, "Who wants to go to heaven with all those beard *wallahs* and *tablighees* (preachers)? Hell will be where all the *sharab* and *taxis* are."

Good. Akbar, Nas and I will be sitting on a *charpoy* with our *Gold Leaf cigarettes, nuswar, charras...* and Khan Baba. At least after Lahore and Dubai, I'll be used to the heat.

I bought a Chinese tape player today in Dubai for Hafez, my travel agent friend in Peshawar. He had humbly asked for one. It came with a 24-hour guarantee!

Called Master Ali Haider in Peshawar today. He asked me if I found Nasreen yet. He said when I got back to Pakistan we would find me another Nasreen soon. I don't think so. I'd like to be optimistic, but I'm just too damn down and out of my mind.

Go to Bangkok? A break from all this. A break from Muslims and Pakistan. A chance to be left alone. Not told what and how to eat, when to sleep or wake or pray. Just lazing in a fresh bed next to Beer watching Thai music videos on TV.

June 18th, 5:00 A.M.
In the middle of a dream... *Bam bam bam!* Pounding on the door—time for morning prayer. Once I'm up, I can't get back to sleep. My mind keeps spinning out. I can't shake the depression. It gets deeper and deeper. I get sadder and sadder and madder and madder. At what? At times I am mad as hell with Pakistan and Islam, but they are just close and comfortable scapegoats right now. It must be true that we only hurt the ones we love. You can't truly hate unless you've loved. I don't want to be so pessimistic, but I am. I've never been like this before in my life. I've always been so optimistic. It was so easy. It was nothing I tried at. It just was. And now this is what is. Nasreen seems to have wiped all my previous life away.

On *Juma* I met Parvez at a Pakistani mosque near where I'm staying for the *Juma* prayer. Parvez comes out here to deliver the Friday Khutba (sermon). Very Pakistani mosque for the Emirates. No AC, older frayed carpets, chipped paint. Lots of worshipers. I arrived late. I could hear the *Azan* coming across the scorching noon sands but it took a little time to find the right street leading to the mosque. Being late, I prayed in the back on the veranda, crowded with other late-comers, on straw mats without even an overhead fan.

After prayer Parvez took me to his house in Ajman (on the Gulf, northeast of Sharja) for lunch. When we arrived at his house, a cozy little bungalow near the beach, he introduced me to his wife and four young children. He, the children and I ate on the floor in the carpeted sitting room. A Pakistani feast of *pilau*, chicken, *seekh kebab*, meat swimming in spicy, greasy gravy, salad, *achar*, *chutney*, *roti*, *qawah*. A pleasant change from the Pathan food I've been eating. After lunch we all took a nap, laying in front of the AC on the carpet in the sitting room. We woke up around 4:00, prayed *Asr* prayer and he drove me home.

Later, as Ahsanullah and I were walking to the taxi stand, a deserted corner near his house, nothing existing except the blazing sun in the blue afternoon sky; the hot, parched desert air; the burning scorched black metaled road and the sandy desert stretching away at our sides, we were talking,

"I didn't like English when I was in school, so I never learned it," he explained. "When people learn English they lose the Islamic customs."

"That's the reason Muslims are so weak today," I complained. "All they have to look up to are donkey brains like Saddam Hussain. The Prophet (PBUH) said education is very important. He said if you need to go to China to get educated, go. You yourself drive a modern Mercedes truck. You have an AC, a fridge and electric lights."

"Noor Mohammad, I also don't like Saddam. Iraq is rich in oil, like the Emirates and Kuwait, but all of the money goes into arms. He may be wrong, but is the United States right? Saddam may be a donkey brain but at least he is our donkey brain. And Kuwait was carved out of Iraq by the *Englaise*. It does belong to Iraq. At least he is not letting them dictate to him. He is standing up to them."

"Yes, it is a difficult thing to say, brother. Being brave is one thing. But jeopardizing innocent people? I don't know the answer."

"God knows better, Noor Mohammad."

I continued with a story I had picked up from Anwar Khan. "Two Pathans were walking next to some railroad tracks. They saw a bull running down the tracks charging an oncoming train. 'He's very brave,' said one of the Pathans. 'Yes, maybe,' said the other, 'but he *is also very stupid.'*" Well, one can't fight city hall, or ignorant rustic beliefs. I'm not blaming Islam, I am blaming (some) Muslims.

"Your friend in America, does he pray?" Ahsanullah asked me, changing the subject from politics to religion, another easy subject to discuss.

"Not all the time," I said, "but he is a very good man."

"Prayer is what is important. Prayer and *wuzu* are obligatory. If he doesn't pray, the rest isn't important."

"You think it is more important to pray than to be a good human?" I asked, continuing, "When I was in Peshawar I heard a story of *Hazrat Ali*. He was in a mosque praying once and a *mullah* was watching him from the back of the mosque. When *Hazrat Ali* went down in *sajdah*, his fingers didn't properly touch the floor. The *mullah* took his shoe and threw it at *Hazrat Ali*, striking him behind the head.

"Then the *mullah* explained to *Hazrat Ali* the mistake he had made in his prayer and told him to do it again. *Hazrat Ali* prayed the prayer again without making one mistake. When he was finished, the *mullah* asked him, 'Now tell me, which time was better, the first or the second?'

"And *Hazrat Ali* answered without a moment's hesitation, 'The first time was better. The first time I was offering my prayers for God and the second time I was offering the prayers for fear of being hit by your shoe again.'"

Ahsanullah agreed it was a very good story and we again changed the subject to easier things to discuss, such as women.

In the evening over dinner, a big plate of meat and gravy, Shireen said to me, "When you get back to Pakistan you have to get married quickly."

"I think I am going to Lahore to check out a Punjabi disco dancer I met at a wedding in Peshawar," I told him matter of factly. "She is in Hira Mandi."

"You like bad women, Noor Mohammad," he stated.

"Yeah, I guess I do.... Bad women are good women."

"Have you done anything with her yet?" Ahsanullah asked me, winking.

"No. Not yet," I answered. There is place in my heart for only one woman. But if I can't find her, I guess I'll have to try to make room for another. It's just I can't seem to think of being with another woman yet. I still love her too strongly. Maybe that is why the culture doesn't like love marriages? That way, one can marry up to four women, have a lot of children, stay away for a year, and spend 10 minutes with a prostitute. I don't know.

I am a bit fed-up with this culture. Is that the price for going so deep? Maybe I got too deep? Is that why now I'm drowning? I agree with this culture and accept (and live) most of it, but not having any *blood* family, the restricted female contact gets to me. Of course I have been lucky living in Bibi Ji's house and knowing all the women of her family and some of the neighbor women who constantly drop by, and then there are some female singers, and my friend Shahnaz and her sister, and of course all the women of Nasreen's house, if I may be so bold in claiming them. But at times, I still miss the free association one can have in the West with a woman.

Maybe I never was as Pakistani as I thought?

June 19th

Why did I do it? Why did I treat her so badly? So callously? Why didn't I appreciate what I had found? Famous last words! I treated it all as a child's game, treated her like a toy. Can she forgive me? It looks like that is a question I may never know the answer to. I hope God can, but then God is supposed to be All Forgiving. Thank God for that. I don't seem to be. Not with myself. From God's side, maybe I just need some more patience? How much do I have?

The pain is sitting deep inside my heart. I still burn inside when I think of her. I guess it is the feeling of telling your wife you don't love her and don't want to be married to her in a fit of anger and then she leaves while you are at work and gets herself killed on the freeway. Burnt to a crisp so you can't even identify the body and you'll never know what was going through her mind there at the end. All you have left is the "if only I hads."

I don't know why I thought everything I had in Pakistan would be ruined if

I married her when what I really mostly had was her? And I really didn't even have her, or if I did, I never knew it. Maybe when I am back in Pakistan I can find someone to learn to love. I can't wait for another Nasreen. There doesn't seem to be any time anymore. Now I know time isn't going to wait for me. It didn't. She took the time and ran.

Pakistan seems so dirty, backward and germ-ridden from here. Here restaurants and butcher shops are so clean, so ordered. There are strict health laws and checking. It doesn't make for such interesting photo ops but I guess it does make for better health. In Pakistan there is no law or efficient checking. Just a 10-rupee note to a cop, or a pistol in the face. All Pakistanis know about it, complain about it, laugh about it, but don't do a thing about it.

Met a pimp on a corner on Nief Road in Dubai this afternoon. A Pathan from Bombay. We went into a juice stall and had ice fruit juices. He told me he had three Indian girls in an apartment close by, behind the gold bazaar. I told him about Nasreen and showed him a photograph. He said he would check around.

He showed me a picture of his girlfriend who also ran away whom he was looking for. I guess these girls have a way of doing that sort of thing. Are they trying to run to something better or just running away from the emptiness of the life they have already known? He said he would meet me at the juice stand at 9:00 in the evening. He didn't show up. People like him, it seems, have a way of doing that.

❖   ❖   ❖

NASREEN IN THE GOLD BAZAAR, IS THAT YOU?

June 21st

Yesterday Ahsanullah and I ran into my street pimp friend. He invited us to come along to his flat. Ahsanullah said, "Why not. Let's go check it out." Obviously, I would never think of doing such a bad thing on my own (*toba*).

We followed the pimp through the gold bazaar and then cut through sandy, narrow, back alleys, water condensation dripping down strings from overhead air-conditioners. Finally we came to the flat: a modern, concrete, newly-finished, six-story apartment building.

We went up the elevator to the fourth floor. Most of the flats were still vacant; his showed only signs of temporary habitation. There were utensils for making tea in the kitchen and low, padded sitting mats on the carpeted floor. There was a telephone, ashtrays and off to the side two flimsily-constructed stalls, the walls not even reaching the ceiling, in which I presumed were mattresses.

The two girls there were speaking Urdu. One looked like one of Bibi Ji's daughters in Peshawar, only younger. She looked too much like somebody I related to as a sister to even consider. The other girl I thought was rather cute. Her dark hair fell half way down her green satin *kameez* covered back. Her dark eyes beckoned me invitingly. The pimp told me she spoke English. I looked at her and asked in English what her name was. Gazing back at me, with nose ring glittering, in a wet, sultry voice she answered, "Nasreen," enticingly drawing out the word.

My *qismet* or had she just been coached?

I arranged to come back and spend the night with her even though she wasn't the Nasreen I was looking for. It is beginning to feel like the quest for her is failing. Only a few days left here anyway. Maybe some special magic will click with her (though with my Nasreen, it happened in a heartbeat—just a look was all it took) and my life can even become more confusing. And anyway, it isn't so often that I get to Dubai.

I was supposed to meet her back at the flat at 8:00. Am I twisted or is it this culture? It felt like I was on my way to a date. On the way, walking through the gold bazaar at 7:00 the *Maghrib Azan* rang out through the streets. I stopped at a gorgeous, large mosque with an immense crystal chandelier hanging from the center of the lofty ceiling. I had prayed the afternoon prayer there once before. Near the doors were polished stainless steel ice-water drinking fountains.

After I left the mosque I had trouble finding the flat, though I thought I had made careful note of corners, shops and signs earlier when I was leaving with Ahsanullah. Walking down the narrow, sandy, darkening lanes between mostly new, multi-storied apartment buildings, I finally found what felt like the right building. It was new and most of the flats were untenanted but when I went up the elevator to the apartment I had been in previously, it too was empty. I left the building and walked around just to make certain I wasn't confusing buildings but I was right. I went back up the elevator to check again. Still empty.

And I was so looking forward to spending a night with someone (a body). It has been five months since I have been with any woman. Feeling completely overdosed on men. I ache for the opportunity to exchange a little intimate energy with a women. My excuse to myself.

This morning I went back to the apartment at 10:30 armed with my trusty knife. I had only given 50 dirhams as a "deposit," so I didn't think it was any big rip off I was walking into, but it just seemed so strange that after making the arrangement the apartment was deserted when I returned last night.

Now the pimp was there but the girls weren't. He said because of the approaching *Eid* holiday the police had come at 3:00 yesterday afternoon. The girls had gone home. He gave me my 50 dirhams back and told me if I wanted to come back on *Eid* day Nasreen would be back then.

At 5:30 Shir Mohammad, Ahsanullah and I drove to the animal bazaar to get a goat to sacrifice for *Eid*. On the way we passed the *tablighee* center. Shir Mohammad started to pull into the parking lot. I commenced to jump out of the car. I didn't come to Dubai to talk to *tablighees*. "I don't want any *tablighee* talk," I yelled. "Let me out of here! I'm going to the Dubai bazaar!"

Ahsanullah calmed me down by telling me we were only dropping off something to Shir Mohammad's father. Ahsanullah and I went in the mosque to pray *Asr*. At least nobody tried to talk to me while we were praying.

Then we went to get our goat. We strolled through the dusty lanes of the makeshift market, between pens of sheep, goats and cows, under the shade of corrugated iron and canvas cloth. We settled on an agreeable price with some *Bedouin* herders and we led the goat out on a piece of frayed twine. We closed it in the desert heated trunk of the car and drove off. I guess they wanted to get it home precooked?

We headed for the vegetable market. Shir Mohammad told me they would drop me in the Dubai bazaar after getting vegetables. The traffic on the wide, divided highway was stop and go, crawling at a snail's pace. On our right the barren sand stretched off to a glassy blue sea (Arabian/Persian Gulf). Several miles ahead of us, standing high modern and massive in the hazy lowering afternoon sunlight was a building appearing to be the Hyatt Regency, marking the start of the Dubai bazaar. Shir Mohammad jokingly told me the buildings in the hazy distance were the Sharja skyline. My tolerance for jokes was at an extreme low and again I almost jumped out of the car until Ahsanullah reassured me it was actually the Hyatt standing in the distance.

At the vegetable market we ran into two other Waziri friends of Ahsanullah. As they chatted, I looked at the traffic going into Dubai, which was only getting worse. I knew Shir Mohammad and Ahsanullah could avoid much of it if they went directly home from here without going into town. Also, it seemed I could walk it as fast as we could drive it in the traffic. And on top of all that, I was starting to totally burn out on quickly spoken Waziri Pashtu and Shir Mohammad's overly friendly, pushy manner.

I'm starting to feel as if I need to get stoned or drunk or committed for shock therapy. I am praying five times a day, but for whose advantage? Ahsanullah very truthfully and sincerely told me the other day that my prayers weren't for his advantage nor were they for God's advantage. It is for my advantage. I am too crazy to see anything and fighting it all the way. Up and down, up and down.

These Waziris are so great to me. God, I must seem so crazy to them. Though I have only known them for such a short time, it feels like we have all known each other for so long. They treat me as if I actually was one of their own family—a commonality with Muslims in general.

❖   ❖   ❖

EID MUBARAK

June 22nd

This morning Ahsanullah and I killed the goat. *"Ai corbaan!"*

First we all drove to the *tablighee* center for the *Eid* prayer, but we arrived just as they finished the prayer. We heard an *Eid Azan* coming across the desert sand from another mosque. We got in the car and headed in that direction. We were early enough to catch the prayer. Shir Mohammad dropped Ahsanullah and I off back at the house. He and Ghulam Ali had to leave on some driving assignments.

Ahsanullah and I went out behind the Sikh's side of the building. In the sand were several old cement slabs. We chose one to sacrifice our goat on. On two of the other slabs other Pathans and a few of their little sons were doing their *Eid* sacrifices. Some of the Sikhs looked on, perched in the windows of their one story apartments.

Ahsanullah had to coach me what to do. The young boys were watching their fathers sacrifice their animals on their slabs. This was something Ahsanullah had been a part of since he was a young child. The closest I had come to anything like this before was killing a few chickens.

We tied the goat's feet and gave him some water. Then we flipped him over on his back. Ahsanullah instructed me to hold him and then he took the knife and saying *"Bismillah"* and *"**Allah Akbar**"* three times,* he ran its sharp edge across the goat's neck. The blood gushed and spurted into the dry sand. A warm, quiet wind blew across the desert. Across from us blood was spurting from the necks of the other sacrifices. We let the blood flow out until the goat stopped his kickings. Then Ahsanullah sharpened the knife on a stone and commenced to cut off the goat's head and feet. He gutted him and cut him into pieces, putting the pieces into a large, dull, aluminum bowl.

By the time Shir Mohammad and Ghulam Ali returned an hour and a half later with Manu Khan and a another friend we had a huge bowl of freshly cooked goat meat waiting. Shireen and Tor Mohammad arrived with a plastic bag of large, flat breads wrapped in newspaper. Neighboring drivers dropped in for *Eid* greetings and to distribute a portion of their sacrifices. With only the ever present ice water bottles, a cardboard crate of Omani grapes and a box of mangos there was plenty of room in the refrigerator to store the abundance of freshly killed meat.

Two of our neighbors stopped by to eat some meat with us. They started talking with me. They had just found out that I wasn't really a beardless Waziri like Shireen. One of them said to me, "Because you have become a Muslim, you are assured to go directly to Paradise."

I looked at Ahsanullah and smiled, "Direct to Paradise, with a stop over in Samnabad and maybe one in Dubai gold bazaar."

He returned the smile and added a wink.

Remembering Nasreen, sitting on a *charpoy* with her last *Eid,* watching her cut strips of freshly slaughtered buffalo meat to hang on a line for jerky. These people I'm living with can't really understand my attachment for her. I'm realizing I spent more time with her, knew her better and more intimately, than they seem to know their own wives. They'd never just sit and watch their wives wash clothes, iron or sweep. We used to get high together, watch TV or videos and go to the bazaar together. *We even made love with the light on.*

When I get back to Pakistan, if she is in Lahore I'll flip. Am I just being self centered? I am so mixed up. Part of me wants to get away from the noise, dust and filth of Pakistan, but then it is all so much like home to me. I still want to

---

* It is regarded inappropriate to use the phrase "Bismillah al Rahman Al Rahim" (In the name of God the Beneficent the Merciful), which is used when starting most actions, in this situation because slaughtering is not considered an act of mercy, though it is to be done with mercy!

stay and continue in my life there. It is the culture I am comfortable in and besides, the chances of Nasreen ever showing up in the United States seem rather nil.

It's *Eid* and a time to be with family or old friends. These Waziris have so taken me in as family it is hard to imagine I have only really been with them such a short time. It feels like I grew up with them. Because they are so Afghan-like, it strengthens the feeling. The customs and ways of Afghanistan feel such a part of my past, my growing up, coming of age in Asia. Yet I keep remembering Nasreen and then I feel so all alone. Not really a true part of any of it. A specter. What can I do to stifle this feeling?

10:30 P.M.
All day I've eaten only meat, as befitting *Eid Corban* I suppose. Remembering an *Eid Corban* in Chitral a couple years back when there wasn't any meat and my main concerns were three gigantic horses and wondering when we would get to Gilgit so I could go to Lahore to see Nasreen. Life shifts so constantly

I'm leaving tomorrow for Pakistan. In my real, or imagined need, for female energy for a change, I finally broke down and went to the Dubai gold bazaar in the evening to see Nasreen. Lesson learned—not all Nasreens are created equal. A Nasreen by the same name, isn't necessarily as sweet. What did I think? I just needed some sort of change from all the bearded men. She was pretty, but being with her only made me sadder in the loss of my Nasreen.

Well, it was a chance. It saddened me just paying to relieve myself with her. I felt bad for her, though she didn't seem to care. Business is business. Very empty feeling. I ended up lecturing her on the necessity of using a condom in her line of work, something she didn't really seem to care about one way or another.

It made me realize how hard my search could be for a replacement Nasreen. Maybe I will just have to wait again for that first magical look. Do those things happen twice in a lifetime? It is that look these Pathans can surely relate to, but is it only in poetry? They just can't seem to believe it is so necessary for me. That I should even want it with a *taxi,* or a wife.

June 23rd, 4:45 A.M.
Shir Mohammad is starting to drive me crazy(ier) and it isn't a very far drive. He jokes with me or talks religion with me when I don't have the patience for it, and in fast Waziri dialect that is hard for me to follow. He sets his alarm for 4:20 and then sleeps through it along with all the rest of them. Besides me, Ghulam Ali, the quietest, is usually the first to get up to pray.

Once I'm up, no matter how little sleep I've gotten, I can't get back to sleep. I go out back to make *wuzu* in the cement and brick trough next to the bathrooms. On cement slabs, similar to the ones we sacrificed our animals on, in the sand between our building and the bathrooms other drivers are praying. Surreal in pre-morning darkness. I offer my prayers in the room next to Ghulam Ali. I make a *dua* that I will see Nasreen again. I make another that I can forget her. I must find some way out of this madness. Then I turn on the tube light. Ahsanullah, Shir Mohammad and Tor Mohammad are still sleeping. I hope they miss prayer. Oh well, at 5:00 I suppose I'll shout, "Get up! Prayer time is going!"

If they are not up by then something like that usually does the job. Then I can reach under Ahsanullah's pillow for a hit of his green *nuswar.*

Shireen and I were eating mangos and talking. "Why don't you grow a beard like all the rest of your villagers?" I asked.

"It is great *sawab* to grow a beard," he agreed. "I'm waiting until I make *Haj.*" I've used the same excuse many times myself.

"Everybody in Pakistan also told me after Nasreen left that it is great *sawab* to marry a prostitute," I began to rant. "But here everybody tells me not to marry a prostitute, but to grow my beard. I guess they are afraid they can't satisfy a woman? A beard you only have to wash once a week (not counting *wuzu*). If they weren't afraid of not satisfying their wives maybe they wouldn't be afraid to let them go out of the house, or talk to men. But then they only go home once a year or so, to get their wives pregnant and that only takes five minutes and they don't even have to waste electricity with the lights on so they don't even have to see how fat she has become."

Shireen must be thinking, "What kind of madman have I befriended?" But they all seem to understand my condition and take all of my ravings with a grain of salt and a lot of brotherly compassion. If I were in Palm Springs and I had picked up some foreigner who turned out like me I'd probably dump him in the desert.

I took a share taxi out toward Dubai and got out at a familiar looking intersection near Overlaunch. Because of *Eid,* shops were closed and the streets were deserted. I started walking, searching for familiar landmarks. Finally I found the house of the fat madame. I took a chance on somebody being there, remembering in Pakistan on the days following *Eid* those types so inclined to such pursuits showing up at Nasreen's house.

The corpulent lady was surprised I had come alone. She was also surprised it wasn't for some of the special *Eid meat* in her establishment. I sat in the air-conditioned sitting room with half a dozen waiting Pathan customers watching a large color TV and chatting, reminiscent of days gone by chatting with waiting customers at Nasreen's. It really made me hope that she had married some nice guy who really loved her instead of being in a room somewhere with a line of hungry men waiting to bed her.

They kept saying I must be an Afghan. I spoke some English to prove I wasn't but switched back to Pashtu as no one there spoke English. I gave the madame Nasreen's photograph. I wrote my address and phone number in Peshawar on the back and Mirza's number in the U.S. in case I should be there. I told her if she found Nas I would come back at once and give her a $1000, though a grand doesn't speak as loud here as it does in Pakistan where people still drool over dollars.

After leaving Overlaunch I went into the Dubai bazaar, to the corner where

I had met the pimp from the gold bazaar. Yesterday I had told him I would probably come back. I had seen a very sexy, long haired slender girl in a pink mirrored embroidered _shalwar kameez_ in his house. On seeing him and after my feelings after yesterday with the other Nasreen I told him I would pass. I gave him a copy of my Nasreen's photo with my address and contact numbers on the back and offered him the same $1000 reward.

If I see a girl as pretty as the girl in his house when I get back to Pakistan I will surely give her a throw, but what is the point of it here? I'm not just looking for some fast sex. I'm looking for something with future potential in it. Obviously I can't afford the fare to fly here every _Juma_. Nor could I afford the visa.

Now it is time to go to the airport. Shireen is waiting to drive me. He just gave me some beautiful, light blue material for a suit (_shalwar kameez_). I'll have a tailor make it for me in Peshawar. He has helped me so much since the day he picked me up walking down the street in front of my hotel in Sharja. The other day in Dubai bazaar I got him a wooden beaded seat cover for his taxi, as most of his time is spent driving it seemed like the perfect practical gift. He accepted it, trying not to show any emotion, folding it and laying it aside against the wall of the room.

I'm doing better now. This morning I was ready to start yanking out beards— but don't push me! When I get back to Peshawar if the neighbors mess with me in any way, I may start blasting pigeon flocks with Mirza's twelve gauge shot gun (inherited from the horse trip). It is sawed off at 18 inches and I imagine I could wipe out half a flock of pigeons at close range. I can imagine the owner's face as he sees half his flock explode into feathers and red droplets.*

❖　❖　❖

FAREWELL TO NASREEN

Arriving back in Peshawar the city was quiet. Not only was it the second day of _Eid,_ but it was early _Juma_ morning. Riding in the _rickshaw_ from the airport we passed piles of stinking offal swarming with flies: the unwanted remains of so many _Eid_ sacrifices.

Unlocking the front door of my house I saw my neighbor's son, Nawazish. He was just leaving with a friend for Lahore. It had been his younger brother's wedding where I had seen the Punjabi disco dancer. He knew how to locate her in Lahore he said, as he had arranged the entertainment for the wedding. We arranged to meet the next evening at 8:00 at the Zamindar Hotel on McCloud Road. Not even a day back and I'm on the Flying Coach to Lahore.

I went out to Nasreen's house. I wondered what I would do if she an-

---

* _People keep flocks of pigeons in cages built on the roofs of their houses called khaboota khanna (pigeon houses). In the afternoons they go up to the roofs to train their flock to fly in circles by whistling and waving nets. The object is to get your flock to mingle with a neighbor's flock and confuse/capture some of the other's flock to come back with yours. Then they are either good-naturedly returned, or a set of complicated negotiations begin._

swered the door, but it wasn't her. She wasn't there and there was no news of her. It was strangely quiet at the house. Not only were there no customers, but there was only one working girl and very few family members.

I called my friends in Gulbarg but a servant said they were taking a nap. Feeling depressed, I went back to the hotel to sleep. At 8:00 I went down to the front desk. Nawazish didn't show up by 8:30 and my heart didn't feel like being in Lahore any longer. I got my bag and walked up to the Flying Coach stands. I caught the next available coach headed for Peshawar. I felt like a yo-yo and GT Road my string.

I didn't expect her to show up in Overlaunch in Dubai either but I gave Islam a call there to check, and I even called Sabor's house. Maybe she really did just get married to some regular guy, but I keep remembering when I was with the gold bazaar Nasreen in Dubai and when we came out of the room she casually handed the money to a fellow, just like I had seen the girls do so often in Lahore with Akbar or Mama. I can't stop imagining Nasreen not having fallen into a similar situation somewhere. But where? Will I ever know? At least I can hope that some nice guy just happened in and fell for her like I had and he could talk properly to her so he siezed the opportunity to get her to leave that life and she slipped out of my life forever. Maybe somebody wiser than I? Maybe somebody not so conspicuous?

"Just enjoy her, just use her, we'll find you a good wife. You can never marry a woman like that," I was told in Peshawar. How I ever listened to that advice, looking back now, it is hard to know. It all just happened. It is the way it was supposed to be. Otherwise, it wouldn't have happened. Acceptance is the hard part.

Now a dead feeling is coming in. At least in Dubai, I had some hope I would find her, see her again, get to talk to her. Now that is over and it all feels so empty. No Nasreen. Pakistan feels so empty. All I've tried to build here seems to be crumbling away.

She was more than a girlfriend (if I may call her that), more than just sex (if I can be so crude). Being with her allowed me to live within Pathan society (albeit, a corrupt section of it) in a way I hadn't imagined. She and the life surrounding her was the entire surrogate Pathan family that I wanted so badly and now I feel may be slipping away with her memory. I can't seem to find what I need to replace it. I would go to her house, staying a day or two, making friends with most of her family. I saw the children growing up. She brought me tea when I came in, lunch when I came in from *Juma* prayer. She washed my shirt when tea spilled on it. We went to the bazaar together. We smoked together, watched TV together and slept together. She was somebody to buy silvery, glittery fabrics for and golden noserings. God, Nasreen, I hope you aren't working somewhere and I just can't find you. What can I do, except go on?

I went with a friend to an orphanage on GT Road. It looked somewhat like a jail. We were told that besides being an orphanage it was a place for boys and girls who have problems at home (i.e: *bad girls*—yeah, yeah). Maybe just the kind of place for future wife material. I am starting to feel I wouldn't mind an orphan. They say you get *sawab* for marrying an orphan and *sawab* for marrying a bad girl. I need all the *sawab* I can get, so as I reason it, the more bad, the more *sawab*. Also it would avoid Pakistani in-laws, something that doesn't feel so unfavorable to me at the moment.

The *chowkidar* told us to go to the orphanage's office in Saddar Bazaar. There we talked to an elderly lady, the president of the organization. She said she would speak to her partner and call me in two days. My friend, who is married to an American, gave me a good introduction. He said what a benefit it would be for any Pakistani girl to marry me. A lucky chance. That I owned a big house in Peshawar. How it offered the opportunity to live a better life, a possibility of getting out of Pakistan to the "golden west."

Two days later I was told I would have to go out to an office near University Town to talk with somebody else. It turned out to be a fellow in his early 20s and the office had nothing to do with the orphanage. He made an arrangement to come over to my house. Good, I thought, they want to check out my house. That evening he arrived with two equally young male friends.

Shortly it became apparent that his two friends had nothing to do with the orphanage at all. They had only come for a chance to talk to the foreigner. When their intention was apparent, I quickly dispatched them. Maybe I can just wait in front of the orphanage and kidnap a girl at my leisure? I'm too tired of all this bull.

Khorshid, my neighbor Arshad's cousin, helped me painstakingly write an ad for the Urdu Jang (Urdu newspaper out of Lahore) matrimonial section. I finally found the word I wanted for liberal thinking. *"Azad khayal"*—literally *free thinking.*

"It doesn't give a good impression here in Pakistan, though," Khorshid warned me. "Here people generally associate *'azad khayal'* with loose."

The next day I took my ad on a small slip of paper to the Peshawar office of the Jang in Saddar Bazaar. I explained to the advertising manager I was an American Muslim and that I had been trying to find a suitable wife, but until now hadn't had much luck. The advertising manager took an instant dislike to me. I couldn't say anything to please him. He told me he would go over my ad and that I should come back tomorrow.

When I came back, he showed me the corrections he had made. There was no mention of *"azad khayal."* When I asked why he had taken it out, he told me that it showed I was advertising for a loose woman.

"Azad khayal doesn't mean loose, it means liberal," I told him. "And if you had educated your mind instead of just going through the formalities of learning to read and write you would realize that!"

"No," he insisted, "it shows you are advertising for a *prost* (prostitute)."

"Maybe you would call a woman with a liberal mind a prostitute. It shows how limited your mind is," I began to argue. "If that is what you would call it, then that is what I want. What is your problem with it? It is for me! Maybe you are afraid of women who can think for themselves. Maybe your mother can find you a girl who won't think on her own. Then she won't say what a jerk you are!"

"Get out of my office!" he shouted from behind his desk.

"Sure. But put my original ad in the paper. It is your job."

"I don't have to put any ad in my paper," he yelled. "Now get out of my office." He called a guard to throw me out. Luckily for him, and for me, I didn't have my gun in my pocket. I had left it at home, along with my sanity.

"Get your hands off me," I told the guard. "I don't want to fight with you. It is your boss who is the idiot. I don't want to make a problem for you. I'm going."

As we walked out the guard closed the door behind me. Then I realized if he wouldn't let me put my ad in the paper here, I'd have to go all the way to Lahore to place my ad at their office there. Feeling frustrated, I turned around and went back to his door. The guard followed me looking worried.

"*You stupid fuck!*" I screamed in English (please excuse the vernacular). I pounded on the wooden veneer door, tearing through the door, leaving a jagged hole. I pulled my hand out and stomped down the stairs, pulling splinters out of my wrist. The guard chuckled, more at his pompous boss than at me... I think.

I'll have to remember to tell Khorshid maybe he was right after all about the word *"azad khayal."*

Chapter 31
Dating

In this world of infinite possibility
I look around for the second step of desire,
All I can see is one footprint.
Mirza Asadullah Ghalib

❖   ❖   ❖

July 7th, 1991
EVENT! Met a girl today.

Hafez, the travel agent, on hearing I hadn't had any luck in finding Nasreen in Dubai said he would see if he could help me to find a wife. Today he called to say I had never given him a picture of myself. It feels like a meat market, but you can't sample the meat. You can barely see the meat until you buy. Before I can meet a girl I have to be the meat; not so much that the girl can see me to approve, but so the family can. We're both meat, before we can meet.

"Noor Mohammad," he said. "Some people are waiting in my office. Can you bring a picture of yourself right now?"

"Okay, I'll leave right now, though it may take 15 or 20 minutes to reach there, what with the construction and traffic nowadays."

Shaheen Bazaar was really crowded as usual during the day, but I needed to walk through it to get to Kalan Bazaar, the closest bazaar large enough to allow anything larger than bicycles or donkeys. Getting through the city even by *rickshaw* is difficult due to so many streets being blocked by construction in Chowk Yadgar and other miscellaneous road repairs. Eventually I managed to walk into Hafez's shop.

His travel agency near Shoba Bazaar is long and narrow inside. There is a long glass-covered desk behind which his two sons (his assistants) sit, with a cushioned bench along the entire wall facing it. At the end of the shop, facing the front door, Hafez reigns from his desk with the agency's sole telephone on it. Next to his desk, on the bench, sat a woman in her late 30s wearing glasses and a white *chaddar* with small red flowers lightly embroidered.

Between her and the end of the bench sat two girls in their early 20s. After shaking his hand and *salaaming* the women I sat on the bench, respectively leaving a few feet between myself and the woman who started right away asking me several questions in Pashtu about myself; my life, my family, my future plans. After several minutes of this informal interrogation, Hafez said in English, "Noor Mohammad, do you like one of these two girls sitting here?"

I looked at them quickly, but a bit closer than I had. It's not polite to look at women too closely, especially when somebody else is watching. The girl in the middle appeared the younger of the two, tall and thin with a long, slender neck and big, brown, doe eyes. Her long dark hair was also covered by a light white *chaddar.* Her still-adolescent skin was a gentle shade of wheat. The other girl sitting farthest from me was shorter, more thick-set and lighter complexioned. She was also wearing a white *chaddar* over short, brown hair.

"Are they for the picking?" I asked.

"One of these girls wants to marry you," he nonchalantly informed me.

I looked closer, trying to be casual, considering for a moment. Here I am, on the spot, being asked to choose right in front of the girls.

"I don't make any commitment," I began, being put on the spot, "but I would consider her, in the middle."

Oops, wrong selection. No prize. All you get is two cups of *qawah.* Hafez refilled my tea cup and asked, "You don't like the other girl? She's the one who wants to marry you. The girl you picked is her cousin. She's engaged already."

"I'll be honest," I answered, hoping the girl didn't speak much English, "I don't even know her of course, so I'm just basing my decision on first look. But she is a bit short for me (and not skinny enough). Besides too light skinned, too English-looking. I'm American, but I want a Pakistani-looking wife."

She was probably 20 or so, though the serious expression on her face made her appear older. I knew this was a serious matter, but there was just nothing appealing to me. No spark. No flash of the eyes.

The women thanked me and left.

Hafez told me the girl could diet and exercise. She looked somewhat like Nargis from Nasreen's house, though not as pretty. If I were married to this girl I would still always be looking at other women. Would that be fair to her? How could I live with that?

July 8th

Juma morning.

The woman from yesterday called me this morning. She wanted to know what I had decided about the girl. It was more embarrassing than yesterday, but at least I wasn't sitting face-to-face with the girl. She told me the girl was very smart. She could diet and exercise. God, I thought, I could get a lady P.E. instructor.

I told her the girl was too light complexioned for me. She didn't think of saying she could go to a tanning studio, not that there are any I know of in Pakistan. I guess she wants to go to the USA badly. I don't blame her. If I were stuck here I'd probably want some way out. She couldn't want my antique house situated right in the heart of that delightful historic slum that is old Peshawar.

She looked so straight, like the kind of girl who would tell you to drive slower on a dangerous mountain road. Nasreen would have laughed and said to floor it. No, she probably would have jammed my foot down on the gas pedal with her own foot, laughing as I tried to control the car with the steering wheel and brake. How do you tell somebody, "Uh, I'm looking for a girl a little more, how you can say, corrupt-looking?"

I miss Nasreen....

WATCH

July 14th

Shah Hussain, Habibullah's cousin, showed up at my house a few days ago and told me to come to his village Saturday. He drew me a diagram on the back of an old envelope. It's approximately one and a half hours from Peshawar by bus, past Utmanzai, to Mandani. Then by *tonga* for 20 minutes more along a canal to a village called Shodag. He has arranged for me to meet two girls that are, as he says, *'azad khayal'*—a word I didn't have very good luck with in the Peshawar Jang office. I hope so. After Nasreen, I realize I'm looking for the type of girl Pakistanis term loose.

Woke up Saturday morning to pleasantly cooler weather and spotty, drizzly rain. I followed Shah Hussain's directions and found myself riding along in a *tonga* on a pothole pocked, rutted dirt road heading north from Mandani along the upper Swat Canal toward Takht-i-Bhai. I got down, as Shah Hussain had instructed me, at the Shodag Boys' Government School. Across the canal from the school was Bachano Kili, Shah Hussain's village. He and two of his brothers were waiting for me as I crossed the canal on a small, wooden foot bridge, a homemade affair made of two crooked logs placed across the 30-foot span with flat boards irregularly placed to step on. We met, hugged and shook hands.

Bachano Kili is four adobe walled houses. The mosque, directly on the canal, is built as part of the front wall of Shah Hussain's house, a typical village mosque with soft straw covering the hard earthen floor. The thick walls have a few tiny windows set high up. In front, a modest courtyard with a hard packed floor is surrounded by low (six feet)) mud walls, serving double duty as his *hujra*. Electricity is supplied by a wire run across the canal from the school.

Something about being in Tribal Territory always feels so natural to me, so invigorating, as if my childhood had been spent there, though now I'm a city dweller. Peshawar has become my home.

We sat on *charpoys* in the front courtyard of the mosque. Habibullah came by. I hadn't seen him since the horse trip. More accurately, since he had deserted us when Mirza and I were stranded in Gupis. He was in a truck with friends on their way down to the Punjab to bring back goods to sell in the village. It was good to see him, Gilgit was a long way in the past.

Lunch was brought. Large elm trees protected us from a cooling drizzle. The air smelled sweetly of damp, dusty earth and cedar wood smoke.

After lunch we sipped tea; Shah Hussain, his three brothers and a doctor friend—one of the people who had arranged a girl for me to meet in his nearby village. Shah Hussain's father also sat with us. The old gentleman farmer, with his white beard and white turban has been an extremely religiously devout Muslim since a fifth son had died several years ago, though Shah Hussain has told me some rather dubious stories of his father's past life.

While we were eating two women came across the fields from a neighboring village, their _chaddars_ swathing them from prying eyes and trailing behind them in the breeze. They went around the back of Shah Hussain's house, presumably entering it to visit his mother and sister-in-law.

After the doctor left for his own village, and Shah Hussain's brothers and father had wandered off, Shah Hussain asked me if I wanted to go around the back of the house to see their crops. We went to the side, then he quickly told me to go inside the house's walled compound. He quickly introduced me to his mother, quite a rare and honored thing in Pathan society. His sister-in-law I saw but wasn't presented to. I was ushered into a room and told to sit on a _charpoy_ in the corner. Across from me in the dimly lit room, on another _charpoy_ a few feet from mine, sat a girl facing me. She was wearing a black _chaddar_ with delicate red and green embroidered flowers centered with small, round mirrors. She was modestly gazing down at the floor. The only light in the room was emitted by a singular low wattage bare dusty bulb hanging from a frayed wire and the sunlight coming in through the doorway. The light from a few small windows in the thick mud walls about five feet from the floor cast golden rays in the dust particles floating in thew air.

I only had a brief chance to greet the girl before a gaunt middle-aged woman with wrinkled yet clear features and the brown, leathery skin of a villager came in and sat in a chair against the wall and between the two _charpoys._ I was vaguely aware of Shah Hussain's mother, father, and his older brother and wife on the other side of the room. The woman sitting by me was the girl's mother. She started talking to me as I nonchalantly eyed the girl, still trying to pay attention to her words.

"You know that we are breaking the Pathan village tradition by letting you two see each other," she started in. "But Shah Hussain says you are his close friend, like a brother. His family is like our family. These are modern times and young people want to meet before they are married. They want to choose on their own.

"Yet if you weren't a foreigner in Pakistan, we never would have arranged this meeting. We came here in secret. My husband and sons do not know. If they did, they would never allow it. It is not the Pathan way.

"I originally came from Dera Ismail Khan. When my husband and I were married, I had never seen him first. They came and brought me here. Then after the marriage, I saw him. That was my great happiness."

She started asking me questions about how I had become a Muslim, about my family, my views on marriage, my future plans. While we talked, the girl got up and left the room. It had been difficult trying to watch her out of the corner of my eye while trying to be polite and pay attention to her mother. I realized what a rare chance this was for me, being here in front of a marriageable Pathan village girl. My mind was starting to wander.

"Well, what do you think?" the mother ended with.

"What?" I said, taken by surprise.

"Have you seen her enough? What do you think? Do you want to marry her?"

"Have I seen her enough? Not enough to marry her. I hardly even spoke with her." (I'd like to see her bare tummy, I thought.)

At first she wouldn't come back in the room. Her mother said it was the first time she had ever had a meeting like this and that was why she was shy.

"Don't worry," I said, "so am I." Later Shah Hussain and his brother, who had gone to school with her, told me she wasn't really so shy, but was acting that way for the benefit of the adults there at the time.

Finally, she let herself be coaxed back into the room. She sat across from me. "What do you want to say?" she asked me rather bluntly.

I realized at a time like this lines like "Do you like sex." or "I want to get my money's worth," just don't seem to make it.

"What do you think about marrying a foreigner?" I asked.

"Whatever my parents say is what I do," she answered complacently.

"No. I want your personal thoughts. What do you think about marrying me?" I asked.

"I'd like it," she smiled. She had a wildish look in her eyes, like Nasreen, which of course I liked.

"Why?"

"I'd like to marry you. I'd like to go and see other places. I'd like to go to *Amerika.*"

"Can you speak Urdu?" I asked.

"Yes. I went to school until the sixth grade. They teach in Urdu. Why?"

"Because my Urdu isn't so good. It would be nice to have a wife that can help me." (also, I feel if someone in Pakistan only speaks one language it shows a rather limited mind and experience because there are so many languages spoken throughout the country)

"Can you read and write?" I asked.

"Somewhat," she said.

"Enough for me," I replied.

"Look, are you looking for a wife or do you want a teacher?" she chided. I liked her attitude and her voice. The sound of a girl's voice speaking native Pashtu is very pleasing to my ears. And Mandani being close to Mardan, her accent was the same Hashtnagar accent as Nasreen's.* Rather different from Peshawari people speaking Pashtu. I liked her energy. Then she asked me, "Why do you want to marry a Pathan girl?"

I was taken aback. I laughed. I wasn't ready for that question. At least not from a girl I was sitting with considering for the part. Otherwise, I might have had a clever answer. "I've been here a long time," I started. "It seems I've become a part of this culture. I don't know if I could have any wife now except a Pathan."

Her name is Zeenat and the village she comes from is Marghano Kili. Shah Hussain and I began using "Watch" as a code name for her, after my watch, a *Zeenat* brand. Using a woman's name in public just isn't done and by

---

* *from the area around Charsadda, Tangi and Takht-i-Bhai are known as Hashtnagar— meaning eight villages).*

calling her *Watch* nobody would know what we were talking about. We called her village "birds' village"—*marghano* meaning birds in Pashtu and *kili* is village.

Later I told Shah Hussain if *Watch* wanted to arrange to meet me somewhere privately, I wouldn't mind talking to her some more. By her smile, her look, her attitude and answers to my questions I feel she has some self will and personal opinions. But such a short meeting for me isn't enough to pick a life partner.

So many people in Pakistan have (maybe are forced to have) their parents pick their spouses. If a boy doesn't like his wife, at least his family will. Chances are they will live with his parents and he can continue hanging out with his buddies and leave his wife at home with those who picked her anyway. Much of the time she is from the same family as well.

Shah Hussain said he would see if he could arrange for us to meet in one of the village fields at night. When I expressed my doubts on this sort of meeting, he assured me it was possible. She could put Ativan, a sleeping pill, in the family's tea at night. They would sleep soundly and she would be able to leave the house for a nocturnal rendezvous. An old village trick. Only the use of Ativan is new.

I still keep hoping one day a girl will walk in the room and I'll look at her and she'll smile at me like when I first met Nasreen, and there will be no second thoughts (will she say 300 rupees, I wonder?). I'll just say, "give me the nikka namma." I'll sign it right on the spot!

I'm at least open to check out this girl again. I forgot to study her fingers. My theory is if the fingers are slender so will be the rest of the girl, since it is difficult to tell accurately what is hidden under loose flowing *shalwar kameez* and *chaddar*. I don't think I'll have many chances in these chaperoned meetings to see a girl's tummy or put my fingers around her ankles to check her bone size. I know I can decide to marry *Watch* if I want and never see her again until after the wedding. Her attitude seemed fine. If Nasreen's memory wasn't so burnt into my mind and eyes maybe I would have liked her more.

Later in the afternoon we walked over to "birds' village," which was also where the doctor's clinic was, basically a small adobe room built onto the front of a house. Inside was his desk, a few rickety chairs and a small cabinet with some dusty medicines in it. We sat with the doctor and a few of his friends drinking tea. He had arranged for me to meet a girl from a village on the other side of the canal from "birds' village." Her name was Sanjeena. We decided to call her "Bayonet" as a code name, bayonet being one English meaning of the word *sanjeena*.

We crossed the canal, following the doctor between mud walls and over little irrigation ditches gurgling with water. We came to a cleared open area with a few *charpoys* placed in it. The doctor told us to have a seat and wait. He left. Some boys brought a small wooden table and a pot of tea, of course. Shah Hussain and I waited alone, chatting. The sun set and the evening sky was darkening and still no *Bayonet*. Finally the doctor returned to apologize, saying that *Bayonet* could not get away from her house to meet me. Shah Hussain became disconcerted,

"I don't know," he complained. "These stupid Pathan people. I don't know why they are always saying they will do something and then they don't. I am very mad at this foolish doctor. He is stupid. Why did he say you could meet *Bayonet* and then she never came? He wasted your time!"

On the way back to Shah Hussain's house his brother Farid met us on the path. As we walked along the canal there was very little light left and though Shah Hussain and Farid didn't seem to have any trouble negotiating the narrow path which they had walked upon since childhood, I had to strain my eyes in the diminishing light to keep from slipping into the murky waters of the canal.

That night we sat around in one of the classrooms of the Boys' Government School across from their village drinking tea and chatting; Shah Hussain, his three brothers and I. The doctor and a friend came by to apologize again because *Bayonet* hadn't shown up. Her older brother was at home so she couldn't leave the house. He said I should come back to the village another time to meet her.

"She's a very forward girl. A good choice for you, I think," the doctor told me. "But you should meet her and make your own opinion. I know little of these things. I am a simple man." The rest of us laughed. Being a simple man was a running joke, used tongue-in-cheek to indicate one does not fully understand a situation or did not want to admit to it.

I had been hearing a lot of stories concerning these "shy" village girls. "Is she a virgin?" I asked the doctor point blank.

"Yes," he said positively.

"I don't mind if she isn't, mind you," I said, "but I want to be told first. I don't want to make an engagement with someone I can barely meet first and that I think is untouched if she isn't. I want to know first. I want to know the truth. I was born in America. I've been around. I've been with numerous women. It's easy to tell if a girl is a virgin before lying with her. I will test on the wedding night. I may be a simple man, but in this matter I'm not that simple!" This statement brought a hearty round of laughter.

That night Shah Hussain, his father and I slept on *charpoys* in the courtyard of the mosque. The tall trees overhead shielded us from the light drizzle. When in the middle of the night a heavy downpour broke upon us, amid flashing lightning and crashing thunder we moved inside the mosque, sleeping on the fragrant, soft, dry straw.

With usual Pathan hospitality in the morning with breakfast of *chai, parattas* and fried eggs, they insisted I spend at least one more day and night in their village. But Shah Hussain understood my need to get back to my complicated life in Peshawar (of doing nothing).

Shah Hussain, Farid and I left in the direction of Mandani. Passing through a graveyard just outside Marghano Kili we stopped at the grave of their brother. We offered a *dua*, our palms raised in front of us in supplication, then continued on the road to Mandani. As we neared the canal we came to a water-powered flour mill. A cement channel brought water into the building where it turned five heavy millstones before rejoining the canal through five smaller cement channels. We looked inside the door of the mill and exchanged greetings with the mill attendants who emerged completely dusted in white, powdery flour. We refused their offers of tea and walked on. After crossing the canal we stood by the road until a *tonga* came by with enough room for me to squeeze into a space. I said my goodbyes and continued on to Mandani and Peshawar alone.

That evening in Peshawar I told Mr. Mahboob about my meeting with *Watch.* I told him I wanted to meet her again to talk to her in private, that I wanted to find out what she really thinks, feels and wants. To get her honest answers, without her mother and other people present. He laughed. "Noor Mohammad, our women are trained to do what their husbands want! She will do what you want, go where you want, like what you want."

"I want a wife that is a friend, not a prisoner," I told him. "I may look for a singer. At least we'll already have some common interests."

"Noor Mohammad, please don't marry a musician! These people are very loose character people. Singer girls are no better than prostitutes," he said. "Really, don't you feel it?"

"I want someone that I will like," I blurted out. "If I find a prostitute I like, I'll marry her. I care about the person, not the position."

Shah Hussain came to Peshawar to see me a few days later. He was still upset with the doctor for just talking and not delivering, as he knew so many other Pakistanis had done concerning my quest for a girl to marry. I told him not to worry, what the doctor did I did not see as any reflection on him. He said it was because he had been the one who had asked me to come to his village and that he had broken his friendship with the doctor.

He asked me about *Watch.* I explained that even though I understood I was very lucky to meet her at all, still the meeting was very short. Also the light wasn't the best and with her mother and the others there it was difficult to tell. Also that Nasreen was strong in my memory still.

"Look, my brother, I really liked her demeanor and attitude, but I would like to see her again. Also I would like to stand directly in front of her while she is standing, to judge her size and stature," I said.

"It will be very difficult with her father to arrange another visit, but I will try," he answered.

"It's not like I want to sleep with her," I pointed out, "though that wouldn't be a bad test either. Need to test her for snoring."

"Okay, Noor Mohammad, now I know that you are crazy," he laughed. "But I like crazies. I think it will be impossible for you to meet her again in the village, but maybe I can make some arrangement to bring her here to Peshawar. I will try for you."

Some days later my telephone rang.

"Noor Mohammad, do you want to meet with *Watch*?" Shah Hussain's voice said on the other end of the line.

"Sure," I replied. "Why? What is possible?"

"If you can pay to hire a car, I can bring *Watch* and her mother by *tonga* to

Tangi, *Insha'Allah*. There I can hire a car to bring them to Peshawar," he told me. "I'm sorry, but I can't bring her to your house alone. Her mother must accompany her. What do you think?"

"It sounds good to me. When?"

"I will try for tomorrow morning. I will call you when we get to Tangi. I'm in Tangi now. It's the closest phone from our village. I will make arrangements with a car and driver now, before going home. But remember, the old woman will be with us. It will be impossible to ditch her."

"No problem. I just want to see *Watch* again."

"Okay. Don't go out. I'll call you in the morning."

"*Insha'Allah*."

"Yes, *Insha'Allah. Khuda hafiz.*"

Early the next morning *Watch* and her mother left their village under the guise of needing to see a doctor in Peshawar. Shah Hussain met them in Tangi. He called me at 7:30 to tell me they were on their way. Having to wait some time for the car and driver he had arranged the day before they arrived at my house after 10:00. I brought them upstairs to my bedroom on the third floor, the first two floors of my house still being almost completely empty. After greeting, Shah Hussain and I chatted as we climbed the stairs. *Watch* and her mother remained silent. We sat in my room.

After some silence *Watch* looked at me and said, "Are your eyes weak?"

"Huh?" I asked, caught off guard.

"Are your eyes weak? You've already seen me one time. And now you want to see me again."

I laughed. I liked her attitude.

"No, my eyes are okay. But it was dark in Shah Hussain's house. And it was my first meeting like that."

"Mine too," she smiled.

"Well, marriage is a serious thing. I wanted to make sure. I don't want to make a mistake."

"*No, whya kena!*" (so, talk then)

I started trying to remember all the questions I had thought over that I wanted to ask. Some of the questions did not be appropriate on this occasion. I mean, how could I ask her, "would you like to sleep with your husband," or "have you ever kissed a boy," with her mother sitting right there? Could we get her away? In English Shah Hussain said to me, realizing the situation, "I will try to get her mother away so you can talk to her in private."

"What are you telling him?" the mother said, turning to Shah Hussain.

"I was just telling him some Pathan traditions I didn't know if he understood or not," Shah Hussain told her.

Looking at *Watch*, I dug in my memory. "Do you speak Urdu?"

"I learned it in school. You already asked me that in Shah Hussain's house. Maybe your ears are also weak?"

"No. I guess I'm just nervous. I'm not used to talking to girls. And my Pashtu is definitely weak. It's hard to remember what I said to you the other day. You did say you'd like to go to America, didn't you?"

"Sure."

"Why?"

"Who (in Pakistan) wouldn't want to go to *Amerika*? I would like to see it. It is a very advanced country, is it not?"

"Yes, in many ways."

"Why did you come to Pakistan?" she asked me.

"I was in Afghanistan before. I became a Muslim there. As a Muslim, I like living in Pakistan. It is a very good country for Muslims. So was Afghanistan, but now is war in Afghanistan," I told her. "Pakistan is the only country in the world created for Muslims. I know there are problems in Pakistan and, of course, Pakistanis aren't perfect Muslims... who in this mortal world is? Except for the Prophet Muhammad, peace be upon Him."

"Peace be upon Him," *Watch* and her mother echoed.

"But, none the less, it is a good country, full of good people, and I would like to remain here and make it my home. If God permits." I looked directly at *Watch*, "How about living in this big old house in Peshawar?"

"It is big."

"You wouldn't be scared?"

"Scared? Why scared? There are ghosts?" she laughed.

"I don't think so, *Insha'Allah*."

I took them upstairs to show them the fourth floor, then up to the main roof. *Watch's* mother didn't want her to climb the stairway to the very top of my house. Even though there is a five foot high brick parapet surrounding that roof and they were wearing their *chaddars* which they had donned for the tour, her mother thought she would be visible to inquisitive neighboring eyes.

I opened a small wooden window so they could look out at the view of Mahabat Khan Mosque's minarets in Ander Sher, Bala Hisar, the top of *Ghanta Ghar's* green dome, the Khyber mountains (Suliman Hills) and the mountains of Mohmand and Bajaur Agencies to the north and Tirah to the south.

As we descended the brick steps back to my bedroom the first of the multitude of *Azans* from my neighborhood mosques began. It was time for midday prayer. Shah Hussain asked mama if she wanted to pray. He told her the bathroom was on the ground floor so she needed to go down to make *wuzu*. *Watch* said she would wait. Shah Hussain winked at me, but mother insisted *Watch* come downstairs to wash and pray with her.

After prayer they left. Shah Hussain went with them. Having brought them, it was his duty to escort them back to Tangi. From there they would have to go on to their own village alone as it was a secret they had gone with him. He told me he would come back the next day.

"Have you come to any conclusions about *Watch*?" he asked me when he returned.

"I really liked her attitude and her personality. I'm just not sure of her look. It's not that she's bad looking or anything, but I'm still so gone on Nasreen. Her color was more red-brown than Nasreen's wheat-brown. More like you, you

Red-Indian. And to be honest, I just didn't feel that special magic in her eyes. It was something I hoped to recognize instantly, like I did with Nasreen, though maybe that only comes once in a lifetime, if ever. I didn't even get a chance to lift her *kameez* and check out her skin."

"These people are backward and stupid people, Noor Mohammad. I don't know why you want to marry a Pathan. All Pathans are cheating people."

"Well, I really did like her. I liked her village, though not her crazy, stupid, backward neighbors in Bachano Kili. I even thought her mom was okay. But you know, Shah Hussain, my brother, I'm just not sure of her look, of her face. I know that is a little thing, but it's important to me. I don't want to marry one girl and then always be looking at other girls. I'm not that Pakistani. That's not my idea of a good marriage."

"This is unusual talk for me to hear, but very smart. But it makes your search twice as hard, you know."

"Yes, I know. They will think I am crazy, but I'd like to look at her again. I know that is virtually impossible."

"Yes, that would be difficult..." he thought a moment. "I don't know, Noor Mohammad, maybe I can arrange something some night in a field."

"No, that's not necessary, but maybe I can get a picture of her face to look at for awhile?"

"This is unusual, but very clever," he said. "This we can try. I can dispatch a boy from our village to her house. He can ask."

"That sounds good. In English they say, 'It doesn't hurt to try'."

"Yes. They can't shoot us for just asking for a picture. *Insha'Allah.*"

I went into one of my cabinets searching for a pair of silver and lapis lazuli Afghani earrings I had saved in a box. I put them in a small, embroidered Turkoman pouch and handed them to him.

"Here. Tell him to give these to her mother as a present for *Watch*," I instructed him. A nice gesture, I thought, but not such a heavy statement as gold, nor as costly. Not ready for gold yet. So the message was run and Shah Hussain returned with two pictures for me: one of *Watch* and her younger sister dressed in brightly colored satin *shalwar kameez* in a garden and another of her alone standing in the garden. In the picture of her standing alone, she was wearing turquoise clothes and sunglasses. It did nothing for me. The way it was taken, she looked somewhat thickset and very white-complexioned. I knew she wasn't near that light nor so stout as the picture, but it made me think. The other photo, a close-up of her and her sister, I kept looking at. There was something about the lower part of her face I personally didn't like. The shape of her mouth or something. I wasn't really sure, but there just wasn't the magnetic feeling I had been hoping for. Maybe it's just too much to hope for a second time?

Haji Mahboob keeps assuring me she sounds like fine wife material and that I shouldn't be so concerned about the way she looks. I told him I don't want to always be looking at women I think are more attractive than my wife. He thinks I'm being a trifle silly. How can I marry someone when I know if

Nasreen ever shows up at my door someday and says, *"Zeh chay zoo"* (let's go), I'd be out the door?

Shah Hussain came around again the end of that week. "Have you made any decision about *Watch*?" he asked me.

"Yeah, I really thought about it a lot," I answered. "There is so much about her I really like. But there is just something about her face. I kept looking at her picture. I'm not sure what it is, she isn't bad looking, but there is something about her face I just don't care for. It's just personal taste, but it is something I have to live with. Also, even though I really like her personality, there just isn't that special spark I was hoping for, like when I first met Nasreen. That goes beyond physical appearances."

"Yeah, but remember, you had sex with Nasreen the first time you met her," he reminded me.

"Are you saying it was just a matter of sex?" I asked him. "That happened after the spark. That is why I picked her. If Watch would have walked in I wouldn't have picked her. Nasreen wasn't exactly what I had had in mind, but from the very first time I looked into her eyes until now I've been gone on her. Lying with her only strengthened it and cemented it. Remember I'm not Pakistani. I have had some experience in the matter. Besides, I've had better lovers than her in my life. The sex was not the magic."

"Well, I'll go and get word to her family," he said. "But I'm happy that you decided no. You wouldn't have been happy with these backward Pathans, Noor Mohammad. I'm sorry. I didn't realize it before, but I think that her family are not good people. I think they just wanted to use you."

"Where can I find honest people in Pakistan then?" I answered. "From my experiences lately, Nasreen and her family weren't such bad people. At least I always knew where they stood. Do I have to look among prostitutes and pimps or in whore houses for some honesty in Pakistan?"

"Maybe, Noor Mohammad. You are a wiser man than I. I'm just a simple man"

The next morning, over breakfast with Anwar Khan in Arif's shop, I told him the situation with *Watch;* that I had decided against the girl from Mandani. He also echoed Shah Hussain's statement that I had had sex with Nasreen the first time I met her. It seems most men in Pakistan think sex and love are things that have nothing to do with marriage.

"Noor Mohammad, do you know about the Pathan boy who went to his father and asked him to make his marriage arrangements?" Anwar asked, leading into a joke. "His father asked him, 'Does your pony reach your ass?' He answered, 'No,' and his father told him to go away and pull on his *pony* every day until it reached his ass. Then come back and ask again."

Anwar paused to put some *nuswar* into his toothless mouth and cackled as he grinned. Arif sat there with a smile on his face, having heard most of Anwar's infinite store of ribald Pathan jokes.

"Yeah?" I queried, "What happened?"

374

"Well, in a year the boy came back to his father." Anwar continued, "He again asked his father if he would make his marriage arrangements. His father again asked him, 'does your pony reach your ass yet?'

"When the boy answered, '*Yes*.' the father said, 'Then go and bugger yourself. There's no need to talk of this marriage nonsense!'"

Arif burst out laughing and slapped me on the back, giving me a bear hug as he continued his high-pitched, infectious, child's laughter.

Several days later, Shah Hussain came to my house again. We had just sat down when there was another ring at my doorbell. I looked out the window of the third floor and down by the door stood a girl in a white *chaddar*, maybe 15 years old, ringing my bell and looking up.

"Who are you?" I yelled down.

"Come down and open the door!" she called back.

Then I saw a lady coming down the street and up to my door. I could see a few of the neighbor women looking out their windows and down into the street. I could almost hear their mental wheels spinning. This was the second time this lady had come to my house, bringing a different girl each time. This is a typical way pimp mothers work in Pakistan I'm told.

"It's *Watch's* mother," I told Shah Hussain. "She's with a girl, but I don't think it's *Watch*. She looks younger than *Watch*. Why don't you go down to let them in? Then they will know you are here from the beginning."

Shah Hussain went down the stairs. In a short while I could hear the sound of my heavy, wooden door closing, echoing up the stairway. I could hear their footsteps and Shah Hussain explaining that he had coincidentally also just arrived.

Watch's mother said they had had to see somebody in the city in the morning. It was *Watch's* younger sister with her. She sat on my bed and I sat on a chair facing her, mother sat in the other chair and Shah Hussain on a red Afghan carpet on the floor, leaning on a red embroidered Turkoman bolster against the wall.

"Why did you reject my sister?" began *Watch's* sister. She used the word *"encar"* for reject, a word I did not know. I looked at Shah Hussain and asked in Pashtu, "What is the meaning of *encar*?"

"I don't know the English for that word," he said, seeming to be forgetting his Pashtu also.

"Excuse me," I told the sister, "but I don't know what *encar* means."

"It means to refuse, to not accept," she explained to me. Reject.

"Well, I just wanted to think about it, to make sure. It's marriage. A big thing. I don't want to make a mistake."

"My daughter says," the mother started in, "'Noor Mohammad has seen me and doesn't want to marry me! I want to kill myself.' She won't sleep. She won't eat. She says if she can't marry Noor Mohammad, then she won't get married!"

"I told you these people are no good," Shah Hussain said quickly to me in English. "She's not telling you the truth. She's lying. They're trying to pressure you. Don't listen to them."

Then he sat there silently and sullenly as *Watch's* mother and sister went on about how they broke all traditions by letting me meet *Watch*. "We even came to your house secretly, without my husband or sons knowing. You gave her these earrings," the mother said, handing me back my earrings. "We gave you her picture. Now you want to break the engagement."

"What engagement? I never said definitely I wanted to marry her. I only said I was interested. That is why I wanted to see her again. I only wanted to make sure before making any decision."

"But you've seen her. We broke *purdah* by going to Shah Hussain's house to meet you. We broke *purdah* in front of his family."

"That's a lie," Shah Hussain said to me. "They've come to my house before to visit my mother and sisters-in-law. We've seen them before. And Farid and I went to school with *Watch*."

"Our honor is at stake," said the mother.

"These people have no honor," Shah Hussain mumbled under his breath, still using English. "Otherwise why did she now bring the other girl?"

The sister said they had heard I said I would take *Watch* to America and have doctors change her face. Plastic surgery. Not a bad idea. Just show them a picture of Nasreen and say, "Make one like this, doc." No, if such a rumor ever started from my lips, it was only in jest.

They noticed an eight by ten framed picture of Nasreen on my wall. I told them she was the Pathan girl I had already told them about, the one who I had known for several years, but was married now. They said she was a Punjabi. I laughed and told them they were wrong.

The mother said how I was unlucky, how their family was a very good, respectable Pathan family. I told them how I understood about the respectability of Pathan families, how Nasreen was from a very respectable Pathan family, also. Shah Hussain looked at me and smiled.

The conversation became a bit heated on both sides, when the mother went to the bathroom downstairs. Shah Hussain told the sister to cut out the crap. "You've come to my house before. We've seen you. You weren't just breaking *purdah* on Noor Mohammad's behalf," he told her. "I don't want to hear any more of this nonsense from you!"

When the mother returned she and Shah Hussain argued more. He told her she knew all along nothing had been agreed upon. After his verbal lashing, the sister kept quiet. I told her I was sorry there had been a misunderstanding, but it's better now than later. End of discussion as far as Shah Hussain and I were concerned. We saw them down the stairs. As they were going, the mother said to me, "Think about it some more."

"Okay, I will," I replied.

At the bottom of the stairs, as I was opening the door, the mother said, "Think about it. We will wait for your answer."

"Wait a minute!" I said quickly. "I said I would think about it... but as of now my answer is the same answer. I can't do it."

"That's not a good answer," both the mother and the girl said.

"I'm sorry, it's the true answer."

We said goodbye. As the heavy door clanged shut I could hear her talking to some of the neighbors.

"Oh, this is very bad," said Shah Hussain. "I knew she was a bad woman. She's telling the neighbors you engaged her daughter and then broke the engagement. She tells lies. She was very rude. If not, I must accompany her and her damn daughter to the bus station. But I let them go. They just came here to bother you, to pressure you. Now I know. They only wanted your money. I think I shall sever ties with their family. They are not good people."

Is he crazy, or are they? Probably just I am for getting involved with these people in the first place. Am I stuck on Pathans because of Nasreen or in spite of her?

❖   ❖   ❖

THE MAGISTRATE

That evening at sunset I went to Bibi Ji's house in Hashtnagri but she and her daughter, Batool, were out. Black Iqbal Shah called me upstairs where he and his family still occupied Zora's old room across from mine on the second floor of the grand old decaying mansion. We sat on a *charpoy* on the second floor patio—my old yard—watching the sun going down over the Peshawar skyline. Troops of pigeons were coming home to roost, their owners perched on their roofs whistling and waving nets to bring their aerial regiments home for the night. Iqbal's wife, a pleasant, round-faced, light-skinned Punjabi lady with blue-gray eyes (who by her appearance looked more Kashmiri than Punjabi) brewed tea for us. The oldest two of their four children brought it.

"Noor Mohammad, are you still looking for a wife?" Iqbal clucked in his raspy, grating voice.

"Yes," I replied, "if I can find the right girl."

"And the Mardan *wallah*? (Nasreen) Is that finished?"

"Yes, it is. I cannot marry her."

"Well, I know a girl. Good for you. She's not Peshawari like the other girl I introduced you to. She is Pathan. Completely! Pure Pathan! One hundred percent. Her uncle is my good friend. He's like my brother. The girl lives in Charsadda with her mother. My friend lives near Swabi. He's a magistrate. A very important person. A very big man. Yes. Very educated man."

"I don't care if her uncle is Ghulam Ishaq (President of Pakistan). You know I want to meet the girl, though. I want to see her. I want to talk to her face to face. I know it is a rare and difficult thing in villages, but that is what I want."

"No, listen my brother, Noor Mohammad," he cackled, coughing and stroking my chin with his black fingers, "This girl will be at his house on *Juma*. We can go there—you, me, my wife and children. You can talk to him directly. See what kind of arrangements he wants. You can meet his wife. You can meet the girl and talk to her. You can decide."

"She says she wants to marry a foreigner. She is a very advanced thinking and capable girl. I think you will like her. If you like her, good, then all work will be taken care of," he said, hacking and spitting phlegm on the roof near our feet.

Pakistanis always seem to think I would see and snap-decide-snap-all-work would be done. Finish. It would be so easy. I guess it is possible. It did just "snap" with Nasreen. But so far, this hasn't been so easy. I'm beginning to think the only ones in Pakistan who know anything about finding a wife are the mothers. Most of the people who have been trying to help me had their own marriages arranged by their mothers. Iqbal's wife being involved made me feel somewhat easier. Up to now even Bibi Ji hasn't been able to help me.

The one girl I had liked in our neighborhood was from a family of proud *Sayids* who would not marry outside of other *Sayid* families. I told Raheel we would tell them I was from a lost tribe descended from the Prophet (PBUH). It seems I have as much proof as many *Sayid* families I have met, but Raheel didn't think it would hold up in Gari Saidan—the Street of the *Sayids*.

So I will have to give up a *Juma* to go with Iqbal and family somewhere near Swabi on the wife search. It's three hours by bus to Swabi from Peshawar. I'd be lucky to escape without spending a night also. At least we're not going by horse. Well, I need to follow up on any chances and also it will help to fill some space. Since Nasreen has been gone my *Jumas* always feel so empty. Visiting Nasreen in Lahore had become such a big part of my Pakistani life.

I arrived at Bibi Ji's one rainy *Juma* morning at 7:00 as planned and sat with Iqbal in his room drinking tea with *parattas.* We piled out of the back streets of Gari Saidan and into Sikunder Pura; Iqbal, the wife, the kids and myself. As usual, there were a few *rickshaws* waiting for riders emerging from the innards of the city. We negotiated with two *rickshaw wallahs* to take us all to the Haji Camp bus stand. From there we could catch a bus in the direction of Swabi.

At a village before Swabi, called Zenda, we disembarked. It had been raining. The unpaved streets were even muddier than the twisted lanes of Hashtnagri. We wandered the main street looking for the magistrate's office trying to avoid the deeper mud. They were in the process of building several new shopping center/market places that all looked alike, so it was with some difficulty that we found the one housing his office. Iqbal said the magistrate had told him he would be in his office on *Juma* before prayer time. He wasn't there. Not a good start, I thought.

We eventually found our way to his house, built into the front walls of a large school compound, presently closed. Downstairs were shops. Upstairs, the magistrate's family occupied an apartment with a large, triangular rooftop yard with several rooms off of it. Across from his apartment was another empty apartment which he used for guests.

A child swept out one of the rooms and Iqbal pulled *charpoys* in. Pillows were brought and soon we were sitting comfortably. A small table—tea and cookies appeared. Iqbal batted his younger kids' hands away from the cookies, he could tell by the gleam in their little brown eyes when the table appeared that they would gobble them all right under my nose. That would never do, after all, I was the guest of honor.

Iqbal kept going into the kitchen. In many Pakistani houses the kitchen is distinguished by a gas fitting, a water tap, a drain in the floor—not by any counters, cupboards or appliances. Of course, if the house is occupied there will be a gas burning stove on the floor (charcoal if there is no gas), utensils and a cabinet to store foodstuffs. The refrigerator is usually in the guest room (livingroom) as mostly ice, cold drinks and occasional leftovers are kept in it. The majority of food items are bought daily and prepared fresh.

Through the glassless windows of the room I was in I could see the kitchen door. By the coughing and rasping echoing from the empty kitchen I knew Iqbal was smoking heroin. The magistrate came in. A rotund little fellow with black hair, streaked with gray, greased back and cut straight across in a line behind his ears. Iqbal took a brief respite from his smoking to introduce us.

After small talk and more tea and cookies the magistrate (he was an irrigation magistrate, settling water disputes in this agricultural area) took a small ball of *charras* from his vest pocket and began to empty a cigarette. Iqbal continued coughing from the other room. We discussed what a shame it was Iqbal had started using heroin again. The magistrate told me how Iqbal's life had gone down since smoking *powder* (heroin), a familiar sad story in present day Pakistan. Iqbal had been a respected goldsmith with shops in Peshawar and Kohat. Now his businesses were closed, his houses in mortgage. I had heard talk in Peshawar that he had also been a dancer in the Punjab with his first wife, but she had died.

We talked about me. Same old information everybody needs to know. About my family. About my becoming a Muslim. What I was doing in Pakistan. Why I wanted to marry a Pakistani girl, etcetera, etcetera. I should just make a cassette tape with the entire story on it. It would save so much repetition.

After lunch the magistrate and I walked to the mosque for *Juma* prayer. Our way led up dirt paths, between rock and mud walls, spiraling as if we were climbing an ancient citadel. On the way the magistrate apologized and informed me the girl wasn't there today. Familiar story. He said he completely approved of me and would arrange to have her there next *Juma*.

We arrived at the mosque along with a few other fellows at 1:30 but the congregational prayer was already over as they had started early. We said our prayers individually. As I was making my *niyat* I remembered the story of why my friend Sayid Hussain's family lived in Kundoz and chuckled to myself.... *

"In Afghanistan, in the time of Amir Abdur Rahman (The Iron Amir), Sayid Hussain's grandfather was an important leader of his tribe in Kabul. One Eid he and some of his followers were five minutes late in reaching the mosque for the Eid prayer. The leader of another important tribe who was their enemy told the mullah to go ahead and proceed with the prayer although the men from Sayid Hussain's side hadn't yet arrived.

When the grandfather and his men reached the mosque they saw that the

---

* *Before prayer one makes "niyat" — intention; denoting which prayer one is intending to make and that it is intended to please **Allah**.*

Eid prayer had just finished. Sayid Hussain's grandfather looked at the mullah and said, 'What has happened? Why did you start the prayer before we got here?' The mullah told him that it was the time for the prayer and his enemy had instructed him to start.

'Is that so?' said the irate grandfather. He pulled out his sword and cut off the mullah's head and his enemy's head. The Amir was very upset with this, but because they were a very important and powerful clan, he couldn't execute him. So he gave his family extensive lands in Kundoz and banished them to the north."

After finishing our prayers we continued up the hill. At the end of the road, at the top of the hill, we came to a large double gate in a white high thick cement wall. Inside was an expansive well-tended lawn and an old British era building.

We sat on chairs set out on the lawn looking down over the town of Zenda. Behind us, up half a dozen wide steps sat the old, well-kept, thick-walled chipped-white building with a wide, column-enclosed veranda and tall arched doorways. Behind the wall we had entered through was a tall, five-storied, pale yellow, cement-block house with a water tank on the roof and plumbing running down the outer walls, obviously constructed at a later date. Close by the table and chairs was an old *kutcha* building that had once been used as a stable.

As we sat a man came across the lawn to join us. He filled a cigarette with charras that the magistrate offered him. Off on the side lawn a gardener tended the flower beds. Another servant was looking after several roosters strutting around the yard—fighting roosters I was informed.

The *Malik* of Zenda appeared. Every man, from the *Malik* down to the gardener, was dressed in the same clothing; *shalwar kameez* and vests. Here a man's wealth is shown by quality of the cloth and the cut of his suit, cleanliness and the lack of wrinkles and wear. The *Malik's* white pressed suit was immaculate. He was approximately 45 years old, tall with very angular features from his long, stiffly-starched *kameez* to his chiseled chin and eagle's beak nose. His abundant, auburn hair was well-styled, his severe beard a slightly darker shade, streaked with silver; his complexion ruddy.

The man with the *charras* moved to a seat next to the *Malik* and handed him the filled cigarette. The *Malik* interrupted the smoking of his imported Dunhills to light it up with his gold lighter and smoke it by himself. Tea and cookies were brought by a servant. After the *Malik* finished his cigarette he proceeded to interview me in flawless English. Rain clouds were building up, the sounds of distant thunder rolling off the mountains ominous. It looked as if I wasn't going to get back to my own bed in Peshawar that evening.

When we got back to the magistrate's house Iqbal and the kids were already comfortably situated. The vacant school's *chowkidar* had opened a door in the massive gates and they had placed *charpoys* on an inside veranda along with two large pedestal fans. This was a summer storm so the air was still muggy. Iqbal knew I had planned to leave before it got dark, that I wanted to be back in Peshawar by nightfall.

"Noor Mohammad, brother, you can't leave now. Much rain is coming," he chuckled. "What can we do? Besides, we've been shopping. We bought meat and vegetables. The rice is already cooking. And tea is just now ready. We'll smoke some _charras_ and you and the magistrate can chat; he's a very smart, educated man. We'll sleep here without any problems or worry."

"I want to go back to Peshawar. I need to be there early in the morning," I protested.

"You can," he said, punctuating the statement by coughing and spitting. "We will sleep here in the open air. Comfortable. Then in the morning, after prayer and tea, you can catch a minivan for Peshawar. Me, my wife and children aren't going back to Peshawar. We're going to Lahore. I'm going to a hospital there for treatment to stop smoking the powder."

"Good for you. _Insha'Allah_, I hope it works."

"_Insha'Allah_. And good for you, Noor Mohammad," he rasped. "The magistrate likes you. Next week you'll get to see his niece face to face as I promised. Then your work will be done. Yes. Yes. _Insha'Allah. Ali madad!_" *

"I hope so. He told me the girl will be here next week. You said she would be here today. I hope this is serious. I am."

"It is. Come to my house early next _Juma_. If I am home from Lahore I will personally take you. If not... you know the way here?"

"I can get here again Iqbal, just no problem. _Insha'Allah_."

The next _Juma_ I went to Zenda alone.

The magistrate and I sat in the guest room again drinking tea. Then he excused himself for a few minutes. Returning he instructed me to follow him into his quarters across the yard and into a room. His wife was sitting there with his twelve-year-old daughter. He sat down.

The girl came in and sat across from me, her head turned over her left shoulder, facing me, though her body was faced away from me. She held a diaphanous red dupatta from her raised left hand to her right hand so I could only see her face through the red veil. We tried to introduce ourselves. It was all a bit awkward with her uncle, her aunt and her cousin sitting there and her holding a veil in front of her face. Eventually her uncle left the room and she loosened up somewhat, lowering the veil, leaving it draped over her shoulders and turning on the _charpoy_ to face me.

She was pretty, though slightly small and she looked her age (did I forget to mention when I arrived the magistrate had informed me she was only sixteen years old?). Her complexion was very light and her orange-henna-streaked brownish hair cut short and falling around her shoulders. Very stylish, as I had been told, though not my style. There were no sparks when I saw her. She didn't have a nose ring, either. The interview was noncommittal.

Later, walking with the magistrate, perched on the raised shoulder of the

---

* _An expression used by Shites, calling on Hazrat Ali, the son-in-law of the Prophet Muhammad (PBUH) and fourth Caliph, for help. Calling on anyone besides God for help is considered sacrilegious by devout Sunni Muslims._

muddy road, an overflowing mud-choked irrigation ditch churning on our right side, he asked me, "What did you think of the girl, Noor Mohammad? She's very *Englaise* looking, eh?"

"Yes, she seemed very nice," I said. "But I don't particularly care for light skin or the English look. It's just my personal taste. Also, don't you think she is a little young for me?"

"Young? She is sixteen. Old enough to have children. And she could go with you when you want—to *Amerika*. She wouldn't have a problem with that."

"How old do you think I am?" I asked him.

"Thirty or thirty-two?" he answered.

"Thank you my friend. I'm almost forty. If I brought a wife who looked that young with me to America people would want to put me in jail."

"She is young, but not too young," he went on. "In a few years she can learn all the things you want her to learn."

And so we parried, I using the age difference as my main thrust. Actually, having been so long in Pakistan, I don't have many concepts concerning age left. Truthfully, my main consideration was the fact there wasn't that first magical look I was dreaming about.

We decided I would think it over and he would contact me the next time he came to Peshawar, in about a week. Also, I was beginning to wonder if I wanted to be so closely related to this *charras*-smoking roly poly little character with his interrogations and his small beady eyes which made me uncomfortable.

Back in Peshawar when I mentioned his name in Arif's shop they chuckled, learning that it was his niece I had gone to see. They knew him. Ten years previously he had been a scribe at the Peshawar courts. "He kept a bloody ledger, *banchod*," Anwar said derogatorily. "Now he's an irrigation magistrate or some such silly post. Where is he now? Swabi?"

"Zenda—before Swabi—this side," I said.

"Well, tell him you don't want to marry the girl and be done with it!" Anwar

382

Khan said bluntly. He considered court scribes as peons and an irrigation magistrate as a low civil service posting. *"Baas!"*

A MEETING IN GUL BAHAR

The next time I saw the magistrate I was on my way out the door of my house with Shah Hussain, who was staying with me because his college examinations had started and it was very difficult to get to the tests on time from his village. Also, the principal reason was, I am sure, to have me help him with his English. Likewise, he was helping me improve my Pashtu, the exchange being fairly mutual.

He was on his way to visit his friend Shah Jan and I was on the way to my former student Shahnaz's house, who had called a few days previously to invite me over to meet a girl from her office who wanted to meet me. All I knew was that she was Pathan and wanted to marry a foreigner. Might as well give it a shot. Always nice to see Shahnaz, anyway.

It was just before sundown when the magistrate and a friend appeared. Shah Hussain was just finishing locking the huge padlock on my front door. The magistrate told me he had received the letter I had sent him explaining that because of the great age difference I didn't think I could marry his niece. No, I hadn't changed my mind and besides, she couldn't be more than a week or so older now.

He kept looking at my house as if he expected me to open it and invite him and his pal in, but I have neither wife, mother nor sisters to make tea for him, nor a younger brother to chat and entertain them until I could return from what I really needed to be doing. The four of us walked down the street. At Shaheen Bazaar the magistrate and his partner went left, into the bazaar and Shah Hussain and I walked into Karimpura. I got a *rickshaw* in Chowk Shadi Pir to take me to Gul Bahar and Shah Hussain continued on to go on his sightseeing tour to Shah Jan's village.

At Shahnaz's house I was let in by one of her younger brothers. In the entrance room two women sat with Rafat, Shahnaz's sister. I hadn't seen her since her marriage the previous year. She stood up, greeted me and told me to wait in Shahnaz's room. I was surprised to be standing there face-to-face talking to her. I figured after her marriage I wouldn't be able to see her again. I was even more surprised when she came in and joined me while I waited. Her mother, one of the ladies sitting in the front room, I have only ever seen from behind. How strange. Although I could see her two daughters, I couldn't see her. Personal cultural values, or choice?

When I had been teaching Shahnaz and Rafat English along with one other pretty, eligible Pathan girl at my friend Professor Soofi's house, it always struck me rather incongruent that when his wife wanted to walk through the yard to go to the kitchen, the three girls and I had to go into the back room. The old woman kept strict *purdah* and God forbid I saw her, yet I could be in the back room alone with three young, pretty, unmarried girls. One of the many contradictions of Pakistan.

Rafat spoke to me in faltering English while her little brother brought in a tray of tea and cookies. She poured the tea, smiling. When I had been her English teacher I was only just starting to learn Pashtu and could only speak minimally. She didn't realize the intensity at which I'd been studying it. "We can talk in Pashtu, I think it will be easier for you," I told her in Pashtu as we shifted languages.

There was the sound of someone arriving at the front door. Voices. Rafat got up and walked to the door, then looked at me. "Shahnaz has come," she said. "Come here, Noor Mohammad."

I got up and stepped into the entrance hall. I saw Shahnaz hugging a lady and another lady hugging a stoutish lady or girl, or was there a girl somewhere I didn't see over the confusion and over Rafat's shoulder? Was I missing something? Shahnaz saw me, bubbled over *salaams* and walked into her room telling me to follow. We sat on the floor. Even though she works in an American aid office and I know she speaks good English, I appreciate that she always uses Pashtu with me.

"Have you had tea?" she asked.

"Yes."

"One cup more is good," she replied as she poured it.

"*Meribani.*"

"What do you think?" she asked out of the blue.

"About what?" I asked, puzzled.

"About the girl. That was her with me when I came in."

"Oh yeah?"

"Did you see her?"

"Well, I saw someone hugging a lady."

"In light orange?"

"Yeah, in light orange clothes."

"That was her. What did you think of her?" Shahnaz asked again as Rafat came in and joined us on the carpet.

"Do you think it might be possible to talk to her, face-to-face, for a bit? I didn't really even see her," I said. Thinking about it, I thought maybe I'd rather not even see her again, though I thought saying that would be impolite.

"I'll go see if she will come into the room," Rafat said. In a few minutes, she came back with the girl. She sat with Shahnaz, Rafat between us. She hardly said a word. I didn't know what to say. It was all quite embarrassing. There was absolutely nothing about this girl I liked. She may have been a sweet girl with a nice personality but not the kind of personality I needed or wanted. Definitely not the look I was stuck on. Having so little time to meet, to talk to prospective brides, I wanted to at least go for looks. This girl didn't do a thing for me, especially seeing her next to Shahnaz and Rafat. There just wasn't that "I must have this one" feeling I've been so desperately seeking.

Being polite, I told Shahnaz when we were again seated alone that I didn't think so but I would call her tomorrow to let her know after I thought about it. I showed her Nasreen's photo in my wallet to reinforce that I was looking for someone pretty, thin, kinda dark and with large dark eyes... none of which fit this girl. Not much to really think over on this one.

I walked home.

Inside the city walls, passing Chowk Shadi Pir, I heard a voice calling me from inside a brightly lit, newly built shopping arcade. There were tailor shops and cassette stores and in the far back the Chowk Shadi Pir P.C.O.*

"Noor Mohammad," I heard, "come here a minute. I want to talk to you."

I walked into the arcade to the call office, shaking hands with Iyas, the proprietor and owner of the arcade.

"*Asalaamo aleikum*," he said.

"*Wa aleikum asalaam*," I responded.

"I haven't seen you in quite some time, Noor Mohammad. Were you gone?"

"No, but I haven't been free, and I have my own phone in my house now."

"*Mubarak* (congratulations)."

"*Khair mubarak.*" That's okay—it cost me 20,000 rupees ($800.00) to not have to wait to have it installed by the phone company. 20,000 rupees and you go to the head of the waiting list.

"Are you still looking for a wife?" he asked. God, am I sick of the question.

"The right girl, yeah."

"You know we now have this marriage business, also?"

I have noticed as I've passed the arcade recently an Urdu sign proclaiming *"Chowk Shadi Pir Marriage Agency."* It looked impressive.

"I have one girl who would be perfect for you. She wants to marry a foreigner."

"She must be a Pathan."

"She is."

It seemed hard to believe that a *Shari* (Peshawari) could arrange the marriage of a Pathan girl, but then, anything is possible.

"And I don't want a white-skinned girl," I stated.

"No. This girl is *ghanum raang* (wheat color)."

"I want to meet the girl face-to-face first. If I have to go through meeting the family first, they are too backward for me. It is my experience."

"No. Don't worry. Come tomorrow at 11:00... no, noon. I'll check and if it's agreed, then I will bring you to see the girl face to face."

The next day I waited until 12:30 for Iyas to come.

But not alone. I sat in the marriage office, behind a glass door with the words *"Chowk Shadi Pir Marriage Agency"* painted on it in white enamel flowing Urdu script with red outlines. The office consisted of a narrow desk with a few straight backed wicker chairs. In front of the desk along the wall was a straight wicker couch. On the desk was a big, heavy, black telephone my mother might have used when she was young. In the chair behind the desk sat a Peshawari

---

* *Public Call Office — In Pakistan there are almost no public telephones and many people don't have phones in their houses. In the last couple of years, dozens of P.C.O.s have sprung up everywhere. Customers pay a fee to use the phone.*

girl with a white *chaddar* covering her hair and shoulders. Two fellows sat on the couch. On the end closest to me sat a young policeman who did most of the talking, asking me all manners of curious questions, not as a cop, but as an inquisitive Pakistani. He said he had seen me around. He was from Hashtnagri Police Tanna and had heard about me somewhat. He was happy to meet me and said he would definitely try to help me arrange my marriage. Iyas's brother sat on the remaining chair in the cramped office. The ceiling fan turned overhead. On the wall, under a calendar with a rainbow colored flowery calligraphic *Kalima,* was a large poster of Malduri Dixit (an Indian rave actress of the day). A large pot of tea arrived and the policeman and Iyas's brother argued over which one would pay. Iyas arrived and apologized for his tardiness. We downed a quick cup of steaming *qawah,* just slow enough to keep from burning our palettes. He knew I wanted to get on with it.

We took a *rickshaw* out to Gul Bahar, then walked down to the end of an unpaved cul-de-sac. We knocked at the metal front gate of a house. A woman came to a second floor window and spoke with Iyas from behind a *chit* in Hindko. A bad sign for me. Pathan women usually speak Pashtu. There was no male relative in the house so we couldn't come in. I grumbled to Iyas about how it looked too backward to me, too traditional.

Iyas said the girl wasn't there anyway. She was at her auntie's house and I should come back to his office at 5:00. It started raining huge cooling raindrops. The ground was turning to mud at our feet. It seems to rain every time I go to meet a girl. Is it an omen, or just traces of the monsoon blowing across the subcontinent?

At 5:00 I returned but Iyas said it was impossible for him to go just then. "Can you come to my office Saturday afternoon?" Iyas asked. "We will be able to go see the girl for sure on Saturday afternoon."

"*Insha'Allah.* I will try," I answered.

It was Thursday afternoon, August 29th.

Chowk Shadi Pir, Karimpura Bazaar (pre 1991)

Roof tops, Ghari Saidan, Hashtnagri

Mohallah Kashmiri, inside Gunj Gate, Peshawar City

"Could I but behold the face of my beloved once more,
I would give thanks unto God until the day of resurrection"
Persian verse

Typical dwelling near Nawa Pass, Bajaur Agency

Pond near Momad Ghat, Bajaur Agency

Chapter 32
Return

"When the Gods want to punish you, they answer your prayer."
Isak Dinesen

August 30th, 1991
Juma morning, 7:30

A bearded fellow appeared at my door, ringing the bell. He was partially expected. Shah Hussain had mentioned to me that before I had returned home last night somebody had called on me. He said his name was Rahmatullah, he had a beard and he had come from somewhere outside Gunj Gate—one of the old city gates not too far from my house. Not familiar. Maybe some *tablighee* religious hawker. He stood five foot eight, eyes of hazel, fair skin, hair and beard a darkish auburn. He looked like he could have been an Afghan, even his Pashtu had an Afghan undertone.

"I have a girl," he stated. "She wants to meet with you. She's like my sister. She knows you. You know her. She's talked to you, you've talked with her. You have seen her with your own eyes." he smiled. "But you haven't seen her in a long time.... Who is your best friend in Pakistan?"

"My best friend?" I asked, surprised he used the female gender of the word friend. In a culture like Pakistan's, for a single male to have a female best friend is almost an impossibility.

"Yes, your best friend," he repeated.

"I only have one best (female) friend in Pakistan. Her name was Nasreen and she lived in Lahore. But she disappeared and she didn't even have my address," I answered, watching his eyes for some sort of recognition at her name. I saw none.

"She wants to meet with you. She wants to come here. But nobody else must be here. And nobody else must know. When you see her you will know and then you will be happy and thank me. But remember, don't tell a soul."

"Okay. When do you want to come?"

"Wait for us on Monday, after noon."

Okay.

Then I'm thinking....

This is Peshawar. What can this mean?

Now it could be Nasreen, but the chance of it being her felt so slim. It could be somebody else who wants to offer me his little sister in marriage, like the fellow who offered his thirteen-year-old sister one rainy night as I came home, *"Fi sabil Allah"* (for God's sake/cause). She didn't quite meet my requirements, but he assured me that she could cook and clean my house, wash my clothes, massage me and have my children. What else could I possibly want?

It could be some girl that wants to meet me, but it can't be anyone I know. The Pakistani girls I know I can count on the fingers of one hand. None of them needed to go to this extent to see me.

Good or bad, it should prove interesting.

My close circle of friends warned me to be careful. It could be someone wanting to kidnap me (or worse, it could be *tablighees* from the mosque). Saturday morning in Khyber Bazaar I bought a new box of Czechoslovakian 32 bore cartridges for my Spanish Llama pistol. I looked closely at the red firing cap seals. They weren't so clear.

"Don't worry. These are original, brother. Everyone will fire for sure," the shopkeeper assured me.

"*Insha'Allah.* They better, friend. I'm not buying them for a wedding. I've got some very special guests coming."

He got my drift.

I walked home through Qissa Khanni Bazaar and Chowk Yadgar. Turning off Karimpura Bazaar I headed up Mohallah Noor Islam toward my house. As I passed the *hammam* the barber hailed me, "Noor Mohammad, please come in. Your guest has arrived."

Wondering just who this guest might be, I stepped up from the street into the shop. There, sitting in the barber's chair just having his hair and beard trim finished, was a friend I hadn't seen in over a year, Ian, who I had originally gone to Lahore with. We greeted in the mirror. He had just come out of Panshir Valley where he had spent six weeks in Afghanistan with Commander Mahsood writing a story for an aid organization.

"Please stay and have tea. It is just now ready," offered the barber.

"Thank you but we must go."

Ian handed him a 10 rupee note. We walked the brief distance to my house. Shah Hussain let us in and returned to his quarters on the second floor. Ian and I climbed the brick stairway to the third floor. We crossed the patio and I unlocked the entrance to my room when the front doorbell rang. I recognized from the way the bell was held down that it must be Rahmatullah. I looked out the window to make sure. On the way down the stairs I met Shah Hussain. "It's him," I said, then I opened the door.

"Can you meet the girl today?" he asked briskly, after *salaams*.

"Can you come back in an hour?" I was taken by surprise. Not ready now. Especially mentally. "I have a guest who has just arrived after a very long time."

"I have a guest for you whom you haven't seen for a long time also. Can whoever is in your house leave now? She wants to meet you now, alone."

I realized whomever it was must be standing out in the street, waiting. "Okay. Bring her in. Wait here in the ground floor *behtak*. I'll go upstairs and tell my friends to leave. They won't be able to see you in the *behtak* as they come down the stairs."

He went back outside and I ran back to the second floor, meeting Shah Hussain on the landing. "It's *coming down*," I said to him in English, having just taught him that bit of American slang. I ran on up to the third floor.

"It's coming down," I told Ian, rushing into the dining room. I quickly explained what was coming down: that some mystery girl was coming and it could be Nasreen. He knew of her since he had been with me in Lahore.

"Sorry, but he's bringing her right now. Can you meet me in the Afghan restaurant at Hashtnagri Chowk on Monday night?" I rushed him down the stairs, joining with Shah Hussain on the second floor landing. I said good-byes and shooed them out the door, then shut it and went into the *behtak*. Her escort was smoking a cigarette, the freshly exhaled tobacco heavy in the air. In the dim light all I could see was a girl standing there in a royal blue *burqa* and swirls of gray-blue smoke. She lifted the veil, smiling at me....

It was Nasreen!

We looked at each other for an endless minute, I was beaming. I didn't know there would be cigarette smoke in heaven (maybe it's not heaven). I was there. She lifted her finger to her lips, "*Bul cha ta na whya,*" she whispered (don't tell anyone).

We went upstairs, sat on my bed, talked and smoked. It was just like old times, only now she was smoking Red and White cigarettes instead of the more costly Gold Leaf and this bearded fellow was sitting with us instead of her husband, Akbar. He was her brother, she said. He lived in Mardan and I had never met him in Lahore.

"Akbar beat me. I ran away," she said. "You've seen him beat me before, huh?"

"Well, sometimes he... " I started to say. He did treat her cruelly.

"Remember how he used to curse me?"

"Yeah, he always treated you badly. The entire family treated you like a servant."

"My brother came to Lahore and found out. He also found out about Akbar's family's work. I ran away and he took me back to Mardan."

"They couldn't find you in Mardan?"

"I hid at a friend's house. And then I spent most of the summer in Bajaur at our *mama's* (Pashtu for maternal uncle) house. Nobody can find me there. And besides, it's cooler there. Just now we are coming from there. The Peshawar—Mardan road is dangerous for us. They could be looking for me on that road. We go to Mardan from the back way, via Timagura."

She looked out the door behind my bed. The roof of the house behind mine has a view of the porch outside my bedroom. She got up to close the door. She obviously didn't want anyone seeing her in my house. Paranoid, but I could understand. She inhaled, threw the butt on the brick floor and then continued, "My brother tried to arrange my marriage in Mardan but there was no one I wanted to marry. I told him I had a friend from when I lived in Lahore, an *Englaise*, and I wanted to marry him. He said he would never wed me to an *Englaise*, but I told him you were a good Muslim and I only wanted to be with you, so he said he would come to find you."

"And I tried to find you for six months," I laughed. "I was crazy. I was so worried for you. I even went to Dubai to look for you. You told me you wanted to go to Dubai and that you were making a passport. How did you find me? And why did you wait six months?"

"You told me that if I wasn't married you'd marry me. I was waiting for my divorce. Also it was hard for my brother to find you. He came to Peshawar many times. Finally I remembered you once told me you knew the owner and the manager of Amin Hotel."

"I went there and asked about you," the brother picked up the story. "They informed me you now live in Karimpura Bazaar. I came up here and a *naan bai* showed me where your house was."

Nasreen took my cigarette from my hand, gave me a sly smile, and put it to her lips taking a drag. She slowly exhaled smoke and said, "He wants to start his own business in Mardan. He only earns 800 rupees a month in a welding shop. It's very little. He has a wife and two little boys. It's very hard. He has someone who wants to marry me in Mardan. They have two *lakh* rupees ready. With that money he could start his own welding shop. But I don't want to marry anyone else. I want to marry you, Noor Mohammad. You are my choice."

"And you are my choice. You know that." I replied.

"What about the money? Do you have it here?"

"What if I did?"

"Then you could give it to him, he will go, and I will be with you."

"I don't have that kind of money here in the house. I will have to make some arrangements. I'll need some time. Can we go in the other room and talk a little privately?"

I'm sitting on a red Turkoman rug in my dining room. She's on a low, square, rainbow-colored, hand turned wood and wicker foot stool. The ceiling fan is turning slowly a story above us and beams of sunlight are streaming down from the clerestory colored glass windows above us.

"I can't believe I'm seeing you. That we're sitting here together, in this house," I say, placing my hand on her knee.

"I love you. I only want to marry you. But what about the money?"

A familiar conversation.

"What about the money? Two *lakh* isn't a lot?" I question.

"Is it?" she seductively smiles. "Didn't you offer Mama two *lakh* for me in Lahore?"

"Yeah, but you said you didn't want to marry me."

"They wanted to cheat you. To take your money."

Now I'd be happy to come up with the money for her, if she were being honest. But her way of asking doesn't seem congruent with the idea that I am the only man she wants to marry. Also, for a Pakistani girl, 26 is old. I know that people of the Afridi tribe sell their marriageable daughters for two and three *lakh* rupees, but Nasreen isn't Afridi, nor by Pakistani standards so marriageable. And now someone is offering two *lakh* rupees for her? Seems highly improbable. But anything is possible.

I'm hooked. She knows the bait.

"Nasreen darling, obviously I don't have that kind of money here. I will call my brother Mirza in America. He's my business partner. Maybe he can raise it. Also, I need to call my lawyer here in Peshawar about either mortgaging or selling my house. Somehow I will get the two *lakh* for you, but it will take a little time. But I want to speak with your mother." — I think if I could see her and this so-called brother together with her mother it would ease my suspicions, but not necessarily. However blinded I have always been by my love for her, I know that these people are not trustworthy. I think she has a spark of goodness inside her. Or should I say, I hope so. I want her to.

Can I be sure? Have I ever been sure?

We decide to go to Bajaur to see the uncle, then to Mardan to see her mother. We walk down Karimpura Bazaar to Chowk Shadi Pir, Nasreen following about 10 paces behind us, now completely covered in the blue *burqa*. I glance behind and catch glimpses of her slender, bangle covered wrists and long, *henna*-orange stained fingers. Occasionally I catch the flash of her dark eyes from under the embroidered grill-work eyepiece of the *burqa*. We take separate *rickshaws* to the Charsadda bus stand. I'm well known and it wouldn't do to be seen getting into a *rickshaw* with a woman. Her family from Lahore could be watching me. Word gets around.

"It's a very difficult journey to Bajaur," the brother was telling me. We were squatting in the dusty dirt under a tattered canvas overhang in front of the Charsadda bus stand.

"He used to come to Lahore every week to see me," she smiled.

"How far is it?" I asked, "I rode over 1000 miles on horseback to Gilgit and back. I even took the bus from Gilgit to Lahore just to see her. I'm used to it. And I did go to Lahore once a week from Peshawar to see her. I'd walk to Bajaur to marry her."

Nasreen nodded, acknowledging my words.

"Well, it's about two hours in a bus and then another two to three hours in a pickup to our uncle's house. In Agency the road is very bad. And much dust. Are you sure you won't get tried?"

"I got tried trying to find her. I got tired of missing her. Now I'm ready to go anywhere if it's with her."

"Maybe it's better if I take her to our uncle's and then to our mother's in Mardan. Then I can come get you. It will be safer for her. And it will give you a few days to make arrangements. Do you think you can have the money in three days?"

"That's very soon. But at least I can start arrangements."

"Good. Then we'll go to Bajaur and you stay in Peshawar to arrange the money. We'll call you in three days. Wait by your telephone from 11:00 A.M. until 2:00 P.M. We have to go far to find a phone, there aren't many in Tribal Territory. And remember, don't tell anybody that you've seen her."

"*Au, bul cha ta ma whya,*" Nasreen repeated. "Don't tell a soul, not even your friends. Understand?"

It made sense not to let word get out due to her position with her family in Lahore and God knows what else she has gotten into since then. I understood. But it did strike me strange how much they kept repeating not to tell anyone, not even my closest friends.

Tuesday the brother called. I had been thinking, and I had discussed the matter with a few close friends despite her warnings.

"Have her bring her *talaq namma* (divorce papers) the next time she comes," my lawyer friend Atique told me. "And any monies exchanging hands must be done in the courts with a magistrate presiding. She should also sign (or put her thumb print on) an *ejaza namma* saying that she isn't married or engaged to anyone."

"*Don't go to Bajaur!*" all my other friends told me. "Not with Nasreen, nor with anyone."

When he called, I had already made up my mind. I told him I needed to speak with her again and that they should bring a copy of her *talaq namma* when they came.

He told me to wait for them tomorrow after noon, but the next morning at 7:00 there was a familiar ring on my doorbell. I looked out the third floor window and saw him. Shah Hussain had left early with his friend Shah Jan for a *chekar* in Charsadda. I rushed down the stairs and opened the door to see Nasreen coming down the street toward my doorway. She was again completely hidden under the blue *burqa* but as she approached my front doorway she lifted the front of the *burqa*. She smiled. I was glad not only to see her, but relieved to know there wasn't somebody hiding under the *burqa* with a machine gun, a common Bajauri trick I'm told.

They came upstairs. There was a little boy with them—Qadeer, their uncle's son. They had come down from Bajaur, not from Mardan. They didn't have a *talaq namma*.

"I don't have one. Akbar and I were never really married," she explained. Only my love for her caused me to believe the lies she was telling me. "Akbar is just my cousin. I just lived there. I was just a working girl for him," she continued. "Just give him the two *lakh* and I will be with you. Easy."

I repeated what Atique had told me.

"No, I don't want anything to do with the courts," she snapped.

"She's afraid to go to the courts. She's afraid of magistrates. She's afraid of them from Lahore," the brother added. "It is very dangerous for her."

She and I went upstairs to talk. I showed her the rooms on the fourth floor. I opened an *almari* in my "office" wall and got out a small embroidered pouch I had been saving for her. In it was a gold nose ring with three small gold balls jangling from it, just like the one she had worn when I first met her. She looked at it and gave me a big smile. "You remembered." She had asked me to get her one like it.

"I had it made specially for you. I even carried it to Dubai, in case I found you." As she put it in her nose, she soothed away my questions in her usual manner; with a smile, a shrug, an impatient comment.

"I saw a picture of you and Akbar when you two were young together."

"I lived there from youth. They are like my family."

"Why did you always say he was your husband?"

"I wanted a husband. He was like my boyfriend. I always told people he was my husband. But he treated me so bad. I couldn't take any more of it."

"Your brother's accent is different from yours."

"He grew up in Mardan and I grew up in Lahore."

"Your family permitted you to live with them, and they never knew you worked?"

"My family and his were very close. Like one family."

"Your family didn't know what their business was?"

"You remember sometimes when you were in Lahore people were there from my family and there was no business? You and I had to be secret. Why so many questions? Stop the questions. Just get the money and we can be together."

"I want to go see your mother. And if we have to go by way of Bajaur, we can see your uncle, too."

She smiled sweetly and asked if I had any *charras*....

We went back down to my bedroom to discuss matters with her brother. He kept insisting the way was difficult and I would get tired. Nasreen and I assured him I had lots of experience on journeys in Pakistan. And my heart was insisting I go with her. We decided to go first to Bajaur to meet the uncle. Then we would continue around the back way to Mardan to see her mother. At least I had seen her mother before. The uncle I wouldn't know. Nasreen I knew. I wanted to believe her, but my trust was not with my heart.

They said they had to say goodbye to the people they were staying with and get some things. They'd come back in an hour, then we would go. I went down to Shah Hussain's room and left a note. I didn't really even know where I was going. I just wrote that I was going to Bajaur with Nasreen and that I should return in a few days, *Insha'Allah*.

I tried to call Master Ali Haider. Having been my close friend for over 10 years he was one of the handful of friends who knew all about Nasreen. I thought it might be beneficial if he could talk to her before we left so he could explain some things to her on my behalf. Also, he is one of my few friends with a telephone. He wasn't there. Gulzar Alam (the singer) answered instead. He also knew much of the story. I told him what was happening.

"Noor Mohammad, please don't go to Bajaur. With Nasreen or with anyone!" he told me explicitly.

"I have to go with her. I must go. Anywhere."

"You're crazy!" he said.

"I know," I answered without hesitation, "but this craziness is enjoyable. She'll be coming back to my house in about half an hour. Then we are going. If Master comes in before that, have him call me."

"Okay, but please don't go to Bajaur!"

It wasn't the first time I had heard the statement. Nor the last.

"Don't tell a soul. Not even your best friends," she again insisted when they returned. "We can get married secretly. No court. No judges. After, we will come to Peshawar and then you can tell your friends. Then it will be too late for them in Lahore. Are you ready? You didn't tell anyone you were going with us?"

"Where are we going?"

"First we will take a minivan from the Charsadda bus stand to Gandao."

"*Gandah!*" I laughed, "Everywhere in Pakistan is *gandah*." (*Gandah* means filth in Pashtu and Urdu.)

"Not *gandah*," she returned the laugh, "to Gandao. That is where the bus ends and we will hire a pickup to take us into Agency."

Again we took separate *rickshaws* to the Charsadda bus stand.

She squatted by the wall on the waiting veranda with the little boy Qadeer. I stood nearby smoking a Red and White cigarette while the brother went off to purchase fruit. They had told me not to talk to anybody as Gandao is in Agency and foreigners aren't allowed to go there.

We boarded a minibus going to Gandao via Shabqadar.

Until Shabqadar the landscape was typical Vale of Peshawar: corn fields and sugar cane, tobacco, dusty roads with the usual roadside businesses— sundry supply stores, cloth, arms, medicos and cassette stores, metal workshops and truck workshops. There were *hammams* with multicolored towels hanging out front for advertisement and to dry in the sun.

We crossed the Kabul River and several tributaries. The road was still fairly well paved. After Shabqadar, we came to the first government militia check post. Soldiers carrying German (Pakistani or Irani made) G-3 automatic rifles checked the bus for arms. I was careful to try to blend in. We had entered Tribal Territory—Mohmand Agency. Nasreen flashed a quick smile at me as the soldiers completed their check of the bus.

Here most of the greenery was left behind. Heading into dry, barren, craggy brown folds of the mountains and brown mud forts. It looked more like Afghanistan. It felt like Afghanistan. Occasionally a group of forts would be alongside the road. Every fort had at least a tower in one corner with metal plate covered shooting loopholes. Other forts were off alone in the jagged rocks and hills. It took over an hour to reach Gandao.

Nasreen, Qadeer and I squatted by a mud wall to the rear of the bus stand while the brother arranged a Datsun (in Tribal Territory any pickup seems to be called a Datsun, regardless of the make) to take us up to Bajaur. I bought them a *Rooh Afza* from a grimy boy wearing a grimy embroidered skullcap carrying a bucket of the drink with a large chunk of dirty ice floating in it and a few besmeared glasses. I smoked a cigarette. She looked around but realized we weren't secluded enough to sneak a puff. We left Gandao in a private Toyota pickup. They reminded me not to talk to anybody.

"Pretend that you are *charra* (speech impaired)," they instructed me. I pantomimed a *charra* trying to ask for a cigarette. We all laughed.

Nasreen and the child sat in the front seat next to the window. The brother sat between them and the driver. I sat in back with two riders we were taking part way and the *kalendar.* *

As we pulled out of Gandao we passed a part of the bazaar that looked as if it had just been bombed. Only the mosque and the school building were not in ruins. It was the section of the bazaar that sold arms, including all sorts of bombs, mines and anti-aircraft weapons from Afghanistan, and drugs—heroin, opium and hashish. Gandao is also a center of the Mohmand car-napping trade (a lucrative trade in Agency—stealing cars from the settled areas and holding them for ransom). Later, I learned that the government militia had come in and bulldozed the bazaar in an "operation cleanup."

We headed up a mountain pass. I saw only one road marking sign, pointing in the direction we were going. All I could make out was the last few faded letters '...*wagai*'. Dust was flying, obscuring my vision and making my teeth gritty. At the top of the pass there was a Mohmand Rifles' check post. In Agency there aren't police. Just Mohmand Rifles in Mohmand Agency and the Bajaur Scouts in Bajaur Agency. Local levies.

We twisted down the steep mountain pass toward a valley ringed with dagger-like mountains. A lunar landscape. As we reached straighter road we raced into the valley with two other Datsuns following at breakneck pace. The drivers charged forward with seemingly no regard for their own lives or the lives of their human cargos. I hoped we wouldn't plunge off the road into the dusty ravine.

Squinting eyes, more dust and grit. After half an hour we stopped for petrol. Here was our two passengers' destination. They took their bundles and left. Nasreen handed me a bunch of cool, sweet grapes through the window as our driver filled the tank, a lit cigarette carelessly dangling from his mouth.

Another half hour and we came to a junction lined with stone open-front shelters, some with canvas stretched over the tops. Some kind of basics stores I presumed. In the dust I didn't have much time to look. We turned left, the only choice besides following the main road, and sped on toward the rugged mountains heading northwest toward Afghanistan. We stopped at another Mohmand

---

* The conductor in Agency is called a "kalendar." It seems to me to be a combination of the Farsi words "kalan," meaning far, and "dar" meaning sight, which is needed in these desolate parts to see tentative riders coming from a distance and hold the vehicle from leaving, though Shah Hussain assures me it is just a local mispronunciation of the English word conductor.

Rifles' check post. Just the *kalendar* and myself sitting in the back. The driver exchanged words with the Levies.

We sped off toward two pointed mountains protruding from the racked landscape like rotted teeth. Behind them was another range of mountains, the Afghan border I assumed. Less than 15 minutes and we were within a few miles of those rotted peaks.

We turned left off the pavement, down a rocky, rutted road through dry, dusty fields of stubble. We were heading due west toward Afghanistan. The only habitations were mud forts, and none were closer than a couple of *furlongs* from each other. The driver had put a new cassette in the tape deck. It was Gulzar and Master. As we bounded along deeper and deeper into Tribal Territory I listened, *"Kusa day lurrey, kor nesdee day—ru ru keda qadamuna, layla (the road is long, the house is near—step slowly, sweetheart)."*

Occasionally Nasreen looked back at me and smiled, her eyes flashing through the grilled eyepiece of her *burqa*. My life was complete....

Twenty minutes later, we pulled off the dirt road, drove through a field and stopped in front of a fort. It was of average size with just a single tower. I climbed out of the back of the Datsun and stood away from it with Nasreen. She faced the fort, away from the driver, as the brother paid. The Datsun drove away, back the way we had come. Nasreen lifted her burqa, free at last. At least from the *burqa*. Still I couldn't believe I was seeing her.

"I bet you wonder what kind of place we've brought you to?" she laughed.

"I've been in desolate, empty areas like this before. Remember, before I lived in Pakistan I spent much time in Afghanistan. This reminds me of Afghanistan," It should have. At most we couldn't have been more than a few miles walk from the Afghan border. Tribal Territory is a shadow zone between Afghanistan and Pakistan, administered by Pakistan, inhabited by tribal Pathans. The Pathans living in it owe their first allegiance to their respective clans and follow the law of the *jirga* (a group of elders). Many are fugitives and outlaws. The government has no power in Tribal Territory, at least not off the few paved roads. If the army comes in, the locals shoot them. They don't keep heavy caliber machine guns mounted in their towers for nothing. Until now, the government tolerates them, a somewhat uneasy status quo.

In front of the fort was a sitting area surrounded by six-foot-high stone walls with a few strategically placed holes for shooting. In the center of this outdoor guestroom grew a dry, gnarled tree covered with a dry grape vine. A young boy brought out two *charpoys* and some pillows. The uncle wasn't home but he should be home by evening the boy, his son, informed us. We sat on the *charpoys* and drank tea. The brother excused himself and went inside the fort's massive wooden doors, set into 20 foot earthen walls, to attend to some family matters. Several younger children kept their distance, silently watching us.

The boy went off into the dry cornfields with his slingshot. Soon he returned with his kill, a black crow. He took it up on a roof inside the fort and hung it from a pole sticking out of the roof. He and the younger children seemed to think it greatly amusing to watch the other birds come to pick at the freshly killed corpse. Then he disappeared into the fields, later returning with two small sparrows he had killed with his sling. I asked Nasreen if they were edible. She said she would cook them for me, getting up and taking them inside.

The brother came out. There was one sparse corn field behind the fort. Another field with the dry stubble of the already harvested wheat crop looking toward the barren mountains of Afghanistan held five grazing donkeys.

There was no irrigation. "If it doesn't rain, the crops will burn (die)," he told me, looking at the field. "All our water here comes from wells. Very deep wells. Ours is 120 feet deep. Dug by hand. The well in that fort is 300 feet deep."

I noticed that the boy was calling the brother Noor Gul. Not so unusual in a suspicious land as this that he would originally come to my house under the guise of another name.

He went inside the fort. I chatted with the boy. "What is your name?"

"Abidullah," he stated.

"Are you in school?"

"I'm in the second class," he told me.

He was probably 12 years old but in Tribal Territory there is much needed to be done around the home. Especially for an eldest son.

"My school is an hour's walk from here. It has four rooms," he boasted. Then he continued in thickly accented English, "Cat-bat-rat-won-tuo-tree-fuor-fibe. Look," he said. Picking up a stick, he scratched his name in the dirt, "ABIDDLAH" in crooked English script. He smiled.

"What is Noor Gul's relation to you?" I checked.

"My cousin."

"And the girl?"

"She's also my cousin. His sister."

"Noor Gul lives here with you?"

"No, he lives in Mardan with his wife and children."

I asked more personal questions but all of his answers were correct. Nasreen came out with the two sparrows skewered and roasted on a gun cleaning rod. Noor Gul brought me a *lota* of water to make *wuzu* for prayer. He told me he had already prayed inside. I prayed with the boy. When we were making *wuzu,* he told me it was *guna* (sin) because I hadn't quite gotten between my toes completely wet. My prayers would not be valid he told me. True in Muslim rules, but then I personally am not sure how God feels about it. But then, every bit gleaned is another bit learned. It fits the form. God is inside. People and forms are outside.

After prayer, more food was brought—a few eggs cooked in grease, spinach and coarse, home-cooked *roti*. Noor Gul said he was sick and not so hungry. He did eat a few bites with me so that I wasn't eating alone. For some reason it relieved me that at least he ate something with me. In this culture, you don't break bread with someone you intend to kill. Inside I knew I couldn't trust Nasreen as far as I could throw her, though I would have rather gone on hearing her lies than go on without her.

The uncle never showed up. Noor Gul and I planned to sleep outside. When night came, we listened to what sounded like thunder from across the mountains. He told me they must be fighting in Afghanistan. Then a dust storm blew in. We hastily retreated into the *hujra*.

In the morning Nasreen brought me *chai* and *parattas* tasting of wood smoke. When I told her I had ventured out in the field at dawn to go to the toilet she said, "I'm afraid to go out at night. The dogs will eat you!"

We spent most of the day sitting on *charpoys* outside the fort in the rock-walled sitting area. We discussed our wedding plans and the future. Talk about being in heaven. Temporary heaven. We could get married, then apply for her visa for America. We would stay part time in Bajaur and part time at my house in Peshawar. Then we would go to America and spend a year or so there. Let things cool down in Pakistan.

Noor Gul and I talked about payment plans for the two *lakh* rupees. If I couldn't get all of the money right away I could give him one *lakh* down, marry her and pay the remaining *lakh* in six months to a year. Or if that was a problem I could pay 50,000 rupees down to assure that they wouldn't marry her off to the suitor in Mardan and after I got another 50,000 to them we could wed. He was rather sure their uncle would agree to those terms. Nasreen and I sat and watched the gray-brown mountains and dry fields. In the distance we could see men working in their fields, rifles or machine guns slung over their shoulders.

We sent Abidullah off to the store for cigarettes and matches. In these backward rural areas stores are commonly just a front room of somebody's house selling a small handful of sundries and essentials. We laughed that we had to smoke Red and White, the more expensive Gold Leaf cigarettes we used to smoke in Lahore not available in remote places such as this. Nobody can spend 20 rupees on a pack of cigarettes here. He returned an hour later. Nothing is close here. I noticed my 10 rupees change in his top shirt pocket. When he saw I didn't ask for it he made a casual, yet noticeable, effort to hide it. Maybe not unusual for a young, dirt poor kid, but rather unusual treatment toward a guest in Pathan society.

Noor Gul was not to be seen most of the morning. Nasreen said he was sick and sleeping. Shortly after noon she disappeared inside the fort. It was *Juma* and the closest neighboring fort, approximately two *furlongs* away, had a mosque built onto it. The *Juma* prayer was starting and the beginning of the *khutba* (sermon) was broadcasting from a scratchy loud speaker perched on the roof of the fort's tower. Abidullah came out with a *lota* of water to make *wuzu*. He said we should pray here as the mosque would be filled with stupid people who would be suspicious as to why I was here. Now, because of the situation with Nasreen, I didn't think it was all that unusual that they were trying to hide me. We made *wuzu*, the water running off and soaking into the fine, dry dust covering the ground. When the final *Azan* sounded, just before the congregational prayer was to start, Abidullah went scampering off across the field of dirt clods and dust to the mosque. Little punk. Left alone and not knowing if it would blow things by following him, I prayed alone. It didn't really matter where I prayed.

A little girl maybe eight and another younger boy with a shaved head were playing nearby. Their faces were snotty and filth-caked. So were their clothes. I tried speaking to them but they acted as if they were deaf or mute, staring at me stupidly. "Tell the girl Nasreen to come here," I told them.

Still they ignored me.

"Nasreena!" I finally shouted.

She came out, bringing me lunch. She was wearing a deep blue shawl wrapped around her shoulders and over her hair. I ate sitting on a *charpoy* under the dry grape arbor. Nasreen sat and kept me company, smoking cigarettes. She looked so thin and dark, her deep brown eyes flashing in the stark, bright sunlight. While we sat there Abidullah returned. I finished eating. He took away the plates. She took a fresh cigarette from the pack, lit it and handed it to me. More talk. I told her more of how crazy I had become when I had found out that she left Lahore. Of my craziness during *Ramazon*. Of chasing her shadow in Dubai. Of my crazy wife search in Peshawar. And back to the marriage....

"We will get married here, in Agency," she repeated. "The people from here will not go to Peshawar. They won't go further down-country than Gandao. And anyway, I'm afraid to get married in Peshawar. I'm afraid to go to the courts. What is wrong with that? People here have plenty of guns. They will come across the fields from neighboring forts. There will be much firing (here joy is expressed by firing guns into the sky—*lethal celebration*). Completely free! Better than Peshawar!"

"But my lawyer said we must do it in the courts for it to be legal. And I need to tell my friends. They should come."

"I'm afraid of courts. We mustn't tell a soul. After we're married we can go to Peshawar, tell your friends, make my American visa. Then we can go to America or anywhere."

"Hmm...."

"Don't say, 'hmm,' Noor Mohammad. You want to marry me. Here is a good place. A free place. Later we can tell people."

I had heard it before.

Noor Gul came out and we went over the financial arrangements again. He agreed with Nasreen that it was important to do the marriage out here. He said he liked me, that I was already like his brother, and for that reason he would talk their uncle into letting him take partial payment now and the rest later. He told me when their uncle arrived I shouldn't let on I've known Nasreen from before. The story would be that I've known Noor Gul for two years. He knew I wanted to marry a Pathan girl so he brought Nasreen to my house in Peshawar for me to meet her. Now we had come to Bajaur to discuss it with the uncle. Supposedly the uncle didn't know what Nasreen had been doing in Lahore. Just your average "shy unmarried cigarette smoking Pathan maiden."

At dusk we heard the sound of a vehicle on the dirt road running near the fort. It stopped. A bearded man carrying a *Kalashnikov* on his back and wearing a bandolier packed with two extra clips (that's over 90 rounds!) and six Russian hand grenades walked into our little walled sitting area. I was sitting on a *charpoy* with Noor Gul. Nasreen was sitting on another *charpoy* across from us smoking a cigarette. She pulled her shawl up over her head and stood up with a "we've been caught" smile as if to go inside. The uncle motioned her to sit back down. She did so, casually dropping her half-finished cigarette in the dirt.

He strode up to me. "I'm Sabut Mafhrul!" he boasted.

"I'm Noor Mohammad Khan. Were you in Peshawar?" I asked. He was a day late.

"I said I'm *mafhrul!* * I don't go to Peshawar!" he snarled. "Pakistan is my enemy. Look at my bombs!"

Nasreen was looking at me, smiling. The uncle looked like a typical backward, rustic Pakistani farmer. He was in his mid 50s, hair and beard black-brown flecked with gray, five foot eight and wiry, with hollow, sunken eyes. He was wearing a coarse, olive green *shalwar kameez* and the same color rough wool *pakul* cap. So this is Nasreen's mother's brother? I'd better get on his good side I thought, if I could find one. Nasreen flashed me her silvery smile, got up and went inside.

Uncle and I walked out to the field behind the fort. Noor Gul and Abidullah brought a large rug and spread it on the dirt. They arranged two *charpoys* on either side of the rug, along with pillows. Uncle started preparing a *chillum*, taking tobacco from a wooden box about the size of a cigar box and packing down the clay bowl with his dirt-hardened hands. As we smoked and coughed I told him the old story of how I'd become a Muslim and of my time in Afghanistan. How I had ended up in Pakistan, about my house and my recording studio business (as to the studio I might as well mentioned something about me landing on the moon).

Abidullah appeared from the fort with the beginning plates of dinner. He came around to each of us with a dented aluminum *lota* of water to wash our hands. He poured it over our hands, the runoff splashing into a basin below, and handed us a well-used towel for drying.

We got down off the *charpoys* and sat on the rug to eat. Abidullah sat close by, not eating, but listening to our talk, on hand in case anything was needed. Proper behavior for a young Pathan boy. After dinner he went inside and reappeared with a tray of tea and a plate of sweet *gor*. We washed our hands and drank tea. After tea and another pipe Noor Gul said he wasn't feeling well and excused himself to go inside to sleep. Uncle and I made *wuzu* and prayed *Isha,* our *qibla* the two jagged, breast like peaks separating us from Afghanistan.

The air was cool, a pleasant respite from the hot summer nights Peshawar was still in the grip of. After prayer we shared the *chillum* again. Uncle told me not to wander around as there were many scorpions at night. A dog was barking off in the corn field.

"Don't wander in the corn fields, either. The dogs don't know you. They will eat you. Good night," he finished as he lay down, hanging his cap over one of the end posts of the *charpoy* and pulling his blanket over his head.

---

* *"Mafhrul" means fugitive in Pashtu — many people hide from the government in Tribal Territory, where there is no government law.*

"Good night." I lay back and watched the stars play hide-and-seek with the clouds and thought of Nasreen and where we were, this uncle and his fort.

Later, the moon came out, beating the stars at their own game, its silvery light magically lining the clouds. Lightning flashed from behind the mountains. I awoke as dawn was just starting to purple the mountains to the east. I took the *lota* and walked into the corn field. After relieving myself I made *wuzu* on the side of the field near the rug.

Finishing my morning prayer I had a hit of *nuswar* and lay back on my *charpoy* to watch the wispy remaining clouds change colors of purple, orange and pink with the idly rising sun. Uncle got up, made *wuzu* and prayed. Then he went inside. Noor Gul and Abidullah brought out tea and *parattas*. Nasreen came out and sat with me. The uncle came back.

"You two go inside," he commanded us. "Some neighbors are approaching. It's not good that they see you. They are suspicious people. They'll ask questions."

We went inside the fort, Nasreen leading me into the *hujra*.

"Give me your shirt," she requested. I had spilled *chai* on it. "The milk will stain. I'll wash it out for you."

"Taking the shirt off my back, as usual," I said in English.

"What?" she looked at me quizzically.

"Nothing." I replied.

The *hujra* had sacks of wheat and barley piled in the center. The walls were of adobe a couple of feet thick, the ceiling supported by four rough hewn wooden pillars. There were two *charpoys*. On one wall were old black and white family photos: men posed in front of painted backdrops of mountains and gardens or the Taj Mahal, Noor Gul in a turban; all men. Another wall displayed two posters of Jamiat Islami Afghanistan.* Two of the walls had one foot square windows about seven feet up with ill-fitting hinged wooden coverings.

I sat in the *hujra* until Nasreen brought lunch, then Abidullah brought us tea. Nasreen told him to bring the cigarettes. We decided it was time to talk to the uncle about money. She went out and didn't return.

I sat on the *charpoy* looking out the door of the *hujra* at the front gate of the fort; thick wooden planks held together with rusty steel plates and bolts. A massive rusty chain hung from it as a latch. An old hag hobbled up to the gate and glanced out to make sure nobody was looking. Back and forth she craned her gray wizened head. Then she hobbled back into the *hujra* on a gnarled walking stick. Her clothes were patches and rags covered in dust. Her hair hung disheveled in dusty gray plaited ropes, her face hung in leathery timeworn wrinkles. She looked at me with wild bloodshot eyes, raised her wrinkled hands and hissed, "*Ubasa, ubasa! Otarel. Ohzah!*" (Get out, get out. They'll tie you. Get out!—as far as I could make out.)

The movie was just beginning....

---

* *Jamiat Islami Afghanistan* — a major mujahideen group in Afghanistan. There is also a Pakistani political party, Jamiat Islami (the Party of Islam).

I went outside the fort. Nasreen, Noor Gul and the uncle were sitting under the dry grape-less arbor, talking.

"What is going on?" I asked.

Noor Gul told me the uncle had accepted the terms we had arrived at yesterday.

"Good," I said to the uncle. "Then I want to go to Peshawar. I'm already a day late. I want to start raising the money."

"I want to talk to him and her some more," the uncle said. "Go inside. We'll drink tea. Then Noor Gul will take you as far as Gandao. The way is dangerous. People here shoot at strangers."

I decided to have tea so went inside. Abidullah brought it; poured and left. I waited, but no one showed up. I drank alone. Tired of waiting, I went outside again. Nasreen, Noor Gul and the uncle were still sitting under the arbor. They were arguing.

"Two years ago this loafer, her brother, got three and a half *lakh* rupees from me," the uncle said, glaring when he saw me, — that is a lot of money in Tribal Territory, where 10,000 rupees buys a Kalashnikov and a few thousand more someone to fire it — "He bought two trucks. Then he sold them and ate my money. I never got any of it," he raged.

"What does that have to do with me?" I asked. "I just want to go to Peshawar to get the money to marry her. You can take it, I don't care. That's between you and him."

"No! I want my money back. I want it now. He did this to me. Her brother. None of you leave here until I get my money."

We stated the obvious. How could we get him any money here? Noor Gul said the man who had bought one of the trucks owed him the final payment now. If he could go to Mardan he could get one and a half *lakh rupees*. I said if I could go to Peshawar I could raise part of the two *lakh* now and the balance shortly after.

"No, I don't trust him anymore. I won't trust him to go to Mardan," the uncle said of Noor Gul.

"Can he and I go inside to talk?" Nasreen asked, pulling me with her eyes.

"Okay. But nobody is going anywhere until I get my money back from your brother, the damn thief."

Noor Gul shrugged his head and remained on his *charpoy*. Nasreen and I went into the *hujra*.

"This is great," I said, "Why didn't you tell me about this?"

"How should I know? I was in Lahore when this happened. Noor Gul never told me. This is the first I've heard of it also."

"I can raise the money. You know for you I will. Maybe I can raise all of it. Noor Gul can pay me back. But I need to get to Peshawar. I can't do anything here."

"I know. We'll have to talk to him. Maybe he'll let you go if we stay here until you get back. How soon can you get back?"

"I'm not sure yet. But I'll come back soon with some money and news about when I can get the rest. What did Noor Gul do with the money anyway?"

"I don't know. Let's go talk to uncle. I'm so sorry."

Before we could get up the uncle came in, sitting on a *charpoy* across the room from us, rocking back and forth, hitting his head with his hand. "I'm sick." he moaned, "Her brother has made my head hurt. I'm becoming crazy,"

We looked at each other. It was getting weird.

"He stole my money. The loafer. Her brother, *khorghod!* He's no good. My family doesn't have food to eat. He ate my money!" He paced in front of us, waving a long handle axe. I exchanged glances with Nasreen, then we heard a machine gun bolt being pulled and snapped into place. A Kalashnikov appeared in the doorway, the wooden butt touching the ground, the barrel pointing to the sky. Someone was obviously squatting just outside the doorway holding it but he was blocked by the thick mud wall. Only the gun could be seen framed in the doorway, like a metal insect crouching in the fading light of dusk.

"What's the point of that?" I asked.

He didn't say a word. Taking the sling from a slingshot hanging from one of the pillars he tied her hands together in front of her. We exchanged glances. I wasn't sure if I should laugh or not. Was this really happening? It was like some movie. Or some kind of joke?

He tied my hands behind my back and sat me in front of her on the *charpoy*, tying my hands to hers. So? There I was with the woman I'd been going crazy trying to find for the past seven months, tied together on a *charpoy*. Life can be strange. Got to remember to watch those desires. He went out, bolting the door chain from the outside. She started to cry softly into her *chaddar*.

"He's not really serious. He's trying to scare us. Look how loose the knots are. He's a stupid man," I soothed, pulling on the cords, loosening them to make them more comfortable on our wrists. I could completely undo them, but I didn't want to upset her uncle. All I wanted was to get out of there with her; to marry her.

"He's crazy," she fretted. "I didn't know about any of this."

"Well it's nice to finally meet your mother's side of the family," I chided. "Thanks."

"I'm sorry, Noor Mohammad. How did I know that Noor Gul did these things? How will we get out?"

"God knows. At least we're alone together. And not in Akbar's house."

In a few hours the uncle came back and untied me. "I don't trust this girl's brother. The liar. The loafer. He's no good. You, I trust."

"Good, if you trust me, then untie her."

He screwed up his face, thinking, then untied her, finally leaving. Later Nasreen left to check on Noor Gul, disappearing into the black night outside the door. Soon she reappeared at the door, looked around and came in. "We were lucky. Noor Gul is tied to a *charpoy* in a room with no light. He is tied very tight."

The uncle came to the door. "What are you two talking about?"

"Can he see Noor Gul?" she asked the mad uncle.

She led me by the hand across the yard to the stone tower in the corner of the fort. The uncle held a lantern, illuminating the dark stone room holding Noor Gul. He was on his side with his arms bound securely behind him, one leg chained to an old broken *charpoy*.

"See, we were lucky," she remarked. Then looking at the uncle, she continued, "Tell him to untie Noor Gul."

"Why don't you untie him, *mama*," I requested. "You have him locked in the room from the outside. He can't go anywhere."

A fellow I hadn't seen before appeared with a Kalashnikov and pulled me away. "He'll be untied when he gives the money," he grunted.

"And like this where will the money come from? The sky?" Nasreen couldn't resist a snicker.

Back to the *hujra*. The boy Abidullah brought me tea.

"My father beat Noor Gul. He's very mad. Noor Gul is crying. Did he beat you?"

"No."

"Drink tea." He poured.

"No. I'm not drinking your tea. Tea is for guests. I'm not a guest. I'm a prisoner. What kind of Muslim is your stupid father?"

"He's a good Muslim. A strong Muslim," he said defensively, giving me a stock answer.

"He's a *Muslim*?" I laughed contemptuously. "He talks about hospitality. It's a sin to make a guest a prisoner."

Until now the boy had been my friend. I could tell my talk was upsetting him. "I'll talk to my father. It's Noor Gul he is mad with. You didn't do anything. He'll let you go tomorrow. Now drink tea."

"I'll drink your tea tomorrow then."

"He will let you go. Someone will take you to the road. It's dangerous to be on the road alone here."

I knew that in Tribal Territory government control ends three feet off the paved road. Or is it three yards? I wasn't worried if it was feet or yards. I was many miles off the paved road. I was even off the dirt road. Later, when I got back to Peshawar I was told that Tribals will shoot people on the road and then drag the body off the road—out of government jurisdiction.

"I'll bring you dinner," Abidullah coaxed.

"No. Tell the girl Nasreen to bring it. I want to talk to her."

Earlier the uncle had told me because I was his guest he would *halal* a chicken in my honor. Nasreen came in the room, followed by Abidullah carrying an aluminum bowl which he placed on the table in front of me. In it was one chicken leg, swimming in an orange soupy greasy gravy. He looked down at it proudly smiling. Nasreen placed a cloth on the table with large flat roti wrapped in it.

"Did the rest of the chicken get away?" I asked, looking in the bowl. She laughed. Even the poorest people when they *halal* a chicken for a guest, serve at least a quarter of it. Usually half, if not the entire bird.

After dinner the uncle came back in the room saying he was sick. He was acting crazy, calling Noor Gul all sorts of foul names. He wanted to chain me to the *charpoy* for the night.

"Why do you want to chain him?" Nasreen asked. "Noor Gul took your money. He didn't know anything about it when he came here with us."

"He's your no-good brother's friend. I'll chain you too, just as your brother will remain chained."

"You say I'm your guest. You say you trust me. This is how much you trust me?" I said, pointing at the three-foot length of chain. "Three feet of trust? I trust on God. If you want, it is your choice. God knows all choices. But first I want to make *wuzu* and say my night prayers.

While I was praying he tied Nasreen's hands in front of her again. It all just seemed a bit too showy for me but I didn't want to blow my chances at getting Nasreen. Quite the movie. Uncle tapped his axe over his shoulder. I knew it could invalidate my prayers but I kept watching him out of the corners of my eyes. Maybe he was joking, maybe not, but I didn't want to chance he'll start swinging on her.

As I finished he told Nasreen to leave the room. Looking over his shoulder he whispered, "I trust you. You are an honest man. But I don't trust them. Her brother is a liar and a thief. I won't tie your hands."

"Thanks," I said as he shackled my leg to the leg of the *charpoy* with the chain and an antiquated heavy rusty padlock. "Thanks for small kindnesses. So you trust me three feet worth? Well, I guess it's more than one foot of your trust." As he left the room I yelled after him, "Untie the girl." It's her brother you're mad with. And besides, she won't go away at night. She's afraid of the dogs."

I heard the door's bolt slam shut.

The next morning as Nasreen and I ate a breakfast of smoky tasting p*arattas* and *chai* in the *hujra* Noor Gul came in the room, taking my hand in supplication. "Noor Mohammad, please accept my apologies. I am so sorry. He is a bad man. He's crazy. This isn't your fault. It was mine. He had no right to tie you. Last year he fired on his own mother."

"*Toba.* Was she injured?"

"No, he missed, *Al-hamdu-lillah.*"

"***Allah** shoker.*" (thank God)

That day we discussed: Noor Gul and I; Nasreen and I; Noor Gul, Nasreen and I; them and uncle; uncle and I; all four of us. I was starting to realize this was my big Pashtu exam and to pass it meant to get out of Bajaur. To get out with Nasreen, now that would be the trick.

"You've waited two years. What's another month?" I asked the uncle.

"No, I can't wait another day. I should kill him," he growled, pointing his gun at Noor Gul.

"The *Qur'an Sharif* says, '***Allah** loves the man who is forgiving.*'"

"If you let me go to Mardan," Noor Gul argued, "I can get the half *lakh* from the man I sold the truck to. Or if not, I can get two *lakh* from the man who wants to marry Nasreen."

"I don't want to marry anybody else," Nasreen interjected, looking to me.

"No," Uncle demanded, "he's cheated me. He can't go. I don't trust him."

"I can to go to Peshawar to arrange the money. Remember, I want to marry her. I'll come back," I told him, in the chance that this was true. I didn't want Noor Gul bringing the two *lakh* of Nasreen's supposed suitor.

"I don't know," said the uncle. "I don't trust them."

"What about me, *Mama*? I might only be a Muslim convert and maybe I've only read the *Qur'an Sharif* in English, but I do know It says that '*God loves the man who is patient.*' You've waited two years. You can't wait one week more? No, five days. I can go to Peshawar, start arrangements for all the money and come back in five days with at least 50,000 rupees. I can get 25,000 on a bank card and I have 15,000 in the bank."

The uncle looked at me as I spoke.

"The other 10,000 I can borrow from a friend, no problem."

"No! Nobody leaves here! Maybe I'll kill you also," he threatened, turning his gun toward us.

"Is that the Islamic way?" I asked.

"Abidullah can take a letter to Mardan and bring money back," Noor Gul added.

"I don't know. I'll think. Can you write a letter to your lawyer in Peshawar? Ask him to send the money?" Uncle asked me. "But write it in Pashtu.... no, I won't be able to read it. We'll borrow a tape recorder. You can make a cassette in Pashtu to send to him."

"And just who will take it to Peshawar, Uncle? You're afraid of Peshawar."

"I'm not afraid. My brother is a *'pole-it-ical'* in Islamabad. I'm not afraid of anyone. One day I will come to your house in Peshawar. I will drink tea in your house."

"*Insha'Allah*." I answered him. "But please don't bring your bombs. We don't like bombs in Peshawar."

Nasreen giggled.

At dusk Noor Gul came in the *hujra* where Nasreen and I were still sitting.

"We need to talk," he said.

"Okay, talk." I'm ready.

"We need to run away tonight, to escape. I'll go to Mardan. I can bring the one *lakh*. That will hold Uncle off until you can raise the rest," he explained. "Nasreen will stay."

"No, I won't go. For one thing, I gave Uncle my word I would not leave without his permission. Also, I won't leave Nasreen with that "*mother-shooting*" nut. Besides, how can we get out? He has us locked in at night."

"The one guarding us is my friend. He will let me out. Then I'll let you out."

"And what's he want?"

"He wants 10,000 rupees. You can bring it from Peshawar. He will do it just before dawn. We'll run across the fields. We'll reach the road by sunrise."

"No, I won't leave Nasreen here with that ignorant crazy fool."

"I'll be all right," Nasreen assured me.

"He shot at his own mother, didn't he? No. It's too dangerous for you here alone."

"He's right," Noor Gul admitted. "We'll have to think of something else."

"At least we're together," I told her.

"Yeah," she laughed, "with *Mama.*"

After dinner the four of us reached an agreement.

Uncle said because of Noor Gul his family doesn't have clothes or decent food to eat. He needs to buy good seeds for the wheat as he only has the old, poor quality Pakistani seeds. He said he doesn't have a rupee in his pocket. I couldn't resist the temptation and as I always carry a few one-rupee notes for beggars in my vest pocket, I found two rupees and pressed them into his pocket. I had no more money as my wallet had been left behind in Peshawar. I looked over his shoulder to catch Nasreen snickering.

We decided I should go to Peshawar in the morning, Noor Gul escorting me as far as Gandao. Uncle had decided to trust him that far. I couldn't go alone he said, as it wasn't safe. In Peshawar I would get him some instant cash to hold him over. Money for clothes, food and seeds. With my credit card, my bank account and friends I could get him 50,000 rupees in a few days. And I would start making arrangements for the rest. That information I would also give him in a few days. Then I would bring the money alone to Gandao. I would give him the money and he would release Nasreen and Noor Gul to me. I promised not to cheat him if he promised not to cheat me.

"I'll come back for you," I told her.

"Are you sure?"

"I'd follow you to hell," I laughed. I already had.

Noor Gul said it would be too dangerous for me to come back to Gandao alone. That somebody should meet me in Peshawar.

Uncle wouldn't let Noor Gul go to Peshawar so in two days I was to go to Phandu Chowk outside the walls of Peshawar at noon where somebody would approach me saying he was from Khan Mama. He would have my picture for identification, one from Nasreen's photo album. I would give him the money and the information about when I'd have the rest. If I didn't fulfill my end of the bargain, then they could get the two *lakh* in Mardan and marry Nasreen to someone else.

In the morning as I was saying goodbye to Nasreen the uncle and Noor Gul came in, followed by Abidullah carrying what appeared to be a *Qur'an* wrapped in a timeworn red cloth. The uncle wanted me to swear on the *Qur'an* that I wouldn't cheat him and run away to America. In return, Noor Gul wanted Uncle to swear that when I gave him the money he would release Nasreen and him to me and let us all go.

Abidullah stood and beamed. "Didn't I tell you that my father would let you go?"

Now, I had been in Pakistan long enough to know that many times when somebody pulls out the *Qur'an Sharif* to swear on, it can be a sure sign they are going to cheat you. I looked at Nasreen, drinking in her face and eyes and wondering if I would ever see her again and quietly said, "I love you," which God knows was true. But I realized I must get away from Bajaur now at all costs. If what happened here was true then I would see her again, *Insha'Allah*. If it wasn't true, if it was a play, I could play too. But for now I needed to get away.

We shook hands.

"I will see you soon," I said, looking at her, trying to memorize every detail of her face, trying to read it, "*Insha'Allah*."

"*Khuda hafiz.*" she answered.

Uncle and Abidullah walked out to the road with Noor Gul and I, then he and I walked down the road for half an hour. Finally a Datsun came by carrying a handful of men, children and a few women completely hidden under their *burqas*. We climbed in. I tried to pay attention to landmarks, reasoning that maybe I would have to find this place again on my own. Our Datsun drove us past the Mohmand Rifles' check post and let us down at the junction on the main road. Noor Gul again impressed on me to keep my talking to a minimum.

We got another Datsun, packed in the back to Gandao which we reached at 11:00. Noor Gul decided to accompany me on to Peshawar as we were so early. He said it would do his heart good to see me safely all the way to Peshawar and he would be able to get vegetables to take back with him. Our minivan boasted relative cramped comfort compared to the hard, narrow, wood benches lining the back of the pickups.

Along the way he told me that all night Nasreen had prayed *nefil* prayers that I would come back and save them, that she and I could get married and we could escape from Pakistan. I have known her almost four years. Her praying all night? I found it hard to believe. God knows better. In Shabqadar, I saw a signboard on a shop. "*Kaka Khel Motors*" it read. It reminded me Nasreen was of the Kaka Khel tribe.

"What is your tribe?" I asked Noor Gul. Maybe I could find a slip.

"Kaka Khel," he answered.

He asked that if I marry Nasreen could I also get him a visa for America. Would he be able to find work in America?

"*Insha'Allah*."

We arrived in Peshawar and took a *rickshaw* to *Ghanta Ghar*. Noor Gul said he would try to get *Mama* to let him come to Peshawar in two days, but he didn't know if the uncle would trust him. I thought that if the uncle trusted him to come to Peshawar on his business it would prove that all things were not as they had tried to make them appear. He had trusted him to go with me to Gandao.

When Nasreen had washed my shirt at the fort she must have left my keys lying by the well. I didn't have them. Now I needed a locksmith to get into my house. Noor Gul and I shook hands and parted.

I went off to Pepal Mandi to fetch the locksmith.

Fort/home, Bajaur Agency

Road from Momand Ghat west to Nawa Pass and Afghanistan

پریدری چه ګرځم لیوني پهٔ غرونه

A map of Bajaur I located and added to when I got back to Peshawar

---

The line of Pushtu at the bottom is from an old song....
"Pregday che gerzoom laywanay pa gharuna"
"Leave me to wander crazily through the mountains."

Chapter 33
The Game

❖ ❖ ❖

There was once a fox who agreed to carry a venomous scorpion across a raging river if the scorpion promised to behave. In the middle of the river the scorpion stung the fox. As they sank below the water's surface the fox cried "Oh, why did you sting me? Now we will both drown."
The scorpion explained that a scorpion cannot change its nature.

❖ ❖ ❖

I was ready to bet 50,000 rupees on the game. On Nasreen. I figured I would need to ante-up in order to stay in the game.

Now to think of a way to stay out of Bajaur and still get her, if I could.

Arriving back in Peshawar I looked like an Afghan refugee who had just made it across the border. My clothes were dirty, wrinkled, travel-stained and I hadn't had a shave in a week. My *chaddar* was wrapped around my head in an impromptu turban, replacing the cap which had blown off while riding in the back of the Datsun on the way down to Gandao from the fort. My *chappals* were caked with mud and dust. When I told the locksmith I had just returned from Bajaur he looked at me as if that explained my appearance.

The boy from the locksmith's followed me home and opened the large padlock on my outer door. Shah Hussain was away. He must have gone somewhere with his friend Shah Jan.

I heated a bucket of water and took a bath, peeling off the caked dirt. I changed my clothes and *chappals*, put my 32 bore Llama in my pocket and went to the barber shop for a shave. Then off to my friend Shiraz Gul in Sarafa Bazaar to change some dollars to rupees. I wrote him a check for $600, all that was left in my Grindley's dollar account. He gave me 15,000 rupees in 100 rupee notes. It was too late to go to the Bank of Oman, the only bank giving cash advances on credit cards, but I would do that in the morning. The other 10,000 I had in my house.

I consulted a close circle of friends....

First I called Mirza in the States. We talked for over an hour—more than a $100 call. If I'm kidnapped to Bajaur who cares about phone bills? Besides, somebody in America had to know what was happening. And people in these *movies* seldom worry about mundane things such as eating, sleeping, paying phone and electric bills or extending expired visas. Mine was expiring any day. A visa would have no meaning in Bajaur anyway.

I walked down to Arif's shop in Kabuli Bazaar and told him, Anwar Khan and our friend Mukhtiare where I had disappeared to and what was happening. They had been worried because I hadn't shown up at the shop for *chai* and *gupshup* in five days. Anwar Khan thought it was a terribly exciting love tragedy drama, but indeed a very dangerous development.

Arif told me the story of Azer and Azra'il (*Azrael*).

"Azer was very afraid of Azra'il, the angel of death. One day Azer was visiting King Suliman (Solomon). Now that very day Azra'il was journeying a very long distance to the 'Place of the Farthest Winds.' He knew that a man would be waiting for him there, but he couldn't imagine how a man would get to such a far off place as that. As he flew past King Suliman's palace, he thought he would stop in to 'salaam' the great Suliman. In a think he flew into the throne room and 'salaamed' Suliman. Then he flew on his way. Azer said to Suliman 'Who was that who just 'salaamed' you?'

Suliman answered, 'That was Azra'il, the angel of death.'

Azer said, 'Oh, from him I am too much afraid. Respected Suliman, you have the power of the winds. Please transport me to the 'Place of the Farthest Winds' so I can hide from Azra'il.'

In the blink of an eye Azer was transported there. And he was waiting there when Azra'il arrived to take him."

"Please, Noor Mohammad," Arif implored, "don't go back to Bajaur, like Azer went to the *'Place of the Farthest Winds.'* Don't go to meet Azra'il."

From Arif's I walked down to Dabgari Bazaar to see Master Ali Haider and Gulzar. The entire band was there.

"You're crazy, Noor Mohammad," Master said, "Mister crazy."

"Maybe," I smiled.

"Completely!"

"Yeah, I guess so. In this, crazy is fun."

Gulzar looked at me with his melancholy, deep brown eyes and sighed.

"Do you really love her that much?" Maz Khan, the *tabla* player, asked.

He didn't know any of the details of our story.

"*Taqriban* (approximately)," I answered seriously.

Everyone laughed.

"I love her enough to bet 50,000 rupees on her," I said, pulling out the wad of 100 rupee notes held together with a rubber band. Everybody looked at me like maybe I really was nuts. When I pulled out my pistol, that clinched it. Gulzar's friend, a lawyer who also spoke English, was there.

"You talk with him in English. Maybe in English you can reason with him," Master begged him. But to no avail. My mind was set. The lawyer agreed with me that if I loved her so strongly, I should take a chance. It is all God's will. He quoted Rahman Baba: *"Che po meena ki, Majnoon ghunday, sadiq vee, Che Layla po darwaza ki, darbon neeshta."* (When you are in love, like Majnoon, when Layla is at the door, there is no guard.)

Master was really upset with me. I'd never seen him like that. He got up and sat on the other side of the room, refusing to speak to me any more. They all warned me not to go to Bajaur again.

Shakeel, my dearest *malangi* brother said, "Who is this brother and uncle? I am from Chowk (Nasir Khan)! *I fuck them!* Noor Mohammad, you don't go to Bajaur alone."

Haji Mahboob, my dear friend and pharmacist said, "Noor Mohammad, just show me this *'Bombuna Mama,'** I shall tell him, *'Just who do you think you are, bugger?'* I will take him by his bandolier of bombs and I will *open the fire!'*

Talking to my lawyer and dear friend Atique, I asked, "Don't you think it strange how I was able to meet and be friends with a Pathan girl like I was with Nasreen? It was in Lahore, right? She worked as a dancer in films. Her family weren't such good character people." I couldn't have put it more polite, under the circumstances, that she had been a *working girl*.

Atique told me not to exchange any monies outside the courts or alone. For some reason, he didn't think that the Bajauris would kidnap me because I was an American. He seemed to overlook the fact that I had just returned from being kidnapped there once.

The general consensus was that I would be foolish to give them any money. And to wait on a corner for some unknown Bajauri with 50,000 rupees in my pocket would be utter insanity. In Agency you can hire an assassin for a mere 5000 rupees. Phandu Chowk, outside the city walls is a good location for murders and kidnapping with a clear run to tribal areas in three directions. People felt fairly certain that I'd be killed or kidnapped for more ransom, or at best, they'd take the money and I'd never see them again. I guess you can say that Bajaur has a certain less-than-savory reputation.

Only Atique didn't agree that if the Bajauris wanted to get me they could

---

* *"una" is used as a suffix of many words in Pashtu to indicate the plural. "Bomb" — bomb in Pashtu and "mama" — maternal uncle, hence "Bombuna Mama" = "Uncle (with) bombs."*

take me even if I came to Gandao with the Army or if I was in lockup in Kabuli Gate Police *Tanna*. Many families in Tribal Territory are better armed than most police.

That night after Shah Hussain went down to his room to sleep, I sat up smoking and thinking. It was strange that when the uncle first arrived, although supposedly I had only just met Nasreen, we were permitted to sit together. I've been in the Frontier long enough and have had enough highly chaperoned meetings with prospective brides to realize that the way I was permitted to be with Nasreen, under normal circumstances would never have happened. The uncle even saw her smoking.

But just what if by some chance it were true? My heart couldn't risk losing Nasreen on inconsistencies of customs.

By morning a plan had come to me. I walked to Arif's shop for my usual morning routine. Walking the streets freely, not knowing what was going to happen, the clear sky above me, I felt a certain thrill. Moment to moment feeling alive and free.

At lunch with Mahboob he kept saying, "Bring that *Bombuna Mama* here, or Nasreen, and I will talk to them. We will catch that *Bombuna Mama* and bring him to Peshawar in chains."

I hadn't the nerve to tell anyone except Shah Hussain that he had tied us up. People would have been too outraged. At noon I didn't go to Phandu Chowk. I was at home with Shah Hussain, waiting by my telephone. Whoever it was that was coming to meet me would have my phone number in case there were any mix-ups. I had thought of a story. Something that would give them leeway if they were being honest with me.

The phone never rang.

At 3:45 my doorbell sounded. A familiar ring—Noor Gul's. It had to be him. Who else could have been sent to do the job? Shah Hussain looked out the third floor window. "Who's there?" he called out to show I wasn't alone.

Yes, it was Noor Gul. So, the crazy untrusting uncle got trusting rather quickly. It didn't bode well for Nasreen. Noor Gul was at my front door, hardly wanting to come in.

"There are some problems," I told him. "You need to come in to talk." As I shook his hand, I brushed the small plastic bag he held. No gun. (I foolishly failed to brush against the *chaddar* hanging over his shoulder.) "Look. I couldn't get the money. And I have a problem with the police. I told you that the bank closed at 12:00. Well, yesterday we arrived too late for me to go. And today, the Special Branch police came to my house at 10:00. They said that the *IB wallahs* (Intelligence Bureau) spotted me at the Charsadda bus stand getting on a minivan headed to Gandao. Then they came to my house every morning looking for me. They wanted to know why I had gone to Agency.

"I told them I had gone to Bajaur to visit a friend. They told me if I had a friend in Bajaur, he must come here to visit me. That as a foreigner I wasn't allowed to go into Agency. They said my visa was expired and if I didn't rectify it immediately they would deport me. I told them I was making my marriage arrangements and I can't leave Pakistan.

"They asked if I were making my arrangements in Bajaur. I told them no, in Mardan. They said don't marry in Bajaur. And if I was, have the girl brought to Peshawar, or I would be arrested and deported. They would be watching me they said. They didn't leave until after 1:00. I was afraid I might have missed whoever was coming to meet me at Phandu Chowk so I waited by the phone."

A very realistic story, giving them a chance if they were being honest and if I were truly "the only man" she wanted to marry, as Nasreen stated.

"How's your crazy uncle?" I asked.

"A bit better."

"And Nasreen?"

"Things are a little better now. He's not as crazy."

I told him that tomorrow I would have to take care of my visa problem and the next day I would go to Grinleys to get the money. Once Noor Gul heard about the police though he just wanted to get out of there. He said he would call me in two days. Before leaving he told me that he had a friend who would buy my house if I signed it over to them. I said that I was ready, but that it would take at least half a day in the courts to arrange the papers. Mention of the courts seemed to greatly dissuade him.

Shah Hussain said that he was sure that Noor Gul's Pashtu was Bajauri. He said when he had heard Nasreen the first time her accent was definitely of Hashtnagar (Mardan area). "Very sweet Pashtu," he noted.

I kept seeing Arif and Anwar Khan, Shakeel and Mahboob as usual. And watching over my shoulders wherever I went. People told me not to go in open places or to wander at night. Mahboob kept telling me that he would bring *"this bloody Bombuna Mama bugger"* to Peshawar in chains.

In Arif's shop, I overheard Anwar Khan discussing with Takhar Khan (Wali Khan's cousin and look-a-like*), "They don't want him to tell anybody. They don't want to go to the courts. They want him to come alone. What is this nonsense, a Pathan marriage, or a heroin deal?"

When I dressed each morning I put on clothes that would be best to be kidnapped in. I made sure I had the few things in my vest pockets I might need; some *nuswar*, a small mirror, a handkerchief. Every time I left my house I found myself wondering if I would end up in Bajaur this time. What were they planning? What if their story was true? How could I leave Nasreen there? Unfortunately, it seemed highly improbable that she wasn't in on it.

That day there was no call from Noor Gul. I had decided I must try to see her again. I wanted to tell her I was open and ready if she ever wanted to come to me. And at least tell her I had enjoyed being with her and thank her for the production she had made for me.

---

* *Takhar Khan looked so much like his cousin, Khan Abdul Wali Khan (President of the Awami National Party and son of Abdul Ghafur Khan) that one time in a procession when he was in the lead car and Wali Khan was in a rear vehicle people went home after they saw him. Wali Khan said he would never let him ride in the lead car again.*

Juma morning at 8:00 the phone rang.

"Who is it?" I asked.

"It is I," Noor Gul's voice said.

"Where are you?"

"I'm close. Can you come see me?"

"No," I answered. "You come see me."

"I'll call you back in half an hour."

Forty-five minutes later he called again. I had Shah Hussain answer the phone so Noor Gul would know I wasn't home alone.

"I want to talk to Noor Mohammad Khan," he said bruskly. When I picked up the phone he asked, "Can you come see me? She's with me."

"Where are you?"

"Outside Gunj Gate." Another excellent kidnapping spot like Phandu Chowk, especially on *Juma* morning when it would be fairly deserted.

"No. There's a lot to talk about. She's a woman. How can we talk at Gunj Gate in the open? Bring her here."

"Can your friend leave?"

"No. He'll be in his room downstairs. He's like my brother. We don't need to keep any secret from him. Are we talking about a clean Muslim marriage or are we talking about a heroin deal?" I heard muffled talking in the background.

"Okay, we are coming."

"Who?"

"Me and my friend."

"Which friend?" I realized he was at a *PCO* (public call office) and he wouldn't use her name in public.

"The same one I was with the last time."

"Okay. You and she can come, but don't bring anyone else."

"We will be there in less than an hour." If she were with him, he would bring her to my house or at least she would speak to me over the phone. She knew that she could wrap me around her little finger. Also Noor Gul would only lie that she was with him when she wasn't if he was prepared to kidnap me back to Bajaur I reasoned.

Shah Hussain and I sat by the phone and waited. He had my 30 bore in his hand and the Llama was in my pocket, ready. I wanted to talk to Nasreen again. Maybe even keep her in my house. We waited.

They never came.

Chapter 34
Bajaur

End of September 1991

I was walking with Shah Hussain on the road coming out of Afghanistan heading toward Momad Ghat, the junction leading north to Bajaur Khar and south to Halki Gandao and on to Peshawar—behind us the jagged, broken-toothed mountains leading up the Nawa Pass out of Pakistan into Afghanistan.

"Are you afraid to die, Noor Mohammad?" he was saying.

"Sometimes," I answered.

"Yes, I am also afraid to die, sometimes. I am afraid to die in a car accident or a house fire. But to die while your enemy is shooting you and you are shooting your enemy, that is beautiful. To have your blood running in the dust and mixing with your enemy's blood, that is not a bad way to die."

"I know. That is why I wish we could have brought some guns," I replied.

"Yes, if he is shooting at us and we don't have any gun to shoot back, that could be a problem."

The previous morning we had left Peshawar for Agency (Bajaur). We had taken a minibus from the Charsadda bus stand to Halki Gandao, via Shabqadar (locally called Dheri). In the bus I was careful to keep conversation light and mumble words I knew I mispronounced. It couldn't be known I was a foreigner. The government doesn't allow foreigners in Tribal Territory. Especially now, at a time when the Mohmands and the government are fighting. And on the road to Momad Ghat which only goes to Afghanistan? No way! I also knew it would be easy to be arrested as a spy checking on the movement of Afghan refugees or on the amount of weapons being smuggled out of Afghanistan.

Shah Hussain was worried that if it was known I was an *"Englaise"* locals could try to kidnap me for ransom. Mainly I was worried that if Noor Gul heard my kind of *"Englaise"* was snooping around Tribal Territory he might get suspicious and hide.

We got down at Gandao. Scanning the faces it felt strange to see the mud wall where Nasreen and I had squatted with the boy Qadeer drinking *Rooh Afza* not too many days before. We walked up and down the bazaar looking for a familiar bearded face. No luck. We went back to the bus stand and sat in a teahouse ordering a pot of tea, then went out on the road to catch a vehicle heading toward Bajaur Khar. We found a Datsun leaving for Nawagai and because there were no women to sit in the front seat, for eight rupees apiece extra we were able to procure seats inside the cab next to the driver. I wanted to be able to see where we were going which I knew would be difficult in the back bed with dust swirling and filling our eyes.

Leaving Gandao, we passed the bulldozed bazaar I had seen two weeks previously. The problem had progressed. There had been fighting on the road for the last four days and it had just opened that morning.

Before reaching the first government check post, just ahead of the Nahakki Pass we passed two tanks, over a dozen armored cars and several heavy pieces of field artillery. The government soldiers were armed with fully automatic G-3 assault rifles, apparently able to outshoot the Kalashnikovs the average tribesmen are armed with. At the check post there were tripod-mounted BMR machineguns on sandbags dug into the earth on either side of the road. Also armored cars had their heavy artillery leveled at our parked pickup. The government didn't want any more trouble. Normally tribals are permitted to carry arms, but right now only the Army could.

Our driver told us the Mohmands had come down at night and attacked the army. Eight people had been killed. The Mohmands are supplied with arms from the Communist regime in Kabul to help stir up trouble for the Pakistani government—a definite bone of contention for the Pakistanis.

"It was a very beautiful fighting," the driver smiled. "The locals fought very beautifully. The government troops also fought very beautifully. Nobody in my family was injured, *al-hamdu-lillah*," he boasted. He looked at Shah Hussain, "You said you are a Mohmand also, did you not brother?"

"Yes, though nobody in my family was injured as well. *Al-hamdu-lillah*." Shah Hussain gave me a wink. We both knew damn well his entire family had been sleeping safely in their village in settled areas near Mandani.

Twenty minutes up the pass.

At the top another government check post.

Mostly checking for heavy weapons.

Twisting back and forth down the pass we could see the familiar lunar landscape of Agency. Mud and stone forts dotted the landscape. Besides the lapis blue sky the predominate color was the gray-brown of the rocks, the dirt and the dwellings. We passed the petrol station where Nasreen had handed me the grapes. An hour and a half after leaving Gandao we passed a junction.

"What is the name of this place?" I asked the driver.

"Momad Ghat," he replied.

"Does that road lead into Afghanistan?"

"Yes," he affirmed. Shah Hussain and I looked at each other. "*Bombuna Mama*," I whispered under my breath.

Fifteen minutes more and we arrived in Nawagai. As in Gandao, we walked up and down the bazaar once, looking in the open shop fronts and on the street for a familiar bearded face. Another teahouse and another pot of tea. As we drank we watched people walking by and the faces filling the backs of pickups.

We found a Datsun leaving for Bajaur Khar and climbed in the back. Almost an hour later we arrived in Khar. We made our usual round, casually looking at every face in the bazaar, then found a teahouse-cum-restaurant and had a lunch of greasy meat *qorma*, sliced raw onions and fresh hot *roti*. It was after 3:00 and we wanted to eat before finding our hosts so we wouldn't imposition them. We were hoping to stay with a teacher friend of Shah Hussain's from Shabqadar who taught at the government school in Khar.

The school/hostel was on the north end of town in the surrounding fields. Like all buildings in Agency (even the hospital) the school was built with loopholes for shooting (*murche-y* in Pashtu) in the outer walls and in the walls encircling the roof. As we walked along the inside veranda I saw a place where the cement was broken out around the lower portion of one of the classrooms' wooden doorjams. The teacher told us that during examinations a student had hidden a grenade there and it accidentally had gone off.

After the dusk prayer we sat in our host's room waiting for dinner and chatting with three students from Bajaur College, slightly further up the road leading toward Timagura. I tried to keep my part in the conversation minimal, which wasn't difficult as Shah Hussain and one of the students dominated the conversation, the two other students being quiet and restrained like myself. They wanted us to visit their village the next day, but on finding out it was north and not in the direction we were interested in we declined, saying we had a friend to visit in Nawagai.

The next morning after prayer and tea we caught a Datsun for Nawagai, sharing the back bed of the pickup with students on their way to school and men carrying metal cans of milk to the Nawagai bazaar. Our blankets, wrapped around us, flapped in the chilly morning air. The rising sun lit the clear azure sky over the hills crisply, the morning was alive. Nawagai town is a cut in the mountains essentially separating Mohmand Agency in the south with Bajaur Agency in the north. The word "*nawagai*" in Pashtu literally means small rain spout. A fitting name.

There a group of raggedy barefoot boys eyed at us suspiciously as we walked the town. We decided we were just a bit too clean cut to fit in properly. I put a wad of *nuswar* in my mouth. As we walked toward the head of the Nawagai bazaar a fellow with skin and hair as light as my own came right up to me. He looked at Shah Hussain briefly, but stood directly in front of me. "*Asalaamo aleikum,*" he said, fixing his gaze upon my face.

"*Wa-aleikum asalaam,*" I replied, exchanging a litany of standard Pashtu greetings.

"Where do I know you from?" he asked suspiciously. "I've seen you somewhere before."

"I don't know. I've never been in Nawagai before."

"But I've seen you," he went on, eyeing me curiously. "Maybe not in Nawagai.... Oh, now I remember, now I remember. I saw you in Peshawar about seven months ago at Sherbaz Music Studio at a Farzana recording session. You're a friend of Master Ali Haider, are you not?"

"Yes," I smiled, relieved, now remembering the meeting. We laughed. Pakistan is a small country and the Frontier Province even smaller. Many times and in many places I run into people I know. Sometimes too often.

Amir Jan has a small medicos shop at the head of Nawagai bazaar where the road comes in from the south from Gandao and Momad Ghat. A good vantage point for us. We sat in his shop and watched people and vehicles passing by, drinking tea and listening to a tape deck play a wobbly cassette of Gulnar Begum: "*Rashah ashna, rashah ashna, sta dedan dapara naray sturgu torauma, ashna.*" (Come on darling, come on darling, for your rendezvous I've made my narrow eyes black.) My *surma* darkened eyes were narrow in the glare of the sun coming into Amir Jan's shop. Well, I'm waiting here; *rasha ashna.*

Shah Hussain told Amir Jan we had come up to Bajaur to visit his friend, the teacher. Also that he wanted to see his family lands in Mohmand Agency. I said I had seen much of Pakistan but never Agency before so I was along for the ride. Having spent so much time in Afghanistan before the war, this area brought back nostalgic memories.

Amir Jan invited us to his village after lunch to spend the night. It was south of Nawagai, but to the east of the main road. We declined the invitation as politely as possible as it would serve our objective no purpose. I told him I wanted to go hang out at Momad Ghat.

"Why? There is nothing there," he puzzled. "It is only the junction to Afghanistan."

"I'm looking for a friend from Afghanistan. I thought just maybe I might run into him there," I answered rather lamely.

"It's a small chance."

"I know. But it is a chance. *Insha'Allah.* God knows better. Also, being from noisy, crowded Peshawar it will be nice just to be somewhere that is open and quiet."

He looked at me strangely, "Noor Mohammad, you are an interesting man. Why are you in such a dirty backward place as this?"

"*Har cha ikhpul waton Kashmir day,*" I answered, quoting an old Pashtu adage ("Everyone's own homeland is Kashmir"—the beauty of Kashmir being famous throughout the subcontinent). "I guess this has become mine."

We laughed.

"Besides, this is a simple country and I am a simple man."

"Every man has his own fate. I hope to see you again."

"Yes, *Insha'Allah*, we will meet again. Now we go."

"Okay friends, goodbye for now, may you go with God."

"Yes. Thank you, *Khuda hafiz.*"

All the vehicles leaving Nawagai heading south were going at least as far as Gandao. Nobody wanted two riders only going as far as Momad Ghat, a meager two rupee ride. We decided to walk. It took us an hour. On the way we passed two huts selling scrap metal. Besides the usual rusty truck and tractor engine parts and old metal drums there were relics from the war across the border—smashed missile launchers, half a tank.

By a stone wall on the side of one of the huts was a well. Beside it on two forked poles of wood was an old, bicycle wheel with bent spokes, a handle coming out of the center. One cranked the handle and it wound up the frayed, knotted rope bringing up a bucket made from old truck tire rubber. The water tasted rubbery and dirty, but it was wet and we were thirsty. On the road Shah Hussain complained about how hungry he was. "How can we ever find anything to eat in this arid, deserted area? Here only owls sing."

"This is nothing compared to when we were riding from Chitral to Gilgit.

422

Ask your cousin Habibullah. I imagine we will be able to find something at Momad Ghat."

"Momad Ghat! We're on foot, Noor Mohammad, not in the Flying Coach. This isn't GT Road. I can't wait." He saw a broken piece of biscuit in the dirt on the side of the road and picked it up, looked it over and ate it.

"I can wait until Momad Ghat, my brother. Especially since you finished the cookie."

Momad Ghat is one of the main junctions on the road running through Agency. It juts off to the west through the mountains via the Nawa Pass to Afghanistan. For the first 50 meters lining the road were rectangular spaces surrounded by three foot high stone walls. A few had canvas tops held up by cut, dried branches and frayed ropes. These were stores selling cigarettes, hard candies, *nuswar* and other sundries. One had a hand-pump kerosine stove and chipped metal enameled teapots. It was a tea house. Others were empty, just places to squat and wait out of the sun, wind and dust. We walked around, sat a bit, walked some more. We had a *qawah*. It tasted like kerosine.

Paying the *chai wallah,* we started walking down the road towards Afghanistan. A few government buildings squatted behind sparse trees but no one was in sight around them. No one was walking.

"I want to see this *Bombuna Mama*," Shah Hussain repeated as we walked.

Datsuns and gaily-painted transport trucks trundled down the road. Men stood by dust covered pickups; loading, going south to Gandao and Peshawar and north to Nawagai, Bajaur Khar, Timagura and Dir, or west to Afghanistan. A few buses with ragged Afghan refugees headed home, their belongings bundled in dusty, tattered rugs tied to the roofs.

"There should be a Mohmand Rifle check post a few *furlongs* from here," I told Shah Hussain. "It's just past where the way turns. I can't believe I am actually seeing those two mountains again."

"I want to see *Bombuna Mama's* house," he laughed. "Noor Mohammad, don't go to Bajaur." Something he knew I had heard from all my friends in Peshawar. With the government check post in sight Shah Hussain suggested we leave the road to circle around it.

"What's the point of that? They've probably already spotted us. And besides," I added, scanning the barren landscape, "where would we hide, unless we could make it to those hills to the north."

"But to reach there without locals shooting us, that is the problem," Shah Hussain pointed out.

"Are Pathans really as good marksmen as I've always heard? I've seen people test firing weapons in Dara, and in Peshawar people only shoot off of their roofs in celebration. I've never seen folks actually practice shooting. Oh well, I have seen a few, though not any shots to brag about."

"Noor Mohammad, in my own village there was an old man who wanted revenge but his enemy would not come out of his fort. He was a clever fellow. He had a well inside for water. When the old man would come, he would sit up in his tower and shoot through a small *murchay.*

"One day the old man came with his son. He had the boy run into the enemy's field. Then the old man watched the hole. When his enemy stuck his gun barrel out the hole the old man shot him. Yes. If people in these backward places are one thing Noor Mohammad, it is good shots. Now let's not talk over much. We're at the check post."

I wasn't as paranoid as my companion about the check post. I had already been through it twice. As we passed, I was within a few feet of one of the Levies standing idly about. I couldn't help but say, "*Asalaamo aleikum.*"

"*Wa-aleikum asalaam,*" he answered.

I could feel Shah Hussain hold his breath.

We walked on, ever closer to those two jagged mountains. They were waxing close when on our right hand we came to a woodcutter's hut. On the left, a dirt road ran off through the fields.

"This is *Bombuna's* address," I excitedly informed Shah Hussain. "It was down that road we went. Their fort is maybe ten kilometers down the road. Shall we go down it?"

"Don't go off the paved road in Bajaur, Noor Mohammad," he voiced the local, well-known and oft repeated advice.

"Yeah, they also said, *'Don't go to Bajaur.'*"

"Yeah, don't go to Bajaur, Noor Mohammad," he chuckled.

We started walking down the road.

"I want to see *Bombuna Mama's* fort," he said again.

Down the road about two furlongs was the first fort. Further down was the large fortress I remembered from the last time. It must have housed a large extended family. It looked like a mud castle with its many towers and high adobe walls.

"You go around that bend, past the big fort," I pointed with my hands. "There are more average size forts and gullies and dried dusty fields."

"Don't make hand signals," Shah Hussain told me. "Here people have enmity. That is why they live in such remote empty places. They sit up in their towers with looking-glasses and big LMG machine guns. Like that *Bombuna Mama*... and don't bring out your pocket mirror. If it looks like we're signaling, someone could start shooting us. Don't go to Bajaur, Noor Mohammad," he repeated, laughing.

Less than a furlong from the fort we realized it would be wise, being unarmed, not to go any further. It wouldn't do to just stroll past the fort, then turn around and stroll back. Surely too spy-like to any prying eyes. I couldn't help thinking that without guns if *Bombuna* should happen by in a Datsun full of people he could just stop and say, "He's an Englaise. He came to my home and insulted one of my women."

What could I say? "They kidnapped me."

Who would they believe? I don't think it would be me.

We walked back to Momad Ghat making all sorts of wild plans of how we were going to get back there to visit *Bombuna.* Right before Momad Ghat on the road back to Nawagai was a small pond. On our way out we had seen

Koochie women in their brightly patterned clothing filling water pots and watering a few gangling cows. Now it was deserted and we decided to sit by its side for a while. The edge of the pond was about 40 feet from the side of the road. We squatted by the side and watched the still water reflecting the mountains. Occasionally a frog would pop out and plop back in, creating little ripples on the surface. "There's your dinner," I told Shah Hussain.

"Before, I was so hungry that I would have eaten it," he told me, "but now I've had kerosine tea and a dirty cookie and am full. Besides, I must save room for dinner. Otherwise teacher will be upset. He's not like your friends. I think he may give us more than just one chicken leg."

As we sat a Datsun stopped and dropped off a fellow. He stood at the side of the road wrapped in his blanket and looked down toward us. He held an AK-47 at his side.

"*Asalaamo aleikum,*" we politely called.

"*Wa-aleikum,*" he answered. "What are you doing?"

"We're just sitting here and resting."

"Is there anything that I can do for you?" The words were friendly, but the feeling antagonistic. The intention was clear: "If you don't belong here, get out!"

"What can you do for us?" Shah Hussain repeated the words to me. "Yeah, you can give us two Kalashnikovs!" he laughed. "From there he must not be able to see our mustaches." *

"If we had Kalashnikovs he'd see our own mustaches," I quipped. "Let's go before I piss in his pool."

"I mount your mother," Shah Hussain said under his breath in the direction of our inhospitable friend.

We got up to go, shortly catching a Datsun at Momand Ghat back to Nawagai. The sun was going down. We climbed in the back of another pickup for Khar. The driver was an Afghan we had met in Amir Jan's shop who warned us he had heard a foreigner had been picked up by the government a couple of days ago near Khar.

We spent the night with the teacher in Khar at the school. The following morning we decided to leave first thing for Momad Ghat. If somebody were leaving the fort, they might arrive at the junction early.

After prayer, chai and sunrise we walked into Khar and found a Datsun back to Nawagai. A militiaman sitting in the back of the pickup with us said that yesterday a truck had come out of Afghanistan. It had stopped in Nawagai for engine repairs. While it was being worked on and the driver and his mate were eating lunch militiamen checked it out and found under the straw in the back two cases of land mines. The driver and his mate absconded, leaving the truck and the bombs behind.

Reaching Nawagai we avoided Amir Jan's shop. We climbed into the first vehicle that would take us the distance to Momad Ghat. We couldn't afford to spend time drinking tea and visiting today.

At Momad Ghat we squatted off the side of the road and told each other

---

* To show one's mustaches is an old Pashtu expression for manliness.

stories in Pashtu and when no one was near in English. We tried to be inconspicuous, joining several Mohmands about 150 feet to the east of the road. They were sitting on rocks talking about a man from Charsadda who arranged a marriage with a Bajauri family. He had paid 80,000 rupees bride price but right after the marriage the bride ran back to Bajaur, and there was nothing he nor the authorities could do. As I was realizing, you can't just go chasing after women in Agency.

Time pass....

At noon a Datsun came up the road from down country. They turned west at Momad Ghat and stopped in a cloud of dust. I thought it was *Bombuna* sitting in the back, but I couldn't be sure as he was facing away from me in the crowded bed of the pickup. I got up and walked quickly toward the junction. As I crossed the paved road I started running. I wasn't sure what I would do but it didn't matter. The truck was too packed to wait for any more riders. They took off in swirling clouds of dust. They were 50 feet away when I saw the side of his face. His sunken eye sockets and hollow cheeks. It was him!

He couldn't hear my voice over the sounds of the vehicle as they drove away in the dust.

❖ ❖ ❖

Tea house in Tribal Territory

426

Chapter 35
Visa Problems

October 1991
Peshawar City

Just got back from Islamabad. I may go back to Bajaur just to escape Pakistan. This must be my year for trouble with visas and women. The clerk from the Chowk Shadi Pir Marriage Agency asked me if he could bring the owner of the agency to my house. They supposedly had another girl for me to meet. But when he came over, after asking if I had any *charras,* all he could talk about was money. Sign your house over to the girl, buy gold, buy clothes. And then there was the matter of his commission, of course.

I told him I was ready for all eventualities if the girl was right. Shah Hussain thinks she is Peshawari. If she speaks tolerable Pashtu and is, of course gorgeous, I won't care. But her father is in Saudi Arabia and won't be back for two weeks. I told them before I would talk any more I needed to see her picture.

I feel better, and safer, going back to Bajaur!

On to matters of visas....

The fellow in the Peshawar Passport Office who wrote me a two week late exit permit when I was leaving for the Emirates told me to come in two weeks before my visa expired. On my registration papers permission for one month was written. I went in two weeks ago.

I told him I had seen a picture of a girl I liked but I needed to wait until her father came back from Saudi Arabia on October 10th, to see if I could arrange to see her. Also I told him I had a ticket booked to the United States on October 14th, which I do unless I change it (I thought it best not to tell him I was mainly waiting to see if my *kanjri* ex-girlfriend and her boyfriend were going to kidnap me back to Bajaur again). He told me to come in on the 23rd, the day before my visa expired.

A few days later Arif told me two agents from the Special Branch (passport control) came by his shop to see me. They said they would come back the next day. It was just a routine report they told Arif. They wanted to see my house. After all these years they were finally dropping in? When I met them the next day they barely spoke any English. They were very petty peon officers and their job was to check on foreigners.

"How do you speak to foreigners?" I asked them.

"Many of the people we check on are Afghan or Pakistanis from abroad," they answered. "And we do know how to speak some English: *'I am a police officer,' 'show me your passport,' 'your passport number?'"* They had 9th grade educations. How Pakistani I thought. One of the reasons I love it here.

Yesterday, I went in to the Passport Office again and spoke with the officer I had seen before. He said it wasn't in his authority to extend my visa and I should go to the office of the Special Branch Police. The way they have been toward me lately I knew they would do little to help, but off I went. I walked in and exchanged greetings with the officer I usually deal with. "My visa expires tomorrow," I told him.

"Do you want to leave the country?" he asked. A normal reply.

"No," I answered. "I would like to explain."

"Then you can speak to our chief," he told me impatiently, gesturing me over to his boss's desk. I've known him for years and he has never seemed to like me much. I've never really seen him do anything more than sit at his desk and sign an occasional stack of papers. Not even sure if he speaks much English. He has never spoken it with me. He once told Mizra *"there is blood between us"* because he was *Shia* and we were *Sunni*. I explained my situation.

"There is nothing I can do to help you," he said, looking away. "Why did you wait until the last day?"

I explained how I was told by the fellow in the Passport Office to come in on the 23rd and he would help, but now he told me to come to them.

"There is nothing I can do to help you," he replied. "Go to Islamabad."

When I rode back to the city the two flunkies from Special Branch who had checked me out the other day shared the *rickshaw* with me. I paid, of course.

"Did you get your exit visa?" they asked me.

"No. I need to go to Islamabad."

"We'll come to your house tomorrow to check if you have gotten it," they told me.

"I'm not even going to Islamabad until tomorrow morning."

"If you don't take care of it we will arrest you," they proclaimed.

Jerks! Special jerks!

In the evening I spoke with Atique, my lawyer friend. I asked him if he had any friends in the Interior Ministry in Islamabad with higher power than a Section Officer (still a fancy pencil-pushing upper-class peon it seems). He gave me the name of a friend, a Joint Secretary, but when I got there I found out he had been transferred to Peshawar like my last friend from Atique. The Section Officer told me I would have to take care of the problem in Peshawar at the Passport Office. He couldn't understand why they had even sent me to Islamabad. Going in circles, as usual. Tomorrow it is back to the Passport Office. My first bid is to try for an extension until November 1st. If that doesn't go over, I'll try for October 15th. If that fails I'll try for a seven-day exit permit (I can go to Delhi for a new visa), and if that fails I'll ask if I can be put in a comfortable cell and given a bag of *nuswar*.

If I could call Nasreen I'd tell her if she still wanted to kidnap me she should have a Datsun waiting at the Passport Office. I'll ask Atique if he knows of an immigration lawyer, but then they might not even have them here. *Who, in their right mind, would want to immigrate here?*

I rode on the Flying Coach back to Peshawar listening to the driver play the same Lata cassette I have heard for the last 15 years, the bus swerving and honking around *tongas*, water buffaloes and pedestrians. I'm so used to it all. It's still so good to be home.

The weather is starting to cool down. Mirza's shotgun is hanging loaded on my wall. My Llama is chambered. When it's not in my pocket, it's right next to my bed. God, I hate to think of leaving here. I am just getting comfortable after all this madness (?). How can I still love that lovely, treacherous bitch? I don't know, but I do. Most people wonder how I can love this dirty, backward country, but I do.

It is nice to be thinking sanely again. If you can call wanting to live in this dirty backward hole, record Pashtu music, become more entangled with this mad culture, and even waiting and hoping that *Jezebel* Nasreen shows up sane?

Maybe I'll just go up to Bajaur with a 1000 rupees, a few suits and a big bag of *subzi*. Tell them I spent all of my money in initiating the sale of my house. That I will pay them on October 15th and try to get her to come to Peshawar with me.

Am I only dreaming?

October 4th
Juma
Had a new visa possibility. A friend's father is a *peer*. He said the head of the Special Branch prays his *Juma* prayer at his father's mosque. He told me it would be a good time to meet with him so we were going today. We would set up a meeting in his office for tomorrow, *Insh'Allah*. It seemed to be looking up. Maybe I could stay until mid-November.

Well, typical to Pakistan the fellow from Special Branch didn't show up at the mosque for *Juma* prayer. Nor did Bacha Peer, my friend's father. He went hunting. The mosque was at a shrine out near *Wazir Bagh*. I prayed next to a close friend of Papu Khan (a well-known, local mafioso who was just gunned down the other day in front of the Peshawar Court House). He kept his bandolier on while he prayed. It held a Mouser fully-automatic pistol and a 30-bore black Chinese pistol. It kept bumping my side as we prostrated ourselves during prayer.

After prayer we went across the road to a garden enclosed by walls. Many men and boys sat around drinking tea, smoking *charras* in *chillums* and singing songs of Sufi poetry. Big trees with birds singing in their twisted, gnarled branches. Dry Asian dusty jungle overhanging garden vines. *Malangs* living in small mud and thatch huts. Many wealthy people with extra land in Peshawar set up places such as this. A good place to hang out with people intoxicated by God and other less subtle substances. You get *sawab* (blessing) for helping the God-intoxicated ones—the ones intoxicated on other substances I'm not so sure about. That, God knows better!

I'm still hoping I can get a few more weeks here to try to get to Nasreen one more time before I have to leave.

I went to Dubai looking for her.

Bajaur is just up the road.

My "All Pakistan" arms licence (good to carry 500 rounds for protection) and my dear brother, Shakeel, playing harmonium for my sweet home's housewarming

Chapter 36
Aftermath

❖ ❖ ❖

It's like a book, I think, this bloomin' world,
Which you can read and care for just so long,
But presently you feel that you will die
Unless you get the page you're readin' done,
And turn another - likely not as good;
But what you're after is to turn 'em all.

Rudyard Kipling;
Sestina of the Tramp-Royal

❖ ❖ ❖

Why Arif doesn't buy a new chair for his shop.

Besides the rickety, wooden slat chair behind his desk that Arif sits on when he is working and the smoothly, age-worn, plank bench in front of the dusty type storage bins that had once been the shop's front step there is one other chair in Arif's shop. It is a wood-framed wicker chair. The wicker work is half unstrung and there is a large hole in the center of the seat where it is completely worn through.

"I won't get another one," Arif said with a laugh. "People still sit in that one. Besides, my customers don't sit in it. That chair costs me money daily. Why spend more? Only friends sit in it and they all drink tea. Noor, do you know the story of the mullah whose clay istidja lota broke?" *

"No, I don't," I answered.

Anwar Khan looked at me, giving me his toothless grin and settled back to listen as Arif narrated. "You see Noor, there was a mullah and he had a favorite clay lota he kept in the mosque which he always used for to make istidja.

"One day, when he went to use it before the prayer he discovered that it was broken. He was crying because of this and the people said, 'Oh mullah, why are you crying so? It was only a clay lota and you can buy another one in the bazaar for a few rupees.' He answered, 'But that lota already saw my private parts!'"

Anwar Khan cackled, coughed and spit on the cement floor. He looked at me as Arif laughed and squeezed me with a tight embrace around the shoulders and explained, "So you see Noor, that is why I don't buy a new chair. This chair has seen our butts!"

He started laughing anew and poured us each a fresh cup of qawah.

❖ ❖ ❖

---

* Istidja — washing of one's private places before prayer; Lota = pot

431

Aftermath

"Kho janana, murg me qabul day, judai ee na kaooma.""
(Oh darling, I accept death, but I do not abide separation)
Pashtu song

Mid-October, 1991

"City people tell me I should just forget it. You don't think that, do you?"

"I was brought up in the village," Shah Hussain replied. "There is a great difference in city people."

"You don't think I should forget it, do you, *yaar*?" I continued, probing for a more definite answer.

"Noor Mohammad, I am young and I've never loved. But I know what love is," he stated. "You cannot forget. In this I am certain. And in this, if you need some help, I am ready for anything."

Pashtu isn't such a great language for practical matters. At least not what most people consider practical. English is practical, a machine language. Pashtu is better suited to evoke mud villages and the barren, desolate rocks and mountains of Tribal Territory. Green fields with flowers blooming gorgeously in the spring. The veiled gaze of a girl's mysterious shy dark eyes and *khaluna* (beauty marks), of unrequited love and revenge. Faith, longing, hardship—things in this day and age quickly being pushed out of this mechanical world.

Maybe Tribal Territory is harsh and violent, but I so feel myself there. I'm going back. Now that I've been on that dirt road leading to their fort how can I stay away? As much as I love her I am bent on teaching her a lesson. And as it has always been, I've just got to see her one more time. The final card may have to wait until I'm back from USA, but I want to get out there once more before I leave.

No definite plans, but just to go up there and play it by ear. Stay at a village closer to the fort. I know it is dangerous for me to go back into Tribal Territory, especially at this time. Even the government would arrest me if they caught me. Not completely sure what I am planning. I don't want to injure her, that much I do know, *Insha'Allah*. I'm aware this is no joke. I am serious. That fort is a good place to hide from me, right on the Afghan border, but not good enough I guess. I was close to knocking on their door last week.

I was visiting *Haji* Makoo in his shop in Ander Sher before I went back to Bajaur with Shah Hussain. *Haji Sahib* is a dear friend I have known closely since my days in Kabul in the '70s when I used to buy most of the embroideries and *Koochie* dresses for my shop in L.A. from him and his family. I told him I had been hanging out with a *mafhrul* girl in Bajaur and that the Bajauris were dirty (not good) people. I left it up to his imagination about what kind of girl I was exactly referring to.

I saw him again a few days ago in his shop. He asked me if I had been back to Bajaur.

"Yeah," I answered. "I've got to find a girl somewhere in Pakistan."

He burst out with the sonorous rolling laugh I've known and loved for so many years. "Noor Mohammad, you have become crazy in Pakistan."

"Yes," I agreed. "And this crazy is fun."

He laughed again.

We sat on a luxuriously rich, red Turkoman carpet in his shop, amid piles of exquisite *Koochie* embroideries and ate skewers of lamb kebab dripping with grease; fresh fragrant *roti,* hot from the *tandoor*; yogurt/mint chutney; and to-mato, cucumber and onion salad brought to us by a local restaurant boy. We then walked over to Mahabat Khan Mosque for *Zohr* prayer. The floors inside the *wuzu* hall had been completely resurfaced in new, pure white marble, as had the fountain and *wuzu* tank in the central courtyard.

At least there is still that here for me. And Ander Sher is a little Kabul, though I must admit lately when I walk through Ander Sher I spend more time looking at gold nose rings and bangles than at Afghan embroidery.

October 14th, 3 P.M.

A gentle balmy breeze is blowing today. From the roof of my house the mountains of Bajaur are lost in a dusty haze. And those *haramis* are up there.

I've got to look her in the eye and tell her, and tell her... what will I tell her? "Thank you for the lovely production you prepared for me in Bajaur. Thank you for the sight-seeing excursion. Thank you for one last adventure." Or should it be slightly more forceful, more Pathan, more like... "I should kill you, bitch"

I sleep with a loaded pistol in the *almari* next to my bed. When I'm not asleep, my gun is in my pocket. Better security than a blanket or a Valium. Could the Bajauris come crawling over the roof and down the walls of my house like the scorpions? I'm not taking any chances.

Maghrib time....

From my roof can be heard the sound of a myriad *of azans* from the many mosques close by and the ever present daily din of Peshawar life. Now I can just make out the Khyber mountains and the mountains of Bajaur in the cloudy haze. I hear my mind saying, "I'll get you, you faithless bitch."

So the *mantra* has finally changed. It used to be, "I love you so much, what am I going to do about you?" Well, the "what am I going to do about you" part is still there. But what I want to do has changed. I hate to say it, but I can't wait to get back in those hard, dry desolate mountains. At least I hear the Mohmands have stopped fighting the government. For now.

The day I came back from Tribal Territory I saw *Haji* Mahboob in his shop. He didn't know I had been to Bajaur again. I don't see him every day and I had only been gone four days.

433

"Noor Mohammad," he asked, "is there any news from that side?"

"No, not yet," I told him. "But I would like to make some of my own. I'd like to go back one time before leaving for the United States."

"If you are going, Noor Mohammad, let me know," he told me. "I'd like to come along and see that *Bombuna Mama*."

Mahboob is a great friend and I love him dearly, but in this matter I knew he was only being polite. His true heart is too gentle and full of **Allah**. But he is a Pathan to the core.

"*Insha'Allah*." I answered him, "Okay. Let's go! I'm going back next week. I just came back from Bajaur this afternoon. I walked on the dirt road to their fort yesterday."

"*Insha'Allah*." he replied.

People seem so civilized, so citified, here in Peshawar. I do understand though, they have responsibilities to their families, their children, their businesses. They all say I'm an "educated, smart American guy," that I should think right and not let my heart make me crazy. But is it maybe my true nature that has pulled me out through the veneers? I would rather be out there. Suddenly Peshawar seems so tame. This isn't buying embroidery in Kabul, nor riding the Flying Coach to Lahore. I understand what this is and it is not a game. And yet, it is....

In this Shah Hussain is at least with me. He is young, unattached and a Mohmand. His roots are in Tribal Territory just a short walk away from their fort. I'm not as young, but I am blind and in love with a faithless Pathan *meteeza* who has nearly gotten me killed trying to steal my money.

The money is the smaller part of it. It is the happiness she dangled in front of me and then treacherously tore away that burns at me so. The happiness I felt sitting on that *charpoy* with her outside that mud fort in Bajaur gazing over dusty fields at the mountains of the Afghan frontier discussing the plans of our marriage to be. I was so ready. We would have our marriage at the fort. The neighbors would come across the fields carrying their guns and firing in the air. None of the crowded city streets nor the crowded city laws of Peshawar. The open spaces and freedom of Tribal Territory.

We would have a house in the city and we would be able to spend time in Tribal Territory with her family. A perfect dream. To have in-laws with a fort in Tribal Territory. Outlaws for in-laws! We could hide from her family in Lahore until her American visa was ready. Then we could go to America for a year or so until the heat (from Akbar's family) cooled down in Lahore. And we would live happily ever after.

And then I was playing a game with her, her supposed brother and mad uncle, to save myself and to get her. Well, I have won the first hand. At least I suppose I have. I'm alive and free, out of Bajaur. Out of their fort. If that is winning. Now to try to arrange the cards. How can I work it to get her and not get myself kidnapped or killed in the process? Can I kidnap her? Could I steal her out of Pakistan and keep her in Thailand until her American visa came through? Then take her to the USA for a year. After, I could bring her back to

Pakistan and tell her, "If you like the dirt and filth of living under a burqa in Tribal Territory, there it is. You can go! You are free!" Ultimately I could never hold her against her will.

And what of the choice I offer her? I myself would prefer life in the Northwest Frontier and in Tribal Territory to the boring, sedate life of America. A fort in Tribal Territory would be nice. But it is nice to be able to visit modern and different places, and I do have a huge house in Peshawar.

Now is time to make plans.

Shah Hussain and I bought cloth to make more Bajauri-looking clothing. We each got a different shade of drab green. Mountain colors. In Tribal Territory most people wear subdued colors: greens, browns or tans; inexpensive cloth. Not my usual expensive city fabrics, but a coarser variety.

"This is really crummy cloth, Noor Mohammad," Riaz, my neighborhood tailor told me. "It is very cheap."

"Yeah, I know," I answered smiling, proud of my wise choice. "It only cost me 12 rupees a meter. I need a special suit. I have some special work up in Tribal Territory."

"Okay, I understand Noor Mohammad. This is cloth a *Muhajir* would wear. I will make you a suit in an Afghan design." He must have thought my work had some connection with Afghanistan and Afghan refugees.

"No. Definitely do not make it look like a *Muhajir*. I don't want to look like an Afghan. I don't want people to think I am an Afghan or that I have anything to do with Afghanistan. My work is in Pakistan." I was mostly thinking of the Pakistani authorities. I not only do not want to be confused for a *Muhajir*, I don't want anyone thinking I am a journalist trying to sneak across the border into Afghanistan. My destination lay just this side of the border, just short of the Nawa Pass. I am after a Pakistani girl, not any news of political portent. But that could never be explained. I can't very well say, "No, I'm not going to Afghanistan. I'm only trying to find a Pathan girl hiding from me in a fort which just happens to be down the road from Afghanistan."

Not a story to be believed. And in Tribal Territory, not a story to be tolerated.

October 17th

At present I'm again in the process of dealing with someone to meet a girl for marriage, this time from Chakdarra on the way to Malakand. He is a Peshawari. I find it hard to believe a Peshawari can help arrange a marriage with a Pathan girl, but no harm in sussing it out. If I am careful.

I am trying to get out of this fatal addiction and another Pathan girl is the only solution I can see. But as learned in the Dubai gold bazaar, it must be the right girl. But I am so tired of it all. At least this weekend I will be relaxing in the mountains of Bajaur. Trying to look up some old friends.

For me being up there and speaking is like walking with a sprained ankle and not wanting anyone to notice. There are certain words I have trouble pronouncing and I have to be careful not to use those words, or to mumble them when they come up.

435

I'm back to loving this *stupid* country, but it seems so many people here have the terrible habit of lying and cheating. I am also dealing with some people from the TV station who want to do a recording studio partnership with me. They want to make a studio for recording commercials and we can record Pashtu music on the side. Both the guy with the girl from Chakdarra and these fellows from the TV station tell me I am their Muslim brother and they just want to help me. They say I should be careful as people here are dishonest, liars and cheats. Obviously the kind of lines that instantly make one suspicious.

Shah Hussain has become my shield in my dealings with people. It is much better with a local obviously in my camp. Otherwise people think I am alone and not really aware of what is going on in Pakistan. After dealing with the Bajauris these Peshawari people don't seem like much.

The other night the fellow with the girl from Chakdarra was giving me a story about wanting to be my friend. For some reason I have trouble believing anybody who tries to speak to me in English. And there has been too much talk of money in our conversations and his story keeps changing. Also, I haven't seen the girl or even anybody from her supposed family.

"I have lots of American friends," he bragged. "I have an MB Degree in English, you know."

We were speaking in Pashtu as he understood my Pashtu better than English. Maybe, because I am such a simple man, my English isn't so easy to understand? I don't usually care for the types that cultivate American friendships though. "I don't have lots of friends," I told him. "I used to have more, but I am getting rid of friends now. I don't need any more. I do have a few good friends, strong friends. I'm not looking for more, especially non-Pathan friends."

"I want to be your friend, Noor Mohammad," he continued.

"Good. I hope so. Because you definitely don't want to be my enemy."

He smiled my craziness away. I feel like I am fencing with him. I feel like I'm fencing with everybody. I'm fencing with myself!

In my fencing with Noor Gul I'm afraid I might have struck too swiftly. Dealt him a fatal blow in unexpected haste and scared him away. He called my house again yesterday. Shah Hussain was sitting in the room with me so he answered the phone.

"Is Noor Mohammad Khan there?" said the voice on the phone.

"Who is calling?" Shah Hussain asked.

"Give the phone to him," the voice demanded.

Shah Hussain handed me the phone. "Yes?" I answered. "Who is this?"

"It is me," said the voice on the other end. I knew the voice. "What have you decided? Do you have the money?"

"No, but I am working on it. But I need to talk to her. I need to see her again."

"That is impossible without the money."

"Is she with you? I want to talk to her."

"No, she isn't with me."

"Well, I need to see her. And as I told you, I need to marry her in Peshawar. We can't do it in Tribal Territory. Besides, I don't think you are really her brother. Your accent is of Bajaur, not of Mardan," I added. Shah Hussain grimaced at my hasty words.

"I will think about it," said the voice on the other end.

"Remember, tell her I want to speak with her. If not face to face, at least on the telephone. If not, I may just come up to Momad Ghat," I added, dropping the hint that I knew how to get to him. Shah Hussain grimaced again.

"I will call you back in a few days." He clicked down the receiver.

"Why did you tell him that?" Shah Hussain complained to me. "Do you want to chase him away? You may as well have told him you were planning to knock on his doorstep."

"I don't know. It just fell out of my mouth. I wasn't expecting him to call. He surprised me."

"Noor Mohammad, maybe now you have become a *sadakhan* (simpleton) like most of us stupid Pathans."

Well, Noor Gul, maybe we'll see you again soon. I'm going back there after *Juma*—in a couple of days. Maybe I am still crazy. Maybe even more crazy. But not the empty crazy I was before I saw her again. Now I'm fully crazy. I want to see her again. To get in the last word. Maybe teach her a lesson. At least she is in my life again.

My thoughts are too tribal for most of my friends in Peshawar. I keep thinking maybe I should just let this go like they all say, but I can't. The emptiness would just return. I want to see her. I guess I'm not so Pathan that I want to kill her. Maybe spank her? I still love her so. I can't stop. It is driving me on. I want to establish if those people in that fort are really bad and crazy or just fakes. Where they live, so far from any police or army or government control they can do anything. I have to be careful they don't as *Haji* Mahboob says, "open the fire" on us when we come knocking on their door. But I am determined to wash my face in the cleansing soap of (some sort of) revenge.

Maybe what I need is to just get away from here? And I am being pulled away from here by certain responsibilities in America beyond my control. I hope not before I can resolve this. I feel an obligation for coming back to my mother alive. She could never understand all this. If she were only Pathan it would make things so much easier. Then she would never let me pass her door until I had avenged myself in this matter.

The thoughts going through my head so sweetly insane are obviously not things I learned while growing up in Los Angeles. But that was such a long time ago. The only growing up I can really remember now are hot, dry, desert nights in Herat (Afghanistan), walking dark, narrow, covered dirt lanes with my *dutar* preciously clutched under my arm. Cold, snowy nights in Kabul listening to my *ustad* play sweet melodies on his *rabab*, a *bukhari* heating the carpet and cushion-strewn room. Shopping for hand grenades and anti-aircraft guns in Dara Adam Khel with Afghan Mujahideen. Two months spent in Rawalpindi prison on false charges and an ensuing two month trial and complete acquittal.

Any other growing up was done at Nasreen's side, in her house, in her arms, in Samnabad. On the Flying Coach. Jangling horse bells in the high mountains. Those are all the memories left to me now that are real.

And then there are my thoughts, my plans....

We could buy a motorcycle, a dirt bike with the strongest tires available. If we couldn't buy two Kalashnikovs in the Nawagai Bazaar for sure we would be able to rent two and leave a 20,000 rupee security deposit. We could pick up a couple fire bombs and half dozen grenades for good measure. After that we wouldn't have to care if the army was checking for weapons on the roads or not. We wouldn't need roads. From Nawagai we could head southwest over the mountains—only one low mountain to cross. Even I could practically get there from Nawagai blind folded.

We'd come down that dirt road leading on to Koda Khel, out of the dry, barren rocks somewhere north of Gandao, cut our engine and silently coast the last 100 yards to their fort. They would think just another vehicle passed by on the road.

If we left Nawagai at the first crack of dawn we would arrive at the fort before they were stirring outside. A few properly thrown fire bombs should bring them running outside and hopefully not kill any innocent people. And then we could shoot down Noor Gul and the uncle. Hopefully we could pull it off without having to shoot any of the women or children. I am not a violent man.

But then these people may really be hard core. Their fort is very remote. They didn't pick such a remote place for meditative purposes. The more remote the residence in Agency, the more desperate the inhabitants. Maybe they would bolt the heavy wooden doors and open fire with their machine guns over the mud walls and from the tower. They do have grenades inside too, that I do know.

And what about the neighbors? What happens in Tribal Territory when a fort is attacked? Do the neighbors bolt their doors and stay inside, uninvolved as most people in Peshawar would? The general consensus from Pathans that I have asked is the neighbors would come to their aid. How would we ride out of there on a motorcycle dodging a hail of machine gun fire? And what if we got Nasreen? The three of us would never make it over the rocky terrain on one motorcycle.

How much money can I scrape together? Enough to get an old Datsun and fit it with heavy steel plates for bullet proofing and a machine gun? I could get a few out of work *Mujahideen*, Peshawar is full of them, and then we could plow down their front gate. We could even make license plates and uniforms so we would appear to be the Frontier Constabulary. That might work.

This will have to be thought out more carefully. Sure, I want my revenge, but more than that, I'd like to get Nasreen and live. If I can just get my hands on her, Shah Hussain has friends with a place in the remote fringes of lawless Baluchistan. Maybe just far enough away to hide her from the Bajauris.

And then what would I do to her? The proof I am not a full-blooded Pathan is that I don't think I could ever bring myself to kill her. I just want her to know that she is in my power. That I have her to do with whatever I like. And what is that? Probably no more than to offer her a life with me, if she wants it. To dangle in front of her a carrot that even I don't really want now. But then for her it is something not yet seen. A kind of freedom—if she wants it.

And if she doesn't want that? What is left? To spank her butt, give her her life and let her go back to the dirt and squalor of Agency? I want to live in Peshawar surrounded by Tribal Territory. It is invigorating to visit Tribal Territory for a while, but to be sequestered there could leave a lot to be desired. But then what good have cities shown her? Maybe she is really tired of all of that?

"Noor Mohammad, you should color your hair and moustache darker and let your beard grow out," Shah Hussain told me. "That way no one will look at you at all."

"Why don't we paint your nose red and your ears black? Then no one will look at me either." I answered, feeling sassy.

We were getting ready to go back to Bajaur again. No course of action had been decided on but we both felt the desire to be in free and open (though dangerous) places again. I had to get back to try to think of what to do. I felt I would only be able to come to a decision in those desolate rocky areas.

"Look, *yaar*," I told Shah Hussain, "I'd love to be here when Shah Jan comes to visit you, but I must go to Arif's shop and tell them I will be away for a few days."

"Noor Mohammad, do you think it is wise to tell anyone where we are going? Maybe you should just say you are going to Lahore?"

"Maybe you are right, but Arif and Anwar Khan know me too well. They will know I am going to Bajaur after her. I can't keep it from them. I see them every day. I can't leave without informing them."

"Okay, you know what is best."

"Of course. I am a perfectly sane, rational man. A smart, educated, American type guy as they say. See you later."

Mukhtiare was very worried. "Please don't go up there *yaar*," he pleaded. "It is so dangerous. And there is nothing we can do if you have any problem. Even the birds will never find your bones there."

"Don't worry. It is safe up there for me now. And I like the fresh air."

"Noor Mohammad," Arif suggested, "you should go see your mother in Amerika. And then, when you leave, tell her not to worry if you don't come back. Then you can go to Bajaur and get yourself killed."

"Don't worry Arif, I promise not to do anything too crazy, *Insha'Allah*. I know your chair and tea is waiting for me. It isn't as if I'm going somewhere really dangerous—like downtown Los Angeles."

Again we traveled in now familiar stages, the words of a well known Pashtu song playing in my head: "*Lar shah Peckhawar la, kameez tor mala rawola... tahza, tahza guluna, dray selor mala rawolla.*" (Go to Peshawar, bring me a black blouse... and fresh, fresh flowers, bring me three or four.)

439

She had asked me to bring her a suit from Peshawar. Was it black or was it red? I had been so busy trying to stay out of Bajaur, when I left Peshawar to go back I had forgotten her orders. The flowers I'd have to get at the Momad Ghat florist.

At the checkpoint before Gandao Shah Hussain elbowed me to look at the large sign on the side of the road. It read, "No foreigners beyond this point, by order of the government."

Don't worry," I whispered to him, "there isn't any government beyond this point. And besides, I won't tell on you."

A swarthy-skinned guard peered into the minivan eyeing me suspiciously.

"What are you looking at *blacky*?" I scowled in my best casually guttural Pashtu. "Where are *you* from, the Punjab?" Some people chuckled. Shah Hussain applied pressure on my foot with his *chappal*.

In Gandao we settled into our routine reconnaissance, ending in the tea house at the bus stand. An old Farzana cassette played on a battered tape player covered in a grease encrusted red and gold embroidered cloth cover. The wooden *charpoys* were dark brown, worn smooth with age. Gnarled wooden posts held up the rickety roof of the wall-less tea house.

While drinking our *qawah* two men got up to leave. Shah Hussain kept his head turned away from them. One was a burly Afghan with a black bushy beard and a dark turban with silver-gray stripes carrying a stick with feathers and balls tied to each end. The other man, Shah Hussain whispered, was from his own area. He didn't want the man to see him as he didn't want word getting back to his family he had been in Tribal Territory. The man was older than his companion, his white beard was cut sharply and he was wearing a white skull cap. He had a falcon perched on his arm. In their village Shah Hussain informed me this man's daughter had made friendship with a man. Her mother knew of it. He had killed his daughter and wife.

The falcon was a hunting falcon. The last time we had been at Momad Ghat, while talking with some fellows off the side of the road four new white Pajaro jeeps passed us and turned off the road to a *Koochie* camp in the dry rocky nearby hills. We were told Arab *sheikhs* pay up to 50 *lakh* (5,000,000 rupees) for a good hunting falcon. Such a fantastic sum seemed hard to believe; maybe they were exaggerating or had their figures mixed up, but then the Arabs do pay a lot for their hunting falcons.

I closely watched every arriving and departing vehicle as we talked. I got up to pay for the tea. I was beginning to enjoy more and more Shah Hussain's nervousness and discomfort when I interacted with local people.

Eventually we found a Datsun headed to Nawagai. We climbed into the seats behind the driver. Two Afghans squeezed into the remaining room next to us. One had a tan turban, black piercing eyes and a dark blue-black beard. He exchanged a few standard words of greeting with Shah Hussain, then focused his attention on me. "Where have you been Noor Mohammad?" he asked, smiling. "I haven't seen you in a long time. Did you go to *Amerika*?"

Shah Hussain and I exchanged a glance. It's hard for you to go anywhere undetected, his eyes told me. I wasn't sure where I knew this fellow from.

"Have you seen Moleem lately?" he asked. Then I realized I knew him from my friend, Haji Makoo's, embroidery shop in Peshawar. "Has Haji Sahib come back from Afghanistan yet?"

"I saw Moleem last week." I answered, "Haji Sahib has come back from Ghazni just recently," We made some more small talk but nobody paid me any attention, I suppose they assumed I must be an Afghan businessman who had been in America.

We topped the Nahakki Pass and sped down into the lunar landscaped bowl of Mohmand Agency. My blood always stirs at the sight of those arid, broken, forsaken mountains. Especially around Momad Ghat. I craned my neck to scan for a familiar face in the forms milling around the junction. I couldn't even see a florist.

My Afghan friend asked the driver to stop as he was headed to Afghanistan. Shah Hussain and I also got out. My friend asked if I was going to Afghanistan.

"No, I have friends down the road I want to see," I told him.

We drank a "kerosine" tea together, squatting next to a stone wall by the roadside, then said goodbyes.

Shah Hussain and I walked down the road heading toward the peaked craggy mountains leading to the Nawa Pass. We passed the check post and came to the dirt road turnoff leading to *Bombuna Mama's* fort. Only I barely recognized it. The wood cutter's hut had been moved several *furlongs* up the road towards Afghanistan. All that remained of its original location were the stones that had comprised its base. Also the large imposing fort that had scared us from going past last time was gone. No, it wasn't actually gone—it was in ruins. Its crumbling mud walls remained standing in places. What had happened? Had a family feud gotten the better of it? We weren't in the kind of place to ask and besides there wasn't anyone around. We could only surmise. We remained on the road until we came to the small village of Shaqak at the foot of the mountains of Afghanistan.

"If we are going to keep walking let us at least go back and walk on the dirt road to *Bombuna's*," I told Shah Hussain. "In fact, we can just cut across from here."

"What about not leaving the road?" Shah Hussain asked, smiling.

"What about not going to Bajaur?" I returned. *"I 'fuck the kus' of their road!"*

"That is a very beautiful use of that expression," Shah Hussain laughed.

"Yeah, I know. I got it from your refined cousin Habibullah. He is a master craftsman with words."

We came onto the dirt road from behind the ruined fort. It was hard to believe all that remained were a few broken mud walls.

"I once had a friend in Kabul named Sharif," I reminisced aloud. "He was a *sharabi* and a philosopher. One time when he was drunk on wine he looked at me, holding a burning match, and said, 'Noor Mohammad, human existence is like this burning match. One day there is fire and then phoof,' he stated, blowing out the match, 'it's gone'."

Five miles down the road we came to a fork in the gravel rutted road. There was an old, mud-caked *mangay* off to the side with a tin bowl covering the top. I tipped water into the bowl and drank.

"How is it?" Shah Hussain asked.

"Muddy, but its cold and refreshing. Have a drink."

"You actually drank it?" he asked in partial disbelief.

"Sure, what is the problem? Do you want me to boil it for you? Come on, drink man. The mud of the mountains of Afghanistan adds the flavor to it."

He drank and gazed where the track we were following divided into two and asked, "Do you remember which way you went when you were with them?"

I thought for a moment. "I don't remember the way dividing. But I think it is the track to the right. I am only judging by the position of the mountains. It is only a guess."

After we followed the track for several more miles it seemed to be heading too much to the north and back around into the far mountains. "We must have taken the wrong turn. We're heading around the backside of the mountain. Their fort was back there," I said, pointing back to the south.

"Let's continue on," he said. "We've already come this far and besides, we may be able to approach their fort from the backside."

"*Ah cha*," I agreed reluctantly. We had gone rather far to turn back and it did seem possible we would be able to double back around the mountain.

As we walked a woman approached us along the trail. Her *chaddar* was over her hair but her face was uncovered. Being completely veiled is more for city women. Out here are less people and most people are related by tribe. As she passed she said *"starray mashi"* (Typical greeting in Tribal Territory meaning "Don't be tired." Very appropriate where any journey is by foot and potentially fatiguing.)

"Ah, this Tribal Territory is very nice," Shah Hussain remarked. "Even the women greet you." (Of course just being there signified we were either Bajauris or Mohmands and, thus, technically related to the woman.)

The piled gray granite rocks of the mountain came down and ended in the brown dirt at our feet. Up the backside of the mountain we could see several tattered green and orange flags on gnarled twisted poles fluttering in the dry wind in the distance.

"It looks like a *zirarat* up ahead," Shah Hussain said.

"Or a Mohmand used car lot."

"Let's go up to it," he continued. "Maybe there is some *malang* there. I am a Mohmand. This is my land. I will ask him to give us lunch. I will demand hospitality."

"That sounds okay to me. At least we can ask where this track leads. I'm not in the mood to visit Afghanistan today."

As we wound our way up the rocky trail the jagged stone walls of the *zirarat* came into view, growing inch by inch out of the chaotically strewn rugged rocks of the mountainside. Squatting on a rock in front of it was a *malang* in a long tattered gown of a multitude of colored dirty patches, his matted hair blowing in the wind. He wore necklaces of large agate beads of many colors and his fingers were covered with rings with equally large agate stones. He spit out his *nuswar,* looked at us with bloodshot eyes and stood.

"*Salaam aleikum,*" he said, raising his hand, holding a *tasbee* of square-cut white agate beads.

"*Wa'leikum asalaam,*" I answered.

"Where are you from?" Shah Hussain asked him.

"Only **Allah** knows," he answered.

"How long have you been here?" Shah Hussain asked.

"That also is known by **Allah**. And where are you going?"

"That also must be known by **Allah**," I echoed his words. "Can we rest here for a while?"

"How long will you stay?" he asked. I thought it rather impolite.

"**Allah** will decide," I answered. "All things are written."

We followed him inside the piled stone walls of the *zirarat*. The rocks shielded us from the wind. He gathered a handful of dry twisted twigs, kindled a small fire, and without speaking began to brew tea in a charcoal-blackened dented aluminum tea pot.

"There is nothing in these mountains," he said as he squatted in the smoke of the fire, fanning it with a frayed woven straw fan. "As we know, **Allah** guides our steps. I assume you must wander in these empty deserted mountains after some enemies. It is the way of Pukhtuns. Is it not?"

"Is it?" I asked, myself not knowing what I was doing there. "Do you know what we know not, brother?"

"This I do know," he continued, "if you will listen to my words."

"Speak."

"Forgiveness is a necessary part of life. A part of growing, a part of living. If we do not forgive others for the wrongs and hurts they have done us, then the pain turns to hate. And just as love is life, so hate is a kind of death. When we hate, a part of us dies. With part of us dead, we cannot grow properly. We grow crookedly, misshapen by hate. Just like these sticks I am burning. We can burn in the fire of that hate. So we must learn to ask others to forgive us and we must learn to forgive others."

"But just as the fire must make the water boil in order to make tea, must we not right a wrong. Must we not cleanse our shame with the soap of revenge? And revenge is permitted in the *Qur'an Sharif,* is it not?" I countered.

"Yes, revenge is permitted for believers. But the Holy Book also says, 'God loves the man who forgives more.' And the Qur'an Sharif also states in Sura The Bee, 'If you punish, let punishment be proportionate to the wrong that has been done to you. But if you are patient, it is certainly best for the patient.'"

"Yes, I realize it does, though sometimes a man wants to forget such wisdoms. When he burns with resentment and his blood boils hot. But I am not out looking for revenge. At least not yet. I am only looking for a friend who is now an enemy. I am only following where my feet are leading."

"Sometimes when we blindly follow our feet on the trail of an enemy we find revenge at the end of our trail. And we must take it or it takes us. He that chooses the devil for his friend chooses an evil friend."

"But I must speak to her one more time," I said more to myself aloud.

"Ah," the *malang* sighed. "I should have known there was a woman in-volved in this. What is the crime that was done against you my brother? Re-member, 'Don't be led by passion,' my friend, 'lest you should swerve from the truth.' The *Qur'an Sharif* states that in the *Sura Women*. I will say no more, my brother. What **Allah** ordains shall be accomplished."

Unfortunately his words rang true, though they were not the words I wanted or expected to find out among those jagged rocks. My dreams shivered like dying reflections in the Kabul River at sunset. Where would I go from here? The page had turned.

My time in Pakistan is so limited now. My visa is running out. How can I extend my already over extended visa any more? That I should even be con-cerned about such mundane things shows that I must be returning from insan-ity. What a sweet carefree garden it was.

And now the words of the *malang* keep coming back to haunt me with their truth and wisdom. And it is the sane who can listen to reason, wisdom and truth. But what is truth? To the insane his own truth is truth enough.

But now I am thinking rationally, logically. Coming so freshly from the freedom of insanity the slavery of sanity feels so painful at times. The pain of ripping off a bandage; draw the pain out slowly or just wrench it off and feel the stinging and the cold air on the wound.

Can I do it? What is my choice? It's God's choice. I have certain respon-sibilities so I must go to America for that reason and that reason only. When will I return? God knows best.

As Shah Hussain and I walked through Shaheen Bazaar, now dark and quiet, toward Kalan Bazaar, I was lost in my thoughts. He broke the silence. "Noor Mohammad, my brother, I have one story to tell you before you leave Pakistan."

"Yes, what is that, *yaar*?"

"There was a very young Pathan boy. Some enemies killed his father. But he was too small to take the revenge. The enemies left the village. When he grew up he could not find them."

"Well, that is a short, and not so good story," I told him.

"But that isn't the end of it," he went on. "You see, his family was very poor and they only had a little piece of land. But he worked hard and one day there was enough money saved for his mother in case something should hap-pen to him. Then he bought a rifle and though it was 40 years after his father's murder he went searching for the enemies."

"Now the story is becoming better."

"Yes. It becomes better. One day he came to the village where the en-emies were living. And he waited in their fields. And when they came out to the fields one morning to work he killed them all. Dead! He had done his revenge."

"Ah, now that sounds more like a Pathan story."

"But that still isn't the end of my story, Noor Mohammad. Do you know what happened after he took his revenge?"

"He ran away to Agency?"

"Maybe. But first he went back to his native village. And there, do you know what the people said to him?"

"No. What? *'Don't go to Bajaur?'*"

"They asked him why he had acted so hastily. Why he had taken the revenge so soon."

"*Ah cha, yaar.* I get your point."

"Yes, Noor Mohammad. A Pathan can wait 100 years for his revenge. In these things the wait does not matter."

We came out into the lights of Kalan Bazaar. Raheel was shuffling from *rickshaw* to *rickshaw* with my 40 kilo over-stuffed suitcase still balanced on his head dickering for one that would take me to the airport for a few rupees less than the others. I glanced at my watch. "Maybe a Pathan can wait 100 years for his revenge, but *PIA* I think won't wait an extra minute for me," I said to Shah Hussain.

"Raheel, what are you doing?" I shouted over the din of *rickshaw* horns, revving engines and *tonga* bells. "I don't have any more time to waste. I will be late for my plane. My people in America will kill me if I don't show up this time."

"I'm sorry, boss," Raheel apologized. "This *banchod rickshaw wallah* wants 30 rupees to go to the airport. I told him not a *paisa* over 20 will you pay."

I looked in at the *rickshaw* driver. "I'll give you 25 rupees to the airport," I said. "Let's go."

"Brother, now is the time of much traffic," he replied, looking at my suitcases and accessing the situation. "Give me 30 rupees."

I thought of how fast I would soon be spending the extra five rupees (20 cents) he wanted. "Okay, *ustada.* But drive me there quickly."

"Yes, we will arrive very quickly. *Insha'Allah.* Get in!"

I looked at Shah Hussain as Raheel squeezed my bags into the tiny *rickshaw.* "Okay, *yaar*, take care of yourself. And be sure to call me instantly if Noor Gul or Nas should call or show up. I am not sure how long I will have to stay in the United States, but it should be less than 40 years, *Insha'Allah.*"

"I sure hope so," he answered. "I will become crazy if I have to wait too much time in your antique house in this backwards and crazy place. You know the only other good friend I have here is my pal Shah Jan."

"I will be back as soon as I am able," I assured him. I hugged him and turned to Raheel. "All right my little brother. You take care. And say my goodbyes to your respected mother Bibi Ji, your sisters, your wife and my little girlfriend Sarosh (his four-year-old daughter). And everyone in the *mohallah.*"

"Okay, boss. We will all do miss with you. And your girlfriend, she will became cried because you are leaved. I will write you all the important news and will keep you informed in all departments. All to all. Not to worry in these matters of mutual interest. Over and out."

We embraced. *"Salaam aleikum."*

"Wa'leikum asalaam."

"Pa makha day kha."

"Pa makha day kha sha."

I crammed into the back seat of the *rickshaw* and off we sped, horn buzzing and blaring, into the dust of a Peshawar evening. I looked back out of the *rickshaw's* door. Shah Hussain and Raheel turned and disappeared into the darkness of Shaheen Bazaar. I glanced one last time at the tower of *Ghanta Ghar* and prayed it would not be long before I saw it again.

Ghanta Ghar, the Clock Tower, Peshawar City

Aash - Afghan noodle soup with legumes, meat, spinach, yogurt, dill and mint

A.C. - government posting - Assistant Commissioner

AC - air conditioner

Achar (Urdu) - a variety of spicy pickled side dishes or condiments popular in the subcontinent, in Southeast Asia and in many other areas among ethnically South Asian communities. The pickle serves as a flavor-enhancer and is eaten typically in small pieces with the rest of the meal. There are a wide variety of different pickles. Each is usually made with a mixture of fruits or vegetables, chopped and marinated in a liquid (often oil or lemon juice) and a variety of spices (often including lots of chili pepper) and salt. *Achar* is quite different from the European pickles in that the pickling is usually done in oil rather than vinegar.

Ah cha - used as "okay" or "uh huh"

Aid wallah - welfare agency worker; see *wallah*

Al-hamdu-lillah (Arabic) - All praise to God.

Allah (Arabic) - name of God; *Al* = the, *Lah* = God

Allah Akbar/Allahu Akbar - God (*Allah*) is great.

Almari - wall cupboard

Asalaam aleikum (Arabic) - Greeting, literally "Peace be upon you."

Asr (Arabic) (**Masdigar** - Pashtu) - Mid afternoon prayer, later part of afternoon; its time is over about 10 minutes before sunset.

Atta (Urdu) - flour

Azan (Arabic - Adhan/Athan) - call to prayer

Badmash - gangster, thug, villain, lout, criminal, ruffian, scoundrel (Hindi-naughty).

Baht - Thai money; At the time of this story, there were about 35 *baht* in $1 U.S.

Banchod (Punjabi, Urdu) - used in general, literally "sister fucker" or as I've heard it more gently put, "lover of your sister." Used as slang much the same as "mother fucker" is used in USA.

Barfi - a sweet from the Indian subcontinent. Plain *barfi* is made from condensed milk cooked with sugar until it solidifies. Other varieties include *besan barfi*, made with *besan* (gram flour) and *pista barfi*, containing ground pistachio nuts *(pista)*. The name is derived from Persian *"barf"* which means ice since *barfi* is similar to ice in appearance.

Baas (Pashtu, Farsi, Urdu, etc) - enough

Bazaari - (slang) pertaining to the bazaar, i.e: common, low caste

Bedouin - predominantly Muslim, desert-dwelling Arab nomadic pastoralist or previously no-madic group found throughout most of the desert belt extending from the Atlantic coast of the Sahara via the Western Desert, Sinai and Negev to the Arabian Desert

Behtak (Urdu, Pashtu—*hujra*) - guest room, sitting room

Bekar - literally "without work" - Can be applied to a worthless object (or person).

Betel - a leaf used in making *Paan*, a South and South East Asian tradition which consists of chewing *Betel* leaf (Piper betel) combined with the areca nut. There are many regional variations. *Paan* is chewed as a palate cleanser and a breath freshener. It is also commonly offered to guests and visitors as a sign of hospitality and as ice breaker to start conversation.

Bhabi (Urdu/Punjabi, Pashtu—*khorandar*) - sister-in-law

Bhang - cannabis, cannabis plants; also a drink (intoxicant) made by pressing the resins out of the plant, flowers and buds with water

Bharat (Urdu; Pashtu—*"janj"*) - wedding parade from groom's home to bride's home

Bindi - lady fingers, okra

Bismillah (Arabic) - "In the name of God," or *Bismil'Allah* "In the name of *Allah.*" Used when starting any action

Bookie - (rifle) scabbard

Boose - straw, wheat chaff

Bukhari (Afghan) - wood burning stove; an important source of heat during cold Afghan winters

Burqa/burka (Arabic—*burqu*) - called *chadri* in Afghanistan - an enveloping outer garment worn by women in some Islamic traditions for the purpose of cloaking the entire body. It is worn over the usual daily clothing (often a long dress or a *shalwar kameez*) and removed when the woman returns to the sanctuary of the household. The full Afghan *chadri* covers the wearer's entire face except for a small region about the eyes, which is covered by a concealing net or embroidered grille.

This type of covering is also common in North Western Pakistan close to the Afghan border. It is frequently referred to as "Shuttlecock Burqa" in Pakistan to differentiate it from other *Burqa* styles due to its resemblance with a badminton shuttlecock or birdie. The garment is usually sewn from light materials and requires many meters of material. Blue is a favorite color for *chadris*. The cap from which the material hangs may be decorated with embroidery. The *chadri* was created by one of Afghanistan's rulers trying to stop anyone from seeing his wives' faces. He came up with the *chadri*, which became a sign of an upper class citizen; however, as times changed, the new government decided that *chadris* weren't modern enough and banned them. The upper class people then gave them to their servants. The *chadris* in those days were made of silk and the mesh at the front was lace.

Buzkashi - Afghan national sport, similar to polo, except played with a goat carcass. Can be played as teams (in Kabul), teams becoming looser getting away from Kabul. The name is Farsi, *"buz"* = goat, and *"kashi"* = drag. The carcass has to be "dragged/carried" across the field and dropped in a circle, no easy feat with 50 to 100 riders charging you from all sides. Competition is typically fierce, as other players may use any force short of tripping the horse in order to thwart scoring attempts. In the past, riders carried knives and chains. Riders usually wear heavy clothing and fur hats to protect themselves against other players' whips and boots. Games can last for several days and the winning team receives a prize, not necessarily money, as a reward for their win. The game consists of two main forms: Tudabarai and Qarajai. Tudabarai is considered to be the simpler form of the game. In this version, the goal is simply to grab the carcass and move in any direction until clear of the other players. In Qarajai, players must carry the carcass around a flag or marker at one end of the field, then throw it into a scoring circle (the "Circle of Justice") at the other end. The riders will carry a whip, often in their teeth, to fend off opposing horses and riders. Buzkashi is often compared to polo. Both games are played between people on horseback, both involve propelling an object toward a goal and both get fairly rough. However, polo is played with a ball, while Buzkashi is played with a dead animal. Polo matches are played for fixed periods totaling about an hour; traditional Buzkashi may continue for days, but in its more regulated tournament version also has a limited match time. The carcass in a Buzkashi game is normally beheaded and disemboweled and has its limbs cut off at the knees. It is then soaked in cold water for 24 hours before play to toughen it. Occasionally sand is packed into the carcass to give it extra weight. Players may not strap the calf to their bodies or saddles. Though a goat is used when no calf is available, a calf is less likely to disintegrate during the game.

Cantt - The section of the city where the British lived: *Cantt* is short for cantonment (derived from the French *"canton"* meaning corner or district).

Chaddar - thin blanket, sheet, shawl, commonly worn as jacket (and used as an all purpose carry all) by both men and women

Chai - tea (any); black tea boiled with sugar and milk (Pashtu— *"tor chai"*)

Chai khanna - tea *(chai)* house *(khanna)*, commonly called "hotel"

Channa - chick-peas, garbanzo beans; see **cholay**

Chapatties - local flat bread (like tortillas) eaten from the Punjab to South India

Chappals - leather sandals

Chappli kebab - The Pathan answer to the Whopper (though it came first). Ground meat, chopped onions and spices (sometimes egg), fried in oil. It is pressed out by hand and the finger marks gives it the appearance of the bottom of a *chappal* (sandal), hence the name.

Charpoy - indigenous bed made from four turned wooden bed posts with rough jute twine woven across instead of a mattress. Nowadays they are also made with metal frames and flat nylon banding or many colored nylon rope in lieu of jute. The name literally means four feet (*char* = four, *poy* = foot).

Charras - hashish (also see **gorda**); The resin of the cannabis plant (Cannabis Sativa or Cannabis Indica). The plant grows wild throughout Northern India, Pakistan and the Himalayas (its putative origin) and is an important cash crop for the local people. Usually smoked mixed with tobacco, it is similar to use of beer in Western culture.

Charrasi - a smoker of *charras*.

Chekar - a tour, walk, excursion

Chillum - water pipe with a bamboo stem (no hose) used to smoke tobacco or hashish

Chit - a written note

Chit - woven wicker screen, used to cover windows and can be doused with water in summer

Cholla/chola - small charcoal burning portable stove

Cholay, choli (Punjabi, Pashtu: Urduduc; *channa* - chick-peas, garbanzo beans. The name is also used in reference to a dish cooked with chick-peas, often eaten at breakfast.

Chowk - intersection, square

Chowkidar - watchman, doorman, caretaker

Chutney - variety of sweet and spicy condiments usually involving a fresh, chopped primary vegetable or fruit with added seasonings. Chutney, as a genre, is often similar to the Indian pickle and the salsa of Latin American cuisine or European relish. In Pakistan many times it refers to yoghurt mixed with mint, coriander, pomegranate seed, cumin, etc.

C.I.D. - Crimes Investigation Department (Pakistan Government)

Click - slang for kilometer

Dacoit - bandit

Dal - pulses (dried beans) which have been stripped of their outer hulls and split. It also refers to the thick, spicy stew prepared therefrom, a mainstay of Indian, Pakistani and Bangladeshi cuisine.

Dari - a rough, thick cloth (flat woven rug). Large ones are usually used at gatherings for a number of people to sit on like marriage or death gatherings (available on rent basis). Also used on tea house floors (where one sits on the floor). Less costly than knotted rugs.

Dari - Afghan dialect of Farsi (Persian)

D.C. - Government posting - District Commissioner

Deg - large cooking pot, usually made of copper with a silver/nickel wash

Deg wallah - the one who supplies the deg; also refers to the cooks who use them

Deja vu - the feeling of thinking a new situation has occurred before

Dholak - double headed (small barrel shape) drum, played on lap or hung over shoulder, sometimes played (beaten) with a stick

Dholey - a palanquin, carried by hand. The bride rides to the groom's house after the wedding in a *dholey*.

Dola - pimp; plural, *dolagaan*.

DSP - Deputy Superintendent Police

Double roti - European loaf-style bread

Dua - prayer, supplication

Duc - a slang for *charras*

Duc cigarette - Pashtu; *"duc"* = fill). A cigarette filled with *charras*; *"duc"* is sometimes used synonymously for *charras*

Dumaan (*Duma*-singular,female) - low caste people, referring particularly to musicians, dancers, actors and prostitutes

Dupatta - long woman's scarf, usually of thin voile type material, worn over and behind shoulders and/or hair

Dutar - Afghan stringed instrument (long necked lute) predominately in Herat (Tajik and Uzbek). *Dutar* literally means two (*du*) string (*tar*), though in Herat they have 3 strings or 13-15 strings.

DWP - Department of Water and Power

Eid (Arabic = celebration; Pashtu = *akhtar*) - a Muslim holiday; there are several Eids: Eid ul-Fitr (the small Eid) at the end of the Holy month of Ramadan (1st day of Shawwal) and Eid ul-Adha (the Big Eid or Eid ul Qurban—the Eid of sacrifice) celebrated at the end of the Haj period, 2 1/2 months after Eid ul Fitr. Also the birthday of the Prophet Muhammad (PBUH) is known as Eid ul-Nabi and is celebrated on the 10th day of the month Rabbi Awal. In many Muslim countries it is not a festive celebration because it is also the date the Prophet (PBUH) died, but in Pakistan and India it is celebrated with much festivities, light shows, street decorations and parades.

Eid Mubarak - Eid congratulations

Ejaza namma - letter of permission; *"ejaza"* = permission, *"namma"* = letter, paper, certificate

Englaise - local pronunciation of the word English

Englaisie - English people

Fajr (Arabic) **(Sahar** - Pashtu-morning) - Dawn Prayer—takes place before sunrise. At moderate latitudes, the time for Fajr begins approximately one hour and twenty minutes before sunrise and ends about ten minutes before sunrise.

Farsi - Persian language; Afghan dialect is known as **Dari**

Ferangi - foreigner; from the word "Frank"

Firman - a decree (by a monarch or government), a letter, a contract

Furlong - a measure of distance in imperial units (British) and U.S. customary units. It is equal to one-eighth of a mile; 220 yards, 660 feet or 201.168 meters.

Gandari - fresh sugar cane stalks which can be bought bagged in peeled one inch sections; popular snack.

Ghanta Ghar - Clock Tower - literally "hour house". There are several *"ghanta ghars"* in

Pakistan: in Karachi (Sindh Province) and in Multan and Faisalabad (in the Punjab). Cunningham Clock Tower in Peshawar, Northwest Frontier Province, was built in 1900 "in Commemoration of the Diamond Jubilee of Her Majesty the Queen Empress." The tower was named after Sir George Cunningham, a former British governor and political agent in the province.

Ghanum (Urdu) - wheat

Ghee - clarified butter used for cooking. Butter is slowly boiled and the solids are skimmed off.

Ghirrat (Pashtu) - honor (respect)

Ghora (Urdu) - foreigner

Ghungrughan - leather leggings worn by dancers, sewed with concentric circles of jangly brass bells, used to stomp the time to the dance

Gold Leaf - The best cigarette in Pakistan (and the world) at the time of this book.

Gor - (jaggery) - sugar cane juice boiled until it solidifies; looks like brown, hard, dirt clods

Gor sherbet - drink made from *"gor"* and water

Gorda - raw *charras* pollen, unpressed

GPO - General Post Office. Post office = *"daak khanna"*

GTS - Government Transport Service

Gujar - ethnic group in India and Pakistan, commonly nomadic shepherds

Gujranwala - city on GT Road between Rawalpindi and Lahore, about 60 miles before Lahore; seventh largest city in Pakistan with over 1,000,000 people (1998 census)

Guna - sin

Gupshup - gossip, chatting

Gurdwara (Punjabi—gurudwara) - meaning "the doorway to the Guru" is the Sikh place of worship and is referred to as a "Sikh temple"

Guru - teacher, instructor, mentor

Haj - the annual pilgrimage to Mecca

Haji/Hajii - one who has made the Haj; people who have made it multiple times are called Al-Haj

Halal - Islamically slaughtered meat. The animal must be treated kindly before slaughter, then the neck is cut with a sharp knife, pronouncing *"Bismillah"* and *"Allahu Akbar"* three times. (**hala-ling** = to make halal).

Hammam - bath house; usually small rooms (part of barber shop) with a hot and a cold tap, two buckets and a scooper; towels and soap are provided; (2) a water storage tank

Haq mahar - the bride price in the wedding; how much the boy is giving the girl

Haram (Arabic) - not permitted, unclean

Harami (Urdu, Pashtu, Punjabi) - bastard (from Arabic *haram* = not permitted)

Harmonium - hand pumped keyboard (organ) usually played on the floor similar to an accordion; some have stops to set drones

Hazrat (Urdu, Arabic—*Hadhrat*) - Hazrat is an honorific Arabic title used to honor a person. The literal translation of Hazrat means "Great Presence."

Hazrat Ali - the cousin and son-in-law of the Prophet Muhammad (PBUH). *Sunni* Muslims consider Ali as the fourth and final *Rashidun* (Rightly Guided Caliph) while *Shia* Muslims regard Ali as the first *Imam* and consider him and his descendants as the rightful successors to Muhammad (PBUH). This disagreement split the Muslim community into the *Sunni* and *Shia* branches. Ali was the only person born in the *Kaaba* sanctuary in Mecca, the holiest place in Islam. When Muhammad (PBUH) reported receiving his divine revelation, Ali was among the first to accept his message, dedicating his life to the cause of Islam.

Henna - hair and skin dye made from powdered plant (Lawsonia inermis); usually orange

Hijra (Urdu, Pashtu) - transgender, transsexual, transvestite. They have a long and colorful history in the Subcontinent and Central Asia. Usually considered a member of "the third gender"—neither man nor woman. Most are physically male or unisex, but some are female. *Hijras* usually refer to themselves linguistically as female and usually dress as women and adopt other feminine gender roles.

Hijra (Arabic) - the migration of the Islamic prophet *Muhammad* and his followers to the city of Medina in 622 (Common Era)

Hindko - the language of citizens of Peshawar and other inhabitants of NWFP. Similar to Punjabi, *Hindko* speakers originally migrated from the Punjab. The *Pashto* word *"Hindko"* (which is a condensation of *"hindaku"*) means "Indian," a term the Pashtun people gave to the people who migrated from *"hind"* which according to them, was immediately east of the Indus River. The word

450

Hindko has also been interpreted to mean the language of India. There are an estimated 2.2 to 4 million speakers of Hindko living primarily in six districts: Mansehra, Abbottabad, Haripur, Peshawar, Nowshera and Kohat in NWFP; Attock and Rawalpindi in Punjab; and parts of Azad Kashmir, including Muzaffarabad. In Peshawar city they are called Peshawari or *"Shari" (Kharay)* by Pashtuns meaning city dwellers or *Hindkowans.*

Hujra (Pashtu) - guest house or guest room. The *Hujra* plays a pivotal role in Pukhtun daily life; it serves as a club, dormitory, guest house and a place for rituals and feastings. The *hujra* is not only a meeting place of villagers, but is also used as a platform for the *jirga's* meetings (grand community meeting) where important decisions are made and family quarrels and tribal disputes are resolved. (2) a separate room or rooms within a mosque for prayer in solitude (Urdu).

Iftari (Urdu; Arabic—*"Iftar"*; Pashtu—*"roja matay"*) - breaking of the Ramadan fast at Maghrib (evening) prayer; from simple dates and water to an elaborate meal (usually both, *Insh'Allah*)

Imam - *mullah,* prayer leader; often the leader of a *mosque* and the community

Isha (Arabic) (Pashtu - Maspikheen) night prayer - begins, at moderate latitudes, when the sky is completely dark and ends just before the Dawn Prayer.

Insh'Allah (Arabic) - God Willing; used often (a good thing), though sometimes to the point of redundancy

Ismaili - an offshoot of Shia Islam, the split having occurred over the recognition of the Seventh Imam. The Shia Ithna Asharia—those who accept the first Twelve Imams, believe that Jafar, the Sixth Imam, passed over his eldest son, Ismail, in favor of Ismail's brother, Musa al Kazim. Ismailis, however, believe that Jafar appointed Ismail to be the Seventh Imam—hence Ismailis are often called Seveners. Little is known of the early history of the sect, but it was firmly established by the end of the ninth century. They are a community of ethnically and culturally diverse peoples living in over 25 countries around the world united in their allegiance to His Highness Prince Karim Aga Khan (known to the *Ismailis* as Mawlana Hizar Imam) as the 49th hereditary *Imam* (spiritual leader) and direct descendant of Prophet Muhammad (PBUH). Their leaders still claim descent, through Nizar, from Ali and Fatima. In 1818, one of them was granted the title Aga Khan by the Shah of Persia. In 1840, after an abortive uprising against the next Shah, this first Aga Khan fled to India. There he and his descendants remained leaders of an *Ismaili* community numbering several million in Syria, Iran, Pakistan, India and elsewhere. The present Aga Khan, born in 1946, is only the fourth in the line. They pray three times a day (not as other Muslims but with *duas* and *tasbees*) in a place called a *Jamat Khanna.* They do not consider it important to face *Qibla* (Mecca) when praying nor do they believe making physical *wudu* is mandatory. Non-Muslims are not let into the *Jamat Khanna* (at least in Northern Pakistan). They celebrate *Eid Fitr* (end of *Ramadan*), though they believe the real and esoteric meaning of fasting is avoiding devilish acts and doing good deeds. Not eating during the month of Ramadan is considered a metaphorical implementation of fasting and is not compulsory, nor do they make Haj. They don't have *Azan (Adhan),* nor do they have *Juma* congregational prayer. Looked down upon by many Sunnis.

Istidja - the first part of *wudu/wuzu,* the washing of one's *private parts.*

Janana (Pashtu) - darling

Jihad (Arabic) - a noun meaning struggle; *Jihad* appears frequently in the *Qur'an* and common usage as the idiomatic expression "striving in the way of Allah *(al-jihad fi sabil Allah)*." A person engaged in *jihad* is called a *mujahid,* the plural is *mujahideen. Jihad* requires Muslims to "struggle in the way of God" or "to struggle to improve one's self and/or society." *Jihad* is directed against *Satan's* inducements, aspects of one's own self or against a visible enemy. The four major categories of *jihad* that are recognized are *Jihad* against one's self *(Jihad al-Nafs), Jihad* of the tongue *(Jihad al-lisan), Jihad* of the hand *(Jihad al-yad),* and *Jihad* of the sword *(Jihad as-sayf).*
(ed. note 2009: not to be confused with what is being called Jihad nowadays)

Jirga (Pashtu) - a tribal assembly of elders which makes decisions by consensus, particularly among the Pashtun people, but also in other ethnic groups near them; they are most common in Afghanistan and among the Pashtuns in Pakistan near its border with Afghanistan and are even held by Pashtuns in Kashmir valley, India. It is similar to that of a town meeting in the United States or a regional assembly in England.

Juma - Friday, Muslim Sabbath

Juma prayer - the Friday afternoon congregational prayer; the one weekly prayer where attendance is incumbent upon all free adults

K2 - the second-highest mountain on Earth, after Mount Everest. With a peak elevation of 8,611 meters (28,251 ft), K2 is part of the Karakoram segment of the Himalayan range and is located in the Northern Areas of Pakistan on the border between Pakistan's northern territories and the Taxkorgan Tajik Autonomous County of Xinjiang, China. K2 is known as the *Savage Mountain*

451

due to the difficulty of ascent and the fact that for every four people who reach the summit, one dies trying. Among the Eight-thousanders, K2 has the third highest climbing mortality rate.

The name K2 is derived from the notation used by the Great Trigonometric Survey. Thomas Montgomerie made the first survey of the Karakoram from *Mount Haramukh*, some 130 miles to the south and sketched the two most prominent peaks, labelling them K1 and K2. The policy of the Great Trigonometric Survey was to use local names for mountains wherever possible and K1 was found to be known locally as *Masherbrum*. K2, however, appeared not to have acquired a local name, possibly due to its remoteness. The mountain is not visible from Askole, the last village to the south or from the nearest habitation to the north, and is only fleetingly glimpsed from the end of the Baltoro Glacier, beyond which few local people would have ventured. The name *Chogori*, derived from two Balti words, *chhogo* (big) and *ri* (mountain) has been suggested as a local name, but evidence for its widespread use is scant. It may have been a compound name invented by Western explorers or simply a bemused reply to the question, "What's it called?" It does, however, form the basis for the name *Qogir* (simplified Chinese) by which Chinese authorities officially refer to the peak. Other local names have been suggested including Lamba Pahar (Tall Mountain, in Urdu) and Dapsang, but are not widely used. Lacking a local name, the name Mount Godwin-Austen was suggested in honour of Henry Godwin-Austen, an early explorer of the area, and while the name was rejected by the Royal Geographical Society, it was used on several maps and continues to be used occasionally. The surveyor's mark, K2, therefore continues to be the name by which the mountain is commonly known. It is now also used in the Balti language, rendered as *Kechu* or *Ketu*.

Kabab/kebab - Barbequed, grilled meats

Kaboota khanna - Pigeon (*kaboota*) house (*khanna*). A popular past time is raising and training flocks of pigeons. They are flown and will mix with other people's flocks trying to capture the other person's pigeon by bringing them back with them to the house. Then a series of negotiations ensues for the original owner to get back their bird.

Kabuli pilau - Afghani rice dish; Basmati rice with julienne carrots, raisins and pine nuts cooked in ghee, usually with a large piece of beef, lamb or chicken under it

Kafir - unbeliever (religiously). Anybody who is not a Muslim (though technically people of "*the Book*"; i.e: Christians and Jews are not kafir).

Kalashnikov - The AK-47 (contraction of Russian: "Kalashnikov's automatic rifle model of year 1947") is a 7.62 mm assault rifle developed in the Soviet Union by Mikhail Kalashnikov in two versions: the fixed stock AK-47 and the AKS-47 variant equipped with an under-folding metal shoulder stock. Both are manufactured in many countries and have seen service with regular armed forces as well as irregular, revolutionary and terrorist organizations worldwide. It is very common in Afghanistan and Pakistan and reverse engineered and manufactured in Dara Adam Khel, a notorious arms and drug bazaar between Peshawar and Kohat.

Kalima (Arabic) - literally "the word." (Shahada) a declaration of faith, Kalima is the first of the five pillars of Islam and belief in the meaning of the Kalima is the primary distinction of what defines a Muslim. The pronunciation is *"la 'ilaha 'illallah muhammadur-rasulullah"* and the translation is "There is no god but God, Muhammad is the Messenger of God."

Kameez - a long shirt or tunic, worn over shalwar

Kanjri/Kanjra (Punjabi) - prostitute

Kanta - a garland, usually super ornate with folded new currency bills, mirrors in colorful plastic borders, fresh marigolds, a clock, etc, sometimes reaching from the neck to the ground; worn in weddings.

Karakoram (or **Karakorum**) - a large mountain range spanning the borders between Pakistan, India and China, located in the regions of Gilgit-Baltistan (Pakistan), Ladakh (India) and Xinjiang region (China). It is one of the Greater Ranges of Asia, a part of the greater Himalaya while north of the actual Himalaya Range. The Karakoram has the highest concentration of peaks over five miles in height on earth, including K2, the second highest peak of the world (8,611 m/28,251 ft). K2 is just 237 m (778 ft) lower than the 8,848 m (29,029 ft) tall Mount Everest. The range is about 500 km (311 mi) in length and is the most heavily glaciated part of the world outside of the polar regions. The Siachen Glacier at 70 km and the Biafo Glacier at 63 km rank as the world's second and third longest glaciers outside the polar regions. The Karakoram is bounded on the northeast by the edge of the Tibetan Plateau and on the north by the Pamir Mountains. The southern boundary of the Karakoram is formed, west to east, by the Gilgit, Indus and Shyok Rivers, which separate the range from the northwestern end of the Himalaya range proper as these rivers converge southwestward towards the plains of Pakistan. Due to its altitude and ruggedness, the Karakoram is much less inhabited than parts of the Himalayas further east. European explorers first visited early in the 19th century, followed by British surveyors starting in 1856.

Keema - ground meat; also a dish of spiced ground meat, sometimes with green peas or potatoes

Khan - Surname of most Pathans; *Khan* is used for big land owners and important people. The title of Khan originated in Turkic and Central Asian traditions, was historically granted to Muslim rulers. Infiltration of the name from Central Asia happened with the coming of Pashtuns into the subcontinent who used this name as a title as well as a suffix to indicate their ethnic identity. The later

Turks and Mughal invaders also brought the name with them. Some of the communities that use the surname Khan include; the Baloch tribes in Balochistan and Sindh; Northern Iranian Turkic tribes; the Mirasis, a community of South Asian musicians; and miscellaneous tribes in northern Asia. It is, however most commonly used as a surname for Pathans throughout the South Asian subcontinent. In India it is referred to as the name for Pathans as a tribe. Today Khan is used for a Pashtuns throughout the subcontinental, ie. a male person of acknowledged Pashtun origin is addressed as Khan Sahib more often than not by a non-Pashtun, whether he has this name formally or not.

Khairiat - charity

Khaluna (Pashtu) - *"khal"*= beauty mark, *"una"*= plural; natural, or applied as tattoos or makeup

Khorghod (Pashtu; Urdu - *banchod*) - *"khor"* = sister, *"ghod"* = fucker

Khutba - sermon usually delivered at Juma (Friday) prayer and on both Eids

Khuda Hafiz (Farsi, Urdu) - goodbye. Literally "in God's protection"

Kilim/kileem - flat woven rug

Koochie - Afghan nomads; from Pashtu verb *"kooch kawal"* meaning "to migrate"

Kotha - rooms where dancing is performed in Hira Mandi.

Kus (Pashtu) - vagina; also used as a derogatory term for a woman depending on the intonation.

Kutcha - uncooked, unripe; adobe bricks for dwellings) are *"kutcha,"* opposed to kiln-fired bricks *"pokh"* (cooked)

Lakh - 100,000

Lassi (Udru; Pashtu—*"shoomlay"*) - cold drink made with yogurt, water, sugar or salt; sometimes cucumber or mint is added to salt *lassi*, especially in Afghanistan (called *dogh* in *Farsi*).

Layla/Majnoon - A classical Arabian love story based on the real story of a young man called *Qays ibn al-Mulawwah* from the northern Arabian Peninsula in the Umayyad era during the 7th century. There were two Arabic versions of the story at the time. In one version, he spent his youth together with Layla tending their flocks. In the other version, upon seeing Layla he fell passionately in love with her. In both versions, however, he went mad when her father prevented him from marrying her; for that reason he came to be called *Majnun Layla*, which means "driven mad by Layla." *Majnoon* is equivalent to "love crazy." An Arabic *Romeo and Juliet* written many centuries before Shakespear's.

Lota - small, personal-sized water pot, sometimes (in Pakistan usually) with a handle and spout. In the Indian subcontinent, where cleaning with water is the usual method for maintaining personal hygiene after defecation or urination, a lota with a spout is widely used as a container for this purpose. Due to the hygienic requirements of ritual ablution, or *wudu* and *ghusl* (bath) in Islam adhered to by many Muslims, the use of a lota has become prevalent throughout the Muslim world, where it is considered to provide a more thorough cleaning than simply using toilet paper.

Mafhrul (Pashtu) - fugitive

Maghrib (Arabic; Pashtu—*"makhum"*; Urdu—*"sham"*) - Sunset time. Maghrib Prayer begins immediately after sunset. At moderate latitudes it ends before complete darkness approaches. It is the forth prayer of the day.

Mahajur/muhajir (Arabic, Farsi, Pashtu) - refugee, emigrant

Mahsoods - a tribe of Waziris (Waziristan); see *Mehsood*

Majnoon/Layla - see *Layla/Majnoon*

Makkah/Mecca - city in Saudi Arabia. Home to the Masjid al-Haram, it is the holiest city in Islam and plays an important role in the faith. It is the city Muslims all over the world turn to in prayer five times a day. (Ed note: as of 2008, the annual Haj yearly pilgrimage attracts two to three million pilgrims to the city.) Culturally the city is modern, cosmopolitan and ethnically diverse. Islamic tradition attributes the beginning of Makkah to Ishmael's descendants. In the 7th century the Prophet Muhammad (PBUH) proclaimed Islam in the city, by then an important trading center. The city played an important role in the early history of Islam. After 966 Makkah was led by local sharifs until 1924, when it came under the rule of the Saudis.

Mal khanna - storeroom, *mal* = stores, material, stuff, *khanna* = house.

Malang - followers of a creed of Sufism. They are usually homeless wanders who praise the Lord through music, dance and smoking *charras*. They wander careless of worldly affairs and desires. People give them charity, food and clothing and they pray for them in return. Similar to the Indian *sadu* or *faqir*. Can be used for people who emulate this lifestyle.

Malik (Arabic) - king. The term Malik is used in Afghanistan and the tribal areas of Pakistan, especially among Pashtuns, for a tribal leader or a chieftain. Maliks serve as *de facto* arbiters in local conflicts, interlocutors in state policy-making, tax-collectors, heads of village and town councils and delegates to provincial and national *jirgas* as well as to Parliament. A landlord, land holder.

Mama (Pashtu) - maternal uncle; paternal uncle is *"tura"*

Mangay - terra-cotta water jug, sometimes used as a drum, with a piece of skin or rubber stretched across the opening

Mantra - a word, phrase or syllable repeated over and over—usually associated with meditation.

Masha'Allah/Mashallah (Arabic) - closest English translation - "God has willed it." Used to indicate appreciation for an aforementioned individual or event. An expression of respect, at the same time serving as a reminder that all accomplishments are achieved by the will of God.

Mastaki - local home made bread eaten in the Northern Areas between Chitral and Gilgit

Maund - a traditional unit of mass used in British India and also in Afghanistan, Persia and Arabia (still in use) and was used in Mughal India. The mass of the maund has varied from as low as 25 pounds (11 kg) to as high as 160 pounds (72½ kg). Approx 80-85 lbs (38 kg) in the areas we were traveling through.

Mazar - a tomb

Mehndi (Urdu; Pashtu = *"narcraizi"*) - see *henna*

Mehsood, Mehsud, Mahsood, Mahsud - The Mehsood tribe lives in the very center of Waziristan, hemmed in on three sides by the *Darwesh Khel Waziris*, and shut off by the *Bhittanis* on the east from the Derajat and Bannu districts. Two Pashtun tribes, *Ahmadzai Wazir* and *Mehsood*, inhabit and dominate South Waziristan. Within the heart of Mehsood territory in South Waziristan lies the influential *Burki* (also known as *Barak/Baraki/Urmar*) tribe's stronghold of Kaniguram. The Burki are considered by other *khels* (tribes) of South Waziristan to be close brethren of the *Mehsood* due to marital and other ties and the fact that the Burki have lived/controlled Kaniguram for over 1000 years. "The Mehsud tribe are a people who can never even think of submitting to a foreign power." Sir Olaf Caroe said (former governor of the British Indian Frontier). From 1860 to 1937, the English forces constantly attacked Mehsud positions in order to subdue them, but never got a foothold in the area. When asked what they would do when the British left they stated, "go back to fighting each other."

Meribani - thank you, literally *"kindness"*

Metaled (road) (British English) - sometimes called *macadam*—paved road. The most common modern paving methods are asphalt and concrete. In the past brick was extensively used, as was metalling. Road metal later became the name of stone chippings mixed with tar to form the road surfacing material "tarmac." The word *metal* is derived from the Latin *metallum*, which means both "mine" and "quarry," hence the roadbuilding terminology.

Mether - the hereditary rulers of Chitral

Meteeza (Pashtu) - harlot

Minar - minaret, tower

Mohallah - block, street, neighborhood

Mohmand - Mohmands are a large Pushtun tribe

Moogays - stakes (our's had rings in the ends for picketing our horses)

Mor ghod (Pashtu) - curse word pretaining to one's mother; literally "mother fucker."

Mr. Jinnah - Muhammad Ali Jinnah (December 25, 1876—September 11, 1948), a 20th century politician and statesman, generally regarded as the father of Pakistan. He served as leader of The Muslim League and served as Pakistan's first Governor-General. He is officially known in Pakistan as *Quaid-e-Azam* (Urdu = "Great Leader"). His birthday is a national holiday in Pakistan.

Mubarak (Arabic, Pashtu, Urdu) - congratulations

Muharram (Arabic) - the first month of the Islamic calendar; the most sacred of all the months, excluding *Ramadan*. The word *"Muharram"* is often considered synonymous with the event of *Ashura*. *Ashura*, which literally means "tenth" in Arabic, refers to the tenth day of *Muharram*. The date is important for all Muslims, especially *Shias*, since Hussain bin Ali (the 2nd Imam of *Shiaism* and the grandson of the Prophet Muhammed *(PBUH)*) was killed on this day. It is also said that in this sacred month *Allah* *(SWT)* created the universe and Adam was created as the first human in the universe and also Musa (Moses) and Issa (Jesus Christ) were born.

Mujahid (Arabic) - literally *"struggler"*; a Muslim involved in a *jihad* (struggle), who is fighting in a war or involved in any other (spiritual) struggle (see *Jihad*).

Mujahideen (Arabic) - plural for *mujahid*; Islamic Freedom Fighters (back in the day when there was a real *jihad* being fought in Afghanistan)

Mullah - imam, prayer leader, priest

Murchay (Pashtu) - shooting loop holes

Musaffar khanna - inexpensive traveler's hotel; *musaffar* = "traveler/wayfarer," and *khanna* = "house"

Naika - female manager of a brothel, a madam

Naan - bread, either round or teardrop shaped, cooked in a tandoor oven (a big clay oven shaped like a pot with a hole in the top)

Naan bai - bakery that bakes *naan;* also the baker who bakes naan is called a *"naan bai"*

Naan nufkar - what the groom offers the bride as a monthly "allowance" for household expenses.

Nal bandi - farrier

Nautch - dance, hence *natch girl* = dancing girl.

Nawab - originally the provincial governor or viceroy of a province or region of the Mughal empire. It has become a high title for Muslim nobles.

Nefil - additional, optional prayers

Nikka/nikkah/nika - the official signing of the marriage papers; Islamic marriage

Nikka namma - Islamic marriage certificate

Nuswar - ground (or powdered) tobacco with lime and ash, similar to snuff or chewing tobacco. In Afghanistan, it is powdered green or dark brown. Usually the green goes under the tongue (takes practice to talk with it there as it makes one salivate profusely); the dark is used in the nose. In Pakistan, green nuswar is mixed with menthol. They also make brown nuswar into blocks or balls. A large pinch/chunk is placed between the cheek and the gums.

NWFP - North West Frontier Province; *(Suba Sarhad)* **Ed note: In 2010 the name of the province was changed to Khyber Pakhtunkhwa. Protests arose among the local ethnic Hazara population and in Chitral due to this name change as they began to demand their own provinces.**

Orbashie (Pashtu) - barley

Paan - South East Asian tradition that dates back thousands of years. Betel nut (*Areca* nut—seed of the *Areca* palm *(Areca catechu,* which grows in much of the tropical Pacific, Asia and parts of east Africa), tobacco and spices wrapped in a betel leaf and chewed. There are many regional variations. Paan is chewed as a palate cleanser and a breath freshener. It is also a light stimulant. It is also commonly offered to guests and visitors as a sign of hospitality and as an "ice breaker" to start conversation. It creates blood red/brown spit and gums.

Paan wallah - *paan* seller, merchant; usually a small, open-fronted shop/stand (sometimes selling cigarettes also) or a portable setup with shoulder straps carried by seller

Pakoras - Asian vegetable fritters made from a batter of *besan* (chick pea flour). *Pakoras* are a fried snack found across South Asia, an integral part of Indian, Pakistani and Punjabi cuisine. Pakoras are also found in other South Asian countries such as Afghanistan, Bangladesh, Nepal and Sri Lanka. Pakoras are created by taking two or three ingredients, such as chicken, onion, aubergine, potato, spinach, cauliflower, tomato or chilli, dipping them in a batter of gram flour and then deep-frying them. Pakoras are usually served as snacks, often taken with *chai* or appetizers. During *Ramadan* pakoras are often eaten by Pakistani Muslims during Iftar (the evening meal to break the fast).

Pakul/pakol/pakool - a soft, round-topped men's hat, typically of coarse wool, found in any of a variety of earthy colors: brown, black, gray or ivory. Before it is fitted, it resembles a bag with a round, flat bottom. The wearer rolls up the sides nearly to the top, forming a thick band, which then rests on the head like a beret or cap. The *pakul* gained some attention in the West in the 1980s as a *Mujahideen* cap, as it was favored by Afghan *mujahideen* from Panjsher (Ahmad Shah Mahsood). The hat originated in the Chitral and Gilgit regions of what is now Northern Pakistan. It gained popularity amongst the Northeastern Pushtun tribes in the early twentieth century largely as a substitute for their large, cumbersome turbans. It also gained popularity amongst the Nuristanis and the Tajiks of Panjsher and Badakhshan. The hat is worn in Afghanistan, Pakistan, Uzbekistan and Tajikistan as well. In Pakistan it is particularly popular in the North West Frontier Province and Northern Areas such as Chitral, Gilgit and Hunza.

Paisa/pesa - one hundredth of a rupee, equivalent to one cent.

Palak aloo - a dish made of *palak* (spinach) and *aloo* (potato)

Pa makha day kha (Pashtu) - goodbye; literally *"Face the good"*

Paneer - most common South Asian and Persian cheese. It is an un-aged, acid-set, non-melting farmer cheese made by curdling heated milk with lemon juice or other food acid, then strained and squeezed.

Parattas - similar to *chapatties* (tortillas), fried in a pan or on a skillet with oil or *ghee*, made from wheat or corn; can have a filling.

Pashtu/Pakhto/Pushto/Pukhto/Pushtu - also known as *Afghani;* an Indo-European language spoken primarily in Afghanistan and Northwestern Pakistan. Pashtu belongs to the Eastern Iranian branch of the Indo-Iranian language family. There are nearly 45 million ethnic Pashtuns. In Afghanistan, Pashtu is primarily spoken in the east, south and southwest, but also in some northern and northwestern areas as a result of recent relocation. No exact numbers are available, but according to "A survey of the Afghan people (Afghanistan in 2006) Pashtu is the first language of 40% of Afghans, while additional 28% also speak Pashtu (combined 68%). In Pakistan, Pashtu is spoken by about 27 million people (15% of the total population) in the North-West Frontier Province, Federally Administered Tribal Areas and Balochistan." Modern "transplant" communities are also found in Sindh (Karachi and Hyderabad). Other communities of Pashtu speakers are found in northeastern Iran, primarily in South Khorasan Province to the east of Qaen, near the Afghan border and in Tajikistan. There are also Pashtun communities in Uttar Pradesh as well as the southwestern part of Jammu & Kashmir in India. Sizable Pashtu speaking communities also exist in the Middle East, especially in the United Arab Emirates and Saudi Arabia, as well as in the United States, particularly California, and in the United Kingdom, Thailand and Australia. (see note at the end of glossary concerning pronunciations of i.e.; Pashtu vs Pakhtu etc.)

Pathans/Pakhtuns/Pashtuns/Pukhtuns/Pashtoons/Pakhtoons - The Pathans live in Northern Pakistan and Afghanistan. Made up of some 60 Pashtu speaking tribes, the Pathans number some 10 million in Pakistan and some 8 million in Afghanistan. They make up the largest ethnocultural group in Afghanistan. The Pathans comprise distinct groups. Some live as nomads in the high mountains with herds of goats and camels; others, such as those living in the Swat Valley, are farmers; and still others are traders or seasonal laborers. However, this ethnographic description defies the fact that they constitute more than 20% of Pakistan's armed forces and dominate Pakistan's transportation industry. The British attacked the Pathans in the late 19th and early 20th century. They were finally forced to offer the Pathans a semiautonomous area between the border of British India and Afghanistan. After the creation of Pakistan in 1947, the new nation annexed the Pathan border regions. In the early 1950s, the Soviet Union, through Afghanistan, supported Pathan ambitions for the creation of an independent *Pushtunistan* (also called *Pakhtunistan*) in the border areas of West Pakistan. Several border clashes and ruptures of diplomatic relations between Afghanistan and Pakistan ensued. The movement was never able to gain popular support considering that Pathans in Pakistan were always better off than Pathans in Afghanistan. Pathans also helped liberate the part of Kashmir which is now under Pakistan's control. Their support and hospitality to more than four million Afghan refugees was crucial in Afghanistan's liberation from the Soviet Union. The Pathans are known as people who are brave, simple, and sincere in their dealings with others. They are noted as fierce fighters and throughout history have offered strong resistance to invaders. They staunchly hold on to their cultural traditions and connect with one another in a visceral way. Most are guided by a tribal code of ethics, *Pakhtunwali*, or "way of the Pakhtun." Tribal customs and traditions make up the biggest part of the Pathan society. The tenets of *Pakhtunwali* show the true essence of Pathan culture and these rules are followed religiously. It incorporates the following major practices: "*melmastia*" (hospitality and protection to every guest), "*nanawati*" (the right of a fugitive to seek a place of refuge and acceptance of his bona fide offer of peace), '*badal*' (the right of blood feuds or revenge), "*tureh*" (bravery), "*sabar*" (steadfastness, patience), "*imandari*" (righteousness), "*isteqamat*" (persistence), "*ghayrat*" (defense of property and honor) and "*mamus*" (defense of one's women).

PBUH - The Prophet Muhammad's (PBUH) name is always followed by "Peace Be Upon Him."

Peer - a religious holy man, a saint

PIA - Pakistan International Airlines (also known as "*Please Inform **Allah***" or "*Pain In the Ass*")

Pilau - rice cooked in ghee or oil and spices; there are a number of variations from region to region, all with a variety of ingredients complementing the essential rice, from chicken and meat to seafood or vegetables. Kabuli Pilau (a popular Afghani pilau) is cooked with raisins, nuts and julienne carrots. Peshawar pilau has raisins and chick peas.

Pindi - short for Rawalpindi, city near Islamabad, Pakistan. The fourth largest city in Pakistan after Karachi and Lahore. In the 1950s Rawalpindi was smaller than Hyderabad and Multan but the building of Islamabad in the 1960s boosted the city's economy, resulting in a tenfold increase in population from 180,000 to over 2.1 million. It is located in the Punjab province, 275 km (171 miles) to the northwest of Lahore and is the military headquarters of the Pakistani Armed Forces

Pita bread - round, brown, wheat flatbread made with yeast. Similar to other double-layered flat or pocket breads, pita is traditional in many Middle Eastern and Mediterranean cuisines. It is prevalent from North Africa through the Levant and the Arabian Peninsula.

PTDC - Pakistan Tourist Development Corporation

Pukhtoonistan/Pashtunistan - the land of (*istan*) the *Pukhtoons/Pashtoons*

Punjab - a region straddling the border between India and Pakistan; "*panch*" = five and "*ab*" = water. The five rivers of the Punjab are: the Jhelum, the Chenab, the Ravi, the Sutlej and the Beas. All are tributaries of the Indus River, the Jhelum being the largest. The *Punjab* has a long history and rich cultural heritage. The people of the *Punjab* are called *Punjabis* and their language is also called *Punjabi*. Lahore is the capitol city of Pakistani Punjab.

Punkah - circular prop ceiling fan; in the past, a large flap hung from the ceiling, pulled up and down with cords by a servant.

Purdah - literally meaning "curtain." The practice of preventing women from being seen by men other than their spouses and immediate family. This takes two forms: physical segregation of the sexes, and the requirement for women to cover their bodies and conceal their form. Purdah exists in various forms in the Islamic world and among Hindu women in parts of India.

Puri - bread, like *chapatti* (tortilla), deep fried until they puff up with hot air

Qawah - popular Pathan drink; green tea (Ceylon little buds are best) boiled with sugar and cardamom. *Qawah* in Arabic countries is coffee.

Qawali/Qawwali - a form of Sufi devotional music popular in South Asia, mostly Pakistan and parts of India), particularly in areas with a historically strong Muslim presence. It's a vibrant musical tradition that stretches back more than 700 years. Often listeners, and even artists themselves, are transported to a state of *wajad*, a trancelike state where they feel at one with God, generally considered to be the height of spiritual ecstasy in Sufism and the ultimate goal of the practice. Originally performed mainly at Sufi shrines or *dargahs* throughout the subcontinent, it has also gained mainstream popularity. Qawwali music received international exposure through the work of the late Pakistani singer Nusrat Fateh Ali Khan.

Qibla - Muslim direction of prayer facing Mecca; in Pakistan basically west

Qissa Khanni (Bazaar) - Market of Storytellers is a famous bazaar of Peshawar. The Qissa Khanni Bazaar; the romantic "Street of Storytellers" extends from west to east in the heart of the city of Peshawar, from Mez Garan (the copper bazaar) to Kabuli Gate. The cosmopolitan character of Qissa Khanni Bazaar is lined with its traditional *qawah khannas, tikka kebab, chapali kebab* and dry fruit shops along with modern showrooms of leatherware and brightly colored garments. In days gone by the bazaar was the site of camping grounds for caravans and military adventures. Professional storytellers recited ballads and tales of war and love to mobs of traders and soldiers. Lowell Thomas and Peshawar's British commissioner, Herbert Edwardes, called it "the Piccadilly of Central Asia" in the 30s. Today, the storytellers and the art of story telling have been replaced with cassette and CD/DVD shops, but the atmosphere of the bazaar is still the same. Bearded tribesmen bargain with city traders over endless cups of green tea. People from everywhere visit the crowded street. Tribesmen still move around with ease and grace in their colorful, native robes and turbans. There are also several publishing houses of books in this bazaar with a long tradition of publishing Pashtu, Urdu and Persian books. Qissa Khanni was the site of a massacre when British soldiers fired upon a crowd of unarmed protesters on April 23, 1930. It was a defining moment in the "nonviolent" struggle to drive the British out of India. It was the first major confrontation between British troops and nonviolent demonstrators in the then peaceful city; some estimates at the time put the death toll from the shooting at nearly 400. The gunning down of unarmed people triggered protests across the subcontinent and catapulted the newly formed Khudai Khidmatgar (now Awami Party) movement onto the national scene.

Quaid-i-Azam - Muhammad Ali Jinnah (December 25, 1876 – September 11, 1948), generally regarded as the founder of Pakistan. He served as leader of The Muslim League and Pakistan's first Governor-General. He is officially known in Pakistan as *Quaid-e-Azam* (Urdu = "Great Leader").

Qurban (Arabic, Pashtu, Urdu) **Corbaan** - sacrifice

Qismet (Arabic) - preordained fate

Qorma/Qurma - meat cooked in a rich spicy sauce, sometimes made with yogurt.

Qur'an - (Arabic - all languages) *Al-Qur'an*; literally "the recitation;" also sometimes transliterated as *Quran, Koran,* or *Alcoran*; the central religious text of Islam. The *Qur'an* is the Muslim book of divine guidance and a direction for mankind. The original Arabic text is the final revelation of God. It was revealed to the Prophet Muhammad (*PBUH*) by the angel Jibril (Gabriel) from 610 CE to his death in 632 CE. and was written down by Muhammad's (*PBUH*) companions while he was alive, although the primary method of transmission was oral. It is maintained that in 633 CE the written text was compiled and in 653 CE it was standardized, distributed in the Islamic empire and produced in large numbers. Academic scholars consider it to still be in the original version revealed to the Prophet Muhammad (*PBUH*). Muslim tradition agrees that it was fixed in writing shortly after Muhammad's (*PBUH*) death by order of Umar and Abu Bakr (the first two Caliphs). The *Qur'an* is the culmination of a series of divine messages that started with those revealed to Adam, regarded in Islam as the first prophet and continued with the Suhuf Ibrahim (Sefer Yetzirah or Scrolls of Abraham), the Tawrat (Torah), the Zabur (Tehillim or Book of Psalms) and the Injeel (Christian Gospel). The contents of the aforementioned books are not physically affixed within the *Qur'an*, but are recognized therein. It also refers to many events from Jewish and Christian scriptures, some of which are retold in comparatively distinctive ways from the Torah and New Testament, while obliquely referring to other events described explicitly in those texts. The *Qur'an* itself expresses that it is the book of guidance, therefore it rarely offers detailed accounts of historical events; the text instead typically places emphasis on the moral significance of an event rather than its narrative sequence. The *Qur'an* itself is considered by Muslims as the main

457

miracle of Muhammad (PBUH) and a proof of his prophethood. Many Muslims (including children as young as five years of age) commit the entire book to memory. They are known as *"Hafiz."*
Qur'an Sharif - (Qur'an) meaning - *Holy Qur'an*, Islam's Holy, Revealed Book

Rabab (rubab/rebab/rabob) - Afghani double chambered lute, precursor of the Indian Sarode. The bowed variety (Arabic) often has a spike at the bottom to rest on the ground and is thus called a spike fiddle in certain areas. **(ed. note):** The *rabab* mentioned in this book is the *Kabuli rabab*, popular in Afghanistan (Kabul), NWFP (Peshawar) and Kashmir (Muzaffarabad and Srinigar). Also played in Northern India and Iran. It is believed to have originated in Afghanistan no later than the 8th century and was spread via Islamic trading routes over much of North Africa, the Middle East, parts of Europe and the Far East. It wasn't until the eighteenth century that it emerged refined to its present form maybe in the Ghazni area. It is plucked with a wood, bone or horn plectrum called a "shahbaz." Its form has been described by some as "boat like." The body of the instrument is heavy, carved wood (usually *dtoot* = mulberry), narrow in the middle, suggesting that it might have been played like a violin at one time, like its bowed cousins. The body is covered with stretched goat skin glued to the body. The neck is very thick and the fretboard is often intricately inlaid with mother of pearl. The pegbox is often topped with intricate carving. The *Kabuli rabab* has three or four main melody strings (with four strings, one is doubled) which are bridged by a carved piece of bone held onto the skin face by pressure. There are also three rhythm strings. The strings are attached to tuning pegs (not machine heads) set in the pegbox and terminate at one or two stout pegs at the bottom of the instrument. Most plucked *rababs* have a number of sympathetic strings (7 to 15, 13 and 15 predominant) stretched underneath the main strings. The sympathetic strings are tuned by pegs set along the neck. In Afghanistan, it is said that when God created Adam he wasn't breathing and the Angel Jibrail (Gabriel) was sent down with a rabab to strum and Adam began to breathe. Also that the sound of rabab is the sound of the music of Paradise. In Arabic *"ru"* means soul and *"bab"* means gateway.

Rahman Baba - *Abdul Rahman Mohmand* (1653—1711) popularly known as *"Rahman Baba"* was called the "Nightingale of Pakhtoonkhwa," the Pashtu speaking region of Afghanistan and Pakistan. Rahman Baba is a legendary Pashtu Sufi poet. His poetry places him alongside Khushal Khan Khattak for his contribution to Pashtu poetry and literature. His mausoleum/shrine and *mazar* (tomb) is located on the outskirts of Peshawar in Hazarkhawni.

Raihal (Arabic) - *Qur'an* holder (so it doesn't rest on the floor); quite often craved wood

Rakat/rakkat - a section of Islamic prayer consisting of *ruku* (bending with hands on knees) and two *sajdah* (bowing with forehead to ground)

Ramazon/Ramadan - ninth month of the Islamic calendar. It is the Islamic month of fasting, in which participating Muslims refrain from eating, drinking, smoking, sex and indulging in anything that is in excess or ill-natured, from dawn until sunset. Fasting is meant to teach patience, modesty and spirituality. Ramadan is a time for Muslims to fast for the sake of **Allah** and to offer more prayer than usual. During Ramadan, Muslims ask forgiveness for past sins, pray for guidance and help in refraining from everyday evils, and try to purify themselves through self-restraint and good deeds. As compared to the solar calendar, the dates of Ramadan vary, moving forward about ten days each year as the Islamic calendar is a lunar calendar. Ramadan was the month in which the first verses of the Qur'an were revealed to the Prophet Muhammad (PBUH).

Rayda - horse cart with two large wooden wheels and a raised platform with a short railing around it, much of the time brightly painted and decorated. The driver sits or stands on the platform.

Rickshaw - actually auto-rickshaw - 3 wheeled cycle/carriage taxi (Vespa powered—not a pedaled rickshaw in these parts of Pakistan!) Runs on a mixture of petrol and oil. (Ed note: CNG was introduced after the writing of this book)

Rooh Afza - a type of sherbet (drink) made from water, sugar, citrus, rose and other flower essences; a cooling summer drink mixed with water, ice, lemon or milk. Similar to grenadine.

Roti - bread. In Peshawar, it is cooked in *tandoor* and slightly leavened (*naan*). In Rawalpindi and Lahore it can be flatter and cooked in a *tandoor* or on a skillet (chapatti/tortilla). *Roti* can be synonymous with food.

Rupee - currency in Pakistan and India. A Rupee is similar to a dollar. At the time of writing of this book the value was 35 to 42 Pak rupees in a U.S. dollar.

Rutter - a pilot's book or seaman's guide carried by early (i.e., middle ages) navigators. The word "rutter" is likely derived from the French word "routier," meaning "something that finds a way."

Sag - greens, usually mustard greens, but can mean spinach or other greens

Sahib (from Arabic) - usually pronounced sa'ab; a term of respect, meaning sir, master or lord. Used in British India for British people and nowadays used for anybody deemed worthy of respect.

Sajdah/Sudjood/sidja (Arabic) - prostration with the forehead, hands and knees on the ground; a part of Muslim prayer

Salaam (Arabic) - greeting, literally "Peace"

Salaam aleikum/salaamu'aliekum (Arabic) - greeting, literally "Peace be on you," answered with *"wa aliekum asalaam,"* = "Onto you be peace."

Samaan/samon - luggage, baggage, belongings

Samaan/samon dapara (Pashtu) - joke name we used for our baggage horse: *samaan* = baggage, *dapara* = for. So when we told their names we could say, "This one *samaan dapara* (for baggage)."

Samosa - a stuffed pastry and a popular snack in South Asia, Southeast Asia, Central Asia, the Horn of Africa and the Arabian Peninsula. It generally consists of a fried, triangular shaped pastry shell with a savory filling of spiced potatoes, onion, peas, coriander, minced meat or sometimes fresh *paneer* (cheese).

Samovar (Russian, literally "self-boiler") - A heated metal container used to heat and boil water, usually for making tea. A traditional samovar consists of a large, metal container with a faucet near the bottom and a metal pipe (flue) running vertically through the middle. Samovars are typically crafted out of copper, brass, bronze, silver, gold, tin or nickel. The pipe is filled with solid fuel, ie: wood and coal, to heat the water in the surrounding container. A small (6 to 8 inch) smokestack is put on the top to ensure draft.

Sarangi - bowed, short-necked lute of the Indian subcontinent. It is an important bowed string instrument of India's Hindustani classical music tradition. Of all Indian instruments it is said to most resemble the sound of the human voice—able to imitate vocal ornaments such as *gamakas* (shakes) and *meend* (sliding movements). The word sarangi is derived from two Hindi words: *sau* = "hundred" and *rang* = "color"). This is because the sound of the *sarangi* is said to be as expressive and evocative as 100 colors.

Sarhad - frontier

Sawab/swab - blessing, benefit

Sayid/Said/Sayed/Syed/Saeed - family related to the family of The Prophet Mohammad (PBUH) through his grandsons Hassan and Hussain, sons of his daughter Fatima Zahra and son-in-law (and nephew) Ali ibn Abi Talib; common first name, especially among Shia

Seekh Kebab - minced meat (lamb/beef) and finely chopped onions marinated in spices and cooked over charcoal fire on a metal skewer (looks like a sausage)

Sehri (Urdu; Arabic—*"sahoor"*; Pashtu—*"peshmanay"* - meal eaten during the Holy Month of Ramadan (or any fast) before sunrise (and morning prayer) signifying the start of the daily fast

Sepoy (Persian; Pushtu—*"sipahi"*) - term used in the British Indian Army for an infantry private (a cavalry trooper was a *sowar*) and still used in the Pakistani, Bangladeshi and Indian Army

Shaitan (Arabic) - Satan, the devil

Shalimar Gardens - a Persian style garden just outside Lahore built by the Mughal emperor Shah Jahan. Construction began in 1641 A.D. (1051 A.H.) and was completed the following year. There is also a famous Mughal garden just outside Srinigar, Indian Kashmir, of the same name..

Shalwar kameez - traditional dress worn by both women and men in South Asia. *Salvars* or *shalvars/shalwar* (Pashtu = *"partoughk"*) are loose pajama-like trousers. The legs are wide at the top and narrow at the bottom. The *kameez* is a long shirt or tunic. The side seams (known as the *chaak*) are left open below the waistline, which gives the wearer greater freedom of movement. In Afghanistan and Pakistan, the garment is worn by both sexes. Men's are usually single colored and women's can be patterned, decorated with embroidery, satin, etc. In India, Bangladesh and Sri Lanka it is most commonly a woman's garment, albeit still worn by some men.

Shamiyana - multi-color patchwork tents used for weddings or other outdoor functions

Sharab - alcohol, alcoholic drinks

Sharabi - alcoholic (person)

Shari (Urdu; Pashtu—*"Kharay"*) - from root *"shar"* = city; a citizen of Peshawar, originally from Punjab, who speaks a language similar to Punjabi called *Hindko*

Sharia Law - the code of law derived from the *Qur'an* and from the teachings and example of the Prophet Muhammad (*PBUH*); *sharia* is only applicable to Muslims. Under Islamic law, there is no separation of church and state.

Sherbet - chilled drinks made from fruit syrups

Shazan (brand name) - a bottled mango drink (the best!)

459

Sheikh (Arabic - pronounced 'shake') - honorific term that literally means "elder." It is commonly used to designate an elder of a tribe, a revered wise man or an Islamic scholar. It can also refer to a man over 40 or 50 years old or to a convert to Islam.

SHO - Station House Officer—usually the head in charge at a police *tanna* (station)

Shokriya (Urdu; from Arabic root *"shokran"*) - thank you

Shia - Shia Islam (sometimes referred to as *Shi'ite*) is the second largest denomination of Islam, after Sunni Islam. Similar to other schools of thought in Islam, Shia Islam is based on the teachings of the Islamic holy book the *Qur'an* and the message of the Prophet of Islam, Muhammad (*PBUH*). In contrast to other schools of thought, Shia Islam holds that Muhammad's (*PBUH*) family, the Ahl al-Bayt (the People of the House) and certain individuals among his descendants, who are known as Imams, have special spiritual and political rule over the community. Shia Muslims further believe that Ali ibn Abi Talib, Muhammad's (*PBUH*) cousin and son-in-law, was the first of these Imams and was the rightful successor to Muhammad and thus reject the legitimacy of the first three Rashidun caliphs, ie: Abu Bakr, Umar and Uthman (Usman).

Sitar - a plucked stringed instrument. It uses sympathetic strings along a long, hollow neck and a gourd resonating chamber to produce a very rich sound with complex harmonic resonance. The neck is fretted with metal frets over the fretboard. Predominantly used in Hindustani classical music, sitar has been ubiquitous in Hindustani classical music since the Middle Ages. It is used throughout the Indian subcontinent, particularly in Northern India, Bangladesh and Pakistan, and popular in Afghanistan.

Special Branch - government office seeing to foreigners; visas, registration, etc

Suba Sarhad - Frontier Province; *"Suba"* = province, *"Sarhad"* = frontier. See **NWFP**.

Subedar - historical rank in the Indian British Army ranking below British commissioned officers and above noncommissioned officers. The rank was otherwise equivalent to a British lieutenant. Still in use.

Subzi - vegetables, greens

Sunat - circumcision, celebrated with rice, prayers, machine guns (firing in the air); traditionally performed by barbers

Sunnah (Arabic) - literally means "trodden path" and, therefore the *sunnah* of the Prophet (*PBUH*) means "the way, words and the manners of the Prophet (*PBUH*)."

Sunni - Sunni Islam is the largest denomination of Islam. The word Sunni comes from the word *Sunnah* (see *sunnah* above).

Surma (*kohl, kajal*) - black eyeliner, also called antimony. The Sunan Abi Dawood (one of the Sunni six major Hadith collections) reports, "Muhammad (*PBUH*) said: 'Among the best types of collyrium use is antimony (*ithmid*) for it clears the vision and makes the hair sprout.'" Used by men and women, liberally applied to infant's eyes. *Surma-dani* - a container for surma.

Sura/surrah (Arabic) - chapter/verse of the *Qur'an*

Surnai - a double reeded horn, like an oboe; indigenous of Afghanistan, Northern Pakistan and India

Swamp-cooler (Anglayzee) - an air-conditioner; a large box with reed mats on four sides and a pump to keep water circulating over them and a fan in the center

SWT - *"Subhanahu Wa Ta'ala,"* which roughly translated means, "The most glorified, the most high." It is a way for Muslims to glorify ***Allah*** when mentioning His name.

Tabla - a popular Indian percussion instrument used in the classical, popular and religious music of the Indian subcontinent and in Hindustani classical music. The instrument consists of a pair of hand drums of contrasting sizes and timbres. The term *tabla* is derived from an Arabic word, *tabl*, which simply means "drum." A set consists of a smaller wooden drum of higher timbre called *"tabla"* and a larger drum made either of wood or metal, of lower timbre called *"bayan."*

Tabligh - preach religion, mostly aimed at strenghtening other Muslims

Tablighee - a person that does *tabligh* (sometimes can become over jealous)

Tabouleh/tabouli - a Levantine Arab dish/salad. Its primary ingredients are bulgur, finely chopped parsley, mint, tomato, scallion and other herbs with lemon juice, olive oil and various seasonings.

Talaq (Arabic, Pashtu, Urdu) - divorce

Talaq namma - divorce certificate; *"talaq"* = divorce, *"namma"* = certificate

Tanda - squash (vegetable)

Tandoor (Pashtu—*"tannur"*) - clay oven for baking bread (naan) and skewered meats (tandoori)

Tanna - station (police)

Taravi - special prayers during the Holy Month of Ramadan immediately after Isha (night) prayer consisting of from 10-20 *rakkats* (in Pakistan 20) in sets of two wherein the entire *Qur'an* is recited, many times more than once in the month

Tasbee - prayer rosary consisting of 99 or 100 beads

Taviz - a religious amulet, usually a small metal, leather or cloth container/pouch, worn on the body or sewn onto clothing with prayers/blessing/*surahs* written on paper and inserted inside

Taxi - Pakistani slang for prostitute

Toba (Arabic/Pashtu/Urdu) - repent, God forbid. *Toba* is usually said accompanied with tugging on the earlobes with the thumb and first finger in Afghanistan and Pakistan.

Tonga - two (wooden) wheeled horse carriage. In Afghanistan called *"gadi"*

Tuareg - a Berber tribe living in the central Sahara. Because of their indigo clothing (which bleeds onto their skin) they are known as "the blue men." They are legendary horsemen.

Urdu - the national language of Pakistan and one of the two official languages (the other being English). It is similar to Hindi and an official language of five Indian states. Its vocabulary developed under Persian, Arabic, Turkic, Hindi and Pashtu influence. Urdu was mainly developed in western Uttar Pradesh, India, which is the seat of Hindustani languages in the Indian Subcontinent, but began taking shape during the Delhi Sultanate as well as Mughal Empire (1526–1858) in South Asia. Urdu or English is the means of communication between the people from various provinces and regions of Pakistan.

Ustad/ustada/ustaz (Persian/Pashtu/Urdu) - master, teacher, maestro

Wa aleikum asalaam (Arabic) - answer to *"Salaam aleikum,"* literally "And on to you, peace."

Walima (Arabic) - the marriage banquet; one of the two traditional parts of an Islamic wedding. The *walima* happens after the *nikka* (marriage ceremony). The word *walima* is derived from *walam*, meaning to gather or assemble. It designates a feast in classical and in newspaper Arabic.

Wallah/walla - to attach someone to a specific task, place or object, i.e: chai wallah (tea maker), tonga wallah (tonga driver), Lahore wallah (someone from Lahore)

WAPDA - Water And Power Development Agency

Water-boilers (special English) - a term applied to foreigners who boil their drinking water and wash vegetables in an iodine solution, etc, out of fear of local bacteria; derogatory classification

Wuzu (Urdu; Arabic—*"wudu"*; Pashtu—*"ohdez"*) - ablutions for prayer; washing the hands, forearms, face, feet and rinsing one's mouth with clean water.

Yar/yaar - friend, buddy, pal; feminine—*"yaara"*

Yarana - darling, love (deep friendship)

Zarri - embroidery with gold or silver thread; traditional on wedding garments

Zendabad - long live; *Pakistan zendabad* = "Long live Pakistan."

Zina (Arabic) - illicit sexual intercourse; adultery or premarital sex.

Zirarat - a shrine (at a grave)

Zohr/Zhuhr (Urdu; Arabic—*"Dhuhr"* (Pashtu—*maazkhawtaan*) - noon prayer, begins just after the sun has passed the meridian. It's time lasts until shortly before the *Asr* prayer begins.

Zoi (Pashtu) - son; plural—*zamon*

Zot (Pashtu) - caste

note: The Arabic letter *"dhal"* (ضْ) is pronounced *"zhal"* in the subcontinent which is why words like *"adhan, wudu, Ramadan, Dhuhr, Abu Dhabi"* become *"azan, wuzu, Ramazan, Zhuhr, Abu Zhabi"* and so on. The Pashtu letter (ښ) is called *"sheen"* (pronounced soft as "sh") in Kandahar, Waziristan and other areas south, though in Peshawar, Jalalabad and other areas north of Peshawar (Yousafzai dialect) is called *"kheen"* (pronounced hard as "kh") hence variations in pronunciations; *Pashtu = Pukhtu, Pushtun = Pukhtun, Peshawar = Pekhawar, shar* (city) = *khar* etc. There are other letters that also vary the pronunciations but as this isn't a book on the *Pashtu* language I just mention these letters here as they are many common words.

461

❖   ❖   ❖

❖   ❖   ❖

توره ږيره مې شوه سپينه زه حيران يم
چې رحمان لانه بالغ شوم نه عاقل

"Tora ghira me shoowa spina zeh hiran yem
Che Rahman la na baligh shoom na ahqal"

"My black beard has become white, I'm surprised,
I am not mature nor wise."
Rahman Baba

❀   ❀   ❀

ABOUT THE AUTHOR

Noor Mohammad Khan has traveled extensively throughout Central Asia and the Indian subcontinent. Born in Los Angeles, he became a Muslim in 1978 in Kabul, Afghanistan. There he submerged himself deeply into the culture; studying music, learning the language, doing field recording and dealing in fine crafts (1975-1979). After years of playing various instruments, his love focused on the Afghan *rabab*.

He resided in Peshawar Pakistan, Northwest Frontier Province, from 1982-1992, where he played with local musicians and had a music recording studio. In 1988-89 he helped organize The Karakoram Equestrian Expedition where he served as a translator and *chargé d'affaires*. With two other American Muslim convert friends and a Pakistani friend he made a 1000 mile (1600 km) five month horse trip through the mountains of Northern Pakistan: Kalash, Chitral, Gilgit, Kaghan Valley and Azad Kashmir.

He currently lives in San Francisco with his wife and son with occasional visits to Pakistan. His deep connection to Pakistan remains unbroken and he hopes to return to live in Peshawar in the near future, *Insh'Allah.*

You can contact the author by leaving a message in his
pbase site's guest book at:
www.pbase.com/noorkhan/profile
or on Facebook at:
http://www.facebook.com/pages/Some-Time-On-the-Frontier-A-Pakistan-Journal/132172606822015

✳   ✳   ✳

Pukhtoon *Zoi* — Adam Khan — 2009

✳   ✳   ✳

Made in the USA
San Bernardino, CA
05 April 2016